Vietnam

Also by Stanley Karnow

Southeast Asia (1962)

Mao and China: From Revolution to Revolution (1972)

Vietnam
A History

Stanley Karnow

The Viking Press   New York

First published in 1983 by The Viking Press
40 West 23rd Street, New York, N.Y. 10010
Published simultaneously in Canada by
Penguin Books Canada Limited

Chapter 5 of this book appeared originally in *Esquire*.

LIBRARY OF CONGRESS CATALOGING IN PUBLICATION DATA
Karnow, Stanley.
   Vietnam: a history.
   Published in conjunction with a 1983 PBS
program: Vietnam, a television history.
   Bibliography: p.
   Includes index.
   1. Vietnamese Conflict, 1961–1975—United States.
2. United States—History—1945–   3. Vietnam—
History.   I. Vietnam, a television history (Television
program).   II. Title.
DS558.K37   1983   959.704′33′73   83-47905
ISBN 0-670-74604-5

Grateful acknowledgment is made to the following for permission to reprint
copyrighted material:
   George Braziller, Inc., New York: Selections from *365 Days* by Ronald J. Glasser.
Copyright © 1971 by Ronald J. Glasser.
   Delacorte Press/Seymour Lawrence: Selection from *If I Die in a Combat Zone, Box Me
Up and Ship Me Home* by Tim O'Brien. Copyright © 1973 by Tim O'Brien.
   Harper & Row, Publishers, Inc.: Abridged excerpts appearing on pp. 320, 321, and 485
from *Lyndon Johnson and the American Dream* by Doris Kearns. Copyright © 1976 by
Doris Kearns.
   Holt, Rinehart & Winston, Publishers: Selections from *A Rumor of War* by Philip
Caputo. Copyright © 1977 by Philip Caputo.
   McGraw-Hill Book Company: Selection from *Born on the Fourth of July* by Ron Kovic.
Copyright © 1976 by Ron Kovic.
   Simon & Schuster, Inc., a Division of Gulf & Western Corporation: Selections from
Westward Ha! by S. J. Perelman. Copyright © 1948, 1975 by S. J. Perelman.

Maps by WGBH Design
Printed in the United States of America
Set in Bembo

For Annette, who was there at the beginning.

They made a wasteland and called it peace.
                              —Tacitus

Preface

The roots of this book reach back to the early 1950s in Paris, where I began my professional career as a journalist. France, supported by the United States, was then fighting to retain its hold in Indochina against the Vietminh, the Communist-led nationalist movement there. As I reported on the French end of the war, I soon became acquainted with the names and places of Vietnam from a distance, but I scarcely imagined that they were to be part of my own experience. Then, in 1959, I was assigned to cover eastern Asia; the region that included Vietnam became my beat for more than two decades thereafter. I visited Vietnam most recently in 1981 for seven weeks, the longest period permitted an American correspondent since the Communists gained control of the entire country in 1975.

Many excellent books have been written on Vietnam, most of them focusing on specific episodes of the American war there or spans of time in its recent history. Given my own background, I considered that I might possess the perspective to produce a panoramic account that, while concentrating primarily on the American intervention, also describes and analyzes at some length the origins of the contemporary conflict. For history is a seamless series of causes and effects, the past, present, and future inexorable. The involvement of the United States in its longest—and undeclared—war did not start when the first American combat battalions splashed ashore at Danang in March 1965. Nor did the Vietnamese struggle against foreign intrusion start with the resistance against French colonial domination. The Southeast Asian peninsula, which the French labeled Indochina, and which encompasses Vietnam, Cambodia, and Laos, has been a battlefield for centuries—as it still is today.

A journalist looking back learns—or ought to learn—that his dispatches from the field were temporal and limited, as befits the nature of his occupation. That is not to say, however, that his observations were necessarily superficial. The Vietnam war was a human tragedy, and I cannot minimize the impact on my mind of having witnessed the ordeal of soldiers and civilians, whatever their allegiance, who lived and died in the conflict. But the role of the historian is to paint a broader canvas, one which also depicts and explains the motives and debates that go into the formulation of policies. It was difficult during the war to penetrate the wall of secrecy behind which decisions were made. Within recent years, however, thousands of confidential documents have been declassified. American and South Vietnamese officials who participated in the process have been receptive to interviews. The Communists in Vietnam in 1981, I discovered, are far more candid than they were at the time of their struggle—as are Soviet and Chinese sources. Nevertheless, memories are selective, and I have approached all recollections with caution.

I undertook this book with no cause to plead. In some instances, fresh evidence compelled me to change or modify a point of view I had previously held. In other cases, new facts reinforced my earlier conclusions. My general attitude, to the extent that I can sum it up succinctly, has been one of humility in the face of a vast and complicated subject.

The book has been linked from its initial conception with "Vietnam: A Television History," a documentary series for television on which I served as chief correspondent. The book and the television series, as different media, parallel each other. The printed word is no match for the intensity of such dramatic film as came out of Vietnam, but on the other hand, the complexities of Vietnam cannot be adequately elucidated on a screen.

The idea for the series, which has been produced under the auspices of WGBH, the public television station in Boston, was originally proposed to me in 1978 by Lawrence Grossman, president of the Public Broadcasting Service. Richard Ellison, an independent producer, had been simultaneously contemplating such a project. It seemed logical for us to collaborate. With the help of Elizabeth Deane of WGBH, we began the arduous task of organizing the enterprise and raising funds. I had not, as a writer, anticipated the intricacies inherent in producing films—especially on a topic so immense in its scope as the Vietnam war. My thanks to Mr. Grossman for introducing me to the field. I am particularly grateful to Mr. Ellison, executive producer of the series, for his patience toward a novice in our cooperative television endeavor.

I am indebted to numerous associates, consultants, and others, whose names are listed in the acknowledgments that follow the text. My special gratitude to Karen Johnson, director of publications at WGBH, and to her deputy, Carol Hills. Elise Katz, photo researcher at WGBH, is responsible for the photographic sections. I depended heavily on Lawrence Lichty of the University of Maryland, director of media research for the television project, who generously put his encyclopedic knowledge at my disposal. Jane Schorall furnished important historical research, for which I am thankful. I cannot sufficiently express my obligation to Gail Lewin, my editorial assistant, for her friendship and aid.

Elisabeth Sifton, editor in chief of The Viking Press, again demonstrated her erudition and skill, providing me with invaluable guidance.

Finally, I relied more than they realize on my wife, Annette, and our children, Curtis Edward, Catherine Anne, and Michael Franklin, for their comments, forbearance, and unflagging encouragement.

S.K.

Potomac, Maryland
May 1983

Contents

Photographs appear at opening of each chapter.
Maps appear on pages 102, 111, 203, 333, 524, 662.

Vietnam

1 The War Nobody Won

The town of Langson, near the border of China, was partly destroyed when Chinese forces invaded Vietnam in early 1979. The Vietnamese preserve the ruins as testimony to what they call Chinese aggression.

The Vietnam memorial in Washington, D.C., a wall of polished black granite bearing the names of 57,939 Americans who died or are missing in action in the Vietnam war, was dedicated in November 1982.

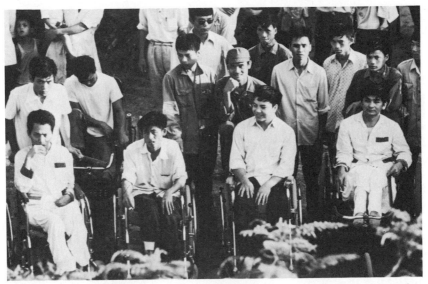

Wounded veterans watch a
soccer match in Vietnam
after the war. Though
Vietnamese authorities
never published the
figures, estimates are that
the Communists lost some
600,000 men in the
struggle.

Thousands of Vietnam
veterans and their families
appeared in Washington in
November 1982 to
commemorate the
American soldiers who
died in the war. They
participated in a parade
and other ceremonies,
including a vigil at the
National Cathedral.

A few of the more than one million Vietnamese who fled Vietnam after the war. These "boat people" languish aboard a ship in Manila Bay, awaiting authorization by the Philippine government to land. Thousands of refugees are still confined to camps throughout Southeast Asia.

A Texan with the family of Vietnamese refugees she has adopted. Nearly a half-million Vietnamese immigrated to the United States following Vietnam's conquest by the Communists in April 1975.

Peasants in Tayninh, a province in the southern part of Vietnam, work in an area defoliated by American herbicides during the war. Many of the 250,000 acres of forest in the area, ruined in 1966 alone, remained barren for years after the war.

The mausoleum in Hanoi containing the embalmed body of Ho Chi Minh is one of the few new structures built in the city. The mausoleum, designed by Soviet architects, was modeled on Lenin's tomb in Moscow. Ho died in September 1969.

A "re-education" camp in southern Vietnam for former Saigon government officers arrested after the war. More than 50,000 political prisoners remain in such camps, many of them suffering from mistreatment and hunger.

Peasants at a "cooperative," the government euphemism for a collective farm, in southern Vietnam. The Communist authorities were compelled to reverse the collectivization programs in the years after the war, when peasant opposition reduced food production.

Young Vietnamese in Ho Chi Minh City continue to defy "socialist transformation." The T-shirt is either a remnant from the American period or a new copy, and the motor scooters are fueled by black-market gasoline.

The manners and mores of the old regime continue in Ho Chi Minh City, formerly Saigon, despite the Communist takeover. Two young prostitutes ply their trade near youths peddling black-market American cigarettes.

One of the saddest legacies of the war are Amerasian children like this girl, the offspring of a GI and a Vietnamese woman. Ostracized by the Communists, they survive by begging or hawking black-market wares.

The skulls piled up in Phnompenh, capital of Cambodia, are those of victims of genocide carried out by the Khmer Rouge, the Cambodian Communist movement. As many as two million people may have been slaughtered in the purge.

Yes, we defeated the United States. But now we are plagued by problems. We do not have enough to eat. We are a poor, underdeveloped nation. Waging a war is simple, but running a country is very difficult.

—Pham Van Dong

Vietnam is still with us. It has created doubts about American judgment, about American credibility, about American power—not only at home, but throughout the world. It has poisoned our domestic debate. So we paid an exorbitant price for the decisions that were made in good faith and for good purpose.

—Henry Kissinger

The memorial, an angle of polished black stone subtly submerged in a gentle slope, is an artistic abstraction. Yet its simplicity dramatizes a grim reality. The names of the dead engraved on the granite record more than lives lost in battle: they represent a sacrifice to a failed crusade, however noble or illusory its motives. In a larger sense they symbolize a faded hope—or perhaps the birth of a new awareness. They bear witness to the end of America's absolute confidence in its moral exclusivity, its military invincibility, its manifest destiny. They are the price, paid in blood and sorrow, for America's awakening to maturity, to the recognition of its limitations. With the young men who died in Vietnam died the dream of an "American century."

Thousands of Vietnam veterans streamed into Washington on a crisp November weekend in 1982, along with their families and the families of the dead, to dedicate the memorial. Some were paraplegics in wheelchairs, others amputees. They wore fatigues or business suits, and several came in full combat gear. There were speeches and reunions and a parade, and a solemn service at the National Cathedral, where volunteers had held a candlelight vigil throughout the week, reciting the names of the nearly fifty-eight thousand killed and missing in action, one by one. From afar, the crowds resembled the demonstrators who had stormed the capital during the Vietnam war to denounce the conflict. But past controversies were conspicuously absent this weekend. Now Americans appeared to be redeeming a debt to the men who had fought and died—saluting their contribution, expiating their suffering. The faces, the words of dedication, and the monument itself seemed to heal wounds. The two names at the head of the memorial—Dale R. Buis and Chester M. Ovnand—evoked my own recollection of a distant event.

I first visited South Vietnam in July 1959, soon after arriving in Asia as chief correspondent for *Time* and *Life* magazines. Insurgents were just emerging to challenge the regime created there five years before, when an international conference held in Geneva had partitioned the country following the French defeat. The term Vietcong, a pejorative label invented by the South Vietnamese government to brand the rebels as Communists, had not yet been conceived—and they were still known as the Vietminh, the movement that had vanquished the French. Several hundred American military advisers had been assigned to train and equip the South Vietnamese army, but signs of serious trouble were rare. Then, on the evening of July 8, an incident occurred at a camp near Bienhoa, the headquarters of a South Vietnamese army division twenty miles northeast of Saigon. I drove there the next day to gather the details.

Six years later, when the United States was pouring men, money, and matériel into an expanding struggle, Bienhoa became the site of a gigantic American base, and the town degenerated into a sleazy tenderloin of bars and brothels. In 1959, however, it was still a sleepy little provincial seat—its church, stucco villas, and tree-lined streets the remnants of a century of French colonial presence. Driving through the heat and humidity of a tropical morning, I caught my first glimpses of a land still undisturbed by war. Peasants in black pajamas and conic straw hats bent over rice stalks in flooded fields, the slow rhythm of their labor testimony to the infinite patience of Asia, and busy village markets along the route advertised the country's fertility. But pulling into the army camp, I could almost taste the start of a war whose eventual magnitude would have then strained my wildest fancies.

The night before, six of the eight American advisers stationed at Bienhoa had settled down in their mess after supper to watch a movie, *The Tattered Dress,* starring Jeanne Crain. One of them had switched on the lights to change a reel when it happened. Guerrillas poked their weapons through the windows and raked the room with automatic fire—instantly slaying Major Buis and Master Sergeant Ovnand, two South Vietnamese guards, and an eight-year-old Vietnamese boy.

The Americans were not the first U.S. soldiers killed in Vietnam. Lieutenant Colonel A. Peter Dewey of the Office of Strategic Services had been gunned down accidentally by a Vietminh band outside Saigon as far back as September 1945. And a daredevil American pilot, Captain

James B. McGovern—nicknamed Earthquake McGoon after a character in the *Li'l Abner* comic strip—crashed to his death while flying supplies to the beleaguered French garrison at Dienbienphu in May 1954. But Buis and Ovnand were the first to die during the Vietnam Era, the official American euphemism for a war that was never formally declared.

My dispatch about the incident at Bienhoa earned only a modest amount of space in *Time* magazine—it deserved no more. For nobody could have imagined then that some three million Americans would serve in Vietnam—or that nearly fifty-eight thousand were to perish in its jungles and rice fields and their names to be etched, twenty-three years after, on a memorial located within sight of the monuments to Washington and Lincoln.

Nor did I then, surveying the bullet-pocked villa at Bienhoa, even remotely envision the holocaust that would devastate Vietnam during the subsequent sixteen years of war. More than four million Vietnamese soldiers and civilians on both sides—roughly 10 percent of the entire population—were to be killed or wounded. Most of the South Vietnamese dead were interred in family plots. Traveling in the north of the country after the war, I observed neat rows of whitewashed slabs in every village cemetery, each bearing the inscription *Liet Si,* "Hero." But the tombs were empty; the bodies had been bulldozed into mass graves in the south, where they had fallen.

In human terms at least, the war in Vietnam was a war that nobody won—a struggle between victims. Its origins were complex, its lessons disputed, its legacy still to be assessed by future generations. But whether a valid venture or a misguided endeavor, it was a tragedy of epic dimensions.

History is an organic process, a continuity of related events, inexorable yet not inevitable. Leaders and the people who follow them make and support choices, but within the context of their experience and aspirations. The roots of the American intervention in Vietnam were planted and nurtured in what Professor Daniel Bell has called America's concept of its own "exceptionalism."

"Westward the course of empire," wrote George Berkeley, the Anglican bishop and philosopher, heralding fresh horizons ahead as he departed from England for America in 1726. And, a century later, other Europeans echoed his celebration of the new society. To Hegel America was "the land of the future," beckoning "all those who are weary" of the old continent, while Tocqueville perceived it to be a beacon, its democratic institutions, natural wealth, and individual opportunities serving as a model for decadent Europe, torn by poverty, frustration, class tensions, and ideological turmoil. The notion of singularity also inspired Americans themselves, and the freighted phrase manifest destiny signified belief in their obligation to export their benefits to less privileged civilizations abroad.

The phrase, coined in 1845 to promote the annexation of Texas, was originally intended to justify America's expansion toward its natural boundaries. It was the slogan of reformers, the sponsors of the Homestead Act, who sought to open new territories to small farmers, among them the German and Irish immigrants who had fled to the young United States in quest of freedom and security. Soon it was amplified by such idealists as Walt Whitman, who foresaw America projecting its "happiness and liberty" to the ancient cultures of Asia. Later, progressives like John F. Kennedy and Lyndon B. Johnson, convinced they were extending their liberal ethic to Vietnam as an antidote to totalitarianism, might have borrowed from Whitman:

Facing west from California's shores,
Inquiring, tireless, seeking what is yet unfound,
I, a child, very old, over waves, towards the house of maternity, the land
  of migrations, look afar,
Look off the shores of my Western sea, the circle almost encircled. . . .

The doctrine of manifest destiny was distinct from the imperialist dynamic that flourished around the turn of the century. The United States did reach out to grab the Hawaiian islands, Guam, and part of Samoa, and it took over Puerto Rico, Cuba, and the Philippines after defeating Spain. But while the European powers were then carving up Asia and Africa, there was little inclination in America for dominating foreign territories. In contrast to the Europeans, who needed overseas raw materials and outlets for their industries, the United States could rely on its own resources and a vast domestic market. Besides, as former rebels against oppressive British colonialism, Americans were instinctively repelled by the idea of governing other peoples. Distinguished molders of opinion at the time, like Andrew Carnegie and President Charles Eliot of Harvard, vigorously opposed imperialism, asserting among their arguments that it violated free trade.

So Cuba was granted independence, and bids by Haiti and San Domingo to become American dominions were rejected. The United

States, unlike the Europeans, refrained from plunging into the plunder of China—and characteristically used an indemnity fund for damages incurred during the Boxer uprising to school Chinese in the United States. The Philippines, the major possession to remain under American tutelage, were finally subdued after a protracted "pacification" campaign which foreshadowed U.S. strategy in Vietnam. But even before that conquest was completed, the Philippines were scheduled for eventual autonomy. Their acquisition had scarcely been hailed with jingoistic fervor, as President William McKinley later confessed: "The truth is, I didn't want the Philippines, and when they came to us as a gift from the gods . . . there was nothing left for us to do but take them all and to educate the Filipinos . . . and, by God's grace, do the best we could do for them."

It would be a gross distortion to suggest that the U.S. presence abroad was consistently prompted by such benign altruism. Big business exploited "our little brown brothers" in the Philippines just as it manipulated the economies of Latin America, often underwriting local despots in order to defend its interests. But a more prevalent strain in American expansionism was evangelical—as if the United States, fulfilling some sacred responsibility, had been singled out by the divinity for the salvation of the planet. The rhetoric of redemption permeated Woodrow Wilson's pledges to "make the world safe for democracy" under American auspices. Franklin D. Roosevelt emphasized the same theme. He encouraged nationalistic self-determination in European colonial areas, while denying that the United States had any hegemonistic ambitions for the period following World War II. Yet, he stressed, international postwar peace and stability would depend on America's global leadership.

These moralistic pronouncements were meanwhile being matched by the zeal of American missionaries, especially in China. There the United States had promulgated an Open Door policy, designed to uphold China's sovereignty against the intrusions of European imperialists. But the missionaries were supposed to work from within to transform China into a Christian nation, thereby spurring the development of its democratic institutions and cementing its ties to America. Quaint though it may seem today, many prominent Americans hoped for a Christian China. Anson Burlingame, a U.S. diplomat and later adviser to the Manchu court, envisioned "the shining cross on every hill and in every valley" of China, and William Jennings Bryan looked forward to a "new Chinese civilization . . . founded upon the Christian movement." Reveries of this kind heightened in the early 1930s, when Generalissimo

Chiang Kai-shek, the Chinese Nationalist leader, converted to a Methodist sect—largely to improve his connections with the West. Many Americans soon saw China becoming a replica of the United States, a hope solemnly expressed by Senator Kenneth Wherry of Nebraska in 1940: "With God's help, we will lift Shanghai up and up, ever up, until it is just like Kansas City."

Exalting the same theme, Henry Luce, the influential proprietor of *Time* and *Life* magazines, unveiled a grand design for America's future on the eve of World War II. He was the son of missionaries and had been born in China. His essay in *Life*, "The American Century," struck a messianic tone: "We need most of all to seek and to bring forth a vision of America as a world power, which is authentically American. . . . America as the dynamic center of ever-widening spheres of enterprise, America as the training center of the skilled servants of mankind, America as the Good Samaritan, really believing again that it is more blessed to give than to receive, and America as the powerhouse of the ideals of Freedom and Justice—out of these elements surely can be fashioned a vision of the 20th century . . . the first great American Century."

Skepticism, even derision, greeted this oracular screed. Luce recanted—particularly in the face of a reply from the eminent theologian Reinhold Niebuhr, who warned against the "egoistic corruption" of nations propelled by such expectations. But the conviction voiced by Luce—the gospel of America's duty to preserve global order—persisted. It acquired fresh urgency after World War II, as the specter of monolithic Communism haunted the United States. Over and over again, successive presidents would explain their foreign policy in cosmic language. "The world today looks to us for leadership," said Harry Truman, and Dwight Eisenhower spoke in similar terms. So did Kennedy, promising in his inaugural address that America would "pay any price, bear any burden, meet any hardship, support any friend, oppose any foe, to assure the survival and the success of liberty." Johnson's goal, as he described it, was to "bring peace and hope to all the peoples of the world," and Richard Nixon portrayed himself as the architect of an international "structure of peace."

The United States thus proceeded on assumptions shared by the government and the public in an atmosphere of bipartisan consensus. The great strategic debates of the postwar period—such as "massive retaliation" versus "flexible response"—focused on means rather than aims. Accordingly, the American involvement in Vietnam was not a quagmire into which the United States stumbled blindly, even less the result of a conspiracy perpetrated by a cabal of warmongers in the White House, the Pentagon, or the State Department. Nor was the nation's slide into the Vietnam war predetermined by historical forces beyond the control of mortals. Legions of civilian and military bureaucrats, armed with tons of data, drafted and discussed plans and options which the president carefully weighed before making choices. The procedure was slow, meticulous, cumbersome, often agonizing.

Inexorably, the decisions reflected America's idea of its global role—a view that the United States could not recoil from world leadership. With the end of the war in Vietnam, however, that view dimmed. The "American Century," Daniel Bell has written, "foundered on the shoals of Vietnam." What remained, as seen in the electorate's support for Ronald Reagan's vow to rebuild the nation's strength, was nostalgia.

Reappraisals of wars tend to be a litany of "what-might-have-beens" which profit from the acuity of hindsight, and the Vietnam experience is no exception. Most Americans, canvassed in the spring of 1965, as Lyndon Johnson sent U.S. ground troops into battle for the first time, supported the commitment. After the war was over, however, Americans overwhelmingly repudiated the intervention as having been a blunder. But roughly the same proportion of the nation holds in retrospect that, once involved, the United States ought to have deployed all its power to succeed. Postwar opinion polls show that Americans blame their political leaders for denying victory to the U.S. forces in Vietnam by imposing restraints on their actions. A survey conducted in 1980 for the Veterans Administration disclosed that 82 percent of former U.S. soldiers engaged in heavy combat there believe that the war was lost because they were not allowed to win—and, astonishingly, 66 percent indicated a willingness to fight again, presumably under fewer limitations. Looking back, too, many senior American officers who served in Vietnam predictably assert that defeat could have been averted had the war been waged more effectively.

General William Westmoreland, who commanded the U.S. forces in Vietnam from 1965 to 1968, compiled a catalogue of grievances in his memoirs. He criticized President Johnson for intensifying the war effort too slowly, refusing to approve incursions against enemy sanctuaries in Laos and Cambodia, giving the South Vietnamese army inadequate equipment, and, among other things, succumbing to the vagaries of domestic opinion by "failing to level" with the American people. He also faulted President Nixon and his national security adviser, Henry

Kissinger, for having "abandoned" the South Vietnamese regime by conceding to a cease-fire accord in January 1973 that permitted North Vietnamese troops to remain in the south. Above all, he denounced American television networks and newspapers for alleged distortions that supposedly turned the people against the war. "A lesson to be learned," he told me in retrospect, "is that young men should never be sent into battle unless the country is going to support them."

Other American military officers are equally troubled as they reassess the war. Like Westmoreland, they rail against the news media, contending that American reporters in Vietnam exaggerated setbacks and atrocities, and thus poisoned opinion at home. For many, though, the culprit was President Johnson, who deliberately declined to rally the U.S. public behind the war effort out of fear that mobilizing the country would doom his domestic economic and social programs. Therefore, they argue, the public's growing disaffection with the conflict eventually disillusioned the American forces in the field. General Fred Weyand, the last American commander in Vietnam, has said, "The American army is really a people's army in the sense that it belongs to the American people, who take a jealous and proprietary interest in its involvement. When the army is committed the American people are committed; when the American people lose their commitment it is futile to try to keep the army committed."

But the professionals also express resentment against their own superiors, and some even argue that the joint chiefs of staff should have resigned in protest against the strictures placed on their prosecution of the war. Air force officers assert, for instance, that full-scale American bombing of North Vietnam from the start would have crushed the enemy. Infantry officers indict the rotation system, under which American troops spent only a year in Vietnam, hardly long enough to develop the *esprit de corps* that boosts morale and combat performance. To retired Brigadier General Robert Montague, who first went to Vietnam in the early 1960s, a crucial error was to have pitched conventional American units, trained to repel Russian aggression in Western Europe, into an unfamiliar terrain of jungles and rice fields, where Vietcong guerrillas could not be distinguished from Vietnamese peasants. Admiral Thomas H. Moorer, a former chairman of the joint chiefs of staff, insisted to me in his damn-the-torpedoes style that the war was waged in the wrong place: "We should have fought in the north, where everyone was the enemy, where you didn't have to worry whether or not you were shooting friendly civilians. In the south, we had to cope with women concealing grenades in their brassieres, or in their baby's diapers. I remember two of our marines being killed by a youngster who they were teaching to play volleyball. But Lyndon Johnson didn't want to overthrow the North Vietnamese government. Well, the only reason to go to war is to overthrow a government you don't like."

Colonel Harry G. Summers, Jr., an instructor at the Army War College, has concluded that the United States won a tactical victory but suffered a strategic failure in Vietnam. A veteran of two tours there, he is less critical of the politicians and the press than many of his fellow officers. He suggests that the basic mistake made by U.S. military planners was to have focused on chasing Vietcong guerrillas, who were deployed to grind down the American forces until big North Vietnamese units were ready to launch major operations. In other words, the Americans exhausted themselves in a costly, futile counterinsurgency effort—"like a bull charging the toreador's cape rather than the toreador." This was Westmoreland's "war of attrition," predicated on the theory that immensely superior U.S. firepower would ultimately wipe out the enemy. "You know," Summers told a North Vietnamese colonel after the war, "you never defeated us on the battlefield." To which his Communist counterpart replied, "That may be so, but it is also irrelevant."

Summers asserts that the Americans should have gone on the offensive late in 1965, after they spoiled a Communist attempt to cut across South Vietnam from the central highlands to the populated areas along the coast. He would have driven through the zone that separated North from South Vietnam, then pushed into neighboring Laos as far as the Thai border on the Mekong in order to seal off the enemy infiltration routes running southward. That alternative, Summers believes, would have required fewer American troops than Westmoreland's grueling "search and destroy" missions, and reduced American losses. The task of fighting the Vietcong guerrillas, in his estimation, should have been relegated to the South Vietnamese army.

But such autopsies are academic exercises, like war games. The essential reality of the struggle was that the Communists, imbued with an almost fanatical sense of dedication to a reunified Vietnam under their control, saw the war against the United States and its South Vietnamese ally as the continuation of two thousand years of resistance to Chinese and later French rule. They were prepared to accept limitless casualties to attain their sacred objective. Ho Chi Minh, their leader, had made that calculation plain to the French as they braced for war in the late 1940s. "You can kill ten of my men for every one I kill of yours," he warned them, "but even at those odds, you will lose and I will win."

"Every minute, hundreds of thousands of people die on this earth," General Vo Nguyen Giap, the Communist commander, once said, and he discounted "the life or death of a hundred, a thousand, tens of thousands of human beings, even our compatriots." During the war against the Americans, he spoke of fighting ten, fifteen, twenty, fifty years, regardless of cost, until "final victory."

American strategists misgauged the North Vietnamese and Vietcong by applying their own values to them. Westmoreland, for example, reckoned that he knew the threshold of their endurance: by "bleeding" them, he would awaken their leaders to the realization that they were draining their population "to the point of national disaster for generations," and thus compel them to sue for peace. Even after the war, he still seemed to have misunderstood the phenomenal discipline and determination of the North Vietnamese. "Any American commander who took the same vast losses as General Giap," he said, "would have been sacked overnight."

Many of the American civilians and soldiers who served in Vietnam were aware of the enemy's perseverance. Patrick J. McGarvey, a CIA analyst, noted in 1969 that no price was too high for Giap as long as he could ravage the American forces, since he measured the situation not by his casualties but by "the traffic in homebound American coffins." Konrad Kellen, a RAND Corporation expert, reached the same conclusion. "Short of being physically destroyed," he wrote of the Communists, "collapse, surrender, or disintegration was—to put it bizarrely— simply not within their capabilities." Lieutenant Colonel Stuart Herrington, a U.S. military adviser in Hau Nghia province in 1971 and 1972, recalled that he "couldn't help admiring the tenacity, aggressiveness, and bravery" of the North Vietnamese troops, who sincerely believed that they were "saving their southern brethren from the clutches of imperialism." An American general who prefers to remain anonymous called them "the best enemy we have faced in our history."

The enemy's intransigence was grotesquely apparent during the war in the spectacle of North Vietnamese and Vietcong corpses stacked up like cordwood following battles. In Vietnam after the war, I interviewed Communist veterans who had spent seven or eight or nine years fighting in the south, their jungle sanctuaries constantly pounded by U.S. bombs and artillery. When I asked them to describe their motives, all replied almost by rote that it had been their duty to "liberate the fatherland." The slogan sounded contrived to my skeptical ears. Yet, as I listened to them, I thought of the old Mathew Brady photographs of Union and

Confederate bodies at Antietam and Manassas and Gettysburg, where thousands of young men had also sacrificed themselves. Theirs had been a cause Americans could comprehend.

Only much later did American officials begin to recognize that the United States had faced a formidable foe. Dean Rusk, secretary of state under Kennedy and Johnson, whose devotion to the anti-Communist crusade in Southeast Asia dated back to the years of the Truman administration, finally admitted in 1971 that he had "personally underestimated" the ability of the North Vietnamese to resist. "They've taken over seven hundred thousand killed, which in relation to population is almost the equivalent of—what? Ten million Americans?" General Maxwell Taylor, who had contributed to Kennedy's decisions on Vietnam and afterward served as Johnson's ambassador in Saigon, had a similar confession to make after the war: "First, we didn't know ourselves. We thought we were going into another Korean war, but this was a different country. Secondly, we didn't know our South Vietnamese allies. We never understood them, and that was another surprise. And we knew even less about North Vietnam. Who was Ho Chi Minh? Nobody really knew. So, until we know the enemy and know our allies and know ourselves, we'd better keep out of this dirty kind of business. It's very dangerous."

President Nixon's chief foreign policy aide, Henry Kissinger, was also baffled and frustrated by the Communists during his secret negotiations with them. Kissinger had tried above all to avoid a repetition of the inconclusive Korean war armistice talks, which had dragged on for two years because, he believed, America had not stiffened its diplomacy with the threat of force. He calculated that the North Vietnamese would compromise only if menaced with total annihilation—an approach that Nixon privately dubbed his "madman theory." But, like his predecessors, Kissinger never found their breaking point. His later claims to the contrary, the Communists agreed to a cease-fire in October 1972 only after he had handed them major concessions that were to jeopardize the future of the South Vietnamese government.

The real pressure on the Nixon administration to reach a settlement in Vietnam came from the American public, which by that time wanted peace at almost any price—for reasons that Kissinger himself had perceived four years before. Early in 1968, on the eve of Tet, the Asian lunar New Year, the Communists had launched a dramatic offensive against towns and cities throughout South Vietnam, which Kissinger saw as the "watershed" of the American effort in Vietnam: "Henceforth, no matter how effective our actions, the prevalent strategy could no longer achieve its objectives within a period or with force levels politically acceptable to the American people."

Americans had been prepared to make sacrifices in blood and treasure, as they had in other wars. But they had to be shown progress, told when the war would end. In World War II, they could trace the advance of their army across Europe; in Vietnam, where there were no fronts, they were only given meaningless enemy "body counts"—and promises. So the United States, which had brought to bear stupendous military power to crack Communist morale, itself shattered under the strain of a struggle that seemed to be interminable. An original aim of the intervention, first enunciated by President Eisenhower, had been to protect all of Southeast Asia, whose countries would presumably "topple like a row of dominoes" were the Communists to take over Vietnam. Ironically, as Leslie Gelb of *The New York Times* observed, the real domino to fall was American public opinion.

The public, distressed by mounting casualties, rising taxes, and no prospect of a solution in sight, turned against the war long before America's political leaders did. Doubts had crept over many members of Congress. Yet except for a handful of senators, among them William Fulbright, Wayne Morse, Ernest Gruening, Gaylord Nelson, and Eugene McCarthy, few translated their private misgivings into open dissent. Not until March 1968, when he decided to run for the presidency, did John F. Kennedy's brother Robert, the senator from New York, denounce the American commitment to South Vietnam—having initially been one of its vocal advocates. Nor was there much dissidence at the upper echelons of the executive branch, apart from George Ball, a senior State Department figure during the Kennedy and Johnson administrations. Ball later looked back on the war as "probably the greatest single error made by America in its history." Robert McNamara, who served both Kennedy and Johnson as defense secretary, may have done more than any other individual to mold U.S. policy in Vietnam, but he lost confidence by late 1967 and came close to an emotional breakdown. He has remained silent on the subject since then.

McNamara's successor, Clark Clifford, had been a strong proponent of a vigorous military approach to Vietnam before taking charge of the Defense Department. A sensitive political animal, his antennae sharply attuned to the national mood, he changed overnight, and played the decisive part in persuading President Johnson to alter his course. In 1981, as I interviewed him in his luxurious Washington law office, he tried to put the Vietnam experience in perspective: "Countries, like human beings, make mistakes. We made an honest mistake. I feel no sense of shame. Nor should the country feel any sense of shame. We felt that we were doing what was necessary. It proved to be unsound."

Such admissions scarcely console the South Vietnamese, who by 1973 had discovered to their dismay that America, after twenty years, would not wage the war indefinitely. Bui Diem, who served as South Vietnam's ambassador to the United States and remained in America, draws a broader lesson from the phenomenon: "Small nations must be wary of the Americans, since U.S. policies shift quickly as domestic politics and public opinion change. The struggle for us was a matter of life or death. But, for the Americans, it was merely an unhappy chapter in their history, and they could turn the page. We were allied, yet we had different interests."

Fortunately, the Vietnam failure has not gripped the United States in a torment of recrimination of the kind that followed China's fall to Communism. No congressional committees have staged inquisitions of allegedly "un-American" citizens. Nor has a demagogue emerged to match Senator Joseph McCarthy, whose cynical witch-hunts in the 1950s put a generation on trial. Despite his portrayal of the struggle as a "noble cause" betrayed by politicians, President Reagan refrained from making it an issue. Perhaps the turmoil that convulsed the nation during the war left Americans too exhausted to embark on a quest for blame. Or perhaps the trauma was so profound that they prefer to forget. Yet, as Kissinger says, "Vietnam is still with us. It has created doubts about American judgment, about American credibility, about American power—not only at home, but throughout the world. It has poisoned our domestic debate. So we paid an exorbitant price for the decisions that were made in good faith and for good purpose."

Few places in America paid as high a price as did Bardstown, a Kentucky community of seven thousand, sixteen of whose boys died in the war. Early in 1983, a decade after the last American troops left Vietnam, a CBS television team visited Bardstown to capture its postwar mood. "I personally can't see that we accomplished anything," said one veteran, and another added: "A lot of people want to make sure that we don't engage in that type of situation again." Gus Wilson, mayor when the young men departed with their national guard unit in 1968, was still mayor: "We believed that the first thing that you did for your country was to defend it. You didn't question that. But I think we realized as we went along—maybe later than we should have—that the government was pulling a bit of a flimflam. We weren't getting the truth. The Vietnam war was being misrepresented to the people—the way it was conducted, its ultimate purpose. Though I'm still a patriot, I ended up very disillusioned."

Millions of Americans share Gus Wilson's sentiment. And their collective disenchantment, known as the Vietnam syndrome, has restrained U.S. leaders from undertaking hazardous ventures since the war ended. Had it not been for Vietnam, the Carter administration might have maneuvered either openly or covertly to thwart the advance of leftist movements in Ethiopia and Angola, or to save the Shah of Iran from collapse. Both President Reagan and the Congress went through a tortured debate before committing U.S. marines to a multinational peacekeeping force in Lebanon. The fear of entanglement in another jungle conflict has also ranged the American people squarely against involvement in the crises testing Central America. Indeed, the divergent attitudes of Americans toward the rebellion in El Salvador today and the growing insurgency in South Vietnam two decades ago exemplify the dramatic difference.

By the end of 1963, American assistance to South Vietnam was costing $400 million annually. Some twelve thousand military advisers were serving there, and fifty of them had been killed during the four previous years—even though their assignment theoretically prohibited their engagement in battle. Yet a poll published at the time disclosed that 63 percent of Americans were paying "little or no attention" to the situation. Nor did Vietnam cause much worry on Capitol Hill. In August 1964, the Congress passed the Tonkin Gulf resolution with barely a murmur of dissent, thereby giving President Johnson what one of his aides was to call "the functional equivalent of a declaration of war." The nation's lack of interest in Vietnam then was equally apparent in the fact that, until the U.S. marines splashed ashore in the spring of 1965, only five American news organizations maintained staff correspondents in Saigon.

Contrast the disregard for Vietnam then with America's jittery focus on El Salvador later. Though only fifty-five U.S. military advisers were serving there in early 1983, American regulations tightly circumscribed their activities in order to avoid incidents that might exacerbate apprehensions at home. The rules barred them from participating in Salvadoran army operations or even from carrying weapons larger than a revolver—and, in February 1983, three American officers discovered on a combat mission were unceremoniously relieved of their duties. Congress bluntly rebuffed President Reagan's first secretary of state, General Alexander Haig, when he attempted to step up the U.S. involvement in Central America in 1981. Opinion surveys two years later divulged that

59 percent of Americans opposed the presence of military advisers in El Salvador, and 72 percent disapproved of an increase in U.S. military aid to the Salvadoran government. Paradoxically, a majority of Americans agreed that a Communist takeover of El Salvador would jeopardize the security of the United States, but that risk seemed to be preferable to American intervention. David Reichhart, a Michigan schoolteacher, told a *New York Times* interviewer: "I don't want Communism to come into this hemisphere, but I don't think the people of this country should be responsible for having to go in and fight."

The echo of Vietnam resonates through these recent surveys. By a margin of two to one, respondents to a *Washington Post* study replied in 1982 that they foresaw El Salvador becoming another Vietnam, and the analogy pervaded a *New York Times* poll. "Vietnam went on year after year," said Carl W. Koch, Jr., of Collingswood, New Jersey, "and I'm afraid that we'll get into El Salvador in the same way." Dennis F. Leary, a Massachusetts air-conditioner repairman, expressed the fear that "maybe we'll take it too lightly, like we did in Vietnam"; "we shouldn't put troops on the line if we're not ready to back them one hundred percent." Mingled in this nervousness, too, was a hint of the isolationism that had permeated America before World War II propelled the nation into assuming global obligations. "It seems like we're always getting pulled in by other people's problems," remarked Cynthia Crone of Payne, Ohio. "We've got enough problems of our own to deal with."

Even if Vietnam had not shaken public confidence in America's role in world affairs, the United States was in no condition following the war to play international gendarme. For the struggle had, along with its other casualties, ruined the nation's military establishment. As late as 1980, army chief of staff General Edward C. Meyer warned Congress that he was presiding over a "hollow" force—short of personnel, experience, and equipment.

The U.S. army in Vietnam was a shambles as the war drew to a close in the early 1970s. With President Nixon then repatriating the Americans, nobody wanted to be the last to perish for a cause that had clearly lost its meaning, and the name of the game for those awaiting withdrawal was survival. Antiwar protests at home had by now spread to the men in the field, many of whom wore peace symbols and refused to go into combat. Race relations, which were good when blacks and whites had earlier shared a sense of purpose, became increasingly brittle. The use of drugs was so widespread that, according to an official estimate made in 1971, nearly one third of the troops were addicted to opium or heroin, and marijuana smoking had become routine. Soldiers not only disobeyed their superiors but, in an alarming number of incidents, actually murdered them with fragmentation grenades—a practice dubbed "fragging." An ugly scandal surfaced after officers and noncoms were arraigned for reaping personal profits from service clubs and post exchanges. Morale also deteriorated following revelations of a massacre in which a U.S. infantry company slaughtered more than three hundred Vietnamese inhabitants of Mylai village in cold blood—an episode that prompted GIs to assume that their commanders were covering up other atrocities.

American strategists were appalled by the broader impact of the struggle on the U.S. armed forces. Between 1965 and the departure of the last American combat soldier in early 1973, the bill for Vietnam had totaled more than $120 billion—much of which would have normally been invested in the modernization of the nation's defenses. As a result, America's security structure had in several respects become an anachronism, its divisions in Western Europe no match for their Warsaw Pact adversaries, in either skill or weapons. Moreover, Lyndon Johnson's reluctance to increase taxes or to impose economic controls to pay for the Vietnam war had caused inflation that the Arab oil embargo of 1973 compounded; the costs of rebuilding the American military establishment soared. By 1975, U.S. defense spending in real terms was roughly $4 billion per year lower than it had been a decade earlier. But inflation was not the only factor.

Richard Nixon ended an inequitable and unpopular draft in order to curry favor with voters. He regretted the move later—as would military professionals and many political figures, both conservative and liberal. For one thing, GI salaries had to be raised to competitive civilian levels to encourage enlistments, and soon the defense budget was consumed by wages. Volunteers were also attracted from among the underprivileged and undereducated—young men often least qualified to handle a modern army's sophisticated technology. Hostility to the war had damaged university and college reserve officer training programs, whose enrollments dropped precipitously from more than two hundred thousand in 1968 to some seventy-five thousand by 1973. An important source of bright, innovative, open-minded leadership narrowed, leaving much of the army's management to superannuated bureaucrats.

American military planners were also influenced by their observations of the Yom Kippur war fought in the Sinai desert between Israel and Egypt at the end of 1973. That collision portended the kind of conflict that the United States might face in Europe—a confrontation waged in open terrain by large infantry units dependent on tanks, tactical missiles, and transport helicopters. As a consequence, they downgraded the counterinsurgency doctrines that had been designed to check guerrillas in the jungles of Asia, Africa, and Latin America and returned to conventional concepts. In the decade since, the American army has regained much of its former strength—though, as General Meyer points out, it is still a force "in transition."

Its social profile has changed. More than 85 percent of army volunteers in 1982 were high school graduates, compared to 67 percent two years before. The economic slump stimulated enlistments among the jobless, who preferred a relatively well-paid stint in uniform to unemployment, and recruiters shifted their drives away from black ghettos to the white suburbs, where they had surprising success in signing up middle-class youths. And, while the memory of Vietnam is still fresh, military service has again acquired a measure of respectability in American eyes. But the army trailed the Reagan administration's list of defense priorities, far behind the development of a strategic nuclear arsenal.

The image of the Vietnam veteran may have benefited from the gradual renewal in public esteem for the armed forces, and it clearly did from the monument in Washington. Yet many veterans feel themselves to be members of a dislocated generation, their place in the society uncomfortable, undefined, almost embarrassing—as if the nation has projected onto them its own sense of guilt or shame or humiliation for the war. Portrayals of the Vietnam veteran in the news media are frequently two-dimensional distortions. He is neither the junkie strumming a guitar in a California commune nor the bustling huckster making millions in Houston real estate. Most GIs returned from Vietnam quietly and unobtrusively, blending back into the population. But the war crippled an unusually high proportion of them, physically and mentally, in ways that are not quickly visible.

Thousands of soldiers in Vietnam were exposed to Agent Orange, a chemical herbicide, which may have afflicted them with cancer, skin disease, and other disorders. A Veterans Administration psychiatrist, Dr. Jack Ewalt, estimates that some seven hundred thousand vets suffer from various forms of "post-traumatic stress disorder," the modern term for "shell shock" in World War I and "battle fatigue" in World War II. Vietnam caused many more cases than those conflicts, however. Its symptoms, which can occur ten or even fifteen years later, range from panic and rage to anxiety, depression, and emotional paralysis. Crime, suicide, alcoholism, narcotics addiction, divorce, and unemployment among Vietnam veterans far outstrip the norm. A massive study published in 1981 by the Center for Policy Research and the City

University of New York concluded that those who served in Vietnam "are plagued by significantly more problems than their peers."

War is war. Why was Vietnam distinctive?

The danger was pervasive and chronic. I spent three years in the army during World War II, much of the time at airfields and supply depots in northeastern India, without ever hearing a shot. But there were no secure areas in Vietnam. A GI assigned to an office in Saigon or a warehouse in Danang could be killed or injured at any moment of the day or night by Communist mortars or rockets. And during his one-year tour an infantryman humping the bush was in combat almost continually—harassed by enemy mines, booby traps, and snipers if not engaged in direct clashes. Philip Caputo, one of the more eloquent chroniclers of the Vietnam war, has noted by comparison that U.S. marine units, celebrated for their exploits against the Japanese in the Pacific campaign, fought for no longer than six or eight weeks during all of World War II.

The average age of the American soldier in Vietnam was nineteen, seven years younger than his father had been in World War II, which made him more vulnerable to the psychological strains of the struggle—strains that were aggravated by the special tension of Vietnam, where every peasant might be a Vietcong terrorist. William Ehrhart, a former marine, recalled a flash of the past that, years after the war, still haunts his dreams: "Whenever you turned around, you'd be taking it in the solar plexus. Then the enemy would disappear, and you'd end up taking out your frustrations on the civilians. The way we operated, any Vietnamese seen running away from Americans was a Vietcong suspect, and we could shoot. It was standard operating procedure. One day I shot a woman in a rice field because she was running—just running away from the Americans. And I killed her. Fifty-five or sixty years old, unarmed, and at the time I didn't even think twice about it."

Paradoxically, the wonders of modern science contributed to the plight of Vietnam veterans. Medical helicopters were so fast and efficient that a GI wounded in action could be on an operating table within fifteen minutes. Statistics tell the story. During World War II, roughly one out of every four U.S. marine casualties died. But survivors in Vietnam outnumbered the dead by a ratio of seven to one, and men who might have perished on the battlefield are now alive—often invalids in need of constant care.

American soldiers in other wars gauged progress by conquering territory; seizing the next town on the route to victory sustained their morale. In Vietnam, by contrast, GIs captured and recaptured the same ground, and not even the generals could explain the aim of the fighting. The only measure of success was the "body count," the pile of enemy slaughtered—a futile standard that made the war as glorious as an abattoir. So homecoming troops were often denounced for bestiality or berated for the defeat—or simply shunned. John Kerry, later elected lieutenant governor of Massachusetts, recalled his return: "There I was, a week out of the jungle, flying from San Francisco to New York. I fell asleep and woke up yelling, probably a nightmare. The other passengers moved away from me—a reaction I noticed more and more in the months ahead. The country didn't give a shit about the guys coming back, or what they'd gone through. The feeling toward them was, 'Stay away—don't contaminate us with whatever you've brought back from Vietnam.' "

Different veterans bear different grievances. Some want more assistance, improved counseling, better jobs. Others continue to wage the war or protest against it; many are still striving to understand what happened. Above all, they seem to be seeking respect and justice—the debt that nations owe their warriors. Monuments and parades and requiems may not be enough.

America's postwar troubles pale in comparison to conditions in Vietnam, which I revisited in early 1981. I rediscovered a land not only ravaged by a generation of almost uninterrupted conflict, but governed by an inept and repressive regime incompetent to cope with the challenge of recovery.

Rebuilding Vietnam would have been a stupendous task under the best of circumstances. The war shattered its economy, disrupted its social texture, and exhausted its population in both the north and the south. But the Communists, showing the same intransigence that inspired them to resist the tremendous U.S. military machine, committed blunders that ruined their chances of winning the peace. Today one of the most impoverished places on earth, Vietnam faces bleak prospects. Prime Minister Pham Van Dong admitted as much as we chatted in French in an ornate salon of a Hanoi mansion that had once housed France's colonial governor. An energetic septuagenarian whose entire life has been devoted to struggle, he appeared to be overwhelmed by Vietnam's present circumstances: "Yes, we defeated the United States. But now we are plagued by problems. We do not have enough to eat.

We are a poor, underdeveloped nation. *Vous savez*, waging a war is simple, but running a country is very difficult."

In 1977, Pham Van Dong and his comrades squandered an opportunity to establish diplomatic ties with the United States. Secretary of State Cyrus Vance and one of his chief aides, Richard Holbrooke, were keen to grant American recognition to Vietnam as a step toward a reconciliation, and President Jimmy Carter favored the move. But Holbrooke promptly ran into a stone wall when the negotiations started in Paris. The Vietnamese insisted, as a precondition, on some $3 billion in "war reparations"—and cited a secret pledge of this aid to them by President Nixon in early 1973 as an incentive to sign the cease-fire agreement. Nixon's promise, which lacked the approval of Congress, was probably illegal, but the Vietnamese stubbornly clung to their demand, having absurdly factored the potential sum into their economic plans. Late in 1978, realizing their miscalculation, they reversed themselves. By then, however, the propitious moment had passed.

At that stage, President Carter's national security adviser, Zbigniew Brzezinski, was eager to taunt the Soviet Union by elevating America's quasi-official relationship with China to a formal level of diplomatic recognition. He argued that a rapprochement with Vietnam would damage the more important Sino-American connection, since the Vietnamese were then antagonizing the Chinese by edging closer to the Soviet Union. Carter's domestic political advisers backed Brzezinski, contending that U.S. public opinion was still hostile to Vietnam—partly because its government had been uncooperative in delivering the remains of more than two thousand Americans missing in action during the war. Meanwhile, thousands of refugees were beginning to flee Vietnam by sea, and the agony of the "boat people" attracted worldwide attention. And U.S. intelligence devices detected reliable signs of an impending Vietnamese invasion of Cambodia. Plans for the American recognition of Vietnam were shelved, and they are still gathering dust.

Because of their mistake, the Vietnamese forfeited American aid, which almost surely would have been forthcoming in one form or another had they established relations with the United States. American loans and investment, bolstered by trade with the United States, would have helped to stimulate the Vietnamese economy—and make it less dependent on the Soviet Union, whose assistance program of about a billion dollars a year is tightly controlled. But the Vietnamese have not given up hope. On more than one occasion during my weeks in Hanoi, my guide pointed to a large gray villa on Hai Ba Trung Street, a busy downtown thoroughfare, reminding me somewhat sorrowfully that it had been cleaned and renovated and its rats exterminated, awaiting the U.S. diplomatic mission that may never arrive.

When the Communists finally conquered Saigon on April 30, 1975, the North Vietnamese officer who took the government's surrender, Colonel Bui Tin, reassured South Vietnamese officials that they had nothing to fear. "All Vietnamese are the victors and only the American imperialists have been vanquished," he told them. "If you love the nation and the people, consider today a happy day." But soon afterward, the Communists proceeded to shunt four hundred thousand South Vietnamese civil servants and army officers as well as doctors, lawyers, teachers, journalists, and other intellectuals into "re-education" centers—and the concentration camps still hold between fifty and a hundred thousand people.

There are about forty of these camps in the south, several of them jails once used by the Saigon regime to detain its critics. The inmates are reported to suffer from malnutrition, malaria, dysentery, and other diseases as a result of inadequate food and medical care, and accounts of torture and summary executions abound. At one large center, located near the town of Tan Hiep, south of Saigon, those charged with infractions of the rules are beaten and shackled in the sun without water. Elsewhere, they are locked in the same "tiger cages" that the South Vietnamese government employed to incarcerate its dissidents—and which aroused protests in America during the war. Ironically, many of the present prisoners, opponents of the Saigon authorities, initially welcomed and later annoyed the Communists, and they include Vietcong veterans. The system may be less savage than the methods of Stalin and Mao Zedong, who slaughtered millions of their adversaries. But it has been denounced by Amnesty International, an organization that monitors human rights violations.

Apart from its inhumanity, the Vietnamese gulag betrays Vietnam's own interests by discarding the skilled people needed for national recovery. During my visit to Ho Chi Minh City, as Saigon was renamed after the war, I encountered a former professor of medicine recently released from a camp. He and his wife, a lawyer, both intense nationalists, had deliberately remained in Vietnam after the Communist takeover in hopes of contributing to their country's reconstruction. Now, their spirit broken, they dream of escape. Many young engineers, accountants, economists, and other technicians have disappeared into "re-education" centers simply because they were educated in America or had held jobs in the discredited South Vietnamese government. A northern Communist official stationed in the south defended the purge, asserting to me that "we must get rid of the bourgeois rubbish." But Dr. Duong Quynh Hoa, a pediatrician who had played a prominent role in the Vietcong, took a different view. "The ideologues are in command," she told me. "We are wasting our best talent."

Antiquated Marxist ideology also prompted the Vietnamese leaders to commit an egregious error immediately after the war, when they launched a five-year plan that concentrated on developing such heavy industries as steel, chemicals, and cement at the expense of agriculture. Under the plan, ample supplies of food would flow from collective farms as peasants dedicated themselves to producing for the state. But the Communist regime could not generate investment capital for industrial development—partly because of its inability to export and also because Nixon's promised "war reparations" never materialized. Its expectation of fat revenues from offshore petroleum also fizzled, when West German, Italian, Canadian, and French oil companies, hamstrung by bureaucratic red tape, dropped their exploration projects. At the same time, farm output faltered, particularly in the fertile Mekong delta, where peasants accustomed to tilling their own soil resisted collectivization. Villagers in many places killed their water buffalo and oxen rather than have them confiscated, and they left large tracts fallow rather than cultivate rice for the government. The five-year plan proved to be disastrous, and the economy has barely improved since.

The rice harvest, scheduled to reach twenty-one million tons annually in 1980, was still five million tons below that target three years later. The official cereal ration during my stay in Vietnam was about thirty pounds per month—and it consisted mostly of wheat, tapioca, and other starches which the Vietnamese detest. Even so, it was five pounds less than the minimum recommended by the World Health Organization, and this was virtually the only item in the Vietnamese diet. Fish, the main protein, has been scarce because fishermen lack fuel and nets—and because thousands of refugees have fled aboard fishing boats—and meat is a rarity. "A whole generation will bear the stigmata of this famine all their lives," observed the late Dr. Ton That Tung in 1981, formerly Ho Chi Minh's personal physician. And Dr. Duong Quynh Hoa illustrated the crisis vividly to me at her hospital in Ho Chi Minh City. Its wards were packed with children on the brink of starvation, some lying two or three to a cot, others sleeping on the floor, their frail bodies bloated and stunted by hunger—a situation she described in French as "*invivable*"—

almost the equivalent of hopeless—adding with a gesture of futility, "Where do we go from here?"

Vietnam's few industries operate in slow motion or not at all. The production of coal, once a major export, has sunk drastically because of a shortage of trucks, conveyers, and other machinery. Plastics factories have been shut down because there is no hard currency to import polyethylene, and other enterprises are paralyzed for lack of raw materials. The most ordinary goods, like soap or needles or envelopes, cannot be found in Hanoi, where the only department store is virtually empty. Inefficiency, confusion, pilferage, and venality are meanwhile endemic—at a heavy cost to the marginal economy.

About thirty thousand tons of freight are landed daily at Haiphong, the nation's principal northern port, most of it aid from the Soviet Union and other Communist nations. But roughly half of it is stolen or left to rot on the wharves. During my visit there, I saw crates that had been unloaded upside down or broken, and equipment rusting from neglect. The components of a complete French cement plant, still in their containers, had been languishing on a dock for two years. The congestion is ghastly—and deliberate. Customs and harbor officials require bribes. Ships must also bribe the authorities to discharge their cargoes, and the illicit tariff is fixed. Japanese vessels, which can afford the top fee of five thousand dollars, usually turn around in three or four days. The less affluent linger for a month, sometimes six months. International proletarian solidarity notwithstanding, Soviet and East European captains are hit for payoffs.

Overall, instead of expanding at a rate of 14 percent a year as envisioned under the ambitious five-year plan, the Vietnamese economy grew by only 2 percent annually—lagging behind a birthrate of 3 percent (one of the highest in the world) and prolonging a trend that has been going on for more than a half century. Despite wars, Vietnam's population has tripled since 1930, while its rice production has barely doubled in that time. The country's average income today is well under two hundred dollars a year, making it one of the poorest on earth. The rest of Asia is booming, but Vietnam remains an island of poverty—a tragedy given the ingenuity and industriousness of its people, who, spurred by incentives, might well match the dynamism of the South Koreans or the Taiwanese.

"It has always been a disaster for Vietnam to rely on one large friend," Pham Van Dong said a few years ago, referring to China, but the comment could also be applied to the Soviet Union. Vietnamese economic setbacks, together with antagonism to China and tensions with the United States, have propelled the Vietnamese squarely into the Soviet orbit.

The Soviets deliver Vietnam two essentials, oil and grain. They have assigned some four thousand advisers to such projects as improving Vietnam's primitive railways and building electric power plants, and they underwrite the Vietnamese army of occupation in Cambodia. But they drive a hard bargain: they compel the Vietnamese to pay for the aid with handicrafts, raw materials, and other commodities, an arrangement that deprives Vietnam of items that might earn it hard currency in the West to buy the technology the Soviets cannot provide. The Soviets have also been known to resell the products on Western markets at lower prices than the Vietnamese quote, thereby undercutting their own dependents. Worse yet, the Vietnamese lack the goods to repay or even service the loans on schedule, and they are digging themselves deeper and deeper into debt to the Soviets, who refuse to sink more money into Vietnam.

Late in 1982, when a high-ranking Vietnamese delegation went to Moscow to appeal for additional help, Leonid Brezhnev, the ailing Soviet president, spurned the plea on the grounds that he had "considerable programs" of his own to fund. Vietnam's number-two leader, Truong Chinh, who headed the group, emphasized that the Soviet Union had always fulfilled its "international obligations." But the Vietnamese went home without an extra ruble.

The Soviet Union has also taken advantage of its assistance to Vietnam to improve its strategic position in Asia. Its aircraft and warships now use the huge complex erected by the United States at Camranh Bay, but the Vietnamese have consistently rebuffed Soviet requests for permanent rights to the base. They recollect numerous instances in the past of Soviet disregard for their interests—such as the occasion in the spring of 1972 when Brezhnev entertained Nixon handsomely in Moscow just as the United States was bombing Hanoi and mining Haiphong harbor for the first time. They were jittery in early 1983 as Brezhnev's successor, Yuri Andropov, resumed negotiations designed to reach a rapprochement with China, their prime enemy. Andropov manifested his priorities bluntly at Brezhnev's funeral—embracing the Chinese foreign minister and brushing off the official Vietnamese representatives.

Though far less obtrusive than Americans were during the war, the Soviet advisers currently in Vietnam are scarcely objects of admiration. The trim, delicate, supple Vietnamese seem to be almost physically repelled by their presence. The Russians resemble caricatures—big, beefy, sweaty men dressed in dowdy clothes unsuited to the tropical climate. I was reminded, as they wandered forlornly around Hanoi or Ho Chi Minh City, of the big, beefy, sweaty American hard hats who used to work for American construction firms in Southeast Asia—but with a couple of differences. Tiny, tarty Vietnamese girls invariably flanked the Americans, while the Russians are usually accompanied by wives as hefty as themselves. The Americans exuded wealth, while the Russians look like muzhiks without two kopecks to rub together—much less spend lavishly in Vietnam. Keenly aware of the distinction, the Vietnamese deride the Russians as "Americans without dollars." When I was in Hanoi, the Vietnamese were also retailing a joke that reflected both their disappointment with Soviet stinginess and their own destitution. Moscow, rejecting a desperate cry for help, cables Vietnam: "Tighten your belts." To which Vietnam replies: "Send belts."

The Vietnamese Communists blame America for their problems, contending that the United States has urged its allies to withhold assistance from Vietnam because of its invasion of Cambodia. And it is true that the Reagan administration has been pressing various United Nations agencies to be stringent with Vietnam, a tactic that has succeeded. But, publicly and privately, Communist officials concede that they themselves are far more to blame for having failed to provide their people with the incentives to boost trade and production. Hoang Tung, the party propaganda boss, rambling on in impeccable French during a chat in his stuffy Hanoi office, acknowledged: "We made mistakes, and we've learned our lesson. We have not used economic levers. Our egalitarianism has sapped the enthusiasm of the workers."

Following a pivotal meeting in 1979, the Vietnamese Communists gingerly introduced flexible economic policies that made the term "profit motive" fashionable, even to their sectarian extremists. Peasants were allowed to cultivate their own crops and raise livestock for sale in free markets, as long as they fulfilled quotas that their collectives could negotiate with the government. Small merchants and artisans were permitted to function as private entrepreneurs, and state factories switched to paying their employees on a piecework basis—a practice once denounced by Marxists as a heinous capitalist evil. Vietnam's economic structure was decentralized in an effort to "widen the power and the responsibility of localities," as Le Duan, the Communist party chief, explained. The new system went into motion gradually, and it caused as many headaches as it was supposed to cure.

Their failures gave the Vietnamese leaders no plausible alternative to offering the material rewards that stimulate trade and production. A dilemma for a Communist regime, however, is to assure that the reforms that encourage workers, peasants, and merchants do not efface its authority. But by 1981, free market forces were swiftly gathering momentum and eroding the Communist party's controls, and they have been unraveling at a rapid pace since then. A liberal economy requires abundance. With scarcities still severe, the reforms have led to spiraling inflation, mounting inequities, growing cynicism, widespread corruption, and a breakdown of the social, cultural, and political values that the Communists are determined to preserve. One Vietnamese official in Hanoi seemed to be almost nostalgic for the war as he recalled the days when the American bombing stiffened the resolve of the northern population. In Ho Chi Minh City, a Communist cadre said, "For most people, the only ideology that counts is a full stomach."

Nothing has dramatized the revulsion against poverty and repression more vividly than the massive exodus from Vietnam—one of the largest migrations of modern times. Nearly a million people have risked their lives to escape from the country, most by sea. Some fifty thousand of them have died from exposure or drowning, or from attacks by pirates who traditionally maraud the waters off Southeast Asia. At least a half million men, women, and children have also fled from Cambodia and Laos, and all except a hundred thousand still languish in squalid camps along the borders of Thailand. Among the first to leave Vietnam were ethnic Chinese. Many of them, expelled when Vietnam and China clashed in early 1979, were fleeced by Vietnamese Communist officials as they departed. I interviewed several of these refugees as their weathered vessel landed at a Hong Kong wharf.

One, a carpenter, revealed that he and some friends had pooled their hoard of gold to make the voyage from the southern port of Danang for themselves and their families, about sixty people in all. They started by paying local Communist officials bribes amounting to some two thousand dollars to look the other way as they prepared for their trip. Then they bought a fishing boat and equipped it with an auxiliary engine and diesel fuel, an expenditure of five thousand dollars more, and finally began the journey that was to take five weeks. The officials confiscated most of their belongings before they embarked, but they were lucky. Many boats crammed with refugees were intercepted by Vietnamese naval ships, whose officers snatched anything they could grab, including wedding rings. In some instances, the Communist authorities connived with Chinese racketeers to bilk the refugees.

Saigon at the height of the war had stunk of decay. Its bars were drug centers, its hotels brothels, its boulevards and squares a sprawling black market hawking everything from sanitary napkins to rifles—all of it purloined from American warehouses. Soldiers from Ohio and Georgia and Oregon, black and white, their pockets filled with cash, strolled streets crowded with whores and pimps, beggars, orphans, cripples, and other victims of devastation. South Vietnamese army generals, enriched by silent Chinese partners, possessed gaudy villas not far from putrid slums packed with refugees, and government officials and businessmen connived constantly, shuffling and reshuffling the seemingly limitless flow of dollars. It was a city for sale—obsessed by greed, oblivious to its impending doom. Returning six years after the end of the war, I found it strangely the same, despite profound changes.

Some changes were cosmetic. The bars and brothels had been closed. The traffic clog of trucks and taxis and motor scooters was gone, and with it the choking gasoline fumes that had once pervaded the town. Like the city itself, streets and buildings had been renamed to herald the revolution. The Hôtel Caravelle, where foreign correspondents huddled during the war, had become the Doc Lap, or Independence, reserved for senior Communist functionaries. The main thoroughfare, Rue Catinat when I first arrived in Saigon in the 1950s, had been altered in the early 1960s to Tu Do, or Freedom. Now it was Dong Khoi, or Uprising, but everyone still called it Catinat. The U.S. embassy had been taken over by the Vietnamese government oil corporation, and the Communist army had seized the American military headquarters with much of its equipment intact. The airport, formerly as busy as Chicago's O'Hare, was asleep.

Within a day or so, though, I began to sniff deeper changes. When the Communists drove into Saigon in 1975, they were prudently greeted by a dazed population yearning for peace and prepared to cooperate. But instead of proceeding gently, they embarked on a program of wholesale repression, creating neighborhood committees of agents and informers to report on citizens, and arresting anyone even remotely affiliated with the *ancien régime*. Thus I sensed a city stifled by fear and cloaked in an eerie mood of melancholy—a ghostly place. And there were the ghosts of the people I had known before.

The bartender at the Hôtel Caravelle is a familiar face. "*C'est bien de vous revoir, monsieur*," he says softly, extending a limp hand and swiftly turning away to polish glasses, perhaps afraid of further talk. The young woman I recognize on the Rue Catinat, once an assistant to a Japanese colleague, is bolder. She proposes a later rendezvous to pass me a letter to smuggle out to her brother, a refugee in Dallas. I suggest that a meeting might endanger her. She persists—then agrees and walks away sadly, the skirt of her gossamer *ao dai* floating behind her. One evening I visit a distinguished lady, formerly a dissident member of the parliament, and the interlude is hallucinatory. As I approach her splendid house, shrouded by a tangle of tropical vegetation, she sits at a piano on the veranda, playing a Mozart sonata. Her husband, also an old foe of the conquered Saigon government, has just been released from prison but must continue to attend seminars in Marxist doctrine to "remold" his bourgeois mentality. She regrets her past opposition to the former regime, explaining that "with all its faults it was preferable to Communism." I try to stress the brighter side, noting that the "bloodbath" forecast by many Americans and South Vietnamese prophets never happened. "So instead of dying quickly," she answers, "we are dying slowly."

I would have hesitated to generalize from such a narrow sampling had not my impression of the gloom and despair been confirmed by even Communist sources. One of them was Nguyen Phung Nam, the official chief of press relations for Ho Chi Minh City and a frequent companion during my sojourn there. A chubby, amiable fellow who chain-smoked my cigarettes, he was a Vietcong veteran whose experience as a guerrilla dated back to the war against the French. One afternoon, over *apéritifs,* he casually disclosed an astounding personal detail. His wife and three daughters lived near Los Angeles, having escaped from Vietnam among the hundreds of thousands of refugees who fled the country after its reunification under Communist control. "Open the doors," he added, "and everyone would leave overnight."

Dr. Duong Quynh Hoa was more outspoken. A chic woman in her fifties, she had been raised in an affluent southern family of *collaborateurs,* the Vietnamese who embraced French colonial rule in exchange for favors. Her father had taught at a French *lycée* in Saigon, a signal honor for a "native" of his generation. She herself, unusually liberated for a Vietnamese woman, went off to medical school in Paris, where she joined the French Communist party. In 1954, back in Saigon, she entered the resistance against South Vietnamese President Ngo Dinh Diem and his U.S. supporters, serving as a covert Vietnamese agent while she practiced medicine. She was afterward appointed deputy minister of health in the "provisional revolutionary government," the

Vietcong's legalistic rival to the Saigon regime, hiding in the jungles and traveling abroad on propaganda missions. One evening in 1981, as we dined in the midst of the exquisite Chinese and Vietnamese porcelains adorning her comfortable villa, she poignantly confessed her disenchantment. "I've been a Communist all my life," she burst out passionately. "But now, for the first time, I have seen the realities of Communism. It is failure—mismanagement, corruption, privilege, repression. My ideals are gone." She decried the northern Communists who now ran the south. She inveighed against their ignorance of local traits and conditions and their heavy-handed methods—citing as an example their attempt to impose collectivization on the peasants of the Mekong delta, whose desire to own property had inspired many of them to side with the Vietcong against the landed gentry of the area. In her view, the northerners resented the southerners for having prospered from the American presence during the war while they, true Communists, had borne the brunt of the struggle. My guide, Nguyen Phung Nam, shared Dr. Hoa's animosity toward northerners. And their attitude prompted me to wonder whether a better understanding of Vietnam's regional differences might have led the United States to explore a sophisticated diplomatic solution to the conflict—rather than to presume that the Communists were a monolithic force in the country.

Focusing on corruption, Dr. Hoa told me about administrators at her hospital who padded payrolls, took kickbacks from suppliers, and pilfered precious pharmaceuticals for resale on the black market. She also pointed to the wives of Communist generals, who regularly flew from Hanoi to Ho Chi Minh City aboard military aircraft to buy up antiques, jewelry, and other valuables from the remnant *bourgeoisie,* which has been surviving by selling off its possessions cheaply. The abuse of rank reminded me of my days in Saigon, when the wives of South Vietnamese generals amassed fortunes by speculating in real estate, gold, import licenses, and other such ventures. "Exactly," Dr. Hoa replied. "This is still very much a feudal society, whatever its ideological labels."

But it was clear as we sipped Italian coffee and French cognac after dinner that Dr. Hoa herself enjoyed special advantages—not to mention political immunity of some sort, since she had criticized the regime to other foreigners. I figured that she could easily supplement her income by selling an occasional ceramic. As for her blunt talk, I could only guess that the authorities either abided her heresy in order to demonstrate their tolerance, or reckoned that silencing her might alienate her southern sympathizers—who included my press official, Nguyen Phung Nam. The morning after, when I cautiously avoided any comment about her, he volunteered his own opinion. Raising a thumb, he said: "*Elle est épatante.*"

One person whose sentiments I had looked forward to hearing was Phan Xuan An, one of my oldest Vietnamese friends—or so I thought. We had met in Saigon twenty years before, when he represented Reuters, the British news service. Judicious and tireless, he had the best Vietnamese sources in town, and he had generously provided me with reliable information. Such was his skill, in fact, that my successors at *Time* hired him as a staff correspondent—the only Vietnamese journalist to attain full status in an American news organization. Knowing that he had stayed behind after Saigon fell in 1975, I had confidently expected to see him. But my requests for an appointment were repeatedly parried with vague excuses until, finally, I was told the truth.

He had been a clandestine Vietcong operative all along. Now, a top security official, he was off limits to foreigners. Hardly had I recovered from that amazing revelation than I learned that another old friend, Colonel Pham Ngoc Thao, a brilliant South Vietnamese officer, had secretly served the Vietcong as well. He had been murdered for entirely different motives during the war by Saigon government rivals, and his remains had been transferred to the "patriots' cemetery" near Ho Chi Minh City not long before my return there. If An and Thao had fooled correspondents like myself, they also duped the U.S. Central Intelligence Agency, which had counted them among its contacts.

I was fed the party line by a senior member of the People's Committee, the Ho Chi Minh City administration, as we sat under a portrait of Ho in a reception chamber of the gingerbread Hôtel de Ville, the town hall, another splendid French colonial relic. A faceless functionary, he assured me that the "socialist transformation" of the south was proceeding apace as the regime, to popular acclaim, "fundamentally" eradicated prostitution, hooliganism, consumerism, and poisons left over from the dark ages of American capitalist influence. I thanked him profusely for the edifying lecture, which we both knew to be a formality.

The same evening, for example, three whores accosted me just outside my hotel with a ferocity unlike anything I had witnessed during the American era, when clients were plentiful. They could not have been more than nineteen or twenty, and they tugged at my sleeves with aggressive desperation, whispering obscenities in a mixture of pidgin English and fractured French perhaps picked up from their older sisters, or maybe even their mothers. Over coffee next morning, I related the incident to my guide, recalling the alderman's assertion that prostitution was being "fundamentally" eliminated. Nam frowned in mock disbelief. " 'Fundamentally'? Did he say 'fundamentally'? *Pas possible.* He must have meant 'theoretically.' "

The official Communist concession to sex, in modified form, is an improbable ritual—a Saturday night ball for "foreign friends" held in the former U.S. officers' club atop the Rex Hotel. The regime recruits the girls—office employees or shop assistants—and pays them a small fee to dance with Russian, French, Scandinavian, and other Westerners, mostly technicians on aid projects. Colored lights beam around the elaborate room as a rock band blares and a singer, sinuous in her clinging gown, belts out the lyrics. The girls, dazzling creatures in stretch jeans and tight blouses, writhe and wriggle with all the verve of New York or London disco addicts. Then suddenly, at midnight, the party is over, and the Cinderellas go home alone—forbidden to fraternize until the next Saturday night. A European acquaintance, understandably smitten, pursued his lovely partner during the week, eventually luring her to a tryst in a secluded café. I indiscreetly prodded him for details later. "We just talked," he said with a sigh.

The puritanical curb strikes me as sound. For a poignant legacy of the French and subsequent American interventions in Vietnam is the unwanted children. The "Amerasian" kids fathered by U.S. troops may number as many as fifty thousand, the majority concentrated in Ho Chi Minh City and other towns where GIs congregated. Showcase orphanages care for a handful, but the xenophobic Vietnamese shun most as outcasts, denying them education, jobs, and even food rations. Those I saw—some with blond hair and blue eyes, others partly black—were peddling or begging on street corners. The mothers, many ostracized by their families, implore international refugee agency officials to locate the fathers—often identifying them simply as Joe or Bill or Mac, to whom they were "married" for six or eight months in Saigon or Danang fourteen or fifteen years ago.

The Communist regime was initially reluctant to release the Amerasian children, calculating that they might serve as chips in diplomatic bargaining with the United States. President Reagan and the Congress were equally slow to revise the U.S. immigration law. But finally it was amended in 1982 to permit a few thousand children to join their fathers in America. Thousands more—neglected in Vietnam and barred from the United States—are doomed.

I have seen socialist principles transgressed by capitalist practice in Moscow, Warsaw, East Berlin, and other Communist cities, but never so flagrantly as in Ho Chi Minh City, where the commercial vitality of the American years still pulsates. Its avenues and alleys teem with stalls offering everything from American cigarettes and Scotch whiskey to French perfume, German cameras, Japanese radios, and a cornucopia of other products, just as in the bad old days. Vietnamese living overseas send the merchandise to their relatives in Ho Chi Minh City; it arrives legally aboard a weekly Air France flight from Paris. Under the regulations, only the recipients are supposed to consume the merchandise. But they sell it to intermediaries, with the Communist apparatus participating in the business. Nguyen Phung Nam, whose wife in California ships him a monthly parcel, candidly disclosed to me that he could not make ends meet without trafficking in its contents. He also exchanged my dollars at the black market rate, presumably taking a commission.

The Vietnamese currency, the *dong,* is so debased that its black market rate oscillates between ten and fifteen times the official rate. Thus, as in Europe after World War II, the value of imported aspirin, vitamins, toothpaste, and especially cigarettes has escalated astronomically in terms of purchasing power—the spiral dramatizing the pressure of demand on supply in a land with a worthless currency. The arithmetic is startling.

A Vietnamese schoolteacher earns two hundred *dong* a month. A pack of American cigarettes fetches one hundred *dong* at a street stall. So, if his sister in Chicago remembers him with a monthly carton of Marlboros, he can quintuple his income. He can afford to buy meat and vegetables on the free market, which is furnished by peasants who are increasingly entering the consumer circuit. He can also pay off the Communist bureaucracy, thereby ensuring himself against harassment, or he can get involved in one or another of several lucrative rackets, like the exit visa scam.

The scheme is based on a regulation that entitles Vietnamese who have been granted exit visas to procure dollars at the fictitiously low official rate of exchange—even though they lack permits for admission to another country and do not intend to leave Vietnam. By prearrangement, the person issued an exit visa kicks back a portion of the dollars to the official who has authorized the departure document. The cheap greenbacks may be traded on the black market for a huge profit, or used to bribe other officials to hand out travel papers to relatives who can then engage in the same machinations. Some of the hard currency is usually converted into gold, to be laid away for future contingencies. Thousands of Vietnamese are involved in these maneuvers. And behind the scenes are the Chinese of Cholon—the mysterious Chinatown of Ho Chi Minh City. Like the Jews of medieval Europe, they are maligned and persecuted but continue to manipulate gold and money rates. The government relies on them as well for a range of other services, from transacting import deals to supplying scarce spare parts for vehicles.

Only a small fraction of the population has a chance to share in this heady action. Plainly, though, Vietnam increasingly displays that familiar symptom of Communist societies, a "new class" of entrenched bureaucrats and their favorites. The phenomenon is particularly apparent in the emergence of a *jeunesse dorée*—young Vietnamese who zip around Ho Chi Minh City on motor scooters fueled by black market gasoline and hang out in cafés that feature pop tunes played on Japanese stereos. A song that I heard frequently during my stay, recorded by a Caribbean combo, evidently owed its popularity to its melancholy lyrics:

> *I see a boat on a river, it's sailing away,*
> *Down to the ocean, where to I can't say.*

Both official U.S. communiqués and press reports asserted during the war that North Vietnam was being blown to smithereens by American air strikes. Visiting the region for the first time, therefore, I expected to observe ruins everywhere. But Hanoi and Haiphong are almost completely unscathed, and the surrounding countryside appears to have been barely touched. I was reminded of General Curtis LeMay's bloodcurdling cry to "bomb them back to the Stone Age." As I looked at the area, the thought crossed my mind that the north had not advanced far since the Stone Age.

If Ho Chi Minh City is sad, Hanoi is miserable. Apart from the mausoleum containing the embalmed body of Ho Chi Minh—a facsimile of Lenin's tomb in Moscow—nothing new has been constructed there for fifty years. Nor is much done to maintain the buildings that stand. Handsome French colonial villas have slid into decrepitude, their windows broken and their walls mildewed. I was luckily housed at the Thong Nhat, or Reunification, once the elegant Metropole, the best hotel in town. Paint flakes from its ceilings; its plumbing fixtures, which bear the proud emblem of the eminent French firm of Jacob Delafonte, are cracked and leaking. Nobody notices when a rat scurries across the floor of the gloomy lobby, where superannuated European leftists and assorted Asian, African, and Latin American insurgents linger over drinks, still conversing in revolutionary jargon. Some are being trained in Hanoi, a certified center of the struggle against imperialism.

A few peasants, who have drifted into the city with nowhere to sleep, huddle on dark sidewalks at night. An occasional beggar is visible but prostitutes are not—though accommodations could be made, a Western diplomat informed me. Bicycles, the main mode of transportation, throng the streets throughout the day. Explaining the heavy traffic, my guide suggested that many people devote hours to the elementary mechanics of survival, going from one place to another to locate a piece to repair a chair, or to negotiate a couple of ounces of meat for dinner. The young foreign ministry employee also confided to me that he was usually so hungry after work that he spent the equivalent of his daily wage on an afternoon snack—an expense he could afford because he lived with his family. He woefully confessed, however, that he would have to marry soon because he was crowded into a couple of rooms with his mother and two sisters. Marriage was the only way he could find the privacy to be alone with his girl friend.

The northern Vietnamese seem to be remarkably cheerful despite their grim poverty—perhaps because they are disciplined after a generation under Communism, and maybe because they never knew the affluence experienced by their southern compatriots during the American era. In an ironic twist, however, the capitalistic propensities that the Communists were supposed to obliterate in the south are instead creeping northward with alarming speed. During my sojourn in Hanoi, the party newspaper *Nhan Dan* published several editorials warning that the "neo-colonialist culture" of the south was "expanding to the north," where it threatened to "spoil our younger generation and wreck our revolution."

The Communists cannot easily stop the trend, having been compelled by the economic crisis to loosen up in order to spur production. Like southern peasants, those in the north have been encouraged to sell their surplus meat and vegetables at free markets, and their earnings are giving them a consumer mentality. Private entrepreneurs are meanwhile emerging in Hanoi, though more cautiously than in Ho Chi Minh City. I dined frequently at a little *bistro* known only as "the French restaurant," concealed in a squalid alley. The proprietor, a former professor of mathematics, serves such superb *specialités de la maison* as *soupe aux crabes* and *pigeon aux champignons,* accompanied by quite respectable French and Bulgarian wines. The place is not only tolerated by the Communist authorities, but patronized by senior political and military figures who spend as much on a single meal as they officially make in a month. One evening, the clients included a prominent Vietnamese general who paid his bill in dollars.

An obligatory journey for foreign visitors takes one to the shabby town of Langson, on the mountainous frontier with China, which the Chinese partly destroyed in February 1979 in retaliation for Vietnam's invasion of Cambodia. The Vietnamese preserve the ruins as evidence of aggression by their neighbors to the north, and distant rumbles of artillery testify to the continued tension. But for me, as an American, the trip to the remote site was significant for another reason. It underlined the ignorance behind the policy that involved the United States in the Vietnam war.

The U.S. commitment to Vietnam, which began as far back as 1950 with President Truman's decision to help the French to retain their hold over Indochina, was designed to prevent Chinese Communist expansion into Southeast Asia. And it was founded on the notion that Ho Chi Minh was a pawn of the Chinese. But Vietnam and China have been enemies for two thousand years, and their traditional conflict could have been exploited. Instead, American intervention in Vietnam united them in a marriage of convenience that fell apart only after President Nixon and the Chinese engineered a reconciliation that left the Vietnamese out in the cold.

Differences were apparent as early as the Geneva Conference of 1954, when the Chinese pushed the Vietnamese Communists to concede to a partition of Vietnam. For years afterward, hoping that a protracted war would drain the United States, the Chinese pressed the North Vietnamese to keep fighting—and, I gathered in Hanoi, actually reduced aid to them after they began diplomatic talks with the United States in Paris in 1968. The Chinese also tried to restrain North Vietnamese plans to conquer South Vietnam following the final withdrawal of U.S. combat forces from South Vietnam in early 1973. Mao Zedong deemed the prospects for Vietnam's reunification to be as implausible as his own dream of capturing the island of Taiwan. At a meeting in Beijing, he told Pham Van Dong: "I don't have a broom long enough to reach Taiwan, and you don't have a broom long enough to reach Saigon."

So America's attempt to "contain" China by checking the North Vietnamese was misguided. The United States could have conceivably taken advantage of Vietnam's historic hostility toward the Chinese, or at least have explored that option—just as, during the late 1940s, Yugoslavia's resistance to Soviet domination was encouraged. Instead, American strategists, hoping to buttress France's position in Europe, casually rejected the possibility that Ho Chi Minh might not be a pliable Chinese tool.

The American crusade, propelled as it was by the "domino theory," and the naive assumption that the entire region would collapse to the Communists if they won in Vietnam, disregarded the complex nationalistic diversity of Southeast Asia. Two "dominoes"—Laos and Cambodia—have toppled since the war in Vietnam. Much of Laos, however, had been a virtual Vietnamese province for years, and Cambodia suffered almost unimaginable horrors—more because of the insane cruelty of its own Communist regime than as a consequence of Vietnamese ambitions.

The full dimensions of Cambodia's martyrdom will probably never be known or understood. Nevertheless, the evidence accumulated until now already makes the Nazi holocaust seem tame by comparison.

Prince Norodom Sihanouk, the shrewd, nimble, tireless ruler of Cambodia, adroitly maneuvered for years to prevent the conflict in Vietnam from engulfing his country—a serene land of placid people. He yielded to the presence of North Vietnamese and Vietcong sanctuaries in territories adjacent to Vietnam, while acquiescing to American air raids against those targets. But in March 1970, while traveling in Europe, he was overthrown, and his ouster furnished President Nixon with the pretext to send American and South Vietnamese troops into Cambodia in pursuit of the enemy, and the war swiftly spread. Sihanouk's recurrent nightmare, he once told me, was that Cambodia would someday become extinct as a nation, remembered only by the mute magnificence of the temples at Angkor Wat. That day was fast approaching.

Sihanouk's successor, the inept and ailing General Lon Nol, shrank into the relative safety of his capital, Phnompenh, relying on American aircraft to bomb the Vietnamese and growing Cambodian Communist forces tightening their hold over the devastated countryside. On April 17, 1975, Phnompenh fell to the Khmer Rouge, the Cambodian Communist insurgents, just as North Vietnamese and Vietcong battalions were sweeping south toward Saigon. In five years, an estimated half million Cambodians had been killed or wounded, most by American bombs. Worse was yet to come.

The Cambodian Communists, originally organized and trained by their Vietnamese comrades, had begun to assert their autonomy during the early 1970s. Like most Cambodians, they distrusted the dynamic Vietnamese, who had repeatedly intruded into Cambodia over the centuries. They were also swayed by Chinese radicals, who preached Mao Zedong's concept of perpetual revolution. And they evolved their own doctrines. Their leader, Saloth Sar, the son of a minor Cambodian official, had gone to Paris to study. There he picked up the undigested notion of an agrarian utopia, to be created by mobilizing the peasants—a reverie of the kind that Lenin had scorned as "infantile leftism." Returning home to adopt a mellifluous but meaningless *nom de guerre,* Pol Pot, he gained command of the Communist movement, and it grew rapidly after the U.S. and South Vietnamese incursions turned Cambodia into a battlefield. Then, triumphant in 1975, he transformed his ideas into reality.

At first, as they emptied Phnompenh and other towns, Pol Pot's legions seemed to be evacuating the refugees who had swollen the cities during the war in order to ease the economic pressure. But reports trickling out of Cambodia soon revealed a diabolically different story, which was confirmed later by the discovery of mass graves, piles of skeletons, and meticulous records, as well as the testimony of survivors.

The Communists were engaged in exterminating as many as two million Cambodians—a quarter of the population. Most, herded into forced marches or slave labor projects, perished from famine, disease, mistreatment, or exhaustion, and the atrocities included instances of cannibalism. Thousands of middle-class citizens, branded as parasite intellectuals merely because they wore spectacles or spoke a foreign language, were systematically liquidated. Several schools and public buildings were converted into torture chambers, among them a Phnompenh *lycée,* Tuol Sleng, which was equipped with electric shock devices, water tubs, and other such instruments. There the deaths soared to an average of a hundred per day during the first half of 1977, husbands and wives slaughtered along with their children—the victims photographed before and after their murders. The Communists proclaimed the advent of their administration Year Zero, the start of a "new community" that would be cleansed of "all sorts of depraved cultures and social blemishes."

The Vietnamese, after driving into Cambodia in late 1978, halted the slaughter and set up a surrogate regime in Phnompenh. But they have never portrayed their invasion as a humanitarian venture designed to rescue the Cambodian people from almost certain genocide. Indeed, they privately admit, despite their knowledge of the holocaust, they refrained from acting. The real motive for the operation, they explain, was their concern that Pol Pot's forces, underwritten by China, intended to embark on a campaign to annex the Mekong delta and other parts of Vietnam that had formerly belonged to the Cambodian empire. "When we look at Cambodia," a Vietnamese official in Hanoi told me, "we see China, China, China."

Cambodia's future still appears to be dim. An army of two hundred thousand Vietnamese, outfitted and financed by the Soviet Union, is skirmishing with a disparate coalition of three Cambodian factions backed by China—with Prince Sihanouk peculiarly aligned to the Pol Pot group even though the Communists killed several members of his family. Peculiarly, too, the United States endorses Pol Pot's representation in the United Nations—partly to placate China and also to penalize Vietnam for its occupation of Cambodia with Soviet support.

Foreign powers have been penetrating Southeast Asia for centuries, searching for wealth or influence, or to counter the lusts of their rivals. No surge in history had a stronger impact on Southeast Asia than European intervention, which transmuted new ideas and new institutions in the crucible of ancient values and traditional customs. The collision of East and West stimulated Asians both to resist and to adapt, infusing them with the vitality to recover their identity and to shape fresh goals. The experience also stirred Vietnam—and sowed the seeds of a struggle that was to culminate in the inscription of nearly fifty-eight thousand American names on a granite memorial in Washington.

2 Piety and Power

Francis Garnier, a heroic French officer, led an attack against the Citadel in Hué. He was killed, as seen here, by mercenaries fighting for the Vietnamese in December 1873. Accounts of his courage spurred the French imperialist drive to conquer Vietnam.

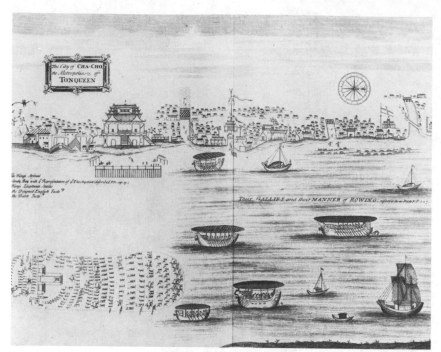

An eighteenth-century
European view of Tonkin,
the northern area of
Vietnam. The British and
Dutch had designated areas
in which foreign traders
were permitted to maintain
commercial posts.

Pierre Pigneau de
Béhaine, bishop of Adran,
the Catholic missionary
who first evoked France's
interest in Vietnam in the
late eighteenth century.
He befriended a pretender
to the Vietnamese throne,
Nguyen Anh (Gia Long),
who founded a dynasty.

Prince Canh, the young
son of Nguyen Anh, who
accompanied Monsignor
Pigneau de Béhaine to the
court of Louis XVI at
Versailles, where he
caused a sensation. His
exotic costume, contrived
for the visit, was more
Indian than Vietnamese.

Alexandre de Rhodes, the
missionary who traveled
through Asia in the
seventeenth century. An
accomplished linguist, he
devised a system, still in
use today, to transcribe the
Vietnamese language in
Roman letters instead of
Chinese ideographs.

Emperor Minh Mang, who ruled Vietnam in the early nineteenth century. The son of Gia Long, founder of the Nguyen dynasty, Minh Mang was a gentle scholar whom French propagandists of the time depicted as a cruel tyrant.

The port of Faifo, on the Vietnamese coast, was one of the first European trading stations in Vietnam. It was founded by Portuguese merchants, but commerce with Vietnam failed to make much headway until the early twentieth century.

Jean-Baptiste de Chaigneau, a French soldier of fortune who entered the service of Emperor Gia Long. Married to a Vietnamese woman, he was promoted by the emperor to the rank of mandarin first class. Many Europeans served Asian rulers as mercenaries.

Admiral Pierre Paul de La Grandière, a French governor of Cochinchina in the mid-nineteenth century. A virtual viceroy, he frequently acted without reference to government policy made in Paris.

A French version of the execution by the Vietnamese of Father Borie, a Catholic missionary. Relatively few European priests were executed in Vietnam, but their martyrdom was publicized in France to stir up religious fervor.

Phan Thanh Giang, a prominent Vietnamese mandarin of the nineteenth century, traveled to Paris to negotiate a treaty with Napoleon II. When the French violated the pact, Phan committed suicide after pledging his sons never to cooperate with France.

An engraving of the Mekong made by a French exploratory expedition. Asian folklore held that the river represented a sacred serpent that wound its way down from Tibet into Southeast Asia.

The French expedition organized in 1868 to explore the Mekong pauses on the steps of Angkor Wat, the great Cambodian temple. The group believed that the Mekong was a waterway to China, and would thus serve as a major trade route, but it was not always navigable and thus poor for trade.

A Vietnamese portrayal of a French battle in Vietnam in 1884. The French soldiers (lower right) are supported by Vietnamese auxiliaries, distinguishable by their bare feet. The fleeing forces (left) are Chinese who have invaded Vietnam to profit from the chaos.

Vietnam at the turn of the century was populated by French adventurers like the weapons merchant Jean Dupuis, dressed here in a Chinese costume. He persuaded the French to launch an attack against Tonkin, the northern part of Vietnam.

No figure during the late nineteenth century did more to promote French imperialism in Vietnam than Prime Minister Jules Ferry. A liberal politician, he considered colonialism to be vital to France's industrial growth.

The French maintained the fiction of "protecting" the areas of Tonkin and Annam through a Vietnamese government. One puppet emperor was Dong Khanh, who was selected to rule because of his docility. The French often sent recalcitrant Vietnamese emperors into exile.

We must, with unquenchable ardor, propagate our sacred religion.
　　　　　　　　　　　　　　　　　　　—Pigneau de Béhaine

Colonial policy is the daughter of industrial policy.
　　　　　　　　　　　　　　　　　　　—Jules Ferry

I n 1787, Monsignor Pierre Joseph Georges Pigneau de Béhaine, bishop of Adran, returned to France after two decades of extraordinary adventures in a remote Asian land, Vietnam, then known to Europe as Cochinchina. A handsome priest in his forties, a large pectoral cross adorning his black silk cassock, he dazzled the courtiers at Versailles, the baroque palace of Louis XVI. His pious demeanor, flavored by a touch of oriental mystery, intrigued the ladies, and his infallible politeness even disarmed potential rivals for royal favors. But he was upstaged by a child whom he had brought with him, Nguyen Canh, the seven-year-old son of a pretender to the throne of Vietnam.

Dressed in red and gold brocade, an incongruous Hindu turban atop his head, the little prince exuded exotic charm. Queen Marie Antoinette bestowed her patronage on the boy by permitting him to play with the Dauphin, the heir apparent, and a court musician composed a hymn to honor the "illustrious infant." Her personal hairdresser celebrated the visitors with a chic new coiffure, *le chignon à la cochinchinoise,* and a court poet acclaimed Pigneau as successor to the legendary missionary Saint Francis Xavier.

Though he welcomed the lavish indulgence, Pigneau had a deeper purpose. He had come to France to lobby for an ambitious scheme—the creation, under French auspices, of a Christian empire in Asia. He died before the dream reached fulfillment, but, through the sheer drive of his personality, he propelled France toward the conquest of Vietnam a hundred years later.

Other Europeans had preceded Pigneau to Southeast Asia. Indeed, for a mixture of motives, Western expansion in Asia had been gaining momentum since the fifteenth century.

The riches of the East, real and fabled, tantalized Europe. Travelers like Marco Polo had returned with breathless tales of Burmese temples "covered with gold a full finger thick," and Indian shores whose "sands sparkled and glittered with gems and precious ores." But no Asian treasure matched its pepper, nutmeg, clove, and other spices essential to preserve food, especially in the warmer climates of southern Europe.

Unlike silks and jewels, which only the affluent could afford, spices were in universal demand, and they yielded profits of a thousandfold or more on European markets. Importing them from Asia, though, was a dangerous business. Merchants braved storms, pirates, and cruel competitors to transport their cargoes, and many perished in the effort. "Where wouldn't they go for pepper!" wrote Joseph Conrad in evocation of their memory: "For a bag of pepper they could cut each other's throats without hesitation, and would forswear their souls. . . . The bizarre obstinacy of that desire made them defy death in a thousand shapes; the unknown seas, the loathsome . . . diseases; wounds, captivity, hunger, pestilence and despair. It made them great! By heavens! it made them heroic; and it made them pathetic, too, in their craving for trade with the inflexible death levying its toll on young and old."

By the late fourteenth century, the dynamic city-state of Venice had cornered the European spice market through shrewd deals with the Muslim powers that controlled the land routes to and from Asia. So rival European powers, determined to shatter the Venetian monopoly, conceived of reaching Asia by sea—either across the Atlantic or eastward around the horn of Africa. Along with spices, religious fervor also obsessed them. Memories of the aborted Crusades still stimulated Europe, whose kings and princes dreamed of outflanking Muslim influence, which extended beyond the Indian Ocean to the Indonesian archipelago, the most abundant source of spices. That spirit fueled nobody more fiercely than Prince Henry the Navigator, the third son of the Portuguese king, John I. By 1450, the Muslims had occupied Spain and Portugal for seven centuries, and to Henry, a militant Catholic mystic, their destruction was a sacred duty. He had fought them in Africa as a youth, but he gradually shaped a geopolitical strategy that also offered commercial advantages: by opening sea lanes to Asia, he would contain Islam, promote Christianity in the East, and further trade. Accordingly, he perfected the Portuguese fleet and he established Europe's first maritime academy to train sailors scientifically.

In 1454, Pope Nicholas V endorsed Henry's enterprise with a bull granting Portugal the exclusive franchise in Asia to "bring under submission . . . the pagans of the countries not yet inflicted with the plague of Islam and give them knowledge of the name of Christ."

Forty years later, after Columbus had discovered America, the Portuguese reconfirmed their Asian domain in a treaty with Spain that recognized Spain's prerogative to exploit the Western Hemisphere. During the century ahead, Portugal would explode out of Europe in a spectacular burst of energy.

Vasco da Gama, the greatest Portuguese explorer, led an armada of four ships around the Cape of Good Hope, landing on the western coast of India in 1498. His armed galleons rapidly enforced Portugal's claim on the area. They intercepted alien vessels, confiscated their goods and burned them, and justified this brigandage with the argument that the "common right to all to navigate the seas . . . does not extend outside Europe." That double standard was to guide Europeans almost to the end of their supremacy in Asia, as they denied their colonial subjects the same legal privileges they reserved for themselves. But the Portuguese, religiously zealous and bluntly greedy, applied it with a crudeness and cruelty equaled only by the barbarity of the Spanish *conquistadores* in America.

Lisbon had supplanted Venice as Europe's main center for Asian products only five years after Vasco da Gama's pioneer journey to India, and the Portuguese could not be stopped. They consolidated Goa as the capital of their Indian territories, then pushed eastward to capture Malacca, the gateway to the China Sea, fanning out from that pivotal Malayan port to assert their presence nearly everywhere in Asia. They journeyed to the distant Ceram and Molucca islands in quest of spices, secured commercial concessions in Burma and Siam, and even sailed to forbidding Japan. Bold Portuguese were probably the earliest Europeans to gaze at Angkor Wat, the fantastic ruins of the vast Cambodian empire. Like many other Europeans after them, some deserted to serve local rulers as mercenaries. In 1557, the Portuguese built a base at Macao, on the southern edge of China, and it remains in their hands to this day—the world's oldest imperial possession.

And they sailed to Vietnam. The area had been visited by traders from ancient Rome, and, in later times, by an occasional Catholic missionary. But the first European to plant a durable settlement there was Antônio Da Faria, who in 1535 found a suitable site for a harbor at Faifo, a coastal village fifteen miles south of Tourane, now the city of Danang. Da Faria had hoped to make it a major Portuguese enclave, like Goa or Malacca, but Faifo never flourished. The Portuguese left a permanent souvenir of their presence there, however, in a misnomer for Vietnam. They labeled the area Cauchichina, deriving "Cauchi" from "Giao Chi," the Chinese characters for Vietnam, and adding "China" to distinguish it from Cochin, another of their colonies in India. Later, the French, to portray Vietnam as disunified, referred only to the southern third of the country as Cochinchina, and called the center "Annam" and the north "Tonkin."

Scarcely a century after their dramatic expansion, the Portuguese began to lose their grasp in Asia, partly because of their own avarice, corruption, and mismanagement, and partly because their fortunes were declining in Europe. Other European powers raced for Asia's wealth. The Dutch took over the spice islands of Indonesia and the English would dominate India. In 1676, the French latecomers to the scene established a station at Pondicherry, on the east coast of India south of Madras. But Europeans made little headway in Vietnam.

As it would be three centuries later, Vietnam was then torn by a civil war between regional factions—the Trinh in the north and the Nguyen in the south. Europeans sold weapons to both sides—a risky business, since supplying one camp antagonized the other. But they could not brutally subdue the Vietnamese as they had more passive Asians, like the Malays and Javanese. Whatever their own differences, all Vietnamese hated foreigners, and their sophisticated administrative structure, modeled on China's, could effectively mobilize resistance against Western intruders. Besides, the Europeans were too preoccupied with fighting among themselves to mount campaigns of the kind that would have been required for conquest.

By the end of the seventeenth century, trade with Vietnam seemed to be pointless. The Dutch and English closed the small offices they had opened earlier in Hanoi, and the French shut down their post at Pho Hien. Only the Portuguese remained where they had started, at Faifo, to fly the flag and carry on their marginal transactions with Macao. But if the merchants had failed, Catholic missionaries evolved a different approach—and greater success.

The Catholic Church left a deeper imprint on Vietnam than on any other Asian country apart from the Philippines, which Spain governed for four hundred years. From the seventeenth century on, hundreds of thousands of Vietnamese embraced the new faith, for diverse reasons. Native merchants were eager to ingratiate themselves with Western traders. To peasants, Christianity also represented freedom from the traditional Confucian system and its oppressive mandarins. The north, where people were impoverished by the pressure of population on scarce land, was especially receptive to Vietnamese priests, who became community leaders. Whole districts turned Catholic, and some became fortified bastions. In 1946, many of these same Catholic districts, still intact, fought against both the French colonial forces and the Communist-led Vietminh nationalists. Nine years later, following the French defeat and the establishment of a Communist government in North Vietnam, entire Catholic villages fled south, attracted by the more congenial regime of Ngo Dinh Diem—whose ancestors, like their own, had been converted to Christianity centuries before.

The Vietnamese emperors pursued contradictory and often unpredictable policies toward Christianity. They welcomed the missionaries' technical advice, as well as their connections to European suppliers of modern arms and other merchandise. But they feared that Western religion, with its accent on individual salvation, would erode the foundation of their society, which was based on the Confucian concept of reverence for authority. As a seventeenth-century emperor proclaimed, a subject could not divide his loyalty between the temporal and spiritual but "owes all his allegiance to the state and his sovereign." The Vietnamese rulers were particularly disturbed by the achievement of Alexandre de Rhodes, the seventeenth-century French Jesuit who perfected the simplified script *quoc ngu,* which transcribed Vietnamese, previously written in arcane Chinese ideographs, into the Roman alphabet. The innovation endangered the traditional Vietnamese structure, for priests could now propagate the gospel to a wide audience, thereby weakening officials whose power reposed largely on their narrow scholarship. But most important, the Vietnamese emperors feared that Christianity might portend European imperialism—as, in fact, it did. Nevertheless, they oscillated between persecuting and tolerating Catholics, and the imperial court was never without a contingent of Jesuit physicians, astronomers, mathematicians, and other scholars.

The earliest Christian missionaries to visit Vietnam were intrepid travelers like Odoric de Pordenone, a fourteenth-century Franciscan who related fanciful accounts of a land where, among other whoppers, turtles were bigger than cathedral domes. Three hundred years later, expelled from Japan, the Jesuits arrived to proselytize, founding the Cochinchina Mission at Faifo, the Portuguese trading station. Though tireless and dedicated, they were all outshone by Alexandre de Rhodes, a uniquely talented figure who opened the gate to French influence in Vietnam.

Born in the southern French town of Avignon, once a papal seat, Rhodes came to Vietnam under Portuguese tutelage in 1627, when he was twenty-eight. At first he recoiled at the language, which sounded to him like "twittering birds." But within six months, he was fluent enough to preach in Vietnamese—and he later mastered Japanese, Chinese, Hindustani, and Persian. And, of course, he revolutionized the Vietnamese tongue with his streamlined alphabet.

Impressed by his linguistic skills, the Jesuit hierarchy assigned Rhodes to Hanoi, where he wooed the northern emperor, Trinh Trang, with such gifts as an intricate clock and a gilded volume on mathematics. The delighted monarch allowed him to stay, and over the next two years, according to his own careful records, Rhodes delivered six sermons a day and baptized 6,700 Vietnamese, including eighteen nobles. But the emperor and his counselors soon reacted against Christian subversion, their suspicions kindled by the court concubines, who denounced the Christian injunction against polygamy as a menace to their position. Banished from the north in 1630, Rhodes retreated south, only to discover that the rival Nguyen dynasty had become equally hostile.

He retired to the Jesuit headquarters in Macao but repeatedly returned to Vietnam during the next decade, risking his life on each trip. In 1645, for instance, he was sentenced to death, then expelled after three weeks in jail; of the nine priests who accompanied him two were beheaded, and each of the other seven had a finger cut off.

Rhodes soon realized that its waning prestige no longer made Portugal a credible patron of Christianity in Asia. He calculated, too, that "hearts and minds" could be won more effectively by Vietnamese priests than European missionaries. He went to Rome to plead his case, arguing in effect for the abrogation of the fifteenth-century papal edicts that had granted Portugal its Asian domain. But he ran into stiff Portuguese opposition and the intractable Vatican bureaucracy, and he turned to his native France for help. To succeed, however, he would have to persuade French religious and commercial leaders to underwrite his project. Thus he lobbied with both, depicting Vietnam as ripe for Christian conversion and portraying it as an Eldorado of boundless wealth where, as one of his accounts put it, Vietnamese fishermen wove their nets of silk.

The Vatican finally accepted his program, though Rhodes died before it went into action. In 1664, four years after his death, French religious leaders and their business backers formed the Society of Foreign Missions to advance Christianity in Asia. In the same year, by no coincidence, French business leaders and their religious backers created the East India Company to increase trade. Their similar aspirations were apparent in their cooperation. A commercial firm established in Rouen at the time paid transportation for missionaries to Vietnam in exchange for their services there as sales agents and bookkeepers. And François Pallu, a founder of the missionary association, pledged to give the East India Company "as many promoters . . . as there will be bishops, priests and believers in Vietnam." Observing this cozy relationship in Vietnam, an English competitor reported home that the French had arrived, "but we cannot make out whether they are here to seek trade or to conduct religious propaganda."

Their objective, of course, was to do both. But they accomplished little during most of the eighteenth century, since the Vietnamese emperors continued to harass or restrict foreign missionaries and merchants. Back in France, moreover, the idea of acquiring overseas territories enthralled neither the public nor government officials. They focused on other concerns, such as France's domestic economic and social problems and its conflicts with England in Europe and America. But the imperial dream was kept alive by a handful of determined individuals and groups which, in present-day jargon, would be called vested interests. In Paris, they were constantly drafting blueprints for the conquest of Vietnam, while irrepressible adventurers in Asia concocted schemes that would prove to be fruitless. One was Pierre Poivre, the son of a prominent Lyons silk tycoon.

In the middle of the eighteenth century, Poivre started out as a missionary in Vietnam, then switched to commerce and obtained a license from the southern Nguyen rulers to open a trading post at Tourane. When the operation collapsed for lack of enthusiasm in France, he blamed local Vietnamese mandarins for swindling him, and decided to punish them. In 1768, he teamed up with Charles Hector d'Estaing, an aristocratic buccaneer whose indirect descendant, Valéry Giscard d'Estaing, became president of France in 1974. Spoiling for action, Hector d'Estaing had earlier been deterred by a storm from mounting an elaborate attack on the palace at Hué, the ancient imperial capital in central Vietnam. He and Poivre proposed to muster a contingent of three thousand troops, seize Tourane, and drive inland to invade the country. The plan was carried out a century later, but at the time it fizzled. D'Estaing transferred his energies to the American War of Independence, in which he distinguished himself by blockading the English fleet outside New York harbor. He died on the guillotine during the French Revolution.

Most foreign descriptions of Vietnam during this period publicized its riches, but there were also gloomy reports of its poverty. One French missionary wrote, for example, that such famine pervaded the country that people practiced cannibalism and entire families were committing suicide "to avoid slow death by starvation." Whatever the truth, periodic revolts testified to Vietnamese restiveness. The most important uprising, the Tayson rebellion, so called for its origin in mountains of that name, offered the French a chance to grab Vietnam. They missed the opportunity, but they gained what some would later consider to be a legitimate claim to intervention.

The Tayson insurrection, which erupted in 1772 against the Nguyen rulers, was ignited by three brothers of a wealthy merchant family said to have been accused of fraud. Their resistance to the kings, at first centered in the region of Quinhon, rapidly grew into a populist movement as peasants, eager for revenge against harsh mandarins, swelled its ranks. Within three years, the Tayson army had captured Saigon, then a tiny port, where the insurgents vented their fury against the town's Chinese inhabitants, who ran its trade, and killed more than ten thousand of them. But the rebels introduced an equitable tax system and an agrarian reform program, distributing land to poor villagers. They also permitted Catholic missionaries to preach publicly and even assigned soldiers to protect them. After subduing the south, they marched north, eventually ousting the Trinh rulers and unifying Vietnam for the first time in a century.

A young survivor of the defeated Nguyen clan, Nguyen Anh, refused to abandon his struggle. He and his sympathizers continued the fight, recapturing and losing Saigon again and again over the next decade. During this turbulence, he met the prodigious French priest Pigneau de Béhaine, who for his own motives rallied to the Nguyen cause. Together they wrote a new and significant chapter in Vietnamese history.

The eldest of nineteen children of a humble tanner, Pigneau later ennobled his name by adding the "de" to Béhaine, his birthplace in Lorraine. He had entered the priesthood against his father's wishes, because, as he told his family, "we must, with unquenchable ardor, propagate our sacred religion." In 1765, when he was twenty-four, the Society of Foreign Missions assigned him to a seminary on Phu Quoc island, in the Gulf of Siam, where, consistent with the policy promoted by Alexandre de Rhodes, he trained some forty Vietnamese, Chinese, and Siamese novices to become native missionaries.

The school was nothing more than a wretched collection of bamboo huts, and young Pigneau quickly faced the hardships that confront a European in that alien environment of unbearable heat, humidity, and chronic disease. Worse, he was caught in the cross fire of local conflicts. Soon after his arrival, he sheltered a Siamese prince, whose enemies appeared in pursuit. They destroyed the seminary, arrested Pigneau, and shackled him in an eighty-pound wood and iron frame. Wracked by fever, he exalted in his martyrdom. "Bless the Lord a thousand times," he wrote to his parents, "that I may suffer or die in His holy name."

Released after three months, he rebuilt the school, only to experience a more harrowing ordeal a year later, when Chinese and Cambodian pirates attacked the place and murdered some of the pupils. Pigneau escaped with a few of the youths and made his way in a frail boat through the Straits of Malacca and across the Bay of Bengal to Pondicherry, the French base in India.

In 1770, Pope Clement XIV appointed him bishop of Adran, an ancient Christian city in the Middle East that had fallen to the Turks during the Crusades. The title was symbolic, the pope having decided that to give him a real diocese in Vietnam would offend the Portuguese, who had still not yielded their claim to Asia.

Five years later, back at the site of his seminary on Phu Quoc island, Pigneau was transformed by a remarkable incident from priest to politician. The Nguyen survivor, Nguyen Anh, had fled to the island with his Tayson foes behind him. As the story goes, Pigneau hid the fugitive prince and became his adviser. Employing guerrilla tactics, Nguyen Anh regained Saigon and its surrounding provinces, but lost it in 1784, when the Tayson forces returned to defeat him. Desperate, he now accepted Pigneau's repeated proposal that he appeal to France to intercede on his behalf. Nguyen Anh authorized Pigneau to negotiate for him, and, in time-honored Asian style, he sent his small son off with the missionary as a sign of his good faith.

At Pondicherry, where Pigneau went first, the French authorities spurned his project as "difficult and useless." He then decided to take his case directly to the French king, Louis XVI. Accompanied by his protégé and a train of Vietnamese flunkies, Pigneau arrived at Versailles in early 1787, his exotic entourage causing a sensation among courtiers always looking for fresh fads.

France was then tottering on the brink of bankruptcy, and Louis XVI, an indecisive man, initially rejected the idea of a costly expedition to Asia. But Pigneau cautioned the king's advisers that England would grab Vietnam should France demur, and he even outlined a precise military plan for conquest. The reluctant Louis XVI finally came around. On November 28, 1787, Pigneau and the Comte de Montmorin, the French foreign minister, signed a treaty. France agreed to furnish Nguyen Anh with 1,650 French officers and men, weapons, ammunition, and transportation, and Vietnam would cede Tourane and the island of Poulo Condore to France in addition to commercial privileges "to the exclusion of all other European nations." Conspicuously absent was any Vietnamese concession permitting the free practice of Christianity in Vietnam—an indication that Pigneau, though still a priest, had really become a diplomat. In another twist, Pigneau abruptly ceased to represent Nguyen Anh and became royal commissioner of France for Cochinchina. In theory, France had created a client relationship that, with variations, would bind the West and Asia for more than a century.

Louis XVI soon had misgivings. He sent a secret message to Thomas de Conway, governor of the French base at Pondicherry, who was to provide the men and ships for the Pigneau expedition. He reminded Conway of France's dismal finances, and instructed him to exercise prudence, even to the extent of canceling the operation. Conway greeted the message as a chance to thwart Pigneau, less out of personal envy than because, to him, Asia was "unhealthy, uninhabitable, and miserable" and not worth the effort of conquest.

Conway, then in his mid-fifties, was a dissolute Irishman at the end of a controversial career. After fighting in the French army in Europe, he had joined the Americans struggling against England, rising to the rank of inspector general of George Washington's forces. But, an inveterate plotter, he conspired in 1777 with several disgruntled Americans, among them Benjamin Rush and Thomas Mifflin of Pennsylvania, to replace Washington with General Horatio Gates. The Marquis de Lafayette foiled the intrigue and denounced Conway as an "ambitious and dangerous man." Nevertheless, Conway returned to France to be hailed as a hero of the American War of Independence, promoted to senior grade in the French army, and assigned to Pondicherry despite his disdain for Asia. When Pigneau arrived there from Versailles, expecting to mobilize his Vietnamese operation, Conway stalled him until the spring of 1789 in the knowledge that, months earlier, Louis XVI had decided to drop the project. The king's timing was fortuitous. In July, a Paris mob stormed the Bastille and sparked the French Revolution.

"I shall lead the expedition alone," announced Pigneau when told that Louis XVI had betrayed him, and he proceeded to fulfill that promise. Offering them trade with Vietnam, he persuaded French merchants in India to buy him two ships, weapons, and ammunition. He also hired nearly four hundred deserters from the French forces and put them at Nguyen Anh's disposal. One of them, Olivier de Puymanel, a twenty-year-old subaltern, trained the Vietnamese army, whose fifty thousand men included a large number of Catholic converts; Jean-Baptiste de Chaigneau, who manned the naval cannon, was later an important figure in Vietnam. At the end of the century, the Tayson challenge waned, fragmented by internal dissension. Despotic officials emerged to supplant the oppressive mandarins they had ousted. The Tayson forces staged their last desperate defense in 1799 at Quinhon, a coastal town, where they were defeated by Nguyen Anh's nineteen-year-old son Canh, the young prince who as a boy had accompanied Pigneau to Versailles.

In 1802, Nguyen Anh crowned himself emperor at Hué, and adopted the title of Gia Long. He showed no mercy to his beaten adversaries, dead or alive. His soldiers exhumed the bones of a deceased Tayson leader and his wife and urinated on them before the eyes of their son, whose limbs were then bound to four elephants and ripped apart. The new ruler revived the name of Vietnam, which the French would soon discard in an effort to efface the country's national cohesion. But the dynasty lasted until 1954, ending with the final Vietnamese emperor, Bao Dai, a French protégé.

Pigneau did not live to see Nguyen Anh's triumph. In 1799, while encamped with Prince Canh's army, he died of dysentery at the age of fifty-seven. He was extolled as no other foreigner in Vietnamese history, before or since, in a funeral of unprecedented splendor. His embalmed body was transported in a teak coffin to Saigon, where both Catholic priests and Buddhist monks conducted rites in his honor; astrologers chose the moment for his burial. Twelve thousand troops, garbed in multicolored uniforms and flanked by elephants, headed a procession of forty thousand mourners, among them Nguyen Anh, borne on a lacquered palanquin, that marched to a bamboo grove outside Saigon, the site that Pigneau had picked for his grave, where Nguyen Anh delivered a eulogy praising his "intimate confidant [and] precious friend," to whom he and his subjects owed an "eternal debt." Nguyen Anh later built a tomb on the spot; the Chinese ideographs on the stele declared that Pigneau's actions "deserve to be transmitted to posterity." The tomb has since disappeared.

Of the four Frenchmen who remained at the court of Gia Long after Pigneau's death, the most prominent was Jean-Baptiste de Chaigneau, the former naval gunner, son of a Breton nobleman and a cousin of the Romantic poet René de Chateaubriand. Chaigneau married a Vietnamese woman, and Gia Long promoted him to the rank of mandarin first-class, inviting him to meetings of the imperial council and exempting him, by special decree, from having to prostrate himself at the emperor's feet. But France failed to benefit from his special position, primarily because Napoleon, by now in power in Paris, was too preoccupied with conquering Europe to focus on Asia.

Nor did Gia Long encourage France. He realized that he owed an "eternal debt" to Pigneau rather than to France, and he discharged the obligation to his late mentor by tolerating Christianity. Also, perceiving that the European powers would sooner or later try to dominate Asia, he prudently avoided any gestures that would give them an advantage. Thus, while he welcomed some Western imports, he granted the French no favors. He deliberately withdrew into the kind of isolation that China had also adopted in defense against the West, even modeling his capital at Hué on Beijing, a walled "forbidden city." As his reign neared its close, he selected an heir whom he knew to be xenophobic. Pigneau's dream of consolidating French influence in Vietnam had evaporated.

In 1819, following the Napoleonic wars, when European merchants again contemplated commerce with Asia, Chaigneau tried to resurrect the dream. But Gia Long died during Chaigneau's absence in the West, and his successor, Minh Mang, sensing that concessions to France would erode his sovereignty, rebuffed proposed pacts. He similarly spurned the first American to set foot in Vietnam, a Captain John White of Salem, whose clipper ship visited Saigon in 1820. He suspected unrestricted commerce might eventually open Vietnam to European domination, and he obliquely communicated his concern in a reply to a request from Louis XVIII that he accord privileges to France: "If your compatriots desire to trade with our kingdom, it is only reasonable that they conform to its laws."

A gentle, almost effeminate scholar, Minh Mang reinforced the Confucian administration he had inherited from his father. Like the Chinese emperor to whom he paid tribute, he was the "Son of Heaven" at the pinnacle of an intricate bureaucracy of civilian and military mandarins whose authority reached down to the provinces and districts. The highest of these officials headed his six central ministries—interior, finance, religion, justice, war, and public works—while those at the lowest echelons managed local government, collected taxes, and commanded troops stationed throughout the country. The establishment contained no department of foreign affairs. The Western "barbarians," as Minh Mang referred to them, were unworthy of institutional attention.

In theory, this hierarchy mirrored a static concept of order and harmony, which required that it be shielded against innovation. For that reason Minh Mang feared potentially disruptive ideas and practices. His code severely punished Buddhists and Taoists, whose beliefs violated the doctrine of the emperor's divinity. The same apprehension prompted his hostility toward Christianity.

At first, Minh Mang tried to control Catholic missionaries by summoning them to his court at Hué on the pretext that he needed their linguistic talents and other skills. But they ignored him, and, in 1825, he issued the first of several harsh edicts banning the further entry of missionaries into Vietnam because, as he put it, "the perverse religion of the Europeans corrupts the hearts of men." One of Gia Long's old advisers, the eunuch Le Van Duyet, reminded Minh Mang of his father's pledge to Pigneau to tolerate Christianity. But revolts against the regime were then spreading, particularly in the south, and Minh Mang suspected that foreign and native Catholics were involved in them.

The emperor saw proof of his suspicion in 1833, when Le Van Duyet's adopted son, Le Van Khoi, rebelled against him with apparent Catholic encouragement. Minh Mang ordered the arrest of both French and Vietnamese priests. Many escaped, but one of them, François Isidore Gagelin, formerly a cartographer at the imperial court, was captured in Binh Dinh province, brought to Hué in irons, and condemned to death for "preaching the religion of Jesus." On the morning of October 17, 1833, six soldiers slowly strangled him as he knelt on a scaffold in the capital. Having read of Christ's resurrection, Minh Mang had the priest's corpse exhumed three days later to determine whether he had truly died. Over the next seven years, ten foreign missionaries were executed, some cruelly.

By modern standards of inhumanity, Minh Mang's anti-Catholic campaign was mild. Moreover, as Vietnamese then observed, the repression hardly matched the persecution by Christians of nonbelievers elsewhere—not to mention the abuses of Christians against each other. But Minh Mang's measures came at an inopportune moment.

In France, religious zeal was again intensifying, in reaction against the secular spirit of the Revolutionary and Napoleonic eras. Missionaries were renewing their efforts to propagate the word of the Church, and they especially sought to intensify their crusade in Vietnam, where martyrs had already suffered for the Christian cause. The navy, the most conservative branch of France's military establishment, was also determined to extend French influence abroad. Thus the navy and the missionaries became natural allies, with a common outlook and a joint goal. By the final decades of the nineteenth century, Vietnam was to be governed by French naval officers. By no coincidence, the French high commissioner for Indochina as late as 1946, Admiral Georges Thierry d'Argenlieu, was a Carmelite monk who had exchanged his cassock for a uniform during World War II.

The pressure for a firmer French presence in Asia mounted after the Opium War of 1841, in which the English opened China to trade.

France's businessmen, whose activities in Asia had been dormant for decades, now reviewed the prospects of the Asian market. But French policy proceeded prudently.

Louis XVIII and Charles X, the Bourbon monarchs who followed Napoleon, had favored the missionary revival, but Louis Philippe, who seized the French throne in 1830, sought to subdue the militant Catholic clergy. His foreign minister, François Guizot, a Protestant, was even cooler toward Catholic aims. Guizot also opposed political and military ventures in the East, because, as he said, "we have sufficiently grave and complicated questions to manage in Europe . . . without throwing ourselves into other hazardous enterprises elsewhere." That theme was repeated later by French enemies of imperialism—but, like Guizot, they would be drawn into "hazardous enterprises" of which they disapproved.

In 1840, his reign almost ended, Minh Mang amended his attitude toward Europe. Viewing England's intervention in China as a portent of a fresh European foray in Asia, he tried to deter a French attack by negotiating. He dispatched two mandarins to France, where their unannounced arrival caused a sensation. Catholic activists took advantage of the occasion to denounce Minh Mang's persecution of Christians, and even the Vatican joined the protest. Louis Philippe, caught up in domestic difficulties, refused to grant the Vietnamese diplomats an audience. An opportunity for compromise was squandered—as would be later chances for reconciliation between France and Vietnam.

Minh Mang died soon afterward, and his successor was even more chauvinistic than he. The new emperor, Thieu Tri, sharing his father's apprehensive view of missionaries, sought to curb them. But he failed to discern that, with European imperialism in Asia gathering momentum, any semblance of anti-Catholic repression would provoke French intervention. Even Guizot now shifted, largely to placate religious and business factions at home, and in 1843 deployed a permanent French fleet in Asian waters "to protect, and if necessary to defend, our political and commercial interests." He also authorized the navy to rescue threatened French missionaries, preferably "without involving the French flag." His policy, however reluctant, gave a green light to French action against Vietnam.

Despite French propaganda portrayals of him as a brutal savage, Thieu Tri initially showed moderation toward missionaries. His aim, after all, was simply to get rid of them. But the priests were passionate men, convinced that God had ordained them to convert pagans. They were also politically astute, aware that a changing mood in France favored them. So they stubbornly pushed on, even though they would collide with the Vietnamese. Thieu Tri tried to avert the clash, as his treatment of Dominique Lefèbvre illustrated.

Arriving in Vietnam in 1835 as a young missionary, Lefèbvre studied the language and began preaching, often covertly to avoid arrest. In 1844, he joined a group of French priests conspiring to replace Thieu Tri with an emperor more receptive to Christianity, as Pigneau de Béhaine had done a generation earlier. Apprised of the plot, Thieu Tri had Lefèbvre caught and condemned to death, but, seeking to avoid trouble, commuted the sentence on the pretense that the missionary was ignorant of the prohibition against Christianity.

Lefèbvre, imprisoned in Hué, now started a chain of errors that would lead to the first direct French assault against Vietnam. One day in the spring of 1845, hearing that a Western warship had anchored at the nearby port of Tourane, he smuggled a message to its commander. The vessel turned out to be "Old Ironsides," the U.S.S. *Constitution,* whose captain, John Percival, was entertaining three or four mandarins when the secret note arrived. Alarmed by the call of a European in danger, Percival promptly held his Vietnamese guests as hostages against Lefèbvre's release. But Thieu Tri declined to bargain, and left Percival no choice but to free the dignitaries and sail away. The United States government quickly disavowed Percival and apologized officially to Thieu Tri, who by then had handed Lefèbvre, along with gifts, over to a French ship in the vicinity.

Lefèbvre went to Singapore while Thieu Tri, now sensitive to Vietnam's vulnerability, considered making a pact with the Europeans. But another incident occurred to prevent an accord, and once more it involved the persistent Lefèbvre. Attempting to re-enter Vietnam, he was again arrested, again sentenced to death, again released, and again deported. This time, though, the French fleet in the area learned of his capture. Admiral Cécille, its commander and a veteran of the region, had long awaited such an occasion: he ordered two warships to Tourane, the *Gloire* and the *Victorieuse,* demanding that Thieu Tri free Lefèbvre and cease repressing Christians.

Unaware that the emperor had released Lefèbvre four weeks earlier, the French force reached Tourane on March 23, 1847. The officers in charge, Captain Lapierre and Captain Charles Rigault de Genouilly, stripped the sails from several Vietnamese boats in the port and bullied the town's recalcitrant mandarins into accepting a letter for Thieu Tri. When the emperor's response came from Hué eighteen days later, the French insisted that, as a gesture of Vietnamese submission, it be brought to one of their ships. Equally proud, the mandarins stalled and a clash occurred.

Who shot first has never been clarified. But within seventy minutes, the French had sunk three Vietnamese vessels, destroyed the harbor forts, and killed hundreds of local inhabitants. They then put out to sea—without evident concern for the fate of the French missionaries left in Vietnam. Nor did they inquire into the fate of Lefèbvre—who had fled to Singapore. He would again return to Vietnam, where he remained for another twenty years.

Thieu Tri reacted angrily to the French attack. He denounced Catholic priests as foreign agents who should be killed on sight. But his fury was only rhetorical. In fact, fearful of French reprisals, he did not execute a single missionary during his reign and he freed those he arrested, as he had repeatedly released the intrepid Lefèbvre. Thieu Tri understood his dilemma. He realized that the French, bent on conquest, were looking for pretexts. He also knew that Vietnam could not protect itself unless it modernized. But he would not break with tradition, for he knew that innovation would bring down his imperial structure.

Nor would his successor, Tu Duc, change the system. Tu Duc, who assumed the throne after his father's death in 1847, clung even more stubbornly to the belief that Vietnam could not disrupt its feudal institutions for the sake of security. Embarking on a fierce campaign to eliminate Christianity, he thereby antagonized the French just as they were exploring ways to escalate their offensive against his country. His myopic intransigence made him the last independent ruler of Vietnam.

Contemporary French publicists depicted Tu Duc, as they had his father and grandfather, as a bloodthirsty beast. But Thieu Tri had chosen him as heir because of his mild disposition, and visitors to his court confirmed his moderation. One French traveler found him to be a "refined and distinguished" person with delicate hands and black eyes of "remarkable profundity," a figure reminiscent of "Egyptian antiquity."

Like his father and grandfather, however, Tu Duc regarded the forty or so Catholic missionaries then in Vietnam to be a menace to his nation, not only because their teachings threatened to subvert the Confucian order, but also because many actually represented French political and military interests. But he cracked down on them only when he calculated that the French were too embroiled in domestic troubles to react effectively. He issued his first anti-Christian edict in 1848, amid the collapse of Louis Philippe's monarchy, and he published a second in 1851 as Louis Napoleon, who had been elected president of France three years earlier, fought the parliament in his bid for absolute power. But Tu Duc miscalculated.

He decreed that Vietnamese Catholics be branded on the left cheek with the characters "*ta dao,*" meaning "infidel," and their properties confiscated. He deemed this punishment reasonable, since native Christians were "poor idiots seduced by priests." On the other hand, European missionaries were to be drowned and Vietnamese priests cut in half lengthwise, and bounties of silver would be paid for their capture. Many baptized Vietnamese suffered, but many others escaped by bribing mandarins. And Tu Duc's wrath intensified when Christians were implicated in an abortive rebellion against him organized by his brother. In 1851, he executed a young French priest, Augustin Schoeffler, and had another missionary, Jean-Louis Bonnard, put to death the next year. Senior French missionaries throughout Asia now called for action, and they were joined by influential French officials in the region.

One of them, Comte de Bourboulon, was a singular specimen. An ugly little man married to an affable American woman a foot taller than himself, Bourboulon professed to be a socialist and an atheist. As France's envoy to China during the early 1850s, he had urged missionaries to behave with "extreme circumspection" lest they transgress local customs. But soon he became a resolute advocate of French vigor and he introduced a new jargon of a kind that would be used by radical French imperialists later in the century. The extension of French power in the East helped "all humanity," he intoned, promising that it put European relations with Asia on a "liberal and equitable basis."

Bourboulon's almost exact opposite, physically and ideologically, was Louis Charles de Montigny, the French consul in Shanghai. A large, imposing man of great energy, fanatically religious, Montigny had carved out the famous French Concession in Shanghai soon after his arrival there in 1848 simply by hoisting the French flag over a district of the city and declaring it to be part of France. He and Bourboulon could work toward the same objective, largely because of political changes then evolving in Paris.

Louis Napoleon, who proclaimed himself Emperor Napoleon III at the end of 1852, had staged his *coup d'état* with the support of the Church. His Spanish wife, Eugénie, was devoutly religious as well. Thus he could not escape a commitment to missionary goals in Asia. That aim also fit his own vision of enhancing France's national grandeur and his own prestige through foreign adventures, as his illustrious uncle, Napoleon I, had done. His priority, however, was to deal with France's alignments in Europe, which were shifting as revolutionary movements spread. He had also cemented a relationship with England that would ally the two nations against Russia in the Crimean War. So he was too distracted by other matters to focus on the East.

In Asia, though, French officials were preparing for intervention. Bourboulon sent a memorandum to the French foreign ministry suggesting that the Vietnamese emperor, Tu Duc, be coerced into ceding Tourane to France as an indemnity for his mistreatment of missionaries—a legitimate project, considering Nguyen Anh's treaty with Louis XVI forty-five years earlier. Bourboulon recommended that a French naval force seize Tourane, and he even outlined battle tactics. A naval operation in Vietnam would be economical, he stressed, since the French fleet "costs almost as much unoccupied as it does active." Admitting that missionaries functioned "at their own risk and peril," he asserted that France nevertheless "shares a responsibility for injuries committed against them."

The foreign ministry's reply arrived in record speed by steamship. It instructed Bourboulon to refine his military plans, noting that the acquisition of Tourane not only would give France a valuable harbor for commerce and a strategic base for war, but would also restore its international "dignity." Meanwhile, Catholic spokesmen in Paris urged Napoleon III to approve the expedition, and they were encouraged by French officers and civilian officials in the field. General Philippe Marie Henri Roussel de Courcy, then in China, took it upon himself to pledge to the Catholic bishops throughout Asia that France would protect missionaries.

In early 1856, after much hesitation, Napoleon III endorsed the proposals put forth by Bourboulon and others. The assignment was entrusted to Montigny, the former French consul in Shanghai, and it gave a renewed impetus to the French drive toward Vietnam.

Montigny was scheduled to proceed to Vietnam accompanied by two French warships that would enforce his demands on Tu Duc. But he was also instructed to negotiate a treaty with Siam. He stopped in Bangkok and afterward dallied in Cambodia, sending the vessels ahead with a letter to the Vietnamese ruler. One of them, the *Catinat,* reached Tourane in mid–September of 1856, meeting the same kind of reception that the French had encountered there nine years before. The local mandarins refused to accept Montigny's message to the emperor. The ship's commander, a Captain Le Lieur, eventually lost patience and fired at the Vietnamese. After destroying the harbor forts, he landed a detachment of marines to occupy the town's citadel. The frightened mandarins agreed to parlay, but Le Lieur stalled, awaiting Montigny. Weeks passed. The other ship, the *Capricieuse*, delayed by a storm, limped in, but still no Montigny. The two vessels, running short of supplies, departed for Macao.

Montigny appeared two months later. But without the warships, he lacked the strength to impose his conditions on Tu Duc. Instead of disenchanting the missionaries and their supporters, the setback fired their enthusiasm to try again. They appealed to French business groups with inflated accounts of Vietnam's wealth in silver, gold, coal, and timber. A pair of veteran priests, the Lazarist Father Huc and Bishop Pellerin, journeyed from Asia to Paris to lobby. Huc told Napoleon III that the treaty of 1787 gave France an incontestable right to Tourane and claimed that the conquest was the "easiest thing in the world," since the Vietnamese would greet the French as "liberators and benefactors." Pellerin, who had narrowly escaped death in Vietnam, preached emotional sermons to Paris congregations on France's duty to aid Vietnamese Christians, and he even obtained the Vatican's blessing for the venture.

The notion of intervention worried several senior French figures. The keeper of the foreign ministry archives, Pierre Cintrat, carefully argued that France had never fulfilled its obligations under the 1787 pact, and therefore an attack against Tourane—which would be costly and dangerous—would also be an illegal act of war. His opinion was backed up by the foreign minister, Comte Alexandre Walewski, the illegitimate son of Napoleon I and his Polish mistress, Marie Walewska.

Walewski judiciously backtracked after Napoleon III personally decided in favor of action. The emperor had succumbed to Catholic pressure as well as to his own obsession with national glory. He also felt encouraged by evidence that England, itself carving out an empire in Asia, would not block a French counterweight in Vietnam. But, as government leaders often do at critical moments, Napoleon III appointed a special committee to provide the rationale for his decision.

The dignitaries on the committee agreed with Cintrat that the 1787 treaty was irrelevant. Nevertheless, it upheld France's right to punish Vietnam for persecuting French missionaries, and it recommended that three Vietnamese ports be occupied and affirmed that a French expedition to Vietnam was consistent with the "force of circumstances" that "propels the nations of the West to expand toward the East." In short, the advisory group concluded, France could not afford to stay behind:

"Will we be the only ones without possessions in Asia, where the English, Dutch, Spanish and even Russians are strengthening their positions?"

If he needed additional justification, Napoleon III received it in a series of dispatches from Bourboulon, then stationed in Canton, who described the alarming repression of Vietnamese Christians in Vietnam, basing his information on biased missionary sources. He also stressed that halfhearted efforts in the past had only dramatized France's weakness and thus prompted the Vietnamese to harden their anti-Catholic policies. The French should now deploy an overwhelming force, he urged, and they could count on the collaboration of a Spanish-led army of Filipinos, disciplined Catholics accustomed to the tropical climate. Spain's wrath had been aroused by the execution of a Spanish Dominican missionary, Father Díaz, in the summer of 1857.

Suspicious of his unenthusiastic foreign ministry, Napoleon III put the expedition under the ministry of the navy. In November 1857, Rigault de Genouilly, now an admiral and commander of the French fleet in Asia, received his orders. A seasoned sea dog who had been involved in the hit-and-run assault against Tourane as a young officer ten years before, he was supposed to grab Tourane and adjacent territories and hold them until Tu Duc conceded to a protectorate that would, in effect, mean French control of Vietnam. Failing that goal, Rigault could settle for a deal that indemnified France for lives and property lost in Vietnam.

The French armada of fourteen vessels and twenty-five hundred men set forth for Tourane the following summer. Rigault strode the bridge of his flagship, the *Nemesis,* with Bishop Pellerin alongside him, puffing choice Manila cigars and dispensing advice in his self-appointed role of political and military counselor. The Spanish initially failed to live up to Bourboulon's expectations, having mobilized fewer than five hundred troops, who had to be transported by the French. Inspired by the government, meanwhile, the Paris press acclaimed the operation in heady superlatives, forecasting that Tourane would become France's Gibraltar in Asia. But the problems encountered by the expedition illustrated the enormous difficulties that beset Western forces in Vietnam.

The fleet reached Tourane on August 31, 1858, and easily subdued the port's defenders. Then the trouble began. Bishop Pellerin's promised Catholic uprising never materialized, presumably because local Christians feared reprisals if the enterprise failed. Pellerin's Vietnamese spies also proved to be purveyors of false intelligence planted by clever mandarins. Nor were his agents able to enlist native laborers. The

French established a beachhead, only to run into two devastating enemies—heat and disease.

Outfitted in heavy uniforms, the French wilted under the searing sun. Many died from dysentery, scurvy, cholera, and fevers that defied diagnosis. Rigault considered a diversionary attack against Hué, but he lacked shallow-draft boats to navigate the Perfume River, and he ruled out an overland alternative, which required vehicles he had not brought along and indigenous porters he could not recruit. So the French remained mired in Tourane for weeks, only to face even worse conditions when the monsoon rains lashed them in late October. Unable to build substantial shelters, they were constantly drenched and vulnerable to infection. Mere scratches led to infections that required amputation; one officer recalled how a slight arm wound became gangrenous. When hitherto cautious Vietnamese soldiers advanced to within two miles of their camp in November, the French were too feeble to do more than hold them off in an indecisive skirmish. The glorious expedition had degenerated into a humiliating disaster.

Rigault and Pellerin inevitably blamed each other for the debacle—Rigault charged Pellerin with misleading him, while Pellerin claimed that Rigault had displayed insufficient vigor. Pellerin urged an attack against the north, where more numerous Catholics would emerge to help them, but Rigault, dismissing the advice, contrived a fresh strategy. His gesture marked a new departure: no longer would French military policy in Vietnam be guided by missionaries, who plainly suffered from what, in later Vietnamese wars, would be termed a "credibility gap." Leaving a small garrison at Tourane, he sailed south to Saigon.

In the cavalier fashion of the period, Rigault acted without official sanction, and his campaign there nearly repeated the Tourane fiasco. Arriving in Saigon in February 1859, his squadron of nine warships and transports managed to dominate the city within two weeks. As in Tourane, however, local Catholics were unwilling to assist him, and the southerners were uncommonly aggressive. Their guerrilla units prevented the French from gaining control of the nearby countryside, and they even staged attacks inside the city. Rigault might have then mobilized for a long struggle to hold Saigon, but he left a small detachment there to return to Tourane.

The French position had deteriorated in Tourane. It had withstood repeated Vietnamese assaults, but illness spread. For every French soldier killed in battle, twenty had died of disease, and the situation became abysmal in the summer of 1859, when epidemics of cholera and typhus broke out. Rigault made a stab at contacting Tu Duc, but the emperor saw no need to talk to the decimated French. Bitter and discouraged, Rigault resigned and returned to France, leaving his successor the embarrassment of evacuating the French garrison. Before leaving, Rigault wrote the whole story of Western intervention in one of his last reports from the fighting front: "Everything here tends toward ruin."

Rigault could have plausibly complained, as so many other officers frustrated in Vietnam would later, that the "politicians back home had let him down." Indeed, Napoleon III had vacillated, shifting his focus to reckless wars in Europe and conflicts in China. But soon the pressure for intervention in Vietnam again built up in Paris, and Napoleon III could not resist it. Manufacturers and merchants seeking overseas markets, officers and officials yearning for adventure—all raised their voices. And the chorus was joined by a new breed of nationalistic intellectual stirred by the dream of carrying French culture to "backward" peoples, just as Rome civilized the "barbarians" beyond its borders.

The call for action sounded even louder in late 1860, when Justin Chasseloup-Laubat became minister of the navy and the colonies, a newly created hybrid post that would generate the main impulses of imperialism. He persuaded Napoleon III to concentrate on Vietnam, and he reinforced an expedition headed by Admiral Léonard Victor Joseph Charner sent to relieve the beleaguered French force in Saigon.

Commanding two thousand men, Charner fought his way slowly inland from the sea, and in July 1861, six months after launching the campaign, he entered Saigon and claimed the city for France. His successors pushed deeper into the Mekong delta, inflicting heavy casualties on the Vietnamese who resisted them. A year later, Tu Duc paid an exorbitant price for peace: he gave France the three provinces adjacent to Saigon in addition to Poulo Condore island, accorded Catholic missionaries the freedom to proselytize, opened three ports to European commerce, and, among other concessions, granted the French the right to forbid Vietnam to cede any part of its territory to another power. Pigneau de Béhaine was more than vindicated seventy-five years after his bold voyage to Versailles.

The surrender of Tu Duc astonished both French and Vietnamese, but the emperor had no other options. France's seizure of Saigon and its surrounding provinces—the rice bowl of Vietnam—was starving his armies. He was also being menaced by rebels in the north, a greater threat in his estimation than the French occupation of the south. His archaic anti-Western policies were bankrupt, he now realized. Against the advice of his more enlightened counselors, he had refused to turn to Europe for help in modernizing Vietnam; now, having isolated his nation, he could not count on any outside power to aid him against France. He showed just how desperate he was on the eve of his capitulation to the French, when he sent a last-minute and futile appeal to Abraham Lincoln for American support.

Vietnam's archaic feudal structure had by this time so decayed that Tu Duc had lost the moral authority to rally his people against the French. Vietnamese peasants may have hated and feared the foreign invaders, who killed and looted indiscriminately, but they also despised their own corrupt and despotic mandarins. Their first priority was survival, not the fate of the regime.

Not that this sentiment always served the French. On the contrary, many Vietnamese patriotically resisted the foreign intruders even though they no longer respected their emperor. Throughout the Mekong delta, local officials who disdained Tu Duc nevertheless quit the provincial administration rather than submit to alien rule. An anonymous poster addressed to the French illustrated the sense of Vietnamese nationalism then emerging: "If you persist in bringing to us your iron and flame, the struggle will be long. But we are guided by the laws of Heaven, and our cause will triumph in the end."

By late 1862, the resistance in the south had spread with such intensity that the French could only crush it with reinforcements from China and the Philippines. But while they fought the southern guerrillas, the French did nothing for the northern rebels, being urged by Christian missionaries to overthrow Tu Duc. Plainly, Catholic pressure had ceased to be a key factor in French policy. Forty years later, a French historian would deny that the missionaries had ever been significant in Vietnam's conquest. As he put it, their persecution had only been "the pretext for our intervention."

The prospect of a protracted Vietnamese conflict especially worried Napoleon III, and he began to display doubts about France's future in Vietnam. He needed funds for another venture—his plan to install Maximilian, the Austrian archduke, on the throne of Mexico. So he not only tried to cut the costs of his force in southern Vietnam, but also showed interest in a Vietnamese proposal to limit French designs on the country as a whole.

Having given them Saigon and its three adjoining provinces, Tu Duc soon sensed that the French would ultimately push on to conquer all of Vietnam and spell doom for his tottering monarchy. He therefore contrived a bargain. In exchange for the return of the three provinces he had ceded to France directly, he would accept a French protectorate over all six provinces of Cochinchina, as southern Vietnam was then called.

He offered France full control over Saigon, commercial advantages in Vietnam, and annual tribute. He sent a prominent mandarin, Phan Thanh Giang, to Paris to promote the package. Napoleon III endorsed it immediately as a cheaper alternative to continued French operations, agreeing to revise the treaty that France had concluded with Tu Duc in 1862.

But Napoleon III had not anticipated the cries of outrage that would come from the champions of French intervention. Naval officers foremost among them, they denounced his decision with such vigor that he quickly scrapped the amended pact and gave free rein to the French forces in Cochinchina.

The French commanders in Vietnam only occasionally sought clearance from Napoleon III. They had learned to employ the *fait accompli,* facing their superiors with the deed already done, a tactic that became standard in Vietnam. Admiral Pierre Paul Marie Benoît de La Grandière, one of the early French governors of Cochinchina, elevated the device to an art. In 1863, he acted on his own authority to extend French control over Cambodia, claiming that France had inherited Vietnam's alleged supremacy over its neighbor. When the Cambodian king tried to flee to Siam, an alert French officer compelled the uncooperative monarch at gunpoint to ratify a French protectorate over his country.

Similarly, in 1867, La Grandière unilaterally occupied the three western provinces of Cochinchina not yet in French hands on the pretense that Vietnamese in the area threatened France's presence in Cambodia. He had secretly prepared the move without advising Napoleon III in advance. Nor did La Grandière warn Phan Thanh Giang, the Vietnamese viceroy in the western provinces, who had negotiated earlier treaties with France. Shocked and shamed, the venerable mandarin committed suicide—after pledging his sons never to collaborate with the French. Tu Duc, equally appalled, published a remarkable confession of his sorrow and his impotence:

> Never has an era seen such sadness, never a year more anguish. Above me, I fear the edicts of heaven. Below, the tribulations of the people trouble my days and nights. Deep in my heart, I tremble and blush, finding neither words nor actions to help my subjects. . . .
>
> Alone, I am speechless. My pulse is feeble, my body pale and thin, my beard and hair white. Though not yet forty, I have already reached old age, so that I lack the strength to pay homage to my ancestors every morning and evening. . . .
>
> Evil must be suppressed and goodness sought. The wise must offer

their counsel, the strong their force, the rich their wealth, and all those with skills should devote them to the needs of the army and the kingdom. Let us, together, mend our errors and rebuild. . . .

Alas! the centuries are fraught with pain, and man is burdened by fear and woe. Thus we express our feelings, that they may be known to the world.

Royal writ. Respect it.

Napoleon III fell in 1870, defeated by Prussia and his own rash gambles, and Paris became a battleground between republicans and monarchists. Nationalist passions concentrated more on demands to recover Alsace and Lorraine from Germany than on efforts to expand France's dominions overseas. French naval officers in Saigon were thus left to promote their own schemes. One, conceived in the mid-1860s, gave the impulse for France later to push northward and dominate all of Vietnam.

Could the mighty Mekong, the sacred serpent of Asian legend, serve as a trade route between its delta in Cochinchina and its upper reaches in the western Chinese province of Yunnan, that misty region of untapped wealth? Would that not validate France's investment in Southeast Asia? To answer those grand questions, Admiral de La Grandière, the dynamic governor in Saigon, organized a voyage of exploration to be led by a subordinate, Captain Doudart de Lagrée, with Lieutenant Francis Garnier as his deputy. Garnier, a promising colonial officer then in his twenties, made the expedition immensely influential—and his heroic exploits came to symbolize the glories of imperialism.

An unalloyed idealist, Garnier fervently believed that France had been divinely designated, as he wrote, to bring "into light and into liberty the races and peoples still enslaved by ignorance and despotism." In pursuit of that *mission civilisatrice,* he had quit the navy to join the corps of "native affairs" officers that administered Cochinchina. The pioneers of Garnier's breed were no routine French functionaries, like those later assigned to Vietnam. They were dedicated men who studied local customs, learned the language, and sincerely considered themselves to be progressive—like America's Green Berets, who a century later believed that "civic action" would win "hearts and minds."

The Mekong expedition fit the great tradition of the period, comparable to John Speke's search for the source of the Nile. Ten French explorers and their native bearers left Saigon in June 1866, paused to gaze at the fantastic temple ruins of the Cambodian empire at Angkor, then proceeded upstream into Laos. Frequently frustrated by rapids and sandbars, they soon surmised that the river had no commercial potential. But Garnier, obsessed by what he himself called an almost maniacal drive, persuaded the group to press on to southern China. Doudart de Lagrée died there, exhausted by fatigue and fever; Garnier took over and led the column down the Yangtze River to Shanghai and back to Saigon. Altogether, the journey took two years, but its full effect would not be felt for another five.

In 1873, Garnier published his two-volume *Voyage d'Exploration,* a sumptuously illustrated collection of historical, anthropological, agricultural, geological, meteorological, and other details amassed during the trip. In it, he expounded his geopolitical theories and warned that decadence awaited France unless it fulfilled its imperial destiny. But most important in practical terms, he concluded that while the Mekong was not navigable, a lucrative trade in Chinese silk, tea, and textiles could be carried along the Red River, which flowed from the heights of Yunnan down through northern Vietnam to Haiphong, a port on the Gulf of Tonkin. France's next step, then, was to reach up from Cochinchina to dominate the rest of the Indochinese peninsula.

Garnier's notion of opening the Red River might have come to naught but for the daring enterprise of Jean Dupuis, a French merchant based in Hankou. The two men had met there during Garnier's journey down the Yangtze. Dupuis, a purveyor of weapons to the warlord of Yunnan province, needed an alternative to the rugged overland route to Indochina. After experimenting successfully on the Red River, as Garnier suggested, he obtained approval to use the waterway from Admiral Jules-Marie Dupré, French governor of Cochinchina, who even guaranteed him a loan from a British bank in Saigon. But the government in Paris reacted cautiously. Vietnam beyond Cochinchina was still a sovereign state, and Dupuis had not acquired its authorization. Besides, the French ministry of foreign affairs, headed by Duc Albert de Broglie, an eminent Catholic scholar, disliked imperialistic gambles. Admiral Dupré, acting on his own, could only deploy the French warships near Haiphong as a gesture of "moral" support for Dupuis.

Bearing Chinese credentials, Dupuis transported his guns and ammunition to Yunnan in March 1873 and returned to Hanoi two months later with a cargo of tin and copper. He was preparing a similar excursion with a shipment of salt when the trouble started. A guild of local mandarins controlled the salt monopoly, and they blocked his departure. Dupuis and his crew of some two hundred armed Europeans, Chinese, and Filipinos promptly occupied a section of Hanoi, raised the French flag, and appealed to Saigon for aid. Tu Duc, in his palace at Hué, complained to Admiral Dupré that Dupuis was violating Vietnam's treaty with France.

Tonkin was in chaos at the time. The Taiping rebellion, which convulsed China for a decade, had been brutally quelled not long before, driving Chinese insurgents into Vietnam, where they plundered defenseless villages. Tu Duc had appealed to Chinese officials for help, but the soldiers they dispatched merely joined the bandits; the French referred to the Chinese regulars and outlaws alike as Black Flag pirates. Their killing and looting, combined with the plight of Dupuis, secretly delighted Admiral Dupré. A foothold near the Chinese frontier, he had written, was a "matter of life or death" for France's future in Asia. Now he could achieve that aim. Employing the new telegraph, he urged Paris to endorse immediate French intervention in Tonkin before the English, Germans, or Americans arrived. And, with overweening optimism of the kind that would later beguile other foreign officers in Vietnam, he added: "Need no assistance. Can act with means at my disposal. Success assured."

The government in Paris warned him against international repercussions, such as Chinese intervention in Vietnam. But Dupré, accomplished in the art of the *fait accompli,* already had a covert plan built around Francis Garnier, whom he had summoned back from a trip to China for the purpose. Dupré sent Garnier and a few French troops to Hanoi, telling Tu Duc that they would evict Dupuis. But once in the city, where he could observe its weak defenses, Garnier dropped all pretense at diplomacy, joined forces with Dupuis, and began issuing orders. He unilaterally declared the Red River open to foreign trade, and he lowered Vietnamese customs tariffs to suit European merchants. When the city's mandarins protested, he stormed the Hanoi citadel. On the same day seventy-three years later, French warships would also seize on a commercial squabble to bomb Haiphong, an action that sparked France's final futile struggle to hold Indochina.

Garnier then fanned out to the east, his ranks reinforced by troops from Saigon as well as Vietnamese Catholics and dynastic foes of Tu Duc. Within a month, he had conquered the region between Hanoi and the sea, including the towns of Haiphong and Nam Dinh. But he suddenly fell victim to his own pride and courage. On December 21, 1873, attacked outside Hanoi by Black Flag mercenaries fighting for the Vietnamese, he impetuously rushed ahead of his men to lead a charge, and crumpled under a hail of bullets. He was only thirty-five years old.

Proponents of imperialism revered Garnier as a martyr later in the century. But just after his death, his expedition aroused misgivings.

Formerly enthusiastic, Saigon businessmen now called for caution, preferring to consolidate their economic gains in Cochinchina. The government in Paris, fearful of escalating costs and possible international complications, ordered Dupré to withdraw the French force from Tonkin. But Tu Duc, having observed Garnier's easy advances in Tonkin, was eager for a pact with France that would guarantee his rule over the region, however nominal it might be.

The man selected by Dupré to sign a new treaty was Paul Louis Philastre, a brilliant scholar who had been one of Garnier's colleagues in the colonial civil service. He had translated Gia Long's elaborate legal code from Chinese characters into French, a feat for which he was promoted to head the indigenous judicial administration. But he made a bigger impact as a rare and eloquent critic of his compatriots in Vietnam. Unlike Garnier, who believed in France's mission to bring sweetness and light to the oppressed, Philastre asserted that the French themselves were the oppressors. He did not entirely reject the French presence. He pleaded, instead, for respect for Vietnamese institutions and aspirations. In 1873, denouncing the imposition of French law in Vietnam, he wrote: "The extraordinary resistance, sometimes violent, sometimes passive in nature, day by day more hateful, which is opposed to us by all classes of the people, is stronger now than at any time since the conquest. We must open our eyes."

Consistent with those sentiments, Philastre expelled Dupuis from Hanoi and evacuated the French force from Tonkin. Then, in Hué, he concluded a treaty with Tu Duc that finally confirmed France's unconditional control over all of Cochinchina, opened the Red River to commerce, allowed the French to establish consulates in three Vietnamese towns, and, among its other provisions, authorized them to help the emperor defend his territories against outside attack.

In conceding to the country's partition, Tu Duc sacrificed the south in order to retain his tenuous hold on central and north Vietnam. Implicitly, though, he recognized a French protectorate over his regime, and that would be confirmed in a later pact. And he had acknowledged direct French control over Cochinchina; this would complicate France's negotiations with the Vietminh seventy years later.

Philastre's flexibility seemed to signal weakness to Tu Duc. He immediately launched a campaign of retaliation against the Vietnamese Catholics who had fought for Garnier, destroying their villages and slaughtering them by the thousands. He also encouraged the Black Flag pirates and other bandits to harass traffic on the Red River, thus nullifying in practice his agreement to permit free trade along the waterway.

And he counterbalanced the French by tightening his links to China, ceremonially paying tribute to Beijing and inviting Chinese troops into Vietnam to maintain order.

The government in Paris, absorbed in internecine political squabbles, neglected Vietnam for the next few years. Imperialist attitudes, always simmering, again boiled up a few years later, but France lacked a towering literary partisan of expansion like Rudyard Kipling, who mobilized England behind his thesis of the "white man's burden." So the colonial issue divided the French in acrimonious controversy. Some argued that rival European nations such as England, Germany, and even little Belgium were outpacing France overseas. They asserted that France's global power would slip unless it offset its loss of Alsace and Lorraine by extending its hegemony elsewhere. The French military establishment, humiliated in France's defeat by Prussia in 1870, also wanted fresh foreign enterprises to salve its wounded pride. And France's businessmen, prospering from industrialization, were captivated by potential investment outlets, raw materials, and markets abroad. The imperialist revival at the time spawned a proliferation of geographical societies, dedicated to publicizing the political, economic, and moral advantages of expansion. A featured speaker at the Paris Geographical Society in 1877, for instance, was Jean Dupuis, the former Hanoi arms peddler, who criticized the pusillanimous French withdrawal from Tonkin.

The most vocal adversary of French expansion was Georges Clemenceau, the famous "Tiger" who would lead France during World War I. Then a left-wing radical, he cursed imperialism as a policy that enriched capitalists and wasted funds that should be spent on domestic social programs. France's security, he insisted, lay in rebuilding its European relationships, and he decried faraway colonial ventures that distracted from the recovery of Alsace and Lorraine. Oddly enough, conservative extremists shared his views, largely for unrelated internal political motives. The strongest expansionists, in contrast, were staunch anticlerical progressives who regarded themselves as the ideological heirs of the French Revolution. With many differences, their contemporary American equivalent might have been the liberals of the Kennedy and Johnson administrations, who went into Vietnam with what they considered to be enlightened intentions.

Their spokesman was Jules Ferry, the first French prime minister to make imperialism his principal platform. Stocky, energetic, and arrogant, he had defied the wrath of the Catholic Church when, as minister of education, he made French schooling secular, free, and obligatory. An intensely nationalistic native of Lorraine, he saw in overseas conquests the compensation for his lost birthplace. His convictions reflected the concept, then prevalent among many French, that it was France's duty "to civilize inferior peoples." But above all, he articulated the aspirations of the burgeoning French business community. Unless manufacturers could sell abroad, their factories would founder, creating unemployment and social unrest of "cataclysmic" proportions. As he put it: "Colonial policy is the daughter of industrial policy."

The rule of the admirals in Saigon ended in 1879 with the appointment of Cochinchina's first civilian governor, Charles Marie Le Myre de Vilers, a seasoned colonial administrator. Even more aggressive than his naval predecessors, he lobbied vigorously for the occupation of Tonkin, asserting that "the moment has come to pluck the ripe fruit." The government in Paris required no encouragement from Saigon. It could count on support from French industrial interests, then concerned that foreign competitors would beat them to Vietnam's resources. French investors who had incorporated to develop the rich anthracite deposits at Hongay, in northern Tonkin, now worried, for example, that Tu Duc might grant the coal-mining concession to an English group. Time was vital.

A pretext was easy. Liberally interpreted, the treaty signed by Tu Duc in 1874 authorized French intervention in Tonkin to quell disorders. Black Flag pirates and other bandits menaced French subjects in Hanoi and trade along the Red River. Paris therefore directed Le Myre de Vilers to defend Vietnam's "sovereignty." He selected Captain Henri Rivière to lead two companies of troops to the north. Rivière's expedition repeated the Garnier operation—but with a different aftermath.

Rivière was an unusual figure in the colonial cast of characters. A career naval officer who wrote plays and novels, he had a list of friends that included Dumas, Flaubert, and other French literati. Unlike Garnier, he had no sense of mission, and in contrast to Philastre, he detested the natives. In his mid-fifties at the time, he was worn out by the tropical climate, which may have explained his volatile conduct.

China, which had not recognized the French pact with Tu Duc, made clear its disapproval of France's aggressive designs against Tonkin. Le Myre de Vilers thus instructed Rivière to proceed "diplomatically and peacefully." But Rivière wanted a "more solid" French presence in Hanoi. So, as Garnier had, he seized on allegedly "belligerent preparations" by local mandarins to storm the Hanoi citadel. The humiliated Vietnamese governor, Hong Dieu, hanged himself in a gesture of shame and protest.

Rivière, leading six hundred men, then followed in Garnier's footsteps by occupying the area between Hanoi and the sea. He took the Hongay coal mines as well, presumably to prevent an English attempt to grab them. But he would share Garnier's fate. Black Flag forces, fighting for the Vietnamese, ambushed and killed him near Hongay—and they carried his head from village to village to symbolize France's defeat. Later, one of his friends commented: "I respect those who have fallen bravely, but they have reaped what they have sown. . . . They attack the Vietnamese, violate their rights, then call them murderers for defending themselves."

Jules Ferry and his associates in Paris disagreed. Though they had hoped for a cheap way to dominate Tonkin, the momentum of Rivière's operation propelled them forward. On May 15, 1883, four days before Rivière's death, the French parliament overwhelmingly voted more than five million francs in appropriations for a full-scale expedition to impose a "protectorate" on Vietnam. One of the few politicians to oppose the decision, the ultraconservative Jules Delafosse, bluntly described its real purpose: "Let us, gentlemen, call things by their name. It is not a protectorate that you want, but a possession."

Tu Duc died two months later, "with curses against the invader on his lips," as a court communiqué put it. His hectic reign had lasted thirty-five years. Probably sterile, he had left no sons, and a struggle for succession promptly ensued at the palace in Hué. Within a year, rival mandarins enthroned and deposed three young princes, poisoning one of them, Hiep Hoa, for capitulating to the French in the final act that deprived Vietnam of its independence.

In August 1883, taking advantage of the confusion after Tu Duc's death, a French fleet appeared at the mouth of the Perfume River, not far from Hué. François Harmand, a "native affairs" official aboard one of the vessels, threatened the Vietnamese with the "worst evils" unless they surrendered within forty-eight hours. "Imagine all that is terrible and it will still be less than reality," he said. "The word 'Vietnam' will be erased from history."

Before the Vietnamese could respond, the French warships opened fire, inflicting such heavy casualties that a chief mandarin emerged personally under a flag of truce to negotiate. Harmand, conducted to the court at Hué, dictated the French terms. He compelled Hiep Hoa to sign a treaty granting France a "protectorate" over all Vietnam with the exception of Cochinchina, already a French colony. Henceforth, the French would install officials and garrisons to exercise jurisdiction over the Vietnamese authorities, including the emperor. They would regulate Vietnam's commerce, collect its customs duties, assure its defense, and manage its foreign relations. In short, as Delafosse had predicted, Vietnam had become an outright French possession. Also, as Harmand had declared in his ultimatum, the name "Vietnam" ceased to exist—at least in French and other Western documents. Divided administratively, the country now comprised three zones—Tonkin, Annam, and Cochinchina—and its people were referred to as Annamites, a term many themselves soon adopted. But the French conquest, though completed on paper, was not over in fact. Protesting against the imposed pact, China sent troops into Tonkin, partly to aid its Vietnamese protégés but also to annex a portion of the area. Soon France and China were waging war in Vietnam.

By the end of 1883, the French had more than twenty thousand men in Tonkin, with Admiral Amédée Anatole Prosper Courbet in charge and three generals each commanding a contingent. Their offensive prefigured the French campaign against the Vietminh two generations later. Spreading north from Hanoi, one column marched up the Red River valley to rout the Chinese at Sontay, while another captured Thai Nguyen and a third took Tuyen Quang, clearing the Black River region. They gave no quarter. One of the French generals, refusing to regard his Chinese and Vietnamese foes as regulars, beheaded all his prisoners as "rebels."

The fighting dragged on for more than a year, even stretching beyond Vietnam. In early 1885, after a fragile accord between France and China collapsed, a French naval squadron under Admiral Courbet bombarded the Chinese coastal city of Fuzhou and then attacked Keelung, a port on the island of Taiwan. The Chinese, their own regime foundering, sued for peace. But other events retarded an agreement.

The French had inched north through a fantastic landscape of sharp limestone hills to occupy Langson, a town strategically situated near the border of China. On March 28, 1885, the Chinese wounded the French general in command while he was out on a reconnaissance mission. A Colonel Herbinger, drunk at the time, thought in his stupor that the enemy had launched a massive attack. He ordered the French force to abandon the town, leave its equipment behind, and flee to the mountains. News of the devastating "defeat" shook Paris.

Facing parliament two days later, Prime Minister Ferry called for the sum of two hundred million more francs to support the military effort in Indochina. But the mood of the legislature had changed since his success with funds two years earlier. The struggle now seemed to offer no end. Clemenceau, more eloquent than ever, accused Ferry of "high treason" for bogging France down in Vietnam; his address foreshadowed speeches that French politicians were to hear, under similar circumstances, sixty years later, and strangely resembled a warning that deputy Secretary of State George Ball would send to Lyndon Johnson in 1965: "When our soldiers are again threatened, as they are today, we will be asked for more money and more men. We will not be able to refuse. And millions upon millions, fresh troops on top of fresh troops will lead to our exhaustion. Gentlemen, we must block this route."

Stirred by Clemenceau's words, parliament rejected Ferry's request and ousted his cabinet—leaving him with the nickname Ferry-the-Tonkinese. By coincidence, the Chinese agreed to recognize France's protectorate over Vietnam in order to preserve their own territory, then being sliced up by the European powers. China's submission revived the imperialist momentum in Paris, and the French forces in Vietnam again intensified their conquest. An incident that occurred at Hué during the summer of 1885 exemplified their renewed ferocity.

Ton That Thuyet, a nationalistic adviser to the thirteen-year-old emperor, Ham Nghi, had objected to French activities in Tonkin, contending that they violated Vietnam's treaty with France. Apprised of the complaint, Foreign Minister Charles de Freycinet, a determined imperialist, decided to "punish" Thuyet. He instructed General Roussel de Courcy, now the French commander in Tonkin, to stage a "military demonstration" unless the dissident mandarin resigned. Roussel thereupon encircled the palace at Hué with a thousand troops and demanded an audience with the boy ruler. Thuyet recklessly ordered an attack against the French, who replied with an orgy of killing and looting that surpassed the notorious sack of the Summer Palace in Beijing by English soldiers under Lord Elgin twenty-five years before. Over three days, according to a French account, French troops burned the Vietnamese imperial library, with its ancient scrolls and manuscripts, and they stripped the palace of gold and silver ornaments, precious stones, carpets, silk curtains, statuary, and even mosquito nets, cuspidors, and toothpicks, the total valued at some twenty-four million francs.

Ham Nghi, accompanied by Thuyet, fled from his capital to the highlands of Laos, and the French supplanted him with a more docile prince, Dong Khanh. Escaping with the imperial seal as well as the deposed emperor himself, Thuyet organized an opposition movement based on Ham Nghi's legitimacy. The former ruler, betrayed by Hmong mountaineers, was captured and exiled, but the Vietnamese resistance continued past the end of the century, plaguing the French nearly everywhere. "We have no friends," noted a ranking French colonial official at the time. "Not even the courtiers surrounding the emperor, our creature, favor us."

The French tightened their hold, assigning civilian agents and soldiers everywhere. In 1887, they created the Indochinese Union, comprised of Cochinchina, Annam, Tonkin, and Cambodia, adding Laos to the cohesive administrative structure six years later. Even so, there remained the prolonged task of "pacification"—a term that would be applied to similar French and American endeavors decades afterward.

That effort would be accomplished by "acts of incredible brutality," as a French civilian governor of the period, Jean-Marie Antoine de Lanessan, recalled. But the French colonial experience would also open Vietnam to Western ideas that, along with the violence and repression and humiliation, rekindled Vietnamese nationalism.

3 The Heritage of Vietnamese Nationalism

趙
嫗
逐
吳
軍

Trieu Au, the Vietnamese equivalent of Joan of Arc, fought for Vietnam's independence against China in the third century A. D. Defeated at the age of twenty-three, she committed suicide. She is still worshiped as a sacred figure.

The economy of Vietnam, like that of all Southeast Asia, is based on the cultivation of rice—a technique learned from the Chinese. Growing rice requires two factors: manual labor and water, both plentiful in Vietnam.

A wealthy Vietnamese couple photographed in front of their luxurious villa in the early twentieth century. The man is wearing his French decoration and Western shoes. His wife's long fingernails denote her unfamiliarity with manual labor.

An early twentieth-century Vietnamese nationalist cartoon depicts peasants routing French colonial troops. The peasants are shouting: "Wipe out the gang of imperialists, mandarins, capitalists, and big landlords!"

Vietnamese prisoners being held in stocks after an attempt to subvert a French army garrison. This plot, uncovered in 1907, led to the execution of several Vietnamese nationalists and the incarceration of many others.

Ho Chi Minh, then known as Nguyen Ai Quoc, at a French Socialist party congress in December 1920. It was here that the Communists broke away to form their own party, and Ho joined them. He was thirty years old.

Ho Chi Minh (back row, third from left) with other Communist agents in Moscow in the mid-1920s. He was then using the name Linh, and his identity papers testified to his fluency in Vietnamese, French, English, Russian, and Chinese.

The French exported the life-style of Paris to Saigon—as they did to all their colonies. The scene here is the terrace of the Continental Palace Hotel, where the French elite met to dine. The hotel is still standing.

French colonial officials, known as "native affairs officers," in a Vietnamese village at the turn of the century. These officials were said to be participating in a local ceremony designed to rid the village of an epidemic.

A handsome Vietnamese prostitute poses in a high-class opium den, presumably in Saigon. The French colonial administration organized the opium traffic in order to raise revenues, and the operation was highly successful.

Paul Doumer, the French governor-general of Indochina around the turn of the century, put the possession on a paying basis by exploiting its resources. Later president of France, he was assassinated in Paris in 1932.

A local caricature spoofs a Vietnamese who has been converted by French culture into a tennis player. In fact, many Vietnamese nationalists who opposed colonial rule were the products of French schools.

Vietnamese art students surround their French teacher in a school in Tonkin. Only a handful of upper-class Vietnamese benefited from French education, which nevertheless contributed to Vietnam's modernization.

When France arrived in Indochina, the Annamites were ripe for servitude.

—Paul Doumer

All subject peoples are filled with hope by the prospect that an era of right and justice is opening for them . . . in the struggle of civilization against barbarism.

—Ho Chi Minh

B ut for his Asian features, he might have been an impoverished young French intellectual, a familiar sight in the Paris of the early 1920s. Small and frail, with a shock of black hair and piercing black eyes, he occupied a shabby room in a hotel on a dead-end street behind Montmartre, eking out a livelihood by enlarging and retouching photographs—"a souvenir of your relatives and friends," his visiting card advertised. He was never without a book, either Shakespeare or Hugo or Zola, and he rarely missed a weekly meeting of the Club du Faubourg, a genteel group that discussed drama, literature, and sometimes even spiritualism, but generally avoided political issues. Earnest yet gentle, reserved yet not timid, he would speak up in fluent French at those sessions, his intensity tempered by wit. Or, as a contemporary French acquaintance recalled later: "He seemed to be mocking the world, and also mocking himself."

But even during those balmy days in Paris, he was a determined revolutionary, devoted to the Vietnamese struggle against French colonialism. He had earlier borne several different names, and he would use many aliases as an underground Communist agent in the years to come. He then called himself Nguyen Ai Quoc, Nguyen the Patriot. Two decades later, during a more tumultuous period, he would assume a more appropriate *nom de guerre*, Ho Chi Minh—the "enlightened" leader of the Vietminh.

Like the other nationalists of his generation, who had lived in France or attended French schools in Vietnam, Nguyen Ai Quoc absorbed the influence of the West but rejected its domination. His experience conformed to Vietnam's past. For long before the French conquest, the Vietnamese had borrowed Chinese culture, institutions, ethics, and even calligraphy while resisting China's efforts to control their country. But French imperialists, in their campaigns to subjugate Vietnam, committed the mistake of believing, as Prime Minister Jules Ferry had put it,

that their Vietnamese foes were merely "bandits" without "any sentiment of patriotism." Similarly, American strategists would later misper-
ceive Ho Chi Minh, though an avowed Communist, as simply a Soviet
instrument. These errors stemmed largely from an ignorance of Vietnam's history, a long and tortuous series of conflicts and accommodations that gave the Vietnamese a profound sense of their own identity.

The Indochinese peninsula, which rounds the southeastern corner of
continental Asia, is a jumbled terrain of towering peaks and deep valleys
reaching down through thick forests to coastal plains. Its earliest inhabitants, Austronesian tribes that had migrated north from the islands of the
Pacific, were later displaced by other peoples. The Khmer, as the
Cambodians refer to themselves, may have come from western India.
The Lao, ethnically related to the Thai, streamed in from the highlands
of China's Yunnan province, and the Vietnamese flowed south as well
from the lower Yangtze valley. The later arrivals occupied the rich river
deltas and fertile shores, forcing the aborigines into the mountains,
where their descendants still survive uneasily in a mosaic of diverse
clans.

Indochina, as its name implies, became the locus for competition
between Asia's two great civilizations, India and China. Merchants and
missionaries from both countries converged on the peninsula, promoting commerce, religion, language, art, and customs. India left its mark
on Laos, Cambodia, and even as far east as Champa, a kingdom that
flourished in central Vietnam until its destruction by the Vietnamese;
China imposed its imprint on Vietnam, which was insulated from
India's sway by topography.

Chronic turmoil plagued the area. The Cambodian empire, which at
its height stretched from the South China Sea into Burma, began to
crumble during the thirteenth century, partly before the onslaught of the
Vietnamese, who wiped out Champa and advanced to the Gulf of Siam
by the middle of the eighteenth century. The Vietnamese also faced
recurrent pressures from China.

Though national personality is difficult to define, two important
elements formed Vietnam's character during those centuries. The original Vietnamese brought with them from China their basic economy,
built around wet rice farming. Rice cultivation, which is dependent on
the vagaries of weather and on complex systems of irrigation, requires
cooperative labor. Vietnamese communities thus developed a strong
collective spirit, and, though autonomous, villages could be mobilized

as a unified chain of separate links to fight against foreign intruders. Their country's frequent wars also infused in the Vietnamese a readiness to defend themselves, so that they evolved into a breed of warriors. Centuries later, during France's war to preserve its hold on Indochina in the 1950s, the French sociologist Paul Mus warned against the "convenient notion" that Vietnamese peasants were a "passive mass, only interested in their daily bowl of rice, and terrorized into subversion by agents." Their commitment to nationhood had been forged long before.

Like most nations, Vietnam traces its genesis to legendary kingdoms ruled by mythical monarchs. The Vietnamese perpetuate this folklore, hoping to demonstrate that their national roots run as deep as those of China, their traditional rival. But their recorded history, as registered in Chinese annals, begins only in 208 B.C., when Trieu Da, a turncoat Chinese general, conquered Au Lac, a domain in the northern mountains of Vietnam populated by Viets, a people of Mongolian origin who had migrated south. Trieu Da, defying the decadent Ch'in dynasty, constructed his capital near the present city of Canton and proclaimed himself emperor of Nam Viet, Land of the Southern Viet, which reached as far south as the present city of Danang. The dynamic Han dynasty, which expanded the Chinese empire across Asia from Turkestan to Korea, annexed Nam Viet a century later as the Chinese province of Giao Chi.

The Chinese integrated the territory in ways that resembled Rome's contemporaneous approach to its dominions—and which the French would emulate millennia later. They created administrative districts under military governors whose civilian Chinese advisers imported Confucian bureaucratic concepts that underlined respect for authority. They established schools to spread the Chinese language, which became the idiom of learned Vietnamese, who even during the days of French supremacy could qualify as officials only by passing the arduous "eight-legged" examination prescribed under Confucian tenets. They also introduced the plow and draft animals, and, to exploit Vietnam for themselves, they built roads, ports, canals, dikes, and dams. At first they ruled Vietnam lightly, co-opting its feudal chiefs rather than subduing them.

But China failed to assimilate the Vietnamese, who retained their ethnic singularity despite their receptivity to Chinese innovations. Indeed, China's superior institutions may have indirectly contributed to Vietnam's cohesion. The Vietnamese, however, soon rebelled against Chinese troop and labor levies, high taxes, and interference in their local affairs. Over the centuries, they would repeatedly challenge Chinese domination. And that hostility entered their historic consciousness. Ho Chi Minh would evoke that memory in 1946 to justify to his own followers a controversial deal with France designed to evict Nationalist China's occupation army from northern Vietnam: "Better to sniff a bit of French shit briefly than eat Chinese shit for the rest of our lives."

A titled lady, Trung Trac, avenging the murder of her dissident husband by a Chinese commander, led the first major Vietnamese insurrection against China. She and her sister, Trung Nhi, mustered other restive nobles and their vassals, including another woman, Phung Thi Chinh, who supposedly gave birth to a baby in the middle of the battle but continued to fight with the infant strapped to her back. They vanquished the Chinese in 40 A.D. and, with the Trung sisters as queens, set up an independent state which stretched from Hué into southern China. But the Chinese crushed it only two years later, and the Trung sisters committed suicide—in aristocratic style—by throwing themselves into a river. The Vietnamese still venerate them at temples in Hanoi and Sontay, and the Communists acclaim them as pioneer nationalists. Madame Ngo Dinh Nhu, the sister-in-law of South Vietnam's President Ngo Dinh Diem, erected a statue in Saigon in 1962 to commemorate their patriotism—and also to promote herself as their reincarnation.

Another woman, Trieu Au, the Vietnamese version of Joan of Arc, launched a revolt against China in 248 A.D., a generation after the collapse of the Han dynasty, wearing golden armor and riding an elephant as she led a thousand men into battle. Gloriously defeated at the age of twenty-three, she committed suicide rather than suffer the shame of surrender. Like the Trung sisters, she is remembered by a temple, and by her words of defiance: "I want to rail against the wind and the tide, kill the whales in the sea, sweep the whole country to save the people from slavery, and I refuse to be abused."

These feminine exploits, doubtless inflated in popular legend, illustrate the unique status of women in Vietnamese society. In contrast to their counterparts elsewhere in Asia and even in Europe, emancipated only recently, they could traditionally inherit land, serve as trustees of ancestral cults, and share their husbands' property.

The Chinese conquerors referred to Vietnam as Annam, the "pacified south." But it was not peaceful. Resistance against China persisted, often led by Chinese colonists who, like English settlers in America many centuries later, fought to free their adopted country. Revolts recurred chronically, and dissident nobles gradually perceived the need to mobilize peasant support. They broadened their movements and stressed that Vietnam's customs, practices, and interests differed from those of China. Even then, a glimmer of Vietnamese nationalism was discernible.

The defiance of Chinese rule accelerated when China's T'ang dynasty began to crumble after three hundred years in power, ravaged by palace conspiracies, corruption, agrarian unrest, and alien incursions from the north. The Vietnamese again struck in the tenth century, this time successfully. Their hero was Ngo Quyen, a provincial mandarin.

China had deployed fresh forces in Vietnam, some arriving by sea. In 938, as a large flotilla of armed Chinese junks approached the Bach Dang River, a tidal waterway in the north, Ngo Quyen resorted to a trick. He ordered his men to drive iron-tipped spikes into the riverbed, their points concealed below the water's surface. Then, at high tide, he engaged the Chinese, his own vessels deliberately retreating as the tide ebbed. The pursuing Chinese ships became impaled, and Ngo Quyen turned back to destroy them. The maneuver was a variation of the guerrilla tactics that the Vietnamese would use again and again in the future as they faced superior foes.

The nature of Vietnamese resistance against China changed in the tenth century. A new emperor, Dinh Bo Linh, ascended the throne in 967, calling his state Dai Co Viet, the Kingdom of the Watchful Hawk. The son of an official, he had organized a peasant army commanded by urban intellectuals. His dynasty lasted only a decade, but it won Chinese recognition of Vietnam's independence in exchange for regular payments of tribute. The tributary arrangement, which was typical of Chinese relations with the other states of Southeast Asia, endured for centuries.

But Sino-Vietnamese relations were recurrently turbulent. During the thirteenth century, the Mongol emperor Kublai Khan invaded Vietnam three times, pushing south to control the spice routes of the Indonesian archipelago. The Vietnamese, commanded by the illustrious Tran Hung Dao, repulsed each offensive. Like outnumbered Vietnamese officers before and since, he relied on mobile methods of warfare, abandoning the cities, avoiding frontal attacks, and harassing his enemies until, confused and exhausted, they were ripe for final attack. In the last great battle, which took place in the Red River valley in 1287, the Vietnamese routed three hundred thousand Mongol troops. In a victory poem, a Vietnamese general affirmed that "this ancient land shall live forever." Seven centuries later, the Vietminh commander Vo Nguyen Giap evoked Tran Hung Dao's memory as he launched an operation against the French in the same area.

The Vietnamese were no less aggressive toward their neighbors. After

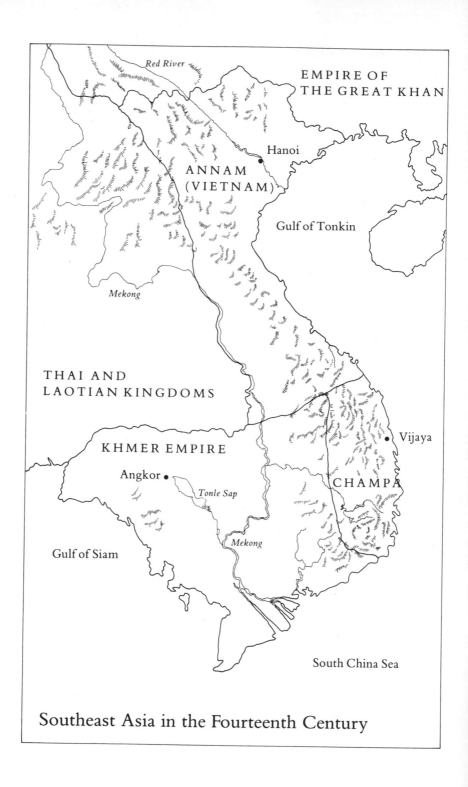

Southeast Asia in the Fourteenth Century

defeating the Mongols, they turned south to conquer Champa, the Indianized kingdom of central Vietnam. The seesaw conflict, which dragged on through the fourteenth and fifteenth centuries, reached its climax in 1471, when the Vietnamese razed the Cham capital of Indrapura, slaughtering forty thousand of its inhabitants. All that remains of Champa today are its magnificent stone sculptures, silent testimony to an extinct society. But its fate has not been forgotten by Cambodians and Laotians, who regard Vietnam's present domination of their countries to be merely the most recent episode in a relentless history of expansion.

Exhausted by their campaigns against Champa, the Vietnamese again fell prey to China, now unified under the Ming dynasty, whose brief rule over Vietnam was probably the harshest in its history. Chinese gauleiters forced Vietnamese peasants to mine for gold and other ores, cut rare woods and grow spices, all to be exported to China along with elephant tusks, rhinoceros horns, pearls, and precious stones. They drastically imposed Chinese culture, confiscated Vietnamese literature and compelled schools to teach in Chinese, suppressed Vietnamese cults and permitted only the worship of Chinese gods. They decreed Chinese dress for women and prohibited men from cutting their hair, and they even outlawed betel nut, the Vietnamese equivalent of chewing gum. They created an administrative grill, issuing identity cards to families, partly to control them and partly to streamline tax collection.

The Ming occupation inevitably provoked an insurrection. Vietnam's savior this time, Le Loi, became its greatest emperor, equal only to Ho Chi Minh in its pantheon of heroes. Not only did he crush the Chinese decisively, but his dynasty, the longest in Vietnamese history, became a model of enlightenment—at least during the early phase of its nearly four-hundred-year span.

The myth of Le Loi, like the Arthurian legend of Excalibur, depicts him as a simple fisherman who one day cast his net into a lake, only to bring up a magic sword that made him superhuman. In reality, he was a wealthy landowner from Thanh Hoa province who rebelled against the Chinese after having served them. "Every man on earth," he said, "ought to accomplish some great enterprise so that he leaves the sweet scent of his name to later generations. How, then, could he willingly be the slave of foreigners?"

In 1418, proclaiming himself the Prince of Pacification, Le Loi raised the banner of revolt. He withdrew to the mountains near his home and rallied relatives, friends, villagers, and even local brigands to his cause, teaching them the guerrilla tactics that had worked for Tran Hung Dao, who had vanquished the Mongols. The Chinese became increasingly insecure as the insurrection spread. They clung to the towns, venturing out only by day, their big battalions sticking to the roads. Adopting a defense that would fail the French five centuries later, they built fortified towers along main routes. Gradually, as the balance of forces tilted his way, Le Loi struck at the Chinese directly, deploying platoons of elephants against their horse cavalry. His adviser, the poet Nguyen Trai, set down the Vietnamese strategy in an essay that shows remarkable similarities to the twentieth-century Communist doctrine of insurgency. Subordinate military action to the political and moral struggle, it stated; "better to conquer hearts than citadels."

In 1426, fighting in rain and mud, the Vietnamese finally routed the Chinese on a field at Tot Dong, west of Hanoi. In an accord signed two years later, the Chinese recognized Vietnam's independence and Le Loi resumed the tributary tie to China as insurance. He generously furnished the Chinese with five hundred junks and thousands of horses to get them home, and apart from a last abortive attempt in 1788, the Chinese never again launched a full-scale assault against Vietnam. Nguyen Trai celebrated the victory with a poem of hope:

> Henceforth our country is safe.
> Our mountains and rivers begin life afresh.
> Peace follows war as day follows night.
> We have purged our shame for a thousand centuries,
> We have regained tranquillity for ten thousand generations.

Le Loi established his capital at Hanoi, calling the city Dong Kinh—hence the name Tonkin, northern Vietnam. He distributed land to poor peasants and rewarded loyal nobles with big estates, and he set up agencies to construct dikes, dams, irrigation systems, and other projects designed to increase agricultural production, which had been harmed by years of war. But one of his successors, Le Thanh Tong, who ascended to the throne in 1460 and ruled for thirty-eight years, lifted Vietnam into its golden age.

The political and bureaucratic structure of Le Thanh Tong's administration in the fifteenth century served Vietnam until its disruption by the French four hundred years later. Modeled along Confucian lines, it consisted of six ministries that shaped policy, each paralleled by a department to implement decisions. A communications network passed decrees to thirteen provincial headquarters, which in turn transmitted them through district offices down to some eight thousand communes, each governed by the equivalent of a mayor. This complex hierarchy was contrived to assure both central authority and local flexibility, and a corps of inspectors toured the country regularly to monitor the civil service and, in theory at least, listen to the complaints of the people.

Le Thanh Tong also created a standing army of nearly two hundred thousand men, organized in units assigned to five military regions. A nationwide census, carried out every three years, was used to draft conscripts. Qualified youths could become officers by taking competitive examinations, which Le Thanh Tong himself devised. Foreshadowing yet another Communist practice, he formed colonies of soldiers to farm virgin areas.

A scholar in the great Confucian tradition, Le Thanh Tong devoted much of his tireless energy to the advancement of learning. He expanded the national university to include a new library and lecture halls, and he perfected examinations through which students could become mandarins, whose ranks were rigorously classified into nine grades, depending on their experience and performance. He encouraged literature, organizing poetry contests in which candidates improvised rhymes in response to his own verses; patronized the publication of mathematical and scientific treatises, anthologies of legends, and a journal of his own reign; and took a special interest in maps, directing provincial officials to prepare charts that featured, along with geographical details, the history and folklore of their localities; and issued the first complete map of Vietnam.

His major achievement was a comprehensive and unusually liberal legal code. It protected citizens against abuse by mandarins, and it entitled women to possess property, share inheritances, and repudiate their husbands under certain conditions. But, consistent with Confucian concepts, it prescribed severe punishment for crimes that threatened order and stability and, by implication, the emperor's divine authority. Disobedience to a teacher or an official could be chastised by banishment—a severe sentence, since it prevented an exiled convict from worshiping at the graves of his ancestors. Strangulation, one of the penalties for treason or rebellion, was considered preferable to decapitation or slow dismemberment, since it left the body intact to join the spirit in the afterlife.

Actors and slaves were virtual outcasts under the code. Male actors could not become mandarins, nor could actresses marry aristocrats. Slaves, either foreign captives or the offspring of criminals condemned to suffer for the guilt of their parents, could be sold, mortgaged, or even put to death for showing disrespect toward their masters. But, in a progressive innovation, the former practice of branding slaves on the face was repealed.

The law's cruel provisions were no harsher than those then being enforced on the scaffolds and in the torture chambers of Europe. They also expressed the constant apprehensions of the Vietnamese emperor, who, his sacred mandate notwithstanding, sat uneasily on a throne that rebels, conspirators, and even his own family could topple overnight. Indeed, court intrigues, regional revolts, and other strife continually menaced Le Thanh Tong's heirs, whose dynasty ruled only nominally after his death.

From the early sixteenth century on, Vietnam tumbled into turmoil as competing families waged arcane power struggles in Vietnam that make the rivalries of Renaissance Italy seem simple by comparison. One clan, the Mac, defied the reigning Le dynasty, thereby antagonizing the Trinh faction, which aspired to power. After subduing the Mac forces, the Trinh effectively governed the north through figurehead Le emperors. But Trinh in-laws, the Nguyen, broke away to set up their own realm in central Vietnam, and they pushed farther south to seize the fertile Mekong delta, until then under feeble Cambodian control.

Civil strife continued in Vietnam for two centuries, as the Trinh and the Nguyen fought each other. Just as the Geneva accords of 1954 divided Vietnam at the seventeenth parallel, so the earlier rivals eventually agreed to a partition along roughly the same line. They also conceded to an expedient truce, each hoping to fight again once it had regained strength. The Nguyen leader of the late eighteenth century, Nguyen Anh, turned to France to bolster his cause. His appeal, carried to Versailles by Pigneau de Béhaine, set the scene for French intervention.

Over the centuries, therefore, Vietnam's attempts to attain political cohesion were repeatedly thwarted by centrifugal forces. The pattern persisted into modern times. The war between North and South Vietnam after 1954 largely expressed ancient regional animosities only newly overlaid with an ideological veneer. And the same tensions continued after 1975 as southerners, Communists among them, balked at northern domination. Equally inimical to Vietnam's unity was the traditional autonomy of its rural communities. Peasants symbolically revered the throne as the divine link between heaven and earth, but they were ruled in practice by their own councils of local dignitaries, selected for their age, education, wealth, and family status. "The edicts of the emperor," went the old Vietnamese adage, "stop at the edge of the village." A sense of Vietnamese national identity nevertheless grew in reaction to foreign intervention—crystallizing during the long resistance against the Chinese. It confronted the French from their first intrusions into Vietnam.

The Vietnamese emperors were too weak to check the French militarily or diplomatically. Assorted armed groups emerged during the nineteenth century, some encouraged by the imperial court, others fighting on their own, that inflicted a heavy toll on the French; yet they failed for lack of a nationwide organization. Even so, the repression of each revolt inspired later uprisings, sowing the seeds of future resistance. General Joseph Gallieni, the great French colonial officer and a hero of World War I, perceived this reality while serving in Vietnam in the late nineteenth century: "A country is not conquered and pacified by crushing its people through terror. After overcoming their initial fear, the masses grow increasingly rebellious, their accumulated bitterness steadily rising in reaction to the brutal use of force."

Vietnamese partisans appeared as early as 1859, when the French captured Saigon, and insurgent movements spread through Cochinchina soon afterward. Buddhist monks led several of these factions. The early guerrillas, elusive and resilient, carved out sanctuaries in such inaccessible zones as the Plain of Reeds, a swampy zone north of Saigon, and the Camau peninsula, an area of marshes located in the southwestern corner of the Mekong delta. They nagged French soldiers then just as the Vietminh and Vietcong would frustrate the French and Americans a century later. Admiral Bonard, the French commander in Cochinchina, issued a report at the end of 1862 that could have been duplicated in 1962: "We have had enormous difficulties in enforcing our authority. . . . Rebel bands disturb the country everywhere. They appear from nowhere in large numbers, destroy everything and then disappear into nowhere."

In 1862, after the emperor Tu Duc reluctantly ceded to France the three provinces adjacent to Saigon, regional dignitaries continued to harass the French despite the ruler's decision. One of them, Truong Cong Dinh, the son of a military mandarin from central Vietnam, mobilized his own peasant units, armed them with spears and swords, and told Tu Duc that "we are determined to disobey your orders as long as you speak of peace and surrender."

Betrayed and killed a year later, Truong Cong Dinh was succeeded by his twenty-year-old son, who himself soon met death when he tried to expand his father's movement through alliances with other partisan groups. His comrades in that venture included a poet, Nguyen Huu Huan, who was later captured and executed by the French; his verses typified the burgeoning nationalistic sentiment of the period:

The more I sense my duty the more I feel
On my shoulders its infinite weight.
A man worthy of the name must blush
If he cannot pay the debt with his life.

Only in the summer of 1885 did the sporadic and disjointed Vietnamese opposition gain broader legitimacy when Ham Nghi, the thirteen-year-old emperor, joined the resistance. His movement collapsed within three years, but his defiance assumed legendary proportions.

The mastermind behind his insurrection was a passionate nationalist, Ton That Thuyet, a scion of the royal family. After 1883, when the French forced a "protectorate" on Vietnam, he smuggled arms, ammunition, food, and money to a secret base north of Hué, the imperial capital. He also disposed of three earlier emperors whose submissiveness to the French exasperated him. When the French imposed their demands at Hué in July 1885, he provoked them into an attack. They pillaged the city and palace; Ton That Thuyet fled to his sanctuary with Ham Nghi, whom the French promptly replaced by a pliant elder brother.

Ton That Thuyet escaped to China, ostensibly to seek aid, while Ham Nghi took refuge in a Hmong village near the Laotian border. The French, who had set the mountain tribes against lowland Vietnamese, bribed the Hmong village chief with money, opium, and a military title to betray the fugitive emperor. They captured him in late 1888, exiled him to Algeria, and executed all his followers except the two sons of Ton That Thuyet—one of whom died defending his monarch; the other strangled himself to death out of shame.

Ham Nghi had issued an edict during his flight from Hué, urging "the rich to give their wealth, the mighty their strength, and the poor their limbs so that the country might be rescued from the invader." The proclamation, known as Can Vuong, or Loyalty to the Emperor, inspired resistance leaders long after his deportation.

In late 1886, for example, a guerrilla chief, Dinh Cong Trang, defended the village complex of Ba Dinh in central Vietnam against murderous onslaughts by a French force of more than three thousand men—among them a young engineer, Captain Joseph Joffre, later to become supreme commander of France's armies in World War I. Another, De Tham, was a former bandit who held sway over three provinces in northern Vietnam and even threatened the approaches to Hanoi. Tracked for years by the French, he fought until 1913. But the most distinguished resistance figure was Phan Dinh Phung, a mandarin from central Vietnam whose virtues were posthumously extolled by a contemporary poet:

A loyal subject between heaven and earth,
His death deprived us of independence.

Phan Dinh Phung had earned immense prestige as the Ngu Su, or Imperial Censor, a position which allowed him to criticize officials and even the emperor for misconduct. He performed his duties with such courage and integrity that, as an adviser to Ham Nghi, he clashed with Ton That Thuyet, whom he regarded as rash and dishonest. But Phan Dinh Phung rallied to the dissident boy ruler and created his own guerrilla army, based on a mountain overlooking a French fortress at Hatinh, near the coast of central Vietnam. For more than seven years, his forays against the French reached as far north as Thanh Hoa province and south to Quang Binh. His organization became a model for future insurgents. He divided his operational zone into twelve districts for the sake of flexibility. His trained and disciplined men manufactured arms and ammunition by copying captured French equipment, and his political cadres levied taxes from local villagers. But even before Phan Dinh Phung's death from dysentery in 1896, the French had begun to overwhelm his followers with their forces, and they bribed his family and friends to betray him. In one act of extreme sacrilege, the French desecrated the tombs of his ancestors and publicly displayed their remains to the town of Hatinh.

Phan Dinh Phung's death ended a phase of Vietnamese resistance that had spanned a generation since 1858, when the French first assaulted Tourane and then occupied Saigon. And though the early opposition failed, its mistakes would educate later nationalists. It had lacked unified direction. Many uncoordinated regional groups were therefore isolated and chopped down by the French. Most partisans had focused mainly on military actions, neglecting political efforts necessary to mobilize mass support. Especially in the north, insurgents had also persecuted Christian communities suspected of pro-French sympathies, thereby alienating Vietnamese Catholics who might have been won over.

The early partisans were also beaten by unvarnished French brutality—carried out beyond the scrutiny of inquisitive journalists. The French subscribed at the time to the principle of "collective responsibility," which meant that any Vietnamese village found sheltering guerrillas could be destroyed and its notables summarily executed. Colonel Fernand Bernard, a French officer of the period, revealed a widespread practice in a brief description of one incident at a place called Haidung: "Our side suffered not a single casualty in the uprising there, but without benefit of trial, sixty-four heads rolled."

Though France had effectively "pacified" Indochina by the twentieth century, the resistance continued, now personified by two Vietnamese with different strategies. Phan Boi Chau, a radical monarchist, held that with Chinese and Japanese help a powerful emperor could crystallize the opposition. Phan Chu Trinh rejected royalism and contended rather that cooperation with progressive elements in the French colonial administration would propel Vietnam toward modern democracy. Neither succeeded, but they inspired a new generation of nationalists.

The son of a poor scholar, Phan Boi Chau was born in Nghe An, a perpetually rebellious province of central Vietnam, also the birthplace of Phan Dinh Phung and Ho Chi Minh. He switched from archaic Confucian studies to politics in 1900, at the ripe age of thirty-three, appalled by the revolts that ravaged his native region. Traveling around Vietnam, he evolved the notion of a royal resistance movement, and he found a candidate for its leader in Prince Cuong De, a direct descendant of the emperor Gia Long. A dramatic event that thrilled nationalists throughout Asia also aroused him: in 1905, Japan defeated Tsarist Russia, the first time an Asian nation had vanquished a European power. He departed for Japan.

There Phan Boi Chau met Japanese political figures and exiled Chinese Nationalists, among them Sun Yatsen, the founder of the Chinese republic in 1911. He wrote books, including a revolutionary history of Vietnam, and he brought Prince Cuong De to Tokyo, later scuttling him as he discarded the idea of a renovated monarchy in favor of a democratic republic. Most important, he formed an up-to-date political organization, the Viet Nam Duy Tan Hoi, or Association for the Modernization of Vietnam, to agitate among merchants, students, and other middle-class Vietnamese at home and abroad. He also helped to create an East Asia United League, composed of Chinese, Japanese, Korean, Indian, and Philippine nationalists. Thus he introduced two innovations to the Vietnamese struggle for independence—a relatively sophisticated vehicle for mobilizing insurgent sympathies and a connection with other Asian militants.

Indochina 1908-1954

Constantly hounded by French agents, Phan Boi Chau lived furtively, traveling from Vietnam to China to Hong Kong to Japan to Siam and back to Vietnam. In 1925, he was still on the run at the age of fifty-eight, when French operatives in Shanghai finally caught him. According to some accounts, he was betrayed by Communist rivals. Tried in Hanoi on charges of sedition, he died under house arrest in Hué fifteen years later.

Phan Chu Trinh, also from central Vietnam, was the son of a rich landowner who had rallied to the dissident emperor Ham Nghi. A senior mandarin, he rose to the rank of minister at the imperial court in Hué, but resigned in 1905 to accompany Phan Boi Chau to Japan. There they parted company. Shrewdly foreseeing the danger of Japanese imperialism, Phan Chu Trinh rebuffed the idea of reliance on Japan. He also rejected even a liberal monarchy as retrogressive. Having returned to Vietnam, he boldly addressed an open letter to the French governor, warning of an eventual upheaval unless the Vietnamese could express themselves politically, economically, and socially. Colonial abuses, he said, violated the democratic principles for which France stood, and his words would be valid a half century later: "In your papers, in your books, in your plans, in your private conversations, there is displayed in all its intensity the profound contempt with which you overwhelm us. In your eyes, we are savages, dumb brutes, incapable of distinguishing between good and evil. Some of us, employed by you, still preserve a certain dignity . . . and it is sadness and shame that fills our hearts when we contemplate our humiliation."

Ignored by the French administration, Phan Chu Trinh started his own progressive programs, among them a school in Hanoi at which local pupils of both sexes, taught in Vietnamese, Chinese, and French, could study modern science and economics along with Asian classics. But he antagonized Vietnamese extremists, who thought him too moderate, and he disturbed moderates, who thought him too extreme. The French authorities also regarded him with suspicion.

They closed his school on a flimsy pretext and, in 1908, during an eruption of tax revolts, they arrested him in a roundup of nationalists, first condemning him to death and later, when his admirers in France protested, commuting the sentence to life imprisonment on the island of Poulo Condore. Released after three years, he was allowed to move to Paris, where, for the next decade, he symbolized the anticolonial resistance for both Vietnamese expatriates and their French sympathizers. He died in Saigon in 1926—the year following Phan Boi Chau's arrest—and teachers and students throughout Vietnam spontaneously shut their schools for a day to mourn him.

Phan Boi Chau failed because his movement lacked broad peasant support and Phan Chu Trinh because he clung to the illusion that the France of Montesquieu and Rousseau would export its enlightened philosophies to Vietnam. But despite their devotion to the *mission civilisatrice,* French colonial officials, soldiers, and businessmen distorted France's lofty ideals in Vietnam, where their primary objective was to exploit the possession for the benefit of the motherland.

The French had faced a choice as they extended their control over Vietnam in the mid-nineteenth century. They could have pursued a policy of "association," as the British did in India, governing indirectly through native institutions. One French expert argued eloquently for this approach, pointing out that the Vietnamese had a national history and ethnic identity "older than our own," and should be respected "with their customs and traditions" rather than forced into a Western mold. But other French specialists pleaded for "assimilation," contending that no greater honor could befall a people than to absorb the ideas and culture of France. Proponents of both these concepts went on debating as long as France remained in Vietnam. In practice, neither thesis prevailed.

Direct French rule took over—as statistics show. In 1925, five thousand British officials governed three hundred million Indians, but it took the same number of French to manage an Indochinese population one tenth that size. Fully half of the French colonial budget went for bureaucratic wages during that year. Even in the 1950s, the French were still unable to delegate authority to indigenous officials, even though they were desperate to counter the Vietminh's nationalist claims. They enthroned Bao Dai as a sovereign emperor, but continued to run his regime. And, as his prime minister, they designated Nguyen Van Xuan, a naturalized French citizen who could barely speak Vietnamese.

When the French first occupied Cochinchina in the 1860s, local mandarins abandoned their posts to join the resistance or, in typical Asian fashion, prudently shifted to the sidelines until the future defined itself. The French admirals then in charge in Saigon coped in two ways, both disastrous. They assigned French officers to run the administration and they recruited Vietnamese collaborators as intermediaries. Apart from some exceptions, the French bureaucrats were unfamiliar with the Vietnamese language or the society's values. They also became preoccupied with routine. They introduced Western methods alien to Vietnam's needs, and they relegated Vietnamese employees to minor functions at minimal salaries. In 1903, the highest ranking Vietnamese in the colonial system earned less than the lowliest French official.

In the provinces, meanwhile, the French relied on village chiefs to collect taxes, mobilize labor for public projects, and other such onerous tasks. The native bosses inevitably used their positions to embezzle funds and oppress peasants, and Frenchmen themselves were frequently involved in the corruption. So the structure was essentially fragile—and the uprisings and insurrections that threatened it could be quelled only by force.

To replace the prominent mandarins who had quit, the early French governors coddled a handful of Vietnamese—many of them Catholic, either by birth or expedient conversion. An impressive prototype was Petrus Truong Vinh Ky, the "most Frenchified" Vietnamese of the time, as one French official called him. A brilliant linguist educated by French and Vietnamese priests, he began his career as an interpreter, and later, as an eminent scholar, he zealously defended France's colonial presence in Vietnam. Equally celebrated was Do Huu Phuong, who administered the Saigon suburb of Cholon and who, it was said, procured girls and perhaps even boys for the French. He had distinguished himself fighting against Vietnamese insurgents, which earned him French citizenship and a *rosette* of the Legion of Honor, and he gained immense wealth. Two of his sons became French army officers and one married a French woman. But he and others like him were too remote from most Vietnamese to serve the colonial administration effectively. One senior French official, Admiral Rieunier, remarked: "On our side, we have only Christians and crooks."

Along with direct rule, the French bought their penal code to Vietnam. Goodwill largely motivated them, since Vietnamese law beheaded thieves and had adulterous women trampled to death by elephants. But French jurisprudence confused and convulsed Vietnam's traditional legal system without creating a viable alternative. It could not handle subtle Vietnamese judicial nuances, such as refraining from pronouncing a defendant's name in court lest he "lose face." It also contributed to the erosion of Vietnamese society in which, according to Confucian tenets, the father arbitrated family altercations or called on a respected dignitary to mediate a dispute informally. Besides, French justice lost its credibility when colonial police could wantonly jail political suspects for years without putting them on trial.

Justly proud of their educational achievements at home, the French planned to revamp the Vietnamese system of schooling, which had been highly developed along Confucian lines. In fact, roughly 80 percent of Vietnam's population was more or less literate in the Chinese ideographs used for written Vietnamese. Aiming to break Vietnam's cultural continuity, the French banned the Chinese characters and replaced them with either French or *quoc ngu,* the romanized alphabet perfected by Alexandre de Rhodes in the seventeenth century. But the French educational reform faltered, largely because young Vietnamese resisted colonial contamination. By the eve of World War II, fewer than one fifth of all school-age boys in Vietnam were attending classes. Earlier, a French governor of Cochinchina had commented: "The Vietnamese can speak their tongue but neither read nor write it. We have been manufacturing illiterates."

There were remarkable exceptions. Vo Nguyen Giap, the Vietminh general who was to defeat France at Dienbienphu, studied law at the University of Hanoi, which had been created by Paul Bert, a liberal French governor of the late nineteenth century. Many young Vietnamese flocked to private institutions like Phan Chu Trinh's school in Hanoi, where French literature and other modern subjects were taught. The unofficial schools attracted Vietnamese youths, partly because they offered sophisticated courses devoid of France's assimilationist doctrine. In 1981, a Communist general, Hoang Anh Tuan, recalled to me the resentment he felt forty years earlier at a French school in Hué, where Vietnamese pupils were obliged to recite the French educational catechism: *"Nos ancêtres les Gaulois habitaient jadis la Gaul."*

A painful experience awaited many young Vietnamese, usually of wealthy origin, who had studied in Paris. Having enjoyed the freedom and comradeship of the Latin Quarter, they would return to Vietnam to have their newspapers and books confiscated by the colonial police, who regarded them as potential subversives. They rarely found jobs that equaled their education, and they could never match the wages of the French. Worse still, minor French officials, to whom all Vietnamese looked alike, would humiliate them by addressing them in the familiar *tu* form reserved for servants and other inferiors. One such returned student, convicted during the 1930s for nationalist agitation, told the judge at his trial that French injustice "turned me into a revolutionary."

But France's biggest impact on Indochina was economic. And one man, Paul Doumer, almost single-handedly transformed Indochina from a financial loss to a profitable enterprise for France. Essentially, he transferred the burden from the French taxpayer to the Vietnamese people, not only saddling them with the costs of supporting their own domination, but also exploiting them in order to gain a fat yield on the colonial investment. He could rightfully claim, as he did at the end of 1902, that "Indochina began to serve France in Asia on the day that it was no longer a poverty-stricken colony, reduced to begging for alms from the motherland. Its strong organization, its financial and economic structures and its great power are being used for the benefit of French prestige."

Like so many dynamic French imperialists of the period, Doumer was a liberal politician who, as France's minister of finance, had antagonized his conservative friends and foes by daring to introduce the income tax. They engineered his promotion and exile to the post of governor-general of Indochina. He went there, not with any romantic notions about the *mission civilisatrice,* but with his eyes fixed on what present-day financiers call the bottom line. His objective: to exploit the country for France's benefit. Looking back, he wrote in his memoirs: "When France arrived in Indochina, the Annamites were ripe for servitude."

The costs of the French conquest of Vietnam had been enormous. And by 1895, Cochinchina, Annam, and Tonkin had slid into huge budget deficits, largely because of disorganization and fiscal mismanagement. Doumer's first priority was to centralize authority. He then proceeded to increase public revenues while developing the economy for France's benefit.

Soon after his arrival in the summer of 1897, Doumer unified the administration by dissolving the powerless Vietnamese emperor's last vestige of sovereignty, the Co Mat, or Cabinet of Mandarins, and supplanting it with a new body containing French advisers. He had a tougher task imposing his will on the French bankers, merchants, landowners, and officials who ran Cochinchina as their own separate colony, but he eventually assumed control of their finances. The Cochinchina clique repeatedly reasserted itself in the years ahead—and its intransigence contributed to the outbreak of France's war with the Vietminh in 1946.

Moving on, Doumer increased his revenues by funneling customs duties and direct taxes into his central treasury. But his most lucrative innovation was the creation of official monopolies to produce and market alcohol, salt, and opium. The opium business was especially notorious because of its human dimensions and complex political ramifications, which entangled Indochina long after Doumer had disappeared from the scene.

Before the French landed, only the Chinese residents of Vietnam had smoked opium, and in such small quantities that it was not worth refining locally. But Doumer built a refinery in Saigon, where a blend was concocted that burned quickly and thus encouraged consumption. Vietnamese addiction soon rose so sharply that opium eventually accounted for one third of the colonial administration's income. Doumer, who would have been horrified by what he wrought, had set in motion a traffic that would attain monstrous proportions. Decades later, with usage still rising, the quest for the drug prompted French agents to manipulate the Hmong tribes of Laos, which traditionally cultivated opium poppies, and the Vietminh intervened to win over certain clans. French counterinsurgency groups also used clandestine opium profits to underwrite operations against the Communists; and the French also backed the Binh Xuyen, drug smugglers who tried to oust South Vietnamese President Ngo Dinh Diem soon after he took office in 1954. Later, too, some Saigon officials imported the narcotics that were to poison American soldiers.

Doumer's land policy, meanwhile, dislocated rural Vietnamese society. Most Vietnamese peasants had owned land before French intervention, but a century of French rule had dispossessed them. Doumer did not begin the process, but he accelerated it as part of his plan to make Vietnam profitable.

The emperors had forbidden rice exports so that surpluses could feed deficit areas or be stored for bad years. To the French, however, rice was a lucrative commodity, and by the eve of World War II they had made Indochina the world's largest rice exporter after Burma and Thailand. But the commercial success paradoxically impoverished the peasantry. By expanding cultivated acreage to stimulate production, the French spurred land grabbing by French speculators and prominent Vietnamese families at the expense of the peasants. During the 1930s, an estimated 70 percent of Vietnam's peasants either were tenants or farmed uneconomically small plots. The pressures of population growth aggravated their plight. Landless peasants suited Doumer; they could be employed in mines or on rubber plantations, or to build roads and railways.

As in colonial areas everywhere, profits in Vietnam depended on mobilizing cheap labor for mining, rubber, construction, and other industries. Most of the companies, connected through interlocking directorates, were also linked to the Bank of Indochina, a financial colossus owned jointly by a consortium of Paris banks and the French government. French officials and private businessmen in Vietnam therefore cooperated closely, leaving no recourse for the Vietnamese to protest legally against exploitation. By no coincidence, one of the most sensational events of the 1920s was the murder by Vietnamese nationalists of a Frenchman, René Bazin, who recruited workers through native agents in a manner reminiscent of the abduction of black slaves by African tribal chieftains.

Conditions in some sectors were appalling. Rubber, the second largest Vietnamese export after rice, was produced by virtually indentured workers so blighted by malaria, dysentery, and malnutrition that at one Michelin company plantation, twelve thousand out of forty-five thousand died between 1917 and 1944. The Hongay coal mines, whose output soared from a half million tons in 1913 to nearly two million tons in 1927, were situated in a self-contained enclave belonging to a syndicate, the *Société Française des Charbonnages du Tonkin,* which, as an American journalist reported at the time, owned "everything from the bowels of the earth to the slightest sprig of grass that may force its way through the coal dust."

Doumer, who established the economic pattern that guided Indochina until the French left in 1954, also built obsessively—opera houses, roads, railways, and the extraordinary bridge across the Red River at Hanoi that bore his name until the Communists took over. But above all, he fulfilled his purpose: he put Indochina in the black, integrating it into the French economic order as an exclusive source of raw materials and a protected market for France's merchandise. And, by relieving French taxpayers of the financial burden, he also reduced anticolonialism in France to a sentiment expressed by only a handful of eccentric intellectuals.

Later elected president of France—and assassinated while in office in 1932—Doumer was followed in Vietnam by liberals who recognized the need for political reform but scored little progress. Even the prestigious Albert Sarraut, who periodically showed an understanding of Vietnamese aspirations, could not buck the powerful French business interests that plundered Indochina. These primitive French capitalists drove Vietnamese nationalists to extremes. Vietnamese moderates were outpaced by the Communists, who became the most tenacious foes of colonialism. Ho Chi Minh personified the phenomenon. He might have been, like Gandhi, an apostle of passive resistance. But French intransigence steered him toward violence.

Ho, originally named Nguyen Sinh Cung, was born in 1890 in a village of Nghe An province in central Vietnam, where shimmering green rice fields stretch from the sea to a hazy horizon of blue mountains. His father, Nguyen Sinh Sac, a concubine's son relegated to menial farm work, had risen to the rank of mandarin through assiduous study. But he quit the imperial court in Hué and, abandoning his wife and three children, roamed the country for the rest of his life as an itinerant teacher and medicine man. Ho inherited his father's wanderlust on a grander scale; he traveled the world in solitude for decades, never married, and rarely contacted his kin. The fate of Vietnam was his obsession, as he revealed in 1950 when, failing to attend his older brother's funeral, he telegraphed relatives to beg forgiveness for having "sacrificed family feelings to state affairs."

Vietnam still churned in dissidence in his youth. In 1907, the French removed the emperor, Thanh Thai, whose sexual fancies they had tolerated as long as he fulfilled his puppet role, and exiled him to the Indian Ocean island of Réunion—just as they would exile his uncooperative son, Duy Tan, a decade later. Tax revolts tore through central Vietnam in 1908, and Vietnamese auxiliaries in the French army mutinied unsuccessfully in Hanoi. Guerrillas continued to operate from mountain lairs, and nationalists like Phan Boi Chau and Phan Chu Trinh spread their gospel. In Hué, young Ho was clashing privately with the French in the person of his schoolteacher, a former Foreign Legionnaire who was avenging his past mistreatment at the hands of native partisans by tyrannizing his Vietnamese pupils.

Ho Chi Minh started his real education at nineteen, when he went south. He taught for a few months at a village school. Then, in Saigon in 1911, he signed on as stoker and galley boy aboard a French freighter, the *Amiral Latouche Tréville*. He called himself Van Ba, *ba* being the Vietnamese term for third child. Thirty years passed before he saw Vietnam again.

Though a prolific pamphleteer, Ho never kept diaries, wrote memoirs, or related his experiences to a biographer, as Mao Zedong did to the American journalist Edgar Snow. His life is therefore filled with mysteries, among them his motives for going to Europe rather than to Japan, then a beacon for Asian nationalists. Perhaps he foresaw then that to count on the Japanese against the French would be, as he warned later, to "drive the tiger out the front door while letting the wolf in through the back." Or perhaps, as a comrade explained, he hoped to learn from the West how to fight against the West.

He spent nearly three years at sea, stopping at ports like Bombay, Oran, and Le Havre, where he worked briefly as a gardener for his ship's captain. In 1913, employed aboard another French vessel, he crossed the Atlantic, visiting Boston and San Francisco before settling in Brooklyn as an itinerant laborer. The skyscrapers of Manhattan dazzled him as emblems of Western industrial progress. He ventured into Harlem, and he was impressed by the fact that Chinese immigrants to the New

World, with whom he chatted in Cantonese, enjoyed the legal rights of American citizens. When he proclaimed Vietnam's independence from France in 1945, his speech would feature an excerpt from the American Declaration of Independence.

After almost a year in the United States, he sailed to London, where he found a job in the kitchen of the elegant Carlton Hotel, whose renowned chef, Georges Auguste Escoffier, promoted him to assistant pastry cook. Now known as Nguyen Tat Thanh, he began to flirt with politics, meeting Irish nationalists, Fabian socialists, and Chinese and Indian workers. He improved his English, and eventually spoke it fluently, along with Russian and at least three Chinese dialects besides French and Vietnamese.

But Paris beckoned. A hundred thousand Vietnamese had arrived in France during World War I as soldiers and laborers, and they were ripe for conversion. Ho adopted a militant new name, Nguyen Ai Quoc, or Nguyen the Patriot. He was to remain in Paris for six years, combining his conspiratorial activities with extraordinarily eclectic cultural pursuits. In 1954, as a young correspondent in *Time* magazine's Paris bureau, I was assigned to retrace Ho's footsteps during the years he resided in the French capital. There were still, surprisingly, many French who remembered him—including my landlord, Jean Longuet, the son of a prominent socialist of the 1920s and great-grandson of Karl Marx. I began my research with Léo Poldès, an elegant and witty gentleman who had run the Club du Faubourg, a polite debating society.

At the club, whose weekly sessions he attended, Ho was entranced by lectures on fashionable occult topics like reincarnation and the metempsychosis of the soul, which suggested to some members that death preoccupied him. One evening in 1921, he disputed with Dr. Emile Coué, the eminent hypnotist, and scoffed at Coué's theory that success and happiness lay in repeating the formula "Every day in every way I am getting better and better." At the Club du Faubourg, too, Ho staged his play *The Bamboo Dragon,* a merciless portrayal of an imaginary Asian king, patterned on the corrupt puppet Vietnamese emperor Khai Dinh. The play's single performance was—as Léo Poldès pompously recalled to me thirty years later—"enlivened by Aristophanic verve and not lacking in scenic qualities."

Ho Chi Minh even wrote an article for a movie magazine, *Cinégraph,* under the pseudonym Guy N'Qua. In May 1922, the French boxer Georges Carpentier trounced the English middleweight champion Ted Lewis in London, and Ho indignantly denounced Parisian sportswriters for truffling their dispatches with what today are referred to as Franglais terms like *"le manager"* and *"le challenger."* He urged Prime Minister Raymond Poincaré to ban foreign words from the French press. Ho displayed the same French cultural chauvinism in an open letter to the Emperor Khai Dinh, the subject of his play, who was then touring France. Besides being the land of racetracks, operas, and other sights shown to foreign dignitaries, Ho said floridly, France was the nation of Voltaire and Victor Hugo, who personified the "spirit of brotherhood and noble love of peace" that pervaded the French people.

But while Ho was converted by France's *mission civilisatrice,* he was also being converted to the revolution. In Paris, the quintessential city of freedom and discretion, he could lead a double life.

One of his early leftist acquaintances was Jules Raveau, a veteran Marxist who had hobnobbed with Lenin before the Russian Revolution. Ho would meet him in the dusty offices of *La Vie Ouvrière,* a labor journal located in a working-class neighborhood, and there Raveau told stirring stories of Europe's socialist struggles, such as battles at the barricades of Paris in 1848 or the martyrdom of the *Communards* in 1871. Ho also spent an occasional evening at a decrepit proletarian hostel run by Voltaire and Renan Radi, brothers who gave him Soviet books and tracts. Another comrade, Jacques Sternel, the editor of an obscure radical weekly, recalled an emotional Ho. "Once," Sternel told me, "he was so overwhelmed by an article that I had written that he asked to kiss my cheek."

In 1919, when President Woodrow Wilson arrived at Versailles for the conference that formally ended World War I, Ho drafted a statement to hand him. Inspired by Wilson's famous doctrine of self-determination, Ho had written that "all subject peoples are filled with hope by the prospect that an era of right and justice is opening to them . . . in the struggle of civilization against barbarism." His appeal to Wilson modestly requested constitutional government, democratic freedoms, and other reforms for Vietnam—conspicuously omitting any reference to independence. Ho never saw Wilson, whose principles presumably applied only to Europe, but his gesture attracted the attention of French socialists like Jean Longuet and Léon Blum, later prime minister. Critics of colonialism, they invited Ho to join them, and, as "representative from Indochina," he attended their congress held in December 1920 at Tours, a charming town in the Loire River valley. It was a decisive moment in his career.

A superb photograph taken at the meeting shows Ho, thin and

intense, addressing a collection of corpulent Frenchmen with walrus mustaches. Speaking without notes, he rebuked the delegates who interrupted him as his speech rose to an impassioned plea: "In the name of all mankind, in the name of all socialists, right wing or left wing, we appeal to you, comrades. Save us!"

The decision that faced Ho at the Tours congress transcended Vietnam. A majority of socialists, enthused by the Russian Revolution, had broken away to form the Communist party. Ho might have preferred to stick with socialists like Longuet and Blum, whose gentle temperament he shared. But he opted for the Communists, figuring that their Soviet patrons had the potential power to spark the global revolution that would liberate Vietnam. As Ho explained years afterward, "it was patriotism and not Communism that originally inspired me."

Ho Chi Minh became a prodigious polemicist during the Paris years. His diatribes contained flashes of acerbic wit, like the remark in his pamphlet, *French Colonialism on Trial*, that "the figure of Justice has had such a rough voyage from France to Indochina that she has lost everything but her sword." He wrote for the French Communist daily, *L'Humanité*, and he edited *Le Paria*, a journal put out by a group of Asian and African nationalists. Smuggled back to Vietnam and circulated secretly, his writings exposed many Vietnamese for the first time to Lenin's thesis that revolution and anticolonial resistance were inseparable. "It opened a new world to us," recalled Tran Van Giau, a veteran Vietnamese Communist.

By the early 1920s, the French police were tracking Ho's movements. He fascinated one of their inspectors, Louis Arnoux, who arranged an informal encounter at a café near the Paris Opéra. The two men, destined to become mortal enemies, thereafter met from time to time, Arnoux listening as Ho recounted his experiences and aspirations. Arnoux urged Albert Sarraut, then minister of colonies, to grant Ho an audience. Sarraut refused, contending that Nguyen Ai Quoc did not exist. He was, said Sarraut, merely an alias of Phan Chu Trinh, the prominent Vietnamese nationalist then still living in exile in Paris.

In 1924, Ho moved to Moscow. Now known as Linh, he met Stalin, Trotsky, and the other Soviet leaders, but decried their lack of sufficient interest in Vietnam. They were busy squabbling over the succession to Lenin, who had just died. Besides, as a Bolshevik analysis put it, Vietnam's nationalists were "disorganized" and its masses "politically inert," and scarcely worth an investment. Still, Ho used his time in the Soviet Union to attend the so-called University of Oriental Workers, an academy for Asian insurgents, where he learned Lenin's key dictum: revolution must be launched under favorable conditions. He was to wait another twenty years before staging his revolution, and even then he may have acted prematurely.

The sojourn in Moscow transformed Ho from a propagandist into a practical organizer, a role that he would begin to play when he traveled to Canton later in 1924. There the Chinese Nationalist Generalissimo Chiang Kai-shek, then allied with the Chinese Communists, had a Soviet adviser, Mikhail Borodin, the classic Russian agent later characterized in André Malraux's novel *Man's Fate*. Ho, now using the alias Ly Thuy, became Borodin's part-time interpreter while peddling cigarettes and newspapers to supplement his income. He also wrote occasionally for a Soviet news agency under the by-line Lou Rosta, and in contacts with foreigners in Canton he posed as a Chinese by the name of Wang, a variation of Vuong, a Vietnamese *nom de plume* he signed to articles that he contributed to a local Chinese newspaper. He sometimes called himself Nilovsky.

During this period, Ho started to mobilize Vietnamese students in southern China, creating the Thanh Nien Cach Mang Dong Chi Hoi, the Revolutionary Youth League. Following classic Communist precepts, he taught his pupils to form small cells to avoid detection and to write tracts for specific audiences, and he inculcated them with the boy scout virtues of thrift, generosity, and perseverance. Above all, he urged them to be concrete. "Peasants," he cautioned, "believe in facts, not theories."

But Ho's prospects suddenly dimmed in 1927, when Chiang Kai-shek slaughtered his Communist associates in a surprise betrayal. Ho fled back to Moscow and then, with little else to do, toured Europe to gaze at castles and cathedrals. He secretly slipped into Paris under the name of Duong, and nostalgia for the city welled up in him. A French Communist friend of the time recalled to me how he met Ho standing on a bridge overlooking the Seine. Ho said to him wistfully, "I always thought I would become a scholar or a writer, but I've become a professional revolutionary. I travel through many countries, but I see nothing. I'm on strict orders, and my itinerary is carefully prescribed, and you cannot deviate from the route, can you?"

A year later, Ho turned up in Bangkok, now a center of Vietnamese dissidence. He shaved his head and donned the saffron robes of a Buddhist monk to proselytize in the temples. Then he went to northeast Siam, the site of a large expatriate Vietnamese community, where he opened a school and published a newspaper. He concealed his identity under a collection of pseudonyms, such as Nguyen Lai, Nam Son, and Thau Chin, which means Old Man Chin in Siamese—another language he mastered. Even after becoming North Vietnam's president in 1954, Ho continued to hide behind aliases, perhaps a holdover from his clandestine past. He wrote articles under such names as Tran Luc, Tuyet Lan, Le Thanh Long, and Dan Viet, the last of them signifying Citizen of Vietnam.

Inside Vietnam in the late 1920s, the revolutionary climate was bleak, as some impatient and impulsive nationalists provoked fierce French repression. In 1929, an agent of one of the most aggressive groups, the Viet Nam Quoc Dan Dang, or VNQDD, created by Chiang Kai-shek's Chinese Nationalists, assassinated Bazin, the hated recruiter of cheap labor, as he was leaving his girl friend's house in Hanoi. The French police arrested scores of VNQDD activists and sympathizers. The movement suffered even more the next year, when its militants incited Vietnamese colonial soldiers to mutiny against their French officers at Yenbay, a garrison town in Tonkin. After killing their superiors, the rebels held out for a night, but fresh French forces arrived, and the retribution was savage. The insurgent troops were executed then and there, and a dozen VNQDD leaders lost their heads on the guillotine. Meanwhile, foreshadowing Vietnam wars to come, French aircraft bombed villages suspected of hiding partisans, and the Foreign Legion gunned down their inhabitants, often indiscriminately. Rural revolts in several other places prompted Edouard Daladier, a future prime minister, to warn the French parliament: "For the first time in a generation armed and unarmed peasants have arisen in Vietnam to press their demands on the French administration."

The disorder was aggravated by the economic depression of the 1930s. World rice and rubber prices plummeted and production was cut. Unemployed workers staged strikes, and hungry peasants in many areas seized estates and took over village councils. In Ho's native Nghe An province, they even set up a "soviet." Ho Chi Minh realized that the moment had come to form a cohesive Communist party out of the three rival Communist factions. He went from Bangkok to Hong Kong. There, in June 1929, he assembled different factional leaders at a local football stadium during a match to avoid detection by the British colonial police, and persuaded them to close ranks. They labeled the new movement the Indochinese Communist party, its name reflecting the ambition of the dynamic Vietnamese to extend their reach over Cambodia and Laos. Its program called for Vietnamese independence and a proletarian government—a far cry from Ho's moderate requests in 1919 of Woodrow Wilson.

At that stage, Ho went through another one of the adventures that make his life seem like the subject of a movie thriller. The Hong Kong police, on a periodic sweep of political troublemakers, arrested him. But a local British lawyer, Frank Loseby, obtained his release on a writ of habeas corpus, a decision upheld by Sir Stafford Cripps, then solicitor general of the Labour government in London. A British doctor had diagnosed Ho as tubercular and now generously sent him to a sanatorium in Britain. The persistent Hong Kong police, however, charged him with illegal departure and had him extradited from Singapore, where his ship had stopped, to Hong Kong, where they put him in a prison infirmary. This time he escaped to China, having persuaded a hospital employee to report him dead. His obituary appeared in the Soviet press and elsewhere, and the French authorities closed his file with the notation: "Died in a Hong Kong jail."

Other Communists inside Vietnam were less fortunate. Pham Van Dong and Le Duc Tho, for example, spent years on the prison island of Poulo Condore. Held in underground cells, they suffered from heat, humidity, and disease. Yet they kept up their morale by teaching each other languages, literature, and science and, in a peculiar tribute to their French jailers, they produced a Molière comedy in handmade costumes and wigs.

In 1932, responding to pressure from liberal opinion in France, the colonial administration loosened the reins on Bao Dai, the eighteen-year-old emperor, who hoped to promote reforms. But Bao Dai, though intelligent, lacked the courage to advance his ideas. Soon he lost his enthusiasm and went back to hunting, gambling, and wenching, which delighted the French. He also lost an able and honest courtier, Ngo Dinh Diem, whose nationalist determination could not abide Bao Dai's weakness.

Ho, the wanderer, meanwhile continued to wander through the 1930s, leaving a trail of legends behind him. One year he would be in Moscow, then China, then in the Soviet Union again—a traveler for weeks aboard cramped freighters that stopped at Asian, African, and Mediterranean ports, or jammed into a squalid compartment of the Trans-Siberian Railway, the temperatures either freezing or torrid, the food inedible and the air polluted by the alcoholic breaths of drunken Russians. On one occasion, he trekked for five days across the mountains of central China to the Chinese Communist stronghold in the caves of Yenan. He was no longer the young seaman of the *Amiral Latouche Tréville,* but a man approaching fifty, tubercular and undoubtedly plagued as well by amebic dysentery and recurrent malaria. A French Communist agent who worked with him then recalled: "He was taut and quivering, with only one thought in his head, his country, Vietnam."

Ho cultivated a reputation for ascetic celibacy during those years, but reality may have been different. One old comrade has claimed that the Russians had furnished him with a "wife" in Moscow. A Communist official in Hanoi in 1981 told me that Ho had loved a Chinese woman, a doctor, who died before they could marry. And yet another story has it that General Lung Yun, the warlord of Yunnan province, who frequently lodged Ho on his estate in Kunming, arranged a liaison for him with a Chinese woman. Whatever the truth, Ho cultivated the image of himself as Uncle Ho, his passions devoted solely to his national family.

In 1940, a tidal wave swept over Southeast Asia. The Japanese, pouring down from China, their offensive timed to Germany's conquest of France, crushed the French administration in Vietnam. They pushed on, driving the British from Malaya, the Dutch from Indonesia, the United States from the Philippines. An Asian nation had destroyed European colonialism.

Native nationalists throughout Southeast Asia rallied to Japan, but Ho feared the Japanese wolf as much as he opposed the French tiger. He aligned himself instead with the Allies, expecting them to defeat Japan, oust the discredited French from Japan, and reward his country with independence. The strategy strained his allegiance to the Soviet Union, which had signed a self-serving pact with Germany and forbade Communists everywhere to resist the Axis powers. But Ho's sole concern was Vietnam.

In early 1941, disguised as a Chinese journalist, he went by foot and sampan into southern China, then slipped across the border back into Vietnam—his first return in thirty years. A comrade had found a cave near Pac Bo, a village nestled amid the strange northern landscape of limestone hills. There Ho met confederates like Pham Van Dong and Vo Nguyen Giap. They called him Uncle, their attitude reverent yet familiar. In the Confucian spirit, he was the respected elder.

The time had come, Ho told them, to form a broad front of "patriots of all ages and all types, peasants, workers, merchants and soldiers," to fight both the Japanese and the French then collaborating with Japan, just as the Vichy regime in France obeyed Germany's dictates. The new organization, led by Communists, appealed to Vietnamese nationalist sentiment. They called it the Viet Nam Doc Lap Dong Minh, the Vietnam Independence League—soon to be simply the Vietminh. Ho borrowed from the movement his official pseudonym, Ho Chi Minh— roughly, Bringer of Light. But decades of dark violence lay ahead.

4 The War with the French

Ho Chi Minh addresses an audience in Paris in 1946, prior to his departure from the French capital following the breakdown of negotiations. Behind him is Admiral Thierry d'Argenlieu, the French governor in southern Vietnam, who had maneuvered to subvert the talks with Ho.

During World War II, the U.S. Office of Strategic Services, precursor of the CIA, trained Ho Chi Minh's forces in the jungles of northern Vietnam. The OSS team, known as the Deer Mission, was headquartered in Kunming, in southwest China.

Lieutenant Colonel Peter Dewey of the OSS, assigned to Saigon in 1945. He alienated French and British officers by contacting the Vietminh. Accidentally killed in a Vietminh ambush, he was the first American to die in Vietnam.

A roundup of Vietnamese nationalists by French troops in Saigon in late 1945. The city was torn by rioting as Vietnamese nationalists tried to prevent the French from re-establishing colonial rule.

On September 2, 1945, Ho Chi Minh declared Vietnam's independence from a platform erected in a Hanoi square. He quoted the American Declaration of Independence, the text of which had been supplied to him by an OSS officer.

Under an agreement to remove the Chinese forces, Ho Chi Minh agreed to the return of the French army to Hanoi in 1946. Troops are seen here re-entering the city. The welcoming crowd was composed mostly of French residents.

In 1946, as they moved to install their new government in northern Vietnam, Ho Chi Minh and his followers organized various associations—including this youth group, whose members were trained to sing political songs extolling Vietnam's independence.

Two senior French officers, General Philippe Leclerc (left) and Admiral Thierry d'Argenlieu, confer in Saigon in 1945 as they plan to reimpose France's rule in Vietnam. Behind d'Argenlieu is General Douglas Gracey, the British commander who was assigned to disarm the Japanese in southern Vietnam.

Ho Chi Minh in 1946 with General Leclerc (left) and Jean Sainteny, a French emissary. Sainteny later acted as an intermediary between President Nixon and the Vietnamese Communists in 1969.

General Vo Nguyen Giap, Vietminh commander, reviewing troops in northern Vietnam in 1951 as the war with France began to gather momentum. The Vietminh sustained serious setbacks during the early period of the war because Giap overextended its forces.

Ho Chi Minh seated, in casual attire, flanked by his senior comrades (left to right) Pham Van Dong, Truong Chinh, and Vo Nguyen Giap. Truong Chinh borrowed his pseudonym, which means Long March, from the famous exploit of the Chinese Communists in 1934.

Armed women warriors of the Hoa Hao, a reformist religious sect founded in the Mekong delta. Like most religious cults in Vietnam, the Hoa Hao rapidly developed into a private army that operated mainly for the benefit of its leaders.

A leader of the Cao Dai religious sect with armed troops of the organization. The ornate temple, located near the southern Vietnamese town of Tayninh, displays statues of the sect's saints, among them Jesus, Buddha, and Joan of Arc.

If those gooks want a fight, they'll get it.
                                    —General Etienne Valluy

If they force us into war, we will fight. The struggle will be atrocious, but the Vietnamese people will suffer anything rather than renounce their freedom.

                                    —Ho Chi Minh

Hanoi awoke to a festive day on September 2, 1945. Young Vietnamese had worked overnight, bedecking drab buildings with lanterns and flowers, red flags and banners bearing nationalist slogans. Shops, offices, and schools had closed for the occasion as hundreds of thousands of people converged throughout the morning on Ba Dinh Square, a large grassy field that lay beyond the handsome French residential district. Peasants in black pajamas and conic straw hats had flowed in from nearby villages to mingle with merchants and mandarins; Vietminh guerrillas, some armed with spears and machetes or primitive flintlocks, marched to the cadence of gongs and drums. Children scurried everywhere, and even Buddhist monks in saffron robes and black-gowned Catholic priests appeared, all for a single purpose—to see the mysterious Ho Chi Minh.

A week earlier, feeble with disease, Ho had been carried on a stretcher from his jungle headquarters to a small house in the city. He set his portable typewriter on the dining room table and began drafting a statement, chain-smoking as he tapped the keys and stopping periodically to nap on a canvas cot in the corner. Comrades bustled in and out, peering over his shoulder to offer suggestions as he polished sentences. Then, on the appointed afternoon, he donned a threadbare khaki tunic and white rubber sandals and was driven to Ba Dinh Square, his little black car wheezing its way through the cheering crowd. There he climbed onto a wooden platform and, speaking into a simple microphone in his reedy rural accent, he asserted Vietnam's independence with phrases unknown to most of his audience: "We hold the truth that all men are created equal, that they are endowed by their Creator with certain unalienable rights, among them life, liberty, and the pursuit of happiness."

Ho had deliberately borrowed the passage from the American Declaration of Independence. Although he had made a futile appeal to Woodrow Wilson a generation before, he believed that he could try again to persuade the United States to underwrite his cause. It seems odd in retrospect that a convinced Communist deeply involved in the global Soviet network should have hoped for American support. But Ho was essentially a pragmatist, principally preoccupied with Vietnam's salvation. While never forgetting that ultimate goal, he constantly shifted tactics to suit changing circumstances. At that time, too, the cold war had not yet polarized the world between the United States and the Soviet Union.

The United States might have plausibly encouraged Ho to emulate Marshal Tito, the Yugoslav Communist leader who was soon to defy Moscow. But American strategists during World War II viewed Indochina only marginally, a minor sideshow to the main Asian theaters in China and the Pacific. Later, as official American political attitudes toward the region matured, they were dictated by two other factors: the U.S. alliance with France, whose fate was deemed vital to the uncertain future of Western Europe; and the fall of China to the Communists, which spurred the foreign policy of "containment," contrived to block what then appeared to be Communist expansion. Within the context of the period, the United States was disinclined to underwrite Ho, a veteran Communist opposed to France. Thus it was that two decades before its commitment of combat troops there, the United States began to sink in the Vietnam quagmire.

Ho had been inspired by the Atlantic Charter, issued during the summer of 1941, in which President Franklin D. Roosevelt and British Prime Minister Winston Churchill pledged "to see sovereign rights and self-government restored to those who have been forcibly deprived of them." Churchill, dedicated to the preservation of the British empire, undoubtedly considered the pronouncement to be idealistic rhetoric. Nor was Roosevelt's position entirely plain, despite his anticolonial reputation. To the extent that he focused on Indochina at all, he was ambivalent.

In 1942, hoping to animate General Charles de Gaulle's Free French in the battle against the Germans, Roosevelt promised them all of France's overseas dominions after the war. The next year, he told his son Elliott that he would work "with all my might and main" against any plan to "further France's imperialistic ambitions." A year after that, he proposed an international trusteeship for postwar Indochina, saying that France had "milked it for one hundred years" and left its people "worse off than they were at the beginning." He amended that idea later, suggesting that the French could repossess the territory by pledging its eventual independence. And in 1945, he offered Indochina to Generalissimo Chiang Kai-shek, the Chinese Nationalist leader, who politely declined the gift on the grounds that the Indochinese "would not assimilate into the Chinese people."

Roosevelt's apparent inconsistencies stemmed in part from his practice of thinking aloud in the presence of visitors, a device he used to test his ideas. But he was basically too concerned with bigger matters during World War II to concentrate on remote Indochina. On January 1, 1945, three months before his death, he told Edward R. Stettinius, his secretary of state, "I still do not want to get mixed up in any Indochina decision. . . . Action at this time is premature."

At the State Department, memorandums flew in opposite directions. Criticizing French colonial rule as the "least satisfactory" in Asia, the Far East division urged that pressure be put on France to grant Indochina "true autonomous self-government"—or else there would be "bloodshed and unrest for many years, threatening the economic and social progress and peace and stability" of the area. Predictably defending their turf, European specialists in the department favored France, and cautioned against any steps that would have a "harmful effect on American relations with the French government and people."

The European faction won. In May 1945, soon after President Harry Truman took office on the death of Roosevelt, Stettinius assured Georges Bidault, then French foreign minister, that the United States recognized France's claim to Indochina. Truman hoped that the French would liberalize their rule, and Americans were to repeat that hope in the years ahead. But the French never created more than a flimsy facade of autonomy in their possession. By 1954, seeing the Indochina war as a struggle against global Communism, the United States had spent $2.5 billion to finance the futile French military effort—more assistance than France received in Marshall Plan aid from America to rebuild its shattered postwar economy.

As he roamed the mountain jungles of northern Vietnam and southern China during the early 1940s, Ho Chi Minh was oblivious to the controversies rippling through Washington. He sought out American officials then in the region, aiming to persuade them to furnish him with arms, ammunition, and other equipment, first to fight the Japanese and later to oust the French from Vietnam. With U.S. aid and encouragement he could also show other Vietnamese nationalists that the world's major power endorsed him, and rally those tempted to join rival movements. And he estimated that the Allies would live up to their vow, publicized in the Atlantic Charter and elsewhere, to free colonial areas.

At its base in Kunming, the capital of China's Yunnan province, the

United States had established the headquarters of the Office of Strategic Services, the wartime precursor of the Central Intelligence Agency. There, during the war, the Allies were caught up in a jumble of intrigue, political romanticism, and oriental exoticism. Clandestine American operatives, many quarreling among themselves, clashed with covert French agents, also locked in factional disputes. Chinese officials manipulated the Westerners and tried to advance their favorite Vietnamese while cashing in on opium sales, gold transactions, arms smuggling, and other maneuvers.

Ho navigated through this Asian thicket, adroitly playing Americans against French, French against Chinese, Chinese against Americans, and even Chinese against each other. But he seemed to prefer the Americans, who represented power, and he made no secret of it. In August 1945, soon after Japan's surrender, the French agent Jean Sainteny arrived in Hanoi accompanied by Major Archimedes L. A. Patti, a minor OSS officer assigned to rescue Allied war prisoners. Ho quickly cozied up to Patti but kept Sainteny at a distance. He chatted with Patti for hours, recollecting his visit to New York as a young seaman, extolling America's colonial tutelage of the Philippines, and minimizing his allegiance to Moscow. He enlisted Patti's help in drafting his declaration of independence, and he transmitted a letter through him to Truman—not the first of such messages he sent to Washington that went unanswered.

But Ho's real feelings toward the United States at the time are difficult to gauge. A master tactician, he was essaying every option. In a conversation with Bao Dai in late 1945, for example, he described the Americans cynically: "They are only interested in replacing the French. . . . They want to reorganize our economy in order to control it. They are capitalists to the core. All that counts for them is business."

Ho had contacted the U.S. consulate in Kunming as early as 1944 to explore the possibility of obtaining a visa for the United States, presumably to plead his cause there. He later went to Kunming, a frail figure in a seamy tunic, to solicit help from Allied officers, offering them the services of his guerrillas, who, he reminded them, had saved an American pilot downed after a raid against Saigon. As a token of gratitude, they ushered him into an audience with General Claire Chennault, the founder of the Flying Tigers, then commander of the U.S. Fourteenth Air Force. Ho humbly asked Chennault for an autographed photograph of himself, and the general magnanimously complied. Returning to the jungle, Ho shrewdly used the portrait to show his skeptical comrades that the United States supported him.

Actually, the OSS did aid Ho Chi Minh in early 1945, when a team code-named Deer parachuted into his jungle camp in northern Vietnam. French intelligence analysts in Kunming had warned the Americans against Ho, calling him "fearless, sly, clever, powerful, deceptive, ruthless—and deadly." At their insistence, the team included a French lieutenant posing as an American. What the OSS men found, lying in a bamboo hut, was a "pile of bones covered with dry yellow skin," as one of them recalled. The team medic, Paul Hoagland, treated Ho for malaria, dysentery, and other tropical diseases, and probably saved his life. Ho spotted the French lieutenant immediately, identified him by name, and ordered him back to China, admonishing the senior OSS officer in colloquial English: "Look, who are you guys trying to kid? This man is not part of the deal."

The proficiency of Ho's intelligence network astonished the Americans, and they were also impressed by his guerrillas, whom they supplied with rifles, mortars, grenades, and other matériel, training them to train other Vietminh partisans. As a member of the OSS team recollected: "They had an uncanny ability to learn and adapt. They learned to pull a rifle apart and put it together again after being shown only a couple of times."

The OSS experience in southern Vietnam was less congenial. While Ho had taken over Hanoi by September 1945, the French and various Vietnamese factions struggled for power in Saigon. Seven OSS agents had landed there to liberate Allied war prisoners, search for missing Americans, and gather intelligence. Their chief, Lieutenant Colonel A. Peter Dewey, the son of a conservative Republican congressman from Chicago, was a remarkably accomplished young man. At twenty-eight, he had already worked as a foreign correspondent in Paris, written a book on the French defeat, fought in the Polish army, and engaged in espionage behind the German lines in France. In Saigon, he soon collided with Major General Douglas D. Gracey, commander of a British force assigned to disarm the Japanese. Dewey, though passionately pro-French, disapproved of Gracey's bias for the French, while Gracey suspected him of conniving with the Vietminh and ordered him out of the country. Before his departure, Dewey summed up the chaotic situation in a prophetic report: "Cochinchina is burning, the French and British are finished here, and we [the United States] ought to clear out of Southeast Asia."

Early on September 26, 1945, Dewey prepared to clear out himself. He went to the Saigon airport with a colleague, Captain Herbert J. Bluechel, only to find that his airplane had been delayed. They came back later in the morning to check on the aircraft, with Dewey behind the wheel of the jeep—which Gracey had forbidden him to identify with a U.S. flag on the grounds that only he, as area commander, was entitled to fly a pennant on his vehicle. Another OSS officer had just been wounded by the Vietminh, and Dewey was upset. He took a shortcut past the Saigon golf course. Suddenly a barrier of logs and brush blocked his path. Braking to swerve around it, he noticed three Vietnamese in a roadside ditch. He shouted angrily at them in French. Presumably mistaking him for a French officer, they replied with a machine-gun burst that blew off the back of his head. Bluechel, unharmed, fled the scene, a bullet knocking off his cap as he ran.

Dewey was the first of nearly sixty thousand Americans to be killed in Vietnam. His body was never recovered. French and Vietminh spokesmen blamed each other for his death, and Ho Chi Minh sent a letter of condolence to the State Department.

The OSS era has been either effaced by Vietnamese Communist historians unwilling to concede that Ho sought the help of U.S. "imperialism" or inflated by French colonial apologists who submit that the United States conspired to deprive France of Indochina. Americans who dealt with Ho directly remember him fondly. But, from an official U.S. perspective, he was then merely a useful expedient, as were so many other local partisans at the time. And his later rise to prominence would not have been possible without the cataclysm that transformed Vietnam during World War II.

When the Japanese invaded Indochina in 1940, they left the French colonial administration intact, directing it from behind the scenes just as Germany obliquely managed Marshal Philippe Pétain's puppet French regime in Vichy. The image of European invincibility was shattered, and Indochina was a potential political vacuum.

Ho, sensing the magnitude of the change, had hastily formed the Vietminh as a nationalist front, masking its Communist leadership in order to appeal to broad patriotic sentiment. He instructed his hard-core militants to mute their radical dogmas and court landowners, village chiefs, merchants, and others who might be troubled by revolutionary slogans whose "time is not yet ripe," as one directive put it. He also needed the cooperation of the Chinese authorities whose territory, adjacent to the Vietnamese border, could be used as sanctuary for his embryonic forces. In late 1941, he set out for China disguised as a blind man, guided by a young comrade over the treacherous mountain trails. Barely had he crossed the frontier than he was detained by soldiers of

Chang Fa-kwei, the warlord who controlled Guangxi province. Learning his real identity, Chang slammed Ho into prison, where he languished for more than a year, weaving Chinese verses in T'ang dynasty style.

Now the wind sharpens its edges on mountain rocks.
The spear of cold pierces tree branches.
The gong from a far-off pagoda hastens
The traveler's steps as boys playing flutes
Drive the buffaloes home across the twilight.

Chang Fa-kwei had jailed Ho out of hatred for Communists, but he had also hoped to emasculate the Vietminh so that he could strengthen his own Vietnamese protégés, most notably the VNQDD, which the Chinese Nationalists had created. But he soon discovered that they lacked the Vietminh's influence. He released Ho and persuaded him to head the Viet Nam Cach Menh Dong Minh Hoi, or Vietnam Revolutionary League, a nationalist coalition. He supplied Ho with money and bases in China in exchange for intelligence on their common enemy, the Japanese. The two men therefore entered into a marriage of convenience despite their ideological differences—a typical practice for Ho, who frequently shelved his Communist principles to attain his goals.

Inside Vietnam, meanwhile, the Vietminh grew under Vo Nguyen Giap, an unusual figure who became one of the century's most spectacular soldiers.

Dynamic and passionate, Giap could also be brutal. In 1969, he admitted to the Italian journalist Oriana Fallaci that North Vietnam had then already lost a half million troops against the United States and its South Vietnamese clients but would continue to fight "as long as necessary—ten, fifteen, twenty, fifty years." A generation earlier, as the war against France began, he said: "Every minute, hundreds of thousands of people die on this earth. The life or death of a hundred, a thousand, tens of thousands of human beings, even our compatriots, means little."

Giap had been embittered by the death of his young wife, also a nationalist militant, who died in a French jail in 1941, along with their infant child. Her sister, arrested for terrorism, was guillotined in Saigon at the same time. Giap was to uncork his emotions to a couple of French officials over drinks one evening five years later, after a day of thorny negotiations on Vietnam's status. He trembled as he related the tragedy that "destroyed my life." Yet, he said, he could distinguish between the

French colonial police and France, which still had his confidence and admiration. To France, he owed much of his cultural formation.

Giap was born in 1912 in Quang Binh province, a poor region of central Vietnam. His peasant father, determined like so many Vietnamese to educate his children, scrounged to send him to a private school in Hué run by Ngo Dinh Kha, the father of Ngo Dinh Diem. Phan Boi Chau, the veteran nationalist then under house arrest in Hué, was allowed to chat informally with students, and young Giap began to acquire political ideas from him. Giap also read Ho's pamphlets, smuggled into Vietnam from abroad. At fourteen, he was already becoming a revolutionary—with a police record to show for his arrest in a protest demonstration.

Too ambitious to remain in Hué, he went to Hanoi in quest of real action. There he graduated from the Lycée Albert Sarraut and earned a law degree at the University of Hanoi—two rigorous French institutions. He wrote for nationalist newspapers in both French and Vietnamese. And, to make ends meet, he taught history at a local private school. Decades later, one of his former students recalled his lectures on Napoleon's campaigns: "He recounted the battles in brilliant detail, as if he were Napoleon himself. Even then he must have been preparing his military career."

Selected by Ho in the early 1940s to shape the Vietminh organization, Giap mobilized his forces carefully. In northern Vietnam, he recruited village chiefs and trained guerrilla bands. He had chosen the region for its proximity to the Chinese border, over which weapons and agents could move easily, and because its terrain of mountain jungles and hidden valleys offered security. He especially cultivated the local tribes, like the Hmong, the Thai, and the Tho, promising them autonomy in an eventually independent Vietnam. The Tho leader Chu Van Tan was to become Ho's first minister of defense, a nominal reward.

On December 22, 1944, Giap formed an armed propaganda brigade, his first major unit, which ranked above district and village groups in the three-tier structure that became Vietnam's Communist military organization. Though the unit comprised only thirty-four men, Giap sought a small victory that would attract support for the Vietminh. On Christmas Eve, he boldly overwhelmed two remote French posts and captured arms and ammunition. He then strengthened his force and attacked larger French installations; within months, the Vietminh's gold-starred red flag flew over communities throughout the zone. In the south, however, the Vietminh was in ragged shape.

The Japanese, originally intending to use Vietnam primarily as a springboard to the rest of Southeast Asia, had left the French colonial structure a degree of freedom. Inevitably, though, Japanese agents began to meddle. Their intelligence agency, the *Kempeitai,* put out feelers to nationalists like Ngo Dinh Diem. Japanese operatives sponsored films and newspapers, and they promoted a local youth movement to spread their message in the villages. They also nourished the Cao Dai and the Hoa Hao, southern religious sects that would complicate Vietnamese politics for years to come.

Founded in 1919 by Ngo Van Chieu, a mystic who claimed to commune with a spirit he called Cao Dai, the Cao Dai cult appealed to the Vietnamese taste for the supernatural and eclectically held that the ideal creed ought to combine the best religious and secular beliefs. Its "saints" included Jesus and Buddha, Joan of Arc, Victor Hugo and Sun Yat-sen, whose effigies graced its main temple, a kind of rococo wax museum located at Tayninh, a town north of Saigon. By 1938, the Cao Dai counted three hundred thousand disciples, a number that quintupled in the years after World War II. Like almost all movements in Vietnam, it became political, turning to the Japanese for protection when the French tried to stifle its activities.

The Hoa Hao, named for a village in the Mekong delta, also emerged in 1919, a brand of reform Buddhism invented by Huynh Phu So, a faith healer with prophetic gifts. The simplicity of the sect attracted thousands of poor peasants. It, too, rapidly became a private army that eluded French control, and the Japanese tried to co-opt it as their own instrument.

Worried by this growing Japanese influence, the French encouraged their own youth groups. But the Vietminh quickly infiltrated them, and also seeded its cadres in Japanese-sponsored associations. So, with no more than five thousand members in early 1945, the Vietminh had a web of activists all across Vietnam, ready to act as events unfolded.

By the end of 1944, U.S. forces under General Douglas MacArthur had fought their way up through the Pacific and were reconquering the Philippines. Rumors spread that they would debark in Indochina in their first assault against the Asian continent. General de Gaulle, determined to regain Indochina for France, feared that the Americans would favor the Vietnamese nationalists. He parachuted French agents and arms into the area with orders to attack the Japanese as the U.S. troops hit the beaches. Soon Saigon buzzed with talk of the forthcoming French operation.

The Japanese lost no time in reacting. On the evening of March 9, 1945, after strategically deploying their forces, they instructed the French governor to place his army under their command. When he failed to respond, they struck at French garrisons. In Hanoi, they ceremoniously interned the French soldiers who had surrendered without fighting. But in other places, those who resisted were wiped out to the man. They imprisoned several hundred French civilians, many of whom were tortured to death by the same native jailers employed by the colonial administration to brutalize Vietnamese nationalists. Overnight, French imperial power had crumbled, and the Japanese seemed to be doomed to defeat. Which Vietnamese faction would fill the void?

Bao Dai, the indolent puppet emperor, had been hunting during the Japanese coup. The next day, back in his palace, a Japanese envoy informed him that Japan had granted Vietnam its freedom. Fearful of retribution if he refused, he consented to reign under the Japanese, just as he had served the French. He formally renounced France's "protectorate" over Vietnam and declared its independence within Japan's Greater East Asian Co-Prosperity Sphere. The Japanese had picked Ngo Dinh Diem as Bao Dai's prime minister but discarded him at the last minute as too truculent. Instead, they designated Tran Trong Kim, a mild and malleable professor. The switch probably saved Diem, whom the United States might not have endorsed later had he been a Japanese collaborator.

Ho, wisely estimating that the Japanese were finished, prepared to greet the Allies in the hope that they would recognize him. He hastened to stiffen the Vietminh's authority for that prospect—and, fortuitously, he was helped by a ghastly famine for which the Japanese were almost entirely responsible.

Earlier in the year, as the Allies cut off their sources of raw materials in Southeast Asia, the Japanese had compelled Vietnamese peasants to plant industrial crops like peanuts and jute instead of rice. They also requisitioned rice, storing it for their troops in case of Allied landings. By the summer of 1945, floods aggravated the already serious food shortage as the Red River dikes, neglected by local officials, burst in several spots. In northern Vietnam, poor in the best of circumstances, two million people out of a population of ten million starved to death. Not far from Hanoi, a leathery old peasant by the name of Duong Van Khang recalled to me years afterward that so many of his fellow villagers died that "we didn't have enough wood for coffins and buried them in bamboo mats." Conditions were no better in the cities. Dr. Tran Duy Hung, mayor of Hanoi at the time, recollected the scene in an interview decades later:

Peasants came in from the nearby provinces on foot, leaning on each other, carrying their children in baskets. They dug in garbage piles, looking for anything at all, banana skins, orange peels, discarded greens. They even ate rats. But they couldn't get enough to keep alive. They tried to beg, but everyone else was hungry, and they would drop dead in the streets. Every morning, when I opened my door, I found five or six corpses on the step. We organized teams of youths to load the bodies on oxcarts and take them to mass graves outside the city. It was terrifying—and yet it helped our cause because we were able to rally the nation.

Starving peasants in several places attacked French posts and stormed Japanese granaries. With the news of Japan's surrender in August, the uprisings spread. Vietminh agents moved quickly to take advantage of the turmoil. A villager recounted the events of that period in a district of Thai Binh province, in the Red River delta:

The village marketplace was jammed. A man in brown pants and a cloth shirt climbed onto a chair, and guards armed with machetes, spears, and sticks surrounded him. He delivered a speech, saying that the Japanese had capitulated to the Allies, and that the time had come for the Vietminh to seize power. I was just a teenager in ragged clothes, and I asked a schoolmate, "Now that we've seized power, who will be the mandarin?" He replied, "Get this. The mandarin is just a peasant—really ordinary."

The Vietminh leader then marched to the district headquarters; the procession behind him swelled as nearby villagers joined in. The local chief had fled. The Vietminh leader seated himself in the district chief's chair to dramatize his new authority. The next day, Vietminh agents put a village official on trial before five thousand people assembled on a soccer field.

They read the charges. He had been an accomplice of the Japanese pirates. He had forced the peasants to pull up their rice and plant jute and peanuts, enriching himself even though the people were miserable and dying. He admitted that he had worked for the Japanese, but claimed that he was just carrying out orders. But they announced that his crime was very serious because he had opposed the revolution and helped the enemy. So they sentenced him to death and shot him right there. . . .This really fired up the people. They went after the henchmen of the Japanese, dragging them out of their houses, making them lower their heads and beating them. That finished their prestige, and the fervor of the masses kept rising.

On August 16, to keep pace with the momentum, Ho Chi Minh summoned sixty comrades to Tran Tao, a village in Thai Nguyen province, north of Hanoi. The time had come to grab power and greet the Allies on their arrival. Ho formed a National Liberation Committee, with himself as president, calling it "the equivalent of a provisional government." Appealing for a general insurrection, he proclaimed in classic revolutionary style, "The oppressed the world over are wresting back their independence. We should not lag behind. Forward! Forward! Under the Vietminh banner, let us valiantly march forward!"

The August Revolution, as the Communists would henceforth dub it, assumed different shapes in different places. Vietminh bands in Saigon clashed with the Cao Dai, the Hoa Hao, and an aggressive Trotskyite faction bearing a French name, La Lutte, the Struggle. Vietminh agents elsewhere embraced their opponents, while others murdered rivals such as Ngo Dinh Diem's older brother, Ngo Dinh Khoi, an influential nationalist in central Vietnam. Some Vietminh guerrillas attacked the Japanese and others made deals for their weapons.

Clad in coarse khaki uniforms or black pajamas, the first Vietminh detachments entered Hanoi on August 16, taking over public buildings as Japanese troops stood by. The emperor's delegate, a symbol of imperial authority, resigned to a Vietminh-run committee of citizens, which promptly announced its seizure of power from a balcony of the Hanoi opera house, a model of French gingerbread architecture. A week later, racing to keep up with events, the sickly Ho Chi Minh arrived to give his declaration of independence.

Nothing had reinforced the Vietminh cause more than the mercurial Bao Dai's decision to abdicate. For his gesture conferred the "mandate of heaven" on Ho, giving him the legitimacy that, in Vietnamese eyes, had traditionally resided in the emperor.

Bao Dai, isolated and confused in his palace in Hué, had received a message from the Vietminh demanding his resignation. He complied—remembering, as he later put it, that King Louis XVI had lost his head for resisting the French Revolution. On August 25, a Vietminh delegation appeared in Hué, claiming to speak for Ho Chi Minh, a name then unknown to Bao Dai. He donned his elaborate court costume and, at an improvised ceremony, read a statement handing over "sovereign power" to the Vietminh, which now proclaimed itself the Democratic Republic of Vietnam. He also relinquished the royal seal and sword, emblems of the monarchy, and he dropped his regal title and became plain Nguyen Vinh Thuy, so that he could "live as a simple citizen in an independent country rather than king of a subjugated nation." He felt relieved and unburdened, he recalled afterward: "I almost wanted to shout—finally free!"

Bao Dai went to Hanoi, where Ho appointed him "supreme adviser" to the new government. He asked to be treated as a "simple citizen," but the Vietminh leaders addressed him as "Sire," and he respectfully referred to Ho as "Venerable." Their modesty impressed him, but they were naive and inexperienced—as if they were running a town council rather than a national government. Even so, he perceived that the Vietminh, despite its flaws, reflected Vietnamese aspirations, and he warned General de Gaulle:

You would understand better if you could see what is happening here, if you could feel this yearning for independence that is in everyone's heart, and which no human force can any longer restrain. Should you re-establish a French administration here, it will not be obeyed. Every village will be a nest of resistance, each former collaborator an enemy, and your officials and colonists will themselves seek to leave this atmosphere, which will choke them.

Ho Chi Minh, hoping for U.S. support, confided to an OSS agent that he would welcome "a million American soldiers . . . but no French." Giap echoed that theme, telling a Hanoi crowd to regard the United States as a "good friend" because "it is a democracy without territorial ambitions." In early September, U.S. intelligence agents in Hanoi reported to Truman's secretary of state, James Byrnes, that the Vietnamese were "determined to maintain their independence even at the cost of their lives," since "they have nothing to lose and all to gain." But the United States and its wartime partners, inexorably if not deliberately, proceeded to restore French rule.

In July, a month before Japan capitulated, the Allied leaders had met in Potsdam, a Berlin suburb, to plan the future. There they had devised a scheme to disarm the Japanese in Vietnam—a minor item on their agenda—by dividing the country at the sixteenth parallel. The British would take the south, the Chinese Nationalists the north. It was a formula for catastrophe.

The British commander, General Gracey, was miscast. A colonial officer with limited political experience but a genuine affection for his Indian troops, he held the paternalistic view that "natives" should not defy Europeans. Officially, his was not to reason why. He had been plainly told by Lord Louis Mountbatten, the Allied commander for Southeast Asia, to avoid Vietnam's internal problems and merely handle the Japanese. But Gracey, guided by his prejudices, violated instructions. Despite Ho's assertion of Vietnam's independence in Hanoi on September 2, he said publicly even before leaving India for Saigon several weeks later that "civil and military control by the French is only a question of weeks."

Saigon was in chaos. The discredited French administration had crumbled, devastated by the defeat of Japan, whose troops in Vietnam were waiting for repatriation. A Vietminh committee set up to govern was wrangling with Jean Cédile, whom de Gaulle had sent to Indochina. French residents, afraid to lose their colonial privileges, were bracing for a fight. The Cao Dai, Hoa Hao, Trotskyites, and others, all striving to outbid the Vietminh, had taken an extremist tack. And tensions spiraled with the emergence of the Binh Xuyen, a gang of guns for hire, which, until its elimination by Ngo Dinh Diem in 1954, would serve the Vietminh and other factions—and even police the south for the French in exchange for the franchise to manage bordellos, casinos, and opium dens.

The violence grew as rival Vietnamese fought each other or clashed with the French. The chances of an accommodation also faded, since Cédile had been ordered to reject the Vietminh's demands for sovereignty, and the Vietminh refused to accept nothing less. Cédile had also succumbed to the spell of veteran French merchants, planters, and officials, who were anxious to safeguard their interests. They urged him to be tough toward the "Viets," as they derisively dubbed the Vietminh, terming them "agitators" and "bandits" who "only understood force." Cédile, originally a moderate, now denounced the Vietminh publicly, claiming that it "did not represent public opinion" and must bow to French control.

Britain's new Labour government was then contemplating independence for India, but Gracey ironically embarked on a different path in Saigon, where he reiterated his desire for the French to return. On September 21, he exceeded his instructions by proclaiming martial law. He banned public meetings, imposed a curfew, and closed down Vietnamese newspapers—though he permitted the French press and radio to function. But with only eighteen hundred British, Indian, and Gurkha soldiers at his disposal, he lacked the muscle to enforce his decree. So, encouraged by Cédile, he released and armed fourteen hundred French army troops, most of them Foreign Legionnaires who had been interned by the Japanese.

The desperate Vietminh leaders thereupon mobilized a massive protest demonstration deliberately designed to provoke British and French reprisals and "cause many casualties and attract world attention," as one of them cynically explained. But a French orgy of violence pre-empted them.

On September 22, a day after their release, French paratroopers and Foreign Legionnaires went on a rampage. Shooting sentries, they poured into the Saigon city hall and ousted the Vietminh's so-called Provisional Executive Committee. They took over police stations and other public buildings, raising the French flag from the rooftops. Then, their ranks swelled by angry French civilians, they coursed through the city, broke into Vietnamese homes and shops, and indiscriminately clubbed men, women, and even children. Gracey and Cédile, appalled by the spectacle that they themselves had inspired, pleaded for calm. But it was too late.

Until then, the Vietminh leaders had calculated that temperance would win them Allied favor. But that prospect had dimmed. More important, they feared losing their militants unless they showed strength. Responding to the French frenzy, therefore, they launched a general strike on September 24. If any one date marks the start of the first Indochina war, it might be that day. For the strike and its aftermath initiated a momentum of conflict that, despite periodic negotiating attempts, could not be stopped.

By morning, Saigon was paralyzed. Electricity and water supplies had halted. Shops were shut and offices closed, trams stood still and even rickshaws had disappeared from the deserted streets. Anticipating the worst, the city's twenty thousand French civilians barricaded their houses or fled in panic to the security of the rambling old Continental Palace Hotel, the billet for French and British officers. The crackle of gunfire and the thud of mortars soon echoed across the city, as armed Vietminh squads attacked the airport, burned the central market, and stormed the local prison to liberate hundreds of Vietnamese inmates.

But the most brutal episode occurred at the Cité Hérault, a residential suburb. At dawn, Binh Xuyen terrorists led by Vietminh agents slipped past Japanese soldiers supposedly guarding the district. Smashing doors and windows, they broke into bedrooms and massacred one hundred and fifty French and Eurasian civilians, sparing neither women nor children. They dragged a hundred more away as hostages, mutilating many before freeing them later. Predictably, Communist historians omit any mention of this atrocity in their accounts of the period.

In London, a senior Foreign Office expert outlined Britain's dilemma in a confidential memorandum. The British could not continue to back the French in Vietnam without alienating China and anticolonial American opinion. But a straightforward retreat from Saigon would dismay the French, and perhaps also spur dissidence in British possessions. He therefore proposed "to get French troops into southern Indochina with the utmost dispatch, and, after turning it over to them, to withdraw our forces as soon as possible"—which is exactly what happened. The United States, while hesitant to get directly involved in Indochina, raised no objections as the British gave their American military equipment to French units and transported them by ship to Indochina.

General de Gaulle, meanwhile, made two appointments that illustrated his determination to reimpose French rule. As high commissioner for Indochina, the equivalent of governor, he selected Admiral Georges Thierry d'Argenlieu, an almost medieval figure who had retired from the navy after World War I to become a Carmelite monk, then shed his robes temporarily to join the Free French. Arrogant and inflexible, d'Argenlieu shared de Gaulle's absolute faith in the grandeur of France, a conviction that set him on a collision course against the Vietminh, whose chauvinistic fervor matched his. As his chief military commander, de Gaulle chose General Jacques Philippe Leclerc, a superb soldier whose tank division had liberated Paris in 1944. Leclerc soon perceived the necessity for a political solution to the chaos in Indochina, but he started out heeding the advice he had solicited from General Douglas MacArthur: "Bring troops, more troops, as many as you can."

Leclerc's forces set forth in October, first cracking a Vietminh blockade around Saigon, then driving through the Mekong delta and up into the highlands. They were constantly harassed by enemy guerrillas: the Vietminh, retreating everywhere, burned villages, destroyed bridges, and terrorized the local population. The ruthless Vietminh leader for the region, Tran Van Giau, weakened his movement by liquidating sympathizers who failed to meet his sectarian standards. Within five months, Leclerc announced victory in the south, but his claim was illusory. The French, like the Americans later, could conquer Vietnamese territory but could not hold it. The French historian Philippe Devillers, who served in Leclerc's army, described the phenomenon: "If we departed, believing a region pacified, the Vietminh would arrive on our heels. . . . There was only one possible defense, to multiply our posts, fortify them, arm and train the villagers, coordinate intelligence and police. What was required was not Leclerc's thirty-five thousand troops but a hundred thousand—and Cochinchina was not the only problem."

On the political side, d'Argenlieu created a new administration in Saigon. No racist, he appointed Vietnamese to positions of authority. But, like the admirals who had governed southern Vietnam in the nineteenth century, his kind of Vietnamese were landowners, doctors, lawyers, and other *évolués*, as the French called them, models of respectability who had an investment in France's presence. An advisory council for Cochinchina, which he formed in early 1946, contained eight Vietnamese and four French members. But seven of the Vietnamese were naturalized French citizens. Their attachment to a separate Cochinchina was calculated to offset the Vietminh's efforts to reunify Vietnam, and it poisoned further attempts to avert war.

The situation differed in the north, where Ho Chi Minh's influence was largely uncontested and his popularity widespread. To project a nationalist rather than ideological image, he had placed Catholics and socialists in his cabinet alongside Communists, and he initiated reformist rather than revolutionary programs. He abolished onerous taxes and puritanically banned prostitution, opium, gambling, and even liquor. He left landowners unmolested and instructed local government committees to make room for the "middle classes." But all was not benign. Vietminh bands in many villages abducted and murdered mandarins, often after staging phony "people's trials," and criminals, indiscriminately released from jails, terrorized the countryside. Like the south, however, the north was soon to be further disrupted by outside intervention.

Under the Potsdam plan, the Chinese Nationalists had been delegated to disarm the Japanese in the north—and the first of their two hundred thousand troops, commanded by General Lu Han, arrived in Hanoi in September. They resembled a horde of human locusts. Hungry, tattered, and even barefoot, many racked with scurvy and other diseases, their ranks included poor peasant boys and ragged soldiers dragging along their wives and children. They had plundered villages during their march down from China, and they carried baskets filled with ducks and chickens, or herded cattle before them. Once in Hanoi, they continued to pillage promiscuously. They barged into private homes and public buildings, stealing light bulbs and unscrewing doorknobs, and they pushed through markets, filching fruit and vegetables, even biting into bars of soap that they mistook for food. Their officers, more sophisticated, were equally rapacious. They cut themselves into Vietnamese and local Chinese business deals, confiscated French property and, among other things, legalized their theft by making the worthless Chinese currency legitimate tender in the area. Ho placated them. Having persuaded the Hanoi population to donate its hidden gold to his regime's depleted treasury, he gave a percentage to the Chinese—and, as a special gift, presented Lu Han with an extravagant set of gilt opium pipes and lamps.

Intricate political maneuvers absorbed Ho and Lu Han. Both wanted to prevent the French, now installed in the south, from regaining the north. But Lu Han sought to promote the VNQDD, his favorite Vietnamese faction. He respected Ho's influence as much as Ho respected his power. So they sealed a bargain. In November 1945, Ho dissolved the Communist party as a gesture of appeasement to Lu Han, who in turn conceded to elections that would yield a coalition government composed of VNQDD and Vietminh members.

The VNQDD leaders, outraged by Lu Han's betrayal, sent out gangs to kidnap and kill their rivals, and Giap barely escaped with his life. Ho now perceived that Lu Han, who had set no time limit on his occupation, might use the disorder as a pretense to keep his forces in northern Vietnam indefinitely. He also learned that Chiang Kai-shek, on a different track, was prepared to withdraw the Chinese troops and allow the French to return to Tonkin in exchange for France's relinquishing its old concessions in Shanghai and other Chinese ports—a pact in fact signed in February 1946.

Ho was trapped. The United States, despite his repeated pleas, had decided to support France. The Soviet Union had neither endorsed his regime nor, he remarked ruefully, even assigned an observer to Hanoi. Nor could he count on the French Communist party, whose boss, Maurice Thorez, then vice-president of General de Gaulle's government, later said that he "did not intend to liquidate the French position in Indochina." In December 1945, Ho confessed to his failures in a remarkable statement:

Though five months have passed since we declared independence, no foreign countries have recognized us. Though our soldiers have fought gloriously, we are still far from victory. Though our administration is honest and efficient, corruption has not been eliminated. Though we have introduced reforms, disorder disturbs several areas. We could ascribe these setbacks to the fact that our regime is young, or make other excuses. But no. Our successes are due to the efforts of our citizens, and our shortcomings are our own fault.

Ho's only alternative at this juncture, he felt, was an accommodation under which the French could come back—on condition that they recognized Vietnam's independence. He signaled his receptivity to such a settlement in interviews with Western correspondents, telling one in early 1946 that "we admire France and have no desire to sever the bonds that unite our two peoples" but that the French should take "a first and sincere step." That invitation and others like it sounded hopeful to Jean Sainteny, who had talked with Ho since his arrival in Hanoi in August as de Gaulle's representative. Sainteny, a former Hanoi banker and son-in-law of Albert Sarraut, the retired governor of Indochina, flew to Saigon to consult with General Leclerc, then acting as high commissioner during Admiral d'Argenlieu's absence. Leclerc preferred a diplomatic solution to a larger conflict. He approved Sainteny's proposal to negotiate.

Leclerc, resorting to something like gunboat diplomacy, dispatched shiploads of French troops to northern Vietnam, ready to attack if the talks failed. Ho and Sainteny argued strenuously, both aware that deadlocked negotiations could spark a war neither one wanted. Sainteny, under pressure from vested French interests in Saigon, insisted on a separate Cochinchina. Ho, committed to Vietnam's national unity, refused. At the last minute, as Leclerc's flotilla steamed into the Gulf of Tonkin, they compromised: the fate of Cochinchina would await a referendum. So, on March 6, 1946, a clash had been prevented. France would recognize Vietnam as a free state within the French Union—the new name for the old French empire—and Ho would permit the presence of twenty-five thousand French troops in Vietnam for the next five years. But the final confirmation of this accord never came.

Ho's balance sheet was mixed. No deadline had been set for a plebiscite, and he had allowed the French army to re-enter the north. But France had confirmed his legitimacy, he had bought time to strengthen the Vietminh, and he had contrived to expel the Chinese—the achievement he considered most important, as he vigorously told his critics at a meeting in Hanoi: "You fools! Don't you realize what it means if the Chinese remain? Don't you remember your history? The last time the Chinese came, they stayed a thousand years. The French are foreigners. They are weak. Colonialism is dying. The white man is finished in Asia. But if the Chinese stay now, they will never go. As for me, I prefer to sniff French shit for five years than eat Chinese shit for the rest of my life."

Ho's immense prestige silenced his disappointed followers. But the agreement split the French. Saigon businessmen, planters, and officials were indignant at the prospect of losing their colonial privileges, and Admiral d'Argenlieu bluntly denounced Leclerc: "I am amazed—yes, that is the word, amazed—that France's fine expeditionary corps in Indochina is commanded by officers who would rather negotiate than fight."

D'Argenlieu went through the motions of further talks with the Vietminh at Dalat, a lovely hill town in the south. But he parried the big issues, like Cochinchina's status and Vietnam's sovereignty, contending that they could only be discussed at a higher level meeting, scheduled to take place in France. On May 31, 1946, Ho departed for Paris—his first trip back to the city of his youth.

No sooner had Ho left Hanoi than d'Argenlieu resorted to the old *fait accompli* ploy. In violation of the March agreement and without informing Paris, he proclaimed a Republic of Cochinchina in the name of France. Ho, arriving in Paris, suffered further humiliation when the French shunted him and his comrades off to Biarritz, in southwest France, ostensibly because an election campaign had delayed the conference, but actually to isolate him from sympathizers in the capital. The French then switched the meeting site to a palace in the forest of Fontainebleau, outside Paris, to remove it from the spotlight. Even worse from Ho's viewpoint, the French delegation contained not a single prominent figure, merely colonial officials and three obscure politicians—one of whom, a Socialist, quit at the start on the grounds that the whole exercise had been rigged in advance to discredit the Vietnamese. A French Communist on the delegation did not resign, however. Years later in Hanoi, a Vietnamese aide to Ho at Fontainebleau admitted to me that Ho was mistaken to have counted on the French Communists to help him; they were more nationalistic than ideological.

The conference coincided with a French political shift to the right, when Georges Bidault, the Christian Democratic leader, became prime minister of a new coalition government. An earnest defender of France's *grandeur,* Bidault had shaped the idea of the French Union as a cohesive group of states "closely linked by common institutions." Ho understandably favored a looser arrangement, like the British Commonwealth, of independent countries connected by treaties respectful of their "right to self-determination." The conceptual difference was crucial, but the tough practical problem was Cochinchina, a question that moved Ho at a press conference to an emotional outburst: "It is Vietnamese soil. It is the flesh of our flesh, the blood of our blood."

The Cochinchina issue also aroused the French in Saigon, who inundated the government in Paris with telegrams and petitions, some even protesting against the presence in France of Ho and his "agitators and troublemakers." At the same time, d'Argenlieu tried to subvert the negotiations by convening his own counterconference in Dalat, to which he invited selected Vietnamese, Cambodians, Laotians, and a delegate from the "Republic of Cochinchina" to discuss Indochina's future. The French government did nothing to disavow him—and may have even secretly approved his machinations.

After eight weeks of haggling, the Fontainebleau conference yielded only a draft accord that reinforced France's economic prerogatives in northern Vietnam without resolving the Cochinchina problem. Ho sent his delegation home and stayed on in Paris alone in a last anguished effort to settle what he publicly glossed over as a "family dispute."

At midnight on September 19, dressed in a thin tunic, he slipped out of his hotel accompanied by a French bodyguard and drove to a building not far away. He took the cage elevator up to the apartment of Marius Moutet, minister of overseas France, another new name for the postwar French empire. In Moutet's study, he initialed a partial agreement, which they entitled a *modus vivendi*, an interim understanding. As he left, Ho murmured to his bodyguard, "I've just signed my death warrant."

Ho's decision to defer to the French on the Cochinchina issue was to obsess him for the rest of his life and made his ambition to reunify Vietnam almost compulsive during his last years. Communist troops were told that the Tet offensive of 1968 was a campaign to "liberate" the south before Ho's death. Similarly, the final Communist drive to take Saigon in 1975 was dubbed the Ho Chi Minh Offensive—and Saigon afterward became Ho Chi Minh City.

In October 1946, when Ho returned to Hanoi, his concessions upset the Vietminh's hard-core militants, some of whom accused him of selling out to the enemy, but the population acclaimed him. Despite his calls for moderation, he must have known that peace would not last. General Etienne Valluy, the French commander who replaced Leclerc, circulated a secret memorandum to his officers proposing a *coup d'état* against Ho, and Giap was girding his forces for a showdown.

French and Vietminh troops, skirmishing against each other in various places, were particularly restive in the port of Haiphong, where they controlled different zones of the city. Their dispute there hinged on the right to collect customs duties, a matter left unclear in the Fontainebleau agreement. When a French patrol boat seized some Chinese smugglers on the morning of November 20, Vietminh militia intercepted the

French craft and arrested its three crew members. At that, the volatile French commander, a Colonel Dèbes, assaulted the Vietminh. By afternoon, fighting lashed the town as French tanks rolled over street barricades and the Vietminh replied with mortars. At the opera house, facing the main square, a troupe of Vietnamese actors held off the French with antique muskets.

A commission of French and Vietnamese officers, assigned to monitor truce violations, managed to impose a cease-fire the next day. That might have ended the flare-up—except for a decision made in Paris by Prime Minister Bidault.

Typically of the Fourth Republic, in which prime ministers rose and fell with tedious regularity, Bidault was teetering. He thus agreed when Admiral d'Argenlieu flew home to remind him that the rising tension in Haiphong offered a pretext to punish the Vietminh. "Can we even use artillery?" asked d'Argenlieu. Bidault answered tersely: "Even that."

D'Argenlieu flashed Bidault's response to Saigon, where General Valluy in turn ordered General Morlière, his representative in Hanoi, to insist that Ho pull all the Vietminh forces out of Haiphong and accede to French control of the city. Morlière, anxious to avert an explosion, reassured Valluy that the ultimatum was unnecessary, since hostilities had stopped. But Valluy, eager to strike, also telegraphed the hawkish Colonel Dèbes: "It appears that we are confronted by premeditated aggression. . . . The moment has come for you to teach a severe lesson to those who have treacherously attacked you. Employ all means at your disposal to master Haiphong completely, and thereby bring the Vietnamese military leaders to a better understanding of the situation."

On the morning of November 23, Dèbes demanded that the Vietminh authorities evacuate their troops from Haiphong within two hours. The Vietnamese, protesting that they were observing the cease-fire, telephoned Hanoi for instructions. Dèbes gave them an additional forty-five minutes, then issued the order.

French infantry and armored units went through the city, fighting house to house against Vietminh squads. French aircraft zoomed in to bomb and strafe while the cruiser *Suffren,* in the harbor, lobbed shells into the city, demolishing whole neighborhoods of flimsy structures. Refugees streamed into nearby provinces with their belongings in baskets and on bicycles, and the naval guns shelled them as well. Days passed before the French finally routed the last Vietminh snipers. The Vietnamese claimed twenty thousand deaths, but a French admiral later estimated "no more" than six thousand. Vu Quoc Uy, then chairman of the Haiphong municipal committee, told me in an interview in 1981 that the toll had been between five hundred and a thousand.

D'Argenlieu, still in Paris, cabled congratulations to Valluy; "we will never retreat or surrender," he assured him. Ho, by now losing hope for an accommodation, radioed an appeal to the French parliament to honor the accord he had signed. He also asserted to a French correspondent that neither France nor Vietnam "can afford the luxury of a bloody war," but he warned that the Vietnamese would endure an "atrocious struggle" rather than "renounce their liberty." In mid-December, his old socialist comrade Léon Blum had become prime minister, and he favored a "sincere" reconciliation with Vietnam "based on independence." Ho sent Blum a set of concrete recommendations for restoring calm. The telegram, transmitted through Saigon, was delayed by French officials there for nine days—during which time the conflict again escalated.

"If those gooks want a fight, they'll get it," said Valluy as he landed in Haiphong on December 17, his temper boiling over the slaughter of three French soldiers by Vietminh militia in Hanoi that day. Incidents were now multiplying in Hanoi and, as they had in Haiphong, the French presented Ho with a demand to disarm the Vietminh and place security in their hands. Ho begged the French to rescind the order. Giap deployed some thirty thousand men at three locations in the suburbs, his plan being to invade Hanoi if the trouble started.

The origin of the events is still murky, but the Vietminh militia probably struck first on the evening of December 19, sabotaging the municipal power plant, then breaking into French homes to murder or abduct their occupants. Alerted in advance by spies, the French counterattacked, and Hanoi became a battleground, its buildings aflame and its tree-lined avenues littered with corpses. Ho Chi Minh, in bed with fever at his modest bungalow behind the French governor's mansion, fled before the French could capture him. At nine P.M., Giap issued a virtual declaration of war: "I order all soldiers and militia in the center, south, and north to stand together, go into battle, destroy the invaders, and save the nation. . . . The resistance will be long and arduous, but our cause is just and we will surely triumph."

Except for a Christmas truce, the battle of Hanoi raged through December. Giap's troops rushed into the city to join the Vietminh, their arms a hodgepodge of ancient French muskets, old American Remington rifles, British Bren automatics, Japanese carbines, and spears, swords, and machetes as well as homemade contrivances called Phan Dinh Phung grenades, after Vietnam's nineteenth-century nationalist hero. They fought from street to street against French tanks, artillery, and machine guns. Dr. Tran Duy Hung, then the Vietminh mayor, described the events to me thirty-five years later:

> We were in Kham Thien Street, a French unit facing us from across the railway tracks. We built a barricade with railroad ties, piling it high with beds, dressers, chairs, tables, whatever. Not even a tank could get through it. Some of our boys—we called them "gentlemen militia"—wore red and yellow shoulder braid captured from the French. People sang revolutionary songs when they charged. We were very optimistic, very romantic. . . .
>
> We were ordered to divert the French until our forces could withdraw from the city. We could only get out by crawling under the Long Bien bridge, which the French controlled. We exploded all the firecrackers we could find. When the noise stopped, the French moved in on us. But we had escaped into the countryside to begin the long war. . . .

Ho had escaped to Hadong, a town six miles south of Hanoi, where he echoed Giap's call to arms—and also appealed to the Western Allies to restrain the French. In Paris, however, Blum had altered his stance. Stressing his commitment to Vietnam's independence within the French Union, he now emphasized that "order must be restored" as a precondition to fresh discussions. He sent Marius Moutet to Vietnam to survey the situation, and Ho promptly offered to talk with the minister in whose apartment he had signed the *modus vivendi* four months earlier. But Moutet rejected the overture as "propaganda," adding ambiguously that France would only deal with "authentic spokesmen for the Vietnamese people." D'Argenlieu, back in Saigon, went further. Conversations with Ho were "henceforth impossible," he asserted, proposing instead that Vietnam return to its "traditional monarchy"—in short, enthrone Bao Dai again, who had by then left Hanoi for Hong Kong. A pattern was emerging that was to be repeated by France and later by the United States: negotiations with the Communists could only be pursued if first the Communists capitulated.

Another familiar pattern emerged as Vietnam refracted domestic French politics. The revolving doors of the Fourth Republic spun again in January 1947, and Paul Ramadier, also a Socialist, supplanted Blum in a coalition government composed of Socialists, Christian Democrats, and Communists. Voicing hope for peace, Ramadier dismissed d'Argenlieu and replaced him as high commissioner in Saigon with Emile

Bollaert, a respected civil servant who appointed as his personal adviser Paul Mus, a scholar of Asian affairs who was sympathetic to the Vietnamese. Ho sensed that reconciliation was possible and proposed an immediate cease-fire to avert a war that, he warned, would "only end in hatred and bitterness between our two peoples." But Ramadier's government was falling apart. In March, the Communists dropped their support over an internal economic matter—though they voted the appropriations to fund the French army in Vietnam. The shift strengthened the Christian Democrats, whose leader, Bidault, favored a tough approach on Vietnam. So, while Ramadier tried to steer a moderate course, Christian Democrats in his cabinet like Bidault and Paul Coste-Floret, the defense minister, were maneuvering to prevent negotiations. Other officials with different views were also subverting them.

In May 1947, instructed to present Ho with a set of suggestions, Paul Mus traveled some sixty miles from Hanoi to the Vietminh's jungle headquarters. There he told Ho that France would agree to a cease-fire on condition that the Vietminh lay down a part of its arms, permit French troops to circulate freely inside its zone, and turn over several German and Austrian deserters from the Foreign Legion. "Would you accept if you were in my place?" Ho asked Mus. "No," replied Mus. Ho thereupon rejected the offer—which was, in any case, a demand for surrender.

Outside pressure was also building up against Ramadier. General de Gaulle had just put his enormous prestige behind a new political party, the Rally of the French People, which strongly opposed retreat from Vietnam. At the time, too, French public opinion favored toughness to regain the national pride they had lost to the Germans in 1940. The French Communists shared that sentiment, and Maurice Thorez, a deputy prime minister in Ramadier's cabinet, countersigned a directive ordering military action against the Vietminh. Not only did Ho Chi Minh seem to be defiant, but French rule was being tested as well by dissident movements in other French possessions—Madagascar, Morocco, and Algeria. Few French, whatever their ideology, could face the rebuff to France's great *mission civilisatrice*. France was thus led into war in Vietnam by a Socialist regime too unstable to withstand the challenge of its conservative critics.

General Leclerc, returned to Paris from Vietnam, now warned that "anti-Communism will be a useless tool unless the problem of nationalism is resolved." But his wisdom was ignored. The French Communists, after breaking with Ramadier, triggered a series of strikes and other disorders that plunged France into civil strife. Though the Soviet

Union then showed little interest in Ho Chi Minh, his Communist record could plausibly be said to link him to a worldwide Soviet plan to dominate the world—or so conservative French politicians began to assert as they equated his resistance against France with Moscow's ambitions elsewhere in the world. And, as the Soviet dictator Joseph Stalin seemed to intensify his threats against the West, the United States gradually accepted the thesis.

In 1947, Truman administration officials conceded that Ho's Communist "connections" might serve the Kremlin's purposes. Two years later, Secretary of State Dean Acheson had no doubts. The question of whether Ho was "as much nationalist as Commie," he said, was "irrelevant," since "all Stalinists in colonial areas are nationalists." France's desperate effort to cling to its Asian possession escalated into an international crisis—and the American commitment took shape.

5 The Light That Failed

Ho Chi Minh and his high command planning the battle of Dienbienphu in their jungle headquarters. At right is General Vo Nguyen Giap, commander of the Vietminh forces.

Bao Dai, chosen by the French to be the puppet emperor of Vietnam, seen here as a boy in Paris, where the French sent him to be educated. He lived with a French family and acquired a particular affection for French girls. He also learned to play tennis.

Late in 1949, Secretary of State Acheson (below, at right) persuaded President Truman to earmark $15 million in aid to the French forces in Indochina. Over the next four years, American assistance for the French war mounted to more than $2 billion.

Bao Dai abdicated in
1945 and then fled to
Hong Kong, where he
was caricatured by Al
Hirschfeld, then on a
world tour with S. J.
Perelman. To Perelman,
the ex-emperor was a
"slippery-looking customer
rather on the pudgy side
and freshly dipped in
Crisco."

General Jean de Lattre de
Tassigny, the dashing
French commander in
Indochina. A Gallic
version of General
Douglas MacArthur, vain
and brilliant, he raised
French morale after
arriving in 1950.

Ho Chi Minh gained a major advantage when the Communists conquered China in 1949: he was then able to obtain modern weapons and other assistance directly. Here he eats with Chinese advisers under portraits of himself and Mao Zedong, the Chinese leader.

The Vietminh forces were meticulous in planning battles. Here, using a sand-table model, they prepare an assault against a village fortified by the French and their Vietnamese auxiliaries. Though outgunned by the French, the Vietminh had the advantage of mobility.

The French commander in Indochina, General Henri Navarre (right), with a deputy, Major General René Cogny. Navarre's plan to pursue the Vietminh forces in the hinterland led him to deploy French units in the remote northeastern valley of Dienbienphu, near the border of Laos.

A Vietminh supply train of bicycles and porters crossing a pontoon bridge en route to Dienbienphu, where Vietnamese forces had encircled a French garrison. The Vietminh also moved cannons onto the hills overlooking the valley of Dienbienphu.

Colonel Christian de Castries, French commander at Dienbienphu, was a romantic cavalry officer who had been wounded and decorated in World War II; he also had a pile of gambling debts and a list of brokenhearted women.

With the Vietminh shelling them from the hazy hills in the distance, the French forces at Dienbienphu tried to survive in trenches reminiscent of World War I. But the Vietminh gradually approached the French garrison by digging tunnels.

A wounded Foreign Legion lieutenant amid the sandbags of a dugout at Dienbienphu. The French were stunned that the Vietminh had managed to haul howitzers onto the ridges overlooking the valley and were pounding its airstrip and fortifications.

Prime Minister Mendès-France poses for photographers with Zhou Enlai, the Chinese foreign minister, at Geneva in 1954. The two men had met secretly beforehand and laid the groundwork for a settlement of the war.

Captain James McGovern, known as "Earthquake McGoon," was one of two Americans killed at Dienbienphu. He and his copilot, Wallace Buford, were shot down by the Vietminh while flying supplies to the French in unmarked U.S. transport planes.

Vietminh troops entering Hanoi in October 1954, following the French evacuation. For many of these soldiers, this was the first time they had penetrated an urban area since the war against the French broke out nine years earlier.

President Eisenhower with Secretary of State Dulles. They regarded the French stand in Indochina as vital to the U.S. policy of "containing" Communism throughout the world, and they financed the war.

Our policy is to support Bao Dai and the French in Indochina until we have time to help them establish a going concern.

—Dean Rusk

A year ago none of us could see victory. There wasn't a prayer. Now we can see it clearly—like light at the end of a tunnel.

—General Henri Navarre

You can kill ten of my men for every one I kill of yours. But even at those odds, you will lose and I will win.

—Ho Chi Minh

On June 25, 1950, North Korean forces surged across the thirty-eighth parallel and four days later captured Seoul, South Korea's capital. Six months earlier, Mao Zedong's Chinese Communist legions had reached the frontiers of Vietnam after conquering all of mainland China. The Soviet Union and China both recognized Ho Chi Minh's regime, the Democratic Republic of Vietnam. President Truman now added a new dimension to American foreign policy: the "containment" of Communism, until then focused on Europe, would be extended to Asia.

Almost overnight, the United States amended its approach to France's war in Indochina against Ho Chi Minh. Dean Rusk, deputy under secretary of state at the time, heralded the change in his characteristically bland style. In late 1949, he announced that "the resources of the United States" would henceforth "be deployed to reserve Indochina and Southeast Asia from further Communist encroachment."

Official American spokesmen had already conceived the "domino theory," warning that if Indochina fell to Communism, so would the other countries of Southeast Asia. But while the French repeated that theme, they were primarily fighting in Indochina to preserve a colonial possession, and their goal was comparatively narrow. The United States, playing for global stakes, therefore became more determined than France to persevere in Indochina. And thus America's view of Indochina as an international cockpit gave the French enormous "leverage," the polite term for blackmail. They repeatedly rejected U.S. attempts to persuade them to conduct the war more effectively, spurned proposals for promoting credible Vietnamese nationalists who might have countered the Communists, and threatened to undermine American military programs in Western Europe unless the United States fulfilled their requests for help in Indochina.

In Washington, right-wing demagogues like Senator Joseph McCarthy meanwhile fueled a febrile atmosphere of anti-Communism, driving normally rational U.S. officials to excessive lengths to prove their devotion to the defeat of the "Red menace." By 1954, consequently, American aid accounted for nearly 80 percent of French expenditures on the conflict, and the compulsion to win created the illusion of imminent success. Admiral Arthur Radford, chairman of the joint chiefs of staff, assured a congressional committee on the eve of France's defeat at Dienbienphu that France had arrived at "a favorable turn in the war." Georges Bidault, the French foreign minister, asserted during the battle: "Ho Chi Minh is about to capitulate. We are going to beat him."

Specialists on Indochina were considerably less optimistic during the early days of the Truman administration. However, their discussions were colored by U.S. policies toward the Soviet Union. A foremost advocate of firmness was Dean Acheson, under secretary of state, who overshadowed his boss, General George C. Marshall, the august secretary of state. Eloquent and elegant, with his crisp mustache and custom-made suits, Acheson personified the Eastern establishment liberal who had urged American intervention in World War II. His memory of the abortive attempts to appease Hitler had ingrained in him a belief that power, rather than negotiations, checked potential aggression, and this guided his attitude toward Russian truculence after the war. So, when the Soviet government appeared to be subverting the postwar regimes in Greece and Turkey, he warned that the Communists would contaminate Western Europe and the Middle East just as bad "apples in a barrel" infect one another. Spurred by him and others, the president appealed to Congress on March 12, 1947, for funds to "support free peoples who are resisting subjugation by armed minorities or by outside pressures."

With this major U.S. initiative—the Truman Doctrine—the cold war between the Soviet Union and America intensified. Later in 1947, the United States launched the Marshall Plan, a colossal economic aid plan for Western Europe largely contrived to curb Communist inroads in France and Italy. The Central Intelligence Agency, recently formed, covertly intervened to block Communist advances in the Italian elections. The Russians staged a Communist *coup d'état* in Czechoslovakia, then barred Western access to Berlin, moving the United States to begin shaping the North Atlantic Treaty Organization as a shield against Moscow. And the prestigious journal *Foreign Affairs* published an article entitled "The Sources of Soviet Conduct," by "X," who was in fact George Kennan, then chief of the State Department's policy planning staff and one of America's leading Kremlinologists.

Kennan described Moscow's strategic behavior as a "fluid stream" that has "filled every nook and cranny available to it in the basin of world power," but that would accommodate to "unassailable barriers in its path." He suggested that Soviet designs be "contained" by the "adroit and vigilant application of counterforce at a series of constantly shifting geographical and political points." In various shapes, "containment" has been a pillar of U.S. foreign policy ever since—though, a quarter century later, Kennan would reflect that his concept had been distorted into a strictly military approach.

To the extent that the Truman administration contemplated Asia at all, its attention was drawn to China, where Mao's Communists were chewing up Chiang Kai-shek's Nationalists in the final phase of a civil war. General Marshall had gone there in 1946 in an attempt to mediate, but recommended that the United States not intervene, since "peace and stability must . . . be achieved by the efforts of the Chinese themselves." Soon afterward, as secretary of state, he took a similar view of the situation in Vietnam. "We have fully recognized France's sovereign position in that area," he advised the American ambassador in Paris, but concluded that it was a matter for the French and the Vietminh "to work out for themselves."

Ho Chi Minh's Communist record was no secret, yet it aroused little alarm among American officials in those days. In 1948, surveying Soviet influence in Southeast Asia, the State Department's specialists estimated that "the Vietnamese Communists are not subservient" to Kremlin directives and, if anything, "it is rather the French colonial press that has been strongly anti-American . . . to the point of approximating the official Moscow position." America's options were therefore restricted, as another State Department analysis of the period tortuously concluded.

The United States ideally preferred Indochina to be a "self-governing nationalist state" uncontaminated by Communism, closely associated with the West and "particularly with France." The French were waging "a desperate and apparently losing struggle," but could not withdraw. Nor could they negotiate with Ho Chi Minh, even though he was "the strongest and perhaps the ablest figure" in the region, and his exclusion from any settlement would be "an expedient of uncertain outcome"—

thus the need for "some solution" that would "strike a balance" between Vietnamese aspirations and French interests. But the State Department experts had no such formula. They shelved their Indochina study.

The French, aware of America's yearning for a truly nationalist Vietnamese regime to rival the Vietminh, reached back to Admiral d'Argenlieu's notion of a return to a "traditional monarchy"—meaning, of course, Bao Dai. No matter that Bao Dai had abdicated in 1945, thereby transmitting the "mandate of heaven" to Ho. Outfitted in his regal trappings, he would symbolize imperial authority; he was easy to manage; and, most important, he had been touted in a *Life* magazine article by William Bullitt, a former U.S. envoy to General de Gaulle during World War II, which plainly indicated that the idea would gain American support—and stimulate Washington to give France help in the war.

Bao Dai had credentials. His ancestor had been Gia Long, the emperor whose cause had been helped by Pigneau de Béhaine. He had been crowned at the death of his father in 1925, when he was twelve, and almost immediately sent to Paris, where he lived with the family of a French colonial official, studied music, learned to play tennis, and attended a public *lycée*. Back in Vietnam seven years later, he ascended the throne and tried to govern with a cabinet of nationalists, among them Ngo Dinh Diem. But the French quickly reminded him that they gave the orders, and his brief dream evaporated. He was even tyrannized by his mother, a betel-chewing crone addicted to gambling. Lonely and powerless, he devoted himself to hunting and wenching. The Japanese had tolerated him during their occupation, and his stint as Ho's "supreme adviser" lasted only a year. In 1946, on the pretext of representing Ho in China, he fled from Hanoi to Hong Kong, where he spent an evening with, of all people, S. J. Perelman:

> The pleasure dome where His Majesty frolicked nightly turned out to be a somewhat sedater version of Broadway's Roseland. . . . Bao Dai was seated in a snug alcove surrounded by several hostesses whose skinny necks and high-pitched avian cackle lent them more than a passing resemblance to a flock of spring fryers. The royal exile, a short, slippery-looking customer rather on the pudgy side and freshly dipped in Crisco, wore a fixed, oily grin that was vaguely reptilian. Since he spoke almost no English, the interview was necessarily limited to pidgin and whatever pathetic scraps of French we could remember from Frazier and Square. To put him at his ease, I inquired sociably whether the pen of his uncle was in the garden. Apparently the query was fraught with delicate implications involving the conflict

in Indochina, for he shrugged evasively and buried his nose in his whiskey-and-soda.

After a short cultural exchange on the subject of films, in which Bao Dai revealed that his favorite actress was Jeanette MacDonald, a silky party appeared to clear up what he termed to be several misconceptions about the emperor:

> For example, he said, certain elements had been circulating tales that His Highness liked to smoke a little pipe or two. He could brand this as a calumny. His Highness was a serious student of international affairs who kept abreast of all the latest political developments and was deeply interested in economics, sociology, archeology, paleontology, epistemology, hagiology and dendrology. Backbiters were also saying that he went to the movies every afternoon. If he did, it was only in an effort to improve his English. . . . At this juncture, a bone-cracking yawn contorted the regal lineaments, clearly signifying that the audience was over. We shook hands formally all around . . . grateful that we had had this rare chance to cement international good-fellowship.

Bao Dai might have been a weak, unpredictable, corruptible playboy, but he was no fool. When the French sent representatives to Hong Kong in early 1947 to lure him back to the throne, he insisted, as Ho did, that France must first accede to Vietnam's independence and unity. His stand heartened anti-Communists like Ngo Dinh Diem, who urged him to stick to his position. It also worried Ho, who ordered the murder of two Vietnamese nationalists engaged in promoting a Bao Dai alternative. Ho engaged in a more moderate maneuver as well, reiterating his eagerness to remain within the French Union if only France would recognize a free and unified Vietnam. He even spoke sweetly about Bao Dai, saying that "he may be far from us in distance, but not in our thoughts." And lastly, he reshuffled his cabinet, confining its Communists to a handful of key posts and ousting Giap, whom the French considered too aggressive.

A possible transaction between Ho and Bao Dai alarmed the French. In September 1947, Emile Bollaert, the French high commissioner, offered to dissolve the separatist "Republic of Cochinchina" invented by Admiral d'Argenlieu and foster a "self-governing" Vietnam, with France responsible for its defense and diplomacy. This was essentially a revival of the nineteenth-century protectorate, and Ho called the proposal "too narrow," but signaled a willingness to bargain. A group of anti-

Communist nationalists, some on the French payroll, rushed to Hong Kong to urge Bao Dai to talk with Bollaert, and they met on December 7, 1947, aboard a French cruiser anchored in the Bay of Along, north of Haiphong, with a spectacular coastline of limestone needles rising from the sea. Bao Dai wanted a firm French pledge of independence, but Bollaert persuaded him to sign a "protocol" that so hedged the magic word with qualifications as to render it meaningless. Bao Dai had been trapped.

A comic sequence followed. Trying to escape his commitment to resume his imperial duties, Bao Dai fled to Europe, where he shifted from one city to another, hiding in cinemas by day and cabarets by night as Bollaert chased him like a process server. Bollaert eventually won, and they returned to the Bay of Along on June 8, 1948. There, in Bao Dai's presence, Bollaert signed an accord with General Nguyen Van Xuan, former head of the "Republic of Cochinchina" and now chief of a new Vietnamese national government. France "solemnly" recognized Vietnam's independence, but would keep control of its army, finances, and foreign affairs. Bao Dai was dissatisfied with this small "step in the negotiations between Vietnam and France" and went back to Europe, asserting that he would not put on the crown until "true unity and real independence" had been attained. The French-sponsored Vietnamese regime lacked credibility from the start.

Nguyen Van Xuan, its prime minister, was a ludicrous choice for the job. Educated at the prestigious Ecole Polytechnique in Paris, he was an exaggerated product of the *mission civilisatrice*. A naturalized French citizen, having spent most of his life in France, he barely spoke Vietnamese. The French had promoted him to general, the first Vietnamese ever elevated to that grade, and as head of Admiral d'Argenlieu's pet project, the "Republic of Cochinchina," he had been an active foe of Vietnamese unity. Even in Vietnam, a nation known for its intrigue and political plots, he was famous for being almost totally untrustworthy. Superficially affable, smooth and cheerful, he devoted nearly all his time to conniving. Soon after concluding the Bay of Along agreement, for example, he confided to the French that the Bao Dai "experiment" would fail.

The Communists branded Xuan a "puppet," but he was also anathema to the colonial French, who feared that a united Vietnam would eliminate their privileges in Cochinchina. In Paris, successive Christian Democratic and Radical Socialist coalitions stalled on granting autonomy to Vietnam. General de Gaulle, pontificating on the sidelines, predicted that "the French solution will be accepted sooner or later."

In late 1948, a new French high commissioner for Indochina took over. Léon Pignon, formerly political aide to Admiral d'Argenlieu, favored firmness. But he foresaw that the Communists, advancing across China, would soon arrive at the Vietnamese frontier to bulwark the Vietminh. He also reckoned that the United States would help France more readily if a liberal French policy were adopted. Thus he carried a set of fresh proposals to Bao Dai, who was lolling at a château on the Côte d'Azur. Bao Dai went to Switzerland to consult with his main American promoter, William Bullitt, who counseled him that he could count on U.S. support if he extracted real concessions from the French. Though Bullitt had no authority to speak for the United States, both Bao Dai and Pignon believed him to be representing the official American view, and this influenced them.

On March 8, 1949, Vietnam's figurehead emperor Bao Dai and France's figurehead president Vincent Auriol signed the Elysée Agreement, so-called for the lavish presidential palace in Paris at which the ceremony took place. The French reconfirmed Vietnam's independence and, going beyond mere promises, outlined measures to incorporate Cochinchina in a cohesive Vietnamese state. But France still retained control of Vietnam's defense, diplomacy, and finances. Helpless and frustrated, Bao Dai remarked soon afterward: "What they call a Bao Dai solution turns out to be just a French solution."

Ho Chi Minh issued a last appeal for compromise, and promised that in the growing conflict between the West and the Communist bloc he would guarantee Vietnam's neutrality. The appeal, which coincided with Mao Zedong's victory in China, evoked no response. In early 1950, abandoning hope of a reconciliation with France, he persuaded Moscow and Beijing to recognize his regime, the Democratic Republic of Vietnam, and his status changed overnight. The West now viewed Ho's government as a satellite in a monolithic Soviet empire. The Soviet endorsement, Dean Acheson said, "should remove any illusions as to the 'nationalist' nature of Ho Chi Minh's aims, and reveals Ho in his true colors as the mortal enemy of native independence in Indochina."

George Kennan had suggested that mainland Asia be omitted from his "containment" concept, since the United States was "greatly overextended in its whole thinking about what we can accomplish and should try to accomplish" in the region. Instead, he recommended that Japan and the Philippines be "the cornerstone of a Pacific security system." The proposal was supported by both Dean Acheson and the joint chiefs of staff, who had originally excluded the Asian continent from the U.S. "defense perimeter"—as did General MacArthur during World War II, when he hopped from island to island in the Pacific rather than fight on a vast land mass and risk stupendous casualties.

By 1949, however, some State Department specialists were warning that "we shall have suffered a major political rout" if Communism "swept" Southeast Asia. They agreed that the United States "should not put itself in a forward position" in the area, whose prospects were "very discouraging," but there was a distinct tone of hostility toward the French for having pursued so archaic a colonial policy in Indochina.

On January 17, 1949, for example, the State Department officials felt that while the United States ought to favor Bao Dai, it could not "irretrievably" support a local administration that "might become virtually a puppet government separated from the people and existing only by the presence of French military forces." Six months later, on July 1, another State Department report acknowledged that the Vietnamese Communists were making progress mainly because the French had been so "niggardly" in their concessions that they "have thus far failed to create an effective puppet regime capable of drawing nationalist elements away from Vietnam." The French military effort had "dwindled to footling punitive campaigns," and not only was this sapping France's strength, but U.S. equipment sent to French troops in Europe was "being squandered in Indochina on a mission that can only be justified in terms of Gallic mystique."

The Elysée Agreement with Bao Dai aroused little enthusiasm among U.S. officials, and the disappointed French intensified their lobbying. Robert Schuman, the Christian Democratic prime minister, personally begged Acheson for help, emphasizing that France was spending nearly $500 million a year, half its total military budget, to "hold the line" against Communism in Asia. Maurice Couve de Murville of the French foreign ministry warned that France might be unable to "hang on alone," and others forecast the possibility of "abandoning Indochina to Moscow."

For a brief moment in early 1950, American experts suddenly wondered whether Ho Chi Minh might not be a Soviet surrogate, since he requested and obtained recognition of his regime from Marshal Tito of Yugoslavia, one of Moscow's principal enemies. But they never explored the mystery further—as they never had in the past. In June 1948, for example, CIA officials had rejected a proposal to contact Ho covertly because "a white man would be very conspicuous. . . . In order to have an effective intelligence officer, he would have to have a little brown blood. Then, we wouldn't be able to trust him."

Acheson had briefly entertained the "theoretical possibility" that Ho might be another Tito, a renegade Communist nationalist. But he dropped the conjecture, concluding that the presence of Mao's legions on the Vietnamese border put the Vietminh under the thumb of "Chi Commie hatchet men and armed forces." However, Acheson was sanguine about Bao Dai's chances, which he described as "fairly fragile."

By late 1949, Acheson and other senior figures in the Truman administration were weighing tangible help for the French in Indochina through a foreign military aid program then being presented to Congress. Most of the aid was earmarked for Western Europe, but the idea arose to provide the president with a "slush fund" of $75 million to spend at his discretion in Asia, mainly for clandestine actions against the Communists in China. A portion might be reserved for the French war against the Vietminh.

Senator Arthur Vandenberg, the powerful chairman of the Senate Foreign Relations Committee, worried aloud about authorizing the president "solely, in his option, to give arms to any country," which would make him the "warlord number one on earth." The influential columnist Walter Lippmann dismissed the project as preposterous, since the promise to contain Communism in Asia for so paltry a sum was an offer to sell "the Brooklyn Bridge to widows and orphans for a down payment of $2.75." But Congress approved the appropriation, and on March 9, 1950, Acheson advised Truman to allocate $15 million to France for Indochina. Six months later, by no coincidence, the "Voice of America" added propaganda programs in the Vietnamese language to its broadcast schedule.

Truman did not actually sign the military aid legislation until July 26, 1950. But on June 28, three days after the Korean war broke out, Acheson persuaded him to order an "acceleration" of assistance to the French. A day after that, and four weeks before the military aid bill became law, eight C-47 cargo aircraft flew across the Pacific to Indochina—not the only time that the United States was to act illegally in Vietnam. During the next four years, the United States was to spend nearly $3 billion to finance the French in Indochina.

The United States then recognized the Bao Dai government in early 1950, but only over the objections of several American officials. Charlton Ogburn, then in the State Department's Bureau of Far Eastern Affairs, excoriated the emperor as "a figure deserving of the ridicule and contempt with which he is generally regarded by the Vietnamese, and any supposition that he could succeed or that a French army in Indochina could possibly be an asset to us could be entertained only by one totally ignorant of Asian realities." Another State Department expert, Raymond B. Fosdick, delivered an even more passionate diatribe in a memorandum that portrayed the Bao Dai regime as "doomed," and went on to foretell the future with remarkable prescience:

> This shabby business . . . probably represents an improvement over the brutal colonialism of earlier years, but it is now too late in the history of the world to settle for the price of this cheap substitute. . . .
>
> Ho Chi Minh as an alternative is decidedly unpleasant, but . . . there may be unpredictable and unseen factors in this situation that in the end will be more favorable to us than now seems probable. The fundamental antipathy of the Indochinese to China is one of the factors. Faced with a dilemma like this, the best possible course is to wait for the breaks. Certainly we should not play our cards in such a way that once again, as in China, we seem to be allied with reaction.
>
> Whether the French like it or not, independence is coming to Indochina. Why, therefore, do we tie ourselves to the tail of their battered kite?

Soon it was clear, however, that support for the French might undermine the global containment of Communism. For one thing, the French were becoming too bogged down in Indochina to meet their military obligations in Western Europe. And the growing burden vexed both soldiers and civilians in the Pentagon. John Ohley, a senior Defense Department official, alerted Acheson in November 1950 to the "urgent necessity for an immediate, thorough and realistic re-examination" of the policy, warning that it "may, without achieving its intended purpose, make impossible the fulfillment of mutual defense objectives elsewhere in the world."

French casualties since 1945 had exceeded fifty thousand, Ohley said, and "officers are being lost . . . at a faster rate than they are being graduated from officer schools in France." The French had pledged to assign twenty-seven divisions to the North Atlantic Treaty Organization by 1954, but "every officer and non-commissioned officer diverted to Indochina materially reduces the prospect that the French can even approximate the present objective." Moreover, France's soaring requirements "cannot be met without a substantial impact" on America's ability to supply its other Western European partners. So, he counseled, the United States ought to consider abandoning the French in Indochina if other goals "of even greater value and importance are to be attained." As it was, "we are gradually increasing our stake in the outcome of the struggle . . . [and] we are dangerously close to the point of being so deeply committed that we may find ourselves completely committed even to direct intervention. These situations, unfortunately, have a way of snowballing."

But new policies, like huge airplanes hurtling down a runway, do not reverse themselves. Acheson's copilot was now Dean Rusk, who had been appointed assistant secretary of state for Far Eastern affairs. He was to be involved in shaping Vietnam policy through three administrations, longer than any major American official, and his views remained extraordinarily consistent for nearly two decades.

In contrast to Acheson, who had attended Groton, Yale, and Harvard despite his family's genteel poverty, Rusk was sheer Horatio Alger stuff. He had grown up barefoot, the son of a tenant farmer in Georgia's Cherokee county, and had worked his way through Davidson, an obscure North Carolina college. Then came the moment that transformed his life and his thinking. He won a Rhodes scholarship to Oxford. More important, his exposure to Europe in the early 1930s, as the Nazis consolidated their power in Germany, scarred his mind, leading him to share Acheson's hostility to appeasement in any form anywhere. In 1981, as a law professor at the University of Georgia, he recalled to me:

I was a senior in college the year that the Japanese seized Manchuria, and I have the picture still etched in my mind from the newsreel of the Chinese ambassador standing before the League of Nations, pleading for help against the Japanese attack. I myself was present in the Oxford Union on that night in 1933, when they passed the motion that "this house will not fight for king and country. . . ."

So one cannot live through those years and not have some pretty strong feelings . . . that it was the failure of the governments of the world to prevent aggression that made the catastrophe of World War II inevitable.

Rusk saw the French effort in Indochina as a stand against Soviet expansion, and he argued in favor of U.S. aid to France in almost the same language he would later use to explain American intervention in Vietnam. In June 1950, addressing the Senate Foreign Relations Committee, he spoke in measured cadence, the faint trace of a southern accent softening his persuasive tone: "This is a civil war that has been in effect captured by the [Soviet] Politburo and, besides, has been turned into a tool of the Politburo. So it isn't a civil war in the usual sense. It is part of an international war. . . . We have to look at it in terms of which side we are on in this particular kind of struggle. . . . Because Ho Chi Minh is tied in with the Politburo, our policy is to support Bao Dai and the French in Indochina until we have time to help them establish a going concern."

With the recognition of Bao Dai's regime, the United States established a full-fledged embassy in Saigon headed by Donald Heath, a veteran diplomat entranced by the French cause. But the French resented intrusion into their affairs. They forbade U.S. military advisers to supervise the use of American equipment and they barred them from planning sessions. They either refused them intelligence or fed them misleading information, and they reacted fiercely to suggestions that they accord more latitude to Vietnamese nationalists. Top French officials even suspected that America's real aim was not to help them, but to supplant France politically and economically.

Nor did the French, despite their "solemn pledges," yield genuine independence to Bao Dai's government. Though they trained a few Vietnamese officers, they kept control of the army. They retained their grip on shipping, mines, plantations, banks, breweries, and factories as well as imports and exports. They also devised a financial arrangement under which piasters, the Vietnamese currency, could be exchanged for French francs at a ridiculously favorable rate, and those with licenses made fortunes. One well-placed figure implicated in the traffic was the son of France's President Auriol.

Not that granting power to Bao Dai at this stage mattered. He spent most of his time at his lodge in Dalat, eluding responsibilities. He had appointed a new prime minister, Tran Van Huu, a rich landowner and naturalized French citizen. But the authority in his entourage belonged to Nguyen Van Tam, his security director, a gnarled creature known as the Tiger of Cailay, his native village in the Mekong delta, where he had served the French by crushing Communist-led peasant uprisings. The Vietminh had killed two of his sons in retaliation, and his specialty in Saigon was tracking down real and innocuous enemies of the French, whom he liquidated brutally. In 1952, when Tam took over as Bao Dai's prime minister, he formed a cabinet described by the U.S. consul in Hanoi as composed of "opportunists, nonentities, extreme reactionaries, assassins, hirelings, and, finally, men of faded mental powers." The minister of youth and sports, Vo Hong Khanh, had been responsible for the murder by garroting of no fewer than ten Frenchmen some years earlier. Not only would the cabinet serve the Vietminh as an indirect "propaganda tool," the consul concluded, but it was "a poor return for French blood and American money."

A huge slice of the American aid went to Bao Dai as a personal allowance. By 1952, according to a secret U.S. report, he was receiving an official stipend of more than $4 million a year. He was not a big spender—his four private airplanes were his major expense—and his wife and children lived in relative modesty on the Côte d'Azur, while his own residence in Dalat was no more lavish than a house in an affluent New York suburb. But he was transferring enormous sums to French and Swiss banks, and investing extravagantly in real estate in France and Morocco—plainly to cushion himself should he one day be forced to go into exile. The annual payment consumed about 5 percent of the regime's total revenues—four times more than the appropriation for the land reform program. Even so, Bao Dai was chronically strapped for funds, and he relied heavily on Bay Vien, the boss of the Binh Xuyen gang, to supplement his finances handsomely.

He had put Bay Vien in charge of Saigon's casinos, bordellos, opium dens, gold smuggling and other rackets, and even promoted him to the rank of general. Soon the French sanctioned Bay Vien's respectability; they employed his hoodlums against the Vietminh and other nationalists. The corruption became institutionalized, making a farce of earnest American hopes for a credible Vietnamese administration that would check the Communists. Indeed, the French and Bao Dai seemed at that stage to have reached a tacit understanding: he played the puppet and they indulged his pleasures. His inner circle at one point included a spectacular French blond courtesan billed as a "member of the imperial film unit." Once, hearing her disparaged, he remarked: "She is only plying her trade. I'm the real whore."

The battlefield was the ground for the ultimate test. Ho Chi Minh called it a conflict "between the elephant and the grasshopper," but the image was not entirely accurate. The French, though far better armed than the Vietminh, were nevertheless short of vital equipment such as aircraft. And the Vietminh, though originally a guerrilla force, gradually grew into a large military unit, able to confront the French in bigger and bigger engagements—mainly in the dense jungles of northern Vietnam.

The area favored the Vietminh, whose troops could disappear and dart out to ambush road-bound French columns. The rugged terrain also offered them secure havens in which to train and rest, and Mao's triumph in China gave them even safer sanctuaries across the border. The Chinese Communists also supplied the Vietminh with advisers and modern American weapons captured from Chiang Kai-shek's routed

Nationalists. Even more important, Ho and his commander, Vo Nguyen Giap, reckoned that time was on their side. A long struggle would exhaust the French—not only on the ground in Vietnam but back in France, where the public would lose patience as the war dragged on.

In preparation for the struggle, Ho and Giap studied both Vietnam's past experiences against China and the lessons that Mao had learned in his protracted conflict. They would wage the war in three phases, starting with hit-and-run guerrilla strikes, then mounting larger actions and, finally, as the balance of force tilted in their direction, staging conventional battles. The schedule seemed doctrinaire on paper, as Communist theories do, but its key in practice was flexibility. Despite his warnings against escalating prematurely, Giap rashly leaped ahead in 1951 and suffered badly. But he regrouped and awaited another chance.

A long struggle required soldiers and civilian supporters braced for enormous losses. The French and later the Americans constantly looked for victories to boost their morale, but the Communists had time on their side, along with a willingness to bear sacrifices. Their troops were not superhuman. They missed their families, whom they would often not hear from for years. They suffered from malaria, dysentery, and other diseases, and they were frequently frightened. Yet they plunged into battle ready to sustain frightful casualties. They had been organized, indoctrinated, and motivated.

Their basic unit was the cell, composed of three, four, or five men responsible to one another—a system designed so that each would fight, not for ideological abstractions, but to gain the respect of his comrades. Their officers shared their hardships, eating the same food, wearing the same clothes, and carrying the same packs as ordinary privates. And they were stiffened by political cadres, commissars who explained their missions, preached their higher purpose, and eliminated those suspected of disloyalty or cowardice. The organization also reached down to a network of sympathetic villages whose chiefs had been won over by persuasion or coercion; the villages were the congenial sea in which the fish could swim, as Mao's famous metaphor put it.

But a strong spirit drove this mechanism. A nationalistic culture, nearly xenophobic in intensity, inspired in Vietminh activists the concept of a virtually holy war against the foreign invaders and their native clients. The fervor scarcely pervaded the Vietnamese masses, which watched and waited in traditional Asian style, bending like bamboo before the prevailing wind. Still, it gave the Vietminh an edge, since its militants would pay heavy costs for their cause, swaying the population as they demonstrated their ability to resist a superior enemy. This Ho knew at the outset of the conflict, when he warned a French visitor: "You can kill ten of my men for every one I kill of yours. But even at those odds, you will lose and I will win."

At the end of 1946, after the Vietminh failed to seize Hanoi, the French expanded along the Red River valley, the region's principal rice-growing area. Constructing towers and blockhouses, they skirmished constantly with Vietminh partisans, who emerged at night to assault their posts, then disappeared into hamlets or fled into the hills overlooking the broad plain of fertile paddy fields. Duong Van Khang had helped to form a small Vietminh unit in his village, Phung Thuong, twenty miles east of Hanoi, and years later, he recalled his exploits at the time.

As a boy before World War II, he had felt no particular resentment against the French, whom he rarely saw. But the famine of 1945 aroused his hostility to both the Japanese and the French, and Vietminh agents entered the villages, urging the peasants to organize. They evoked Ho Chi Minh, a name then unknown to Khang. Even so, he agreed to head a platoon of seventy peasants armed with machetes and scythes, with only two muskets among them. They fortified the villages, building fences and digging tunnels, and laying traps of pointed bamboo staves in holes covered with foliage. One night, in an ambitious endeavor, they stalked a French tank at a bridge two miles away, fleeing after they had fired six of their seven bullets. In 1947, they guided a team of Vietminh sappers back to the bridge and blew it up. Early in 1981, when I visited the area, the twisted remains of the steel bridge still littered the dry riverbed—as if the incident had occurred the day before.

During the years that followed, the French frequently attacked Khang's village, confiscating its rice and water buffalo, and burning its huts. They withdrew after each foray, and the Vietminh returned. Khang summed up the story of the war in a sentence: "We couldn't protect it, and they couldn't hold it."

The Vietminh also recruited women, among them Khang's wife, who served as a courier. She would collect intelligence from Vietminh spies inside French installations:

I would resort to all kinds of tricks to get near the posts. I would pretend to cut grass around the post, and our man inside would come out shouting for me to go away. He would push and shove me, passing me a message with information on the number of French troops in the post and how many guns they had. Or I would make believe he owed me money. I would cry insults at him, and he would finally give me a ten-piaster note. I would return him a five-piaster note in change with a message folded into it, warning him, say, that we were planning an attack. Sometimes, when I had to deliver bundles of documents, I would put them in my shoulder baskets and cover them with manure.

The Vietminh force had established a base in the Viet Bac, eighty miles to the north, in a landscape of jungle-clad mountains honeycombed with caves. Heavy monsoon rains drenched the region for half the year, covering it with a protective mist against air raids. The French encircled the area in 1947 by securing its only two roads and dropping in paratroopers. They almost captured Ho Chi Minh, who slipped into a camouflaged hole at the last minute. But the French commander, General Etienne Valluy, whose experience until then had been in Europe, quickly sized up his effort as impossible. With a total of some fifteen thousand men, he was trying to defeat sixty thousand enemy troops over nearly eighty thousand square miles of almost impenetrable forest. Unlike his nineteenth-century predecessors, he was up against not small insurgent bands but a disciplined army. He could only withdraw to a thin string of forts along Route 4, a twisting road running through ravines and over high passes between the towns of Langson and Caobang. Chronically exposed to Vietminh ambushes, French soldiers dubbed it the *Rue sans Joie*, or Street without Joy.

Giap had bought time to enlarge his forces. He promoted local guerrillas to regional units and assigned regional officers and noncoms to bigger detachments. Between 1949 and 1950, he quadrupled the number of regular Vietminh battalions to one hundred and seventeen. But his army never exceeded three hundred thousand men—fewer than that of France, which comprised more than one hundred thousand French, Foreign Legion, and African colonial troops in addition to three hundred thousand Vietnamese. Giap's ability to recruit more soldiers was limited by French control of most of Vietnam's populated areas.

The situation changed drastically in 1949, when the Chinese Communists reached the Vietnamese border. China could now provide the Vietminh with automatic weapons, mortars, howitzers, and even trucks, most of it captured American matériel, some of it Soviet equipment earmarked for the Korean war. Chinese advisers joined Vietminh detachments, and Vietminh units crossed into China to train at camps near Nanning and Ching Hsi. Giap swiftly expanded his battalions into regiments, and soon he had mobilized six divisions, each numbering ten thousand men, among them a "heavy division" composed of artillery and engineering regiments. The image of ragtag Vietminh guerrillas persisted, but it was pure romanticism. Giap now commanded a real army, backed up by China's enormous weight. As a veteran Vietminh officer, recollecting the period after 1949, told me: "It was a significant moment. We were no longer isolated from the Communist camp."

The Vietminh relied at first exclusively on porters to deliver their Chinese supplies, and the manpower needs were immense. To sustain an infantry division, for example, required forty thousand coolies, crawling like ants through jungle trails and over mountain passes. One of Giap's initial aims, therefore, was to open the roads to China, which meant ousting the French from their pivotal positions near the border. Some French strategists urged the evacuation of these overextended posts, arguing that Hanoi and the Red River rice bowl be more heavily protected. But the French command stubbornly clung to fortified positions, courting catastrophe.

Giap began his drive gradually in 1949 by harassing the most isolated French garrisons, bottling up their defenders and leaving the countryside open to the Vietminh. Then, accelerating as his strength increased, he directed his offensive against larger French garrisons. In September 1950, after the summer rains had subsided, he took Dongkhe, located on Route 4 between Caobang and Langson, wiping out two French columns as they rushed to its rescue. A month later, having cut the French supply line from Langson, Giap attacked Caobang, ambushing its defenders as they fled south to Langson. Panicked by the collapse of Caobang, the French withdrew from Langson, abandoning precious artillery, mortars, eight thousand rifles, and more than a thousand tons of ammunition. Soon afterward, they pulled out of Laokay and Thai Nguyen, two other key posts in the vicinity. Some six thousand French army troops were killed or captured in the engagements. France lost the crucial Chinese frontier section—and, with it, any chance of victory in Indochina. Looking back, the French scholar Bernard Fall called the series of setbacks France's greatest colonial defeat since the fall of Quebec to the British in 1759. By now, a CIA report described the French hold on Indochina as "precarious."

The stunned government in Paris dismissed its senior officers and civilian officials in Indochina, and conferred both military and political responsibility on General Jean de Lattre de Tassigny, one of France's most prominent soldiers. The appointment represented an extraordinary compliment to Giap, the former schoolteacher. He responded to the honor, gallantly proclaiming that his army would now face "an adversary worthy of its steel."

De Lattre was a Gallic version of MacArthur—handsome, stylish, sometimes charming, yet egocentric to the point of megalomania. His flash of glory in Indochina ended abruptly and tragically: his only son, Bernard, was killed in action, and he died of cancer less than a year after assuming his new command. But, for a few months, de Lattre infused his troops with the conviction that they might redress the dismal situation.

The spark of hope was largely rekindled by Giap's blunders, however. By late 1950, Giap perceived that his gains in the sparsely inhabited zone adjacent to China left him with two principal problems: to assert the Vietminh's political authority, he had to conquer the main population centers around Hanoi and Saigon; and to get the food his men desperately needed, he had to take over the rich rice fields of the Red River valley in the north and the Mekong delta in the south. The French dominated both areas, and they could protect them better with their armor and artillery than they had the Chinese border sector. Nevertheless, Giap planned a big campaign against the Red River valley, ambitiously forecasting Ho Chi Minh's arrival in Hanoi for Tet, the lunar New Year, beginning in February 1951.

Giap's plan may have been influenced by General Lo Guipo, a Chinese Communist veteran whom Mao had assigned to the Vietminh as diplomatic representative and military adviser. Years later, the Vietnamese blamed the Chinese for exerting pressure on them to escalate too soon from guerrilla warfare to larger offensives. But Giap was himself a gambler.

Anticipating the attacks, de Lattre had strengthened the Red River valley with hundreds of cement blockhouses and new airfields. He was prepared in January 1951, when two Vietminh divisions, comprising twenty thousand men, swept down from the Tam Dao mountains and stormed Vinhyen, a town situated amid flooded rice fields thirty miles northwest of Hanoi. Outnumbered, the French defenders initially fell back. But de Lattre, personally taking charge, flew in reinforcements and mustered every available aircraft to bomb the massive Vietminh formations. Giap retreated after three days of fierce combat, leaving six thousand Vietminh dead and carrying off another eight thousand wounded. He was determined to try again.

Late in March, he focused on the port of Haiphong, through which the French brought in supplies, and once more he miscalculated, underestimating the ability of the French to deploy naval guns and move reinforcements aboard assault boats on the estuaries and canals. When he launched an initial attack against Maokhe, northwest of Haiphong, the French again fought him off.

In late May, in yet another attempt, Giap attacked with three divisions along the Day River, southeast of Hanoi, aiming to dramatize his supremacy over the French and thereby sway Vietnamese inclined to lean toward the victor. Heavy rains complicated his supply movements, and he encountered stiff resistance from Vietnamese Catholic communities in the area, which had organized their own militia. The French also defended their positions stubbornly, especially at the town of Nam Dinh, where Bernard de Lattre died obeying his father's orders to hold at all costs. After three weeks, Giap pulled back his force, his initiative blunted. Both the Vietminh and the French were exhausted.

De Lattre, now eager to go on the offensive, flew to Washington to request more American aid, and there he portrayed the importance of Indochina in lurid geopolitical terms. Speaking at the Pentagon on September 20, 1951, he warned that the loss of northern Vietnam would open the rest of Southeast Asia to the advance of Communism, which would then engulf the Middle East and Africa, and eventually "outflank" Europe. But the United States, by now committed to the Korean war and other responsibilities abroad, could only partially help. De Lattre got more American transport airplanes, trucks, and other equipment—a significant contribution to his arsenal—but it was scarcely enough to turn the tide for France. Five months later, he died in a Paris hospital, raised to the dignity of Marshal on his last day. The war was deadlocked for the next two years.

Just as President Nixon began a "Vietnamization" program in 1969 to lend credibility to the Saigon government, so the French in 1952 strengthened the Vietnamese units serving with their forces, to counter the Vietminh's claim to represent true nationalism. They dubbed the policy *jaunissement*, or yellowing. But, like the Bao Dai regime itself, the "yellowed" army lacked credibility. Its commander, General Nguyen Van Hinh, the son of Bao Dai's former prime minister, Nguyen Van Xuan, was a French army officer, a French citizen, married to a French woman. In any event, the French distrusted these Vietnamese soldiers, fearing they might defect to the Vietminh, and assigned most of them to static defense duties. The innovation of transferring responsibility to an indigenous anti-Communist corps had been started too late. Recruiting and training its leaders would require time and effort, as General Hinh estimated, saying that it would be seven years before his battalions were ready to relieve the French and participate on their own in offensive operations.

Nor had Bao Dai's administration made much progress in winning over the "hearts and minds" of the average Vietnamese. Composed principally of urban elite and wealthy landowners, it resembled the French bureaucracy it was supposed to replace. Or, as a senior American aid official, R. Allen Griffith, observed in late 1951:

> It is in no sense the servant of the people. It has no grass roots. It therefore has no appeal whatsoever to the masses. It evokes no popular support because the nature of its leaders tends to an attitude that this would be a "concession." . . . Revolution will continue and Ho Chi Minh will remain a popular hero so long as "independence" leaders with French support are simply native mandarins who are succeeding foreign mandarins. . . . The present type of government in Vietnam is a relic of the past as much as French colonialism.

By late 1952, French dead, wounded, missing, and captured totaled more than ninety thousand since the war had begun six years earlier, and France had spent twice the sum it had received in U.S. aid under the Marshall Plan. Public enthusiasm for *la sale guerre*, the dirty war, had long ago waned in France, and the unease had penetrated the National Assembly—the "house without windows," as the French mocked it. There, in December 1952, a debate over fresh appropriations for the Indochina conflict sparked almost the same controversy that it had seventy years earlier, when Georges Clemenceau accused Jules Ferry of squandering funds in Indochina to the detriment of domestic needs and France's commitments in Europe. Now a foremost critic was Pierre Mendès-France, a maverick respected for his nonconformist courage. He warned that the soaring cost of the war threatened "rising prices and further social unrest" that would be exploited by the Communists: "You will never succeed in organizing our defenses in Europe if you continue to send all your cadres to Asia, to sacrifice them every year without any result. . . ."

Though the Vietminh could outlast the French, even when Giap expended thousands of lives in his reckless campaigns. Ho Chi Minh worked tirelessly to mobilize the population by emphasizing the nationalist character of the war: he changed the name of the Communist party to the Lao Dong, or Workers party, and he merged it with the Lien Viet, the National United Front, a movement designed to attract wide support; he introduced land reform, education, health care, and other programs in the areas under Vietminh control that would broaden participation in the struggle. Even so, he knew that only a spectacular military victory would make the French negotiate on his terms.

By 1952, Giap had partly regained his lost momentum by compelling the new French commander, General Raoul Salan, to withdraw from Haobinh, a key position southeast of Hanoi. But Giap dreamed of a more ambitious target, and he contemplated different regions in which to launch a major offensive. Laos looked promising for several reasons. He could rely on its mountain tribes, many of them related to the ethnic minorities he had cultivated in northwestern Vietnam. And the French garrisons in Laos, outside of the principal Mekong towns, like Vientiane and Luang Prabang, were scattered and vulnerable. He estimated that the French would fight to protect Laos, whose king genuinely believed in their cause. But he was less interested in taking over Laos itself than in snaring the French in the region along the Laotian border where their supply lines were stretched thin.

In October, moving three divisions toward Laos, he occupied a wretched village near the frontier that had been evacuated by a Laotian battalion cooperating with the French. The village, located in a valley eleven miles long and five miles wide, belonged to an ethnic minority, the T'ai, who farmed rice and marketed opium brought down from the surrounding mountains by Hmong tribes. The T'ai called the place Muong Thanh. It was known to the Vietnamese, who bought opium there, as Dienbienphu.

After a series of clashes in the sector, Giap drove into Laos in April 1953. He skirted the French fortifications on the Plain of Jars, a plateau strewn with prehistoric urns, and reached the outskirts of Luang Prabang, the royal capital, whose inhabitants had been alerted in advance by a blind soothsayer. Then, fearful of being trapped by rains, he pulled back. But he had demonstrated that he could march into Laos with relative impunity, and might attack again following the end of the wet season. In French eyes, Dienbienphu became the vital barrier at which to block the Vietminh's future access to Laos.

General Salan was supplanted in May 1953 by General Henri Navarre, another peculiar choice as French commander. A career officer who had fought in two world wars, Navarre was cold and solitary, "physically and morally feline," as a French writer described him. He also exuded optimism, forecasting success with an image that would be repeated with sardonic regularity during the years ahead in Vietnam: "Now we can see it clearly—like light at the end of a tunnel."

Navarre's chief subordinate was Major General René Cogny, a towering figure with graduate degrees in law and political science and a tendency to dispute his boss. Another adviser, Colonel Louis Berteil, was a jovial theorist with literary aspirations. These men outlined a grand design for Navarre that promised to regain the initiative for the

French. It included the idea of a *môle d'amarrage*, or mooring point, from which the French and their native auxiliaries could penetrate the Vietminh's rear areas. Cogny proposed Dienbienphu as such a base, since T'ai and Hmong mountaineers could be recruited to fight against the Vietminh. But Dienbienphu would first have to be recaptured.

Navarre flew to Paris in July to present his plan to the French government, whose prime minister, Joseph Laniel, had just been revolved into office by the Fourth Republic turnstile. Predictably, there was something of a mix-up. Navarre arrived with a formula for victory, but Laniel never explained plainly that he merely wanted to stabilize the situation in Vietnam, so that peace talks could begin, as they had in Korea. Nor did he make it clear to Navarre that Laos could be abandoned if the price of its defense was too high. Thus Navarre returned to the field convinced that he had been directed to prevent Giap from invading Laos. His conviction was reinforced in October 1953, when France implied in a treaty its readiness to protect Laos as a member of the French Union. The next month, Navarre ordered preparations for Operation Castor, in which Dienbienphu would be retaken by five battalions of French troops.

Colonel Jean-Louis Nicot, head of France's air transport unit in Indochina, immediately objected on the grounds that bad weather would hamper the endeavor. Cogny, assigned to command the overall assault, also changed his mind, warning that Dienbienphu would become a "meat grinder" of French battalions rather than a "mooring point" from which they could pursue the Vietminh. But Navarre, by now wedded to his strategy, disregarded their misgivings. Besides, he was persuaded that Giap could not respond in strength.

Giap had deliberately created that impression by staging diversionary actions around the country. His scattered assaults also tied down the French in different areas, so that they could not reinforce one threatened spot without inviting an attack on another. Vietminh terrorists stepped up their assassinations of pro-French officials, and guerrillas constantly harassed French convoys transporting supplies inland from Haiphong. Vietminh regulars struck along the coast of central Vietnam, and some crossed the frontier of Laos to besiege towns in the southern Laotian panhandle. Meanwhile, Giap steadily built up his detachments around Dienbienphu, having now chosen his arena for a set-piece confrontation. As he assessed it in retrospect, the French were in a "completely isolated position," dependent on airlifted supplies only, which meant that their initiative could be easily blunted. The Vietminh, in contrast, had the advantage of being in the mountains dominating the valley, to which food and ammunition could be brought in from the rear. Consequently, Giap wrote afterward, italicizing his words: *"We decided to wipe out at all costs the whole enemy force at Dienbienphu."*

Starting in November, soon after the French paratroopers had dropped into the valley, Giap moved thirty-three infantry battalions, six artillery regiments, and a regiment of engineers toward Dienbienphu, some over long distances, proving to military historians that in a conflict like the Indochina war the mobility of individual soldiers outweighs the mobility of armies. Cao Xuan Nghia, then a Vietminh infantryman, traveled for forty-five days with his company from Thai Nguyen, north of Hanoi, reaching the hills overlooking Dienbienphu in late 1953. He later related the experience to me:

> We had to cross mountains and jungles, marching at night and sleeping by day to avoid enemy bombing. We sometimes slept in foxholes, or just by the trail. We each carried a rifle, ammunition, and hand grenades, and our packs contained a blanket, a mosquito net, and a change of clothes. We each had a week's supply of rice, which we refilled at depots along the way. We ate greens and bamboo shoots that we picked in the jungle, and occasionally villagers would give us a bit of meat. I'd been in the Vietminh for nine years by then, and I was accustomed to it.

As French and Vietminh troops prepared to slaughter each other at Dienbienphu, fresh factors added a sense of urgency to their confrontation. After three years of bitter fighting in Korea, an armistice had finally been reached, and the notion swiftly spread among the big powers that the Indochina conflict should be settled as well. Following the death of Stalin in March 1953, the new Soviet leaders were also seeking to relax world tensions. And the French were sick of the war. Mendès-France, who had consistently called for negotiations, was joined by influential figures like Albert Sarraut, the former colonial governor of Indochina. Even Georges Bidault, an advocate of firmness, said on July 13, 1953, two weeks before the signing of the Korean cease-fire, that France would be in an "untenable position" if "peace were re-established in Korea while the war continued in Indochina." In November, Prime Minister Laniel made what amounted to an offer: "If an honorable settlement were in sight, on either the local or the international level, France would be happy to accept a diplomatic solution to the conflict."

The Soviet Union was on a similar track. Stalin's successors had issued a statement as early as August 4, eight days after the Korean agreement was signed, proposing discussions to resolve conflicts in Asia. Such a meeting, they later suggested, could proceed from a conference scheduled to explore ways to settle differences over Germany. Their conciliatory gesture was partly designed to disavow the late Soviet dictator's belligerence and promote themselves as partisans of "peaceful coexistence." They hoped as well that, by extending an olive branch to the French, they might dissuade France from joining the European Defense Community, an American plan to bring a rearmed West Germany into a Western military pact. They also insisted that China be included in talks on Asia.

The Chinese Communists, who had gained control in Beijing only three years earlier, were then eager to play a role on the international scene—largely to dilute their almost exclusive reliance on the Soviet Union. Their economic programs were also faltering, and they felt that they might benefit from trade with the West. And, by projecting an image of moderation, they hoped to win sympathy from the nonaligned countries of Africa and Asia, and perhaps gain recognition from Western Europe, even if the United States continued to spurn them. Above all, they were worried about their own security.

Prime Minister Zhou Enlai, who directed Chinese foreign policy, had concluded by 1953 that France would sooner or later scuttle its commitment in Indochina. He estimated, however, that the United States might step in, thus menacing China on its own doorstep. So he favored a negotiated settlement that would give the French a future stake in their former colonial possession and prevent the United States from filling the vacuum left by their departure. He would work for such an accord, even at the expense of the Vietminh.

These trends troubled both Bao Dai and his anti-Communist Vietnamese adversaries, who feared that the French might sell them out for the sake of a deal with Ho Chi Minh. A vocal spokesman for the "third force" nationalists was Ngo Dinh Diem's brother, Ngo Dinh Nhu, a fiery intellectual who in September 1953 organized a demonstration in Saigon to denounce France. The protests, amply reported in Paris newspapers, further confused and alienated the French public, which had been told that France's only foes in Indochina were Communists, and the clamor for withdrawal mounted. Prime Minister Laniel himself declared in a parliamentary speech that France "has no reason to prolong its sacrifices if the very people for whom they are being made disdain those sacrifices and betray them."

Nowhere did the drift toward negotiations raise more alarm than in Washington, where President Eisenhower's secretary of state, John

Foster Dulles, saw the U.S. policy of containment crumbling. In his view, the Chinese Communists had only conceded to a truce in Korea in order to redirect their aggression against Southeast Asia. He therefore leaned on the French to delay making any diplomatic moves until they had improved their military posture in Indochina, and he pledged $500 million to sweeten his plea. The French took the money but rebuffed his advice—even to the point of threatening to sabotage the projected European Defense Community unless he supported their efforts to achieve what Prime Minister Laniel had called an "honorable settlement."

Ho Chi Minh, having been betrayed by France in the past, was suspicious of negotiations. His strategy was to continue fighting until he had worn down French opinion to the point at which he could dictate the terms of an armistice. In a statement issued on September 2, the eighth anniversary of his declaration of independence, he cautioned against a premature cessation of hostilities, saying that "only when our long and hard resistance is victorious can we win peace." But both Moscow and Beijing were urging him to show flexibility, and the Chinese in particular could exert leverage.

They had trained his troops at camps in China, and they had stiffened his ranks with advisers. Though they probably never intended to intervene directly, they had massed two hundred thousand men on the Vietnamese border, thereby frightening the weary French public into seeking an exit from Indochina rather than risk a wider war. They had furnished him with at least fifty thousand tons of military hardware since 1950, and he knew that their heavy artillery, antiaircraft guns, mortars, and ammunition would be crucial to the outcome of the confrontation then shaping up at Dienbienphu. Since the Korean truce, indeed, the Chinese had vastly increased its supplies, providing him with four thousand tons of equipment and two thousand tons of food per month. Later, Beijing would threaten to curtail its aid unless Ho compromised with the French—just as, in 1972, both the Chinese and Russians used the same pressure to compel his successors to make concessions to the United States. For all his claims to independence, Ho was essentially reliant on his Communist patrons, who did not hesitate to subvert his goals to advance their own interests.

Under this pressure, Ho turned to diplomacy. On November 29, 1953, the Swedish newspaper *Expressen* published his answers to questions posed by Sven Löfgren, its enterprising correspondent in Paris. He would be willing, Ho wrote, to end the war "by peaceful means."

Löfgren had cabled his questions through Beijing weeks earlier and the Chinese, aware of them, certainly informed the Soviets of the opportunity to benefit from the interview. Thus, two days before *Expressen* printed Ho's replies, the Russians accepted an old Western proposal for discussions on Germany among the United States, Britain, France, and the Soviet Union: by implication, the meeting would go on in larger form to deal with Indochina.

The situation had changed drastically. Both the French and Vietminh forces now faced a deadline at Dienbienphu. And, in the words of General Walter Bedell Smith, who headed the U.S. delegation to the Geneva talks: "You don't win at the conference table what you've lost on the battlefield."

Actually, the French did not lose at Dienbienphu itself, but in General Navarre's air-conditioned headquarters in Saigon, where he had woefully miscalculated Giap's intentions and capabilities even before the shooting started. Afterward, summing up Navarre's fundamental error, a French War College study concluded that he and his staff had wrongly disregarded intelligence that did not fit their prejudices, and instead "substituted their preconceived idea of the Vietminh for the facts."

Navarre, declining to credit Giap with plans for a major test at Dienbienphu, had committed large units to central Vietnam, and even refused to shift them once the bigger encounter began. He misread Giap's ability to move a huge force rapidly, so that his own troops were outnumbered by a ratio of more than five to one during the trial by fire. He rejected the notion that the Vietminh could devastate his men with artillery deployed on the hills above Dienbienphu, nor did he foresee that the enemy emplacements would be protected by camouflage and antiaircraft guns against bombing from the air. He failed to anticipate that Giap's howitzers, poised within easy range of his airstrip, would cut off flights in and out of the valley, making it difficult for his besieged soldiers to receive supplies or evacuate wounded—much less withdraw themselves. He also chose a terrain presumed suitable for tanks only to discover that, unlike its description on his maps, its cover of thick bush entangled armored vehicles and its monsoon rains flooded the plain in the spring.

Expecting to use tanks, Navarre picked a cavalry officer to command. Colonel Christian Marie Ferdinand de La Croix de Castries, then fifty-two, was a lean aristocrat with a Roman profile whose ancestors had soldiered since the Crusades. Irresistible to women and ridden with gambling debts, he had been a champion horseman, daredevil pilot, and courageous commando, his body scarred by three wounds earned during World War II and earlier in Indochina. His deputy, Colonel Charles Piroth, was a one-armed gunnery expert who had predicted that "no Vietminh cannon will be able to fire three rounds before being destroyed by my artillery." At dawn on March 15, 1954, two days after the Vietminh had wiped out the second of three key French artillery positions, Piroth pulled the safety pin out of a grenade with his teeth and blew himself to bits, having said the evening before, "I am completely dishonored."

The French, awaiting a direct Vietminh assault against their garrison in the middle of the valley, had built three artillery bases, supposedly named for Castries's current mistresses. They situated two of them, Gabrielle and Béatrice, to the north, and the third, Isabelle, to the south. Again they had erred. Instead of storming the center, the Vietminh attacked Gabrielle and Béatrice first. Not only was Isabelle located too far away to give them fire support, but by protecting it they tied down one third of the total French combat force, which could not be moved to rescue threatened posts elsewhere.

Navarre underestimated the Vietminh in another respect. Recalling Giap's reckless Red River campaign of 1951, he anticipated a swift and headlong Vietminh charge. But Giap had become prudent as negotiations approached.

> By launching a big offensive with fresh troops, we could have foreshortened the duration of the campaign, and avoided the wear and tear of a long operation. . . . [But] we saw that these tactics had a very great, basic disadvantage. Our troops lacked experience in attacking fortified entrenched camps. If we wanted to win swiftly, success could not be assured. . . . Consequently, *we resolutely chose to strike and advance surely . . . strike to win, strike only when success is certain. If it is not, then do not strike.*

In 1961, when he wrote that retrospective analysis, Giap did not mention that he had originally unleashed a "human wave" assault against the French at the urging of Chinese advisers at Dienbienphu, among them General Wei Guoqing, a native of nearby Guangxi province and later chief political commissar of China's army. After initially sustaining fearful losses, Giap called a halt to the fighting and issued the order to "strangle" the French by encircling them with tunnels and trenches. Colonel Bui Tin, a Communist veteran of the battle, recalled the experience to me years later:

> General Giap changed the entire plan. He stopped the attack and pulled back our artillery. Now the shovel became our most important weapon. Everyone dug tunnels and trenches under fire, sometimes hitting hard soil and only advancing five or six yards a day. But we gradually surrounded Dienbienphu with an underground network several hundred miles long, and we could tighten the noose around the French.

Giap, contrary to Navarre's estimates, had spent more than three months deploying his men before beginning his assault. He had positioned fifty thousand men at the site, with another twenty thousand strung out along his communications lines—while the French force numbered thirteen thousand, about half of it qualified for combat. Equally important, Vietminh soldiers, cadres, and coolies had demonstrated phenomenal muscle in dragging artillery up to the heights above the valley. On the afternoon of March 13, Giap switched from siege to attack.

His first target, Béatrice, fell immediately, and Gabrielle collapsed the next day, as Vietminh guns raked the airstrip and pinpointed other French posts. Soon afterward, however, Giap interrupted the blistering offensive to shift to a less costly strategy of attrition for two weeks. The French figured that the oncoming rains would mire him in mud, but just the opposite occurred. The lowering clouds hindered French aircraft from bombing and strafing the Vietminh, and made parachuting supplies to the beleaguered garrison difficult. The French now knew that, on the eve of negotiations, they were doomed on the battlefield and also at the conference table—unless they received a formidable dose of outside help. Only the United States could furnish that aid quickly and effectively. So another engagement had to be fought in Washington.

After Giap's opening salvos at Dienbienphu, the French claimed that only American military aid for the battle would bolster their diplomacy at Geneva. General Paul Ely, the French chief of staff, carried that message to Washington on March 20, winning over Admiral Arthur Radford, chairman of the joint chiefs of staff. Radford proposed that sixty B-29 bombers based in the Philippines, escorted by fighter aircraft of the U.S. Seventh Fleet, conduct night raids against the Vietminh perimeter around Dienbienphu. Ely returned to Paris with the plan, labeled Operation Vulture, and the French government welcomed it.

Another member of the joint chiefs, General Nathan Twining of the air force, endorsed the idea. But General Matthew Ridgway, army chief of staff, had no faith in air strikes—and no taste for a fight on the mainland of Asia. An old-fashioned infantryman who had commanded the U.S. forces in Korea, he argued that even atomic weapons would not reduce the need for seven American combat divisions to assure French success in Indochina—twelve divisions if the Chinese intervened. The other members of the joint chiefs agreed with him that the Indochina conflict was the wrong war in the wrong place. As they stated shortly afterward, "Indochina is devoid of decisive military objectives" and involvement there "would be a serious diversion of limited U.S. capabilities."

The French, disappointed by that verdict, were further discouraged by President Eisenhower's insistence that he would not even ponder Radford's project without its approval by Congress as well as by America's allies, especially Britain. Radford, backed by Dulles and Vice-President Richard Nixon, tried to get legislative authorization for the president to employ air power at his discretion, but the request was rejected by several influential senators and representatives—among them, Senator Lyndon Johnson of Texas. The members of Congress allowed, however, that they might reconsider if, among other things, the British joined an endeavor to rescue the French.

A Pentagon study group at the time concluded that three tactical atomic weapons, "properly employed," would suffice to smash the Vietminh forces at Dienbienphu. The idea tantalized Radford, and he favored its proposal to the French. But the notion alarmed senior State Department officials, one of whom warned that, if the French were approached, "the story would certainly leak" and spark "a great hue and cry throughout the parliaments of the free world." Georges Bidault disclosed some months later that he had turned down an offer by Dulles for atomic weapons during talks the previous April. Dulles denied the account, and the French confirmed his denial, saying that Bidault had been "jittery" and "overwrought," and had misunderstood. Bidault nevertheless repeated the account in his memoirs.

Contrary to portrayals that depict him as a "dove," Eisenhower did not completely oppose U.S. intervention. But recalling his command of the Allies during World War II, he refused to commit America alone. "Without allies and associates," he told his staff at one meeting, "the leader is just an adventurer, like Genghis Khan." Besides, he had been elected on a pledge to end the war in Korea, which might have spiraled into a bigger confrontation with China—and as his closest aide, Sherman

Adams, observed: "Having avoided one total war with Red China the year before in Korea, when he had United Nations support, he was in no mood to provoke another one in Indochina . . . without the British and other Western allies."

Eisenhower appealed to Prime Minister Churchill to participate, and reminded him of the failure to stop Hitler "by not acting in unit and in time." He sent Dulles to London to plead his case, but the British spurned him. Churchill told the House of Commons that Britain "was not prepared to give any undertakings . . . in Indochina in advance of the results of Geneva," and Foreign Secretary Anthony Eden, who was to cochair the conference with Vyacheslav Molotov, Soviet foreign minister, simply refused to be "hustled into injudicious military decisions." The best that Dulles could achieve was a British promise to contemplate a future security arrangement, which eventually became the Southeast Asia Treaty Organization.

By late April, it was clear that there would be no attempt to salvage the French at Dienbienphu. Strangely, though, their imminent defeat was now accepted with relative equanimity in Washington. Dulles tried to present the coming debacle as a blessing in disguise, saying that it would arouse the rest of Southeast Asia "to measures that we hope will be sufficiently timely and vigorous to preserve [them] from Communist domination." And Eisenhower seemed to shrug off what had loomed as a huge crisis; he told a press conference on April 29, "You certainly cannot hope at the present state of our relations in the world for a completely satisfactory answer with the Communists. The most you can work out is a practical way of getting along."

Giap's timing was perfect. On the afternoon of May 7, 1954, the Vietminh's red flag went up over the French command bunker at Dienbienphu. The next morning in Geneva, nine delegations assembled around a horseshoe-shaped table at the old League of Nations building to open their discussions of the Indochina problem.

Except for Dulles, who checked into a hotel and stayed only a week, the chief delegates at Geneva rented residences, as if they intended to remain forever. The Chinese, as befitting their debut on the international stage, arrived with a mission of two hundred and ensconced Zhou Enlai in a lavish estate, Grand Mont-Fleuri, decorating it with antiques and carpets brought from China. Eden lived in equal splendor amid the velvet upholstery of Reposoir, an eighteenth-century mansion set in a park, while Georges Bidault occupied Joli-Port, a modest villa next door to

Pham Van Dong, the Vietminh leader. But despite their seventy-four days together in the placid Swiss city, the diplomats never cleared the prevailing atmosphere of distrust and tension.

The Vietminh's officials avoided Bao Dai's representatives and spurned the envoys from Cambodia and Laos; they also boycotted the French, who did not encounter the Chinese until late in the episode. The Russians dropped disparaging remarks about the Chinese. The Americans had been ordered to shun the Chinese, lest a smile be interpreted as formal recognition, and Dulles even refused to shake hands with Zhou Enlai, saying grumpily that they might possibly meet if their cars collided. The French resented American attempts to use them as intermediaries, and the Americans blamed the French for keeping their maneuvers secret. The Americans also expressed impatience with the British, who they felt were not sufficiently tough. Eden struggled heroically to hold them all together, observing afterward: "I had never known a conference of this kind. The parties would not make direct contact, and we were in constant danger of one or another backing out the door."

In the end, the Geneva Conference produced no durable solution to the Indochina conflict, only a military truce that awaited a political settlement, which never really happened. So the conference was merely an interlude between two wars—or, rather, a lull in the same war.

The American delegation, headed by Bedell Smith, the unflappable under secretary of state, limped into the meeting, its legs shackled by Eisenhower and Dulles. Eisenhower, having failed to mobilize a Western coalition, had publicly ruled out a unilateral U.S. military alternative in Southeast Asia if the talks foundered. So American appeals to resist Communist demands lacked substance. At the same time, Dulles had instructed Smith to stand aloof from the negotiations—partly because he considered concessions to Communists to be sacrilegious, and also because he was reluctant to link the United States to any agreement that already looked as if it would be unsatisfactory. Smith, therefore, could only keep the French representatives from betraying American interests. That meant, among other things, keeping them from making any deal that gave real estate to the Vietminh.

Bidault, puffy and dissolute, started out by proclaiming that he would not accept a divided Vietnam as a solution, but would work solely for a cease-fire. He simply hoped to stop the fighting, placate French public opinion, and save Laniel's tottering government—postponing a political agreement for a later date. Without informing the United States, however, the French had already begun to toy with the concept of partition, figuring that they might induce Ho Chi Minh to halt the hostilities in exchange for granting some measure of legitimacy to his regime.

Since the Vietminh had prevailed at Dienbienphu and still menaced the French elsewhere in Indochina, Pham Van Dong predictably came on strong. He insisted on a political settlement first, under which the French would withdraw and leave the Vietnamese to resolve their own differences—a formula calculated to panic the Bao Dai regime and virtually guarantee a Communist triumph. He also argued for recognition of the Pathet Lao and the Free Khmer, resistance movements backed by the Communists in Laos and Cambodia supported by the Vietminh, contending that they deserved legal status and control of territory in their countries. The French rejected these demands, and Pham Van Dong refused to budge. The conference slid to a standstill.

There it remained until the middle of June, when two major events occurred. The French parliament, reflecting the public's impatience with the immobility at Geneva, ousted Prime Minister Laniel and replaced him with Mendès-France—in effect, challenging the critic to do better. And Zhou Enlai, grabbing a chance to break the deadlock, stepped in to take charge of the talks for the Communists. From then on, Mendès-France and Zhou negotiated covertly, the ritual speeches around the conference table serving only as a facade for their transactions. In the end, both men realized for their own reasons that an imperfect compromise was preferable to a prolonged war that could escalate.

Zhou Enlai, then fifty-six, showed at Geneva for the first time the skills that made him one of the most brilliant diplomats of the century. Urbane, subtle, tough, and determined, he was a unique blend of Chinese mandarin and Communist commissar, and he had a special affinity for the French, having spent his youth in Paris. The Chinese had just suffered a million casualties in Korea, and the conflict had nearly spilled over their border. Zhou's primary aim at Geneva was to carve out an agreement that would deny the United States a pretext to intervene in Indochina and again threaten China. Thus he sought a settlement that would keep the French in their former possession, to the exclusion of the Americans.

Such an accommodation inevitably required a sacrifice of the Vietminh's objectives. But Zhou put China's priorities first. Besides, Chinese foreign policy throughout the centuries had been to fragment Southeast Asia in order to influence its states, and Zhou subscribed to that tradition. A divided Vietnam suited the Chinese better than a unified neighbor—particularly one that had quarreled with China for two thousand years. Similarly, China's security would be served by restraining Vietnamese ambitions in Laos and Cambodia. By curbing the Vietminh, moreover, Zhou hoped to display his moderation to India, Indonesia, and the other nonaligned countries of Asia. Indeed, his appearance at Geneva was a prelude to his performance soon afterward at the Bandung Conference, where he and Indian Prime Minister Jawaharlal Nehru launched their campaign to preach the *pantjasila*, the "principles of peaceful coexistence."

As early as May 18, ten days after the start of the conference, one of Zhou's deputies explained to a French delegate over dinner that "we are here to re-establish peace, not to back the Vietminh." Soon, Zhou confided to Eden and Bidault separately that he opposed the Vietminh's attempts to control Laos and Cambodia. He further annoyed the Vietminh leaders by taking a furlough to visit India and Burma, whose governments did not recognize their regime. During that trip, he met with Ho Chi Minh in southern China, evidently telling him not to expect further Chinese economic aid unless the Vietminh behaved more flexibly at Geneva. By this time, Zhou was beginning to clear the air with Mendès-France.

Mendès-France, then forty-seven, was Jewish, rather a rarity in French politics; even more rare, he could be bravely candid. He had been denouncing the Indochina war for years. Now he would try to end it— and he publicly handed himself an ultimatum. On June 17, asked by the president of France to form a cabinet, he ascended the rostrum of the National Assembly to seek a vote of confidence. He dramatized the danger of an international, perhaps even atomic war in Asia unless he obtained a cease-fire, and he set a deadline. "My government will give itself—and its adversaries—four weeks. . . . If no satisfactory solution can be achieved by then, I will resign."

His task was daunting. The Vietminh showed no signs of elasticity, and Bao Dai had just appointed the intractable Ngo Dinh Diem to be his prime minister. But Zhou Enlai intervened. He arranged to meet Mendès-France covertly on June 23, at the French embassy in Bern, the Swiss capital.

Zhou had discarded his usual severe tunic for a gray Western business suit, and he meant business. He told Mendès-France that, in contrast to the demands of the Vietminh, he favored a cease-fire first and political accord afterward. He would urge the Vietminh to stop meddling in Laos and Cambodia, and to respect the sovereignty of these two countries. Most astonishingly, the foresaw the probability of "two Vietnams"—a direct blow to he Vietminh's dream of unification. The possibility of American military bases in Indochina worried him. Beyond that, he said, China's only aim was peace in the region, adding that it had "no other ambitions [and] poses no conditions."

Dulles, hypnotized by his own vision of monolithic Communism bent on world domination, fretted over the meeting between Zhou and Mendès-France. He considered pulling the U.S. delegation out of Geneva, as he informed Douglas Dillon, the American ambassador in Paris: "These negotiations appear to have gone underground, and we have little reliable knowledge of what is really in the minds of the French government. . . . We fear that the French may in fact, without prior consultations with us . . . agree to a settlement that . . . contains such political clauses and restrictions that Laos, Cambodia, and southern Vietnam will almost surely fall in a few months under Communist control."

Encouraged by Zhou Enlai's apparent willingness to cut Vietnam into two zones, Mendès-France, too, came around to the idea of partition. But how? Pham Van Dong had finally acceded to the principle under both Chinese and Soviet pressure, but he argued that the line should be drawn at the thirteenth parallel, which would give the Vietminh two thirds of the country. Mendès-France suggested the eighteenth parallel. On July 12, he again met in Bern with Zhou Enlai, who hinted at a pro-French tilt: "The two parties should take a few steps toward each other—which doesn't mean that each has to take the same number of steps."

Zhou had earlier persuaded the Vietminh to drop its demand that the Pathet Lao and Free Khmer occupy parts of Laos and Cambodia, but another snag developed. Partition, a temporary expedient designed to separate the belligerents, would be followed by elections to unify Vietnam. But when? Pham Van Dong, eager to take advantage of the Vietminh's military momentum, called for six months from the date of a cease-fire; this was much too soon for the French. The haggling continued as Mendès-France raced the clock.

Now Molotov, the grim old Bolshevik, would arbitrate—at the last minute. On the afternoon of July 20, Mendès-France's deadline, Molotov convened a meeting at his villa, Le Bocage. He conspicuously excluded Bedell Smith and Bao Dai's delegate, but Mendès-France, Zhou, Eden, and Pham Van Dong assembled in the salon, and they bargained. Pham Van Dong, perspiring as the heavyweights encircled him, now accepted a partition at the sixteenth parallel. Mendès-France stuck to the eighteenth. "Let's agree on the seventeenth," announced

Indochina   1953–1954

✹ Major Battles

Molotov, then moved on to the election schedule. Mendès-France wanted the timetable left open. Pham Van Dong amended his demand for six months, offering a year, maybe even eighteen months. Molotov, his round face motionless, delivered the verdict with a rhetorical question: "Shall we say two years?" Mendès-France had slipped under the wire, having completed the onerous job that no other French politician had the courage to undertake. He had won more for France at the conference table than its generals had won on the battlefield; the Vietminh had gained less in the talks than in combat. Pham Van Dong, furious with Zhou, walked away from the last round of haggling and muttered to an aide, "He has double-crossed us."

Worse awaited the Vietminh leader two evenings later, at a farewell dinner organized by Zhou. The guests included a member of Bao Dai's delegation, Ngo Dinh Luyen, the younger brother of Ngo Dinh Diem. Pham Van Dong was astonished and dismayed that Zhou, a Communist comrade, should have invited a "puppet" of the French. But Zhou went even further, obliquely indicating in his silky manner that China favored a permanent partition of Vietnam. Turning to Luyen during the evening, he suggested almost casually that the government to be established in Saigon open a diplomatic mission in Beijing: "Of course, Pham Van Dong is closer to us ideologically, but that doesn't rule out representation from the south. After all, aren't you both Vietnamese, and aren't we all Asians?"

The conclusion at Geneva was to be misinterpreted, if not misunderstood, for years to come. The only documents signed were cease-fire accords ending the hostilities in Vietnam, Cambodia, and Laos. The agreement between France and the Democratic Republic of Vietnam, as the Vietminh officially called itself, was not a political settlement. It provided for the temporary division of Vietnam pending a nationwide election to be held in the summer of 1956. The French forces would meanwhile withdraw from the north, and the Vietminh from the south. Except for the United States and the Saigon regime, the other participants merely gave their oral endorsement to a final declaration noting the understandings.

The Eisenhower administration, crusading against its foggy notion of an international Communist conspiracy, reluctantly pledged to abide by the Geneva agreement. In a separate statement, however, Bedell Smith warned that the United States would view "with grave concern . . . any renewal of aggression"—a caveat President Kennedy used seven years later to justify his commitment to the Ngo Dinh Diem government.

Diem also rejected the Geneva accords, which put half of Vietnam under Communist control, and he predicted that "another more deadly war" lay ahead for Vietnam. His forecast was prescient: after eight years of conflict and four hundred thousand soldiers and civilians dead, the agony was far from finished.

6 America's Mandarin

Ngo Dinh Diem in a characteristic meditative pose in his palace in Saigon. Aloof and austere, he mingled poorly with people, preferring instead to isolate himself with his family and close aides.

In June 1954, when Diem
returned to Vietnam as
prime minister, he was
met at the Saigon airport
by only a handful of
enthusiasts, most of them
Catholics like himself.
Though a veteran
nationalist, he was a
virtually unknown figure.

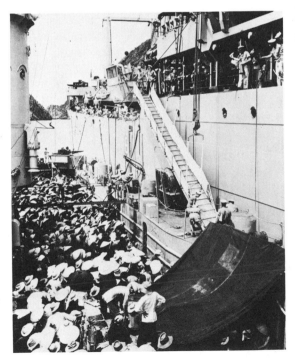

Nearly a million refugees,
a large proportion of them
Catholic, fleeing from
northern Vietnam in late
1954 as the Communists
prepared their takeover. In
many instances, as here,
the evacuation was han-
dled by the U.S. navy.

Not long after his return to Vietnam as prime minister, Ngo Dinh Diem organized a referendum to oust Emperor Bao Dai. Diem received almost all the votes, the result of electoral devices contrived by his American advisers.

Ngo Dinh Diem consolidated his power by defeating the Binh Xuyen, a private gang supported by the French. Diem's forces clashed with the Binh Xuyen in the streets of Saigon, devastating the city.

Ngo Dinh Diem owed his political survival largely to Colonel Edward Lansdale (near left), an air force officer attached to the CIA. Lansdale, a former San Francisco advertising man, was portrayed as Colonel Hillendale in the 1965 best-seller The Ugly American.

Ngo Dinh Diem posing with his immediate family. Behind him stands his brother and chief adviser, Ngo Dinh Nhu; the woman in the center is Madame Nhu, his powerful sister-in-law. The most influential figure, however, is Archbishop Thuc, the oldest brother.

A meeting of the Lao Dong in 1961, as the North Vietnamese Workers party called itself. By the 1960s, the North Vietnamese had decided to step up the insurgency against the Diem regime in Saigon.

A peasant woman mourns her husband, murdered by Vietcong terrorists in the Mekong delta. He was selected for assassination because he had informed on the Vietcong, whose terrorists tended to be selective in eliminating Saigon government officials and sympathizers.

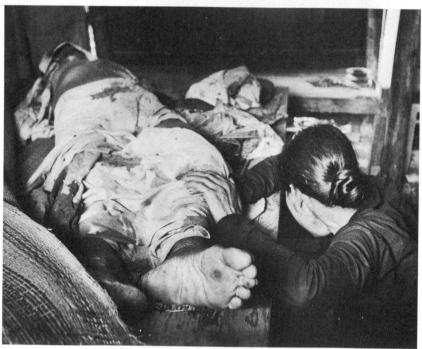

Nguyen Huu Tho (below), head of the National Liberation Front, as the Vietcong was officially called. The movement was formed in 1960 on directives from Hanoi.

Ngo Dinh Diem on one of his early trips into the South Vietnamese countryside. Despite his cheerful expression, Diem disliked such expeditions, which were urged on him by his American advisers, who thought he lacked the "common touch."

Ngo Dinh Diem waves to a New York City lunchtime crowd as a parade in his honor proceeds up Broadway in May 1957. Very few Americans could have then found Vietnam on a map.

Soon after consolidating its power in Saigon, the Diem regime embarked on a massive campaign to liquidate the remaining Vietminh elements in South Vietnam. Many were imprisoned in re-education camps, as seen here. By 1958, almost all the residual insurgents had been wiped out.

Not long after establishing their government in North Vietnam, the Vietnamese Communists launched a brutal land reform program in which thousands of landlords were executed. Ho Chi Minh later apologized for the excesses of the episode. Here "Nguyen Van Dinh, landless peasant," as his sign identifies him, attends a land reform meeting with his family.

A sacred respect is due the person of the sovereign. . . . He is the mediator between the people and heaven as he celebrates the national cult.

—Ngo Dinh Diem

President Diem is the Churchill of the decade . . . in the vanguard of those leaders who stand for freedom.

—Lyndon B. Johnson

By 1954, following the Geneva Conference, reputable Vietnamese nationalists outside the ranks of the Vietminh were scarce. Many had been liquidated by the Communists, killed by the French, or had withdrawn from politics to private occupations in Saigon. Some had even moved to France to become dilettante activists—holding sterile meetings, issuing meaningless manifestos, and conspiring constantly in the comfort of sidewalk cafés. Ngo Dinh Diem filled a vacuum, but despite his record of integrity, he was hardly a national leader.

An ascetic Catholic steeped in Confucian tradition, a mixture of monk and mandarin, he was honest, courageous, and fervent in his fidelity to Vietnam's national cause; even Ho Chi Minh respected his patriotism. But he was no match for Ho, whom even anti-Communists regarded as a hero. Imbued with a sense of his own infallibility, as if he were an ancient emperor ordained to govern, Diem expected obedience. Distrustful of everyone outside his family, he declined to delegate authority, nor was he able to build a constituency that reached beyond his fellow Catholics and natives of central Vietnam. Above all, he could not comprehend the dimensions of the political, social, and economic revolution being promoted by his Communist foes. He saw their uprising in narrow military terms—a misperception shared by his American patrons. Limited thus, he could not effectively mobilize the South Vietnamese people to cope with the growing Vietcong insurgency, nor could he check the mounting opposition of his critics, whose frustrations with his regime were only aggravated by his inability to check the Communists.

The flawed Geneva accommodation had postponed rather than achieved a settlement. Hastily contrived to prevent a wider war, it was merely a temporary truce between France and the Vietminh—to be honored until a durable political solution could be reached. Diem, having rejected it, refused to cooperate, and the United States backed him. But the Communists, who had fought to unify Vietnam, would not accept the prospect of permanent partition; they prepared to renew their struggle, again challenging the policy of containment that had initially involved the United States in Indochina.

The Americans had underwritten Diem "because we knew of no one better," as John Foster Dulles put it. But while they publicly extolled him, U.S. officials were not deluded by their own rhetoric and privately conceded, as Dulles had, that they could find no alternative. Carried away by oratorical hyperbole during a visit to Saigon in 1961, Lyndon Johnson, then vice-president, had compared Diem to Churchill. "Did you really mean it?" I asked Johnson aboard his airplane later. "Shit," he drawled, "Diem's the only boy we got out there."

Lavish praise only reinforced Diem's belief in his importance to the United States, and he defied American advice to reform his administration. It also stiffened his intransigence toward his internal critics, and their resistance to him. Gradually, the United States concluded that the conflict could not be won with Diem. For nine years, though, Diem served as America's surrogate in Vietnam—and through him the U.S. commitment in Southeast Asia deepened.

As a foreign correspondent, I first met Diem in Paris in the spring of 1954, on the eve of his return to South Vietnam as Bao Dai's prime minister, and I later spent hours with him in Saigon after he had become president. Invariably dressed in an immaculate white sharkskin suit—the sartorial status symbol of Vietnamese officialdom—he was a rotund little figure whose feet barely touched the floor when he sat on the elegant chairs in a salon of the Gia Long palace, the former French governor's residence. He looked as fragile as porcelain, with delicate features and ivory skin, but his black eyes projected a fanatical faith in his crusade. Pausing only to light one cigarette from another, he would talk tirelessly in a high-pitched voice, recalling his life in excruciating detail. Once, after an entire afternoon of listening to his monologue, I stepped into the fading tropical twilight bewildered by the fact that, with his country in crisis, he could devote half a day to a reporter. But that was part of his problem. Outside, on the veranda, a crowd of officials, army officers, and politicians were waiting impatiently, their urgent business delayed by my lengthy audience.

Diem traced his roots back to the village of Phu Cam, in central Vietnam, where the Ngo Dinh clan, converted to Christianity by seventeenth-century Portuguese missionaries, had suffered persecution. Nevertheless, the Ngo served as mandarins at the imperial court in Hué, and

Diem's father, Ngo Dinh Kha, carried on the tradition, rising to the grade of counselor to the Emperor Thanh Thai, whom the French deposed in 1907 on the pretext of insanity. Quitting in protest, Kha retired to the countryside to meditate and farm a few rented acres; though virtually penniless, he scraped together the money to educate his six sons.

The third boy, Diem, was born in 1901 and christened Jean-Baptiste in the cathedral at Hué. He labored in the family's rice fields while attending a French Catholic school nearby, and he later entered a private school opened by his father. He declined a scholarship to study in France, contemplated the priesthood, and then dropped the notion because, he told me, the discipline was too rigorous. Like his older brother Thuc, who became a worldly priest, Diem might have led a less monastic existence if he had joined the clergy, which at least deals directly with people. As an adolescent, he had a mild flirtation with a girl, but she jilted him for a convent, and he probably remained chaste for the rest of his life. An old acquaintance of his once remarked: "A woman might have tempered his character."

Following in the footsteps of an older brother, Khoi, who had enrolled in the civil service, Diem entered the School of Law and Administration, a French institution for training native bureaucrats. Promoted rapidly after graduation, he became a provincial governor at the age of twenty-five, and that may have been the happiest period of his career. He rode horseback through the rice fields and mountains, and it was then that he first encountered local Communist agents distributing propaganda. He tried to fight it by publishing his own pamphlets, eradicating corruption, and improving the conditions of peasants in his area but, as he later recollected, "I was working with advanced ideas in very small dimensions."

In 1933, the French advised Bao Dai, just back from France to ascend the throne, to name Diem his minister of interior. They also appointed him to a commission to examine administrative reforms. Diem hesitated, asking how far the reforms would go. "You have a difficult character," a senior French official replied. "Take the job, and don't complain."

Diem took the job, and complained. He insisted that the French invest real influence in a Vietnamese legislature, but his demands were rebuffed. He resigned in disgust after only three months, publicly proclaiming that he could not "act against the interests of my country." The French stripped him of his decorations and titles, and even threatened him with arrest. Summing up the experience, Diem made a prophetic comment at the time: "The Communists will defeat us, not by virtue of their strength, but because of our weakness. They will win by default."

Over the next decade, Diem vegetated in Hué at the home of his mother and a younger brother, Can, the least educated of the Ngo sons, occasionally contacting nationalist comrades. The French kept him under surveillance and harassed his family by dismissing his oldest brother, Khoi, from the post of governor of Quangnam province. When the Japanese occupied Indochina in 1942, Diem tried to persuade them to declare Vietnam's freedom, but they preferred to function through the Vichy French colonial administration. The Japanese spurned him again three years later when they selected a more docile prime minister to head the "independent" government they had set up under Bao Dai. Vietminh agents captured him in September 1945 as he was traveling from Saigon to Hué to warn Bao Dai against joining Ho Chi Minh, then in Hanoi. They exiled him to a primitive highland village near the Chinese border, where he might have died of malaria had not local tribesmen nursed him back to health. While there, he learned that the Vietminh had shot his brother Khoi and Khoi's son. Six months later, he was taken to Hanoi to meet Ho Chi Minh for the first time.

Fifteen years afterward, Diem painted an almost sympathetic portrait of Ho, a cigarette dangling from his lips as he spoke gently. Their conversation, as Diem recalled it, was candid.

DIEM: What do you want of me?

HO: I want of you what you have always wanted of me—your cooperation in gaining independence. We seek the same thing. We should work together.

DIEM: You are a criminal who has burned and destroyed the country, and you have held me prisoner.

HO: I apologize for that unfortunate incident. When people who have been oppressed revolt, mistakes are inevitable, and tragedies occur. But always, I believe that the welfare of the people outweighs such errors. You have grievances against us, but let's forget them.

DIEM: You want me to forget that your followers killed my brother?

HO: I knew nothing of it. I had nothing to do with your brother's death. I deplore such excesses as much as you do. How could I have done such a thing, when I gave the order to have you brought here? Not only that, but I have brought you here to take a position of high importance in our government.

DIEM: My brother and his son are only two of the hundreds who have died—and hundreds more who have been betrayed. How can you dare to invite me to work with you?

HO: Your mind is focused on the past. Think of the future—education, improved standards of living for the people.

DIEM: You speak a language without conscience. I work for the good of the nation, but I cannot be influenced by pressure. I am a free man. I shall always be a free man. Look me in the face. Am I a man who fears oppression or death?

HO: You are a free man.

With that, Diem walked out. In early 1981, I talked with the Vietnamese Communist party propaganda chief Hoang Tung, who criticized Ho for his leniency. "Considering the events that followed," he said, "releasing Diem was a blunder."

During the late 1940s, Diem's efforts to muster support for himself were fruitless. Even so, the Vietminh deemed him enough of a nuisance to be condemned to death *in absentia*, and, reversing Ho's verdict, its agents tried to kill him as he was traveling to visit his brother Thuc, by now bishop of Vinh Long diocese, in the Mekong delta. Brave but not foolhardy, Diem left Vietnam in 1950, ostensibly to attend the Holy Year celebration at the Vatican. He eventually went to the United States, where he spent two years at the Maryknoll Seminary in Lakewood, New Jersey, washing dishes, scrubbing floors, and praying, like any novice, and he even watched a football game at Princeton. More important, he gained introductions to such prominent Americans as Francis Cardinal Spellman of New York, Justice William O. Douglas, and Senators Mike Mansfield and John F. Kennedy. Diem pleaded his case with a simplistic if compelling logic that appealed to conservatives and liberals alike. He opposed both Communist domination and French colonialism; thus he represented true nationalism. The added attraction for Cardinal Spellman was Diem's Catholicism, and he became one of his active promoters.

Diem made no headway with the Eisenhower administration, then committed to the French. In May 1953, he quit the United States for a Benedictine monastery in Belgium, but he shuttled frequently to Paris. His guide there was his youngest brother, Luyen, an engineer, who had been lobbying for him among exiled Vietnamese in France. Diem needed French endorsement, American approval, and an official appointment from Bao Dai. A year later, as the Geneva Conference augured a settlement in Vietnam, the pieces fit together.

Bao Dai was still residing at his château near Cannes with his wife and five children. He kept a Vietnamese mistress in Paris, and his aides supplemented that diet with elegant French courtesans. He also spent his evenings at the roulette wheels of Monte Carlo, squandering extravagant sums. He had sunk into an intellectual torpor, yet his political interest in Vietnam could be aroused if he felt that events might affect him directly. As the Geneva negotiations approached a denouement, he finally realized that his own status hung dangerously in the balance. He summoned Diem.

The playboy and the puritan made an odd couple, but they could use each other. Diem perceived Bao Dai to be his path to power. And Bao Dai saw two advantages in Diem. For one thing, Diem's brother Nhu in Saigon had organized the Front for National Salvation, which appeared to be a plausible political coalition. Bao Dai also estimated that Diem, having sojourned in the United States, would bring America onto the Vietnamese scene to supplant the French, whose days seemed to be numbered. But contrary to the legend that Dulles, Cardinal Spellman, and other Americans were then pushing for Diem, the United States had not yet anointed him. Indeed, American officials in Geneva politely brushed off his brother Luyen, who was urging them to meet Diem. The French government, meanwhile, regarded Diem with indifference.

Bao Dai, a captive of his own fancies, nevertheless believed Diem to be America's challenge to France when he called him to his château. There, on June 18, 1954, Bao Dai placed Diem before a crucifix and persuaded him to swear to defend Vietnam "against the Communists and, if necessary, against the French." He thereupon named him prime minister—and, unwittingly, dug his own political grave.

Diem's new prestige scarcely altered him. Back in Paris as he prepared to return to Vietnam, he consented to hold formal audiences at the ornate Hôtel Palais d'Orsay, but insisted on sleeping every night in a room without bath at the sordid Hôtel de la Gare, located in a slum neighborhood near the Austerlitz railroad station. When I interviewed him at the time, he sounded like a Vietnamese version of Joan of Arc, forecasting that the national army he planned to mobilize "will inspire the people to flock to us." He had a long road ahead. On June 26, 1954, when he landed in Saigon, a group of barely five hundred, mostly Catholics, greeted him at the airport. The rest of the city stayed home.

Just as generals face each new war with the strategies of the last war, so Dulles now feared a repetition of the Korean conflict in Southeast Asia, with Communist hordes sweeping southward. He conceived the Southeast Asia Treaty Organization, composed of the United States, Britain, France, Australia, New Zealand, Thailand, and Pakistan, to defend the region, and a protocol to the treaty put South Vietnam, Cambodia, and Laos under its protection. The alliance proved to be irrelevant, since its signatories had different—often divergent—priorities. More to the point, South Vietnam was threatened not by outright aggression, but by a combination of internal instability and subversion. From the start, consequently, uncertainties confronted the Eisenhower administration as it contemplated Diem's government in Saigon.

Under the Geneva agreement, a French force was supposed to remain in South Vietnam to guarantee the armistice until nationwide elections took place in July 1956. But Diem, aware of his weakness, had no intention of participating in elections. He made it equally plain that he aimed to replace the French with American patrons. His demands increased tension between the United States and France, and sparked a dispute between the secretary of state and the joint chiefs of staff of the kind that would persist, with variations, through several administrations.

The joint chiefs, as reluctant as ever to invest in a shaky cause, asserted as early as August 1954 that the United States ought not assume the burden of training the South Vietnamese army until Diem demonstrated that he had a "stable" government. Dulles replied that training Diem's army was "one of the most efficient means" of strengthening his government. Senator Mansfield complicated their differences by reporting, after a quick trip to Vietnam, that there was no alternative to Diem, whose program "represents genuine nationalism." Eisenhower, caught in the cross fire, seemed to arbitrate the squabble by telling Diem that U.S. aid would depend on his "standards of performance." In fact, plans to furnish direct American assistance to Diem were already taking shape, without regard to his performance. But the debate continued among senior U.S. representatives in Saigon.

Diem was plagued by chaos throughout the summer. General Nguyen Van Hinh, the irreverent army chief of staff and a French protégé, had attempted to oust him, contending that South Vietnam needed a "strong and popular" leader like himself. Diem ordered him out of the country, but Hinh defied the directive by charging around Saigon on his motorcycle, displaying the expulsion notice. Finally, under American pressure, Bao Dai eliminated Hinh by inviting him to France for "consultations." Now Diem, facing the challenge of the Cao

Dai, Hoa Hao, and Binh Xuyen factions, tightened the circle around himself to his family and close friends, as he always would under pressure.

General J. Lawton "Lightning Joe" Collins, the former army chief of staff, arrived in Saigon in December as Eisenhower's personal emissary. Sensing the confusion, he concurred with the French that Diem was hopeless. He proposed that limits should be put on aid, even suggesting American withdrawal unless the situation improved. Donald Heath, the U.S. ambassador, disagreed. Underwriting Diem was a "gamble," he said, but denying him help would have "a far worse effect." Dulles sided with Heath, arguing that the United States had "no choice" except to bolster Diem, "if only to buy time." The time-buying operation opened with $300 million in American assistance.

Dulles used the same argument that month in Paris against Prime Minister Mendès-France, who described Diem as "wholly negative." The following May, a similar dispute was to set Dulles against Mendès-France's successor, Edgar Faure, who called Diem "not only incapable but mad." Faure's fury secretly delighted Dulles, since it precipitated a French decision to pull out of Vietnam prematurely—which they might have done anyway to redirect their resources to the war that had broken out in Algeria.

The U.S. commitment in Vietnam hardened, but American sway over Diem was always ephemeral. The plaintive tone of a message from General Collins to Washington at the time expresses the chronic U.S. diplomatic headache: "He pays more attention to the advice of his brothers . . . than he does to me."

One American did influence Diem in those days, though his clout has been exaggerated by both his admirers and critics. Colonel Edward G. Lansdale had served with the Office of Strategic Services during World War II, and he afterward helped Ramón Magsaysay, the Philippine leader, to crush the Communist-led Hukbalahap rebels. A deceptively mild, self-effacing former advertising executive, Lansdale counted on "psychological warfare" techniques that resembled advertising gimmicks. He also exuded a brand of artless goodwill that overlooked the deeper dynamics of revolutionary upheavals, and he seemed to be oblivious to the social and cultural complexities of Asia. William J. Lederer and Eugene Burdick, the authors of The Ugly American, glorified him as Colonel Edwin Hillendale, who captured "hearts and minds" with his harmonica. Graham Greene depicted him in The Quiet American as Alden Pyle, the naive U.S. official who believed that Vietnamese peasants instilled with the precepts of town hall democracy would resist

Communism. Lansdale made it all sound simple, as he did in a "counter-insurgency" training course for Americans years later: "Just remember this," he advised. "Communist guerrillas hide among the people. If you win the people over to your side, the Communist guerrillas have no place to hide. With no place to hide, you can find them. Then, as military men, fix them . . . finish them!"

Lansdale had landed in Vietnam in June 1954, nearly a month before Diem's return as prime minister. He set up the Saigon Military Mission, a covert American group of a dozen soldiers and intelligence agents who were specialists in "dirty tricks." To sow dissension between the Viet-minh and China, for instance, they spread rumors that Chinese Communist troops had pillaged Vietnamese villages in the north. They counterfeited Vietminh documents to frighten peasants, and they recruited soothsayers to create fake forecasts of doom under Communism. The Central Intelligence Agency furnished Lansdale with funds to bring in Philippine auxiliaries, and it also subsidized his clandestine operations in Hanoi, which had not yet come under full Vietminh control as prescribed under the Geneva agreement timetable. Heading the northern team was Major Lucien Conein, a rough-and-tumble officer of French birth who had fought against the Germans with the French resistance during World War II, and had worked with the OSS in Vietnam a decade earlier. He was to be a decisive figure in the *coup d'état* against Diem in 1963.

Instructed to sabotage the transportation network in the north in anticipation of the Vietminh takeover, Conein and his colleagues laced the oil destined for Hanoi's trams with acid, and they concealed explosives in the piles of coal that fueled railway locomotives. Conein proposed blowing up the Standard Oil and Shell storage tanks located at Haiphong, but his idea was rejected on the grounds that "we'll need them when we go back."

In violation of the Geneva accords, Conein and his team also formed secret squads of Vietnamese composed of anti-Communist political activists. These so-called stay-behind squads, comprising about two hundred men split into two groups, code-named the Hoa and the Binh, were intended to harass the Vietminh. They were trained at Clark Air Field, an American base in the Philippines, and infiltrated back to Vietnam aboard U.S. navy vessels. The Conein team hid their arms and ammunition along the Red River as well as in Hanoi cemeteries by organizing phony funerals and burying the equipment in tightly sealed coffins. The undercover squads were not expected to stage major uprisings, but merely foment unrest that could be exploited for psychological purposes. Their other function was to gather information, again to be employed for propaganda. They accomplished little. Most of them were eventually rounded up and tried, thus giving the regime in Hanoi a chance to denounce the United States and its Saigon clients for subversion. Other such squads would be deployed in North Vietnam in later years, but the early effort failed, Conein recalled to me, because "we did it all too quickly."

Lansdale played a part in the massive movement of refugees from north to south—though, again, his role has been inflated in some accounts. Nearly a million Vietnamese made the journey—a forerunner of the tremendous flight of "boat people" from Vietnam after the Communists gained control of the entire country in 1975. The majority were Catholics, whole communities of whom fled, their priests in the lead; others included various factions that had opposed the Vietminh. The United States and France provided ships and aircraft for their voyage. The refugees from the north were to furnish Diem with a fiercely anti-Communist constituency in the south, and thus their exodus was politically important. Lansdale encouraged the Catholics by broadcasting slogans like "the Virgin Mary is going south," but he put his own contribution in perspective, as he explained: "People just don't pull up their roots and transplant themselves because of slogans. They honestly feared what might happen to them, and the emotion was strong enough to overcome their attachment to their land, their homes, and their ancestral graves. So the initiative was very much theirs—and we mainly made the transportation possible."

Lansdale also helped Diem to outsmart his domestic adversaries. He nipped General Nguyen Van Hinh's planned *coup d'état* in the bud, for example, by hustling his chief lieutenants off on a trip to Manila. And when the Cao Dai and Hoa Hao defied the regime, Lansdale bribed several of their leaders to rally to Diem, paying them as much as $3 million each out of CIA funds. General Duong Van Minh, a Diem loyalist, finally subdued the sects in early 1956 by capturing the fanatical Hoa Hao guerrilla commander, Ba Cut, who was publicly guillotined. Minh, a burly figure known as Big Minh, was to head the conspiracy that overthrew Diem seven years later.

The big trial for Diem, however, was his showdown with the Binh Xuyen force of forty thousand, which challenged him in the spring of 1955. Lansdale had dangled a deal before Bay Vien, the Binh Xuyen boss, but Diem rejected it, and skirmishing began in Saigon in March. The French, who openly favored the Binh Xuyen, fed its officers with intelligence and threw up road barriers against Diem's troops. The

French government in Paris meanwhile denounced Diem, and Bao Dai entered the fray from his château on the Côte d'Azur, attempting to manipulate factions in Saigon. Diem seemed to be finished by late April. Reporting from Saigon, the influential newspaper columnist Joseph Alsop wrote him off as "virtually impotent." As was often the case, Alsop erred.

On April 27, Diem ordered the Binh Xuyen to cease its deployments in the city. The Binh Xuyen disobeyed and Diem's army attacked its strongholds the next day. The Binh Xuyen riposted by firing shells into the park around the presidential palace, and soon Saigon was a battleground as the rival forces fought street by street. Artillery and mortars obliterated the city's poor districts, killing five hundred civilians and rendering some twenty thousand homeless. As the fighting raged, Bao Dai summoned Diem to France, hoping to neutralize him. Diem refused to budge. When Bao Dai's officers tried to oust him, Diem turned his generals against them. By the end of May, the Binh Xuyen had been routed and its boss, Bay Vien, flew to asylum in Paris. Diem had prevailed—but at a cost that he would have to pay later. Nearly two thousand defeated Binh Xuyen, Hoa Hao, and Cao Dai fighters joined the underground Communist forces concealed in the recesses of the Mekong delta, and they would emerge afterward among the Vietcong guerrillas.

The United States rewarded Diem for his stubborn courage. A new American ambassador, G. Frederick Reinhardt, landed in Saigon to express unequivocal U.S. confidence in the regime. Five months later, Diem consolidated his power. With Lansdale and other Americans helping, he deposed Bao Dai in a referendum, and promoted himself to the rank of chief of state.

The election, like others to follow, was a test of authority rather than an exercise in democracy. With Bao Dai far away, Diem's activists could easily exert pressure on the voters. Lansdale, with his talent for advertising, showed them how to design the ballots in order to sway the electorate. Those for Diem were red, which signified good luck, and those for Bao Dai green, the color of misfortune. Diem's agents were present at the polling stations. One voter recalled the scene in a village near Hué: "They told us to put the red ballot into envelopes and throw the green ones into the wastebasket. A few people, faithful to Bao Dai, disobeyed. As soon as they left, the agents went after them, and roughed them up. The agents poured pepper sauce down their nostrils, or forced water down their throats. They beat one of my relatives to a pulp."

In several places, including Saigon, the tally of votes for Diem exceeded the number of registered voters. He claimed to have won 98.2 percent of the vote—having spurned American advice to aim for a more plausible 60 or 70 percent. What the Americans failed to understand was that his mandarin mentality could not accept the idea of even minority resistance to his rule. With no compunctions whatsoever, Diem again renounced the nationwide elections prescribed by the Geneva agreement because, he said, they could not be "absolutely free."

If the Communist takeover of the north alarmed Washington and worried Diem, it only partially satisfied Ho Chi Minh and his comrades, who had been denied complete victory at the Geneva conference table. Within a year of the accord, moreover, they could sense that the elections scheduled to unify Vietnam would never take place. Diem refused to discuss election preparations, and the United States indirectly backed him, saying that the matter "should be left up to the Vietnamese themselves." The Soviet Union and China did nothing to press for a political settlement. So the deadline, July 1956, passed without any action to fulfill the most important clause in the Geneva agreement, and it looked as if Vietnam would become another truncated nation, like Germany and Korea. Indeed, the Soviet Union even suggested a permanent partition by proposing in early 1957 that both North and South Vietnam be admitted to the United Nations as "two separate states . . . which differ from one another in political and economic structure." The United States, unwilling to recognize a Communist regime, rebuffed the initiative—-a grievous mistake. For international endorsement of "two Vietnams" might have averted the later confrontation.

When Ho Chi Minh returned to Hanoi in October 1954, after eight years in the jungle, his problems differed from those that faced Diem. There were no fractious sects and gangsters to challenge his authority. The French army was leaving the north in orderly fashion, and the massive flight of the Catholics to the south made his control easier, since their fanatical anti-Communism would not nag him. He could also count on the fidelity of his soldiers and civilian cadres, whose loyalty had been tested during the struggle against France. But he was beset by severe economic difficulties.

The war against the French had devastated the north. Railways had been disrupted, bridges blown up, buildings destroyed. On Diem's orders, departing anti-Communist Vietnamese had dismantled harbor installations, post offices, libraries, and hospitals, and stripped factories of tools and machinery. Most critically, the separation from the south deprived the north of its traditional source of rice. In 1955, only emergency rice imports from Burma, financed by the Soviet Union, prevented a recurrence of the disastrous famine of a decade before.

Had Ho been as realistic in coping with the economy as he was in waging war, he would have offered incentives to his people to spur production. Instead, motivated by ideology, he proceeded to categorize peasants in five classes, ranging from "landlord" to "farm worker"; the idea was insane. In contrast to the south, where large holdings were common, very few peasants in the north possessed more than three or four acres. But the Communist leaders concluded that "landlords" and other "feudal" elements represented 2 percent of the rural population, and they dispatched teams of cadres to liquidate them.

Starting in 1955, cadres set up Agricultural Reform Tribunals, and zealously began to fulfill their quotas. In a village of two thousand inhabitants, for example, they had to arraign twenty alleged "landlords." The program touched off atrocities throughout the country. Anxious to avoid indictment, peasants trumped up charges against their neighbors, while others accused their rivals of imaginary crimes. Anyone suspected of having worked for the French was executed as a "traitor," and other victims included those who had shown insufficient ardor toward the Vietminh. The cadres, under pressure, singled out alleged culprits on no pretext at all. One group of cadres, reporting that it could discover only two "landlords" in a certain village, was ordered back to find six more, which it did by selecting a half dozen peasants at random. Many cadres themselves seized the property of the condemned, or spared relatives.

The Communists have never published an official count of those killed in the land reform, but thousands died. And thousands more were interned in forced labor camps. In August 1956, a year after the campaign, Ho publicly confessed that "errors have been committed," and promised that "those who have been wrongly classified as landlords and rich peasants will be correctly reclassified." The Communists dutifully echoed his admission, disclosing that even loyal Vietminh veterans had been unjustly tried and executed. Thousands of survivors were released and sent back to their villages amid exhortations to the nation to forgive and forget. But tensions continued as victims of the repression took revenge against the cadres who had persecuted them. In several areas, peasants refused to obey directives, and North Vietnam foundered in an atmosphere of suspicion and apprehension. Describing the mood, the official Hanoi newspaper, *Nhan Dan,* wrote that "brothers no longer dare to visit each other, and people dare not greet each other in the street."

Ho's appeal came too late to prevent an eruption of indignation in his native Nhge An province, where peasants had spontaneously defied the French twenty-six years before. The new uprising started on November 2, 1956, when local peasants presented a protest petition to Canadian members of the International Control Commission, the group created by the Geneva Conference to monitor the armistice. Soldiers dispersed the peasants with rifle butts, and by nightfall, violence was sweeping through the province. Ho responded exactly as the French had to the earlier insurrection. He sent a division of troops out to quell the disorders, and they killed or deported some six thousand peasants. The world, then focused on the Hungarian uprising against Soviet domination, paid no attention to the episode. Nor did the International Control Commission, which included Indian and Polish representatives, investigate the incident thoroughly. But Ho, realizing that his own reputation for moderation was at stake, introduced further liberal measures—conceding, however, that they were inadequate to repair the damage. "One cannot awaken the dead," he said. Giap made a similar *mea culpa:* "We attacked on too large a front, and, seeing enemies everywhere, resorted to terror, which became far too widespread. . . . Instead of recognizing education to be the first essential, we relied exclusively on organizational methods such as disciplinary punishments, expulsion from the party, executions. . . . Worse still, torture came to be regarded as normal practice."

The regime, seeking a scapegoat, placed the blame on a veteran Communist figure, Truong Chinh, and dismissed him from the post of secretary-general of the Lao Dong, the Workers party. But he retained his membership in the party's politburo; the leadership thus acknowledged obliquely its collective responsibility for the brutal campaign. Years later, the Vietnamese Communists would contend that they had been pushed into the program by Chinese advisers, who had imposed a devastating land reform effort on China a couple of years before.

The Hanoi government, having expected the 1956 nationwide elections to reunify the country, had transferred about a hundred thousand southern Vietminh activists to the north in conformity with the Geneva accords, leaving others in their native areas. After Diem reneged on the elections, Ho told the southern comrades to be patient. The policy was first to "firmly consolidate the north," they were informed, which emphasized the Soviet party line: "all conflicts can be resolved by peaceful negotiations." So the Vietminh militants in the south were exposed to Diem's retribution. As early as January 1956, having beaten his adversaries in Saigon, Diem launched a drive against Vietminh remnants in the countryside, his offensive a mirror image of the repression then going on in the north.

A "Vietminh suspect" might be anyone who had fought against the French or even counted a relative in the resistance. As in the north, numbers of innocent peasants were denounced by jealous neighbors or arrested by corrupt officials who coveted their property. Prisoners were tried not in formal courts, but by "security committees" headed by province chiefs personally appointed by Diem. Denied counsel, the defendants were often tortured.

I myself watched an interrogation in a Mekong delta town on a blistering hot day in the late 1950s. Soldiers had brought in a lean youth in black cotton pajamas who looked like any peasant. He squatted impassively, as if stoically awaiting a fate he could not avoid. The soldiers wired his fingers to a field telephone, then cranked it as an officer spoke with surprising gentleness to the youth, trying to extract either information or a confession. The youth gritted his teeth, his facial muscles taut as the electricity coursed through his body, and he finally blurted out a few words, perhaps only to stop the ordeal. I was relieved when he talked, but the officer refused to tell me what he had said, nor where the youth was being taken as the soldiers led him away. He may have been released. He may have been executed. He may have been banished to Poulo Condore, the island prison formerly used by the French to cage Vietnamese nationalists. I also knew that Diem's police frequently shot prisoners—reporting that they had been killed attempting to escape.

The cruelty worked. By 1956, Diem had smashed 90 percent of the former Vietminh cells in the Mekong delta, and those that survived retreated into remote swamps. They moved constantly and furtively, covering their tracks and contacting nobody. Ultimately, though, Diem's severity probably created more enemies than it crushed. For his indiscriminate offensive against former members of the Vietminh drove many back into the underground who would have preferred to live in peace and might have even rallied to his colors.

Such was the case of Tran Van Bo, a captured Vietcong cadre whom I interviewed at length in the early 1960s in his Saigon prison cell. Then in his late thirties, he was educated and articulate, though it took days of quiet persuasion before he consented to relate his experiences. Bo scarcely fit the image of the "oppressed" peasant portrayed in Communist propaganda. He had grown up in Ba Xuyen province, a lush area of the Mekong delta, where his father owned twenty-five acres of farmland, a sizable holding. After graduation from high school, he went to work for his uncle, an affluent rice wholesaler. Under other circumstances, he might have become a wealthy merchant. But the French presence aroused his nationalistic sentiments; he resented their possession of vast estates by virtue of their colonial status, and they had slighted his family. "They were rude and overbearing when they came into our village," he recalled. "They looked down on us even though we were rich."

He welcomed the Japanese troops who occupied the area during World War II because, for the first time, they made the French appear inferior. Soon after Japan's defeat, he quit his uncle's business and returned to his village, where the Vietminh had already set up an assortment of peasant, religious, youth, and other associations. Many of his relatives belonged to one or another of the groups. One, who called himself a Communist, urged Bo to join his youth organization. That started Bo's career in the *khang chien*, or resistance, as he referred to the Vietminh.

His village, Long Dien, comprised twenty-two hamlets, and its population swelled to some twenty thousand as refugees streamed in to escape the war in other parts of the Mekong delta. The local Vietminh leader, a peasant named Hoa, assigned Bo to mobilize meetings and spread propaganda, a function known in Communist jargon as agitprop. Bo formed a team of three men, none of them armed. They distributed books and leaflets sent to them from the Vietminh province committee or passed out tracts which they ran off on a crude mimeograph machine carried from place to place to avoid detection. But most peasants were illiterate, and Bo delivered speeches that usually stressed the importance of unity in the struggle against the French. He lived in an ordinary hut; sympathetic villagers fed him, and his family furnished his clothes. He had become a professional revolutionary.

Bo rose rapidly in the movement. After a year, he was selected for membership in the Communist party, which still existed covertly despite its official dissolution. He attended classes in Marxist theory held at the Vietminh regional headquarters in nearby Bac Lieu province, and not long afterward he became a delegate to the Youth Liberation League for the Nambo, as the Communists had designated the Mekong delta. He married the daughter of a prominent dignitary in his native village. She had also become a Vietminh militant and, with some misgivings, her father had thrown in his lot with the resistance. By the early 1950s, the whole village had come under Vietminh control. As Bo explained it to me, "There was no way for anyone to remain neutral."

But about that time, presumably anticipating an early victory, the Communists imposed class distinctions on the movement. The phase coincided with an agrarian reform then being conducted by the Vietminh in the regions under its domination, and Bo fared badly as the son of a big landowner. Demoted because he lacked a "poor peasant" background, he quit to take up farming in the Camau peninsula, a remote sector at the westernmost end of the Mekong delta. Surprisingly, the Vietminh did not harass him for his decision. "I claimed that my health had failed, and they left me alone," he recalled.

The Diem regime would not leave him alone, however. One night in 1956, four years after his resignation from the Vietminh, a platoon of Saigon government troops arrived at his house to arrest him. He had gone fishing, and neighbors warned him. He sent a message to his wife, telling her to go to her father's place, and he fled to another hamlet, where he hid with friends. Before long, he received a visit from a couple of old Vietminh comrades, who spent hours describing the iniquities of the Diem regime and its American supporters. Bo listened intently, and finally agreed to return to the fold, for a mixture of motives: "As a Vietnamese, I was saddened by the partition of the country and Diem's refusal to discuss reunification. That was wrong, and I figured that the Americans were to blame for backing him. So the resistance was correct to oppose him. But I also joined out of self-preservation. Diem's soldiers would have killed me if I had simply tried to continue living as a simple peasant. I really had no choice."

The movement at that stage was far more clandestine than it had ever been, since Diem's forces scoured the area more thoroughly than the French had done. Police and informers pervaded every village, and many remembered Bo from his Vietminh days. He assumed an alias, Hai Cao, or "second tall one," a reference to his height and to his status as second son in his family, and he operated through an intricate command system for the sake of security. Nobody knew the names of the entire apparatus. Bo's contact in the village under his supervision was one agent who communicated with another agent, and so forth through the network. Nor did Bo ever meet his superior, who passed him messages through an intermediary. His responsibility, as it had been before, was propaganda. But gradually, as the war intensified, he joined a squad armed with various French, American, and German weapons, most of them acquired by ambushing government self-defense units.

"Our long-range objective," Bo told me, "was to liberate South Vietnam. First, however, we had to liberate the nearest hamlet."

Bo was eventually arrested, along with three other cadres, as they carried two million piasters in Vietcong tax revenues across the Mekong delta to a clandestine headquarters in Tayninh province, adjacent to Cambodia. But Vietminh veterans like him became the nucleus of the National Liberation Front, which the Communists organized at the end of 1960. Diem's publicists gave it a pejorative label, the Vietcong, or Vietnamese Communists, and the name stuck.

In May 1957, Diem paid a state visit to the United States, where President Eisenhower hailed him as the "miracle man" of Asia. The remains of the Vietminh in the south had "disintegrated," Diem asserted, and he was not entirely wrong. At that stage, he might have sealed his control over his half of Vietnam had he not made a series of errors that revealed the nature of his regime and his own lack of understanding of the challenge that confronted him.

His government had become a narrow oligarchy composed of his brothers and other relatives. The brothers rivaled each other for power and influence and operated through separate factions that resembled traditional Vietnamese secret societies. Nhu, for example, ran the Can Lao Nhan Vi Dang, or Personalist Labor party, whose members, many of them Catholics, held key posts in the government bureaucracy. His undercover police were directed by Dr. Tran Kim Tuyen, a northern Catholic who also directed an intelligence network with the guidance of CIA advisers. But Nhu's men could not intrude into central Vietnam, the fiefdom of brother Can, a virtual warlord. The two brothers competed through their business agents for the rice trade and American aid contracts. Nephews, cousins, and in-laws, granted special licenses because of family connections, underwrote the Ngo clan with money as well, and Diem's brother Thuc, the bishop, had a hand in making investments on behalf of the Catholic Church. As much as they squabbled among themselves, however, the brothers stuck together under pressure, and Diem's refusal to delegate power beyond his kinship circle limited his popular appeal.

From the outset, Diem sought the support of the affluent landowners of the Mekong delta, whose families were influential in Saigon, and he balked at imposing a rigorous agrarian reform program there that might have won him peasant sympathies. He brought in prominent American experts like Wolf Ladejinsky, who had planned successful land reforms in Japan and Taiwan, but he discarded their advice. He permitted landlords to retain large holdings, so that little acreage was available for distribution. In Long An province, adjacent to Saigon, for example, fewer than one thousand out of thirty-five thousand tenants received property. The minister in charge of the program, himself a big landlord, delayed its implementation. Even worse, Diem antagonized peasants by requiring them to pay for land that they had been given free by the Vietminh during the war against the French, and the Communists capitalized on his crude policy.

Another blunder at the time was the creation of Khu Tru Mat, known as *agrovilles*, farm communities designed mainly to isolate the rural population from the Communists. These centers, later to be called strategic hamlets, showed Diem's conventional misconception of the problem as simply one of security. In any event, they were built and managed in such a way that they alienated peasants, as I learned on a trip during the spring of 1959 to Vi Thanh, in the heart of the Mekong delta.

Guerrillas were then beginning to snipe at travelers, and I drove into the countryside accompanied by a pair of sleepy South Vietnamese soldiers for protection. The Mekong delta, as flat as a billiard table, seemed peaceful on that warm morning: peasants tended their rice stalks and children splashed in the irrigation ditches that separated the flooded fields. The *agroville* near Vi Thanh, when we reached it, looked magnificent compared to the scrubby villages along the road. Flanking a canal, it was enclosed by a bamboo fence, and neat rows of thatched-roof huts had been laid out. Its director, an army major by the name of Tran Cuu Thien, showed me its school, dispensary, and power plant, which would furnish peasants with electricity for the first time in their lives, and he described plans to give them incomes between harvests by setting up cottage industries. He boasted that he had completed the project in fifty days on Diem's personal instructions, and it was plainly the kind of place to warm the hearts of visiting American congressmen. In reality, it was a disaster.

For one thing, peasants assigned to the *agroville* had been uprooted from their native villages and ancestral graves, and their traditional social pattern disrupted, for reasons that they could not fathom. Worse still, Major Thien had rushed to comply with Diem's order by mobilizing twenty thousand peasants to construct a project that could only accommodate six thousand. Thus, fourteen thousand men and women had been compelled to abandon their crops and work without pay for others. Major Thien explained to me that the program would educate peasants in their "civic duties." In their eyes, it was merely forced labor, however, and though they did not shift their support to the Vietcong immediately, their attitudes toward the Diem regime soured.

Then, as later in the war, every statement coming out of both Saigon and Hanoi repeated the same stereotype—that the struggle could not be won without the peasants, who comprised the majority of Vietnam's population. About that time, accompanied by an interpreter, I wandered into hamlets and villages in the Mekong delta, along the coast of central Vietnam, and in the highlands near the Laotian border, trying to assess peasant attitudes. Questions were more easily posed than answered, since Vietnamese peasants, like farmers everywhere, tend to distrust strangers—and especially foreigners. Even so, I learned a few things that could not be charted on graphs in Washington offices.

The lives of peasants are dictated by the arduous and endless cycle of their crops. They plow, sow, and harvest, resigned to the droughts, floods, pests, and diseases that blight their rice, corn, sugar, peanuts, and potatoes. Their daily tasks bend their backs and age their wives far beyond their years, and the hunger of each day stunts their children. Their every waking hour is concerned with survival. But in Vietnam, along with the ancient toil and the whims of nature, peasants had borne the burden of war for a generation.

I found them to be muddled, frightened, weary. Again and again as they spoke, one thread seemed to run through their conversation. They were not participants in the conflict, but its victims. They sympathized with neither Diem nor the Vietcong, only leaning to the side that harassed them less. Squatting in his muddy field, the smoke of a hand-rolled cigarette clouding his eyes, an old man in black cotton pajamas summed up the view in a metaphor: "If a son is mistreated by his father, he may adopt another."

In some areas, I discovered, peasants welcomed Vietcong agents and referred to them as "liberators" or "resistants." The Vietcong benefited from the image of the Vietminh, who had distributed land to the poor, and their promise of a better future was enticing. Often, too, the agents helped peasants at their labors. Even an affluent miller in a Quangngai province village had been swayed. "If they win," he told me, "I'll probably be left alone. They're against the government, not the people. We have nothing to fear."

But the Vietcong's velvet touch often concealed talons of steel, and its terrorists were merciless in their murder of government officials and informers, their actions earning them a reputation for omnipotence and omnipresence. Yet for all its brutality, Vietcong terrorism was usually selective, as a bus driver in Long Khanh province, northeast of Saigon, recounted.

Five or six Vietcong guys stopped my bus one morning to check the identity cards of the passengers. They dragged two men off the bus, and their chief said to them: "We've been waiting for you. We've warned you many times to leave your jobs, but you haven't obeyed. So now we must carry out the sentence."

They forced the two men to kneel by the roadside, and one of the Vietcong guys chopped off their heads with a machete. They then pinned verdicts to their shirts saying that the murdered men were policemen. The verdicts had been written out beforehand. It was horrible to watch.

Afterward, the Vietcong guys gave the passengers back their identity cards, saying: "You'll get into trouble with the authorities without these, and we don't want that to happen."

We picked up the bodies of the two cops and took them to the nearest town.

By contrast, peasants said, they had little contact with the Saigon authorities or even district chiefs. One Bienhoa province youth recollected that "Mr. Government," as he called Diem, had once driven past his village, so surrounded by soldiers that he could not be seen. But the absence of government troops was a blessing, since they often pilfered rice, pigs, and chickens. Worse yet, their presence frequently meant indiscriminate artillery bombardments against innocent villages suspected of harboring the Vietcong. As we chatted over tea in his Mekong delta hamlet, a leathery peasant offered his opinion: "Personally, I think that the 'resistance' has made many mistakes. But we dread the army's cannon shells, which fall anywhere."

The South Vietnamese regime was then organizing the Dan Ve, village self-defense units that evoked mixed reactions from the peasants. In some places, the militiamen protected villages against Vietcong attacks even though they carried antiquated French muskets and only earned the equivalent of ten dollars a month for their services, which diverted them from their own farming. Elsewhere, however, they behaved badly. Many deserted to the Vietcong, and others became petty tyrants. "As soon as one of them gets a gun, he can rob any house he wants," one peasant complained. "One day they're our friends, and the next day they're enemies."

Though few peasants identified with the Vietcong—or would admit to me that they did—few appeared to feel much affinity for the Diem government. For the regime, with its focus on security, had spent little on schools, medical care, or other tangible social services. In a coastal village of Quangngai province, I encountered a peasant woman with a baby astride her hip, its face a mass of sores. She could not afford the bus fare to see a doctor, much less his fee. At a hamlet not far away, a peasant was tutoring his children, since the place lacked a school, and to send them to town by bus would be too expensive.

And, nearly everywhere, I met corruption. In parts of Binh Dinh province, huge rats were eating up the crops. Two brands of poison could be bought: one from a government agency, which seemed to make the rats grow bigger; and the other from private entrepreneurs at twice the price. They were actually the same poison in the same bag, the cheaper version diluted by local officials who then sold the full-strength pesticide on the black market. I found a similar situation in Kontum, a mountainous province, where peasants had been resettled from the poor lowlands of central Vietnam. Crouching in the doorway of his shack to shield himself against the dusty wind, one peasant explained forlornly that his rice ration had been trimmed and that he had not received the allowance he had been promised to cover the cost of building his hut. "I can't understand what has happened," he said.

A local supervisor disclosed what had gone on: "The rice and cash grants are being stolen by officials, who also rob the fertilizer sent here and sell it. I'd like to tell President Diem how they are profiting from the sweat of the people."

"Have you protested?" I asked. "Yes," he replied, "and I'm due to be transferred to another district."

Several peasants sounded a note of fatalism, and that sentiment worked to Diem's detriment, since even popular neutrality deprived him of the support his regime needed. My small sampling convinced me then that he could not mobilize that support, and one peasant put that conclusion into words: "We are always for the government—no matter which government is in control. But in our hearts we like the government that takes the least from the people, and gives them abundance and happiness. We do not yet have that government."

More vocal disenchantment in Saigon paralleled the peasant dissatisfaction. Doctors, lawyers, teachers, and other professionals, most of them educated under the French, were disturbed less by the lack of genuine democracy than by Diem's rigidity. The grumbling rose to an audible pitch in August 1959, when he organized legislative elections, mainly as window dressing for his American patrons. The contest, arranged under U.S. auspices, was designed to replicate a Western political exercise. The government registered voters, vowed to respect the secret ballot, and even invited critics to run against the regime. But the election was a sham. In the countryside, Diem's officials coerced peasants into voting for the government candidates or simply stuffed the ballot boxes. In Saigon, where rigging was more difficult, they resorted to other techniques, such as disqualifying uncongenial politicians for "irregularities." On election day, the regime brought contingents of troops into the city to vote for its candidates.

Diem's repression only stimulated his domestic adversaries. In April 1960, eighteen distinguished nationalists, including several former members of his cabinet, signed a petition urging him to reform. Their requests were modest; they merely asked him to broaden his entourage, and they even offered to serve him. To Diem, however, their gesture amounted to *lèse majesté*. Instead of liberalizing, he closed opposition newspapers and arrested a number of journalists, students, and other intellectuals, accusing them of "Communist affiliations." And he turned more and more to his brother Nhu.

Though the United States had by then sunk more than a billion dollars into South Vietnam, its leverage over Diem was diminishing. Elbridge Durbrow, the American ambassador in Saigon, was a chubby figure with a Rotarian manner whose gawky wife insisted on wearing an *ao dai*, the gossamer Vietnamese dress. But Durbrow was a shrewd diplomat. He warned Diem that Nhu and his wife were damaging the government's reputation and tactfully suggested that they be sent abroad. Diem dismissed the criticism of his brother as "Communist propaganda." In a message to Washington on December 4, 1960, Durbrow floated an idea that, three years later, would become U.S. policy: "We may well be forced, in the not too distant future, to undertake the difficult task of identifying and supporting alternative leadership."

During that period, though, Diem knew that he could resist American pressures for reform because the United States needed his regime as an anti-Communist bastion. He was, as one American official then in Saigon put it, "a puppet who pulled his own strings." He channeled the bulk of U.S. aid into his own priority, South Vietnam's military and police machinery, leaving only a small fraction for economic development; and he was less interested in building an army to fight Vietcong guerrillas than in forming conventional units that would protect him against his rivals in Saigon.

Diem's instinct proved to be prescient in November 1960, when three crack paratrooper battalions and a marine unit surrounded his palace in an effort to force him to reform. The instigator of the revolt, Lieutenant Colonel Vuong Van Dong, was a young northerner who had fought with the French against the Vietminh. Lean and intense, he had trained afterward at Fort Leavenworth, Kansas, and his American advisers in Vietnam regarded him highly. Fiercely anti-Communist, he had become irritated with Diem's arbitrary rule—especially his meddling in army operations. It was common for Diem to deploy detachments around the country without informing the general staff; he promoted favorites; and he played senior soldiers against each other in order to prevent the army from challenging his power. Years later, Dong disclosed to me his objective had simply been to force Diem to change. But the naiveté of that hope was reflected in the inefficiency of his maneuver.

A year earlier, Dong had lined up other disgruntled officers, among them his commander, Colonel Nguyen Chanh Thi, who had fought for Diem against the sects in 1955. Dong also enlisted the cooperation of an armored regiment. But the operation, launched at five o'clock on the morning of November 11, was off course at the start. The rebels failed to follow the most elementary procedures, such as seizing the radio station and blocking the roads into the city. They left telephone lines at the presidential palace intact, allowing Diem to appeal to loyal units to rescue him. And they refrained from attacking for thirty-six hours in the expectation that Diem would comply with their demands. During that time, Dong called on Ambassador Durbrow to intervene on his behalf. But Durbrow, though he had no love for Diem, equivocated. "We support this government until it fails," he told Dong.

Cleverly using the time at his disposal, Diem outwitted the dissident soldiers. Descending into the cellar of the palace, he taped a speech agreeing to free elections and other liberal measures. The stall worked. Just as his concessions were being broadcast, loyal contingents rolled into Saigon. The clash was brief but bloody; the four hundred dead included many inquisitive civilians who had streamed into the streets to watch the confrontation. Dong, Thi, and their officers fled to asylum in Cambodia, and Diem promptly reneged on his promises. He also rounded up numbers of innocuous critics, among them several former members of his cabinet.

Not long afterward, Nhu invited me to his office to reveal the "real" story behind the attempted coup. Cluttered with mounted animal heads and tiger skins, the study resembled a den in a hunting lodge. Nhu chain-smoked as he spoke in shrill French. Plainly referring to Durbrow's equivocation, he asserted that the regime's enemies were "not only Communists, but foreigners who claim to be our friends." He would repeat that accusation until it finally came true in 1963, when

Ambassador Henry Cabot Lodge encouraged a cabal of South Vietnamese generals to oust Diem.

Dong's abortive effort was a pivotal event. From then on, many of Diem's former disciples began to plot against him. They included his secret police chief, Dr. Tran Kim Tuyen, who quietly consulted with military and civilian officials, and several senior South Vietnamese officers. Also among them was Colonel Pham Ngoc Thao, a southern Catholic and former Vietminh intelligence agent—and a clandestine Communist agent.

As early as October 1957, on instructions from Hanoi, the Communists in the south organized thirty-seven armed companies, most of them in the impenetrable forests and marshes of the western fringe of the Mekong delta. In May 1959, the North Vietnamese leadership created a unit called Group 559, its task to begin enlarging the traditional Communist infiltration route, the Ho Chi Minh Trail, into the south. Two months later, another logistical unit, Group 759, was formed to study ways to ship men and especially supplies from North Vietnam to the south by sea. "Absolute secrecy, absolute security, were our watchwords," recalled the Communist oficer in charge in an interview after the war. His motives were clear. At the time, the Communists were determined to foster the impression of total adherence to the terms of the Geneva agreement, which banned military buildups by either of the two Vietnamese regimes in each other's zone. The Communist moves then, however, were largely precautionary.

Until 1959, Ho Chi Minh had discouraged his southern comrades from engaging in armed attacks against the Diem regime, arguing that the situation was "not ripe" for insurrection. He warned against "reckless" actions, contending that they would provoke Diem to repress the population and thus impede the construction of a solid political organization. A contemporary Communist document typified the plea for prudence: "At the present time, we are still in an indecisive back-and-forth period. . . . We must accumulate our forces and develop our apparatus . . . preserve the legal status of the masses, not eliminating the government but just crippling it. . . . To ignore the balance of forces and rashly call for a general uprising is to commit the error of speculative adventurism, leading to premature violence and driving us into a very dangerous position."

That directive disconcerted Vietcong activists in the south, who were being decimated by Diem. They objected, and their case was supported in Hanoi by Le Duan, secretary-general of the Lao Dong party and a native of central Vietnam. He had covertly gone south to analyze the situation, and he returned to argue that the already tattered Vietcong structure would be completely wiped out unless it resorted to violence. Indeed, Vietcong groups in parts of the Mekong delta were then assaulting government units in defiance of Hanoi's orders. As a result, the northern leaders issued new instructions, authorizing limited "armed struggle" in the south as a way of intensifying the "political struggle." The directive did not yet call for guerrilla warfare. It signified, in simple language, that the Vietcong could now terrorize Diem's officials and other "traitors"—the assassination campaign was to focus particularly on honest hamlet chiefs and schoolteachers whose popularity represented a threat to the Communists.

Statistics reflected the toll of Vietcong terrorism. Between 1959 and 1961, the number of South Vietnamese government officials assassinated soared from twelve hundred to four thousand a year, and the murders evoked precisely the reaction from Diem that the Vietcong wanted. Predictably perceiving the problem in security terms, Diem appointed army officers to manage the rural bureaucracy, so that by 1962, thirty-six out of forty-one province chiefs were military men; soldiers pervaded the administration down to the district level. Many of them, northern Catholics or natives of central Vietnam whom Diem could trust, were alien to their areas of responsibility. Not only did they neglect the economic and social needs of the local population, they operated as if they were in enemy territory—living in fortified garrisons protected by blockhouses and barbed wire, venturing into the countryside only under heavy guard, often accompanied by American advisers whose presence lent substance to Vietcong denunciations of the "My-Diem clique," a slogan standing for the "neocolonial" collaboration between America and Diem. The villages, open to Diem's troops by day, were run by the Vietcong at night, which meant that the regime could not rely on their loyalty. One of Diem's aides confessed at the time: "Except for the color of our skin, we are no different from the French."

In December 1960, Hanoi decided that the moment had arrived to announce a new organization in the south, the National Liberation Front. The classic Communist ploy was reminiscent of the formation of the Vietminh twenty years before. As a "front," its aim was to bring together a disparate collection of elements opposed to Diem: various peasant, youth, religious, cultural, and other associations founded by the Vietminh during the war against the French; and remnants of the Cao

Dai, Hoa Hao, and Binh Xuyen, which had retreated into their sanctuaries in the Mekong delta after their defeat by Diem five years earlier. As a southern movement, it was intended to serve to underpin Hanoi's claim that North Vietnam was not violating the Geneva agreement by sending forces into the south. Its chairman, Nguyen Huu Tho, was a French-educated Saigon lawyer who had demonstrated against France during the early 1950s and had later been jailed by Diem for mildly left-wing activities. His benign middle-class credentials were supposed to attract a wide spectrum of supporters, but he was merely a figurehead. The front's real leadership resided in the People's Revolutionary party and the Liberation army, its Communist components, which took their orders from the politburo in Hanoi.

But to label the National Liberation Front as simply a satellite of Ho Chi Minh's regime, as American spokesmen were to do, was to miss a key point. For there were serious divergences between the northern and southern Communists in a society as pluralistic as Vietnam, and perhaps they could have been exploited. Following the reunification of Vietnam in 1975, the southerners became increasingly antagonized by northern carpetbaggers—an indication that Vietnamese regionalism was strong. But the entire history of Vietnam is a series of lost opportunities that might have averted the worst.

7 Vietnam Is the Place

An American adviser, Lieutenant Colonel William Dickerson, supervises the abandonment of an untenable outpost in the jungle. American helicopters flown by American pilots helped evacuate the South Vietnamese troops.

President Kennedy and two of his principal advisers on Vietnam—Secretary of Defense McNamara (left) and Secretary of State Rusk. Rusk's experience in Asian affairs dated back to his military service during World War II.

Vice-President Johnson chatting with Ngo Dinh Diem in Saigon in May 1961. Johnson, whom Kennedy had sent on an ambassadorial world tour, exuberantly praised Diem as the "Winston Churchill of Asia," which reassured Diem of American support.

Captain Gerald Kilburn (left), an American adviser, leads South Vietnamese troops into action in the Mekong delta in 1963. American advisers then in Vietnam were supposed to avoid combat, but many participated in battle nevertheless.

Frederick Nolting (left), American ambassador to South Vietnam, chats with General Paul Harkins, commander of the U.S. military advisory mission. Nolting's previous diplomatic experience had been in Europe. Harkins had once played minor roles in the movies.

In February 1962, two insurgent South Vietnamese air force pilots bombed Diem's palace. Diem and his family miraculously escaped injury, but Madame Nhu was slightly hurt. Here, sometime later, Madame Nhu inspects the bombed palace.

Madame Ngo Dinh Nhu, President Diem's beautiful and impetuous sister-in-law, who considered herself South Vietnam's First Lady. She was an active feminist who organized her own corps of women warriors, to whom she here gives a lesson in target practice.

Diem's younger brother, Ngo Dinh Nhu. An erratic figure with scholarly pretensions, Nhu evolved an arcane doctrine called Personalism, which rejected both capitalism and socialism. It was understood by very few Vietnamese.

A South Vietnamese peasant helps a Vietcong guerrilla make traps to be used against Saigon government troops. These devices, made of barbed nails capable of penetrating the sole of a boot, were concealed in flooded rice fields or on jungle trails.

Beginning in the late 1950s, North Vietnam sent supplies to Vietcong insurgents in the south. Porters carried the equipment along the Ho Chi Minh Trail, which threaded through the mountains and jungles of adjacent Laos.

An American adviser trains a South Vietnamese soldier in the use of a bayonet. Despite training and equipment, the South Vietnamese troops were frequently no match for the highly organized and motivated Vietcong guerrillas.

U.S. advisers also tried to teach the benefits of American civilization to local youths. The effort was known as "nation-building"; it made only a superficial dent in Vietnamese culture.

To isolate peasants from the Vietcong guerrillas, the South Vietnamese government built fortified enclosures called "strategic hamlets." But this alienated many peasants, who resented being moved from their native villages.

Both the South Vietnamese army and the Vietcong guerrillas frequently tortured peasants, either to extract information or in retaliation for sympathizing with one side or the other.

Now we have a problem in making our power credible, and Vietnam is the place.

—John F. Kennedy

These people may be the world's greatest lovers, but they're not the world's greatest fighters. But they're good people, and they can win a war if someone shows them how.

—Colonel John Paul Vann

As his term neared its end, President Eisenhower was troubled less by the growing insurgency in Vietnam than by a minicrisis in adjacent Laos, where the Soviet Union had stepped in to take advantage of a confused civil war. On January 19, 1961, on the eve of his retirement, Eisenhower cautioned his young successor, John F. Kennedy, that Laos was "the key to the entire area of Southeast Asia" and might even require the introduction of American combat troops. Kennedy listened warily. Foreign policy topped his agenda, as he dramatized in his inaugural promise to "pay any price, bear any burden, meet any hardship, support any friend, oppose any foe to assure the survival and success of liberty." But Europe and Latin America loomed larger than Asia in his sights.

Kennedy, a student during the 1930s, recalled the appeasement of Hitler that had led to World War II, and as a member of Congress he had uttered all the fashionable cold war platitudes. He had favored funding the French war in Indochina, asserting that the United States must prevent "the onrushing tide of Communism from engulfing all Asia." He had been an early enthusiast for Diem's regime, describing it in a mixture of metaphors as "the cornerstone of the Free World in Southeast Asia, the keystone to the arch, the finger in the dike," and he had portrayed Vietnam as not only "a proving ground for democracy in Asia," but a "test of American responsibility and determination." He fully subscribed to the policy of containment, arguing that the line had to be held against "the relentless pressure of the Chinese Communists." And, along with most of his American contemporaries, he feared the menace of monolithic Communism directed from Moscow, citing Soviet support for "wars of national liberation" as evidence of their plans for global domination. Reiterating the domino theory, he said: "No other challenge is more deserving of our every effort and energy. . . . Our security may be lost piece by piece, country by country."

But behind the facade of his New Frontier, with its brash buoyancy, Kennedy was far from self-confident during his first year in office. He had scored an uncomfortably thin margin of victory over Richard Nixon, who had assailed him during the presidential election campaign for being "soft" on Communism. He was shattered at the Bay of Pigs, where his Cuban exile surrogates were defeated by Fidel Castro's forces, and he confronted the Kremlin over divided Berlin. He was further shaken five months after entering office when Soviet Prime Minister Nikita Khrushchev bullied him at their summit meeting in Vienna. Coming out of that encounter, he confided to James Reston of *The New York Times*: "Now we have a problem in making our power credible, and Vietnam is the place."

Spurning Eisenhower's advice, Kennedy sidestepped Laos, whose rugged terrain was no battleground for American soldiers. He assigned W. Averell Harriman, a seasoned and sagacious diplomat and negotiator, to another Geneva conference that brought about an agreement by the major powers to honor a "neutral and independent" Laos. But Kennedy rejected neutrality for South Vietnam, even though Hanoi was prepared to accept it, if only as a device to forestall American intervention. His decision was upheld by nearly every senior official in his inner circle. One exception was Chester Bowles, under secretary of state, who recommended that the Laotian formula be extended to all of Southeast Asia. Bowles's proposal was "either too early or too late," as the historian Arthur Schlesinger, Jr., then a White House aide, later wrote. Kennedy dumped Bowles soon afterward. He also rebuffed President de Gaulle, who warned him that Vietnam would trap him in "a bottomless military and political swamp."

Still, Kennedy was not quite prepared to pay any price or bear any burden to protect South Vietnam. He seemed to be persuaded from the start that he could deal inexpensively with the threat of Communism there. Besides, he had other priorities. His brother, Attorney General Robert Kennedy, refused to dwell on Vietnam when I raised it during a chat in his Washington office about that time. "We've got twenty Vietnams a day to handle," he said impatiently.

Not long after his inauguration, Kennedy had perused an analysis of conditions in South Vietnam by Colonel Edward Lansdale, now a Pentagon specialist, who had just returned from a mission there. Lansdale, alarmed by the deteriorating situation, urged that aid to Diem be increased. He also depicted his old protégé as a victim of American abuse, submitting that U.S. influence could become "effective again" if only "we . . . show him by deeds, not words alone, that we are his friend." Lansdale's warning jolted Kennedy. Turning to Walt Rostow, a State Department official who had urged him to read Lansdale's report, he said: "This is the worst one we've got, isn't it?"

But Kennedy preferred to tailor American commitments to immediate circumstances. Thus he continued the pattern that the United States had followed during the years before—and would follow in the years ahead. He rejected withdrawal from Vietnam, yet he balked at plunging into total war, a prospect he could not even envision. When George Ball, another dissenter in his entourage, conservatively predicted that Vietnam might one day demand as many as three hundred thousand U.S. troops, Kennedy laughed and replied: "Well, George, you're supposed to be one of the smartest guys in town, but you're crazier than hell. That will never happen."

Kennedy, like any president, tried to juggle the pressures brought on him by different aides. These pressures often expressed both bureaucratic rivalries and personal attitudes. Yet they were real. Dean Rusk, his secretary of state, a veteran exponent of toughness toward Asian Communism, was also a disciplined civil servant determined to promote the State Department's supremacy in the formulation of foreign policy. He frequently allied himself with Robert McNamara, the defense secretary, a former Ford Motor Company executive who believed, as a businessman, that the proper investments would produce the desired results. Both Rusk and McNamara were sensitive to the joint chiefs of staff, which predictably adopted a belligerent posture in concert with such hawkish civilians as Rostow, an articulate armchair tactician, whose aggressiveness they worked to curb. Nor could Kennedy neglect Congress, where he counted on J. William Fulbright, chairman of the Senate Foreign Relations Committee, then a firm supporter of U.S. involvement in Vietnam.

In the process tons of memorandums were ground out—only a tiny fraction of which would later be disclosed publicly in the *Pentagon Papers*, the compilation of documents purloined by Daniel Ellsberg, a Lansdale assistant who turned against the war. And there were endless meetings and private conversations and arcane machinations, many never recorded. Ultimately, however, Kennedy made the decisions—sometimes on the basis of advice, sometimes by sheer instinct.

He had been unhappy with the Eisenhower administration's policy of "massive retaliation," an abstract notion nicknamed the "bigger bang for a buck," which had been contrived to curtail defense expenditures by threatening the Soviet Union with nuclear conflict rather than maintaining a large and costly conventional force. Kennedy was influenced in this respect by his favorite general, Maxwell Taylor, who advocated a "flexible response" as a way of dealing with so-called brushfire wars, especially in developing areas of the world. The Taylor concept encouraged Kennedy's fascination with "counterinsurgency," which became the obvious approach to Vietnam.

In April 1961, Kennedy created a "task force" to prepare economic, social, political, and military programs aimed at preventing Communist "domination" of South Vietnam. George Ball, now deputy under secretary of state, soon took over the project, and diluted some of its original statements of unqualified commitment. Nevertheless, Kennedy accepted its proposals, among them a plan to strengthen the Saigon regime's army of one hundred and fifty thousand by twenty thousand men. He also agreed to send an additional hundred American military advisers to Vietnam, to bring the total up to nearly eight hundred—a decision that posed a legal problem, since the Geneva agreement specified that foreign military personnel could be assigned to Vietnam only as replacements. Rusk recommended that they be deployed without consulting Britain, cochairman of the Geneva Conference, or the International Control Commission, which was supposed to monitor the accords. He also suggested that they "be placed in varied locations to avoid attention."

At the same time, Kennedy replaced Ambassador Durbrow, who had annoyed Diem, with Frederick Nolting, a scholarly diplomat with no experience in Asia. Whatever Diem's shortcomings, the United States would "sink or swim" with him. Diem now began to view himself as indispensable, and this notion was reinforced by Vice-President Johnson, whom Kennedy dispatched to Asia in May 1961. Acting as if he were endorsing county sheriffs in a Texas election campaign, Johnson swept into Saigon and hailed Diem as the reincarnation of Winston Churchill. Returning home, Johnson echoed the domino theorists in a message that foreshadowed his later contention that the loss of Vietnam would compel America to fight "on the beaches of Waikiki." "The battle against Communism must be joined in Southeast Asia with strength and determination . . . or the United States, inevitably, must surrender the Pacific and take up our defenses on our own shores."

During Johnson's hectic Saigon visit, Diem had responded unenthusiastically to the idea of U.S. combat troops in his country. A larger American presence in Vietnam would compromise his nationalistic pretensions, and it might also give the United States greater leverage over his government. But the question of deploying American fighting units in Vietnam recurred throughout the year; it was finally resolved in

October, when Kennedy sent Maxwell Taylor to Saigon on a crucial mission.

Taylor, officially titled the president's special military representative, was Kennedy's kind of soldier—a World War II hero who spoke several languages and had written a book, thus combining courage with culture. Handsome and charming, he even resembled a character out of Camelot. One day in the summer of 1961, Kennedy casually stopped him in a White House corridor and handed him a voluminous letter from Diem. "How do I answer this?" Kennedy asked, and strolled away.

At Johnson's suggestion, Diem had again proposed that the size of the South Vietnamese armed forces be increased, now by one hundred thousand to a total of two hundred and seventy thousand men. This would demand an expanded American advisory group, more U.S. equipment, and additional financial aid, not a package to be considered lightly. Taylor and Rostow were instructed to go to Saigon to make an assessment. Kennedy was succinct: he wanted to "avoid a further deterioration of the situation" but, he reminded Taylor, the "initial responsibility" for South Vietnam's fate lay with its own government and people. In short, he opposed the introduction of American combat troops into Vietnam, though he had no intention of accepting defeat. Or, as Taylor put it afterward: "The question was how to change a losing game and begin to win, not how to call it off."

Taylor prepared to reach Saigon in mid-October, and the weeks before his arrival were filled with fresh events that seemed to augur change. As a gesture of defiance, large Vietcong contingents attacked South Vietnamese army posts in Phuoc Thanh and Darlac provinces, inflicting heavy casualties. Diem, declaring that a "real war" was developing, reversed himself. He now told Nolting that he would welcome American combat soldiers as a "symbolic" presence, and he also requested a bilateral defense pact between the United States and South Vietnam. In Washington, the joint chiefs of staff recommended a U.S. troop commitment, and they were seconded by William P. Bundy, then acting assistant secretary of defense, who argued for an "early and hard-hitting operation" that would give Diem "a chance to do better." Kennedy, seeking to deflate the pressure, resorted to a tricky tactic. He planted a fake story in *The New York Times*, which reported without attribution that "military leaders at the Pentagon, no less than General Taylor himself, are understood to be reluctant to send organized U.S. combat units into Southeast Asia." The article silenced Diem, who had immediately surmised its source, but it did not sway Taylor.

After a two-week tour of South Vietnam, he and his team repaired to Baguio, a cool mountain town in the Philippines, to draft a series of memorandums. They restated the basic tenets of the domino theory, warning that "if Vietnam goes, it will be exceedingly difficult if not impossible to hold Southeast Asia," whose loss would shatter "the faith that the United States has the will and the capacity to deal with the Communist offensive in that area." Then, outlining practical measures, they recommended an increase in the number of U.S. military advisers, and they urged that three squadrons of helicopters, manned by American pilots, be deployed in Vietnam to give mobility to the Saigon regime's forces. These and other steps, they said, would make the relationship between the United States and South Vietnam a "limited partnership" in which the American military advisory group would become "something nearer—but not quite—an operational headquarters in a theater of war."

But Taylor's most significant message to Kennedy—for the president's "eyes only"—proposed an initial commitment of eight thousand U.S. combat troops to Vietnam disguised as logistical legions to deal with a flood then ravaging the Mekong delta. Taylor would later explain that this was a "deliberate straddle," meaning that he had merely offered Kennedy an option. His cables to the White House at the time, however, plainly indicate that he favored direct American intervention. The U.S. soldiers would "act as an advance party of such additional forces as may be introduced," and he minimized potential fighting conditions, saying that South Vietnam "is not an excessively difficult or unpleasant place to operate." And, foreshadowing his later advice to President Johnson, he brushed aside the risk of a major response from North Vietnam to an American buildup, presuming that it could be discouraged by U.S. bombing of its territory: "North Vietnam is extremely vulnerable to conventional bombing. . . . There is no case for fearing a mass onslaught of Communist manpower into South Vietnam and its neighboring states, particularly if our air power is allowed a free hand against logistical targets."

Thus Taylor started out with the same misperception held by his French and American predecessors in appraising the conflict in strictly military terms. Long after the war had ended, he had not altered his opinion, telling an interviewer that the Kennedy administration should have deployed "a strong American combat force right then, and see whether that wouldn't deter the enemy when they saw that indeed the United States was ready to fight for this place if necessary."

Taylor's less prominent companions on the voyage to Vietnam in

1961 saw the problem in broader dimensions. William Jorden, a former newspaperman who had joined the State Department, observed with alarm that numbers of South Vietnamese officials, soldiers, and ordinary citizens had "lost confidence" in Diem. Another State Department specialist, Sterling Cottrell, emphasized that the war was being waged in the villages, where "foreign military forces themselves cannot win," and he questioned whether the Diem regime could succeed even with American assistance. "It would be a mistake," he warned, "for the United States to commit itself irrevocably to the defeat of the Communists."

In Washington, McNamara and the joint chiefs of staff rejected Taylor's proposal as inadequate. The expedition of only eight thousand American combat troops to Vietnam, they said, "probably will not tip the scales decisively [and] we would be almost certain to get increasingly mired down in an inclusive struggle." To show that "we mean business," they urged the deployment of six U.S. divisions—some two hundred thousand men. The recommendation put President Kennedy in a quandary. He could not alienate the Pentagon, which had powerful sympathizers in Congress, but he would not make such a commitment. Juggling, he persuaded McNamara to join Rusk in drafting a less aggressive memorandum that approved more aid to Diem, but deferred the combat option. So Kennedy, while refusing to quit, was clearly afraid to speed up the process of escalation. Or, as he confided to Arthur Schlesinger: "The troops will march in, the bands will play, the crowds will cheer, and in four days everyone will have forgotten. Then we will be told we have to send in more troops. It's like taking a drink. The effect wears off, and you have to take another."

But Kennedy's restraint was illusory. All the rhetoric now emanating from his administration reiterated its resolve to stop Communism in Southeast Asia, so that he could not backtrack without jeopardizing the American government's prestige—and in time that consideration would become the main motive for the U.S. commitment in Vietnam. The involvement also deepened with the rapid arrival of more and more American advisers and equipment to shore up the Diem regime. The number of advisers had already quadrupled before the Taylor mission from fewer than seven hundred to some three thousand, and the figure climbed to sixteen thousand over the next two years. American pilots began to fly combat sorties out of Bienhoa, an air base north of Saigon, their flights camouflaged as training exercises for Vietnamese.

The growing U.S. military investment in Vietnam was kept secret, partly because it violated the Geneva agreement, and partly to deceive the American public. One morning in December 1961, I was sipping coffee with a U.S. army press officer on the terrace of Saigon's Majestic Hotel as an American aircraft carrier, the *Core*, turned a bend in the river and steamed toward us, the first shipment of forty-seven helicopters strapped to its deck. Astonished, I grabbed the officer's arm, shouting: "Look at that carrier." He directed a mock squint in the direction of the gigantic vessel and replied: "I don't see nothing."

McNamara had been a brilliant corporation executive who could scan a balance sheet with unerring speed and skill. When he made the first of his many trips to Vietnam in May 1962, he looked at the figures and concluded optimistically after only forty-eight hours in the country that "every quantitative measurement . . . shows that we are winning the war."

No conflict in history was studied in such detail as it was being waged. Military and civilian officials from nearly every Washington agency would sooner or later conduct surveys in Vietnam, along with specialists from dozens of private think tanks, like the RAND Corporation and the Stanford Research Institute. They included weapons technicians, economists, sociologists, political scientists, anthropologists, agronomists, biologists, chemists, and public opinion pollsters. They investigated the effects of defoliants, the impact of bombs, the efficiency of cannon. They scoured villages and interviewed peasants. They interrogated enemy defectors and prisoners. They pored over captured Communist documents and scrutinized Hanoi statements—and they produced voluminous graphs, charts, pamphlets, brochures, and books. But the statistics somehow failed to convey an accurate picture of the problem, much less offer solutions.

For the missing element in the "quantitative measurement" that guided McNamara and other U.S. policy makers was the qualitative dimension that could not easily be recorded. There was no way to calibrate the motivation of Vietcong guerrillas. Nor could computers be programmed to describe the hopes and fears of Vietnamese peasants. The arcane maneuvers of Diem and his family also baffled U.S. diplomats, who were even less equipped to influence their decisions.

As the war intensified, American civilian officials and soldiers were spurred on by a myopic sense of "can-doism"—the conviction that, as Americans, they could achieve anything anywhere. Their belief in their own omnipotence was stimulated, too, by pressures from their superiors in Saigon and Washington. To adopt a negative attitude was defeatism, and there were no promotions for defeatists. In contrast, positive reports were rewarded, even if they bore little resemblance to the truth.

Yet another impulse that generated Americans in Vietnam was a brand of missionary zeal, not unlike the credo that had inspired early French imperialists. But Americans gave it a different guise. They were not imposing colonialism but, rather, helping the Vietnamese to perfect their institutions. They called it "nation-building," and they would have been arrogant had they not been utterly sincere in their naive belief that they could really reconstruct Vietnamese society along Western lines. As they sought to teach Diem's bureaucrats the intricacies of government procedure or economic planning, however, they soon discovered to their chagrin that the Vietnamese marched to a melody alien to Western ears. During the American presidential election of 1960, for instance, the U.S. Information Service tabulated the incoming returns in the window of its Saigon library in an effort to publicize democracy in action. American officials were ecstatic at the turnout—until they learned that the crowd of Vietnamese had assembled solely to lay bets on the numbers appearing on the scoreboard.

But U.S. withdrawal was unthinkable. Beginning in late 1961, the flow of American advisers and matériel increased—along with a rising crescendo of declarations hardening the U.S. commitment. On a trip to Saigon in early 1962, Robert Kennedy affirmed that "we are going to win," and that theme was echoed at the time by his brother's political adversary, Richard Nixon, who asserted that the United States ought to allocate "all the resources of which it is capable" to attain victory. Almost every American newspaper agreed with *The New York Times*, which stated in an editorial that the Vietnam war "is a struggle this country cannot shirk."

Despite their verbal devotion to a common goal, the Kennedy administration and the Diem regime were proceeding along separate tracks. The U.S. establishment was also split, with one faction stressing the need for a stronger political, economic, and social focus to America's involvement in Southeast Asia, and the other favoring a largely military approach. The discord was evident, in part at least, in divergent attitudes taken toward the "strategic hamlet" program, a vast and expensive enterprise launched in early 1962.

The plan was to corral peasants into armed stockades, thereby depriving the Vietcong of their support, which could not survive without the population just as fish die outside water, as Mao Zedong's image put it. The *agroville* scheme, a similar effort three years earlier, had been a botch, yet Diem and his brother Nhu clung to their brainchild, and they were encouraged by Robert Thompson, a British counterinsurgency specialist who had successfully promoted a similar program in the fight against Communist guerrillas in Malaya. But the Malayan experience did not quite fit Vietnam. The insurgents in Malaya had been predominantly ethnic Chinese detested by the Malays, while Vietnamese peasants and Vietcong were indistinguishable from one another. Malaya was chronically short of rice, so that the enemy could be starved into submission, while South Vietnam was a granary in which food could not easily be denied to the Vietcong. And there was the question of objectives.

Diem and Nhu saw the strategic hamlet program as essentially a means to spread their influence rather than a device to infuse peasants with the will to resist the Vietcong. Nhu, personally taking charge, was obsessed by numbers. He tried to build stockades as fast as possible, and Thompson himself would afterward disavow them: "No attention was paid to their purpose. Their creation became the purpose in itself."

A pilot project dubbed Operation Sunrise was launched in March 1962 in Binh Duong province, a landscape of jungles and rubber plantations north of Saigon. Vietcong units, strong in the area, melted away as government troops poured in to set up five strategic hamlets in Ben Cat district. The Vietcong stood back, watching the regime fumble. The first stockade, for example, was situated so far from the nearest market that only seventy out of two hundred peasant families moved voluntarily, carrying their meager belongings on bicycles or on their backs. They were soon disappointed when the government withheld the funds promised them until it was sure they would not bolt. The peasants were supposed to defend the hamlet themselves, but most of the able-bodied men had rallied to the Vietcong, perhaps less out of conviction than in defiance of the regime's coercive methods.

Two Vietnamese-speaking RAND researchers, John Donnell and Gerald Hickey, concluded after observing the Ben Cat test that it was being bungled. But with U.S. approval and financing, the government continued to commit the same errors elsewhere. Given catchy titles in different sectors, like Operation Sea Swallow or Operation Royal Phoenix, the program surged ahead; the regime announced with dubious precision at the end of September 1962 that 4,322,034 people, or 33.39 percent of the population, were in strategic hamlets—with more scheduled to move. Donnell later called the figure "statistical razzle-dazzle" of the kind that pleased McNamara. It also nourished Nhu's fantasy that he had sparked a rural revolution that would undermine the Vietcong.

In reality, the program often converted peasants into Vietcong sympathizers. Peasants in many places resented working without pay to dig moats, implant bamboo stakes, and erect fences against an enemy that did not threaten them but directed its sights against government officials. Numbers of strategic hamlets, therefore, were Potemkin villages mainly designed to impress visiting dignitaries. Even peasants who agreed to join local self-defense groups were disenchanted when the government failed to furnish them with weapons, and many were antagonized by corrupt officials who embezzled money earmarked for seed, fertilizer, and irrigation as well as medical care, education, and other social benefits.

Nhu, an unleavened intellectual who was more at home in the Latin Quarter than in Vietnam, neither understood the countryside nor really cared about the peasants. He issued instructions based on his theories, and the South Vietnamese bureaucracy, much of it composed of remnants from the French colonial period, routinely obeyed. Ancient patterns were wantonly disrupted in many areas. In the Mekong delta, for instance, where communities were traditionally strung out along canals, sometimes for miles, villagers were concentrated, often under duress, in barbed wire enclosures from which they had to walk long distances to their fields. Frequently, strategic hamlets were thrown together in such slapdash fashion that Vietcong agents remained inside, acting as informers for their comrades.

Interestingly, Nhu's chief lieutenant in carrying out the strategic hamlet program was Colonel Pham Ngoc Thao, the secret Communist operative. Years afterward, Communist sources would disclose to me that Thao had deliberately propelled the program ahead at breakneck speed in order to estrange South Vietnam's peasants and drive them into the arms of the Vietcong. Nhu had been duped.

At the working level, American soldiers and civilians in Vietnam decried the strategic hamlet scheme. One U.S. officer in the Mekong delta criticized Diem's lopsided priorities, saying that he was "trying to hold everything and thus holding very little." Another asserted that the strategic hamlets were paralyzing South Vietnamese forces that ought to be fighting the Vietcong, and yet another pointed out that Diem's officials totally misconstrued the program. "They only want to please the regime. They haven't the faintest idea what makes peasants tick—and how can they? They're city boys who earned promotions by kissing the asses of their bosses, and all they care about is getting back to Saigon to get promoted again." Diem predictably dismissed such misgivings, describing the strategic hamlets as "a means to institute basic democracy" in Vietnam, and Nhu termed them "an enthusiastic movement of solidarity and self-sufficiency."

Despite negative appraisals from the field, senior Kennedy administration figures hailed the program. Roger Hilsman, then the State Department intelligence director, called it "an effective strategic concept," and McNamara praised its progress in "countering subversion." But these accolades mainly reflected a yearning at the upper echelons of the U.S. establishment for positive signs. General Paul Harkins, head of the American military assistance command in South Vietnam, fed Washington rosy reports, saying openly that "I am an optimist, and I am not going to allow my staff to be pessimistic."

Hopes were no substitute for reality, however, and the strategic hamlets soon crumbled. In late 1962, though, the introduction of U.S. helicopters and other equipment into Vietnam did seem to make a difference—for a while.

The U.S. helicopters, piloted by Americans, had two tasks. Some ferried South Vietnamese troops into action, while others, bristling with machine guns and rockets, flanked the airlift to attack the battlefield before the landing. I participated in such an operation at the time aboard a UH 1-B, or "Huey," one of a fleet of six armed choppers accompanying three South Vietnamese battalions in an assault against suspected Vietcong positions in the Camau peninsula, at the southernmost tip of the Mekong delta.

We took off in a cloud of dust from Saigon's Tonsonhut airport at sunrise, the crew consisting of two American officers, one at the controls and the other directing fire, and two enlisted men as spotters. We wore bulletproof vests and sat on heavy flak jackets, and this helicopter mission, like others I later experienced, would be hours of boredom punctuated by a few minutes of fright.

The Mekong delta lay below us, an intricate tapestry of canals and irrigation ditches. The crew members chatted casually, one of them snapping photos as if he were a tourist on an excursion. Soon we observed the target ahead, an area already bombed and strafed by artillery and fighter aircraft. We circled over the site as the troop carriers descended like giant birds to a landing zone. Peering out the open helicopter door, I could discern figures in black pajamas on the ground, scurrying in different directions. It was impossible to determine whether they were guerrillas or ordinary peasants, but the Vietcong was certainly in the vicinity. Tracer bullets came toward us, rising in arcs, and the chopper shook as the crew replied with a salvo of rockets and the rattle of machine guns. I held my breath, fearful of a hit. But we were spared, and soon cruised lazily back to Saigon as the crew consumed box lunches of fried chicken and lemonade. When we landed at Tonsonhut airport, one of the officers relieved the tension with a quip: "Now how much do you suppose that outing cost the American taxpayers?"

Television screens and publications in the United States were then already portraying Americans in combat, but the public at home had not yet grasped the implications of the phenomenon, perhaps because casualties were small. The country was also prepared to trust the president, even though he blatantly dissembled. For example, there was no further inquiry when Kennedy, asked at a news conference on January 15, 1962, if U.S. troops were engaged in fighting in Vietnam, delivered a one-word answer: "No."

The heliborne deployments initially lacerated the Vietcong, whose remote sanctuaries could now be penetrated, but the guerrillas gradually adapted to the new challenge. They dug trenches and tunnels as shelters against helicopter raids, and they methodically practiced assaults against full-scale mock-ups of choppers constructed in jungle clearings. They also acquired more sophisticated weapons, either infiltrated from North Vietnam or by ambushing South Vietnamese units. Soon they were able to mortar helicopters on the ground or pepper them aloft with automatic fire. As we nursed our beers at a Saigon officers' club, one American chopper pilot was still shaking after a night flight back from the Mekong delta. Bad weather had forced him to cruise at low altitude, and he said: "Man, it was the Fourth of July—tracers coming up everywhere."

The influx of U.S. hardware at that time was tiny compared to the later vast flow of matériel into Vietnam. But the equipment paradoxically sapped the Diem regime. For the aid, overwhelmingly military, confirmed Diem's conviction that he was waging a conventional conflict, and it stiffened his resistance to political, economic, and social reforms. Moreover, his battalions became more and more reluctant to confront the Vietcong squarely, relying instead on American air strikes and artillery shells to do their job for them. This suited Diem, who instructed his officers to avoid casualties. Their primary role, in his view, was not to fight the Vietcong, but to protect him against possible coups in Saigon.

The Diem army's shortcomings became dramatically apparent in January 1963 near Ap Bac, a village in the Mekong delta forty miles southwest of Saigon, where an inferior Vietcong contingent mauled a South Vietnamese division that could have scored a victory had it not been led by pusillanimous officers. But the officers, personally picked by Diem, exemplified his regime. So their defeat was less a military catastrophe than a reflection of his convoluted priorities.

General Huynh Van Cao, the South Vietnamese commander of the Fourth Corps, which embraced the whole of the Mekong delta, was a classic Diem loyalist whose fidelity had earned him promotion over more competent colleagues. A Catholic from Hué, he belonged to Nhu's secret political organization, the Can Lao, and he rarely saw action, preferring instead to intrigue in Saigon, where choice appointments could be gained. He had recently turned over the Seventh Division, the principal South Vietnamese unit in the area, to a protégé, Colonel Bui Dinh Dam, also a Catholic high on Diem's list of favorites. Dam theoretically exercised authority over the province chief, Major Lam Quang Tho, whose local troops were supposed to beef up the regulars. In practice, however, Tho took his orders directly from Diem, usually without Dam's knowledge. Diem constantly played his subordinates off against each other in this way, believing that he could thus prevent conspiracies to oust him.

The American in the middle of the muddle was Lieutenant Colonel John Paul Vann, the top U.S. adviser with the Seventh Division, a controversial figure who would soon become even more controversial after the Ap Bac debacle. Vann's irreverent candor was a refreshing antidote to the overweening optimism of prominent American officials in both Saigon and Washington, and it endeared him to American correspondents. But Vann also patronized the Vietnamese in a manner that characterized many Americans in Vietnam, who considered it their duty to educate the "natives"—just as, in their day, French administrators were committed to the *mission civilisatrice*. As Vann once told David Halberstam, then a *New York Times* reporter: "These people may be the world's greatest lovers, but they're not the world's greatest fighters. But they're good people, and they can win a war if someone shows them how."

Vann and other American advisers had repeatedly boasted that the elusive Vietcong guerrillas could be whipped "if they would only stand and fight." The chance for such an encounter finally loomed in late December 1962, when reliable intelligence located three Vietcong companies reinforced by local partisans in the neighborhood of Ap Bac. Vann urged Colonel Dam to move on January 1, 1963. But Dam considerately delayed for a day so that the American chopper pilots could sleep off New Year's Eve. The Vietcong, learning of the imminent operation, prepared defensive positions along a canal running for roughly a mile from Ap Bac to the next hamlet, Ap Tan Thoi. The canal, bordered by trees and shrubs, offered the Vietcong both conceal-ment and a clear range of fire across rice fields. The French had fought the Vietminh on almost the same terrain a decade earlier—and lost.

The South Vietnamese Seventh Division and its auxiliary units, which outnumbered the Vietcong by a ratio of ten to one, planned a three-pronged pincer. An infantry regiment would be landed to the north by helicopter while two regional battalions approached by foot from the south and a rifle squadron advanced from the west aboard armored personnel carriers, which functioned as the equivalent of light tanks. Three additional South Vietnamese companies remained in reserve, and the entire force had artillery and air support. By any calculation, the Vietcong should have been doomed. The Vietcong commander expect-ed defeat, having written in his diary, which was later found: "Better to fight and die than run and be slaughtered."

Patiently waiting until the government troops came into their sights, the Vietcong guerrillas held their fire as the first three waves of helicop-ters lifted the infantry regiment into the zone. Then, as a fourth wave arrived bearing reserves, the guerrillas opened up with automatic weap-ons. By noon, five choppers had been downed, three of them on return trips to save the crews of two helicopters that had been crippled earlier. For the next three hours, despite pleas by his American adviser, the South Vietnamese armored commander balked at rescuing the crews. When he finally moved, he deployed the vehicles slowly and separately, so that they were easy targets for the Vietcong, which raked them mercilessly, killing fourteen of the South Vietnamese machine gunners. Three Americans, all helicopter crew members, also died.

The spectacle was equally grim to the south. Major Tho, the province chief in charge of the two regional battalions on that flank, had abruptly halted his units after losing an officer. Colonel Vann, flying over the scene in an observation plane, radioed him to continue, but Tho refused to budge. Nor would he heed the orders of Colonel Dam, the Seventh Division commander. He had, in effect, opted out of the battle. By early afternoon, it was clear that the Vietcong could not be overrun.

The eastern side of the combat area, mostly open farmland, had deliberately been left unguarded to permit artillery and aircraft to deci-mate the Vietcong guerrillas if they tried to flee across the exposed terrain. The challenge now was to block their avenue of retreat until morning, and Vann advised that paratroopers be deployed for that purpose. But his proposal provoked yet another squabble with the South Vietnamese. General Cao, the Fourth Corps commander, felt that his army had already sustained too many casualties, and he waffled. Finally, with dusk coming on fast, as it does in the tropics, he agreed to bring in an airborne battalion—but to the west, where its presence would be useless. He prevailed over American protests, and the worst occurred. Landing at twilight, when it was difficult to distinguish friend from foe, the paratroopers quickly found themselves skirmishing with other South Vietnamese in the confusion.

By nightfall, the shooting had ended. A total of sixty-one government soldiers had been killed and a hundred had been wounded. The Vietcong had evaporated into the darkness, leaving only three bodies behind. Now the investigations and recriminations would begin.

"A miserable fucking performance, just like it always is," said Vann, excoriating the South Vietnamese officers. Several months afterward, having quit in disgust, he publicly charged that Diem wanted the war to stumble along inconclusively so that he could continue to receive American aid. That accusation, however valid, reflected Vann's fundamentally sanguine view that the conflict could be won, and he would later return to Vietnam and be killed—the apotheosis of the American for whom the anti-Communist struggle had become a crusade.

The U.S. top brass refused to see the Ap Bac episode as a disaster. Admiral Harry Felt, the American commander for the Pacific, flew into Saigon two days later and called it a South Vietnamese triumph because, as he pointed out, the Vietcong had abandoned its positions. His assessment, shared by other senior U.S. officers and civilians, again underlined their concept of the conflict: a conventional contest for territory, like World War II or the Korean war, the experiences that marked them.

The outcome at Ap Bac aggravated the friction then growing between the American government and the news media. Neither Kennedy nor his successors would impose censorship, which would have required them to acknowledge that a real war was being waged. Instead, they wanted journalists to cooperate by accentuating the positive. Just after the Ap Bac battle, when Peter Arnett of the Associated Press asked him a tough question, Admiral Felt shot back: "Get on the team."

Following his resignation, Vann reproved his superiors in Washington and Saigon for their "tendency to play down the real picture" in Vietnam because of a "consuming desire . . . to show some palpable results." The remark went to the heart of the matter, which was not a simple debate between army officers and civilian officials. American advisers in the field, such as Vann, mostly concurred with their middle-level State Department and CIA counterparts that South Vietnam's prospects were dim unless Diem overhauled his regime. But they came up against Nolting and Harkins in Saigon as well as higher ranking Washington figures like Rusk, McNamara, Taylor, and Rostow, who contended that the war could be effectively waged without pressing Diem to change. Nor did the debate merely focus on the question of whether the conflict was strictly military or purely political. Both sides realized that it was a mixture, but they disagreed over emphasis. With variations, the dispute persisted throughout the next decade.

Frederick Nolting, the U.S. ambassador in Saigon, had been miscast. A tall and gracious Virginian, known as Fritz to his friends, he had previously served in the chanceries of Europe, where diplomats played by the rules. He abhorred untidy discord—so much so that he once asked a television interviewer to replace a portrait of Jefferson on the wall behind him with Washington, who was "less controversial." Straightforward and guileless, he could not quite adapt to Vietnam. Not that he was blind to Diem's shortcomings, but in his opinion the military effort came first, and he repeatedly recommended to Washington, as he said in one cable in 1961, that "efficiency" was more important than the "nebulous concept" of political reform. Consistent with that view, he also believed that South Vietnam's dissidents were at fault for not cooperating with the regime—even though it was Diem who refused to broaden his administration to include dissenters. On February 15, 1962, in an astonishing display of naiveté, Nolting publicly admonished the cream of Saigon society, telling the local Rotary club: "What a marvelous transformation would take place in this country if all those who criticize their government would decide to work with it and for it."

His speech disturbed numbers of South Vietnamese middle-class professionals, who had hoped that the United States would lean on Diem to liberalize. And it was followed one morning a week later by a dramatic incident.

I awoke suddenly at seven o'clock that morning in February 1962 to the thud of bombs and the rattle of automatic weapons. Years afterward it might have been a Communist attack, but I knew then that the Vietcong lacked the strength to assault Saigon. Rushing to my hotel room window, I peered across the city to see smoke billowing above the presidential palace, nine or ten blocks away. I pulled on my clothes, ran downstairs, and sprinted up Tu Do, the main street, to the Boulevard Norodom, a handsome avenue that opened onto the palace, an imposing structure that dated back to French colonial days. It was now a flaming shambles. Overhead, beneath a low cloud cover, two fighter aircraft were circling in an almost leisurely racetrack pattern. I recognized them as AD-6s, World War II models given to the South Vietnamese air force by the United States. They were dropping napalm and bombs, and as I watched, sprawled on the sidewalk a hundred yards from the palace, they came around again and again to strafe their target with machine-gun fire. I presumed that Diem and his family were inside, probably dead.

The Saigon garrison, not knowing whether the airplanes were acting alone or in concert with a ground force, was caught off balance. Tanks and truckloads of troops sped to battle stations, and antiaircraft batteries began to fill the sky with flak, nearly hitting loyal fighter airplanes that had taken off in pursuit of the attackers. Sirens screamed as police cars careered around the city, and the heavy scent of cordite pervaded the air. Amid the uproar, though, I noticed that the population seemed to be strangely calm, almost detached. Girls in *ao dais* pedaled their bicycles through the streets as always, their silk skirts billowing behind them, and motorists even stopped for traffic lights.

The storm ended within an hour—miraculously for Diem and his family. An early riser, Diem had been perusing a biography of George Washington, a gift from an American visitor, when the first bomb fell into his wing of the palace. It failed to explode. He dashed to a fortified cellar, where he had survived the attempted coup in 1960, and there he was joined by his brother Thuc, as well as Nhu, with his wife and children, who had been in other parts of the building. Madame Nhu had fractured her arm tumbling downstairs, and she wept through the ordeal. Three guards and servants died, and thirty were injured. But the family emerged alive and Diem, in a brief radio announcement, attributed his escape to "divine protection."

It had not been a plot, but an aborted aerial assassination. The two insurgent pilots, trained in France and the United States, were among South Vietnam's finest. They had taken off that morning on a mission against the Vietcong in the Mekong delta, but had turned back to stage their assault. One of them, who had bailed out over the Saigon River after his airplane had been nicked by flak, survived imprisonment and died in a raid on North Vietnam in 1965. The other, Lieutenant Nguyen Van Cu, flew on to Cambodia, believing he had killed Diem. He explained his motives to me when he returned to Vietnam after Diem's overthrow the next year. He had been denied promotion for six years, he said, because his father had belonged to a dissident political party. The war against the Vietcong, he complained, was not being prosecuted with sufficient vigor. And, in a reference to Nolting's speech to the Rotary club, he added: "I felt that the Americans had slammed the door on those of us who really wanted to fight against the Communists."

Diem's extraordinary experience reconfirmed his conviction that his domestic adversaries were his real danger. He dug himself deeper into his family, whom he could trust. He also receded from running the country's daily affairs, delegating more and more authority to his brother Nhu, who became the regime's principal theoretician and manager. As one American diplomat then in Saigon quipped: "Until surgery invents a technique for operating on Siamese twins, they cannot be separated."

I saw Nhu periodically in those days, and he appeared to me to be approaching madness. I could not substantiate the allegation of his critics that he smoked opium, though he often ranted and raved like a drug addict. He had graduated from the Ecole Nationale des Chartes, an elite French school for archivists, and he returned to Vietnam before the outbreak of World War II filled with assorted notions picked up in the Latin Quarter. Foremost among them was "personalism," a philosophy conceived in France during the 1930s by Emmanuel Mounier and other Catholic progressives. Analogous to the ideas of thinkers like Karl Jaspers and Martin Buber, who had emphasized human dignity as an alternative to modern materialism, it was never intended to be more than an abstraction. But it became Nhu's response to both Communist autocracy and Western liberalism. As the Diem government's official ideology, however, the doctrine suffered from two flaws. It was incomprehensible to South Vietnam's intelligentsia, much less to its masses. Clearly, too, Nhu was striving to put a gloss of respectability on his various clandestine activities. Mounier's heirs in Paris, who edited the left-wing Catholic review *Esprit*, denounced Nhu as a fraud.

Nhu's real talent was organizational. He had formed student movements in his youth, and, under Diem, he created a web of covert political, security, labor, and other groups, all in the tradition of the secret societies that had flourished in Asia for centuries. Emulating the Communists, he built a structure of five-man cells inside the South Vietnamese army and bureaucracy to spy on dissidents and to advance those loyal to the regime. But the system had no other purpose than to preserve Diem's administration, a narrow objective that limited its ability to inspire popular support.

If Nhu's intrigues blemished the Saigon government's credibility, its reputation was tarnished even more egregiously by Madame Nhu, who soared into notoriety as her husband's influence heightened. She promoted herself as the reincarnation of the legendary Trung sisters, who had led Vietnam's struggle against China in the first century, and the statue that she had erected in their honor was plainly a monument to herself. Sexually suggestive in her décolleté gowns, which shocked old-fashioned Vietnamese, she occupied a peculiar place as the only woman close to the misogynic Diem. She often infuriated him in private and embarrassed him publicly with her provocative remarks, but he tolerated her out of fidelity to the family. She became more and more outspoken as he sank into seclusion. Her power, however, signaled a regime in decay—just as, to cite contemporary Chinese parallels, the rise of Madame Chiang Kai-shek hastened her husband's collapse, and the growing sway of Mao Zedong's wife, Jiang Qing, mirrored his decline. Ironically, Diem himself had written long before he took office that "the history of China bears witness to the grave crises brought on by the empresses and their relatives." Now, in Madame Nhu, he had his empress.

Named Le Xuan, or Beautiful Spring, she was born in 1924, the second of three children. Her paternal grandfather had collaborated with the French, working his way up in the colonial administration and amassing a fortune in the process. Her father, Tran Van Chuong, studied law in Paris and returned to practice in Vietnam, where he wed an aristocratic lady related to the imperial family. They settled in Hanoi, where Madame Chuong became a glittering hostess, entertaining the French and the Frenchified Vietnamese at her lavish villa. A renowned beauty, she reputedly had a series of lovers, among them the handsome Ngo Dinh Nhu, just back from France and employed at the National Library. Nhu was six years her junior, but fourteen years older than Le Xuan, her daughter, whom he married in 1943. Le Xuan had dropped out of the Lycée Albert Sarraut, the prestigious French high school in Hanoi, where she had been a mediocre student. Fluent in French, the language spoken at home, she never learned to write in her native tongue. In later years, she would draft her speeches in French and have them translated into Vietnamese.

When the French dismissed Nhu, penalizing him for Diem's nationalist activities, he took his bride to Dalat, where they lived comfortably during France's war against the Vietminh. He edited a newspaper and dabbled in politics and she gave birth to four children. In 1955, after Diem ousted Bao Dai in the rigged referendum, the Nhus moved into the presidential palace in Saigon and Madame Nhu quickly adopted an imperious manner as South Vietnam's First Lady. She also began to display the spunkiness that later became her hallmark, annoying Diem to such an extent that he nearly took the advice of General J. Lawton Collins, then U.S. ambassador, who bluntly told him that she was a "troublemaker" and should be sent away. But Diem would not act without consulting Thuc, his older brother and head of the clan. Thuc, though a Catholic clergyman, offered Confucian counsel. The family must be kept intact.

Recalling Collins's attempt to oust her, Madame Nhu fiercely reproached the United States during the years that followed, alleging on more than one occasion that Americans were plotting with Vietnamese dissidents to topple Diem. She also became South Vietnam's most dynamic bluestocking. She promoted an edict abolishing divorce and making adultery a crime, and, in the name of protecting Vietnam's "traditional virtue," she banned abortions, contraceptives, beauty contests, and boxing matches. She closed Saigon's nightclubs and ballrooms, asserting that "dancing with death is enough," but she allowed cafés to remain open—on condition that bar girls, most of them prostitutes, wear white tunics that made them look like dental assistants. The permissive Vietnamese scorned her sanctimonious decrees, especially since her own siblings were scarcely models of rectitude. Her playboy brother, Khiem, used his lofty connections to extort money from wealthy merchants. Her stringent divorce law had also been designed to prevent her sister, Le Chi, who had a French lover, from breaking with her husband, whose enormous riches would have been denied to the family.

Though I cannot pretend to have been prescient, I sensed the rot then eroding the Diem regime during a conversation with Nhu in his den one day in early 1963. I had asked him to comment on the charge, swirling through Saigon, that he and his wife were corrupt. It was an outrageous question, but the kind that had to be posed. To my surprise, he replied softly and persuasively.

"It's not true. We have nothing. You can examine our bank accounts. We are poor."

"But people think you're dishonest," I pressed.

"I don't care what the people think," he said.

Approaching the Vietnam challenge like industrial managers, Washington strategists reckoned that larger investments of men, money, and matériel in 1962 would logically yield larger results. Indeed, they euphorically began to plan a phased withdrawal of U.S. personnel and a reduction of American subsidies. According to their timetable, the number of advisers would decline from twelve thousand in 1964 to a spare training mission of only fifteen hundred four years later, and aid would drop proportionately. The word "victory" now popped up in many utterances made by prominent American military and civilian officials. "There is a new feeling of confidence that victory is possible," said McNamara, and Admiral Felt predicted "victory in three years." But President Kennedy was prudent: "We don't see the end of the tunnel, but I must say I don't think it is darker than it was a year ago, and in some ways [it is] lighter."

Actually, a thousand U.S. advisers went home in December 1963, but their departure from Vietnam was essentially a bureaucratic accounting exercise. A year later, contrary to Washington's plan, the American contingent in Vietnam swelled to twenty-three thousand, and further deployments were in the offing.

Mike Mansfield, the Senate majority leader, clearly saw the danger ahead and its causes. A liberal Catholic who had initially sponsored Diem, he was a lean, leathery, laconic politician from Montana with the acuity and courage to change his mind. So when Kennedy sent him to Vietnam in late 1962 to survey the scene, he returned with brutally frank conclusions. The United States had spent $2 billion in seven years, yet "substantially the same difficulties remain if, indeed, they have not been compounded." The fault lay not only in the Vietcong threat, but also in the shortcomings of U.S. policy—and with the Diem regime, for its failure to share political power. Mansfield recommended a careful reassessment of American interests in Southeast Asia to avoid deeper U.S. involvement in Vietnam, where the "primary responsibility" rests with the South Vietnamese themselves. And he warned: "It is their country, their future that is at stake, not ours. To ignore that reality will not only be immensely costly in terms of American lives and resources, but it may also draw us inexorably into some variation of the unenviable position in Vietnam that was formerly occupied by the French. . . . The great increase in American military commitment this year has tended to point us in that general direction."

Shortly afterward, at a party aboard his yacht, Kennedy rebutted Mansfield's gloomy report. "You asked me to go out there," answered Mansfield, to which Kennedy replied frostily: "Well, I'll read it again." Later, Kennedy confided to Kenneth O'Donnell, an assistant: "I got angry with Mike for disagreeing with our policy so completely, and I got angry with myself because I found myself agreeing with him."

Kennedy also intimated to O'Donnell that he would have the Americans withdraw from Vietnam after his re-election in 1964, even at the risk of being "damned everywhere as a Communist appeaser." But whatever he said privately, Kennedy's actions and statements at the time were tough. In 1963, for example, he responded to a flare-up in Laos by sending three thousand troops into northeastern Thailand near the Laotian border. He could not see "the burden being lightened" in Southeast Asia during the coming year, he declared. Nor would he retreat from South Vietnam, even though a series of internal convulsions there in 1963 were to implicate him in one of the strangest episodes in the annals of American foreign policy and practice.

8 The End of Diem

The Brahmin and the Mandarin: Henry Cabot Lodge, American ambassador to Saigon, with President Diem in 1963. Lodge had little patience for Diem, whom he felt was hindering the American effort to help South Vietnam fight the Communists.

A Buddhist monk burns himself to death in Saigon in June 1963 in protest against the South Vietnamese government's mistreatment of Buddhists. This suicide, the first of several by Buddhist militants, sparked widespread demonstrations against the government.

Tri Quang (left), a Buddhist monk, displayed phenomenal skill in mobilizing South Vietnam's Buddhists to protest against the Diem regime. He and other monks here stage a sit-down strike on a street in Saigon.

Dr. Tran Kim Tuyen, a
northern Catholic who
relied heavily on CIA
advice and funds, was not
only head of Diem's secret
police but also one of the
earliest plotters against the
regime. He was later
arrested and jailed by some
of his co-conspirators.

One of the early plotters
against the Diem regime,
Colonel Pham Ngoc
Thao, was revealed after
the war to have been a
secret Communist agent.
The son of an upper-class
southern Catholic family,
he had served with the
Vietminh in the war
against the French.

General Duong Van Minh, who was chosen to head the officers plotting against Diem because of his popularity with the South Vietnamese army. Minh's real passions in life were orchids and tennis.

Lieutenant Colonel Lucien Conein (rear), a CIA agent who served as liaison with the generals who conspired to overthrow Diem. His special contact was General Tran Van Don (center). Both were born in France and had been friends for years. Others (left to right) are Generals Le Van Kim, Ton That Dinh, Nguyen Van Vy, and Mai Huu Xuan.

Ngo Dinh Diem's brother Nhu in his cluttered study in the presidential palace. He tried to organize a counterconspiracy, but his complicated maneuver failed when he was double-crossed by General Ton That Dinh, who he believed was on his side.

General Dinh, commander of the Saigon military region and thus a key figure in the Diem coup. A bombastic character, he was distrusted by nearly everyone.

The streets of Saigon were littered when opponents of Diem broke into the office of a newspaper sympathetic to the government. Diem's overthrow was greeted with jubilation by the Saigon populace, which had hated his harsh rule.

A mutinous South Vietnamese soldier inside the presidential palace on the morning of November 2, 1963, after Diem and Nhu had fled to a hiding place in the Saigon suburbs.

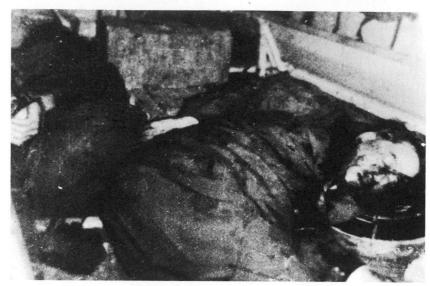

The bodies of Diem and Nhu in the back of an armored personnel carrier, in which they were murdered by two insurgent officers after their capture on November 2. They had surrendered, hoping to be permitted to leave the country.

Three weeks after Diem's death, President Kennedy was assassinated in Dallas. Kennedy's flag-draped coffin is seen here before the steps of the Capitol. The deaths of Kennedy and Diem led to a new phase in the American involvement in Vietnam.

This is an underdeveloped country economically, but a highly developed country politically.

—Tran Kim Tuyen

We are launched on a course from which there is no respectable turning back: the overthrow of the Diem government. . . . There is no possibility, in my view, that the war can be won under a Diem administration.

—Henry Cabot Lodge

At Saint Francis Xavier, a French mission church in Saigon's Chinese district of Cholon, the early morning Mass had just celebrated All Souls' Day, the day of the dead. A few minutes later, the congregation gone, two men in dark gray suits walked quickly through the shaded courtyard and entered the church. South Vietnam's President Ngo Dinh Diem and his brother Nhu, haggard after a sleepless night, were fugitives in the capital they had once commanded.

A few hours earlier, rebel soldiers had crushed the last of their loyal guards. The remote church was their final haven. They prayed and took Communion, their ultimate sacrament. Soon their crumpled corpses would be sprawled ignominiously across the deck of an armored car that rumbled through the streets of Saigon as the people cheered their downfall.

Diem, though dedicated, was doomed by his inflexible pride and the unbridled ambitions of his family. Ruling like an ancient emperor, he could not deal effectively with either the mounting Communist threat to his regime or the opposition of South Vietnam's turbulent factions alienated by his autocracy. His generals—some greedy for power, others antagonized by his style—turned against him. His end, after eight years in office, came amid a tangle of intrigue and violence as improbable as the most imaginative of melodramas.

His collapse would have been impossible without American complicity. President Kennedy, frustrated by Diem's inability to conciliate dissident groups in the face of the growing Communist challenge, conceded that the war could not be won under his aegis. Kennedy deferred to Henry Cabot Lodge, the U.S. ambassador in Saigon, who encouraged Diem's senior officers to stage a *coup d'état*. Once in motion, the plot spiraled out of control. Kennedy, shocked by Diem's murder, would also be assassinated—three weeks later.

America's responsibility for Diem's death haunted U.S. leaders during the years ahead, prompting them to assume a larger burden in Vietnam. Inefficient as Diem had been, his successors were worse. They squabbled among themselves, and the chronic turmoil in Saigon dashed America's hopes for progress on the battlefield as the Communists escalated their offensive. The U.S. commitment inexorably deepened. Diem's demise, then, marked a fresh phase in the conflict.

The end to the Diem regime began with a religious controversy that seemed, at first, to be trivial. But it quickly crystallized the accumulated other grievances against the government and swelled into a political upheaval.

The Vietnamese are not passionately spiritual. Like the Chinese, whose beliefs they have borrowed, they venerate scholars rather than priests, seeking harmony in the present rather than salvation in a hereafter. Thus they put a premium on ethics rather than on faith, and they can blend elements of Buddhism, Confucianism, and Taoism, their three pillars of wisdom, with animism, superstition, various forms of magic, idolatry, and, above all, ancestor worship. But the Mahayana school of Vietnamese Buddhism, gaudier than the Hinayana version found elsewhere in Southeast Asia, has tried more than the other creeds to adopt the trappings of a formal religion—partly in reaction to past repression and partly under the tutelage of modern reformers.

The ancient emperors of Vietnam recurrently persecuted Buddhists as a menace to their Confucian system of authority. The French, equally suspicious of potential threats to their power, limited the Buddhist clergy and curbed the construction of temples. Having ostensibly invaded Vietnam to spread Christianity, they favored Catholics. The Catholic Church became the largest landowner in the country. The French also imposed a "private" status on Buddhism, requiring its adherents to obtain official permission to conduct public activities. Diem never repealed that statute.

Diem counted on the thousands of Catholics who had fled south after the 1954 partition as his core constituency. He coddled them with key military and civilian posts, business deals, and property privileges. He underwrote Madame Nhu's puritanical campaigns as manifestations of Catholic morality, and he lobbied in Rome for his brother Thuc's appointment as archbishop of Saigon. The Vatican, loath to endorse the Ngo oligarchy too openly, assigned Ngo Dinh Thuc to Hué. But he spent most of his time in the capital, managing the Church's real estate—

and helping Diem and Nhu to manage the country. As the senior member, Thuc was pre-eminent inside the family.

Though Buddhist activists resented Catholic supremacy, they mainly focused on improving their own organization in an endeavor to match the Church's strength. They initiated recruitment drives, appealed for national cohesion, and affiliated with international Buddhist associations. Their antipathy toward Diem might have remained latent had he not committed a blunder which, given his own intransigence, was probably inevitable.

On May 8, 1963, as Buddhists assembled in Hué to celebrate the 2527th birthday of the Buddha, the deputy province chief, a Catholic by the name of Major Dang Xi, enforced an old decree prohibiting them from flying their multicolored flag. A week earlier, however, he had encouraged Catholics there to display blue and white papal banners to commemorate the 25th anniversary of Thuc's ordination. The discrimination dismayed the Buddhists. Several thousand gathered peacefully in front of the city's radio station to listen to loudspeakers broadcast a speech by Tri Quang, a Buddhist leader. The station director canceled the address, claiming that it had not been censored. He also telephoned Major Xi, who dispatched five armored cars to the scene. The commander ordered the crowd to disperse, then told his men to fire. The people stampeded. A woman and eight children died, either shot or trampled in the melee. Buddhist protests multiplied during the weeks that followed, and government troops aggravated the unrest by quelling them, sometimes brutally.

Diem's regime blamed the whole incident on the Vietcong, but a distinguished physician who had examined the victims confirmed the Buddhist account of their deaths; the government suppressed his report. Outraged, the Buddhists demanded among other things that the officials responsible for the killings be punished. Diem ignored them.

The Buddhists now mobilized with astounding speed and efficiency. They were not linked to the Communists, but they adopted Communist techniques. They formed honeycombs of three-member cells, set up headquarters in temples, and conducted crash courses in drafting tracts, slogans, and other propaganda, which they ground out on mimeograph machines. They agitated among relatives in the army and the bureaucracy, and they coordinated rallies and hunger strikes with remarkable precision. Some who had studied abroad briefed foreign journalists, arranged interviews, and distributed English-language copies of their manifestos. They put out daily news bulletins, even sending couriers to the U.S. Information Service office for daily American press accounts of the crisis. Dr. Tran Kim Tuyen, the regime's secret police chief, who by now was plotting against Diem, made a perceptive remark amid this ferment. "You know," he said, as we sat among the atrocious *objets d'art* cluttering his living room, "this is an underdeveloped country economically, but a highly developed country politically."

A force behind the aggressive Buddhist push was Tri Quang, a swarthy monk in his early forties. With his shaved head, saffron robe, and elliptical speaking style, he exuded mysticism, but he was a shrewd and tireless political operator. During his youth the French had jailed him as a Communist—a gross distortion, since his views tended to be right wing. He had been introduced to dynamic Buddhism as a novice in Ceylon, and he returned to Vietnam to await the chance to act. It came in Hué in May 1963. He toured the city in a sound truck on the night of the demonstration and killings, stirring up the people against Diem. Then he embarked on a trip around South Vietnam to enlist support. He met covertly in Saigon with U.S. officials, cautioning them: "The United States must either make Diem reform or get rid of him. If not, the situation will degenerate, and you worthy gentlemen will suffer most. You are responsible for the present trouble because you back Diem and his government of ignoramuses."

Ambassador Nolting, on instructions from Washington, urged Diem to conciliate. But Diem, who seemed to have slid into a trance, refused to retreat even privately from his contention that the Vietcong had caused the Hué incident. On June 7, Madame Nhu contradicted him and further aggravated the crisis by publicly alleging that the Buddhists as well were being manipulated by the Americans. Diem had known in advance that she intended to publish the charge, but he was too numb to stop her. He consulted Nhu, who endorsed his wife's accusation— probably having helped her to draft it.

The United States now rebuked Diem more sharply than ever. Nolting, bewildered that his gentle approach had not yielded results, had left on vacation. His deputy, William Trueheart, temporarily replacing him, was made of sterner fiber despite his outwardly mild demeanor. He bluntly warned Diem that the regime might lose U.S. support if the repression of the Buddhists continued. Madame Nhu screamed "blackmail" in response to the threat. Diem, stalling for time, created a cosmetic committee to investigate the Buddhist complaints.

The tough American initiative reflected shifts in the State Department. Averell Harriman had recently become under secretary and Roger Hilsman head of the Far Eastern bureau, and both favored firmness toward Diem. In Saigon, Trueheart was delighted to scuttle Nolting's appeasement policy, which in his estimation had encouraged Diem's excesses—even though he and Nolting had been close personal friends since college. After Vietnam, they never again exchanged a word.

As Diem procrastinated, the Buddhists burst a bombshell. On the morning of June 11, a motorcade pulled up at a busy Saigon intersection and an elderly Buddhist monk climbed out of one of the cars. He sat down on the asphalt and crossed his legs as other monks and nuns encircled him. One of them doused him with gasoline while another ignited him with a lighter. He pressed his palms together in prayer as a sheet of flame the color of his orange robe enveloped him. Pedestrians, amazed by the awesome sight, prostrated themselves in reverence, and even a nearby policeman threw himself to the ground. Trucks and automobiles stopped, snarling traffic. By the time an ambulance arrived, the old man had fallen over, still burning as the fire consumed his flesh. Only his heart remained intact.

A photograph of the grisly spectacle leaped off every front page in the world the next morning. Buddhist militants had tipped off Malcolm Browne, an Associated Press correspondent, who arrived with a camera. They also handed reporters copies of a biography of the suicide, Quang Duc, a sixty-six-year-old monk who had been in the Buddhist clergy since the age of fifteen. The document included his last words, a "respectful" plea to Diem to show "charity and compassion" to all religions. A Buddhist student who had driven Quang Duc to the site later recalled the events preceding the self-immolation with disarming serenity. His act was not unique, he explained, since monks often burned a finger or toe as a gesture of protest. Two monks had volunteered, but Quang Duc's seniority prevailed. Had someone tried to stop Quang Duc? "It was his own choice," the student replied.

Repeated American entreaties failed to shake Diem's stubbornness, even after the immolation. The committee of inquiry reconfirmed his thesis that the Vietcong had caused the Hué incident—and more Buddhist monks went up in flames. Madame Nhu became increasingly shrill, which only exacerbated the crisis. The self-immolations were a "barbecue," she said, and told one interviewer, "Let them burn, and we shall clap our hands."

At sixty-two, with a lifetime of public service behind him, Henry Cabot Lodge was healthy, vigorous, and looking for work. He struck Dean Rusk as an ideal successor to Ambassador Nolting. Lodge had visited Vietnam during the 1930s as a young newspaper reporter, and he spoke fluent French, having served as a liaison officer with the French army in World War II. The idea tantalized President Kennedy. He could be magnanimous to an old foe whom he had defeated for senator in Massachusetts and again as Nixon's running mate. Besides, a Republican in Saigon was insurance against recrimination should Vietnam go down the drain. So, on June 27, 1963, Kennedy named Lodge his envoy, scheduling him to start in September. A week later, Kennedy summoned a few aides to the Oval Office to discuss Vietnam. They included Harriman, Hilsman, and George Ball, now deputy secretary of state. They concurred that Nhu was the culprit, but they also agreed that Diem would never jettison him. For the first time in Kennedy's hearing, they speculated on the likelihood of a *coup d'état* against Diem.

On the same evening in Saigon, the same topic was discussed by General Tran Van Don, figurehead commander of the South Vietnamese army, and Lucien Conein, the veteran CIA operative, now a lieutenant colonel. A few nightclubs were thriving despite Madame Nhu's ban, and they had gone to a noisy *boîte* after a Fourth of July reception at the U.S. embassy, reckoning that the music would muffle their conversation.

Don, then in his late forties, was smooth, handsome, and more French than Vietnamese. Indeed, he had been born in Bordeaux, where his father, the son of a rich Mekong delta landowner, was studying medicine. Back in France as a university student, he became a French army officer when World War II erupted. He later returned to Vietnam, rising rapidly in the French-sponsored Vietnamese forces. He rose in rank under Diem, but gradually soured on the regime as he observed its shortcomings, and he began to share his doubts with other senior officers. His closest confidant was his brother-in-law, General Le Van Kim, the brainiest of South Vietnam's top soldiers. Kim had also been raised in France, where he had worked as an assistant film director before joining the French army. Though he recognized Kim's talents, Diem distrusted him, and had kicked him upstairs as head of South Vietnam's military academy. Don and Kim would later recruit another dissatisfied colleague, General Duong Van Minh, the hefty southerner known as "Big" Minh who had helped Diem to eliminate the sects. Minh was too popular with the troops for Diem, who a couple of years earlier had named him a "special adviser," a job without authority. Don had sounded out other discontented officers, and now he was ready to consult his old *copain*, "Lulu" Conein, whom he rated as "the only American I could really trust."

An eccentric, boisterous, often uncontrollable yet deeply sensitive and thoroughly professional agent, Conein inspired confidence in his Vietnamese contacts, who in typically Asian fashion placed more faith in personal ties than in institutional relationships. He and Don had not only fought and boozed and wenched together, but also shared a peculiar cultural bond. Just as Don was a Frenchified Vietnamese, so Conein was an Americanized Frenchman.

Born in Paris, he had been shipped alone at the age of five by his widowed French mother to live in Kansas City with her sister, the wife of a World War I doughboy. He grew up speaking with a Missouri accent, but he retained his French citizenship. He enlisted in the French army at the outbreak of World War II, deserting when France surrendered in 1940. He managed to escape from Europe to the United States, where the OSS recruited him to parachute back into France, this time to link up with a French resistance unit. When the war ended in Europe, he transferred to Asia to join a company of French and Vietnamese commandos harassing Japanese posts in northern Vietnam. He entered Hanoi after Japan's defeat with the OSS team that dealt with Ho Chi Minh and the other Vietminh leaders, and he returned there nine years later on a furtive mission to sabotage the Communist transportation system. During those early days in Vietnam, he befriended many young Vietnamese officers and political figures who later became his informants. He also married his third wife, a pretty Eurasian.

One of the star performers in the CIA's "department of dirty tricks," Conein had also infiltrated saboteurs and other covert agents into Eastern Europe, and he had trained paramilitary forces in Iran. The only physical scars of his perilous career were two missing fingers, absurdly cut off by the fan of an automobile engine he was trying to repair. E. Howard Hunt, a former CIA colleague, nearly hired him later for the group that bungled the Watergate burglary and sparked the scandal that led to Richard Nixon's resignation. "If I'd been involved," Conein once assured me, "we'd have done it right."

Reassigned to Vietnam in early 1962, Conein masqueraded as an adviser to the Saigon ministry of interior, a "cover" that allowed him to roam the country and gather intelligence on the conspiracies against the government. His job was delicate. He had to be careful that his reports on close friends, like Don, were not leaked to Diem and Nhu by the regime's American sympathizers. His own life was in jeopardy, since Nhu could have liquidated him for intriguing and attributed his death to the Vietcong. Most important, Conein had to get his facts straight, a normally difficult task in Vietnam, now even more complicated by the proliferation of plots and rumors of plots. Dozens of different factions were scheming, and not until late 1963 would they become a single conspiracy.

An early plotter was Dr. Tran Kim Tuyen, a tiny man with a squeaky voice who scarcely seemed like one of Saigon's most sinister figures. He ran the Office of Political and Social Studies, the secret government apparatus organized with CIA assistance to keep tabs on dissenters. A northern Catholic who had fled south in 1954, Tuyen feared that Diem's failings would bring about a Communist takeover. Ironically, he filled his faction with dissidents he had blacklisted, and he also attracted disgruntled junior officers. He teamed up as well with Colonel Pham Ngoc Thao, unaware of his clandestine Communist ties. Thao's followers included a young air force pilot, Nguyen Cao Ky.

Tuyen and Thao had planned a quick coup against Diem which, they hoped, would pre-empt other plotters. But Conein, getting wind of their project, tipped off General Tran Thien Khiem, the army chief of staff, who stopped the premature action; Nhu then exiled Tuyen to Cairo as consul general. Tuyen went no farther than Hong Kong, where he continued to plot long distance. Thao thereupon joined Khiem's insurgent group, which eventually was folded into the mainstream conspiracy.

With the pieces of the puzzle not yet fit together, Don had few details to offer Conein as they talked in the noisy nightclub after the Fourth of July party. He could only hint to Conein that a coup was in the making. And he had a crucial question to ask him: "What will the American reaction be if we go all the way?"

The question revealed the conspirators' basic preoccupation, which persisted as they prepared the coup. Inexperienced politically, tutored first by the French and later reliant on Diem, they were eager for American approbation—partly because they were accustomed to acting on orders and also because they would need U.S. aid if they succeeded. So the United States probably could have prevented Diem's downfall by disapproving of the plot. While no U.S. officials of any rank considered Diem ideal, some foresaw disaster in his continued leadership; others predicted chaos without it. Either way, the dilemma illustrated the danger of underwriting a client who refused to behave like a client.

The problem of the recalcitrant protégé was not confined to Vietnam. In varying degrees and at different times, such states as Israel, Taiwan, and South Korea manipulated the United States, so Diem was not the only "puppet who pulled his own strings." But, in exerting leverage, he ran the risk of exasperating an American government no longer willing to be a captive of its dependent.

Conein could not furnish Don with a clue to U.S. intentions in early July because, at that stage, Kennedy still hoped that Diem might be persuaded to compromise with the Buddhists. Kennedy sent Nolting back to Saigon with instructions to "get that guy out there to play ball." But Nolting, fearful of weakening the regime, refused to prod Diem, who did little to resolve the crisis. Four more monks burned themselves to death during the first half of August as Madame Nhu applauded the suicides.

Nolting finally went home in the middle of August, still extolling Diem's devotion to "democratic principles" and "social justice," even asserting that he had "never seen any evidence of religious persecution" during his two years in Vietnam. A week after his departure, the tottering U.S. policy toward Diem fell into shambles.

On August 20, Don and other generals proposed to Diem that he declare martial law so that they could prosecute the war more effectively despite the political turmoil. Their real purpose was to strengthen their control for a coup. Surprisingly, Diem acquiesced, but for another purpose: by imposing martial law, he aimed to implicate the army in a scheme then being designed by Nhu—to crack down on the Buddhists with his own loyal forces disguised as regular soldiers. Thus, he calculated, he could turn the Buddhists and their sympathizers against the army and to his own advantage. He struck shortly after midnight on August 21.

Armed with rifles, submachine guns, and tear gas grenades, truckloads of Nhu's men raced through the silent streets of Saigon to surround the Xa Loi temple, the city's principal Buddhist sanctuary. They attacked without warning, ransacked the ornate pagoda, and arrested some four hundred monks and nuns, among them Vietnam's eighty-year-old Buddhist patriarch. But the Saigon raid paled in comparison to events in Hué, where monks and nuns barricaded inside the Dieude temple fought off Nhu's assailants for eight hours as nearly two thousand townspeople rioted in protest. Nhu staged similar assaults in other cities, rounding up more than a thousand monks, nuns, student activists, and ordinary citizens. Many were injured and others disappeared, presumably killed in the melees.

Vietnamese reacted in dismay. Urban youths, most of them the sons and daughters of the middle-class families that made up the bureaucracy and army leadership, poured into the streets to demonstrate against the regime. Madame Nhu's father, Tran Van Chuong, the South Vietnamese ambassador in Washington, quit his post to denounce the government. Foreign Minister Vu Van Mau resigned and shaved his head like a

Buddhist monk as a gesture of protest. Tri Quang, the Buddhist leader, took refuge in the U.S. embassy—belying the government's allegation that he was a Communist.

The CIA was supposed to track Nhu's every move, but its agents had been caught off balance by the attacks. Nhu had cut the U.S. embassy and residential telephone lines when he launched his raids, gulling American officials into the belief that the army had attacked the Buddhist temples. The "Voice of America" at first broadcast that version of the event, which infuriated the generals; the Vietnamese listened to its Vietnamese-language news programs, their only unbiased source of information. Don summoned Conein to his headquarters near the Saigon airport and denied that the generals had suppressed the Buddhists. But despite Don's demands, the "Voice of America" refrained from broadcasting a retraction.

Henry Cabot Lodge, en route to Vietnam, was conferring in Honolulu when the crackdowns against the Buddhists occurred. On instructions from Washington, he sped to Saigon, landing on August 22. Awaiting him was a cable from the State Department requesting his immediate appraisal of the situation. After he was briefed by his staff, he reported that Nhu had planned the move against the Buddhists, "probably" with Diem's "full support." He also confirmed that the generals had sought American support for a coup against the brothers, but he counseled prudence; immediate action would be a "shot in the dark." At the same time, Admiral Felt, commander for the Pacific, telephoned Washington from Honolulu to urge that the American government act tough to Nhu; two of Diem's close civilian aides, upset by the repression, made the same recommendation to their American contacts in Saigon.

These and other messages, heightened by dramatic newspaper headlines and television accounts of the situation, pushed the Kennedy administration toward a prompt response. On Saturday, August 24, an American policy decision went back to Lodge, and it was to be the focus of controversy and recrimination for years afterward.

Roger Hilsman, head of the State Department's Far Eastern bureau, considered himself a counterinsurgency expert, having served as a commando in Burma during World War II. He had long criticized the Saigon regime's competence to wage an essentially political struggle. Now, he believed, the moment had come to exert maximum pressure on Diem. Asserting that the United States "cannot tolerate a situation in which power lies in Nhu's hands," Hilsman proposed that Diem be "given the chance" to jettison his brother. If Diem "remains obdurate and refuses," the directive continued, "we must face the possibility that Diem himself cannot be preserved." The message to Lodge further advised him to pass on this decision to the dissident generals—in effect, to assure them of American support for a coup against Diem unless he removed Nhu.

Thus Hilsman was recommending that the Kennedy administration encourage the overthrow of an uncooperative ally, a proposal whose significance far transcended Vietnam. For it meant, in theory at least, that the United States reserved the right to manipulate a dependent government that failed to conform to its standards.

Hilsman drafted the cable with the collaboration of Averell Harriman and Michael Forrestal, an aide to McGeorge Bundy, the president's national security adviser. Their next step was to obtain approval from their superiors—late on a hot Saturday afternoon in August.

George Ball, deputy secretary of state, was playing golf at a Washington club, and Harriman and Hilsman drove up just as he had completed the ninth hole. Ball took them to his house to study the message. He favored its firmness, but insisted that it be cleared with President Kennedy, who was spending the weekend in Hyannis Port at his Cape Cod estate. It has never been established whether Kennedy received the text before by teletype, as Hilsman has claimed, or was merely read the "relevant passages" over the telephone, as Ball has recollected. Kennedy could not have assumed that all his advisers had approved the cable, as his brother Robert recalled, since he endorsed it on condition that Ball get the concurrence of Secretary of State Rusk and of Roswell Gilpatric, the deputy secretary of defense acting for McNamara, who was on vacation. Most probably, Kennedy was not paying close attention to the details.

What followed was a series of misunderstandings. Rusk, telephoned in New York, where he had gone for a special United Nations session, cautiously endorsed the directive under the impression that Kennedy had approved it. Gilpatric similarly assented in the belief that both Kennedy and Rusk had agreed, but he later telephoned Maxwell Taylor, chairman of the joint chiefs of staff, to register his misgivings. Taylor, who had been dining in a restaurant and could not be immediately located, said afterward that this was the first he heard of it. But one of his deputies, General Victor Krulak, had earlier cleared it on his behalf without notifying him. In years to come, Taylor branded Ball, Harriman, Hilsman, and Forrestal as "anti-Diem activists" whose maneuver had been an "egregious end-run." McGeorge Bundy, however, later summed up the lesson of the improvised process: "Never do business on the weekend."

Everyone involved gathered with Kennedy at the White House on Monday morning for the first of four days of stormy meetings. Kennedy opened by lashing out at Ball, Harriman, Hilsman, and Forrestal for their impulsiveness. Soon they were locked in a fierce dispute with Taylor, McNamara, Lyndon Johnson, and John McCone, the CIA director, all of whom argued against a coup; Rusk characteristically played safe by remaining silent. A day later, Kennedy invited Nolting to present his ideas; predictably, he opposed taking action against Diem. Incensed, Harriman unleashed a tirade against Nolting and even refused afterward to drive him back to the State Department in his limousine. The upper echelons of the administration were split as never before. "My God!" Kennedy confided to a friend, "my government is coming apart!"

While the acrimonious White House debate droned on, U.S. officials began to resemble the Vietnamese plotters, as they deviously jockeyed to advance their views. Taylor and Harkins, both opposing a coup, were surreptitiously communicating with each other over a "back channel" Pentagon line between Washington and Saigon. At Lodge's request, Hilsman now authorized the "Voice of America" to broadcast a report absolving the South Vietnamese army of responsibility for attacking the temples. The radio went even further, citing American press speculation that the United States "may sharply reduce its aid" to Diem unless he dismissed the organizers of the anti-Buddhist raids. Though this was promptly denied, the broadcast plainly indicated to Diem that the Kennedy administration was turning against him. It also worried the Saigon conspirators, who feared that their intrigue would be tainted if U.S. support was displayed too publicly.

Originally cautious, Lodge now pleaded for giving the rebel generals the green light. He told Washington that delays would only strengthen Nhu and diminish the prospects for an effective coup. He also doubted that Diem could be persuaded to drop Nhu, an impression he confirmed on August 26, when he met Diem for the first time to present his credentials. Both Brahmins in their way, they sat stiffly over their ritual tea in the presidential palace, neither one willing to yield to the other. As Lodge recalled the scene to me years later: "I could see a cloud pass across his face when I suggested that he get rid of Nhu and improve his government. He absolutely refused to discuss any of the topics that President Kennedy had instructed me to raise, and that frankly jolted me. He looked up at the ceiling and talked about irrelevant subjects. I thought it was deplorable."

John Richardson, the CIA chief in Saigon, backed up Lodge. Basing his assessment on intelligence that Conein and other clandestine agents had gathered, he reported to Washington that the situation had reached a "point of no return." The generals "must proceed quickly," he said, recommending that they be given covert U.S. help, since Vietnam's fate hinged on their success. "It is obviously preferable that the generals conduct this effort without apparent American assistance. . . . Nevertheless, we all understand that the effort must succeed and that whatever needs to be done on our part must be done. If this attempt by the generals does not take place, or if it fails, we believe it no exaggeration to say that Vietnam runs a serious risk of being lost over the course of time."

Harkins demurred. He privately warned Taylor against "crash approval" for the conspirators, pointing out that they lacked the force to defeat the government's units. He also perceived, accurately, as it turned out, that the plotters would not move without a U.S. signal. Harkins would continue to try to foil the coup, clashing with Lodge's endeavors to push the generals into action.

By late August, the generals had not yet divulged their plans to Conein and other CIA operatives. They feared betrayal; they also wanted visible evidence of American endorsement, such as a halt in U.S. economic aid to Diem. Kennedy was not yet ready for so strong a gesture of reproval, but Lodge took an unusual step, designed to demonstrate his sympathy. He ordered the CIA to furnish them with information on a secret base used by the special forces, a unit loyal to Nhu.

On August 29, impatient at Washington's waffling, Lodge sent a cable demanding decisive measures.

We are launched on a course from which there is no respectable turning back: the overthrow of the Diem government. There is no turning back because U.S. prestige is already publicly committed to this end in large measure, and will become more so as the facts leak out. In a more fundamental sense, there is no turning back because there is no possibility, in my view, that the war can be won under a Diem administration.

Lodge proposed that U.S. aid to Diem be halted—the signal awaited by the generals to spark their coup. And, with uncharacteristic emotion, he urged an "all-out effort" to make the insurgents "move promptly," stressing that the outcome of the action would depend "at least as much on us" as on them. Otherwise, he warned, dissatisfaction with the Diem regime might explode in violence, bringing in a "pro-Communist or at best a neutralist set of politicians." America's investment in Vietnam entitled the United States to intervene: "Our help to the regime in past years inescapably gives us a responsibility that we cannot avoid."

Kennedy approved Lodge's recommendations, giving him complete discretion to suspend U.S. aid to Diem. So Lodge was handed the mandate to manage American policy in Vietnam. And the policy, as Lodge defined it, was to topple the Diem regime.

What inspired Kennedy to delegate such power to Lodge remains a mystery that has not been adequately unraveled by any of the self-serving memoirs of the period. It may be, as Arthur Schlesinger, Jr., wrote, that Lodge was "a strong man with the bit between his teeth" who eluded Kennedy's control. On the other hand, Kennedy may have agreed with Lodge on the need to oust Diem, but preferred to give the Republican a messy job that might backfire politically.

Kennedy would later have reservations about the coup. But on September 2, in a prime-time television interview with Walter Cronkite, he publicly backed Lodge's approach. Repeating Lodge's private warning almost word for word, Kennedy doubted that the war could be prosecuted effectively "unless a greater effort is made by the [Diem] government to win popular support." He bluntly added that the regime had "gotten out of touch with the people." And he also called for changes in "policy and personnel," meaning that Diem had to conciliate the Buddhists and dump the Nhus. None of this signified, however, that he contemplated a retreat from Vietnam. "I don't agree with those who say we should withdraw. That would be a great mistake. We must be patient. We must persist."

But Lodge, for all his determination and dynamism, could not get the conspirators to "move promptly." On the contrary, he predicted, getting them to move at all would be like "pushing a piece of spaghetti."

At the beginning of September, to Lodge's consternation, the rebel officers abruptly postponed their coup planning amid clouds of suspicion and uncertainty. Some suspected that Richardson, the CIA chief, was informing on them to Nhu, with whom he maintained close contacts, while others suspected Harkins of betraying them to Diem. Don suspected Khiem, who had rescued Diem from the insurgent paratroopers three years before, and Khiem suspected Thao because of his Vietminh past. Most had misgivings about Minh's nominal leadership, since he seemed to be more interested in playing tennis and raising orchids than in directing a revolt. Above all, they sensed at that stage that they lacked the strength for a showdown.

The principal plotters, Minh, Don, Kim, and Khiem, were prestigious figures, but they did not themselves command troops. They had lined up infantry battalions around the country as well as air and naval units. The key to success, however, lay in Saigon. There Diem could count on the special forces headed by Colonel Le Quang Tung, a Catholic from central Vietnam who had been trained by the CIA in the United States. To counter him, the conspirators had to win over General Ton That Dinh, the commander of the Saigon military region, a swaggering prima donna whose loyalties were then in doubt. The generals had delayed the coup in order to cultivate Dinh, and their stalling frustrated Lodge, who concluded bitterly that they had "neither the will nor the organization . . . to accomplish anything." Harkins, delighted by Lodge's disappointment, misquoted Kipling in a sardonic remark to Taylor: "You can't hurry the East."

Nhu, aware of the American dealings with the plotters, meanwhile began to make roundabout overtures to the Communists. One of his key contacts was Mieczyslaw Maneli, chief of the Polish delegation to the International Control Commission, the vestigial group set up under the Geneva accords to monitor violations of the peace. Its Indian, Canadian, and Polish members could travel freely between the two zones of Vietnam. As a Communist official, Maneli had special access to the North Vietnamese hierarchy. When he first arrived in Hanoi in early 1963, Ho Chi Minh and his comrades were closely watching the growing tensions between Diem and the Americans, hoping to drive a wedge between them. Maneli, who later defected to the United States, recalled Hanoi's policy at that time: "Our real enemies are the Americans. Get rid of them, and we can cope with Diem and Nhu afterward."

Diem, and particularly Nhu, had never foreclosed on the possibility of an accommodation with Hanoi, despite their anti-Communist rhetoric. One of their intermediaries was Buu Hoi, a distinguished scientist and former adviser to Ho, who lived in Paris, where he had contacts with de Gaulle. The French president then favored neutrality for Indochina and, at Buu Hoi's urging, he instructed Roger Lalouette, his ambassador in Saigon, to promote the concept with Diem and Nhu. They sounded receptive, and Lalouette secretly commissioned Maneli to sound out the Communists about economic and cultural exchanges between North and South Vietnam as a prelude to an eventual political deal. Maneli carried this proposal to North Vietnamese Prime Minister Pham Van

Dong, who reminded him that the Communists had made such a recommendation years before. Once the Americans were out, said Pham Van Dong, "we can come to an agreement with any Vietnamese."

Maneli returned to Saigon, where Lalouette introduced him to Nhu. At a private meeting in Nhu's palace office on September 2, Maneli disclosed his conversation with Pham Van Dong. Nhu expressed interest. Maneli shuttled back to Hanoi, where the Communists reiterated that their principal foe was U.S. "imperialism," not the Diem regime. They even authorized Maneli to inform Nhu that he could rely on their help in the event of a clash with the United States. Maneli never relayed the message. Diem and Nhu were dead by the time he got back to Saigon.

Were these maneuvers serious, or merely a smoke screen? In Vietnam, where nothing is simple, they were probably a combination of both. Hoang Tung, the Communist party propaganda boss, confirmed to me in Hanoi in 1981 that the North Vietnamese had in fact tried to "probe the depth of the differences" between Diem and the United States. Madame Nhu, who later was to affirm that talks had been going on, even revealed that she was prepared to send her two oldest children to Hanoi as a "fraternal gesture." But Nhu's machinations were also contrived to blackmail the Americans. Among other things, he leaked the story to columnist Joseph Alsop, in an obvious attempt to scare Washington. "He was," as Maneli put it, "playing on many instruments at the same time."

To some American officials, these schemes were an added reason for Diem's ouster. Hilsman, in a top-secret memorandum to Rusk, suggested that the rebel generals be spurred to "move promptly with a coup" if the Diem regime negotiated with Hanoi; and also recommended that U.S. military strikes be staged against North Vietnam if the Communists sent troops south to rescue Diem. Hilsman later explained to me that his memorandum had simply listed "options."

Perhaps an opportunity was lost for a marriage of convenience between the two Vietnams. But, given the U.S. mood of the period, an American withdrawal was unthinkable.

Robert Kennedy floated that notion at a White House meeting in September. He wondered aloud whether a Communist takeover "could be successfully resisted with any government" in Saigon, and if not, perhaps "now was the time to get out of Vietnam entirely." As Arthur Schlesinger, Jr., recalled, however, the speculative question "hovered for a moment, then died away, a hopelessly alien thought in a field of unexamined assumptions and entrenched convictions."

The idea had also been raised at a national security council session on August 31 by Paul Kattenburg, a perceptive State Department veteran of Vietnam. He had just returned from Saigon, where he had found opinion so hostile to Diem that, he forecast, the United States would be compelled to leave in six months if it continued to back him. So, he went on, perhaps it was preferable now "for us to make the decision to get out honorably." His view stunned the assemblage. Rusk asserted that "we will not pull out . . . until the war is won." McNamara affirmed that "we have been winning the war," and Lyndon Johnson added, "We should stop playing cops and robbers [and] go about winning the war." That took care of Kattenburg, who was to terminate his government career at the U.S. embassy in Guyana—not far from Devil's Island.

But while getting out of Vietnam was excluded, nobody could come up with suggestions for relaxing the tensions in Saigon. On McNamara's advice, President Kennedy did what is usually done in times of indecision: he sent out a "fact-finding mission." This one, composed of General Victor Krulak and Joseph Mendenhall, a State Department official who had served in Vietnam, flew a total of twenty-four thousand miles for a four-day survey to confirm their prejudices. An optimist, Krulak concluded from speaking almost exclusively with American and South Vietnamese army officers that "the shooting war is still going ahead at an impressive pace." A pessimist, Mendenhall concluded from talks primarily with urban bureaucrats and politicians that the Diem government was near collapse. After they presented their divergent reports to him on September 10, Kennedy quipped: "You two did visit the same country, didn't you?"

Undeterred, Kennedy decided to send McNamara and Taylor on a voyage to Vietnam in late September. Ambassador Lodge objected, contending that Diem would construe the high-level mission as U.S. endorsement, but Kennedy had bureaucratic motives: the Pentagon brass opposed the attempts by American diplomats to reform Diem, believing they were impeding the war effort; what Kennedy wanted from McNamara and Taylor was a negative assessment of the military situation, so that he could justify the pressures being exerted on the Saigon regime. But Taylor and McNamara would only further complicate Kennedy's problems.

They listened to a spectrum of opinions during their exhausting ten-day tour, and their conclusions were riddled with contradictions and compromises. To placate Harkins and the other optimists, they hailed the "great progress" of the military campaign, proposing that a thousand U.S. advisers be pulled out by the end of the year. They even predicted that the "bulk" of the American force could be withdrawn by 1965—a prophecy evidently made for domestic political consumption at Kennedy's insistence. At the same time, they did their best to satisfy Diem's critics by decrying his intransigence, and they proposed taking limited sanctions against him. Among other steps, they suggested that Colonel Tung's special forces be deprived of American funding unless they were deployed outside Saigon, where Nhu was using them to repress dissidents. Kennedy approved the document except for one nuance. He deleted a phrase calling the U.S. commitment to Vietnam an "overriding" American goal, terming it instead a part of his worldwide aim to "defeat aggression." He wanted to preserve his flexibility.

Taylor, hoping to get "Big" Minh's views, had invited him to play tennis at the Cercle Sportif, the old French club now frequented by Saigon's elite. The place was crawling with Nhu's secret police, and Minh prudently avoided mention of the conspiracy. Taylor presumed that the coup had been canceled. Acting on that presumption, Kennedy cabled Lodge on October 2: "No initiative should now be taken to give any covert encouragement to a coup. There should, however, be an urgent effort . . . to identify and build contacts with possible alternative leadership as and when it appears."

Three days later, however, Lodge reported to Kennedy that the on-again, off-again coup was on again. The generals had been quietly organizing over the past month and were now ready to share some of their thoughts with the Americans. Don arranged a meeting between Conein and Minh for the morning of October 5 at Le Van Duyet, Saigon garrison headquarters, a sprawl of mildewed bungalows built by the French.

Conein groaned at the prospect of an encounter with Minh, whom he considered to be a "glorified French army corporal." But Minh was now unusually articulate. Speaking in French, he told Conein that the generals did not expect tangible American support for a coup, but merely assurances that the United States would "not thwart" it. They also wanted a pledge of continued U.S. military and economic aid—it was then running to more than $500 million per year—after they seized power. Minh identified the other principal plotters as Don and Le Van Kim, adding that he distrusted Khiem; he emphasized the urgency. Conspiracies were mushrooming everywhere, and the wrong attempt made by the wrong group could cause a "catastrophe."

The generals were contemplating three possible strategies. The "easiest" would be to assassinate Nhu and Ngo Dinh Can, the brother in

Hué, leaving Diem in office. Or they could strangle the regime by encircling Saigon, a maneuver that required the cooperation of General Ton That Dinh, the area commander. Or they could directly confront the government troops in the capital, dividing the city into sectors and "cleaning it out pocket by pocket" in street fighting. A key figure to eliminate was Colonel Tung, head of the special forces, whose five thousand men were sure to defend the Ngo brothers. Conein agreed, calling Tung "one of the more dangerous individuals."

Minh's talk with Conein at last gave Lodge the formula he was looking for to encourage the conspiracy without overt American complicity. He recommended to Kennedy that Minh be told that the United States "will not attempt to thwart" the coup. Kennedy approved the convoluted language—cautioning only that Americans refrain from direct involvement in the plot: "While we do not wish to stimulate a coup, we also do not wish to leave the impression that the United States would thwart a change of government. . . . But we should avoid being drawn into reviewing or advising on operational plans, or any other act that might tend to identify the United States too closely."

A few days later, Conein conveyed the substance of that message to Minh. The green light had been flashed. Minh designated Don to keep in touch with Conein, and from then on, Conein and Don met secretly at a Saigon dentist's office: "Whatever else happened," Conein recalled to me later, "I certainly had a lot of work done on my teeth."

Lodge was now armed with the rationale he would employ publicly in the years ahead to deny his responsibility for Diem's downfall: he had not promoted the coup, but simply had "not thwarted" it. Or, as he commented to *The New York Times* on June 30, 1964, eight months after the episode: "The overthrow . . . of the Diem regime was purely a Vietnamese affair. We never participated in the planning. We never gave any advice. We had nothing whatever to do with it." But in a cable to Washington on November 6, 1963, four days after Diem's murder, Lodge privately offered Kennedy a somewhat different assessment. The coup, he said, had been a Vietnamese action that "we could neither manage nor stop after it got started." Nevertheless, he added, "It is equally certain that the ground in which the coup seed grew into a robust plant was prepared by us, and that the coup would not have happened [as] it did without our preparation."

Saigon seemed to have gone haywire during the early weeks of October 1963. Nhu's influence was now predominant, and though martial law had been lifted, political repression intensified after another Buddhist monk burned himself to death near the central market at noon on October 5—the first self-immolation since the summer. Hardly a day passed without Nhu's secret police arresting scores of dissidents, among them children caught distributing antigovernment tracts or scrawling slogans on walls. Bureaucrats were ordered to boycott their American advisers as Nhu issued almost daily denunciations of the United States, in both private and public. He charged American officials with "destroying the psychology of our country" and "initiating a process of disintegration," and he described Lodge as a "man of no morality." He had managed to install electronic eavesdropping devices into the U.S. embassy and was thus able to publish remarkably accurate accounts of confidential American discussions in his English-language newspaper, the *Times of Vietnam*. And he spread rumors of his covert contacts with the Communists, claiming that "the Americans have done everything to push me into their arms." The turmoil even spilled into the United States when Madame Nhu went on a speaking tour during which she shrilly excoriated American liberals as worse than Communists and dismissed Buddhist monks as "hooligans in robes." Following her around the country was her father, Tran Van Chuong, the former South Vietnamese ambassador in Washington. Acting as a one-man "truth squad," he would contradict her statements, criticize the Diem government's "injustice and oppression," and warn that the Saigon regime "has become unwittingly the greatest asset to the Communists." A similar squabble meanwhile intruded into the American media.

The Vietnam drama at the time was a journalist's dream, but a nightmare for U.S. officials, who feared that accounts of events in Vietnam would turn the American public against the war effort. Censorship was still ruled out, but without censorship it was difficult to control dynamic young correspondents in Saigon like David Halberstam of *The New York Times*, Neil Sheehan of United Press International, and Malcolm Browne of the Associated Press, who were deluged with real and imaginary details fed them by adversaries of the regime. Even Lodge, who could be as devious as any Vietnamese, leaked information aimed at tarnishing Diem's image. Kennedy tried to have Halberstam transferred, but he was rebuffed by the publisher of the *Times*. Carl Rowan, then director of the U.S. Information Agency in Washington, instructed the U.S. mission in Saigon to steer the news media away from events that "are likely to result in undesirable stories." Like so many other embarrassing documents, his classified memorandum on this subject found its way into print.

The nastiest diatribes against reporters in Saigon, however, came from journalistic purveyors of the official line. Joseph Alsop, for example, accused his young colleagues of carrying on "egregious crusades" against Diem, and he compared them to Chiang Kai-shek's press critics, whom he blamed for China's fall to the Communists. An equally vitriolic assault was inspired by Otto Fuerbringer, then managing editor of *Time* magazine, who commissioned an article charging the Saigon press corps with pooling its "convictions, information, misinformation and grievances" to distort the truth. Charles Mohr and Mert Perry, two *Time* correspondents in Vietnam, promptly resigned, protesting that the article had been cooked up in New York.

The U.S. mission in Saigon was also roiled by internal disputes over whether the rebel generals ought to be encouraged to topple Diem. Lodge had heartened the Vietnamese insurgents in early October by dismissing John Richardson, the CIA chief, who had begun to express doubts about a coup. But Lodge still had to contend with Harkins, who opposed the conspiracy and was, besides, complicating an already complicated situation with his indiscretions. On the evening of October 22, at a British embassy reception, Harkins drew General Don aside to tell him that he had heard that a coup was imminent and that he considered it a mistake. Alarmed, Don left the party early and summoned Conein to the dentist's office the next morning. Unusually excited, Don told Conein that the coup had been scheduled for October 26, Armed Forces Day, when rebel military units could be deployed in Saigon without attracting attention, but that he had hastily postponed the plan after listening to Harkins. He then bombarded Conein with questions. How did Harkins know about the plot, when only Lodge and Conein were supposed to be privy to it? Did Harkins mean that the insurgents could no longer count on American support? What was the U.S. attitude now?

Don's questions were crucial. For they suggested, once again, that the conspirators were desperately anxious for U.S. approval and might cancel the coup were it not forthcoming. Interviewed years later, Conein disagreed: "At that point, they would have gone ahead even without American acquiescence. Their necks were stretched too far. If the generals hadn't done it, the colonels would have, and if the colonels got cold feet, someone else would have pulled the coup."

As they talked in the dentist's office, Don gradually relaxed; Conein reassured him that the United States would "not thwart" a coup. He guaranteed that neither he nor Lodge was consulting Harkins and that no information on the plot was seeping out. "*Mon vieux*, I love my lily-white skin as much as you love your yellow skin, and I'm not going to take any chances. They can bump me off and call it a Vietcong incident, and nobody'll know the difference."

Don promised to show Conein the plans for the coup, insisting that they be shared only with Lodge. But two days later, when they met again at the dentist's office, Don was empty-handed. He had accidentally seen Harkins the previous night, and he still feared betrayal. Don again pledged to give the Americans an outline of the rebel military tactics and a blueprint of the political organization that the insurgents intended to set up after they won, and he vaguely informed Conein that the coup would take place before November 2.

Harkins was still jockeying behind Lodge's back. In private communication with Taylor, he continued to warn that an attempt to destroy Diem could wreck the war effort against the Vietcong. Indeed, intelligence estimates already indicated that the Vietcong was taking advantage of the unrest and escalating its activities. Taylor passed on Harkins's misgivings to Kennedy, who began to get last-minute jitters.

Kennedy was troubled that the U.S. mission in Saigon did not have the coup plans. Suspicious of romantic CIA agents, he wanted more details on Conein's peculiar relationship with Don. Above all, an aborted plot conjured up his memories of the Bay of Pigs disaster. McGeorge Bundy transmitted these worries to Lodge on October 25: "We are particularly concerned about the hazard that an unsuccessful coup, however carefully we avoid direct engagement, will be laid at our door by public opinion almost everywhere. Therefore, while sharing your view that we should not be in a position of thwarting a coup, we would like to have the option of judging and warning on any plan with poor prospects of success."

Lodge, replying immediately, tried hard to allay Kennedy's apprehensions. He admitted the risks but argued that "it seems at least an even bet that the next government would not bungle and fumble as the present one has." Besides, he contended, to prevent a coup was to assume "an undue responsibility for keeping the incumbents in office," which represented "judgment over the affairs of Vietnam." That said, Lodge then violated his own principle of noninterference by proposing the composition of a future Saigon regime to include the Buddhist militant Tri Quang, and Tran Quoc Buu, a labor leader with close ties to the CIA.

On the morning of October 28, behaving as if nothing were amiss, Diem assembled the diplomatic corps at the Saigon airport; he was leaving for a visit to Dalat to open an atomic energy installation there. General Don, a member of his entourage, decided to take a bold step: he steered Lodge into a corner and questioned him directly for the first time about America's attitude toward the conspiracy. Did Harkins or Conein reflect the official U.S. position? Lodge told Don to ignore Harkins and listen to Conein, thus obliquely confirming that America would "not thwart" the coup.

Back in Saigon that evening, Don again met Conein at the dentist's office; this time he disclosed which military units would be involved in the revolt. Conein pointed out that Lodge, who was due to fly to Washington in three days for consultations, wanted to review the coup preparations before his departure. But the plans might not be available until four hours before the action began, Don explained; he advised that Lodge leave on schedule, nonetheless, to avoid arousing suspicion. Lodge, who had no intention of missing the spectacle, found a pretext to postpone his trip: he stayed on to greet Admiral Felt, arriving on a routine visit.

That night, Lodge told Washington that a coup was "imminent." It could be stopped only by betraying the insurgent officers to Diem, which was unacceptable. He would have only four hours' notice before the action started, which "rules out my checking with you" in advance. In short, it was too late for second thoughts. He, Lodge, would alone steer U.S. policy in Vietnam.

But there were second thoughts at the White House the following day, October 29, when Kennedy convened the national security council. Harkins had sent more angry messages to Taylor, who brought them to the meeting to reinforce his own objections to Lodge's conduct. Harkins distrusted Conein's accounts of the conversations with Don, who was "either lying or playing both ends against the middle." He challenged Lodge's bleak appraisal of Diem's performance and once more asserted that "we are gaining in the contest" against the Vietcong—again reviving the issue of whether the struggle was primarily political or fundamentally military. "There is a basic difference apparently between the ambassador's thinking and mine," Harkins said, outlining his own attitude with emotion unusual for a soldier.

In my contacts here, I have seen no one with the strength of character of Diem, at least in fighting Communists. Clearly, there are no generals qualified to take over. . . . I would suggest that we not try to change horses too quickly. That we continue to take persuasive actions that will make the horses change their course and methods of action. That we win the military effort as quickly as possible, then let them make any and all the changes they want.

After all, rightly or wrongly, we have backed Diem for eight long hard years. To me it seems incongruous now to get him down, kick him around and get rid of him.

Harkins's plea shook Robert Kennedy, who warned the national security council that a coup "risks so much," and the president also shifted. McGeorge Bundy, speaking for him, renewed his misgivings in a cable to Lodge. The president was "deeply concerned" that Conein was the only link to the conspirators; he wanted Harkins to take charge of the U.S. mission in Saigon if the revolt should begin during Lodge's scheduled trip to Washington. Above all, Bundy made plain, Kennedy doubted that a coup could succeed. The insurgents were apparently too weak to vanquish Diem's forces, and "the substantial possibility of serious and prolonged fighting or even defeat . . . could be serious or even disastrous for U.S. interests." Bundy instructed Lodge to direct Conein to inform Don that "we do not find that the presently revealed plans give a clear prospect of quick results." The generals were to be told, at least implicitly, that the United States favored postponement if not cancellation of the coup.

Lodge never conveyed that order to Conein. Nor was General Don advised through any other channel. The rebel generals continued to believe, as Lodge wanted them to believe, that the Americans would "not thwart" their bid for power.

Answering Bundy the same day, Lodge parried the president's instructions. He refused to widen the American contacts with the plotters, since the link between Conein and Don was, he said, "an appropriate security measure"; besides, the generals distrusted U.S. officers. He also spurned the idea of putting Harkins in charge of the American mission during an episode "so profoundly political as a change of government." As for blocking the coup itself, Lodge again argued, the action could be stopped only by betraying the insurgents to Diem, which would "make traitors out of us" as well as sacrifice the "civilian and military leadership needed to carry the war . . . to its successful conclusion."

Once again, Lodge contradicted his principle of nonintervention. He would grant asylum to Diem and his supporters in the wake of a coup, but he flatly opposed any help for them against the insurgents. On the other hand, he proposed that the rebel generals be "discreetly" furnished with U.S. funds "to buy off potential opposition," and he further recommended that they be promptly rewarded with American recognition and aid after they overthrew Diem. Lodge made it clear that his management of events fit his own concept of "nation building": "My general view is that the United States is trying to bring this medieval country into the twentieth century. . . . We have made considerable progress in military and economic ways, but to gain victory we must also bring them into the twentieth century politically, and that can only be done by either a thoroughgoing change in the behavior of the present government, or by another government."

Bundy insisted that "we do not accept as a basis for U.S. policy that we have no power to delay or discourage a coup." Once more, however, the main concern in the White House was pragmatic rather than ethical—not whether the United States ought to be involved in the plot, but whether it would work. Despite the gravity of the matter, Kennedy finally left the judgment to Lodge: "If you should conclude that there is not clearly a high prospect of success, you should communicate this doubt to the generals in a way calculated to persuade them to desist at least until chances are better. . . . But once a coup under responsible leadership has begun . . . it is in the interest of the U.S. government that it should succeed."

Lodge had, of course, made up his mind long before. It now remained to the rebel officers to fulfill his faith in them—though Lodge and his aides were only dimly aware at the time of the tangled maneuvers going on among the assorted dissident groups.

If the insurgent generals had been proceeding prudently toward a coup, it was not only because of their uncertainties about U.S. policy. They also faced an array of other problems that threatened to subvert their effort. Saigon was seething with intrigues within intrigues, many of them so obscure, complex, and quixotic that the various conspirators suspected each other as much as they distrusted their potential adversaries in Diem's regime.

The generals had become particularly worried by Colonel Pham Ngoc Thao's faction, composed of infantry, marine, paratroop, and armored elements comprising some three thousand men. Dissuaded from acting in August, his group was now preparing to strike on October 24, two days before the generals' deadline. They again stopped him, and after considerable haggling, Thao agreed to place his units under their direction, but they could not be sure of his fidelity.

An even more difficult hurdle was winning over General Ton That Dinh, the Saigon region commander, without whose cooperation a coup would be impossible. Unusually young for a South Vietnamese general—he was then only thirty-seven—Dinh had risen rapidly. He had been trained in France, later becoming the protégé of Diem's brother Can, the boss of central Vietnam, who had been impressed by his courage. But Dinh's bravery as a soldier was matched by his ambition, vanity, and impulsiveness, and Don skillfully played on those character flaws to draw him into the conspiracy. Indeed, no factor in the coup was more important than Dinh's conversion, which dramatized his extraordinary talent for duplicity.

The crackdowns on the Buddhist temples in August had been carried out by Colonel Tung's special forces on orders from Nhu. But General Dinh, who had approved of the raids as Saigon commander, claimed credit for them, boasting that he had rescued South Vietnam from Buddhists, Communists, and "foreign adventurers," his transparent euphemism for Americans. "I have defeated Henry Cabot Lodge," he announced. "He came here to stage a *coup d'état*, but I, Ton That Dinh, have conquered him and saved the country."

Don saw an opportunity to snare Dinh in his own inflated ego. The senior South Vietnamese officers, a lusty lot, frequently drank and whored together, and Don arranged such a series of binges for Dinh in early September. Embarking together on an "inspection tour" of the provinces, they flew from town to town, visiting military units during the day and carousing throughout the evening. Night after night, after polishing off sumptuous dinners and dallying with local prostitutes, they talked endlessly over Scotch whiskey and French brandy. Don assured Dinh that he was a national hero worthy of political authority, and the flattery worked. Dinh now saw himself as a cabinet member, and his favorite fortune-teller further puffed him up by predicting his forthcoming elevation to prominence. Dinh did not know, of course, that Don had bribed the soothsayer to fabricate the prophecy.

His ego inflated, Dinh asked Diem to name him minister of interior. As Don anticipated, Diem not only rejected the request as preposterous, but scolded Dinh for proposing it. Dinh went off in a sulk, and Don grabbed his chance. He persuaded Dinh to join the conspiracy, promising him the ministry of interior in a successor regime.

Even so, the rebel officers continued to doubt Dinh. They calculated that he would cooperate only as long as the coup promised to be successful. As a precaution, they assigned a hit squad to liquidate him if he wavered.

Meanwhile, the generals had to cope with Huynh Van Cao, the Mekong delta commander, a Diem loyalist. His three divisions, deployed close to Saigon, could not only tip the scales in Diem's favor, but transform the city into a bloody battleground. To avert that possibility, Don and Dinh devised a stratagem: Dinh's deputy, Colonel Nguyen Huu Co, would take charge of the division stationed nearest Saigon at Mytho, a town on the Mekong; he would use these troops to prevent

General Cao's forces to the south from moving into Saigon to save Diem. But Nhu heard of the maneuver from one of his spies, and a decisive scene ensued.

Summoning General Dinh to his office in the presidential palace, Nhu confronted Dinh with his knowledge of Co's assignment. Dinh, knowing this was a test, performed to the hilt. Feigning astonishment at his deputy's betrayal, he flew into a tantrum, shouting: "The little traitor! I'll chop the bastard's head off!"

The act convinced Nhu of Dinh's sincerity. Taking him into his confidence, he disclosed that he knew of the generals' plot against him and his brother. But instead of arresting them, he had conceived an elaborate project, presumably with Diem's approval. He would launch his own pre-emptive coup, defeat the conspirators, and in the process strengthen the American commitment to his regime. "Coups, like eggs, must be smashed before they are hatched," Nhu told Dinh.

Nhu's fantastic machination consisted of two operations, Bravo I and Bravo II, and he delegated General Dinh to play a pivotal role in both. As Saigon commander, Dinh would deploy Colonel Tung's special forces in the nearby countryside in early November on the pretext of pursuing the Vietcong. During their absence, Bravo I would begin, as loyal soldiers and police disguised as insurgents staged a "revolt." Diem and Nhu would flee to a prepared refuge at Vung Tau, a coastal resort southeast of the capital, while mob violence "spontaneously" shook the city. Gangs of hoodlums would murder several prominent Vietnamese and American officials, and, amid the chaos, the Saigon radio station was to proclaim the creation of a "revolutionary government" dedicated to evicting the Americans and making a deal with the Communists. This charade would last a few days, and then Bravo II would unfold.

Dinh, with Colonel Tung's special forces and other units faithful to Diem, would march into Saigon and easily crush the "uprising." Diem would return in triumph to reaffirm his legitimacy, having "proved" that only he was capable of subduing a pro-Communist challenge to his government, and the Americans would embrace him as a savior. Nhu calculated as well that the phony coup would flush out his opponents, whom he could arrest. He had also drafted a list of innocuous dissidents, planning to indict them on charges of involvement in the fake rebellion.

The principal defect in Nhu's bizarre intrigue was its reliance on General Dinh—who promptly confided the details of the scheme to Don and the other mutinous generals. But they still distrusted him, fearing that he might betray them just as he was betraying Nhu. They were racing the clock, however. If Nhu planned to pre-empt them, they had to pre-empt him. They had fixed their coup for October 26, then delayed it until October 31 because of Harkins's indiscretion. Heeding an astrologer's warning, they changed it again to a more auspicious moment, one thirty on the afternoon of November 1.

Nhu, learning of the generals' timetable from his informants, moved up his own schedule. He could turn their coup into his pseudocoup, he figured, and he instructed General Dinh to set his project in motion. On October 29, consequently, Dinh ordered Colonel Tung's special forces out of Saigon. But then Dinh pulled another trick. Explaining that Bravo II could be conducted more effectively under his overall direction, he persuaded the regime also to give him command of the Mekong delta forces headed by General Cao. Thus he gained control of nearly all the military units in and around Saigon.

Believing him to be on their side, Diem and Nhu authorized Dinh to deploy troops as he saw fit during the days that followed. Accordingly, Dinh positioned rebel forces inside the capital to attack such key government installations as the radio station, police headquarters, and presidential palace. Except for a few senior officers, most of the soldiers entering Saigon were unaware that a coup was under way. A paratroop lieutenant asked the major in charge of his battalion, "Who is the enemy?" Replied the major, "Anyone who opposes us is the enemy."

At ten o'clock on the morning of November 1, Ambassador Lodge and Admiral Felt paid a courtesy call on Diem. The ritual was the same as always. They sat in brocade armchairs in an ornate salon of the palace and listened wearily as Diem delivered one of his marathon monologues. At one point, Diem referred to rumors of a coup against him, but he seemed unperturbed, probably because he expected Nhu's countercoup to succeed; possibly, too, he expected Nhu's devious scheme to restore him to America's good graces, and as the two-hour session ended, he suggested to Lodge that they meet again soon to resolve their differences.

Lodge retired to his residence for lunch and his customary siesta, leaving Felt to drive to the airport with Generals Harkins and Don. As Felt prepared to board his airplane, Harkins rambled on about the military situation. Don glanced nervously at his watch. The coup was due to begin in an hour, and the other insurgent generals awaited him at the officers' club inside the compound of the staff headquarters near the airport.

The generals and other senior officers, not all of them involved in the plot, had been gathering at the club since noon. They included Colonel Tung, commander of the special forces, who had been told to report to what was described as a routine meeting. Conspicuously absent, however, was Diem's loyal navy commander, Captain Ho Tan Quyen. An hour earlier, his suspicions aroused by unaccountable troop movements around Saigon, he had driven off to consult a fellow officer outside the capital. A jeep filled with rebel marines followed him, blocking his car on a deserted road beyond the city. Leaping from his vehicle, Quyen dashed across an open field, the marines in pursuit. He stumbled and fell. One of the marines reached him as he lay on the ground, placed a pistol against his head, hesitated for a second, and fired. Quyen was the first casualty of the coup—which had not yet officially begun.

Conein had been summoned to the headquarters by the dentist whose office he and General Don had used for their furtive meetings. Wearing his uniform, an ivory-handled .375 magnum frontier-model revolver strapped to his waist, Conein carried a satchel containing three million piasters, the equivalent of $40,000, in case the insurgents needed funds. The generals equipped him with two telephones, one linked to the main CIA office and the other to his villa, where a squad of American Green Berets were guarding his wife and children. Conein also had a radio in his jeep. As he drove to the headquarters, he transmitted to his superiors the prearranged cipher that signaled the imminent start of the coup: "nine, nine, nine, nine, nine, nine. . . ."

Accompanied by a platoon of troops, Colonel Co had driven that morning from Saigon to Mytho, the Mekong delta town. General Dinh, whose writ now extended into the area, had given him official orders to take over the division based there. The division's officers considered Co's arrival to be a normal change of command, not suspecting that his real purpose was to turn them against General Cao's loyalist forces if they tried to rescue Diem. Reaching Mytho two hours before the start of the coup, Co stalled for time by staging an elaborate ceremony in a local hall, which his soldiers surrounded. At precisely one thirty, they burst through the doors, waving their automatic weapons at the officers present. Co thereupon revealed that the coup had begun in Saigon, adding: "Please remain seated quietly. Anyone who rises will be instantly shot."

At that moment, mutinous units went into action in Saigon. Some encircled Diem's palace and his guards' barracks, while others quickly captured the police headquarters and the radio station, where an insurgent officer promptly began to broadcast tapes proclaiming the "revolution." General Don announced to the officers assembled at staff headquarters that a military revolutionary council was seizing power, and he invited them to swear allegiance to the new body. Many had not known of the impending coup; now all but one of them stood up to applaud. The exception was Colonel Tung. Tung's fate had been decided beforehand. Minh's bodyguard, a Captain Nguyen Van Nhung, took him to another room in the building. Tung's brother, Major Le Quang Trieu, was also arrested, later in the day, and at nightfall Captain Nhung drove them both to a spot outside the headquarters compound and shot them. One of the officers present at the compound afterward recalled to me Tung's searing words as Nhung led him away. Denouncing the generals for betraying Diem, he shouted, "Remember who gave you your stars!"

Ensconced in the air-conditioned cellar of the presidential palace, where they had survived earlier threats against them, Diem and Nhu at first reacted calmly to the events, confident that their Bravo operations were unfolding according to plan. Within an hour or so, though, they sensed that something was wrong. They could not reach General Dinh, and refusing to imagine that he was double-crossing them, they conjectured that he might have been captured by the insurgents. But they rejected the generals' appeals to surrender. At about three o'clock, however, Diem abruptly changed his tactics. He had outwitted the rebel paratroopers in November 1960, and he could repeat that performance. He telephoned General Don.

DIEM: What are you generals doing?
DON: Sir, we have proposed to you many times that you reform your policy to conform with the wishes of the people. . . . The time has come for the army to respond to the wishes of the people. Please understand us.
DIEM: Why don't we sit down together? We could talk about the strengths and weaknesses of the regime, and seek ways to improve it.
DON: It may be too late for that.
DIEM: It's never too late. I hereby invite you all to the palace to discuss the matter together, and find a solution acceptable to both sides.
DON: Sir, let me see what the others think.

The others, recollecting Diem's persuasive skills, spurned the offer. But the insurgent leaders, having agreed in advance to spare Diem's life, refrained from shelling his palace. Instead, they directed artillery fire against the presidential guard barracks nearby.

At four thirty in the afternoon, Diem telephoned Lodge. He was too proud to plead for American assistance, and Lodge, having helped to set the coup in motion, was not about to stop it.

DIEM: Some units have made a rebellion, and I want to know what is the attitude of the United States.

LODGE: I do not feel well enough informed to be able to tell you. I have heard the shooting, but am not acquainted with all the facts. Also, it is four thirty A.M. in Washington, and the U.S. government cannot possibly have a view.

DIEM: But you must have some general ideas. After all, I am a chief of state. I have tried to do my duty. I want to do now what duty and good sense require. I believe in duty above all.

LODGE: You have certainly done your duty. As I told you only this morning, I admire your courage and your great contribution to your country. No one can take away from you the credit for all you have done. Now I am worried about your physical safety. I have a report that those in charge of the current activity offer you and your brother safe-conduct out of the country if you resign. Had you heard this?

DIEM: No. [And then, after a pause] You have my telephone number.

LODGE: Yes. If I can do anything for your physical safety, please call me.

DIEM: I am trying to re-establish order.

Soon afterward, the generals telephoned Diem, promising to allow him and Nhu to leave the country unharmed if they capitulated. Otherwise, they warned, they would attack the palace. But Diem, his intransigence stiffened by Nhu, refused to yield. Using his private transmitter, he radioed to his handpicked province chiefs for assistance, and he even appealed to his youth and women's organizations for aid. Nobody responded. His messages were either jammed by the insurgents, or his supporters had rallied to the rebels to save themselves. General Cao, one of his few hopes, had been blocked deep in the Mekong delta since midday.

Realizing that they could not hold out for long, Diem and Nhu made a desperate move. At about eight o'clock in the evening, accompanied by two aides, they slipped out of the palace to a nearby street. There they climbed into a waiting Land Rover and drove to Cholon, the Chinese suburb of Saigon, where they switched to a black Citroën sedan. A curfew had been imposed, and they zigzagged around the deserted city, luckily managing to avoid rebel troop patrols. Finally, they pulled up at a large villa belonging to a wealthy Chinese merchant, Ma Tuyen, who had financed their covert political network for years. Nhu's secret agents had equipped the villa for just such an emergency. One of its telephones was connected to the palace communications system, so that the insurgent generals did not know that Diem had escaped their siege as they talked with him later in the night. Nor were the generals aware, when they issued the order to assault the palace at nine o'clock, that they were about to stage a battle for an empty building. Tragically, the presidential guards were also under the illusion that they were protecting Diem, and they died defending the palace he had fled earlier.

The insurgents triggered the attack with an artillery barrage, but it failed to break the presidential guard battalion. An infantry division commanded by Colonel Nguyen Van Thieu—later to become South Vietnam's chief of state—then attempted to storm the shattered building. Again the defenders clung tenaciously to their positions; the futile fighting went on for hours.

As the battle seesawed, Diem and Nhu doggedly continued their efforts to contact General Dinh, still believing him to be loyal. At midnight, they finally reached him for the first time since the uprising had begun. With the other generals hovering over him as he picked up the telephone at staff headquarters, Dinh was anxious to dispel any doubts about his commitment to the coup. Selecting a choice vocabulary of Vietnamese obscenities, he barked at Diem, "I've saved you mother-fuckers many times, but not now, you bastards. You shits are finished. It's all over."

Not quite. At three o'clock in the morning, November 2, the generals received a telephone call from one of the two aides who had left the palace with Diem and Nhu. Having decided to shift to the winning side, he whispered that the brothers were in Cholon, but he would not pinpoint their exact location. The generals, uncertain whether to trust the disclosure, nevertheless dispatched search parties to the Chinese district—a labyrinth in which fugitives could, unless betrayed precisely, hide out for weeks.

A couple of hours later, the rebel troops besieging the palace noticed a white flag fluttering from a window. Assuming it meant surrender, they advanced in the open toward the building. A fusillade of automatic fire broke out, and one of the advancing officers fell dead. At that, the insurgents intensified their attack. They captured the palace in forty-five minutes, and then proceeded to loot, stealing Madame Nhu's negligees and Nhu's whiskey. Piles of American adventure magazines littered Diem's bedroom; on Nhu's desk, strangely, were several copies of the same book, a thriller entitled *Shoot to Kill*. The brothers, as Diem's turncoat aide had reported, were gone.

At six A.M., Diem telephoned Minh, his voice husky with fatigue. He was prepared to negotiate, but he refused to reveal his whereabouts. He would resign, but only on condition that authority be transferred either to the vice-president or the speaker of the legislature, in accordance with the constitution. The generals, conferring hastily amid the empty beer bottles and cigarette butts that cluttered staff headquarters, quickly rejected the terms, suspecting that he had a trick up his sleeve. At six thirty, when Diem called back, Don informed him of the rebuff, suggesting instead that he and Nhu simply leave the country. Diem agreed. Again, however, he posed a condition—or, as he put it, a "special favor."

DIEM: I am the elected president of the nation. I am ready to resign publicly, and I am also ready to leave the country. But I ask you to reserve for me the honors due a departing president.
DON: [After a pause] Really, I must say that we cannot satisfy you on that point.
DIEM: It's all right. Thank you.

Diem hung up, but he called Don back a few minutes later. He would now surrender unconditionally, and he disclosed that he and Nhu were at Saint Francis Xavier, a French church in Cholon, waiting to be fetched.

General Don was worried. He had guaranteed Diem's security. Now he had to fulfill the pledge. The generals had forgotten to make arrangements to transport Diem and Nhu from Vietnam. They turned for help to Conein, and he explained the complications involved. A long-range aircraft had to be requisitioned, probably from the American base on Okinawa, which meant a delay of at least twenty-four hours. And where would the brothers go? The Kennedy administration, fearful of their embarrassing propaganda potential in the United States, would not give them asylum. Finding another haven would require diplomatic exploration. The generals would have to keep the brothers out of danger until they could be exiled.

Not all the generals favored leniency. Some argued for expelling Diem and holding Nhu for trial, while others wanted both to face a court-martial. They debated the issue and finally decided that their first priority was to escort the Ngos from Cholon to staff headquarters in Saigon. They entrusted the assignment to General Mai Huu Xuan, an unsavory figure who had worked for the French as a secret police agent and afterward served Diem in the same capacity. He detested Diem for having shunted him into a minor job—but then, most of the insurgent officers had similar grievances against the regime they had just deposed.

The generals provided Xuan with an M-113 armored personnel carrier and four jeeps containing several soldiers, among them a tank officer by the name of Major Duong Huu Nghia, and Minh's bodyguard, Captain Nhung, who had murdered the Tung brothers the previous evening. Before the group left headquarters, Minh gestured to Nhung by raising two fingers of his right hand—the signal to kill them both.

At the church, the Ngo brothers politely shook Xuan's hand. Diem appeared to be disappointed that a limousine befitting his rank had not been dispatched, but Xuan advised him that the armored car had been deliberately chosen for his protection against "extremists." Acquiescing, Diem and Nhu boarded the vehicle. Nghia climbed into the gun turret overlooking them, while Nhung sat near them below. Xuan and the other officers got into jeeps, and the motorcade drove off.

What occurred after that has been related in various versions, but most of the details concur. The convoy headed toward Saigon and stopped at a railroad crossing. There, by every account, the assassinations took place. General Don's later investigation determined that Nghia shot the brothers point-blank from the gun turret with an automatic weapon, while Nhung sprayed them with bullets, then stabbed their bodies repeatedly with a knife. Awash with blood, the armored car went on, preceded by the jeeps, whose passengers had not looked back.

Don and the other officers were stunned when the corpses arrived at headquarters. Barging into Minh's office, he demanded an explanation; Minh parried him, and Don began to insist. At that moment the door opened and Xuan entered. Unaware of Don's presence, he snapped to attention and said, *"Mission accomplie."*

The report of Diem's death, flashed to Washington, caught Kennedy in a meeting with Maxwell Taylor and other aides. Kennedy leaped to his feet and, as Taylor later recalled, "rushed from the room with a look of shock and dismay on his face." Soon afterward, the White House requested further information from Lodge, who directed Conein to see Minh. Conein, who had gone home to bed, returned to staff headquarters—less to gather intelligence than to scold Minh for inventing a lame alibi.

MINH: He committed suicide.
CONEIN: Where?
MINH: Well, he was at a Catholic church, and—
CONEIN: Listen, this is your affair, but I'll tell you something as a Catholic. If a priest holds mass for him tonight, everybody is going to know that he didn't commit suicide. Therefore, your story doesn't sound right.
MINH: Would you like to see him? We have him here.
CONEIN: No. There's a one-in-a-million chance that people will believe your story. But if the truth gets out, I don't want to be blamed for leaking it.

Kennedy's assassination, which occurred only three weeks afterward, would be exhaustively investigated by official commissions. But neither the American nor South Vietnamese government ever conducted a public inquiry into Diem's death.

At the time, Saigon welcomed his downfall. Crowds tore up his portrait and slogans. Political prisoners, many scarred by torture, emerged from his jails. The city's nightclubs reopened with a vengeance. In the countryside, peasants demolished the strategic hamlets. Elated and unrepentant, Lodge invited the insurgent generals to his office to congratulate them on their victory, which was his triumph as well. A few days later, he cabled Kennedy: "The prospects now are for a shorter war."

9 The Commitments Deepen

South Vietnamese women were issued American flags in order to greet Secretary of Defense McNamara during his visit to Saigon in February 1964. McNamara toured the countryside with General Nguyen Khanh, the new leader, to whip up support for the regime.

Lyndon Baines Johnson, a young Texas congressman who aspired to emulate President Roosevelt (left), with his idol in Galveston in 1937, shortly after Roosevelt was elected to the second of his four terms.

Johnson, soon after taking office as president in 1963, with his advisers on Vietnam (left to right): Ambassador Lodge, Secretary of State Rusk, Secretary of Defense McNamara, and George Ball, under secretary of state.

General Minh, head of
the group that ousted
Diem, never liked the
responsibilities of power.
He did little to govern
South Vietnam after
becoming its head of state,
and was himself over-
thrown in late January
1964.

General Khanh, who
overthrew General Minh
in January 1964, quickly
received support from the
United States. He is seen
here with (left to right)
Secretary of Defense
McNamara and General
Taylor, who were visiting
Vietnam in February
1964, and Ambassador
Lodge.

After Diem's
assassination, the
"strategic hamlet"
program was disrupted—
either by the Vietcong or
by the peasants them-
selves. This hamlet in the
Mekong delta was aban-
doned by its inhabitants.

President Johnson with
Senator Mike Mansfield,
the majority leader.
Mansfield, an early
supporter of the American
involvement in Vietnam,
lost his enthusiasm for the
commitment, but, loyal to
Johnson, limited his criticism to private memoran-
dums.

Ambassador Lodge dons a South Vietnamese costume as he bids farewell to the people of Saigon in the spring of 1964. He had decided to return home to run for the presidency.

General Taylor (below, at right), who replaced Lodge as ambassador in Saigon in June 1964, with General William Westmoreland, commander of the American military advisory mission. Their dual appointments reflected the importance President Johnson attached to Vietnam.

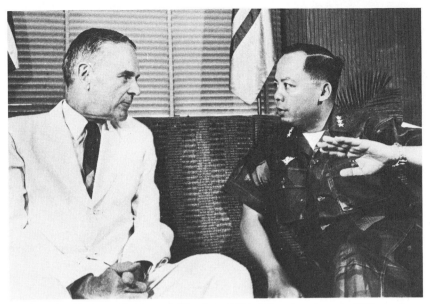

Ambassador Taylor with General Khanh in 1964. These two grew to dislike each other intensely, and Taylor tried to have Khanh removed from office, claiming he was unreliable.

As the American presence in Vietnam expanded, USO appearances became a familiar sight there. Bob Hope, on one of his annual trips to Southeast Asia, entertains the troops with the actress Jill St. John, Christmas 1964.

An American medic examines a peasant child—one of the many civic action projects undertaken by American troops to win the "hearts and minds" of the South Vietnamese people. Peasants often welcomed American help but sympathized with the Vietcong.

The Communists enlarged the Ho Chi Minh Trail during 1964 and were sending big units along it by the end of the year. Their aim was to crush the South Vietnamese army as quickly as possible and force the creation of a coalition government in Saigon.

We should watch the situation very carefully, running scared, hoping for the best, but preparing for more forceful moves if the situation does not show early signs of improvement.
—Robert McNamara

Only by revolutionary violence can the masses defeat aggressive imperialism and its lackeys, and overthrow the reactionary administration to take power.
—Vo Nguyen Giap

L yndon Baines Johnson, a consummate politician, was a kaleidoscopic personality, forever changing as he sought to dominate or persuade or placate or frighten his friends and foes. A gigantic figure whose extravagant moods matched his size, he could be cruel and kind, violent and gentle, petty, generous, cunning, naive, crude, candid, and frankly dishonest. He commanded the blind loyalty of his aides, some of whom worshiped him, and he sparked bitter derision or fierce hatred that he never quite fathomed. And he oscillated between peaks of confidence and depths of doubt, constantly accommodating his lofty ideals to the struggle for influence and authority. But his excesses reflected America's dramas during his lifetime, among them the dramas he himself created. Or, as Hubert Humphrey, the vice-president he both respected and abused, put it, "He was an All-American president. He was really the history of this country, with all of the turmoil, the bombast, the sentiments, the passions. It was all there. All in one man."

Raised in the harsh hills of eastern Texas, the elder son of a protective mother and a brutish father, Johnson early acquired an elemental faith in rugged individualism. He pulled himself up by his own bootstraps—a thrifty, industrious, sincere, ambitious Horatio Alger hero. At college, he excelled as a campus operator, and after graduation he briefly taught high school before grabbing the chance to go to Washington as a congressman's assistant. Using a job in the Roosevelt administration as a springboard, he won election to Congress, where he mastered the arcane art of politics as few of his colleagues would. By 1955, he was the Senate Democratic majority leader and one of the most powerful forces on Capitol Hill. Then, unpredictably, he accepted an offer to stand as John F. Kennedy's running mate, and the vice-presidency spelled oblivion—until Lee Harvey Oswald's bullets propelled him into the White House.

Now, in 1964, he was president, but he never learned that the politician's virtues can become the statesman's vices, as Professor Hans J. Morgenthau once observed. As a representative and senator, Johnson could maneuver, dissemble, break promises, and still escape retribution. As president, by contrast, his every word and action were accountable.

The Depression and his formative New Deal years had ingrained in him an obsession to perpetuate Franklin D. Roosevelt's reforms. He labeled his vehicle the Great Society, and he fought dynamically for social justice, economic equity, and racial equality, promoting the most progressive legislation in those fields in decades. But Vietnam intervened, and he was to explain his decision to wage war in Southeast Asia as inextricably linked to his determination to carry on in Roosevelt's footsteps. Doris Kearns, the most intimate of his biographers, recorded the arguments he advanced, following his retirement:

I knew from the start that I was bound to be crucified either way I moved. If I left the woman I really loved—the Great Society—in order to get involved with that bitch of a war on the other side of the world, then I would lose everything at home. All my programs. All my hopes to feed the hungry and shelter the homeless. All my dreams to provide education and medical care to the browns and the blacks and the lame and the poor. But if I left that war and let the Communists take over South Vietnam, then I would be seen as a coward and my nation would be seen as an appeaser, and we would both find it impossible to accomplish anything for anybody anywhere on the entire globe.

Johnson especially feared that right-wing adversaries would prevail over him should South Vietnam fall to Communism, just as Harry Truman had been hounded by Senator Joseph McCarthy and other demagogues after the Communists engulfed China. Recollecting McCarthy's witch-hunts, he foresaw the danger of another "mean and destructive debate" that would "shatter my presidency, kill my administration and damage our democracy." If a Communist victory in Vietnam knocked over the dominoes, Johnson would be the biggest domino to topple—or so he believed.

This real or imaginary prospect haunted him during the summer of 1964, as he campaigned for election against Senator Barry Goldwater, the conservative Republican with stridently anti-Communist rhetoric. But despite his political acuity, Johnson balked at mobilizing public support for the war in Vietnam. Instead, he manipulated the news media, evidently presuming that his measures would not be noticed. He may have initially expected to avoid full-scale intervention, or perhaps he estimated that most Americans were too concerned with other problems to protest, as opinion surveys showed. He was certainly anxious to avert gestures that might encourage the Soviet Union or China to launch a variation of the Korean conflict in Vietnam or stage a diversionary crisis elsewhere. Whatever his motives, he refused to admit that he was going to war, yet he would never disavow his commitment, as he told Kearns: "Losing the Great Society was a terrible thought, but not so terrible as the thought of being responsible for America's losing a war to the Communists. Nothing would be worse than that."

Such assertions revealed Johnson's basic conviction that America, the beacon of liberty, should never surrender. He had inherited the mythology of the Alamo, where Texas boys had "fought for freedom," and he was not contaminated by the cynicism that affected youths after World War I, claiming, as he wrote in his college newspaper in 1927, that it had been necessary to "make the world safe for democracy." The same concept had guided him as a young congressman, when he labored to back Roosevelt's attempts to prepare the United States for World War II. The memory of the Munich pact—Britain's retreat from the Nazis—made him a staunch cold warrior in the struggle against Communism, and it molded his attitude toward the challenge in Vietnam. He would not reward "aggression" with "appeasement," as he declared in a typically vulgar analogy: "If you let a bully come into your front yard one day, the next day he'll be up on your porch, and the day after that he'll rape your wife in your own bed."

That primitive bluster also masked Johnson's discomfort in the complicated realm of international affairs. The strange names, places, and customs puzzled him. During a visit to Bangkok, he flew into a rage when a staff member of the American embassy counseled him against shaking hands with the Thais, who traditionally recoil from physical contact with strangers. Dammit, Johnson exploded, he shook hands with people everywhere, and they loved it. Nor could he comprehend his inability to bargain with foreign leaders the way he haggled with American politicians, businessmen, and labor negotiators. In 1965, to cite an example, he was baffled by Ho Chi Minh's rejection of his offer of a huge economic project to develop the Mekong valley in exchange for concessions to end the Vietnam war. "Old Ho can't turn me down, old Ho can't turn me down," he repeated after making the offer. In his mind, Ho was no different from labor leader George Meany, with whom he regularly struck such deals.

Equally alien to Johnson was the Eastern establishment that monopolized American foreign policy. The Bundys and Harrimans and Achesons were not his breed, nor were the State Department "cookie pushers" with Ivy League credentials. They spoke a language of their own, the shorthand of New York and Boston, which sounded fake and affected to a Texan. They frequented the affluent salons of Georgetown, which derided him and his "white socks" cronies, and they vacationed on Martha's Vineyard—that "female island," as he scornfully called it. Besides, he had inherited them, along with Rusk and McNamara and Taylor, from Kennedy, whose inner circle he had never penetrated, and that was reason enough to suspect their fidelity. Yet he could not function without them, any more than he could do without the generals and admirals, whom he coddled mainly because they had confederates among his crusty rivals in Congress. So he consulted with them all continually, convening meeting after meeting and insisting on studies and analyses that mounted into millions of pages. To outsiders, it seemed, he was always in search of "consensus."

But he alone exercised control—and with prodigious attention to detail. He made appointments, approved promotions, reviewed troop requests, determined deployments, selected bombing targets, and restricted aircraft sorties. Night after night, wearing a dressing gown and carrying a flashlight, he would descend into the White House basement "situation room" to monitor the conduct of the conflict, hovering above the military and civilian specialists collating reports from Saigon or Danang or Bienhoa. Often, too, he would doze by his bedside telephone, waiting to hear the outcome of a mission to rescue one of "my pilots" shot down over Haiphong or Vinh or Thai Nguyen. It was his war.

At about eleven o'clock on the night of November 22, 1963, Johnson arrived back in Washington from Dallas, where he had gone to campaign with Kennedy. Now Kennedy was dead and he was president. Exhausted after the ghastly day but too nervous to sleep, he drove home. He sprawled across his bed, talking for hours as his assistants listened. He was going to revolutionize America with federal aid to education, tax cuts to stimulate business, civil rights legislation, conservation programs. He barely mentioned Vietnam. As Jack Valenti, one of those present, recalled: "Vietnam at the time was a cloud no bigger than a man's fist on the horizon. We hardly discussed it because it wasn't worth discussing."

But Johnson was not oblivious to Vietnam. To the extent that he had focused on the problem as vice-president, he had been a partisan of firmness, having argued after his whirlwind trip through Southeast Asia in 1961 that the "battle against Communism" in the area "must be joined . . . with strength and determination." He had also been impatient with the attempts to compel Diem to behave more flexibly, saying that "we should stop playing cops and robbers and get back to . . . winning the war." On November 24, two days after succeeding Kennedy, he invited a small group to talk with Henry Cabot Lodge, who was in Washington for consultations following Diem's assassination. He would not "lose Vietnam," Johnson asserted, and he instructed Lodge to "tell those generals in Saigon that Lyndon Johnson intends to stand by our word." He translated his affirmation into an official national security council "action memorandum," which reiterated that the United States would assist the South Vietnamese to "win their contest against the externally directed and supported Communist conspiracy."

The pledge, Johnson's first formal decision on Vietnam, essentially signaled a continuation of Kennedy's policy. But how long could American involvement remain at the present level? For not only had the situation in South Vietnam worsened in the weeks since Diem's downfall, but irrefutable evidence now indicated that it had been degenerating since the summer.

Conditions were particularly perilous in the Mekong delta, the rice basket of South Vietnam, where 40 percent of the population lived. About that time, curious to observe the situation firsthand, I drove south from Saigon into Long An, a province I had visited before. There I found the strategic hamlet program begun during the Diem regime in shambles. At a place called Hoa Phu, for example, the strategic hamlet built during the previous summer now looked like it had been hit by a hurricane. The barbed wire fence around the enclosure had been ripped apart, the watchtowers were demolished, and only a few of its original thousand residents remained, sheltered in lean-tos. Speaking through an interpreter, a local guard explained to me that a handful of Vietcong agents had entered the hamlet one night and told the peasants to tear it down and return to their native villages. The peasants complied without question. From the start, in Hoa Phu and elsewhere, they had hated the strategic hamlets, many of which they had been forced to construct by corrupt officials who had pocketed a percentage of the money allocated for the projects. Besides, there were virtually no government troops in the sector to keep them from leaving. If the war was a battle for "hearts and minds," as the popular platitude went, the United States and its South Vietnamese clients had certainly lost Long An.

My cursory impression, I later discovered, was confirmed in a more extensive survey conducted by Earl Young, the senior U.S. representative in the province. He reported in early December that three quarters of the two hundred strategic hamlets in Long An had been destroyed since the summer, either by the Vietcong or by their own occupants, or by a combination of both. He also contradicted the American and South Vietnamese optimists in Saigon, who had been heralding the decline in enemy activity, by pointing out that Vietcong attacks in the province had subsided primarily because there were no longer any strategic hamlets worth attacking. "The only progress made in Long An province," he concluded, "has been by the Vietcong."

Young's survey, along with other similarly downbeat accounts forwarded to Washington by Ambassador Lodge, unnerved the Johnson administration—as did the initial performance of the generals who had overthrown Diem. They rapidly disrupted the South Vietnamese administrative structure by replacing Diem's officials with their own cronies, many of them not only inexperienced but, hungry for graft, even more corrupt than their predecessors.

In Saigon, meanwhile, the ruling generals were paralyzed by ineptitude. They had formed a military revolutionary council, composed of twelve members who bickered endlessly. Their nominal chairman, General Minh, boasted that the collegial arrangement would guarantee against the autocratic excesses of the old regime. In reality, Minh had contrived the committee in order to bolster his prestige without increasing his responsibility. He was a model of lethargy, lacking both the skill and the inclination to govern. As he confided one morning as we chatted in his headquarters, he preferred to play tennis and tend to his orchids and exotic birds than to preside over tedious meetings and unravel bureaucratic tangles. His junta was to be ousted in late January by General Nguyen Khanh, who was equally incompetent, despite his shrewdness. Until then, Lodge tried to guide Minh. But though Lodge was hardly dynamic himself, his patience soon wore thin. In a cable to Washington, he described Minh as a "good, well-intentioned man," but added a prophetic note: "Will he be strong enough to get on top of things?"

Even at that early stage, Johnson could sense eventual doom. Over dinner one evening not long after he took office, he confessed to his press secretary, Bill Moyers, that he had "the terrible feeling that something has grabbed me around the ankles and won't let go." Unsure how to proceed, he did what Kennedy had done when in doubt: he sent McNamara, his secretary of defense, to Vietnam.

"I am optimistic as to the progress that can be made in the coming year," intoned McNamara following his arrival in Saigon on December 19. But, as usual, his public utterances bore no resemblance to his real estimate. The situation was "very disturbing," he privately told Johnson, predicting that "current trends, unless reversed in the next two or three months, will lead to neutralization at best or more likely to a Communist-controlled state." On his previous journey to Vietnam in October, he had assured Kennedy that "the military campaign has made great progress and continues to progress." Now, in a startling turnabout, he acknowledged that the statistics on which he had based that conclusion had been "grossly in error." Since July, the regime's hold over the countryside had "in fact been deteriorating . . . to a far greater extent than we realized." The Vietcong controlled "larger percentages of the population, greater amounts of territory and have destroyed or occupied more strategic hamlets than expected." The South Vietnamese army was losing more weapons to the Vietcong than it was capturing, and its casualties were also rising. And the slide had accelerated since the coup against Diem.

One "major weakness," McNamara went on, was the official American team in Saigon, which "lacks leadership, has been poorly informed and is not working to a common plan." Lodge was still squabbling with General Paul Harkins, the American military commander, even to the point of excluding him from the embassy's communications with Washington, and their subordinates were also wrangling. Worse yet, "there is no organized government in South Vietnam." The junta was "indecisive and drifting," its generals "so preoccupied with essentially political affairs" in the capital that their troops and provincial officials were "not being effectively directed." Thus, McNamara stated, "there are more reasons to doubt the future of the effort . . . than there are reasons to be optimistic about the future of our cause." But he could not offer a precise prescription: "We should watch the situation very carefully, running scared, hoping for the best, but preparing for more forceful moves if the situation does not show early signs of improvement."

Predictably, the joint chiefs of staff were preparing for "more forceful moves." General Curtis LeMay, the outspoken commander of the air force, had already begun to argue that North Vietnam should be bombed on the grounds that "we are swatting flies when we should be going after the manure pile," and his colleagues were no less bellicose, even though they employed more respectable language. Early in 1964, they handed Johnson a series of suggestions that then seemed drastic, but he would gradually adopt many of them.

The joint chiefs prefaced their plan with an inflated version of the "domino theory." South Vietnam was "pivotal" to America's "worldwide confrontation" with Communism, and a defeat there would deal a blow to U.S. "durability, resolution, and trustworthiness" throughout Asia as well as erode "our image" in Africa and Latin America. Given its importance, the conflict could not be confined to South Vietnam, where "we are fighting . . . on the enemy's terms" and under "self-imposed restrictions." The United States should undertake "increasingly bolder" measures, among them, joint actions with the South Vietnamese to stage air strikes and commando raids against North Vietnam, and flights over Cambodia and Laos to gather intelligence. American combat forces might also be necessary. But above all, a U.S. commander must assume "the actual direction of the war." In short, they were ready to "Americanize" the struggle.

Johnson subscribed to the adage that "wars are too serious to be entrusted to generals." He knew, as he once put it, that armed forces "need battles and bombs and bullets in order to be heroic," and that they would drag him into a military conflict if they could. But he also knew that Pentagon lobbyists, among the best in the business, could persuade conservatives in Congress to sabotage his social legislation unless he satisfied their demands. As he girded himself for the 1964 presidential campaign, he was especially sensitive to the jingoists who might brand him "soft on Communism" were he to back away from the challenge in Vietnam. So, politician that he was, he assuaged the brass and the braid with promises he may have never intended to keep. At a White House reception on Christmas Eve 1963, for example, he told the joint chiefs of staff: "Just let me get elected, and then you can have your war."

At the same time, though, Johnson was loath to alienate old friends like Senator Richard Russell of Georgia, who had coached him during his early days in the Senate, and Mike Mansfield, his successor as Senate majority leader. He genuinely admired them, and he also counted on their support to promote the Great Society. He could not ignore their concerns about the growing U.S. involvement in Vietnam. In particular, he listened to Mansfield, a former professor of Asian history who, after all, had been instrumental in pushing for the original American commitment to South Vietnam a decade before. Now the course of events troubled Mansfield, who voiced his anguish to Johnson in private conversations and memorandums—just as he had cautioned Kennedy a year earlier.

Mansfield agreed with the joint chiefs of staff that the war could not be confined to South Vietnam. But while they favored its extension into North Vietnam, Cambodia, and Laos, he warned Johnson that the conflict might spread to include China, thereby crushing the United States with "massive costs." A "deeper military plunge" neither was in the U.S. "national interest" nor would "settle the question," he argued; it threatened to "enlarge the morass in which we are now already on the verge of indefinite entrapment." As an alternative, Mansfield recommended an "astute diplomatic offensive" based on President Charles de Gaulle's recent appeals for a neutral Vietnam, and he urged Johnson to solicit French help even if this approach offered only a "faint glimmer of hope."

On July 27, 1965, in a last-ditch attempt to change Johnson's mind, Mansfield and Russell were to press him again to "concentrate on finding a way out" of Vietnam—"a place where we ought not to be," and where "the situation is rapidly going out of control." But the next day, Johnson announced his decision to add forty-four American combat battalions to the relatively small U.S. contingents already there. He had not been deaf to Mansfield's pleas, nor had he simply swallowed the Pentagon's plans. He had waffled and agonized during his nineteen months in the White House, but eventually this was his final judgment. As he would later explain: "There are many, many people who can recommend and advise, and a few of them consent. But there is only one who has been chosen by the American people to decide."

Early in December 1963, Ho Chi Minh and his senior comrades in Hanoi assembled to evaluate their past accomplishments and chart their future strategy. Though they shared the conviction that Vietnam must be reunited under their aegis, they were unsure how to proceed. A new group had seized power in Saigon and a new administration had taken over in Washington. As couched in their jargon, they anticipated a "transitional period that entails complex forms and methods of struggle." True, the Vietcong insurgency had made strides within recent months, having benefited from the turmoil that convulsed South Vietnam during Diem's final days and right after his collapse. From Hanoi's viewpoint, however, the prospects of rapid victory were still remote.

Peasants throughout South Vietnam were abandoning the hated strategic hamlets for their native villages, yet their rejection of the Saigon regime reflected weariness with war rather than a vote of confidence in the Vietcong. Similarly, the swelling numbers of South Vietnamese army deserters were not defecting to the Vietcong, but merely going home. Nor did the Saigon government officials, Buddhist militants, student activists, and others who had opposed Diem respond to Communist suggestions for a compromise. Most were at least as anti-Communist as Diem's family had been, having counted among their grievances with Diem his inability to cope with the Vietcong. And with Diem gone, the Communists could no longer focus their propaganda on the abuses of an autocratic oligarchy. Despite their flaws, the generals enjoyed a measure of popularity, especially in Saigon and other cities, where their benign if inept rule was a welcome change from Diem's severity.

North Vietnam's difficulties were also exacerbated by the dispute between its Communist "big brothers," the Soviet Union and China, whose ideological, strategic, national, and even racial differences had by then degenerated into a bitter quarrel. The Hanoi leaders trusted neither the Russians nor the Chinese, both of whom were essentially motivated by their own interests. But the Sino-Soviet squabble was crucial to the North Vietnamese war effort, since Russian and Chinese economic and military aid would be vital if the conflict intensified. Indeed, if later Chinese claims can be believed, China armed the Vietcong guerrillas in 1962 alone with more than ninety thousand rifles and machine guns. Thus the North Vietnamese alternated between trying to patch up the quarrel and shifting to the side that best suited their goals.

Considering themselves to be in the vanguard of the fight against American "imperialism," the North Vietnamese had been disappointed and dismayed by Soviet Prime Minister Khrushchev's attempts to promote "peaceful coexistence" with the United States, their principal enemy. Soviet policy was directly detrimental to their designs to the extent that, while publicly extolling "wars of national liberation," Khrushchev had privately leaned on them to refrain from seeking to "liberate" South Vietnam out of fear that a bigger conflict might burden the Soviet Union—and poison the Kremlin's relations with the United States. Making no secret of their sentiments, the North Vietnamese assailed Khrushchev for retreating in his clash with the Kennedy administration during the Cuban missile crisis of 1962, and they criticized his decision to sign the nuclear test ban treaty the following year. By late 1963, consequently, they had edged toward China, which was castigating Moscow on the same issues, and they continued to echo the Chinese line until Khrushchev's dismissal a year later.

But the Chinese camp was uncomfortable for the Vietnamese Communists, who, like all Vietnamese, recalled centuries of tensions with China. Fresh in their minds as well was China's betrayal at the Geneva Conference. Now they resented the pressures being put on them by Chairman Mao Zedong, who was exhorting them to wage the war in Vietnam according to his formula. He urged them to conduct a protracted conflict, as he had done against Japan and later against Chiang Kai-shek's Nationalists, cloaking his counsel in one of his typical homilies: "A long road tests a horse's strength, and a long march proves a man's heart."

Mao's advice concealed an ulterior purpose. He had not forgotten the Korean war, in which a million Chinese had died, among them his own son, and he was eager to avert a major conflict in Southeast Asia that might again pit China against overwhelming U.S. technology. He was then also contemplating a showdown against adversaries within his own Chinese Communist party, and he intended to use the Chinese army as his instrument for that enterprise rather than in an external venture. Besides, he calculated, a drawn-out war contained within Vietnam's boundaries would fulfill two other objectives: it would gradually weaken the Vietnamese, who had traditionally been a nuisance to China; and it would slowly drain America's resources without posing a serious risk to China's security. So at the time Mao saw the Vietnamese as proxies in his struggle against the United States—just as, a decade later, he would forsake them in order to purchase a rapprochement with President Nixon.

The Vietnamese Communists were never blind to Mao's duplicity. Out of necessity, though, their propaganda during the early 1960s proclaimed their bonds with China to be "as close as lips and teeth." It was not until much later, after the war, that they uncorked their real feelings—with a vengeance. As we chatted in Hanoi in 1981, Vietnam's Prime Minister Pham Van Dong delivered a tirade against Mao, saying: "He was always ready to fight to the last Vietnamese."

Above all, the Vietnamese Communist leaders in late 1963 grimly concluded that Lyndon Johnson had no intention of dropping the American commitment to South Vietnam or negotiating a settlement acceptable to them. Weighing his possible options, they reckoned that he would continue to bulwark the Saigon regime with American advisers and equipment and might, at worst, deploy as many as one hundred thousand U.S. combat troops in Vietnam—though, like the American public during that period, they myopically dismissed that eventuality as "remote." But either way, the Vietcong could not deal with such a challenge alone. Until then, the North Vietnamese had stiffened the Vietcong's ranks with experienced cadres, most of them southern veterans of the war against the French who had gone north after the Geneva agreement. Now, they estimated, their only alternative was to send larger North Vietnamese detachments into the south. The move would require no small investment. They would have to revamp their economic and social priorities as they mobilized North Vietnam's entire population for an expanded conflict. Yet they resolved to make the sacrifice, having learned painfully over the years that the battlefield was decisive. So they declared: "The key point at present is to make outstanding efforts to strengthen rapidly our military forces in order to create a basic change in the balance of forces between the enemy and ourselves in South Vietnam."

During the years that followed, Hanoi's leaders were to issue contradictory statements on their role in South Vietnam. On the one hand, they affirmed the principle that they had the right to intervene there. Ho Chi Minh, in an interview in late 1965, for example, contended that "our people in the north are bound to extend wholehearted support to the patriotic struggle waged by the people of the south," since "Vietnam is one [and] the Vietnamese people are one." At the same time, though, they consistently and vehemently denied the presence of North Vietnamese army regulars in South Vietnam, since an acknowledgment would serve to validate American involvement. Such allegations, asserted Prime Minister Pham Van Dong in January 1966, were "a myth fabricated by the U.S. imperialists to justify their war of aggression." But after the war, when it no longer mattered, the Communists openly admitted the truth. In early 1981, Pham Van Dong told me that "weapons, ammunition, and other military supplies as well as tens of thousands of soldiers were moved into the south for combat" along the so-called Ho Chi Minh Trail—the elaborate communications network that cut through Laos and Cambodia.

A question repeatedly raised during the war—and one that has been repeatedly debated since—is whether major North Vietnamese units went south prior to the arrival of American combat forces in Vietnam or in response to their deployment there. Among the authoritative Communist informants for me on that subject was Colonel Bui Tin, deputy editor of *Quan Doi Nhan Dan*, the official Vietnamese army newspaper, with whom I talked at length in Hanoi in February 1981. His military career had spanned a generation. He had left his aristocratic Hué family in 1945 to join the Vietminh in its struggle against the French, and it was he who accepted the surrender of the shattered South Vietnamese government in Saigon thirty years later. A short, sinewy soldier, he spoke in fluent French as we nursed beers in the squalid bar of the Thong Nhat Hotel in Hanoi, disclosing to me that preparations to send North Vietnamese troops south had begun long before Lyndon Johnson seriously considered the introduction of American battalions into Vietnam. And the North Vietnamese were engaged in battle against Saigon government detachments months before the U.S. marines splashed ashore at Danang in March 1965. Bui Tin, according to his own account, played an important part in the plans to escalate the conflict.

Just as Johnson rarely acted without consulting studies and analyses fed to him by advisers, so the senior Communist commanders in Hanoi were prudent. Before infiltrating troops into the south, they formed a team to survey the situation there, assigning Bui Tin to the mission. It was his first journey to the south since he had left his family eighteen years earlier. Accompanied by a dozen military specialists and civilian cadres, he began the trek down the Ho Chi Minh Trail in late 1963 and, as he recalled, the trip was "extremely arduous." For a veteran of his military experience to so describe it, the ordeal must have been extraordinary.

The trail, which threaded through southern Laos and northeastern Cambodia into the highlands of South Vietnam, was not a single track, but a complex web of jungle paths. When I frequently scanned the region from helicopters during the 1960s, nothing was discernible, even at low altitudes, beneath the green canopy that seemed to stretch on endlessly. Aboriginal tribes who had inhabited the area for centuries, hunting its tigers and elephants and other wild beasts, had carved out the paths in their migrations, and for millennia they had also served traders, as caravans of coolies transported gold and opium from China to the cities of Southeast Asia. The Vietminh had used the Ho Chi Minh Trail as a communications link in the war against the French and, in the initial stages of the southern insurgency, it became the route through which North Vietnam infiltrated cadres as well as modest shipments of arms, ammunition, and other matériel to the Vietcong. Later, it grew into a highway, but as Bui Tin and his comrades embarked on their march, the Ho Chi Minh Trail was still primitive.

They traveled by foot, sweating as they plodded through damp forests and shivering as they forded icy mountain streams. They were plagued by mosquitoes and leeches and other insects that they could not even identify, and some came down with malaria. They carried socks of rice around their torsos, and each bore a knapsack with thirty or forty pounds of food, medicine, extra clothes, a hammock, and a waterproof sheet. There were few villages in the wasteland, but they could replenish their supplies from stocks stored for that purpose at isolated outposts. They sometimes spent the night at these dismal spots, which were manned by lonely North Vietnamese or Vietcong soldiers or their Laotian allies. More often they slept in jungle clearings. After five weeks, they reached their destination inside South Vietnam—a strategic hamlet in Quangngai province that had fallen into Vietcong hands. There the group split up.

Donning black pajamas to avoid detection, Bui Tin went farther south, furtively moving from one Vietcong unit to another to conduct his investigation. He found them unprepared for an intensive campaign. They had lost ground in several areas after Diem's collapse—partly because the government army had regained a measure of morale and partly because peasant grievances against the regime had diminished. They were also poorly organized and lacking in leadership; the Vietcong ranks thinned as many youths dropped out to work with their families in the rice fields. To train the Vietcong for a larger conflict would have been impossible. Bui Tin concluded that the only choice for the Communists was to send sizable North Vietnamese contingents into the south. "We had to move from the guerrilla phase into conventional war," he explained. "Otherwise, our future would have been bleak."

In the spring of 1964, after five months in the south, Bui Tin laboriously retraced his footsteps back to Hanoi. Like the many Americans who returned to Washington with reports on their "fact-finding" missions to Vietnam, he merely confirmed a decision that had already been made by his superiors. North Vietnamese troops were mobilized for deployment in the south, and their units were laced with southern Vietminh veterans to guide them in the unfamiliar area. In order to furnish the force with hundreds of thousands of tons of weapons, ammunition, food, and the other necessities vital for major battles, the Hanoi high command set in motion a vast and ambitious scheme to turn the Ho Chi Minh Trail into a modern logistical system. As Bui Tin put it: "We would no longer carry supplies into the south on our backs and shoulders, like ants filling anthills."

The immense project, which began in the middle of 1964, continued until hostilities ceased a decade later. Its architect was Colonel Dong Si Nguyen, who was to become minister of construction in Hanoi after the war, and he spared no expense. He brought in engineer battalions

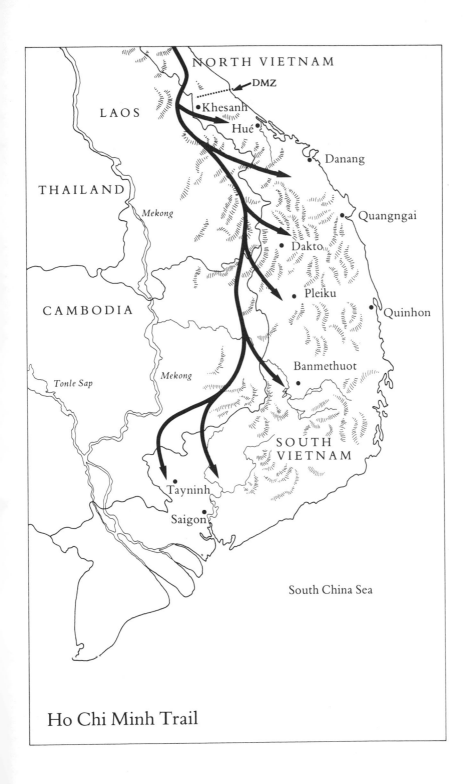

NORTH VIETNAM

DMZ

LAOS

•Khesanh

Hué•

•Danang

THAILAND

Mekong

•Quangngai

•Dakto

CAMBODIA

•Pleiku

•Quinhon

Mekong

Tonle Sap

Banmethuot

SOUTH
VIETNAM

•Tayninh

Saigon•

South China Sea

Ho Chi Minh Trail

equipped with up-to-date Soviet and Chinese machinery to build roads and bridges that could handle heavy trucks and other vehicles. Anticipating the likelihood of relentless American bombings, he erected sophisticated antiaircraft defenses. He dug underground barracks, workshops, hospitals, storage facilities, and fuel depots—further precautions against air raids—and platoons of drivers, mechanics, radio operators, ordnance experts, traffic managers, doctors, nurses, and other personnel were recruited to support the North Vietnamese army in the field.

The few thousand Communist soldiers and civilian cadres who had infiltrated into South Vietnam during previous years had mostly been indigenous southerners, returning home to aid the Vietcong. By April 1964, northern regulars were headed down the enlarged trail, and they were followed by the first complete North Vietnamese tactical units at the end of the year. Throughout 1964, an estimated ten thousand North Vietnamese troops went south—a trickle compared to the numbers three years later, when they were pouring into South Vietnam at the rate of twenty thousand or more per month. The Communists had added a new and significant dimension to the struggle. Henceforth, in their view, there could be no substitute for military victory: the strategy that had succeeded against the French would work again. As General Vo Nguyen Giap asserted at the time: "The most correct path to be pursued by the people to liberate themselves is revolutionary violence and revolutionary war. . . . Only by revolutionary violence can the masses defeat aggressive imperialism and its lackeys, and overthrow the reactionary administration to take power." Throughout the Vietnam war, as in all wars, the protagonists persistently perceived their fortunes differently. So while the Communist leaders in Hanoi felt in 1964 that only a swift military triumph could crush their South Vietnamese enemies, the view from Washington during the same period was that the tottering Saigon government would crumble at any moment in confused turmoil. Neither side was willing to consider a compromise, since each sought to improve its bargaining posture. Each escalated in hopes of negotiating from strength and imposing its conditions on the other.

Lyndon Johnson certainly had cause for concern as he observed the scene in Vietnam from the Oval Office. He had opposed the plot to overthrow Diem, fearing that it would damage the war effort, and his apprehensions seemed to be coming true. As reports of the chronic ferment in Saigon reached his ears, he barked at his White House aides that he was fed up with "this coup shit." But Diem's successors continued to squabble among themselves; the regime would be revamped seven times in 1964, even though the same faces reappeared like a reshuffled pack of cards. With each change, the government's authority dwindled, and its influence further declined with its inability to check the Vietcong's progress on the battlefield. By early 1965, after he won his own mandate as president, Johnson concluded that only direct American intervention could prevent a Communist takeover of South Vietnam—and, more importantly, shield him against charges of having been "the first president to lose a war."

Late in January 1964, a thirty-seven-year-old field commander, General Nguyen Khanh, toppled the junta that had ousted Diem only three months before. A jaunty figure with darting eyes and a goatee, Khanh strutted and swaggered like a character in a Chinese opera, and his performance in power sometimes bordered on the comic. But he was shrewd and energetic. Even in a society where scruples were scarce, he was distrusted, having built his career on switching his allegiance to whichever faction promised to fulfill his limitless ambitions.

I had occasionally chatted with Khanh in those days, but I interviewed him at length only after the war, when he had immigrated to the United States. He was then managing a shabby little oriental restaurant amid the service stations and used-car lots of a tawdry boulevard in West Palm Beach, Florida, and he lived nearby in a humble little house cluttered with flags, emblems, autographed photographs, and other souvenirs of his former prominence. We slouched in plastic-covered armchairs in that melancholy atmosphere of faded glory as he reminisced in fluent French, and I knew as I listened that I would later have to separate the fact from the fiction in his "war stories." But whatever the truth of his account, it seemed, in retrospect, to be almost beyond belief that America's crusade in Vietnam could have hinged on so sleazy a surrogate.

Khanh began his career as a soldier at the age of sixteen, after what must have been a troubled childhood. His mother, who ran a nightclub in Dalat frequented by roistering French, had sent him off as a boy to reside with his father, a wealthy southern landowner, and he was raised by his father's mistress, a popular Vietnamese actress and singer. Yearning for adventure, young Khanh left school in Saigon to join a crudely armed Vietminh band harassing the French in the Mekong delta. He later claimed that he soon abandoned the Vietminh when he learned of its Communist coloration, but I suspect that he quit because the French had more to offer. They enrolled him in their military academy for Vietnamese officers, gave him advanced training in France, and made him a platoon leader in a mobile combat unit. A tough fighter, he was wounded twice in battles against the Vietminh. He recalled during our talk in Florida that he eventually became disillusioned with the French and considered forming his own "third force." But in a conversation we had fifteen years before in Vietnam, he had expressed pride at having served under General Jean de Lattre de Tassigny. "We campaigned together all over the country," he told me then, as if he and the flamboyant French commander had been buddies.

Following the partition of Vietnam in 1954, Khanh rallied to Ngo Dinh Diem, who desperately needed seasoned officers. He became deputy chief of staff in the South Vietnamese army, but his fidelity to Diem was open to question. In November 1960, when rebel paratroopers staged a revolt, Khanh parlayed with them long enough for loyal forces to arrive from the provinces to crush the uprising, but on the other hand, his critics contended, Khanh was himself waiting to see which way the wind blew. Three years later, Khanh participated in the coup that culminated in Diem's murder. Though his role was minor, he expected a big reward, but the junta instead assigned him command of the First Corps, the northernmost area of South Vietnam. Nobody wanted a mischief-maker in Saigon.

Even so, Khanh demonstrated that his reach was long. His ego bruised, he began to conspire against the junta. He recruited other disgruntled officers, among them General Tran Thien Khiem, commander of the Saigon region, who also felt that his contribution to Diem's downfall had not been adequately recompensed. Starting in early January 1964, they met covertly with confederates in Saigon or at Khanh's headquarters at Hué, and finally arranged to launch their coup at four o'clock on the morning of January 30. According to the plan, Khiem's forces in the capital would surround the homes of the sleeping junta as Khanh, leading a paratrooper unit, occupied the general staff headquarters near the airport. On January 28, dressed in civilian clothes, Khanh flew from Hué to Saigon aboard a commercial airliner. He was accompanied by his American military adviser, Colonel Jasper Wilson, and he put out the story that he had arrived to visit the dentist. He went to the home of a friend to wait. As the appointed hour approached, he donned his uniform and drove with an aide to staff headquarters, where the paratrooper unit was scheduled to meet him. But the headquarters area was dark and deserted except for a few guards. What ensued, as Khanh recalled it in 1981, typified the inefficiency of South Vietnam's high command: "Here I was, at the staff headquarters, and nothing was happening. No troops, no action, nothing. So I telephoned my friend, General Khiem, and I asked him, 'What are you doing? Nothing is moving.' He answered, 'Oh, I must have forgotten to set my alarm clock, and I overslept. But don't worry, we have the situation in hand. There's no problem.' "

Khiem was correct. By daybreak, Khanh had taken over the government without firing a shot, asserting in a morning radio broadcast that he had conducted his "purge" because the junta had failed to make any progress against the Communists. The Saigon population went about its business, apparently oblivious to the event.

Ambassador Lodge had been aware of Khanh's plans in advance, but he did nothing to squelch the plot. Following the coup, moreover, U.S. officials boosted Khanh as South Vietnam's new hope. It seemed at the time, therefore, that the United States, having lost confidence in the junta, encouraged Khanh to seize power. But as usual in Vietnam, appearances blurred reality. Lodge and his staff had in fact dismissed Khanh's signals as mere products of Saigon's prolific rumor mill, and had been caught by surprise. The episode further illustrated how little the Americans could monitor, much less control, the arcane political maneuvers of their South Vietnamese clients. President Johnson, in Washington, could demand stability in Saigon, but in Saigon itself, the "puppets" were still pulling their own strings.

As early as the first week in December, a month after Diem's collapse, Khanh had divulged his intentions to Lieutenant Colonel Conein, the ubiquitous CIA agent. Conein dutifully reported the conversation to his superiors, who filed it along with the multitude of other rumors then sweeping through the capital. Undeterred, Khanh and his fellow conspirators continued to badger almost any American official they could find. Like the generals who had overthrown Diem, they were anxious to obtain American approval as an assurance of future support. But nearly every South Vietnamese officer was involved in a plot of one sort or another, and some were enmeshed in several intrigues. The American intelligence establishment in Saigon simply could not cope.

In one respect, Khanh struck a chord with the Americans. President de Gaulle, then contemplating the recognition of China, favored the neutralization of Southeast Asia as part of his grand design. The concept alarmed the United States, but Khanh saw it as a chance to advance his own aims. He spread the word around Saigon that French agents were behind a conspiracy to install a South Vietnamese government that would carry out de Gaulle's policy. The principal plotters, he alleged, were Generals Tran Van Don and Le Van Kim, both of whom had served in the French colonial administration—as, indeed, he himself had. American intelligence operatives regarded these allegations as flimsy.

Yet Lodge gave them credence, possibly because he heard them from European diplomats he respected. After the coup, he welcomed Khanh as a convenient antidote to the dreaded virus of neutralism. He tortuously explained his sentiments in a confidential cable to Washington: "To overthrow a government that was progressing fairly satisfactorily seemed like a violent and disorderly procedure. . . . On second thought, however, one realized that Generals Don and Kim had never at any time forsworn the possibility of a neutral solution."

As regimes rose and fell in Saigon, nothing alarmed American strategists more than the prospect of a change that would bring to power South Vietnamese leaders prepared to reach an accommodation with the Communists. Ironically, Khanh was to attempt to make such a deal years later, after he had been exiled to Paris, and he actually held a press conference to reveal his secret correspondence with the Vietcong. But in early 1964, it suited his aims to appear fiercely anti-Communist. Lodge was somewhat skeptical at that stage, and his diagnosis of the situation once again mirrored the fatal American flaw of thinking that the challenge in Vietnam was essentially a management problem: "We have everything we need in Vietnam. The United States has provided military advice, training, equipment, economic and social help, and political advice. The government of Vietnam has put a relatively large number of good men into important positions and has evolved civil and military procedures that seem to be workable. Therefore, our side knows how to do it. We have the means with which to do it. We simply need to do it. This requires a tough and ruthless commander. Perhaps Khanh is it."

The uncertain note in Lodge's appraisal was prescient. For it quickly became apparent that Khanh would perform no better than his predecessors—and might even be worse. No sooner had he seized authority than he ordered the liquidation of Major Nguyen Van Nhung, one of the officers who had murdered Diem and Nhu three months earlier. The job was done surgically by one of Khanh's henchmen, who quietly led Nhung to a garden behind a Saigon villa on the evening of January 31, forced him to kneel, and put a single bullet through the back of his head. Nhung probably deserved the punishment, having himself snuffed out dozens of lives as a professional assassin. Khanh's aides circulated the story that Nhung, overcome with remorse at having killed Diem, had hanged himself. Not only did this ring hollow, but Nhung's summary execution sparked a series of complicated political reactions—he was, despite his unsavory record, a symbol.

In the first place, he had worked for General Duong Van Minh. Thus, apart from any personal grievances Minh might have felt, Nhung's death suggested to him that Khanh intended to repudiate the coup against Diem and reinstate those who had served the old regime. Lodge and his aides in Saigon, fearful that a feud between Minh and Khanh would divide the South Vietnamese army, persuaded the two men to cooperate. Minh sullenly accepted Khanh's offer to become titular head of state. But soon South Vietnam tumbled into a year of upheavals nearly as chaotic as Diem's battles against the dissident religious and gangster factions a decade earlier.

Militant Buddhist groups, to whom Nhung's elimination also portended a return to power of Catholics and others faithful to Diem, exacerbated the turbulence. The heads of eleven of South Vietnam's fourteen different Buddhist sects had agreed to cease their bickering and form an alliance designed to exert political influence. Tri Quang, the monk who had first mobilized the Buddhist campaign against the Diem regime the year before, lobbied for a key post in the coalition. But his dynamism worried his rivals, some of whom also suspected that he had Vietcong connections, and they instead gave the direction of the movement's secular affairs to Tam Chau, a North Vietnamese refugee and fierce anti-Communist. Frustrated, Tri Quang decided to go on a pilgrimage to India, Ceylon, and Japan—to "bury my life" in faraway monasteries, as he put it to friends. He was raising funds for the journey in late January, when Khanh had Nhung shot. He abruptly canceled his travel plans and moved to Hué, the scene of the initial Buddhist uprising against Diem. There he began to organize his acolytes, warning them that Diem's disciples were conspiring to regain authority. He soon persuaded Tam Chau and other Buddhists to embark on an offensive that would challenge Khanh and his successors.

Khanh had also blundered by detaining Generals Don and Kim, whom he banished to Dalat to await trial for allegedly plotting with French agents to establish a neutralist government in Saigon. Unable to produce a shred of evidence to substantiate the accusation, Khanh ended up looking petty and foolish. Indeed, a court-martial afterward rejected the indictment and merely reprimanded the two officers for such infractions as "lax morality," a ruling that sounded to the permissive Vietnamese like an indirect jibe at Khanh. More important, the transparently phony case turned many officers against Khanh, further dividing the upper echelons of the South Vietnamese army at a time when it badly lacked cohesion. Khanh later tried to repair his error by appointing Don and Kim to advisory jobs, but the damage had been done.

Khanh made yet another mistake by seeking support from remnants of the Dai Viet Quoc Gia Lien Minh, or Greater Vietnam party, a nationalist movement that had been largely shattered by the Vietminh and the French. One of its surviving leaders, Dr. Nguyen Ton Hoan, a deceptively mild-looking Catholic physician, had fled to Paris in 1955 after staging an abortive bid to unseat Diem. Typically, he opened a restaurant, meanwhile maneuvering from afar to influence events inside South Vietnam through a clandestine network of associates there. Khanh, figuring that he could play off the Dai Viet against competing factions to his own advantage, summoned Hoan home to become prime minister, but the ploy misfired. The Dai Viet was so splintered that Hoan could not harness its assorted cliques; other parties, hungry for a share of power, resented his appointment; and younger political activists protested, complaining that the country needed fresh blood rather than superannuated exiles. Khanh backtracked, and made himself prime minister and named Hoan his deputy. Hoan, feeling betrayed, began to conspire against Khanh, who had also become a target for Buddhist, Catholic, and other groups, which spilled into the streets to demonstrate against each other. Saigon again spiraled into confusion, and its population grew still wearier of a war that had, at that stage, only started to intensify.

"One clear victory would do wonders for this government right now," an American military adviser told me at the time, but the South Vietnamese army was no match for the Vietcong, which stepped up its operations in the countryside and even staged a series of terrorist attacks in Saigon, one of them killing three Americans and injuring forty others in a downtown movie theater. Khanh's forces suffered a particularly humiliating setback in the Mekong delta in late February, when a Vietcong battalion eluded three thousand of his best troops. The government units had encircled the enemy but balked at advancing, once again calling for air and artillery strikes to avoid casualties. Stung by the failure, Khanh peremptorily dismissed three of his four corps commanders and five of his nine division commanders. The gesture eroded the army's morale. Meanwhile, he had shattered the rural administrative structure by replacing most of the province and district chiefs appointed after the coup against Diem.

Gloom pervaded the U.S. mission in Saigon. Lyman Kirkpatrick, a senior CIA official, reported after a visit there in February that he was "shocked by the number of our people and of the military, even those whose job is always to say we are winning, who feel that the tide is against us." Other American officials echoed his pessimism, estimating that "unless there is a marked improvement in the effectiveness of the South Vietnamese government and armed forces," the country had only "an even chance of withstanding the insurgency menace during the next few weeks or months." Lyndon Johnson had ruled out withdrawal, nor would he contemplate a compromise with the Communists. But how could he halt the drift toward defeat?

Roger Hilsman, an assistant secretary of state held over from the Kennedy era, had never abandoned his belief in counterinsurgency. He proposed that the United States train South Vietnamese soldiers as guerrillas to fight the Communists at their own game, and he outlined an "ink blot" plan under which Saigon government partisans would secure villages one by one, extending the regime's control over the countryside like a spreading blot of ink. But, during the early months of 1964, the situation was too desperate for such a slow strategy, whose results could not be guaranteed. Besides, Johnson distrusted Hilsman— partly because of his Kennedy connection and partly because of his role in the ouster of Diem. He forced Hilsman to resign and leaned instead toward the blunt military approach recommended by the joint chiefs of staff, now headed by Maxwell Taylor. Johnson sent McNamara and Taylor back to Vietnam in early March, and their trip deepened the U.S. commitment.

To the extent that Congress was paying attention to Vietnam in those days, its mood seemed to be ambivalent. Members of the House Armed Services Committee, grilling McNamara in late January, expressed concern at the possibility of greater U.S. involvement, yet they were also impatient at the visible lack of progress. McNamara tried to reassure them by promising that American intervention would be limited merely to "logistical and training support," that it was "a Vietnamese war . . . that can only be won by the Vietnamese themselves." And he optimistically forecast the eventual withdrawal of U.S. military advisers, explaining that by "keeping the crutch there too long we would weaken the Vietnamese rather than strengthen them."

But McNamara's behavior during his trip to South Vietnam, combined with the decisions taken in Washington after his return, pointed the Johnson administration in a different direction. "We shall stay for as long as it takes to . . . win the battle against the Communist insurgents," he pledged as he landed in Saigon on March 8. In addition to giving the usual briefings and conferences, he stepped out of character to stage a public relations act designed to put America's imprimatur on Khanh, and the theatrical performance dramatized the absurdity of the U.S. role in Vietnam. Here was McNamara, the quintessential American businessman, incongruously barnstorming this strange Asian land in an attempt to promote Khanh to his own people. Heavily protected by troops and helicopters, they toured the Mekong delta and flew up to Hué; McNamara, fumbling with the difficult tonal language, uttered memorized Vietnamese phrases extolling Khanh as the country's "best possible leader." No matter that he might be debauching Khanh's nationalist pretensions by thus presenting him as a protégé of the United States. He was really talking to Lyndon Johnson, who firmly believed that the South Vietnamese would make the necessary sacrifices if only they knew that the United States stood behind them.

Back in Washington five days later, McNamara produced contrasting public and private accounts—as he had after his trip in December. He issued a confident statement for public consumption, declaring that Khanh was "acting vigorously and effectively" and predicting that "the war can be won." But to Johnson he reported that the situation had "unquestionably been growing worse" since his last trip. About 40 percent of the countryside was now under Vietcong "control or predominant influence," the figure running as high as 90 percent in such provinces as Long An and Kien Tuong, not far from Saigon. South Vietnamese army desertions were "high and increasing," while the Vietcong was "recruiting energetically." Much of the population was overcome by "apathy and indifference," and "signs of frustration" were apparent in demoralized American officials. The "greatest weakness," however, was the "uncertain viability" of Khanh's regime, which might crumble at any moment in another coup.

McNamara urged that South Vietnam be put on a rigorous "war footing," with the United States making "emphatically clear" its readiness to give Khanh an open-ended pledge of assistance. Among other things, the United States should finance an increase in the size of his army, provide him with more modern aircraft and other equipment, and underwrite the expansion of his rural administration. Johnson approved these proposals, which were formally restated in a national security council "action memorandum."

The decision to furnish Khanh with additional aid, while significant, was less important than the strategic goals it redefined. Until then, the U.S. aim had been limited to helping the Saigon government defeat the Vietcong. Now the administration broadened the objective. More was involved than just South Vietnam or even Asia, the national security council document asserted; a Communist victory would damage the reputation of the United States throughout the world. The conflict was a "test case" of America's capacity to cope with a Communist "war of liberation," and the whole of U.S. foreign policy faced a trial.

The flaw was Khanh, who was more preoccupied with protecting than exercising his authority. He spent most of his time maneuvering against internal rivals, with the result that he neglected his administrative duties, which bored him anyway. Though the United States was now pouring in aid at the rate of nearly $2 million a day, South Vietnamese army officers and civil servants were being paid late and often not at all, projects to train soldiers and civilian officials had fallen into disarray, and funds were not reaching peasants who had been promised subsidies to relocate as part of the "pacification" program. Nor did Khanh put the country on a "war footing," as he had assured McNamara he would. He introduced a national service law but never fully implemented it, and blamed delays on "complicated bureaucratic procedures" allegedly inherited from the French. In reality, he had no intention of antagonizing influential urban families by conscripting their sons—just as, ironically, Johnson generously deferred U.S. college students from the draft to avoid alienating the American middle classes.

To demonstrate his aggressivity, however, Khanh began to thump for an offensive against North Vietnam. His campaign rattled Johnson, who feared a clash with China or the Soviet Union. It also evoked little enthusiasm from American officials in Vietnam, who saw it as primarily a device to avoid a long and tedious war in the south. By coincidence, Ho Chi Minh reached a similar conclusion. Calling Khanh's threat to invade the north "sheer stupidity," Ho asked, "How can he talk about marching north when he cannot even control areas in the immediate vicinity of Saigon?"

But even as the U.S. mission in Saigon tried to restrain Khanh, planners in Washington were exploring ways to extend the hostilities beyond South Vietnam's boundaries. In the middle of March, for example, Johnson authorized Lodge to flash the green light to Khanh to stage covert cross-border raids against Communist sanctuaries in Laos—on condition that Prince Souvanna Phouma, the Laotian prime minister, endorsed the operations. He also approved additional American reconnaissance flights over Laos, and ordered studies to be made for possible incursions into Cambodia, where the North Vietnamese and Vietcong were just beginning to lengthen their web of supply routes. Meanwhile, Pentagon specialists were pinpointing targets in North Vietnam for potential American air strikes.

Johnson was then divesting himself of Kennedy administration figures like Hilsman and Harriman, who had favored a more political approach to Vietnam, and the locus of planning shifted to one of McNamara's top subordinates, William P. Bundy, the assistant secretary of defense who was to supplant Hilsman as assistant secretary of state for the Far East. A lean patrician with a lockjaw accent, Bundy, like his younger brother McGeorge, had attended the Groton School and Yale University; he had graduated from Harvard Law School before joining the CIA—at a time when the agency was virtually an Ivy League alumni association. Like McGeorge, who now headed Johnson's national security council staff, his connections were impeccable. He had married Dean Acheson's daughter, and his patrons included such Washington luminaries as Allen Dulles, the legendary CIA director. But in contrast to his brother, a brilliant scholar with a penchant for power, Bill was the classic bureaucrat—the kind of man whose lifetime of faceless public service would have been capped with a knighthood in Britain. One unfortunate incident marred his otherwise seamless career. During the early 1950s, as a CIA operative in Germany, he had been singled out for attack as a Communist sympathizer by the demagogic Senator McCarthy, who was indirectly trying to smear Acheson. Bundy's prominent protectors defended him and the ugly charge evaporated, as did McCarthy. Still, the episode seemed to have wounded Bundy, and though his instincts were liberal, he advocated a hard line toward Vietnam, as if striving to compensate for his vulnerability.

On March 1, following up earlier Pentagon proposals, Bundy sent Johnson an elaborate new set of recommendations for punishing North Vietnam. As an opening gambit, the United States ought to blockade Haiphong harbor—less to destroy the traffic there than to hit "at the sovereignty of North Vietnam" and to warn that "we would go further." The next steps would be to bomb North Vietnamese railways, roads, industrial complexes, and training camps, the purpose being as much political as military: the air raids would compel Hanoi to "stop or at least sharply cut down" its assistance to the Vietcong, but equally important, they would "stiffen the Khanh government, completely assure it of our determination, and discourage moves toward neutralism" in Saigon, as well as "show all of Southeast Asia . . . that we will take strong measures to prevent the spread of Communism specifically, and the grab of territory generally, in the area."

Bundy focused on an issue that until now had been overlooked. To launch operations against North Vietnam, he noted, would "normally require" a declaration of war under the U.S. Constitution, and that might spark domestic controversy. Yet to proceed without legislative endorsement would be "unsatisfactory." The "best answer," therefore, was a congressional resolution of the sort that had freed President Eisenhower's hands to act in 1955, when the Chinese Communists menaced the offshore islands of Quemoy and Matsu. It was unclear how

Johnson could persuade Congress to pass the resolution. But his aides soon began to draft a document that, in murky circumstances five months later, would overwhelmingly win the approval he needed to fulfill nearly all the Pentagon's dreams.

In June 1964, claiming that a letter from an American enlisted man in Vietnam had inspired him, Lodge resigned as ambassador to seek the Republican nomination in the presidential campaign. Johnson cast about for a successor, and there was no shortage of candidates. Rusk, McNamara, and McGeorge Bundy volunteered, and so did Robert Kennedy, who told Johnson in a handwritten note that Vietnam was "obviously the most important problem facing the United States and . . . I am at your service." But, in an election year, Johnson wanted prominent representatives in Saigon who would reassure the hawks in Congress and still heed his wish to keep the war within bounds. He selected General Maxwell Taylor, chairman of the joint chiefs of staff, naming as his deputy U. Alexis Johnson, a veteran diplomat and then the State Department's fourth-ranking official. And he promoted Lieutenant General William C. Westmoreland to replace Harkins as commander of the U.S. military advisory group. Never before in history had such a distinguished array of talent been assigned to cope with a conflict that was not being directly conducted by the United States.

Westmoreland, who had been in Vietnam since January as deputy to Harkins, was then nearly fifty years old, and he looked like the model of a modern American general. A tall, erect, handsome West Pointer with narrow eyes and a chiseled chin, he had earned a chestful of ribbons during World War II and in Korea, and he exuded the same virtuous resolve he had displayed as an eagle scout during his boyhood in South Carolina. But Johnson had not chosen him for his physique or his purity. Westy was a corporation executive in uniform, a diligent, disciplined organization man who would obey orders. Like Taylor, he saw the war as essentially an exercise in management—and together they began to "Americanize" the effort.

Even before Taylor and Westmoreland assumed their new jobs, frustrated officials in Washington had been contemplating a fresh approach that would give the United States greater leverage in Vietnam. In a cable to the U.S. embassy in Saigon, Secretary of State Rusk speculated on possible ways to "shake" the South Vietnamese leaders "by the scruff of the neck and insist that they put aside all bickering and lesser differences." He suggested that "somehow we must change the pace at which these people move," musing that perhaps "this can only be done with a pervasive intrusion of Americans into their affairs." William Sullivan, one of Rusk's assistants, spelled out the notion more precisely. Until then, he said, the United States had expected the Saigon regime to enforce more programs than it was "technically and administratively capable of handling." Accordingly, he proposed a revision of the "ground rules" under which the United States had tried to wage the war through its Vietnamese clients. He recommended the creation of a "coordinated executive direction," with American military and civilian officials squarely integrated into the South Vietnamese government structure from the central down to the district level. Such an arrangement risked creating the "stigma of colonialism," he conceded, but a desperate situation required desperate measures. The country could only be saved from the Communists by a more efficient system of management under closer American supervision.

Lodge had never been a team player. Almost as arcane and secretive as the Vietnamese, he had relied on two or three intimate aides to assist him. Taylor, in contrast, reorganized the American mission the moment he arrived in Saigon. He tightened the apparatus around the "mission council," whose members were the political, military, intelligence, aid, and information officers. They would attend weekly meetings to discuss possible programs, and, if an idea sounded plausible, the ambassador would order it "staffed"; a committee of subordinates then prepared a detailed outline of the project, eventually sending it back to the council for a verdict—or what was called, in bureaucratic jargon, concurrence or nonconcurrence. But the council's decision was not enough. A proposal approved in Saigon would be referred to Washington for further examination by other committees—a procedure that could consume weeks, during which time it might be amended over and over again. The final plan would be presented to a parallel South Vietnamese government panel, a stage of the process that was usually smooth. For as long as the United States was willing to foot the bill for any given program, the Vietnamese rarely rejected it.

The difficulty, however, was to measure results. Or, as a U.S. official in Saigon explained it to me at the time: "Say, for instance, that we hand them a plan to distribute ten thousand radios to villages so that peasants can listen to Saigon propaganda broadcasts. They respond enthusiastically, and we deliver the radios. A few months later, when we inquire, they tell us what we want to hear: peasants are being converted to the government cause, and we're winning the war. But what has really happened? Have all the radios reached the villages, or have half of them been sold on the black market? Are peasants listening to Saigon radio, or to Hanoi radio? We don't know. We're in the mysterious East. We report progress to Washington because Washington demands progress."

By the middle of 1964, the United States had formed in South Vietnam the most formidable American team ever assembled abroad in "peacetime"—and it was only a hint of things to come. American experts in the provinces were teaching Vietnamese peasants to breed pigs, dig wells, and build houses. There were American doctors and schoolteachers, accountants, mechanics, and even disc jockeys running an American radio station in Saigon. American ordnance technicians were testing high-velocity rifles, weird needle bombs, and infrared cameras to peer through camouflage. Covert American operatives were involved in a dozen secret intelligence networks, including a special detachment that spied on spies. All these and other American activities were financed by U.S. aid, which also underwrote weapons as well as imports of medicine, milk, gasoline, fertilizer, and other products, sold locally to generate the cash to pay the Saigon government and its armed forces, then expanding to six hundred thousand men. The war, in short, had become the principal pillar of the South Vietnamese economy.

As it grew, the cumbersome American complex in Vietnam was roiled by intramural squabbles among its various agencies, each striving to promote itself. The CIA, arguing that counterinsurgency was the answer, criticized the conventional tactics favored by the military advisers. State Department officials questioned the intelligence estimates of CIA analysts, who moaned that their evaluations were being ignored. Civilian aid operatives resented interference in their economic and social projects by military officers, who quarreled over the relative merits of different weapons. Taylor, in chairmanlike fashion, tried to arbitrate these inevitable squabbles. But as one member of the embassy staff put it: "We criticize the Vietnamese for their rivalries, but we're not exactly setting an example."

But nothing troubled Taylor and his associates more than dealing with the rambunctious, unruly, intriguing South Vietnamese leaders. Westmoreland, who habitually understated his feelings, obliquely disclosed his perplexity when he conceded to me at the time that he found the situation "more complex than I ever visualized it would be." Taylor was equally baffled. After his first month on the job, he described Khanh's regime as an "ineffective government beset by inexperienced ministers who are also jealous and suspicious of each other." Yet he feared that another change of authority in Saigon would be disastrous, and he clung to Khanh as America's only hope.

Lyndon Johnson was then inaugurating the first of several secret diplomatic attempts to induce North Vietnam to halt the war in the south. His confidential emissary in the initial overture was J. Blair Seaborn, chief Canadian delegate to the International Control Commission, the toothless body set up to deal with infractions of the Geneva accords, and he carried a carrot-and-stick offer: if the Communists agreed to cease their assistance to the Vietcong and end the conflict, the United States would provide them with economic aid and even diplomatic recognition. If not, they could anticipate American air and naval attacks against North Vietnam. Prime Minister Pham Van Dong reacted predictably. No deal was conceivable, he told Seaborn, unless the Americans withdrew from Vietnam and accepted Vietcong participation in a neutral South Vietnamese coalition government. "I suffer to see the war go on, develop, intensify," he said, "yet our people are determined to struggle."

The same kind of dialogue continued for another decade as the war ravaged Vietnam. But in the summer of 1964, as the Saigon regime seemed to be crumbling, a curious incident furnished the Johnson administration with the occasion to widen the conflict.

10 Disorder and Decision

Senator Fulbright (left), chairman of the Senate Foreign Relations Committee, helped President Johnson secure passage of the Tonkin Gulf resolution. Fulbright, later an opponent of the war, afterward tried to repeal the resolution.

The U.S.S. Maddox, one of two destroyers assigned to carry out electronic intelligence activities in the Tonkin Gulf in 1964. The destroyers were also involved in covert attacks by South Vietnamese commandos against North Vietnamese coastal installations.

On August 4, 1964, the Maddox clashed with North Vietnamese patrol boats in the Tonkin Gulf, one of them seen here. A second incident was also reported, but many American officials doubt that it occurred.

Three of President Johnson's close advisers on Vietnam (left to right): William Bundy,
assistant secretary of state; Secretary of State Rusk; and Walt Rostow, national
security adviser. Rostow conceived a plan for Johnson to obtain a "blank check" from
Congress to conduct the war.

A bitter opponent of the Vietnam war from the start was Senator Morse of Oregon,
seen here with Johnson. A garrulous independent, Morse exerted little influence on
Capitol Hill but was respected for his knowledge of social issues.

Lieutenant Everett Alvarez, shot down in an air raid against North Vietnam following the Tonkin Gulf incident, was the first American prisoner to be taken in the war. The Communists used him for propaganda purposes, as in this photograph taken in Hanoi.

Lyndon Johnson campaigned for the presidency in late 1964, promising to keep young Americans out of Vietnam. He sought to counter his Republican opponent, Senator Barry Goldwater, a strident anti-Communist, by portraying himself as a moderate.

Students clash with South Vietnamese troops in Saigon. The student groups were manipulated by various political factions attempting to oust General Khanh, but there was little evidence of Vietcong penetration.

Throughout 1964, students in Saigon demanded that General Nguyen Khanh reform his government. Here Khanh tries to placate a crowd of them assembled to demand his resignation.

Buddhist monks are routed by police during a demonstration in Saigon. The Buddhists resented the return to authority of certain Catholic politicians, and the convulsions caused by the constant unrest shook South Vietnam throughout 1964.

The internal ferment in South Vietnam brought to the fore Air Vice Marshal Nguyen Cao Ky, a flamboyant pilot, seen here with his wife. They habitually dressed in garish costumes that showed an effort to present themselves as fashion plates.

In one of Saigon's political upheavals in 1964, a compromise was reached by naming Phan Khac Suu (at front, right) president and Tran Van Huong prime minister. These decrepit characters were unable to control the various political factions bidding for power, and soon in turn gave way to the next regime.

Vietcong terrorists stepped up their attacks in Saigon, bombing the U.S. embassy in 1967. An embassy employee, Eva Kim, here aids an injured American diplomat, James Rosenthal. Behind them is John Condon, the labor attaché. A new embassy building was constructed soon afterward.

In Vietnam, too, we work for world order. . . . Let no one doubt for a moment that we have the resources and the will to follow this course as long as it may take. No one should think for a moment that we will be worn down, nor will we be driven out, and we will not be provoked into rashness.

—Lyndon Johnson

The United States has not provided massive assistance to South Vietnam, in military equipment, economic resources, and personnel in order to subsidize continuing quarrels among South Vietnamese leaders.

—Dean Rusk

Nothing mattered more to Lyndon Johnson during the summer of 1964 than the approaching presidential election. Having been accidentally propelled into the White House, he wanted to win a mandate that would make him president in his own right—and he wanted to win big. A resounding victory at the polls would exorcise the ghost of Kennedy, which continued to exacerbate the sense of inferiority that had nagged him during the glamorous days of Camelot, when he had been shunted offstage as an uncouth provincial—a "freckle-belly," as the Kennedy courtiers derided him. Johnson yearned to rise to the stature of his hero, Franklin D. Roosevelt, and confirm his conviction that the Great Society was heir to the New Deal. He took heart in the public opinion surveys that showed him to be surprisingly popular among voters who had supported Richard Nixon in 1960—which meant that he could triumph despite the defection from the Democratic ranks of the Deep South, where George Wallace, governor of Alabama, was mobilizing white racists against his civil liberties programs. Even so, Johnson had been in politics long enough to be wary of complacency, especially with his administration committed to a small but unpredictable war in Southeast Asia. His concern sharpened in late July 1964, when the Republican convention rejected Governor Nelson Rockefeller of New York, a moderate, and nominated as its presidential candidate Senator Barry Goldwater of Arizona, a craggy ultraconservative who held a major general's commission in the air force reserve.

"Extremism in the defense of liberty is no vice," Goldwater proclaimed in his acceptance speech at the convention in San Francisco, using the line to punctuate denunciation of the Democrats for being "soft" on Communism. But Johnson's aides had taken precautions. They had drafted a legislative resolution that would serve a dual purpose: by giving Johnson a free hand to conduct the war in Southeast Asia as he saw fit, it would strengthen his international credibility; more important, its passage by a substantial majority in Congress would assure him bipartisan endorsement and thereby remove the Vietnam issue from the election campaign.

The idea of such a legislative resolution had been suggested as early as February by Walt Rostow, then head of the State Department's policy planning staff. The son of an idealistic Russian-Jewish immigrant father who had celebrated his adopted land by naming his three sons after Walt Whitman, Eugene Debs, and Ralph Waldo Emerson, the young Rostow had been precociously brilliant. He was graduated from Yale, attended Oxford as a Rhodes scholar, and became a professor at the Massachusetts Institute of Technology at the age of thirty-four; his specialty was the economics of underdeveloped countries. Like many other academics attracted by power, he made himself available to several administrations. He had skirted the fringe of the Eisenhower administration before switching to Kennedy, who made him one of his foreign affairs advisers. Rostow quickly earned a reputation as an effervescent idea man whose memorable phrases included the "New Frontier," which became the Kennedy administration's slogan. Kennedy had sent him with Maxwell Taylor on a mission to Vietnam in late 1961, and Rostow returned full of zeal for a larger U.S. commitment, asserting that the conflict in Southeast Asia "might be the last great confrontation" with Communism. Recalling his service during World War II, when he had helped to select bombing targets in Europe, he soon began to speak military jargon as he enthusiastically advanced his strategic and tactical concepts. Eventually he seemed to revel in the war, as if trying to prove that a short, bespectacled intellectual could be tough.

Nearly every senior official concurred with Rostow on the need for some kind of congressional prop to underpin the administration as it laid plans for a larger U.S. presence in Vietnam. But Rostow's suggestion raised a cloudy legal question, one that had been examined and debated throughout the course of American history: Who had the power to involve the United States in a foreign conflict?

In 1787, the framers of the Constitution had devised a flexible formula: they designated the president to be commander in chief of the armed forces in order to guarantee civilian control over the military; but they vested the power to declare war in Congress. Thomas Jefferson noted the important distinction at the time. By giving that power to initiate hostilities to the legislative rather than the executive branch, he observed, the authority to unleash the "dog of war" had been transferred "from those who are to spend to those who are to pay."

Rigorously respecting the Constitution, America's early presidents obtained congressional approval for such ventures abroad as the naval skirmishes with France and the pursuit of the Barbary pirates. Gradually, though, their successors stretched the rules. Ulysses Grant acted on his own when he attempted to annex the Dominican Republic, and McKinley landed five thousand troops in China to help quell the Boxer uprising without consulting Congress in advance. Theodore Roosevelt and Woodrow Wilson went further, disregarding Capitol Hill as they sent forces into the Caribbean and Mexico to coerce or occupy sovereign states. By the middle of the twentieth century, the president had largely usurped the constitutional powers of the legislature in the realm of foreign affairs. Franklin Roosevelt steered the United States into a sea war against Germany before the nation formally declared war. And Truman, terming the intervention a "police action," plunged into Korea without authorization from Congress.

This trend toward unshackled presidential power in foreign affairs was spurred throughout the 1950s and early 1960s by congressional, academic, and media liberals whose minds had been molded during the Roosevelt era. They believed that World War II could have been averted had the United States and its allies moved earlier to stop the Nazis, and they applied the same logic to the Communist threat. So they favored a strong and active executive force capable of confronting that danger, and they battled against congressional conservatives who sought to limit the president's prerogatives and whom they branded antiquated isolationists. Later, many of these liberals were to blame the Vietnam war on a presidency gone wild. But even Senator J. William Fulbright at first argued that the president lacked sufficient authority to deal with America's enormous international responsibilities. Writing in the *Cornell Law Quarterly* in the fall of 1961, Fulbright advocated an overhaul of the nation's "basic constitutional machinery," adding, "I wonder whether the time has not arrived, or indeed already passed, when we must give the executive a measure of power in the conduct of our foreign affairs that we have hitherto jealously withheld."

Lyndon Johnson had voiced a variation of that view nearly a decade earlier, soon after becoming Senate majority leader. Senator McCarthy had just died, having unscrupulously exploited the fall of China and the deadlocked conflict in Korea to spark an explosion of anti-Communist paranoia aimed at promoting his own influence. Johnson, fearful that another demagogue might seize the same pretext to sow dissension and recrimination, believed that rational Democrats and Republicans ought to bury their differences in a bipartisan foreign policy that would, as he put it, discourage "the public's tendency to go off on a jag, paralyzing itself in endless debate and stampeding us in panic." Though a fervent Democrat, he rallied behind Eisenhower and scrapped the old theory that "the duty of the opposition is to oppose." He spelled out his position on the floor of the Senate in February 1953: "I want to make absolutely sure that the Communists don't play one branch of government against the other, or one party against the other. . . . The danger is they'll think we're fat and fifty and fighting among ourselves about free enterprise and socialism and all that. We might mislead them so they'll think these Americans are just the country club crowd. That's a mistake our enemies have made before. If you're in an airplane, and you're flying somewhere, you don't run up to the cockpit and attack the pilot. Mr. Eisenhower is the only president we've got."

As president, Johnson expected bipartisan support, but it was not to come easily. Government officials, sensitive to the possible snares that may entrap them, approach problems slowly and prudently. Closeted in monotone offices, committees prepare options that are weighed at meetings that in turn yield revised alternatives that are further refined at other meetings, so that an apparently casual suggestion can represent weeks, even months, of labor.

A prodigious producer of bureaucratic paper, William Bundy incorporated his thoughts on Rostow's notion for mobilizing congressional cooperation in the same verbose memorandum to Johnson that had outlined plans for striking against North Vietnam—actions which, he explained, would "normally require" a declaration of war. To ask Congress for such a "blunt instrument," as Bundy put it, might set off a domestic political squabble, since the administration claimed to be proceeding toward only "selective" goals in Vietnam, yet it would be "unsatisfactory" to bypass legislative endorsement, since the recommended military moves were plainly not a response to an attack or to a "sudden change of events," and the administration could be accused of wantonly escalating the conflict. Hence the "best answer," Bundy advised Johnson, seemed to be a resolution such as Eisenhower had gotten from the Senate and the House in January 1955. Passed almost unanimously by both chambers, it had mandated him to deploy U.S. forces "as he deems necessary" to protect Taiwan as well as Quemoy and Matsu against a putative Chinese Communist assault. Johnson, who vividly remembered his Senate career, recalled the resolution. Then hospitalized for a kidney stone operation, he had paired with another hospitalized senator, John F. Kennedy, to cast a vote *in absentia* giving Eisenhower the same power he now sought for himself.

Despite his enormous prestige, Eisenhower had won his special authority only after several days of debate, and that recollection worried Bundy. He knew that Mike Mansfield, the Senate majority leader, favored a compromise settlement of the war, and he anticipated fierce resistance from Senator Wayne Morse of Oregon, a cantankerous character who had consistently battled over the years against according extraordinary powers to presidents. Bundy therefore warned Johnson that "doubtful friends" on Capitol Hill might delay passage of such a resolution, which would cede to both America's allies and adversaries the time to build up "tremendous pressure" on the United States "to stop and negotiate" an end to the conflict. But Johnson, undaunted, demanded a congressional resolution.

The rough draft, completed by Bundy and other aides in late May, gave Johnson the right to commit U.S. forces to the defense of any nation in Southeast Asia menaced by Communist "aggression or subversion"—and it also gave him the discretion to determine the extent of the threat.

Bundy reckoned that a propitious period to present the resolution to Congress would be during the week of June 22, after a civil rights bill had cleared the Senate floor and the Democrats were feeling virtuous. But he emphasized the need for the resolution to gain rapid approval "by a very substantial majority," and proposed a major promotional effort, with public statements by high officials and a presidential message to Congress. Urging the administration to gird itself, he even prepared a "scenario" of suggested replies to the "disagreeable questions":

Does this resolution imply a blank check for the president to go to war over Southeast Asia?
The resolution will indeed permit selective use of force, but hostilities on a larger scale are not envisaged and, in any case, any large escalation would require a call-up of reserves and thus a further appeal to the Congress. . . .
What kinds of force, if any, are possible under this authorization?
No force will be used if the president can avoid it. If the continued aggression of others should require a limited response, that response will be carefully aimed at installations and activities that directly support covert aggression. . . .

What change in the situation requires such a resolution now?
This answer should include a candid account of the existing situation and hazard and growing dangers both in Laos and in South Vietnam [and] refer to the need for international awareness that the United States is not immobilized by a political campaign. . . .
Does Southeast Asia matter all that much?
Yes—because of the rights of the people there, because of our own commitments, because of the far-reaching effect of a failure, and because we can win if we stay with it.

The resolution was ready by the beginning of June—and so were the administration's top civilian and military officials. Relying on high-altitude reconnaissance airplanes and other sources of intelligence, Pentagon planners had pinpointed ninety-four bombing targets in North Vietnam; they had also made provisions for suppressing flak, rescuing downed pilots, and coping with other tactical problems. Aircraft carriers, poised to cruise into the Tonkin Gulf off the North Vietnamese coast, had been instructed to brace themselves to stage "reprisal" raids within seventy-two hours of receiving orders, and the diplomatic apparatus was prepared to explain the actions to governments around the world. But suddenly, at a meeting on June 15, Johnson's national security adviser, McGeorge Bundy, informed Secretary of State Rusk, Defense Secretary McNamara, and other senior figures that everything was being postponed.

Johnson had changed his mind. Though the situation in South Vietnam was deteriorating, it did not yet look sufficiently critical for him to court the risk of appearing like a warmonger to American voters. Nor did he have the hard evidence to prove that North Vietnam merited the bombing. He could probably get his resolution, but only at the cost of damaging the image of moderation he was striving to project. Better to wait until after the November election.

Years later, when American casualties in Vietnam had finally aroused Congress, McNamara still blandly denied to a Senate committee that the Pentagon had drawn up a bombing program as early as the spring of 1964. And, in subsequent testimony, William Bundy dismissed his elaborate preparations for the resolution as "normal contingency planning," adding that he was "not sure that my drafts were even known to others"—as if he had improvised them in the solitude of his office in his spare time. The fact is that by the summer of 1964 Johnson had a document that Nicholas Katzenbach, then acting attorney general, was later to call the "functional equivalent of a declaration of war." It required only approval by Congress, and a dubious incident assured its endorsement.

Ever since the Geneva agreement had partitioned Vietnam into two zones in 1954, covert American agents had been helping the Saigon government to carry on clandestine activities against North Vietnam. Though the North Vietnamese authorities were aware of these activities, the United States and its South Vietnamese clients kept them secret in order to be able to refute charges of violating the accords. The practice of dissimulation, loftily termed the "principle of plausible denial," is still pursued today to shroud undercover operations that may create diplomatic complications.

The hush-hush scheme began right after the Geneva Conference, when a handful of U.S. operatives headed by the intrepid CIA veteran Lucien Conein surreptitiously formed squads of anti-Communist Vietnamese to organize guerrillas, abduct or assassinate officials, disrupt installations, establish espionage networks, and distribute propaganda in the north—just as former Vietminh militants stayed in the south to conduct the same activities against the Saigon regime. But the rigid Communist control structure, a tightly knit web of local cadres and informers, pervaded almost every North Vietnamese town and village, and few of Conein's teams survived. Conein himself, recognizing the failure of his venture, soon went on to other CIA jobs in Vietnam and elsewhere. Yet the enterprise continued—a futile endeavor designed mainly to gratify the Saigon leaders, who derived satisfaction from the illusion that they were avenging themselves against their northern foes. Of more than eighty groups sent into North Vietnam in 1963, for instance, nearly all were killed or captured. The prisoners invariably repented at showcase trials organized in Hanoi, and their testimony fueled Communist radio broadcasts that were beamed to South Vietnam. One CIA agent, who quit the project in disgust, later told me: "I didn't mind butchering the enemy, but we were butchering our own allies."

Under Diem's regime, the covert program was officially directed by Colonel Le Quang Tung, the northern Catholic who commanded the government's special forces and who was murdered by the insurgent generals during their coup against Diem on November 1, 1963. In fact, CIA experts ran the operation—though none actually participated in the forays. The commandos were South Vietnamese army volunteers, most of them northern refugees supposedly able to blend into their native regions and count on relatives or friends for assistance. They were trained by CIA instructors at camps near Danang and Nhatrang, or at

American bases on Taiwan, Guam, and Okinawa, where they learned to sabotage factories, blow up bridges and communications lines, gather intelligence, and defend themselves with light weapons or their bare hands. Then, garbed in black peasant pajamas to avoid detection, they were infiltrated into North Vietnam, usually in groups of six or seven. They might be landed by junk or sampan at night along the North Vietnamese coast, or parachuted into the country's mountain jungles from unmarked transports belonging to Air America, a CIA subsidiary headquartered on Taiwan and used for furtive activities throughout Asia. American and Chinese Nationalist mercenaries piloted the planes; to boost their morale, South Vietnamese officers were occasionally allowed to fly missions. Air Vice Marshal Nguyen Cao Ky boasted to reporters in July 1964 that he had flown several—a revelation that embarrassed American officials, who were then striving to promote the line that the Communists alone were transgressing the Geneva agreement.

These ineffectual "dirty tricks" had been conducted only intermittently before Lyndon Johnson entered office in late 1963. At that point, the joint chiefs of staff conceived a more ambitious and systematic plan for covert operations against North Vietnam, typically giving it an acronym: OPLAN 34-A. Major clandestine innovations required clearance by the ultrasecret 303 Committee, so named because it had once met in Room 303 of the Executive Office Building, the wedding cake next to the White House that accommodates the president's aides. The committee, headed by McGeorge Bundy and composed of senior State Department, Pentagon, and CIA representatives, endorsed the proposal in January 1964, and Johnson cautiously approved a four-month experimental phase to begin on February 1. The Pentagon delegated day-to-day direction to a unit of the U.S. military command in Saigon, the studies and operations group, which in turn enlisted CIA advisers.

The program prescribed larger South Vietnamese intrusions into the north as well as a bigger propaganda effort, such as leaflet drops contrived to stimulate a sense of fear and foreboding among the populace. It also included maritime activities designed to intercept Communist ships delivering matériel to the Vietcong in the south and to kidnap fishermen for interrogation. But the most important aspect of the marine operation was related to plans then being refined by Pentagon experts for eventual strategic air and naval attacks against North Vietnam. Among these plans was a blueprint for an amphibious invasion by U.S. and South Vietnamese ground troops—an idea particularly favored in subsequent years by Rostow and the more vigorous members of the American military establishment.

The Communist leaders in North Vietnam, anticipating an escalation of the war into their territory, had recently persuaded the Soviet Union to bolster their defenses, and the Russians had begun to install modern antiaircraft missiles and radar stations around North Vietnam's main cities and along its ragged coastline of bays and islands on the Tonkin Gulf. The United States needed precise information on this protective network for its contingency plans to bomb, blockade, or invade the north. The inland sites could be detected by sophisticated high-altitude espionage airplanes like the U-2, but another approach was developed to profile the shore facilities. Covert South Vietnamese commandos would harass the enemy radar transmitters, thereby activating them so that American electronic intelligence vessels cruising in the Tonkin Gulf could learn their locations and measure their frequencies. In addition, the American ships could chart and photograph the coastal region, and monitor its traffic. Similar operations, code-named DeSoto missions, had been going on for years off the coasts of China, North Korea, and the Soviet Union, and a few had been briefly carried out in North Vietnam. Whatever else it achieved, the program offered the U.S. navy its first chance to get involved in Vietnam.

The maritime project had to be organized from scratch. American purchasing agents acquired a small fleet of Norwegian-built patrol boats—aluminum craft dubbed Swifts and Nasties, armed with automatic weapons and light cannon, and capable of speeds exceeding fifty knots. Their South Vietnamese crews were trained at Danang by U.S. naval teams: Seals. The principal adviser engaged in the operation was a tough CIA soldier of fortune, Tucker Gougelmann. A former marine officer, severely wounded in the Pacific campaign during World War II, he had conducted covert missions in Eastern Europe, Afghanistan, and Korea before moving to Vietnam. There he adopted the children of his Vietnamese mistress, and his attachment to them was to cost him his life. In the spring of 1975, shortly after Saigon fell to the North Vietnamese, he secretly went back into Vietnam from Bangkok in an attempt to rescue the family. The Communists arrested him, and he died in captivity. His remains, returned to the United States two years later, were buried in Arlington National Cemetery.

The Tonkin Gulf is one of the world's scenic wonders. Junks and sampans ply its blue waters, silhouetted against a horizon of sharp karsts rising strangely from the sea, their peaks shrouded in gray mist. But this placid picture, depicted in soft brushstrokes by painters over the centuries, is deceptive. Invaders and marauders had struck at Vietnam through here for thousands of years. And now it seemed to Hanoi's Communist rulers, with their keen historical memory, that the same threatening pattern was being repeated by a fresh breed of aggressors, the Americans and their South Vietnamese henchmen.

The first DeSoto mission under the new U.S. plan, to be undertaken in March 1964 by the destroyer *Craig*, was quickly canceled because of bad weather. Covert South Vietnamese raids were also delayed while the commandos trained and tested their boats. But soon President Johnson extended the program's four-month experimental phase by a year, and the combined operations resumed in July 1965 on instructions from the joint chiefs of staff. Admiral Ulysses Grant Sharp, Jr., now American commander for the Pacific, sent out the order from his Honolulu headquarters to the Seventh Fleet to deploy the aircraft carrier *Ticonderoga* and its ancillary force at the entrance to the Tonkin Gulf. The destroyer *Maddox,* then in Japan, was assigned to the area to revive the DeSoto electronic eavesdropping activities. Coincidentally, the vessel would have delighted Lyndon Johnson, named as it was for Captain William Maddox, a marine hero of the Mexican war. Its chief officer, Captain John J. Herrick, was an Annapolis graduate and a veteran of World War II and Korea.

Admiral Sharp cautioned Captain Herrick to get no closer than eight miles from North Vietnam's coast and four miles from its islands—the assumption being that the Communists, who had never officially defined their territorial waters, still adhered to the three-mile limit set by the French during the colonial period. Yet it could have been equally assumed that they had switched to a twelve-mile limit such as China observed. Indeed, the U.S. director of naval intelligence had anticipated in a memorandum more than a year earlier that "there is a good possibility" that North Vietnam "will subscribe to the twelve-mile limit claimed by other Communist nations if the issue were raised." On July 10, as Herrick headed the *Maddox* toward Vietnam, he was also authorized to maintain contact with the U.S. military command in Saigon for information on the South Vietnamese commando movements, so that they could avoid "mutual interference" and arrange "such communications . . . as may be desired." Thus the destroyer was conceivably violating North Vietnam's sovereignty in connection with a clandestine South Vietnamese operation.

Herrick stopped the *Maddox* at the Taiwan port of Keelung, where he picked up a huge van outfitted with electronic gear and seventeen specialists to operate the equipment. He then steamed south toward the Tonkin Gulf to start scanning the North Vietnamese littoral. By the afternoon of August 1, the ship was cruising a zigzag course, seven to nine miles from the coast and four to six miles from the islands. The climate was unbearably hot and humid, and Herrick and his crew felt nervous in the alien waters. On his way into the zone, Herrick had sighted patrol boats in the distance, which he identified in a radio message to the Seventh Fleet as Soviet-made craft, presumably manned by North Vietnamese. A reassuring message came back. They were Swifts, returning from an undercover South Vietnamese mission.

On the afternoon of July 30, two days before, four Swifts filled with South Vietnamese commandos had left their base at Danang, going northward. Just after midnight, two of the boats tried to storm Hon Me, an island seven miles offshore, their aim to demolish a Communist radar installation there with satchel charges. But the resistance was too strong for a landing, and the raiders instead raked the island from afar with machine-gun and cannon fire. At the same time, the two other boats bombarded Hon Ngu, an island about three miles from Vinh, one of North Vietnam's busiest ports. The crackle of North Vietnamese radar signals and radio traffic triggered by the attacks was monitored aboard the *Maddox* and transmitted to a special American intelligence center in the Philippines, which in turn relayed the information to CIA headquarters outside Washington.

The North Vietnamese immediately sent a formal protest to the International Control Commission. But the *Maddox* remained in the vicinity and continued to monitor the coastal facilities through the next day and into the night. Before dawn on August 2, however, the destroyer encountered hundreds of North Vietnamese junks. Captain Herrick, fearing they might be armed, sounded a general quarters alarm and radioed to the Seventh Fleet that he expected "possible hostile action." Soon afterward, as he steered the *Maddox* eastward to avert a clash, his technicians intercepted a North Vietnamese message indicating that the Communists were preparing for "military operations." They may have been planning strictly defensive measures, but Herrick read the message to mean attack. He now reported that his itinerary presented an "unacceptable risk" and recommended that it be abandoned. His superiors rejected the proposal, instructed him to resume the mission, and advised that he exercise prudence.

By eleven o'clock on the morning of August 2, the *Maddox* had come within ten miles of the Red River delta, the northernmost point of its circuit. The day was clear and calm, and the danger seemed to Herrick to have subsided—even though he spotted three Communist patrol boats emerge from the estuary and disappear behind Hon Me, one of the islands that had been raided by South Vietnamese commandos two nights before. Herrick, confident that he was in international waters, doubted that they would strike. But his technicians now intercepted another order to the North Vietnamese boats instructing them to attack after they had refueled. "The next thing we knew," Herrick later recalled, "they came out at us."

The *Maddox* turned toward the sea as the North Vietnamese boats, going at nearly twice its speed, followed in pursuit. Tracking them on his radarscope, Herrick directed his crew to commence firing if the craft came within ten thousand yards. He contended afterward that he meant the initial salvo as a warning, but he recorded no such entry in his log. His deck officer also recollected later that the *Maddox* was "shooting to kill" when, just after three in the afternoon, it opened fire. Herrick radioed the *Ticonderoga* for air support.

Undaunted, the North Vietnamese boats clung to their course. Two of them, closing in at a range of five thousand yards, each launched a torpedo—both missing the *Maddox*. The third, its weapons pumping away, sped directly at the destroyer to discharge its torpedo, which turned out to be a dud. Herrick's gunners hit one of the craft as three needle-nosed Crusader jets from the *Ticonderoga* arrived overhead to strafe the other enemy boats. To a *Maddox* crew member, radar man James Stankevitz, it was "like trying to swat mosquitoes with a big fly swatter." But the tenacity and discipline of the North Vietnamese impressed Herrick.

The skirmish, which lasted a bare twenty minutes, ended in a clear U.S. victory. Only one North Vietnamese bullet had struck the *Maddox;* no casualties occurred. In contrast, the destroyer had crippled two Communist craft and sunk the third. Herrick wanted to finish off the surviving boats, but he was ordered to withdraw to await further instructions. Ten days later, Hanoi Radio's self-serving version of the event omitted any mention of losses, claiming instead that the North Vietnamese vessels had downed one American airplane and damaged two others before "chasing away the U.S. pirates . . . on the sea and in the air." On one point, however, the American and North Vietnamese accounts agreed. An incident had occurred.

Washington is twelve hours behind Vietnam, and reports of the incident reached Lyndon Johnson on the morning of the same day, Sunday, August 2. Then preoccupied mainly by the presidential election campaign, he calibrated his reaction accordingly: he knew that the voters would not take kindly to a candidate who appeared to be heading toward war, but Goldwater was pressing for a tougher approach to Vietnam, and Johnson also wanted to look firm.

Since no Americans had been hurt, he told his staff, further action was unnecessary—and he specifically rejected reprisals against North Vietnam. He instructed his spokesmen to play down the matter, so that the initial Pentagon press release on the subject did not even identify the North Vietnamese as having been involved. And, in his first use of the "hot line" to Moscow, he sent a personal message to Prime Minister Khrushchev stating that he had no wish to widen the conflict, but hoped that North Vietnam would not molest U.S. vessels in international waters. At the same time, however, Johnson directed the *Maddox* and another destroyer, as well as protective aircraft, to return to the Tonkin Gulf, their orders to "attack any force that attacks them." He also approved the first U.S. diplomatic note ever sent to Hanoi, warning the Communist regime that "grave consequences would inevitably result from any further unprovoked offensive military action" against American ships deployed "on the high seas" off North Vietnam.

Though Johnson may have believed that his stern rhetoric would end the affair, his aides behaved differently. William Bundy was away on vacation, but Dean Rusk told his State Department staff to "pull together" Bundy's draft resolution, just in case the president's authority to deal with Southeast Asia had to be broadened. Rusk also sounded an ominous chord in a chat with reporters, saying that "the other side got a sting out of this [and] if they do it again, they'll get another sting."

Meanwhile, the joint chiefs of staff and their far-flung commanders began to unveil plans to give the North Vietnamese more than a sting. They dispatched additional American fighter-bombers to South Vietnam and Thailand, and they placed U.S. combat troops on alert. On their maps of North Vietnam, they pinpointed such targets as harbor installations and oil depots while Admiral Sharp arranged for possible air strikes by ordering the carrier *Constellation* to the South China Sea to join the *Ticonderoga*. He also outlined a new mission for the *Maddox* and a second destroyer, the *C. Turner Joy*. The DeSoto electronic intelligence patrols were to be superseded by more vigorous maneuvers contrived to "assert the right of freedom of the seas." The two destroyers would stage direct daylight runs to within eight miles of North Vietnam's coast and four miles off its islands, as if defying the Communists to "play chicken." Rear Admiral Robert B. Moore, head of the *Ticonderoga* task force, virtually preordained another clash. He radioed Captain Herrick and advised him that the North Vietnamese had "thrown down the gauntlet" and should be "treated as belligerents from first detection."

So the *Maddox* and the *Turner Joy* were effectively being used to bait the Communists. And the bait was sweetened by the covert South Vietnamese commandos, who returned to the scene; the Swifts and Nasties again departed from Danang on the afternoon of August 3—just as the American ships were beginning their zigzags off the North Vietnamese coast. This time the South Vietnamese sped toward mainland objectives at Cape Vinhson and at Cua Ron, about seventy-five miles above the seventeenth parallel. Herrick knew from monitoring the North Vietnamese radar and radio traffic that the Communists were aware of these clandestine movements, and that they connected his presence in the area to the commando forays, as they had the day before. Wanting no part of another incident in that unfriendly area, he proposed that the destroyers retreat to sea. But Admiral Sharp rejected the proposal, replying testily that to terminate the mission so soon "does not in my view adequately demonstrate United States resolve to assert our legitimate rights in these international waters." He ordered Herrick to continue the patrols and suggested that the American vessels might serve as decoys to distract the Communists from the nearby South Vietnamese operations.

The summer climate in the Tonkin Gulf is volatile, and thunderstorms throughout the next night buffeted the destroyers as their crews, blind in the inky darkness, sat glued to their instruments. The sonar aboard the *Maddox* was functioning erratically, and atmospheric conditions were distorting the radar beams reaching both vessels. The technicians on the two ships, trying to track North Vietnamese movements, could have been registering anything from rain and waves to the whir of their own propellers.

At about eight o'clock, Herrick intercepted radio messages that gave him the "impression" that Communist patrol boats were bracing for an assault. He appealed to the *Ticonderoga* for air support. Soon eight Crusader jets were circling overhead, but their pilots saw nothing. An hour later, the two destroyers started firing in all directions, gyrating wildly to avoid what they believed to be North Vietnamese torpedoes racing toward them. Their sonars counted a total of twenty-two enemy torpedoes, none of which scored a hit, and their officers reported sinking two or perhaps three Communist craft during the hectic engagement, which went on past midnight. But hardly had the shooting stopped than Herrick and his men began to have second thoughts.

Steaming away from the site, Herrick immediately communicated his qualms to his superiors. He said that the "entire action leaves many doubts," and he urged a "thorough reconnaissance in daylight" from the air. He then ordered officers on both ships to quiz the crews, and his skepticism mounted as he listened to the accounts. Not a single sailor on either vessel had seen or heard Communist gunfire. Those who claimed to have observed anything at all, such as the lights or shadows of North Vietnamese boats, were not really sure. The Crusader pilots were equally baffled, having detected no enemy craft during their forty minutes of flying over the area.

Herrick reiterated his doubts in another report. The *Maddox* had not made any "actual visual sightings" of Communist patrol boats. The radarscope blips apparently showing the enemy had been due to "freak weather effects," and an "overeager" young sonar operator was responsible for recording the torpedoes. Herrick suggested again that a "complete evaluation" of the event be conducted before further measures were pursued. His report went to Admiral Sharp, who relayed it to Washington.

Presidents usually rush into decisions without waiting for all the details, and Lyndon Johnson was no different. Though his information was sketchy, he announced to key Democratic members of Congress on the morning of August 4 that the U.S. destroyers in the Tonkin Gulf had definitely been attacked. This time, he said, he would retaliate against North Vietnam—and he would ask Congress for a resolution of support. Not a congressman present demurred.

Johnson strolled back from the meeting to his desk with Kenneth O'Donnell, a former Kennedy disciple who had stayed on as a White House aide. Speculating on the potential domestic political effect of the crisis, they agreed that Johnson was "being tested" and would have to respond firmly to defend himself against Goldwater and the Republican right wing. As O'Donnell later wrote, they felt that Johnson "must not allow them to accuse him of vacillating or being an indecisive leader."

Yet Johnson was anxious for some verification of the incident—if only to guard against possible future charges of having acted precipitously. He leaned on McNamara, the cabinet officer he then trusted most. McNamara, aware of Captain Herrick's equivocal reports, telephoned Admiral Sharp to stress that retaliation could not be justified "unless we are damned sure what happened." A stream of messages now flowed back and forth from Washington to Hawaii to the South China Sea. Herrick had been under constant tension for five days, and now Sharp was exerting pressure on him to "confirm absolutely" that the attack had taken place. Again Herrick canvassed his officers and men, but they could produce only inconclusive fragments from their memories of the frantic night.

In Washington, however, the need for a major move was generating its own momentum, eclipsing the mysteries of Tonkin. Since early on the morning of August 4, administration officials had been braced for a move. They advised the ambassadors of allies like Britain and West Germany to be ready for secret briefings, and they drew up arguments to be presented to the United Nations. They contacted important congressmen, telling them to stand by for an "urgent" meeting with the president. Johnson, hunched over maps in a secluded White House dining room, listened as McNamara pointed to the North Vietnamese targets recommended by the joint chiefs of staff—four patrol boat bases and an oil depot. Johnson approved. At six o'clock in the evening, while Herrick was still struggling to furnish additional evidence, a Pentagon spokesman declared that "a second deliberate attack" had occurred. Just before midnight, nearly an hour after the carriers *Ticonderoga* and *Constellation* had sent off their jets on the first U.S. bombing mission of North Vietnamese territory, Lyndon Johnson appeared on television screens across the nation, his manner sober and solemn: "Repeated acts of violence against the armed forces of the United States must be met not only with alert defense, but with positive reply. That reply is being given as I speak to you tonight."

Johnson's spokesmen described the reprisals as "limited in scale." But American aircraft flew sixty-four sorties against four North Vietnamese patrol boat bases and a major oil storage depot, "severely" hitting all the targets. An estimated twenty-five vessels were destroyed or damaged. Two American airplanes were lost, the pilot of one having reported as he went down that he was parachuting. "His whereabouts is at present listed as unknown," stated a Pentagon communiqué.

The missing pilot was Lieutenant (jg) Everett Alvarez, Jr., of San Jose, California. Stationed aboard the *Constellation*, he had been assigned his objective in advance, a patrol boat base near the coal-mining town of Hongay, northeast of Hanoi. Years afterward, he would recollect the experience that was to begin one of the worst ordeals for any American in the war:

I was among the first to launch off the carrier. Our squadron, ten airplanes, headed toward the target about four hundred miles away—a good two hours there and two hours back. It was sort of like a dream. We were actually going to war, into combat. I never thought it would happen, but all of a sudden here we were, and I was in it. I felt a little nervous. We made an identification pass, then came around and made an actual pass, firing. I was very low, just skimming the trees at about five hundred knots. Then I had the weirdest feeling. My airplane was hit and started to fall apart, rolling and burning. I knew I wouldn't live if I stayed with the airplane, so I ejected, and luckily I cleared a cliff.

He landed in shallow water, fracturing his back in the drop. Local North Vietnamese militia soon arrived and took him to a nearby jail, where he was briefly visited by Prime Minister Pham Van Dong, who had been coincidentally touring the region at the time. Alvarez became something of a celebrity—the first of nearly six hundred American airmen to be captured by the Communists during the Vietnam conflict. Transferred to the "Hanoi Hilton," as U.S. prisoners of war dubbed their grim internment center, he was held until the signing of the cease-fire agreement more than eight years later.

Subsequent research by both official and unofficial investigators has indicated with almost total certainty that the second Communist attack in the Tonkin Gulf never happened. It had not been deliberately faked, but Johnson and his staff, desperately seeking a pretext to act vigorously, had seized upon a fuzzy set of circumstances to fulfill a contingency plan. Much of the truth was to trickle out in the years ahead—yet some relevant evidence has remained confidential, presumably to spare prominent U.S. bureaucrats who concealed or twisted the facts, either intentionally or inadvertently, then and later.

McNamara, for example, was probably sincere when he told Admiral Sharp that reprisals against North Vietnam could not be carried out until "we are damned sure" what happened on the night of August 4. Testifying before the Senate Foreign Relations Committee in early 1968, he divulged that he had seen "unimpeachable" proof: four intercepted North Vietnamese radio messages revealing Communist intentions to attack the U.S. destroyers on that fateful night, messages that he could not make public because they might compromise secret intelligence methods. The intercepts are still classified. But reliable sources have since concluded that McNamara was still mistaken—if not dissimulating—when he testified more than three years after the controversial incident.

The intercepts were not "attack orders," as he termed them, but instructions from a North Vietnamese shore command to its patrol boats to prepare for "military operations" that may well have been defensive—especially since the Communists believed the *Maddox* was linked to the covert South Vietnamese raiders. Moreover, the "time-date groups" on the messages referred to the first engagement and not, as McNamara contended, to the second event.

Ray Cline, then deputy director of the CIA, had discerned the crucial difference at the time, as he recalled to me years later: "I felt from the start that the second incident had been questionable, but I simply wasn't sure. However, after a number of days of collating and examining the reports relating to the second incident, I concluded that they were either unsound or that they dealt with the first incident." Even Johnson privately expressed doubts only a few days after the second attack supposedly took place, confiding to an aide, "Hell, those dumb stupid sailors were just shooting at flying fish."

Despite his misgivings, Johnson was not about to forgo the chance to gain bipartisan support on Capitol Hill for whatever policies he chose to pursue in Southeast Asia. His aides had broadened the draft of the proposed congressional resolution so that it now authorized him to "take all necessary measures" to repel attacks against U.S. forces and to "prevent further aggression" as well as determine when "peace and security" in the area had been attained. In short, as Johnson later quipped, the resolution was "like grandma's nightshirt—it covered everything."

He now mobilized two men to promote the document. One was McNamara, who could dazzle legislators with his maps and flip-charts. The other was Fulbright, chairman of the Senate Foreign Relations Committee.

On August 5, though the Tonkin Gulf puzzle had not yet been pieced together, Johnson sent his resolution to Congress for approval. A day later, McNamara appeared before a joint session of the Senate Foreign Relations and Armed Services committees to persuade their members to endorse the resolution rapidly. It was plain from the beginning that he would face little opposition. Opinion polls showed that 85 percent of the American public stood behind the administration, and most newspaper editorials faithfully reflected this support. So did the senators. With Fulbright in the lead, they commended Johnson for his prudence and decisiveness. But Wayne Morse of Oregon stubbornly refused to go along. And his loud dissent was to haunt Congress for years to come.

Morse was the Typhoid Mary of Capitol Hill. A lean, humorless teetotaler, he had arrived in Washington in 1945 as a progressive Republican determined to steer his party toward enlightened positions on such issues as education and labor relations, which he knew intimately.

Frustration prompted him to switch to the Democrats, who rewarded him with choice committee appointments. By the 1960s, however, he had become a sanctimonious bore, a garrulous orator whose gravel voice would drone on over trivia. By the time he confronted McNamara on August 6, he had lost his credibility. His colleagues would tolerate him for five or ten minutes, since they respected the ritual courtesies of the Senate, but he rarely changed votes. He lacked influence.

Early that morning, a Pentagon officer telephoned a startling tip to Morse. The officer, whose identity Morse would never divulge, revealed that the *Maddox* had indeed been involved in the covert South Vietnamese raids against North Vietnam. Thus the administration had been disingenuous in describing the Communist attack against the destroyer as "unprovoked." But at the joint committee meeting, when Morse suggested that there was a connection between the American ship and the South Vietnamese commandos, McNamara gave him a steely glare and a duplicitous answer: "Our navy played absolutely no part in, was not associated with, was not aware of, any South Vietnamese actions, if there were any. . . . I say this flatly. This is a fact."

At fresh Senate Foreign Relations Committee hearings in 1968, challenged by documents that disclosed a different story, McNamara awkwardly amended his earlier denial. The *Maddox* captain had known about the clandestine South Vietnamese operations, he conceded, but was not aware of the "details." But at the same hearings, McNamara and General Earle Wheeler suffered memory lapses when asked about the Pentagon's plans to bomb North Vietnam, which had been drawn up in early 1964. McNamara said he would "have to check the record," while Wheeler opined evasively that "to the best of my knowledge and belief . . . there was no thought of extending the war into the north."

His colleagues ignored Morse, as did the full Senate when it convened on the afternoon of August 6, 1964, to debate Johnson's proposed resolution. Speaking to an almost empty chamber, Morse asserted that "the place to settle the controversy is not on the battlefield but around the conference table." He was joined in opposition by only one other senator, Ernest Gruening of Alaska, a veteran liberal who warned that "all Vietnam is not worth the life of a single American boy." But their voices were drowned out by a din of patriotism. Even Senator Richard Russell of Georgia, who had long harbored reservations about the U.S. pledge to Southeast Asia, cast aside his doubts. "Our national honor is at stake," he intoned. "We cannot and we will not shrink from defending it."

Though the resolution was never in jeopardy, Johnson had told

Fulbright to secure its passage as fast as possible by the largest possible vote. Anything less, Johnson explained, would tarnish the image of unity so important to America's international reputation. Also implicit in Johnson's demand for overwhelming congressional endorsement was his constant preoccupation with Goldwater. Johnson knew that the Republican hard-liners would back him, but he worried that he might become their captive unless liberals rallied to his side as well. The liberals respected Fulbright. It was his job to bring them aboard.

Fulbright portrayed the resolution as a moderate measure "calculated to prevent the spread of war." He began to work on doubters like George McGovern of South Dakota and John Sherman Cooper of Kentucky, allaying their fears that the president would be accorded excessive power. In particular, Fulbright dissuaded Wisconsin Senator Gaylord Nelson from introducing an amendment calling for efforts to "avoid a direct military involvement" in Southeast Asia. Such a codicil was superfluous, he assured Nelson, since "the last thing we want to do is become involved in a land war in Asia."

So the Senate approved the resolution with only Morse and Gruening dissenting, while the House of Representatives passed it unanimously. Morse predicted that its supporters "will live to regret it," and he was vindicated in May 1970, when the resolution was repealed—on the initiative, ironically, of a loyal Richard Nixon disciple, Senator Robert Dole of Kansas, who figured that it had become obsolete. The outcome of the vote pleased nobody more than it did Walt Rostow, who had originally conceived the idea. Looking back on the Tonkin Gulf incident and its aftermath, he remarked, "We don't know what happened, but it had the desired result."

To the Hanoi leaders, the U.S. air strikes dramatized their vulnerability to American military might. Stressing in internal directives that "our initial experiences in fighting were inadequate," they redeployed their defense forces and tightened discipline. Worried by the prospect of future reprisals, they also began to probe the possibility of negotiating an end to the war—at least as one of their options.

J. Blair Seaborn, chief Canadian member of the International Control Commission, who had for months been secretly carrying sweet-and-sour messages from Washington to Hanoi, met with Pham Van Dong again on August 13 to outline the deal that the Johnson administration was repeatedly to offer the Communists. They could count on "economic and other benefits" if they abandoned the insurgency in the south, but they would "suffer the consequences" if they persisted in their "present course." Infuriated, Pham Van Dong warned that sustained American attacks against North Vietnam would spread the war "to the whole of Southeast Asia." Then, changing his tone, he gently advised Seaborn to return with fresh American proposals, perhaps based on the 1954 Geneva accords.

And other intermediaries were getting into the act. The United Nations secretary-general, U Thant, flew to Washington with a suggestion for Johnson. A former foreign minister of Burma with impeccable neutralist credentials, he proposed to organize talks with the North Vietnamese. Johnson could not afford to rebuff him. Accordingly, Thant proceeded to make arrangements for an exploratory meeting in Rangoon, the Burmese capital, relying on the Soviet Union to transmit his message to Hanoi. His initiative coincided with an attempt by Prime Minister Khrushchev to bring the North Vietnamese to the conference table. Though they distrusted Khrushchev, who had capitulated to the United States in the Cuban missile crisis and subscribed to President Kennedy's nuclear test ban treaty, and though they had shifted their sympathy to China, the North Vietnamese realized that there was no firepower in Chinese rhetoric. Only the Soviet Union could supply them with the sophisticated surface-to-air missiles and other equipment they needed. Backtracking, they appealed to Khrushchev for heavier doses of aid. He agreed—on condition that they consider negotiations.

The faint glimmer of hope for a negotiated settlement faded in October 1964, when Khrushchev was ousted by his Kremlin rivals, who promptly increased Soviet assistance to the North Vietnamese. But the prospects for peace had never been strong. Even before Khrushchev's fall, American officials had rejected diplomacy: in September, when U Thant received a receptive response from Hanoi, administration officials withheld the information from Johnson. To open talks with North Vietnam, explained Dean Rusk, would have signified "the acceptance or the confirmation of aggression."

Johnson was not wedded to the idea of war. On the contrary, he exercised caution immediately after the Tonkin Gulf affair. He restricted U.S. air strikes against North Vietnam to that single day, and he temporarily suspended both the DeSoto missions and the covert South Vietnamese raids. Yet he and his entourage could not concede to a diplomatic alternative, given foreign policy goals and their appraisal of the situation in South Vietnam itself.

Johnson and his advisers shared the fundamental assumption, inherited from Eisenhower and Kennedy, that an independent South Vietnam was vital to the defense of Southeast Asia—and, more important, to America's global credibility. In short, they clung to the domino theory, unable to contemplate negotiations that might eventually give the Vietcong a recognized political role in South Vietnam. They knew that the Saigon regime was too weak to survive a compromise settlement. The top priority must be, they concluded, to stabilize the South Vietnamese government and redress its military position in the field.

That objective was to be unattainable. Therefore, despite their awareness of the pitfalls, Johnson and his aides took over the management of the war. If the recalcitrant natives could not be prodded, they would have to be supplanted. As Rusk put it: "Somehow we must change the pace at which these people move, and I suspect that this can only be done with a pervasive intrusion of Americans into their affairs." But unless they were to suffer the opprobium of total colonialism, Americans would have to work through a client South Vietnamese government. And throughout the latter half of 1964, General Maxwell Taylor bore the brunt of that task as U.S. ambassador in Saigon.

A former chairman of the joint chiefs of staff, Taylor had been selected by Johnson for the job primarily to placate the U.S. military establishment. But the choice had been a poor one. Taylor, though intelligent, was a conventional soldier with little patience for Vietnam's political complexities. Nor could he understand the vendettas being waged by South Vietnam's various factions against each other. In his view, the South Vietnamese needed leadership, discipline, cohesion, and a sense of purpose—qualities they could acquire by heeding his advice. Unfortunately, they marched to their own tune, and Taylor later reflected on his frustrations at the time. "One of the facts of life about Vietnam was that it was never difficult to decide what should be done, but it was almost impossible to get it done."

Nothing bedeviled Taylor more than trying to guide Prime Minister Nguyen Khanh. By the early summer of 1964, with his internal opponents plotting against him, Khanh was heading toward collapse, and thus pleading for an extension of the war into the north as a distraction from his problems. Suddenly, the American reprisal raids following the Tonkin Gulf incident infused him with fresh confidence. He declared a state of emergency, reimposed censorship, and announced other controls. Then he hastily drafted a new constitution for South Vietnam, promoting himself to the presidency and dismissing his principal rival, General Duong Van Minh, the nominal chief of state, whom the Americans had counseled him to include in the government. Taylor had cautioned against making "sweeping changes" that might spark disorder. But Khanh disregarded the warning, and Saigon went into spasms of protest.

Beginning on August 21, students streamed through the city demanding that Khanh ease his restrictive new laws. Soon they were joined by Buddhist militants, who insisted, among their other grievances, that too many former Diem supporters still held official jobs. Khanh met with the Buddhist leaders Tri Quang and Tam Chau, but virtually admitted his incompetence by telling them that he would discuss their complaints with Ambassador Taylor—who, in turn, urged him not to knuckle under to any minority. Caught between conflicting pressures, Khanh relented. On the morning of August 25, after four frenetic days, he promised to "revise" his constitution and introduce other liberal measures. But his adversaries, now certain that they had him on the run, continued their pursuit.

A crowd of twenty-five thousand massed outside his office, clamoring for his resignation. Bravely facing the mob, Khanh denied that he was trying to establish a dictatorship. But that afternoon, he quit. His stillborn constitution was scrapped and the government's advisory body, the military revolutionary council, met the next day to choose another chief of state.

Officers at the meeting wept and confessed their shortcomings. But the political theater was only a charade contrived to conceal their maneuvers. General Tran Thien Khiem, who had helped Khanh seize power in January, now turned against him, and Minh also jockeyed for position. After lengthy haggling, the council finally created a compromise triumvirate of Khanh, Khiem, and Minh to rule until a permanent government could be formed. Khanh, who still retained the rank of prime minister in the flimsy coalition, flew off to recuperate in the mountain air of Dalat, and anarchy overtook Saigon.

Catholic activists, spilling into the streets to check the Buddhists, converged on the military headquarters near the airport where the council had been in session. As they approached the gates, many of them riding or wheeling bicycles, nervous soldiers behind coils of barbed wire started to shoot wildly. Their bullets killed six demonstrators and wounded dozens of others. Exaggerated accounts of a massacre swept across Saigon, always receptive to rumors, and by evening, gangs of frenzied kids armed with sticks and clubs were coursing through the city, smashing shop windows or battling one another in apparently mindless outbursts of violence as the police fled before them. I had witnessed uncontrolled mobs committing horrors in places like Baghdad and Calcutta—and even in Saigon on earlier occasions—and I knew they could be murderous. I retreated to the safety of my hotel to observe these youths from afar as they streamed along Tu Do, the principal thoroughfare, and it occurred to me as I watched them that South Vietnam's feeble authority was perhaps less threatened by Vietcong guerrillas in the countryside than by this whirlpool of factional chaos.

Only after two days did paratroopers, their bayonets fixed, restore order. Meanwhile, Khanh had appointed an amiable Harvard-educated economist, Nguyen Xuan Oanh, to act as prime minister in his absence. Oanh's prospects were dim from the start. For one thing, he spoke fluent English, which tainted his nationalist pretensions. And American officials in Saigon did not help by calling him "Jack Owen."

The turbulence persisted into early September. Dissident army units periodically menaced Saigon from the Mekong delta as the Buddhists threatened the regime from their stronghold in Hué. Potential military insurgents could be blocked by guns or bribed with money, but the Buddhists were harder to handle. Now a potent political force with disciplined followers throughout the country, they wanted far more than their routine demand that Diem's residual sympathizers be purged from positions of authority. Their aim was to exercise a veto over all government decisions, so that Buddhism, which had suffered persecution under the French and later under Diem, could flourish as both a religious and a secular movement. As he braced for a comeback, Khanh met with Tri Quang and Tam Chau to exchange pledges of mutual support. Khanh sealed the bargain by contributing the equivalent of $200,000 to the Buddhists, which was, in a reversal of Western practice, like a politician paying off a lobby.

Returning to Saigon from Dalat, Khanh displaced Oanh with the promise to retire in favor of a civilian regime as soon as he had stabilized the administration. Nobody was optimistic—least of all Ambassador Taylor, who reported that "we need two or three months to get any sort of government going that has any chance of maintaining order."

In fact, fresh disorders were about to erupt, provoked by a couple of disgruntled officers. General Lam Van Phat had recently been dismissed as minister of interior, and General Duong Van Duc was due to be relieved as commander in the Mekong delta. On September 13, they drove their troops into Saigon and took over the usual key points. The coup attempt, which collapsed within twenty-four hours, was notable in only one respect: it marked the first major appearance in the Saigon political arena of Air Vice Marshal Nguyen Cao Ky, commander of the South Vietnamese air force, who had celebrated his thirty-fourth birthday the week before.

Ky, a lean figure with a hairline mustache who wore purple jump suits and carried pearl-handled revolvers, was as daring as his garb was colorful. A northerner trained by the French as a pilot, he later operated under CIA auspices, flying secret agents into North Vietnam. He was bluntly outspoken, and Americans liked his candor—even though his impetuous style sometimes scared them, as it did on that September day. Instead of offering to negotiate with the insurgent generals, he sent his aircraft over their headquarters and threatened to blast it to bits unless they surrendered. They complied.

The abortive coup also damaged Khanh's already tarnished prestige. Indeed, many Vietnamese regarded the whole episode as having been an elaborate ploy designed by American officials so that Ky and other young officers could upstage Khanh. But just the contrary was true. Secretary of State Rusk directed the American embassy to "make it emphatically clear" to the South Vietnamese that their internecine squabbling was eroding the patience of the Johnson administration. Implicit in his message was the warning that U.S. aid might be curbed unless the chaos stopped: "The United States has not provided massive assistance to South Vietnam, in military equipment, economic resources, and personnel in order to subsidize continuing quarrels among South Vietnamese leaders."

Ky and other young officers, among them the armed forces chief of staff General Nguyen Van Thieu, soon posed a challenge to Khanh. For the moment, though, the Americans were stuck with him—even though he continually confused and disheartened them. An inveterate intriguer, he could never be trusted. Though he had resigned as prime minister, he retained real power for himself by taking over as commander in chief of the armed forces and getting rid of his two main rivals, Khiem and Minh. He sent Khiem into honorable exile as South Vietnamese ambassador to Washington, and he dispatched Minh abroad on a "goodwill" tour. On October 20, with his approval, a rubber-stamp council of seventeen notables proclaimed the creation of a civilian regime headed by a couple of decrepit dignitaries.

The new chief of state, Phan Khac Suu, was an octogenarian who advertised his obsolescence by dressing in a black mandarin gown. A French-trained agricultural engineer who vaguely belonged to the Cao Dai sect, he had once served the Emperor Bao Dai and was briefly jailed by Ngo Dinh Diem for mild dissidence. The prime minister, Tran Van Huong, a schoolteacher and former mayor of Saigon, seemed equally out-of-date—or so he struck me during a chat we had one morning in his shabby office. A pleasant gentleman in his early sixties, with close-cropped white hair and a ruddy complexion, he might have been a *petit fonctionnaire* in a French provincial town. Yet, speaking in flawless French, he evoked his Asian identity in an appeal to some vague divinity that would rescue South Vietnam: "I am completely tranquil, as I must be to have faith in this country's future. You know, we Asians are fatalistic. I believe in providential assistance."

The gods did little to help Huong during his three months in office. Soon Saigon's factions, the Buddhists in the forefront, were again on the rampage. They staged protest demonstrations, went on hunger strikes, and repeated their charge that the government still employed pro–Diem elements. After appealing in vain for calm, Huong declared martial law—a move that Khanh and the Ky group interpreted, possibly with good reason, to be a device to put General Minh back in power. They again began to plot.

Rumors of their conspiracy alarmed Ambassador Taylor. He had just returned from a quick trip to Washington, where President Johnson had insisted that he stem the instability in Saigon. On December 8, over steak and red wine at General Westmoreland's villa, Taylor frankly warned Ky, Thieu, and a few other young officers that the chronic disorder not only "dismayed the staunchest friends of South Vietnam," but might even discourage Congress from increasing U.S. aid. The officers left, apparently chastened. Within two weeks, however, they were again hectoring Huong. They demanded that he forcibly retire nine "old guard" generals, including Minh, now back from his tour abroad, charging them with "fomenting unrest." Huong predictably refused, and they set their plan in motion. Early on the morning of Sunday, December 20, they rounded up Minh and four other generals at their homes and flew them to confinement in Pleiku, a squalid town in the central highlands. They also arrested thirty other officers and civilian politicians and set up an Armed Forces Council as the real authority in Saigon, with Khanh its titular head. Confident that they could control Huong, they left him undisturbed.

Taylor, usually unflappable, was now frustrated to the point of despair. On December 21, he summoned Khanh and the young officers to his office at the U.S. embassy, an ugly new building designed by the noted architect Edward Durell Stone. Only Ky, Thieu, and two others appeared. Taylor motioned them to seats in the spacious room, its picture window looking out on a courtyard graced by a giant tamarind tree. "Do all of you understand English?" he began abruptly, his voice taut. They nodded. He then launched into a tirade, scolding them as if he were still superintendent of West Point and they a group of cadets caught cheating: "I told you all clearly at General Westmoreland's dinner that we Americans were tired of coups. Apparently I wasted my words. . . . Now you have made a real mess. We cannot carry you forever if you do things like this."

Taylor had committed a cardinal sin. By humiliating the young officers, he had made them "lose face"—the most demeaning of experiences for an Asian. The incident so rankled Ky that, a decade later, he bitterly remembered Taylor as "the sort of man who addressed people rather than talked to them." More significant, Taylor's performance revealed a deeper error. The South Vietnamese were competing against a Communist movement that, having defeated the French, could rightly claim to represent the vanguard of Vietnamese nationalism. For the sake of their own pride, they resented being treated in ways that reminded them of their almost total dependence on an alien power. How could they preserve a sense of sovereignty when Taylor, striving to push them into "getting things done," behaved like a viceroy?

Khanh reacted angrily. In an interview with the *New York Herald Tribune* correspondent in Saigon, he denounced Taylor for meddling in South Vietnam's internal affairs. The Americans were trying to remold Vietnam in their own image, he said, and unless Taylor acted "more intelligently," the United States "will lose Southeast Asia and we will lose our freedom." He went even further in a radio broadcast, implying that the American effort to manage him was a form of "colonialism" as dangerous as the Communist threat: "We make sacrifices for the nation's independence and the people's liberty, not to pursue the policy of any foreign country."

Stung by the attack, Taylor advised Khanh to resign and go abroad. Khanh replied by hinting that he might expel Taylor. That, said Taylor, would spell the end of America's responsibility for South Vietnam. To make his warning credible, he suspended certain U.S. military and civilian programs. Once again, though, America lacked leverage, as it had when Henry Cabot Lodge quarreled with Ngo Dinh Diem. For the South Vietnamese knew that the United States could not abandon them without damaging its own prestige. So despite their reliance on American aid, now more than a half-billion dollars a year, they could safely defy American dictates. In short, their weakness was their strength. As a Saigon government official privately explained it to me at the time, "Our big advantage over the Americans is that they want to win the war more than we do."

But Khanh, realizing that the Americans could play his rivals against him, tempered his squabble with Taylor and agreed to respect Huong's civilian government. His compromise gesture, however, was part of a maneuver.

By early January 1965, the Buddhists were again demanding Huong's ouster, and Khanh saw this as a chance to advance his own ambitions. He offered to protect Huong on condition that four army officers, among them Ky and Thieu, be given cabinet posts. But he also encouraged the Buddhist protests, now beginning to turn against the United States. Buddhist militants had mobilized a mob of five thousand students to sack an American library in Hué, and they organized a demonstration against the U.S. embassy in Saigon. As the unrest spread, Khanh stepped in as the only person capable of restoring order. On January 27, his military colleagues deposed Huong and returned him to power. He retained the facade of civilian government by keeping the aged Phan Khac Suu as figurehead chief of state and by reappointing as acting prime minister Nguyen Xuan Oanh, whose previous tenure in the job had lasted five days.

Taylor's first instinct was to withhold U.S. recognition from Khanh—not only for personal reasons but also because he was beginning to doubt Khanh's fidelity to the anti-Communist cause. Taylor's suspicions were not unfounded. Khanh, increasingly exasperated by American attempts to restrain him, had in fact been covertly exploring a possible accommodation with the Vietcong. But Taylor was overruled in Washington. President Johnson and his aides remembered the vacuum after Diem's overthrow, and they were unwilling to unseat Khanh in favor of an unknown alternative. McGeorge Bundy even believed that Khanh was "still the best hope" and could be handled. Nevertheless, Taylor signaled to Khanh's rivals that he would welcome a change. As he confided to one of my colleagues at the time, "We haven't told Khanh to go, but we've made our wishes known to the Vietnamese, and we're leaving it up to them."

An American intelligence agent then trying to monitor the political machinations shaking Saigon referred to the city as "the capital of the double cross." Factions and individuals constantly switched sides as they jockeyed for power. So it was that Ky, Thieu, and others, having risen to prominence as protégés of Khanh, in early 1965 began to plan his downfall. They were not directly spurred into action by the U.S. mission, but they assumed that Taylor's hostility to Khanh would gain them American support.

On February 16, Khanh replaced the hapless Oanh with a new prime minister, Phan Huy Quat, a physician of northern origin with years of political experience behind him. Quat invited representatives from nearly all of South Vietnam's feuding political, religious, and military factions into his cabinet. But Khanh soon started to manipulate the coalition—and the inevitable occurred.

Hardly had Quat taken office than several battalions of troops entered Saigon. In familiar fashion, they occupied army headquarters, the radio station and post office, and encircled Khanh's house. Khanh escaped through a back gate and telephoned Ky, who flew him to Dalat. Then Ky returned to the Bienhoa air base, where a group of his own comrades had gathered. Resorting to his favorite tactic, he called General Robert Rowland, U.S. adviser to the South Vietnamese air force, and asked him to deliver an ultimatum to the conspirators. Unless they capitulated within four hours, he would bomb Saigon.

The plot had been concocted by a pair of irrepressible schemers—General Lam Van Phat, whose bid to grab power in September had fizzled, and Colonel Pham Ngoc Thao, the clandestine Communist operative assigned to stir up trouble of any kind. Thao, a charter organizer of the coup against Diem, had also been involved in an earlier attempt to topple Khanh, who had dispatched him to the South Vietnamese embassy in Washington to keep him out of mischief, and then, fearing his conspiratorial skills even at that distance, summoned him home in late December to entrap him. Thao, tipped off as he landed in Saigon, immediately went underground. He contacted Phat, and they planned the challenge. Now, however, they were confronted with Ky's threat. Knowing him to be impulsive, they were reluctant to call his bluff.

On the evening of February 19, within minutes of the deadline, Rowland telephoned Ky to say that Phat and Thao were ready to fly to the Bienhoa air base to negotiate. Ky quickly rescinded his bombing orders, and the three men met. Phat and Thao, whose troops still held vital positions in Saigon, agreed to surrender—but only on condition that Khanh be dismissed and sent into exile. Nothing suited Ky better. Indeed, many American officials believed—though he later denied it—that Ky had surreptitiously engineered the attempted coup in order to dramatize that Khanh had lost the confidence of the armed forces and was thus unfit to rule.

Whatever the truth, South Vietnam's senior officers voted the next morning to strip Khanh of his authority and, as a face-saving device, to appoint him ambassador-at-large. Three days later, after a ceremonial airport farewell, Khanh left Saigon, never to return. Taylor, present at the departure, could scarcely conceal his pleasure. It had been, he informed President Johnson, the "most topsy-turvy week since I came to this post."

The veneer of a civilian government remained for another four months, but gradually peeled off as Buddhist, Catholic, and other factions defied the prime minister, Dr. Quat. In early June, the generals ousted him along with the moribund chief of state, Phan Khac Suu. Ky thereupon became prime minister, with Thieu as chief of state; the combination seemed to President Johnson and his staff to be, as William Bundy afterward put it, "the bottom of the barrel, absolutely the bottom of the barrel."

Having hoped to limit America's involvement, Johnson now realized that he could not count on the undisciplined South Vietnamese, who plainly possessed neither the will nor the capacity to block what then appeared to be an almost inevitable Communist victory. The honor of the United States—and his own reputation—were at stake. He had no choice. He would have to Americanize the war: "Power. Power on the land, power in the air, power wherever it's necessary. We've got to commit it. . . ."

11 LBJ Goes to War

The first American combat troops arrived in Vietnam in March 1965, when U.S. marines waded ashore near the coastal city of Danang. Their initial assignment was to protect a big American airfield.

Lyndon Johnson was elected president in his own right in November 1964 by a landslide vote. He was determined to promote the Great Society, his progressive economic and social programs, but equally determined to prevail in Vietnam.

A familiar Washington scene as President Johnson discusses the Vietnam situation with his advisers in the White House. Seated at his right is Secretary of State Rusk; at his left, Secretary of Defense McNamara. Both strongly supported the war.

On Christmas Eve 1964, Vietcong terrorists bombed a hotel in Saigon housing American officers. President Johnson refrained from taking reprisals so as not to jar the U.S. public during the holiday season.

On February 7, 1965, when the Vietcong attacked the American base near Pleiku in the central highlands of South Vietnam, Johnson responded with American air raids against North Vietnam.

President Johnson's national security adviser, McGeorge Bundy (left), arrived in Saigon in early February 1965. He is greeted by General Westmoreland as Ambassador Taylor looks on. While Bundy was there, the Communists staged an attack against an American camp at Pleiku.

American aircraft bombed North Vietnam just as Soviet Prime Minister Aleksei Kosygin (left) was meeting with Ho Chi Minh. The bombing undercut Kosygin's attempts to persuade Ho to negotiate with the United States.

An American pilot, Commander George Jacobson, Jr., following an air raid against North Vietnam in early 1965. Operation Rolling Thunder continued until November 1968, but it did not deter North Vietnam from pursuing the war.

U.S. troops in South Vietnam were soon deployed in the countryside on offensive operations. A marine general said they could not win the war by "sitting on their ditty box."

In April 1965, President Johnson unveiled a peace plan in a speech at Johns Hopkins University in Baltimore. His proposal for a huge economic aid package to the Communists in exchange for a compromise was spurned by the Hanoi leaders.

Two press critics of the Vietnam war: Walter Lippmann, the elder statesman of the news media; and Art Buchwald, the satirical columnist. Both annoyed the president.

General Tran Do, deputy commander of the Vietcong forces, spent most of his time concealed in villages near the Cambodian border. He claimed later that Vietcong spies in Saigon kept him informed of American and South Vietnamese army deployments.

A Vietcong camp in the south, where guerrillas and their sympathizers assemble shells and rockets. Large Communist units, then moving south, carried heavy equipment along the Ho Chi Minh Trail, while the guerrillas often relied on small arms manufactured locally or captured from American troops and the South Vietnamese army.

Once on the tiger's back, we cannot be sure of picking the place to dismount.

—George Ball

I have asked the commanding general, General Westmoreland, what more he needs to meet this mounting aggression. He has told me. And we will meet his needs. We cannot be defeated by force of arms. We will stand in Vietnam.

—Lyndon Johnson

The trend was clear before midnight on November 3, 1964, and it fulfilled Johnson's most optimistic expectations. He had crushed Barry Goldwater by a margin of sixteen million votes, the highest proportion ever scored by a presidential candidate. The spectacular landslide swept along the rest of his party and gave the Democrats huge majorities in both chambers of Congress. Now he could make the Great Society a reality.

But there was the war in that "damn little pissant country," as he called Vietnam. Johnson had shrewdly and skillfully prevented the war from becoming a divisive political issue. He had deflected Goldwater's early attempts to rally right-wing sentiment against him, and his readiness to bomb North Vietnam had immunized him against charges of being "soft" on Communism. At the same time, he had pledged that "we are not about to send American boys nine or ten thousand miles away from home to do what Asian boys ought to be doing for themselves." But even as he campaigned—rushing from city to city to attend dinners, deliver speeches, and shake hands in a prodigious demonstration of raw energy—his civilian and military advisers in Saigon and Washington were charting plans that soon brought the United States directly into the conflict.

Some historians hold that events enveloped Johnson in the war. Others portray him as the victim of duplicitous aides, while still others contend that he consciously chose involvement. No single theory tells the entire story, yet each contains a grain of truth.

Johnson was an immensely complicated figure, confronted by a challenge of enormous complexity. Vietnam was not his kind of problem, and he constantly tried to mobilize a consensus among his advisers before he acted. The specialists may have deceived him—but only to the extent that they deluded themselves. Ultimately, though, he bore the responsibility.

Given his view of America's position in the world, Johnson could not envisage anything less in Vietnam than an outcome that stopped Communist "aggression"; in that respect he shared the same hope that had guided Truman, Eisenhower, and Kennedy. His purpose was to compel the leaders of North Vietnam to abandon the insurgency in South Vietnam—in short, to deny them victory. And he insisted that he was waging only a "limited" conflict, saying again and again: "We seek no wider war."

What limitations? Johnson began by exerting gradual pressure on North Vietnam, though he was uncertain the strategy would work. With each new step, he perceived that additional manpower, money, and matériel might be necessary. So he entered the war fully aware of the dangers ahead. He eventually failed because he misjudged the enemy's capacity to withstand pain, believing there was a threshold to their endurance. But, as Ho Chi Minh had warned the French, the Vietnamese Communists would risk annihilation rather than capitulate. That concept was beyond the comprehension of Johnson and his advisers, who mistakenly imputed their own values to the Communists. Paul Warnke, an assistant secretary of defense, was to reflect on this crucial error after leaving office: "The trouble with our policy in Vietnam has been that we guessed wrong with respect to what the North Vietnamese reaction would be. We anticipated that they would respond like reasonable people."

Johnson's strategy had an inexorable downward curve. Having discarded diplomacy, he narrowed his choices to only one option—war. He was not blind to the tragedy. But he closed his eyes to the possibility of other alternatives, and seemed to have persuaded himself that his plight was inevitable. As he told his press secretary, Bill Moyers, "I feel like a hitchhiker caught in a hailstorm on a Texas highway. I can't run. I can't hide. And I can't make it stop."

If Johnson had wanted bipartisan congressional endorsement for domestic political reasons, his advisers welcomed it as an opportunity to intensify U.S. activities in Southeast Asia. As usual, Bill Bundy, assistant secretary of state for Far Eastern affairs, took the lead. On August 11, 1964, four days after the legislature handed Johnson the Tonkin Gulf resolution—a virtual blank check to conduct the war as he saw fit— Bundy circulated a memorandum outlining the "next course of action."

Unless South Vietnamese "morale and momentum" were maintained, he warned, General Nguyen Khanh's fragile regime would crumble and local politicians or soldiers would either negotiate or embark on armed adventures without American "consent." He therefore proposed intensive military pressures against the North Vietnamese until they accepted "the idea of getting out." Bundy conceded that too bold an approach "would be difficult to justify to the American public." His blueprint was calculated to achieve "maximum results for minimal risks," and it stressed caution: "Probably the sequence should be played somewhat by ear, with the aim of producing a slightly increased tempo, but one that does not commit us prematurely to stronger actions."

During the first phase, to run through August, the United States would refrain from belligerent gestures that might "take the onus off the Communist side for escalation." Then tougher actions could slowly be introduced: the resumption of South Vietnamese commando forays against North Vietnamese coastal bases, the redeployment of DeSoto patrols in the Tonkin Gulf, and U.S. and South Vietnamese air strikes at Communist infiltration routes in southern Laos, these last carefully camouflaged "so as not to embarrass" the neutralist Laotian prime minister, Prince Souvanna Phouma.

The "next move upward" would begin in January 1965 with the regular U.S. bombing of North Vietnamese bridges, railroads, and oil storage facilities as well as the mining of Haiphong harbor. "Beyond these points," Bundy added, "it is probably not useful to think at the present time."

Ambassador Taylor in Saigon was thinking beyond those points. He foresaw the probability of a U.S. troop commitment to Vietnam—and it rattled him. He subscribed to the doctrine that there should be no American land wars in Asia. He now feared that a big U.S. effort against North Vietnam, such as Bundy suggested, would provoke a Communist reaction in the south that the feeble Saigon government could not handle—and that would require direct American combat intervention. Give the Khanh regime the time to strengthen itself, he argued: "We should not get involved militarily with North Vietnam and possibly with Red China if our base in South Vietnam is insecure and Khanh's army is tied down everywhere by the Vietcong insurgency."

The joint chiefs of staff shared Taylor's concern about sending U.S. troops to Vietnam, but they criticized his reluctance to bomb North Vietnam, contending that only such "significantly stronger military pressures" against the Hanoi regime would give the Saigon government the "relief and psychological boost" it required to attain "stability and viability." They favored immediate air strikes against the targets in the north they had pinpointed six months earlier, and they also proposed, among other things, clandestine incursions against suspected Communist sanctuaries in Cambodia.

They were seconded by John McNaughton, a former Harvard Law School professor who was a key civilian aide to McNamara. Though later skeptical, he then believed that only a more dynamic involvement could save South Vietnam. He called for a bigger American military commitment in Vietnam, including combat divisions, and the construction of a U.S. naval complex, perhaps at Danang. He suggested that American ships reassigned to the Tonkin Gulf patrols deliberately provoke a Communist response, which could be met by a "crescendo" of U.S. air raids and other actions against North Vietnam. Since reports of these initiatives, "distorted" by the media, might poison the election campaign at home, McNaughton advised that "we must act with special care" to assure the American public that "we are behaving with good purpose and restraint." Still, McNaughton was as uncertain as his colleagues. At worst, South Vietnam might "disintegrate," leaving the United States to claim that "the patient . . . died despite the extraordinary efforts of a good doctor."

A disservice done by the *Pentagon Papers,* the purloined collection of secret Vietnam war documents published in 1971, was to convey the idea that plans drafted by bureaucrats all reflect official policy. In fact, Washington is always awash with proposals and projects, some incredible. But they do not become policy without the president's approval. This was especially true under Johnson. Ultimately, Lyndon Johnson endorsed most of the schemes for stepping up the U.S. commitment to Southeast Asia. In the late summer of 1964, however, he was in no hurry to plunge into a conflict.

On September 7, he assembled his top aides at the White House to canvass their opinions. Among those present were Secretaries Rusk and McNamara, the Bundy brothers, General Earle Wheeler of the joint chiefs, and Ambassador Taylor, who had just flown in from Saigon. As the discussion started in the cabinet room, Johnson interrupted to ask whether Vietnam was "worth all this effort." His advisers knew that the question was rhetorical, and Johnson knew they knew it, but typically, he wanted to hear the explicit consensus—partly because he thought of himself as a pragmatist, receptive to many ideas, but also perhaps because his inner doubts compelled him to validate his views in the concurrence of others.

Johnson later claimed that he always listened carefully to his staff, inviting each assistant to voice objections or advance alternatives. But his aides could rarely resist the sheer weight of his personality, compounded as it was by the awesome power of the presidency. Johnson did not bully recalcitrant advisers into submission: on the contrary, they shared his fundamental assumption that America's credibility was at stake in the crusade to contain Communism. Though they might differ over tactics, they came to the White House meeting in agreement that only vigorous measures could now avert catastrophe in Southeast Asia.

Most of the participants performed predictably. Wheeler suggested that North Vietnam be bombed as soon as possible, while Rusk urged that other options be explored first. Taylor, having earlier pleaded that the Saigon regime be given time to stiffen itself, now conceded that "only the emergence of an exceptional leader could improve the situation and no George Washington is in sight." So he favored "increased pressure" against the north, to begin about December 1, and dutifully recited the dogma of the domino theory: "If we leave Vietnam with our tail between our legs, the consequences of this defeat in the rest of Asia, Africa, and Latin America would be disastrous."

Johnson, still hoping to delay or even avoid direct U.S. intervention, remained cool. On September 12, he ordered American vessels back into the Tonkin Gulf but withdrew them after another dubious clash with Communist patrol boats six days later—and kept them out of the area until February. And he also put the South Vietnamese commando raids against the North Vietnamese coast under strict American supervision. Right after the meeting, however, he approved a contingency plan that then seemed ambiguous, but which turned out to be a crucially important trip wire. The United States, it stated, would react "as appropriate" against North Vietnam in retaliation for "any" Communist attack against American units in Vietnam.

A year before, seeking to measure the cost of "victory," the joint chiefs of staff had conducted a "war game" code-named Sigma I. Its outcome was discouraging: at least a half-million U.S. combat troops would be necessary. Now, in September, they organized a sequel, Sigma II, to gauge the potential impact of an air offensive against North Vietnam. The players, which included McGeorge Bundy, McNaughton, Wheeler, and General Curtis LeMay, formed two teams, one representing the United States and the other North Vietnam. Again the results were depressing: no amount of American pressure could stop the Communists.

The conclusion should have been self-evident. North Vietnam, a predominantly rural society with an apparently inexhaustible people prepared to die for their cause, could not be blasted "back to the Stone Age," as Curtis LeMay wanted to do. Neither Britain nor Germany had been bombed to its knees during World War II, and Japan had succumbed only to the atomic weapon—hardly an option in Vietnam. Some senior officials, McNamara among them, later recognized this reality. But in late 1964, despite the lessons of the "war game," the Washington planners continued to refine their program for air strikes.

In Vietnam itself, though covert Vietcong agents may have been exacerbating the chaos then engulfing Saigon, the Communists in Hanoi were not counting on the disarray in the south to gain their objectives. For one thing, they tended to trust only movements they had themselves organized and disciplined, and they were reluctant to associate with the unruly factions defying the South Vietnamese government. More important, their basic strategy stemmed from Mao Zedong's famous dictum: "political power grows out of the barrel of a gun." The real arena was the battlefield. Throughout 1964, they buttressed their forces with that in mind.

They built the Ho Chi Minh Trail into an elaborate logistical network that could funnel modern equipment into the south. Vietcong battalions that until then had relied mainly on old French and Japanese weapons or on U.S. arms captured from the South Vietnamese were now strengthened with mortars and rocket launchers, AK-47 automatic rifles, and machine guns using the same caliber ammunition. The sophisticated weaponry, provided by the Soviet Union and China, made for resupply problems, but that drawback was more than offset by its superior effectiveness.

Vietcong strength during 1964 doubled to a total of one hundred and seventy thousand men, most of them recruited in the south. About thirty thousand were incorporated into fifty hard-core battalions, elite units equipped with these new modern weapons and stiffened by northern veterans. Their objective was to chew up the South Vietnamese army. And, by shattering the Saigon regime, they hoped that some of its leaders would concede to the formation of a coalition government containing Vietcong representatives—its aim to break with the United States and create a neutral state that could eventually come under Communist tutelage.

The Hanoi regime also sent seasoned officers to the south, among them General Tran Do, one of North Vietnam's most distinguished soldiers, then a mysterious figure cloaked in pseudonyms who was reportedly killed several times.

During an interview in Hanoi in 1981, Tran Do recalled the Communist strategy of the period. I discerned in his tone the regional tensions that still divide northern and southern Vietnamese despite their common allegiance to national unity. The Vietcong guerrillas, he explained, lacked the skill and experience to wage the conventional war the Communist leadership then foresaw. By the fall of 1964, northern troops infiltrating into the south were enlarging the Vietcong contingents and strengthening them with commanders, political commissars, communications experts, ordnance technicians, and other specialists. The first complete North Vietnamese unit, a regiment of the Three Hundred and Twenty-fifth Division, had already departed for the south, and the overall Communist command structure was tightened. The Vietcong forces, officially entitled the People's Revolutionary Army, were responsible to a headquarters in the south known in Vietnamese as the Truong Uong Cuc—the Central Office for South Vietnam, or COSVN. But, Tran Do told me, instructions came from the Communist hierarchy in Hanoi. He thus dispelled the myth, in which many Westerners then believed, that the Vietcong was essentially an indigenous and autonomous insurgent movement.

American officials, characteristically committing the error of ascribing their own practices to the enemy, often envisioned the Communist headquarters as a miniature Pentagon, hidden away in the jungle like a sort of Shangri-la. Some even naively imagined that it was staffed by platoons of bureaucrats and stenographers, furnished with desks and typewriters and filing cabinets and duplicating machines, as their offices were. In fact, as Tran Do described it, the Communist command base was a shadow flitting from one tiny hamlet to another to elude detection. When he first reached South Vietnam at the end of 1964, it was located in a corner of Tayninh province, conveniently near the Cambodian border.

We slept in hammocks in small thatched bamboo huts, and we held our meetings in deep underground tunnels, which also served as shelter against air raids. Informers in Saigon passed us intelligence, so we were able to decamp whenever the Americans and their South Vietnamese puppets planned operations in the area. Anyway, we could hear them coming, because big modern armies cannot move quietly. Still, we had some close shaves. Once, soon after I arrived, American airplanes dropped thousands of tons of bombs around us, but we weren't even scratched.

American intelligence experts were "almost certain" that the U.S. air strikes against North Vietnam would deter the enemy. The CIA estimated that the Communists, though they would exploit the chaos in Saigon, would "probably avoid actions" that might bring "the great weight of U.S. weaponry" down on them. On November 1, 1964, three weeks after that confident forecast, the Vietcong was to prove the CIA wrong and, for the first time, stage a major attack against the Americans.

Three months earlier, the joint chiefs of staff had ordered a squadron of vintage American B-57 jet bombers from Clark Field in the Philippines to Bienhoa air base, twelve miles north of Saigon, for the purpose of training South Vietnamese pilots. State Department officials had protested that the introduction of jets into Vietnam would further destroy the already tattered Geneva accords of 1954, which the United States theoretically claimed to respect. McNamara shared their misgivings, but he was preoccupied by so many other disputes with the joint chiefs that he preferred to sidestep this one. The B-57s had been duly flown to Bienhoa and, as a precaution against sabotage, lined up in the open like sitting ducks.

Late in October, a hundred Vietcong troops armed with mortars slipped into the surrounding area of rice fields, palm groves, and placid villages. Though they were dressed in black peasant pajamas, the local peasants knew their identity, yet not a hint of their presence reached the authorities. Before dawn on November 1, a shower of shells fell on the base, the explosions shattering the still darkness. South Vietnamese pilots and technicians and their U.S. advisers tumbled out of bed, running in all directions as gasoline tanks erupted in flames and debris flew everywhere. Search parties immediately fanned out through the neighborhood in quest of the assailants, but they had vanished without a trace. By daylight, when the losses were tabulated, six B-57s had been destroyed and more than twenty other aircraft damaged; five Americans and two South Vietnamese were dead, and nearly a hundred injured.

Taylor, outraged, could no longer restrain himself. In September, he recollected, the president had approved reprisals for "any" Communist actions taken against American units. Now he cabled Washington to urge that air raids against selected North Vietnamese targets should be promptly initiated, with warnings that bombing would occur again in the event of future Communist assaults. Too mild, the joint chiefs of staff complained; Taylor's "tit-for-tat" approach was "unduly restrictive." The moment had come for a relentless bombing offensive, they said. Indeed, aircraft carriers deployed off North Vietnam were poised to strike.

President Johnson did nothing. With the presidential election three days away, he was wary of a dramatic venture that might either dismay voters or offend them, if they construed it as a cheap expedient to deflate Goldwater. Curiously, however, Johnson told the joint chiefs he was contemplating sending an expedition of U.S. combat troops to Vietnam to protect American families and installations. The idea alarmed Taylor, who was puzzled that Johnson could "casually" make a decision so much more difficult than the bombing of North Vietnam.

On November 3, just after the polls confirmed his election, Johnson created a "working group" composed of eight middle-level State Department, Pentagon, and CIA officials, with William Bundy as chairman, to study "immediately and intensively" the U.S. options in Southeast Asia. Its conclusions were to be reported to a panel of ten "principals"—Rusk, McNamara, McGeorge Bundy, Wheeler, Taylor, and five others—who would in turn transmit an array of refined proposals to the president. The bureaucratic layer cake suited Johnson, since it offered him the chance to create unanimity, but in the end, the final choices were to be his—and his alone.

The research and discussion done by the committees throughout November were interestingly circumscribed. The fundamental issues had ceased to be whether Vietnam was vital to America's national interests or whether the United States could succeed there. The issue now was, starkly, what to do. A sense of urgency animated Bill Bundy's group: another Vietcong attack like the one against Bienhoa could occur at any moment, or the South Vietnamese regime might fall. The Johnson administration was on trial before the world—its credibility, in Bundy's words, hinging on its "determination to take risks if necessary to maintain our position in Southeast Asia."

But certain of his colleagues had doubts. Many CIA analysts had been consistently gloomy. One, Willard Matthias, had forecast in June 1964 that the situation in Vietnam at best augured a "prolonged stalemate," and he had suggested a negotiated settlement "based upon neutralization" of Southeast Asia. The Bundy group's intelligence expert, Harold Ford, now offered a similar prognosis. The Vietcong, he pointed out, could carry on the insurgency even if North Vietnam were "severely damaged" by U.S. bombing. He saw no early end to the war.

The Pentagon representative, Vice Admiral Lloyd Mustin, disagreed. He argued that "something far less" than the total annihilation of North

Vietnam would work. How much less he could not say, but he proposed a "progressively increasing squeeze"—inflicting "substantial levels of military, industrial, and governmental destruction" on the north. In any case, there was no choice. The only alternative to success in Vietnam, he concluded apocalyptically, was "abject humiliation."

After three weeks, Bundy boiled down the group's reports into three broad options: to continue the present policy of moderation; to launch bold attacks against North Vietnam immediately; and to make "graduated military moves," initially in Laos and then against North Vietnam, so designed as to give the United States the flexibility at any time "to escalate or not, and to quicken the pace or not." Bundy had resorted to a classic bureaucratic device known as the "Goldilocks Principle." By including one choice "too soft" and one "too hard," he could plausibly expect the upper-echelon "principals" to go for the "just right" option—in this case the third, which he himself favored.

In late November, the president's top advisers met to shape the recommendations they would give him after he returned from a Thanksgiving holiday at his Texas ranch. The foremost partisan of prudence among them was George Ball, under secretary of state. A bulky bear of a man, Ball firmly believed in the primacy of America's relations with Europe—a concept that bucked the then fashionable trend of focusing on Asia, Africa, and Latin America, where Communist-led "wars of national liberation" were frequent. That trend, exemplified in the fixation on Vietnam, alarmed Ball, and he had told Kennedy as much; Johnson was also aware of his dissidence. But Ball was valuable as a "devil's advocate." He kept other officials alert by testing their conformism, and particularly comforted Johnson, who liked to hear different sides of an issue. Besides, Ball was a discreet team player. He might quarrel internally, yet he would never openly wash the dirty linen.

Years later, when he had become a New York investment banker, I asked him why he had stayed in government service long after his views on Vietnam had been spurned, rather than resign and speak out. His somewhat awkward reply obliquely explained how it was that not a single high-level American bureaucrat walked out in protest against the war, even though many were disgusted with it: "I figured that I could do better by remaining on the inside. Had I quit, the story would have made the front page of *The New York Times* next day—and then I would have been promptly forgotten."

A liberal New Deal lawyer, Ball had served on a mission to survey the effect of the Allied bombing of Germany during World War II. The raids, he learned, had barely dented German industry, and he could not imagine that bombing rural North Vietnam would be any more effective. He had also conversed frequently with de Gaulle, who had warned him that the United States was courting the risk of repeating France's tragic experience in Indochina—"*ce pays pourri*," as de Gaulle called it. Now, in the fall of 1964, Ball was acutely worried, and in early October he dictated a sixty-seven-page memorandum—a "challenge to the assumptions of our current Vietnam policy."

"Once on the tiger's back, we cannot be sure of picking the place to dismount," he wrote, and argued that a U.S. air offensive against North Vietnam would induce escalation on both sides. The Communists would step up their attacks on the flimsy Saigon regime, which could be rescued only by the introduction of American forces. But the United States "cannot substitute its presence for an effective South Vietnamese government . . . over a sustained period of time." The spreading conflict would threaten to "set in train a series of events leading, at the end of the road, to the direct intervention of China and nuclear war." The sanest approach, Ball asserted, was "an immediate political solution that would avoid deeper U.S. involvement." Refuting the notion that America's global credibility stood to suffer as a consequence, he added: "What we might gain by establishing the steadfastness of our commitments, we could lose by an erosion of confidence in our judgments."

Johnson did not see the memo until February 1965. But Ball had addressed personal copies to "Dean, Bob, and Mac"—Rusk, McNamara, and McGeorge Bundy. McNamara was shocked by the document, less by Ball's apostasy than by his rashness in putting such heretical thoughts on paper, which might be leaked to the press. The others, as Ball recalled, dismissed the critique as "merely an idiosyncratic diversion" from the basic problem of "how to win the war."

Walt Rostow, at the other extreme, urged audacity. Send American troops to Vietnam promptly, he asserted, and the Communists would understand that "we are prepared to face down any form of escalation" they might mount. "Massive" U.S. air and naval forces should be deployed in the Pacific to strike at North Vietnam and even China should either or both react. Only a stupendous display of American muscle would drive the Communists into submission. "They will not actually accept a setback until they are sure that we mean it," Rostow affirmed, and they had to be told bluntly that "they now confront an LBJ who has made up his mind."

Not even the joint chiefs of staff were ready to go so far—though General Wheeler repeated Johnson's ambiguous suggestion that American combat units be sent to Vietnam to guard U.S. installations there, an idea to which McNamara and McGeorge Bundy were cool. So was Taylor, once again in Washington. If the administration hoped to compel the Hanoi leaders to abandon the insurgency in the south, Taylor reasoned, "too much" coercion could be dangerous. Again he recommended "measured military pressures," among them the bombing of Communist infiltration routes in Laos, and selective air raids against North Vietnam in retaliation for specific incidents like the Bienhoa attack. But short of a complete American takeover, an unappealing alternative, Taylor could not promise that moderation would succeed. The key, he said, was a solid regime in Saigon, without which American aid was only a "spinning wheel unable to transmit impulsion" to the effort to beat the Communists. No such regime was visible. "It is impossible to foresee a stable and effective government under any name in anything like the near future. . . .We sense the mounting feeling of war weariness and hopelessness that pervade South Vietnam. . . .There is chronic discouragement."

In contrast, Taylor could not conceal a sneaking admiration for the enemy: "The ability of the Vietcong continuously to rebuild their units and to make good their losses is one of the mysteries of this guerrilla war. . . . Not only do the Vietcong units have the recuperative powers of the phoenix, but they have an amazing ability to maintain morale."

Rusk, McNamara, McGeorge Bundy, and the other advisers knew that Johnson was virtually resigned to the direct use of American force, but they also knew that he was reluctant to act drastically. When they conferred with him at the White House on December 1, they recommended a diluted version of Bill Bundy's "just right" option—a program to escalate the U.S. involvement in Vietnam in gradual phases.

A first step would be Barrel Roll, a secret bombing campaign against the Communist infiltration routes in southern Laos from aircraft carriers in the South China Sea. Johnson, relieved that it was being conducted outside Vietnam, where it would not attract media attention and raise questions at home about his intentions, approved the plan to begin promptly. He also agreed to additional covert South Vietnamese commando raids against the North Vietnamese coast.

Johnson fretted over the shakiness of the Saigon regime, remarking on the hazards of extending the conflict if the South Vietnamese could not cope with a vigorous enemy response. He told a visitor: "If one little general in shirt sleeves can take Saigon, think about two hundred million Chinese coming down those trails. No sir! I don't want to fight them." He sent Taylor back to Saigon with a proposal for the obstreperous South Vietnamese generals: if they stopped bickering among themselves, the United States would accelerate a series of air attacks against North Vietnam. But the endeavor was futile. The Saigon generals, Taylor discovered, were more fractious than ever.

The Communists, meanwhile, were gambling that Johnson would not intervene in strength. He had refrained from reacting to their assault against Bienhoa, and he had procrastinated since then. Perhaps they could step up their offensives without provoking him into enlarging the American commitment. Beginning in December, they launched coordinated attacks throughout South Vietnam—the largest against Binh Gia, a Catholic village only forty miles southeast of Saigon in coastal Phuoc Tuy province.

Never before in the war had the Vietcong been deployed in such size. Two battalions and ancillary units comprising more than a thousand men had started out weeks earlier from a sanctuary in Tayninh province, northwest of Saigon. The troops, divided into small groups to avoid detection, trekked across rice fields and through jungles, relying on an elaborate network of friendly hamlets for food and shelter. By late November, having silently completed an arc around the capital, they reached Phuoc Tuy, presumably a "pacified" area. There, after picking up fresh weapons brought in by sea from North Vietnam, they retired to hidden encampments to plan the operation with meticulous care. What followed was not a set-piece confrontation, but an array of dazzling movements devised to ensnare and destroy the South Vietnamese forces.

As usual, the South Vietnamese had advantages—tanks, armored personnel carriers, heavy artillery, and helicopters flown by American pilots. But the superior equipment made them complacent in contrast to the Vietcong, which had learned to be fast and flexible. In typical style, Vietcong soldiers would hit a target while their comrades ambushed South Vietnamese convoys speeding to the rescue along exposed roads.

On the night of December 28, 1964, after sporadic actions in the region, the Vietcong occupied the village of Binh Gia for eight hours to dramatize its prowess, then faded into the jungle to elude pursuit. Five days later, the South Vietnamese army suffered a devastating blow as two companies of crack rangers, accompanied by tanks, ran into a Vietcong ambush inside a nearby rubber plantation: the Vietcong, armed with recoilless rifles and other sophisticated weapons, had waited patiently in the trees before raking the rangers from both sides of a narrow road. Surprised and confused, the rangers valiantly tried to fight back but were cut to pieces.

Altogether, seven battalions of South Vietnam's best troops were thrown into the Binh Gia engagement; nearly two hundred were killed, along with five American advisers. The enemy had tightened the noose around Saigon. Senior U.S. officers in the city were both awed and astonished. As one of them said at the time: "The Vietcong fought magnificently, as well as any infantry anywhere. But the big question for me is how its troops, a thousand or more of them, could wander around the countryside so close to Saigon without being discovered. That tells something about this war. You can only beat the other guy if you isolate him from the population."

American officials had been even more stunned on Christmas Eve, when Vietcong terrorists penetrated Saigon itself and planted a bomb in the Brinks Hotel, which housed U.S. officers. The explosion had killed two Americans and injured fifty-eight others. The Vietcong commanders had planned the daring venture with two aims in mind: by attacking an American installation located in the very core of the heavily guarded capital, the Vietcong demonstrated its ability to react in South Vietnam should the United States begin air raids against North Vietnam; equally important, the South Vietnamese population would be shown that the Americans, with all their pretense of power, were vulnerable and could not be counted on for protection.

The two Vietcong agents who performed the operation and escaped unscathed had prepared it with painstaking care. One of them, Nguyen Thanh Xuan, recollected the episode with professional coolness during an interview in 1981 in Ho Chi Minh City. He and a comrade had received orders for the mission from an intermediary in late November 1964. They reconnoitered the target, mixing easily with the crowds that filled the busy street outside and noting, among other details, that South Vietnamese officers mingled freely with the Americans. That determined their first move. Obtaining the proper uniforms from the city's ubiquitous black market, where nearly anything could be bought, Xuan's comrade disguised himself as a South Vietnamese army major while Xuan dressed as his military chauffeur. Next they observed the mannerisms of South Vietnamese soldiers. "We spent several days following the puppet soldiers around to watch their behavior—how they talked to people and to each other, how they got in and out of their cars, even how they smoked cigarettes."

Xuan had meanwhile procured two automobiles and the explosives for the job—again, not a difficult task in Saigon, where the Vietcong had a clandestine logistical labyrinth. Then, on the afternoon of December 24, they went into action.

They stashed the explosives in the trunk of one of their cars, setting a timing device to trigger at exactly 5:45 P.M. They drove both automobiles to the Brinks Hotel, and there the "major" played a persuasive scene. A Vietcong spy inside the South Vietnamese government had told them that a certain American colonel had left for the United States. Armed with that intelligence, the "major" told the desk clerk he had an appointment with the colonel, who was arriving soon from Dalat. The clerk replied that the colonel had left Vietnam, but the "major" insisted otherwise. Finally, turning to his "chauffeur," he ordered him to wait; he, the "major," would drive home in his own car and the "chauffeur" was to bring the American along in the other automobile. After that, as Xuan recalled, "I parked the car in the lot beneath the building. Then I went to the front gate, where a cop was on duty. I hadn't eaten all day, I told him. If the American colonel showed up, could he tell him that I'd gone for a bite and would be back soon. The cop agreed. I strolled over to a nearby café, sat down at a table and waited. The explosion came right on time."

Ambassador Taylor, backed up by General Westmoreland and every other senior American officer in Saigon and Washington, urged President Johnson to authorize retaliatory raids against North Vietnam. But Johnson still demurred. He did not want to intensify the war during the Christmas season, and there were practical considerations, which he explained to Taylor in an unusually long cable—a "full and frank statement of the way I see it. . . . The final responsibility is mine and the stakes are very high indeed," Johnson wrote.

Raising many of the same doubts that Taylor had expressed earlier, and observing that "our own security seems at first glance to be very weak," Johnson was worried that reprisals might spark a Communist response which the U.S. advisory force of twenty-three thousand then in Vietnam could not withstand. The political disarray in Saigon also troubled him, and he rather peevishly chided Taylor for failing to communicate "sensitively and persuasively" to the South Vietnamese generals the importance of unity and efficiency. To Taylor's surprise, Johnson's cable went on to state more explicitly than ever before that he was contemplating a U.S. combat troop commitment: "I have never felt that this war will be won from the air, and it seems to me that what is much more needed and would be more effective is a larger and stronger use of rangers and special forces and marines, or other appropriate military strength on the ground and on the scene. . . . I know that it might involve the acceptance of larger American sacrifices [but] I myself am ready to substantially increase the number of Americans in Vietnam if it is necessary to provide this kind of fighting force against the Vietcong."

Taylor replied in early January 1965 in a series of despondent messages. "We are presently on a losing track," he said. "To take no positive action now is to accept defeat in the fairly near future." But what could be done? First, it was hopeless to expect the South Vietnamese regime to improve. He could see nothing ahead but continued "political turmoil, irresponsibility, and division . . . lethargy [and] deepening loss of morale and discouragement," and an eventual move by some Saigon faction to make a deal with the Communists. So the United States had a choice, either to consider "ultimate withdrawal" or to introduce a "new element or elements." Rejecting the first, Taylor proffered two options: either put in American combat troops or step up the bombing of North Vietnam.

To send over U.S. soldiers would be a mistake, he argued. With Americans there to "carry the ball," the South Vietnamese would fight even less. A large American presence might evoke memories of colonialism and encourage Vietnamese hostility to Americans. As for using U.S. military units simply to protect American installations, Taylor figured that seventy-five thousand men would be needed—and even that number might not prevent a repetition of the Vietcong attacks against Bienhoa and the Brinks Hotel. By default, then, an air offensive against the north was the only alternative. It would not win "this guerrilla war," Taylor agreed, but nothing else seemed plausible.

Johnson appeared to feel that doom awaited him whatever he did. Chatting privately with a few reporters, he portrayed himself almost surrealistically as a man standing on a newspaper in the middle of the ocean. David Wise, then a *New York Herald Tribune* correspondent, recalled Johnson's tormented mood: " 'If I go this way,' he said, tilting his hand to the right, 'I'll topple over, and if I go this way'—he tilted his hand to the left—'I'll topple over, and if I stay where I am, the paper will be soaked up and I'll sink slowly to the bottom of the sea.' As he said this, he lowered his hand slowly to the floor."

A politician with keen antennae, Johnson sensed the uneasiness then creeping into congressional, press, and public attitudes toward Vietnam. He was distressed that a figure he deeply respected, Senator Richard Russell of Georgia, now argued that the time had come to "re-evaluate our position" in Vietnam. The influential columnist Walter Lippmann irked him by asserting that the president was transgressing "our own vital interests" and stretching "the limitations of our power" in trying to defend Southeast Asia. And he was disturbed by public opinion surveys, which showed growing dissatisfaction among Americans with his handling of the Vietnam predicament. The polls also indicated, as they frequently did throughout the war, that it was uncertainty that unsettled people; they consistently rallied behind the president, the commander in chief, when he acted decisively. Johnson edged toward such action. He refrained for the moment from deploying U.S. combat forces in Vietnam. But he approved retaliatory bombings of North Vietnam "immediately following the occurrence of a spectacular enemy action"—even though he was unsure that any tactic would "produce the necessary turnaround in South Vietnam in the coming months." He and his aides, poised to escalate the war, awaited the pretext to strike. It was, McGeorge Bundy said, like waiting for a "streetcar."

In pressing the president to make a decision, Taylor had recommended that Mac Bundy visit Vietnam to appraise the situation. Bundy had never been there and was "physically detached from the local scene," and he might assure Johnson that "we are missing no real bets in the political field." So Bundy scheduled a trip for the beginning of February 1965. But he was scarcely going with an open mind.

Late in January, after conferring with McNamara, he addressed a memorandum to Johnson stressing that "both of us are now pretty well convinced that our present policy can lead only to disastrous defeat." To expect the emergence of a stable regime in Saigon was futile. The Vietcong, encouraged by America's "unwillingness to take serious risks," was "gaining in the countryside." The worst course was to continue "this essentially passive role." The United States could either negotiate and "salvage what little can be preserved," or resort to armed power to "force a change" of Communist strategy. They favored the military alternative, though, they added, other plans ought to be "carefully studied." Either way, "the time has come for hard choices."

Mac Bundy departed for Saigon, coincidentally, just as the new Soviet prime minister, Aleksei Kosygin, left Moscow for Hanoi. Kosygin had embarked on his journey at the invitation of the North Vietnamese leaders, who were then angling for more Soviet military aid. He was prepared to fulfill their request—but on condition that they follow Soviet rather than Chinese guidance. Fearing that a wider war might jeopardize the Soviet policy of "peaceful coexistence" with the United States, he also tried to persuade them to consider a compromise solution. His talks in Hanoi, ironically, were as stormy as Taylor's wrangles in Saigon. One Soviet participant later described the North Vietnamese to me as a "bunch of stubborn bastards."

A Vietcong attack against a U.S. base near Pleiku, in the central highlands of South Vietnam, was to have a shattering impact on both Kosygin's and Bundy's journeys—and propel the conflict into a fresh phase.

Pleiku, traditionally a market town for the region's mountain tribes, had become the site of a South Vietnamese army headquarters that directed patrols against Communist infiltration routes threading through the jungles from Laos and Cambodia. A detachment of American special forces and other military advisers was billeted three miles away at Camp Holloway, whose perimeter was heavily protected by barbed wire and sandbag bunkers. A fleet of U.S. transport and observation aircraft and helicopters was parked at a nearby strip, and both South Vietnamese and American soldiers guarded the area.

Specialist Fourth Class Jesse Pyle of Morina, California, on sentry duty, sat shivering in a trench during the cold night of February 6–7. A nearby noise jarred him at about 2:00 A.M. Clambering out to investigate, he spotted shadows crossing the compound. He shouted, then started shooting. At that instant, a hail of mortar shells exploded, and the rattle of automatic fire could also be heard. An American screamed in the darkness: "We're going to die. We're all going to die."

Eight Americans died and more than a hundred others were wounded, and ten U.S. aircraft were destroyed. Nearly all the Vietcong assailants escaped. The body of one, found inside the enclosure, contained a detailed map of the camp—testimony to a meticulous job of espionage.

Mac Bundy, his mission completed, was packing to leave Vietnam that February morning when news of the Pleiku attack reached him. Joining Taylor and Westmoreland at U.S. military headquarters in Saigon, he was tense and abrupt—behaving, as Westmoreland afterward recalled, like many civilians in authority who display a "field marshal psychosis" once they have "smelled a little gunpowder." They quickly agreed that the "streetcar" had arrived. Bundy telephoned the White House to urge that American air raids against North Vietnam begin promptly, in accordance with the long-standing Pentagon plan quaintly entitled "Punitive and Crippling Reprisal Actions on Targets in North Vietnam." Contrary to most accounts, Bundy did not make his proposal under emotional stress on the spur of the moment. "That's nonsense," he explained to me years later. "I had already recommended retaliation beforehand."

Bundy also cabled President Johnson to make clear his conviction that a tough U.S. move was imperative. His message confirmed what he had told Johnson before going to Vietnam: the prospects there were "grim," the Vietcong's "energy and persistence are astonishing," and both the

Vietnamese and Americans he saw were uncertain "whether a Communist victory can be prevented." The "one grave weakness" in the U.S. posture was "a widespread belief that we do not have the will and force and patience and determination to take the necessary action and stay the course." To negotiate an American withdrawal "would mean surrender on the installment plan." So the only alternative was "continuous" bombing of North Vietnam—not merely "episodic responses geared on a one-for-one basis to 'spectacular' outrages," which would "lack the persuasive force of sustained pressure." The United States could anticipate "significant" losses, yet the program "seems cheap . . . measured against the costs of defeat." The Pleiku attack, Bundy concluded, had "produced a practicable point of departure."

Johnson convened his national security advisers, expanding the group to include Mike Mansfield, Senate majority leader, and John McCormack, speaker of the House of Representatives. Johnson plainly announced at the outset his intention to punish the North Vietnamese—as if they had struck him personally. "I've gone far enough," he barked. "I've had enough of this." Most of those present concurred, among them George Ball, who felt that at this juncture discretion was the better part of valor. But Mansfield and Vice-President Hubert Humphrey dissented. Johnson banished Humphrey from Vietnam deliberations for the next year, and quietly rehabilitated him only after Humphrey pledged to subscribe to the official administration line. Humphrey, the prototype of the unalloyed liberal, was tormented by Vietnam for the rest of his life.

Within hours, Operation Flaming Dart was under way, as the carrier *Ranger* launched its jets to bomb a North Vietnamese army camp near Dong Hoi, a coastal town sixty miles above the seventeenth parallel dividing North and South Vietnam. The South Vietnamese were brought into the first mission to boost their morale, and Air Vice Marshal Nguyen Cao Ky interrupted his political maneuverings in Saigon to lead their aircraft. But the initial raid fizzled because of foul weather.

A major casualty of the attack was Kosygin's initiative to persuade the North Vietnamese leaders to consider negotiations. Now they could claim to be victims of U.S. "aggression," worthy of total support from the Communist powers. And Kosygin, compelled to defend the Soviet Union's "anti-imperialist" image, had no choice but to fulfill their requests for unconditional military aid. They may have planned the Pleiku assault to incite an American reaction that would put him on the spot. In any case, new shipments of sophisticated Soviet surface-to-air missiles began to arrive at the port of Haiphong ten days after Kosygin's return to Moscow.

Mac Bundy had cautioned Johnson to alert the American people to the "fundamental fact" that "the struggle in Vietnam will be long" and that "there is no shortcut to success." Johnson disregarded the advice. He shrouded himself in silence—or, on occasion, privately told visitors to ignore the histrionic newspaper headlines and television broadcasts that, as usual, exaggerated events. Unwittingly, he was broadening the "credibility gap" that had dogged his White House years and would eventually prove politically fatal. By the middle of February, for example, James Reston of *The New York Times* was already denouncing his duplicity: "The time has come to call a spade a bloody shovel. This country is in an undeclared and unexplained war in Vietnam. Our masters have a lot of long and fancy names for it, like escalation and retaliation, but it is a war just the same."

But Johnson knew better than Reston that Americans placed their faith in the president in difficult moments, and the opinion surveys bore him out. Almost 70 percent of the nation gave him a "positive" rating, with the same proportion supporting a bombing strategy as the "only way" to "save" Vietnam. Nearly 80 percent believed that an American withdrawal would open Southeast Asia to Communist domination, and an equal proportion favored a U.S. combat troop commitment to block that possibility. So Johnson, whose pockets always bulged with the latest polls, felt confident that the public would uphold him whatever the journalists said.

As he intensified the war in early 1965, Johnson tried to manage the nation's perception of his policies—and his aides devoted as much attention to vocabulary as they did to strategy. To mute anxieties, his spokesmen withheld the real dimensions of the conflict from the American people, pursuing what one of them termed "a policy of minimum candor": a deliberate tactic to disclose only the barest essentials without blatantly lying. The president also wanted to warn the North Vietnamese that worse lay ahead unless they met his demands, but he was wary of resorting to belligerent rhetoric that might provoke drastic Soviet or Chinese intervention. So as the war grew, so did a lexicon of special phrases contrived to convey particular signals to the enemy.

American officials said that the bombing of North Vietnam after the Pleiku attack was "appropriate and fitting," which is how they had described the raid after the Tonkin Gulf incident six months earlier. On February 11, describing the next strike against the north, they referred to "air operations" designed to stop the "pattern of aggression"—thereby suggesting that a prolonged offensive was about to supersede individual reprisals. The labels changed as Johnson retired Flaming Dart, which had been retaliatory, and authorized Rolling Thunder, a continuous bombing program that would go on for three years, its name borrowed from the words of a hymn.

Started on March 2, as more than a hundred U.S. aircraft raided a North Vietnamese ammunition dump, Rolling Thunder was originally scheduled to last eight weeks. Johnson himself closely supervised it, boasting that "they can't even bomb an outhouse without my approval." But by April, as General Wheeler told McNamara, the strikes had "not reduced in any major way" North Vietnam's military capabilities or seriously damaged its economy, and the Hanoi regime "continues to maintain, at least publicly, stoical determination." The air offensive had failed.

The answer was typically American: more and bigger. Soon the operation became "sustained pressure," and B-52s armed with napalm and cluster bombs joined the action. By the time the Nixon administration signed a cease-fire agreement in January 1973, the United States had dropped on North Vietnam, an area the size of Texas, triple the bomb tonnage dropped on Europe, Asia, and Africa during World War II. Yet Vietnam was different. The dikes along the Red River, whose destruction would have flooded the valley and killed hundreds of thousands of people, were never targeted. Nor were North Vietnam's cities subjected to the kind of "carpet bombing" that obliterated Dresden and Tokyo. Bombs devastated parts of North Vietnam, particularly the area above the seventeenth parallel, where troops and supplies were massed to move south, but Hanoi and Haiphong were hardly bruised.

Wars generate their own momentum, and, as the bombing of North Vietnam accelerated, a related problem arose. The U.S. carriers in the South China Sea were obviously safe from North Vietnam's mosquito navy, but the American airfield at Danang was vulnerable to attack by some six thousand Vietcong guerrillas in the vicinity. On February 22, 1965, Westmorcland asked Johnson for two marine battalions to protect the base. Westmoreland later claimed that he had not at the time considered the request the "first step in a growing American commitment" that would swell to nearly two hundred thousand U.S. troops by the end of the year. But Taylor did, and he promptly objected.

The introduction of thirty-five hundred marines was the start of an "ever increasing" U.S. combat involvement in "an essentially hostile foreign country," Taylor warned, and "it will be very difficult to hold the line" once the deployment began. Three years before, he had said that Vietnam was "not an excessively difficult or unpleasant place to operate," but now he emphasized that "white-faced" soldiers were unsuited to "Asian forests and jungles." He doubted they "could do much better" than the French, who had "tried to adapt their forces to this mission and failed." Moreover, there was the "ever present question" of how Americans in that alien environment "would distinguish between a Vietcong and a friendly Vietnamese farmer." In short, he viewed Westmoreland's proposal with "grave reservations."

Johnson quickly overruled him. On the morning of March 8, marines in full battle regalia splashed ashore at Danang, the first American combat troops to set foot on the Asian mainland since the end of the Korean conflict. They rushed onto the beach, just as their fathers had stormed Pacific atolls during World War II—to be greeted by grinning Vietnamese girls distributing garlands of flowers and a poster proclaiming: "Welcome to the Gallant Marines."

The flamboyant arrival, arranged by the U.S. navy, appalled Westmoreland, who had expected the marines to maintain a "low profile." Two days earlier, a Pentagon press release had declared that the marines were being sent at the "request" of the South Vietnamese government, but the regime had been neither consulted nor informed in advance. Bui Diem, then an aide to Prime Minister Phan Huy Quat and later South Vietnam's ambassador to Washington, described it later: "That day, March 8, Dr. Quat summoned me to his office, where I found an American officer. We were supposed to draft a joint communiqué in Vietnamese and English to announce the marine landing. I asked Dr. Quat if he had known about it beforehand. Not exactly, he replied. There had been a general understanding, but he only learned the details at the last minute."

The marine deployment was one of the crucial decisions of the war, yet it hardly stirred a ripple, either in Congress or in the American press—largely because Johnson had skillfully presented it as simply a short-term expedient. He even deceived the Communist strategists in Hanoi. They feared that an American troop buildup in Vietnam would cause them "new difficulties," but they doubted that Johnson would authorize such "enormous expenditures in money and matériel" without being "certain of victory." They miscalculated.

Disappointed by the lack of results from the air strikes against the north, Johnson vented his frustrations on his military staff. He wanted fresh "ideas and solutions," he said, not merely proposals for more bombing, and over breakfast in the White House family quarters, he ordered General Harold K. Johnson, army chief of staff, to go to Vietnam and come back with the answers. As they descended in the elevator following the meeting, the president leaned close to the military aide and thrust an index finger into his chest, saying: "You get things bubbling, general."

The president meanwhile sent Westmoreland a blank check, telling him to "assume no limitation on funds, equipment, or personnel" for any requests that he and General Johnson might recommend. Westmoreland wanted more manpower, and, at his behest, General Johnson returned to Washington a week later with a proposal for a division of American troops to be deployed to protect U.S. bases in South Vietnam. Predictably, Ambassador Taylor disagreed; again he stressed that a big American commitment would encourage the South Vietnamese army to "let the United States do it," and he repeated his warning that it would look as if Americans had inherited "the old French role of alien colonizer and conqueror." This time the president sided with Taylor—but only briefly. He deferred approval of a U.S. division and instead authorized more bombing over North Vietnam.

Back in Washington for consultations in late March, however, Taylor sensed that the administration was edging toward a decision to put more American troops into Vietnam. Mac Bundy, for example, had advised the president that additional U.S. units would improve America's "eventual bargaining position" in negotiations. John McNaughton asserted that only American combat forces could prevent a "humiliating U.S. defeat." The joint chiefs of staff, outdoing General Johnson, called for three divisions, including one from South Korea—and Westmoreland, now pessimistic about the usefulness of air strikes against the north, endorsed the suggestion. At the Pentagon, where the nostrils of military planners flare at the scent of a buildup, rival services were competing furiously for a piece of the action.

At a high-level White House meeting on April 1, 1965, President Johnson decided to give Westmoreland two more marine battalions as well as eighteen to twenty thousand logistical troops—since Americans never fight abroad without ample supplies of arms and ammunition, and vast quantities of beer, chocolate bars, shaving cream, and their favorite brands of cigarettes. The president also dictated an important tactical change. Taylor, now resigned to having the marines in Vietnam, had insisted that they be restricted to defending U.S. bases and other installations along the coast. But Westmoreland, arguing that "a good offense is the best defense," wanted them out patrolling the countryside. Johnson backed Westmoreland. And the marines, as one of their commanders put it, would henceforth "start killing the Vietcong instead of just sitting on their ditty box."

Johnson concealed the momentous step from the public. He told reporters that "no far-reaching strategy . . . is being suggested or promulgated." He also instructed his staff to avoid "premature publicity . . . by all possible precautions" in order to "minimize any appearance of sudden changes in policy." Not until June was the decision to send U.S. troops into offensive operations in Vietnam officially revealed—and then almost casually at the State Department. The lack of candor was later criticized by many of Johnson's wartime associates, among them Westmoreland: "It was a masterpiece of obliquity, and I was unhappy about it. To my mind the American people had a right to know forthrightly, within the actual limits of military security, what we were calling on their sons to do, and to presume that it could be concealed despite the open eyes of press and television was folly."

Even so, rising concern in Congress about the war worried Johnson. The list of opponents to the war, though still short, had grown to include Senators Frank Church of Idaho and George McGovern of South Dakota. And William Fulbright, chairman of the Senate Foreign Relations Committee, seemed to be shifting. In late March, he was sufficiently troubled to caution Johnson that a "massive ground and air war in Southeast Asia" would be a "disaster" for the United States. Johnson ignored the warning, but directed his aides to draft a major speech to assuage his domestic doubters.

Written by Richard Goodwin, the most talented wordsmith in Washington at the time, the speech was both stick and carrot. The United States "will not be defeated" or "withdraw, either openly or under the cloak of a meaningless agreement," said the president, but he appealed to the North Vietnamese to concede to "unconditional discussions" and offered them a share of a huge Mekong development project to be financed with American funds. Once again he was imputing his own values to the Communists, figuring he could buy their cooperation with a bit of old-fashioned pork-barrel patronage.

Mac Bundy had counseled Johnson to show an advance text of the speech to Walter Lippmann in the hope that it would "plug his guns." Johnson did better. He invited Lippmann to the White House on April 6, the day before the speech was scheduled for delivery at Johns Hopkins University in Baltimore, and assured him that he was "going to hold out that carrot you keep talking to me about." But soon he was bellowing, "I'm not just going to pull up my pants and run out on Vietnam. Don't you know the church is on fire over there, and we've got to find a way out? . . . You say to negotiate, but there's nobody over there to negotiate with. So the only thing there is to do is to hang on. And that's what I'm going to do."

Characteristically, though, Johnson was nagged by doubts. As he flew back to Washington following the Johns Hopkins speech, he told Bill Moyers that "old Ho can't turn me down." But he grudgingly respected North Vietnam's stubborn courage, and he would also confide to members of his staff: "If I were Ho Chi Minh, I would never negotiate."

The North Vietnamese prime minister, Pham Van Dong, insisted that discussions, unconditional or otherwise, could not be held unless the U.S. bombing ended; any settlement would also require the creation in Saigon of a neutral coalition government that included Vietcong representatives. Linking the military and political issues was characteristic of the Communists, and they stuck to that position until late 1972. They may have erred, though, in spurning Johnson's offer to talk. For one thing, they might have deterred the U.S. military buildup and strengthened themselves in the interval. By appearing receptive they would have certainly demoralized the Saigon regime. But, like Johnson, they were prisoners of their experience—as Pham Van Dong plainly disclosed during the summer of 1965: "We entered into negotiations with the French colonialists on many occasions, and concluded with them several agreements in an effort to preserve peace," he said. "To them, however, the signing of agreements was only designed to gain time to prepare their military forces for further aggression. . . . This is a clear lesson of history, a lesson on relations with the imperialists, which our people will never forget."

The Vietcong was relatively subdued during the early spring of 1965 as its forces regrouped in central Vietnam and in the region around Saigon, stiffened by four North Vietnamese regiments that had trekked into the south since the start of the year, despite air strikes against their infiltration routes. President Johnson, anticipating an enemy offensive, cabled Ambassador Taylor on April 15. Besides bombing the north, he said, "something new must be added in the south." He was ready to Americanize the war. He proposed sending out a U.S. brigade to protect the Bienhoa air base, lacing South Vietnamese army units with regular U.S. troops and, among other innovations, introducing U.S. officials into South Vietnam's provincial administration to manage its machinery.

Taylor again objected, sarcastically attributing the initiatives to "a new level of creativity by a president determined to get prompt results." He termed the idea of Americans running the South Vietnamese administration "disastrous," since it would erode the regime's already ragged nationalist credentials. He again protested against committing more U.S. troops until they were absolutely necessary. He detected a different Johnson, now racing into an American ground war, and he later summoned up a classical allusion to describe the moment: having "crossed the Rubicon" by starting his bombing campaign, he said, Johnson "was now off to Rome on the double."

The unflappable Mac Bundy advised Johnson to be patient. Taylor could be persuaded to "come aboard." Bundy was correct. Peer pressure works wonders inside the government, and at a hastily convened gathering in Honolulu on April 20, McNamara, Wheeler, Westmoreland, and Bill Bundy brought Taylor into the fold. He upheld their plan to send an additional forty thousand U.S. troops to Vietnam by June—double the number already there. But even that force might not do the trick, and they left the door ajar to "possible later deployments."

Johnson endorsed the proposal—his instinct for action encouraged by one trusted intimate, Abe Fortas, a Washington lawyer whom he was soon to appoint to the Supreme Court. Fortas, a friend of Johnson's from the New Deal, was a hard-line Jewish progressive—a man with an unsurpassed record of struggle for social justice and civil liberties who still retained the foreign policy outlook of the 1940s, when liberals abhorred "appeasement." He has not been mentioned earlier in these pages because he played only a shadowy role; he rarely gave interviews, and put his imprint on few formal documents. Yet he talked on the telephone almost daily with Johnson, and influenced him perhaps more than any other person on a range of topics, including Vietnam. Or perhaps, as courtiers do, he simply confirmed Johnson's own intuition. Once, over lunch in Washington in 1966, a senior State Department official challenged me to identify the single individual who exerted the most influence on Johnson's policies toward Vietnam. McNamara? Rusk? Mac Bundy? None of them. Abe Fortas. "But Fortas doesn't know anything about Vietnam," I remonstrated. "True," the official replied, "but he knows a lot about Lyndon Johnson."

Yet Johnson demanded approval from everyone, and dissidents irritated him even if they were numerically inconsequential. They now included Clark Clifford, the powerful Washington attorney and a close friend, who privately warned him that a "substantial" U.S. troop commitment to Vietnam "could be a quagmire . . . without realistic hope of ultimate victory." Capitol Hill also buzzed with murmurs of concern from senators like Jacob Javits of New York and George Aiken of Vermont, who until then had displayed few misgivings about the war. Johnson was especially annoyed when Frank Church publicly urged negotiations with North Vietnam. Singling out Church one evening at a crowded White House dinner, Johnson asked him whom he had consulted in preparing his speech. Church mentioned Walter Lippmann, and Johnson snapped: "All right, Frank, next time you want a dam for Idaho, you go talk to Walter Lippmann."

Despite his reservations, Church fell into line with nearly the entire Senate to grant Johnson's request for $700 million in appropriations to conduct the war; the House went along with only seven nays. Johnson had not needed the funds, but he wanted a reaffirmation of congressional assent for his Vietnam policy, and he lobbied strenuously—even prevailing upon former President Eisenhower to issue a statement declaring that "none of us should try to divide the support that citizens owe their head of state in critical international situations."

Then, on May 13, Johnson floated Operation Mayflower, the first of several ill-fated diplomatic overtures, all code-named for flora. He announced a "pause" in the bombing of North Vietnam, having instructed Foy Kohler, his ambassador in Moscow, to inform the North Vietnamese legation there that the United States expected "equally constructive" gestures in exchange. The North Vietnamese not only refused to receive Kohler, but returned his message unopened. Nor would Soviet officials intercede on his behalf. Two days later, Hanoi Radio denounced the bombing halt as a "worn-out trick," and Johnson ordered the air strikes resumed.

The purpose of his maneuver, Johnson explained to aides, had been "to clear a path either toward the restoration of peace or toward increased military action, depending upon the reaction of the Communists." He should have expected a rebuff from the North Vietnamese. They, like Johnson himself, could conceive of negotiations only on their own terms. Besides, they had just launched their biggest offensive to date in the south in hopes of improving their bargaining position.

Countrywide attacks erupted on May 11 as more than a thousand Vietcong troops overran Songbe, the Phuoc Long province capital, about fifty miles north of Saigon and not far from the Cambodian border. Soon afterward, the Vietcong destroyed two South Vietnamese battalions near the city of Quangngai, in central Vietnam. Then two Vietcong regiments struck again in Phuoc Long, raiding the government military headquarters inside the town of Dong Xoai and hitting a U.S. special forces camp a mile away. Exceeding their mandate, American advisers often took command of shattered South Vietnamese units whose officers had fled in panic. At Dong Xoai, for example, Second Lieutenant Charles Q. Williams single-handedly knocked out a Vietcong machine gun and guided helicopters into the area to evacuate the wounded. Himself wounded four times in the engagement, he was awarded the congressional Medal of Honor.

By the middle of June, the South Vietnamese army had lost its best mobile battalions. At the same time, the government crumbled. Catholic militants engineered the ouster of Prime Minister Quat, and a faction of young officers named General Nguyen Van Thieu chief of state and Air Vice Marshal Nguyen Cao Ky prime minister.

Westmoreland, appalled by the disintegration, confronted Johnson with an urgent appeal. "The South Vietnamese armed forces," he reported, "cannot stand up to this pressure without substantial U.S. combat support on the ground." To prevent South Vietnam's "collapse" he needed more than double the number of U.S. troops already in the pipeline. He wanted a total of one hundred and eighty thousand men—thirty-four U.S. battalions and ten battalions to be provided, at American expense, by South Korea. And they would only serve as a "stopgap" to avert imminent catastrophe. Another hundred thousand Americans, perhaps more, would be required in 1966—and maybe even more afterward, "to seize the initiative from the enemy." Westmoreland was steeped in gloom. "We are in for the long pull," he bluntly told Johnson. "I see no likelihood of achieving a quick, favorable end to the war."

For Johnson, the choices were simple: either the United States plunged into war or faced defeat. Once again, he canvassed opinions and got a predictable range of views. No outsider, unfamiliar with the governmental process, could even faintly imagine the mountains of memorandums and hours of dialogue consumed in the tortured deliberations.

Senator Fulbright went to the White House at Johnson's invitation. He sat silently, trying to stay attentive as Johnson droned on, explaining how he had offered peace to the Communists but had been spurned, had been spit in the eye. Now, with the Vietcong attacking and the South Vietnamese about to cave in, his only choice was to send American boys out there. He hoped that Bill Fulbright would stand up and tell the Senate how patient he had been. Fulbright's eventual Senate speech disappointed Johnson. Though he opposed America's "unconditional" withdrawal from Vietnam, he also opposed "further escalation" that threatened to drag the nation into "a bloody and protracted jungle war in which the strategic advantages would be with the other side." The Communists should be offered a "reasonable and attractive alternative to military victory" through negotiations. Johnson never forgot or forgave this "betrayal," and the two southern Democrats, Senate colleagues for years, ceased to speak to each other.

George Ball, keeping his misgivings private, handed Johnson another set of dire premonitions. An "investment trap" loomed: American soldiers would "begin to take heavy casualties in a war they are ill-equipped to fight in a noncooperative if not downright hostile countryside"; to compensate for the losses, more troops would be sent out, and eventually the involvement would be "so great that we cannot—without national humiliation—stop." Still, Ball predicted, "humiliation would be more likely than the achievement of our objectives—even after we have paid terrible costs." So, he urged, maintain the U.S. force pledged at its current level, but start an active search for a "compromise settlement."

Other Johnson aides were also uncertain. Rusk, always sensitive to global consequences, linked America's presence in Vietnam to "the integrity of the U.S. commitment" throughout the world, yet he wondered whether Westmoreland was not exaggerating the danger. Taylor continued to vacillate—a hint, perhaps, that a year in Saigon was unhinging him. In early June, he conceded that American combat troops "will probably be necessary," but now, at the end of the month, he questioned the need for them, saying that the best they could do was to hold a few enclaves. The CIA echoed his sentiment; their latest study concluded that a large U.S. force would fail to halt the Communists, who clung to the conviction that "their staying power is inherently superior" to that of the Americans and South Vietnamese. The Communists would thus intensify "their present strategy of attrition and subversion," aiming to undermine the Saigon government "through exhaustion and internal collapse."

Bill Bundy proposed a "middle way." He ruled out withdrawal, but he also doubted that an American buildup would work. Unless the South Vietnamese army performed better, "our own intervention would appear to be turning the conflict into a white man's war, with the United States in the shoes of the French." He recommended that no more than a hundred thousand American troops be committed, both to hold the line and to be tested in the coming months. And after that? Perhaps the "Vietcong tide could be stemmed." The North Vietnamese, facing a "stalemate," might compromise. Or maybe the Saigon regime would "throw in the sponge and make a deal" with the Communists.

His "middle way," at least in the short term, avoided the "clear pitfalls" of either quitting or brutal escalation. He, too, was unsure.

Not so McNamara and the Pentagon brass. They pleaded with Johnson to grant Westmoreland's troop request, and McNamara went even further. He stressed that Johnson had to call up the reserves—the force of former servicemen—a politically explosive step tantamount to an announcement of full-scale war. He also proposed a massive offensive against North Vietnam—mining its harbors, destroying its airfields, obliterating its rail and road bridges, and wiping out every installation of military value, from ammunition dumps and oil storage facilities to power plants and barracks. He suggested a few token diplomatic gestures, like enlisting Soviet help in the quest for accommodation, but only to sanctify an armed approach designed to dramatize to the Communists that "the odds are against their winning."

Mac Bundy recoiled at the program, terming it "rash to the point of folly." Not only was an extravagant campaign against North Vietnam preposterous, but putting a huge American force into Vietnam was "a slippery slope toward total U.S. responsibility and corresponding fecklessness on the Vietnamese side." What, Bundy asked, was the ceiling on the American liability? Could U.S. troops wage an antiguerrilla war, the "central problem" in South Vietnam? And above all, what was "the real object of the exercise"? To get to the conference table? If so, "What results do we seek there?" Or was the investment simply intended "to cover an eventual retreat"? In that case, "Can we not do that just as well where we are?"

The younger Bundy was not being gratuitously tough on McNamara, one of his close friends. Nor was he a cut-and-run type. He shared the assumption that Vietnam was vital to America's interests. But as chief of Johnson's national security staff, he wanted the president's cabinet—and the president himself—to ponder the crucial questions. The questions were posed, but they were never deeply examined.

After screening the assorted ideas that cluttered his desk, Mac Bundy counseled Johnson to "listen hard" to Ball but to discard his proposal—and then "move to the narrower choice" between the Bill Bundy and McNamara options. Their recommendations were to be discussed toward the end of July, the deadline for a final decision. "I was not about to send additional men without the most detailed analysis," Johnson later recalled. But he had already made up his mind—and his apparent probe of the issues was largely contrived.

Johnson ordered McNamara back to Vietnam to reassess the situation. McNamara arrived on July 16, accompanied by Wheeler and Henry

Cabot Lodge, who had just agreed to return to Saigon for another tour as ambassador, succeeding Taylor. The group went to dinner that evening with Ky and Thieu, who had grabbed power a few weeks earlier. Ky showed up in a tight white jacket, tapered trousers, patent leather shoes, and red socks, looking like a saxophone player in a second-rate nightclub. McNamara did a double take at the sight of the new South Vietnamese leader on whom America's fate hung so precariously. One U.S. official in the party muttered, "At least no one could confuse him with Uncle Ho."

McNamara was supposed to devote several days to his "fact-finding" mission. But a day after his arrival, he received an ultrasecret cable over the CIA's "back channel" from his deputy, Cyrus Vance. President Johnson had decided to go ahead with Westmoreland's troop request, and he wanted McNamara to return to Washington immediately. As Westmoreland noted afterward, the policy debate "turned out, in a way, to be moot."

McNamara came back with a lengthy memorandum, and his confidential comments again bore little resemblance to his public remarks. He told reporters that the U.S. forces in Vietnam were inflicting "increasingly heavy losses" on the Vietcong, but he informed Johnson privately that conditions were "worse than a year ago." Communist infiltration into the south had not been daunted by the American bombing, and the Saigon government's chances for survival over the next six months were "less than even." Then he gave Johnson the bad news. By early 1966, he said, Vietnam would need not only the number of U.S. soldiers Westmoreland requested, but another hundred thousand or more. And that meant, McNamara again stressed, mobilizing the reserves and the national guard—putting the country on a war footing, in effect. Otherwise, America could not meet its global security responsibilities.

Johnson could see even farther ahead. Though he never revealed it publicly, he already sensed by July 1965 that Vietnam would require six hundred thousand American men and cost billions of dollars. But as he opened a week-long series of White House sessions on July 21, Johnson fostered the impression that he was groping for answers. "I want this discussed in full detail," he said, his narrow eyes darting around the table at Rusk, McNamara, Wheeler, Mac and Bill Bundy, and the others. He wanted to weigh all the options. What results can we expect? Do we have to defend the world? Who else can help? What are the alternatives?

Relentlessly, almost plaintively, he went through the motion of firing questions, particularly at Ball, his devil's advocate. And he continued the next day with his generals and admirals. Can American boys fight

Asians in the jungle? Will the North Vietnamese pour in more men? Might they call for Chinese or Russian volunteers? How much will this cost us? Are we getting into something we cannot finish? Johnson convened other meetings with only two or three aides, and he consulted outsiders like John McCloy, the distinguished New York banker who had advised presidents since the Roosevelt era. Edging closer to the deadline, he communed with Abe Fortas.

Johnson wanted to portray himself as a model of moderation—partly to reassure the American people that he was not going to war, partly to avoid a Soviet or Chinese response. He rejected McNamara's plea to call up the reserves, and he parceled out the American troop shipments to Vietnam. He could not conceal his decision, but he could muffle it. On July 28, 1965, at midday, when the television audience is smallest, he soberly announced, "I have asked the commanding general, General Westmoreland, what more he needs to meet this mounting aggression. He has told me. And we will meet his needs. We cannot be defeated by force of arms. We will stand in Vietnam."

12 Escalation

For most American combat troops, the Vietnam war was endless plodding across flooded rice fields and tangled jungle trails in search of an elusive enemy. Most often, the soldiers were harassed more by heat and leeches than by the Communists.

The biggest revolution to hit South Vietnam during the war was the consumer revolution. The streets of Saigon were jammed with black marketeers selling everything from cigarettes and hair spray to guns; most of the merchandise was pilfered from American warehouses.

One of America's most potent weapons in Vietnam was the B-52, which flew strategic and tactical bombing missions from bases in Thailand and Guam. Here, on Guam, American technicians prepare to load the aircraft with what was called "ordnance."

Sexual encounters between GIs and Vietnamese girls were frequent in Saigon and other South Vietnamese cities.

In Vietnam, as in other wars, a soldier's life was filled with hours of monotony punctuated by moments of sheer terror. Here, at a remote camp, GIs languish in the heat, but the barbed wire testifies to the constant danger.

At a meeting in Honolulu in February 1966, President Johnson was gratified when Prime Minister Nguyen Cao Ky delivered a speech filled with phrases reminiscent of his own about the Great Society. Ky's speech had been written for him by his American advisers.

As they had before, Buddhist militants demonstrated against the Saigon government, claiming that their own movement was insufficiently recognized. They protest here in Danang, where a clash between rival South Vietnamese army factions erupted in 1966.

In contrast to the generals, some Pentagon civilians began to realize that bombing North Vietnam was futile because of the regime's ability to keep supplies moving south via such simple conveyances as bicycles.

North Vietnam's principal capital was its population. The Hanoi regime was able to mobilize people rapidly to repair the damage caused by bombing, seen here on an irrigation canal.

Most North Vietnamese cities were evacuated as the American bombing intensified. Individual shelters were built for those who remained in urban areas. President Johnson carefully controlled the bombing, restraining the air force from targeting many populated regions.

The biggest dilemma for American soldiers in Vietnam was distinguishing friendly from hostile peasants. Here they conduct an operation in a village suspected of harboring Vietcong sympathizers, even probing a haystack for the enemy, as a peasant goes about her business.

An American soldier reaches out to a wounded buddy. Unlike previous wars, the conflict in Vietnam was not fought at the front lines. Americans could be wounded or killed by enemy terrorists anywhere, in the countryside or within cities.

There was extraordinary fervor then. The Americans thought that the more bombs they dropped, the quicker we would fall to our knees and surrender. But the bombs heightened rather than dampened our spirit.

—Ton That Tung

When we marched into the rice paddies on that damp March afternoon, we carried, along with our packs and rifles, the implicit convictions that the Vietcong could be quickly beaten. We kept the packs and rifles; the convictions, we lost.

—Philip Caputo

General Westmoreland had conceived a long-range strategy even before Lyndon Johnson fulfilled his request for more American battalions. He would first deploy the American troops to protect the U.S. air and supply bases along the South Vietnamese coast and around Saigon. At the same time, he would send units into the central highlands in order to block any attempt made by the North Vietnamese and Vietcong to sweep across to the sea and slice the country in two. Then, having gained the initiative, he planned to launch a series of "search-and-destroy" operations in which the American forces, with their vastly superior mobility and firepower, would relentlessly grind down the enemy. And finally, as he put it, he would "mop up" the remaining Communists to achieve "victory." Meanwhile, he counted on two further efforts to contribute to success.

One was the intensive bombing of North Vietnam. The other was "pacification," an ambitious military, economic, and social program pursued under American tutelage, which would help the Saigon government to control South Vietnam's rural population. Official pronouncements still paid lip service to the need to "win the hearts and minds" of the people. But the new approach was essentially predicated on muscle. Or as American officers summed it up: "Grab 'em by the balls, and their hearts and minds will follow."

So American soldiers went into action in Vietnam with the gigantic weight of American industry behind them. Never before in history was so much strength amassed in such a small corner of the globe against an opponent apparently so inconsequential. If Ho Chi Minh had described his war with France as a struggle between "grasshoppers and elephants," he was now a microbe facing a leviathan.

As a correspondent, I observed the change with astonishment. During the late 1950s, when I began to report from Southeast Asia, the American imprint on South Vietnam was barely visible. Saigon still resembled a French provincial city—its acacia-shaded streets lined with quiet shops and sleepy sidewalk cafés, its residential district of handsome villas wallowing in lush tropical gardens of jasmine, mimosa, and brilliant red and purple bougainvillea. Danang and Nhatrang and Vung Tau were lovely little seaside towns, scarcely bigger than fishing villages, and the towns of the Mekong delta, like Mytho and Cantho, stirred only once a week, when peasants brought their rice and vegetables and pigs to market. But starting in the summer of 1965, as American troops landed, South Vietnam underwent a convulsive transformation.

Westmoreland gambled by bringing in his forces before he had developed a system to support them. The gamble paid off. Within two years, he had achieved a logistical miracle.

American army engineers and private contractors labored around the clock, often accomplishing stupendous tasks in a matter of months. Their giant tractors and bulldozers and cranes carved out roads and put up bridges, and at one place in the Mekong delta they dredged the river to create a six-hundred-acre island as a secure campsite. They erected mammoth fuel depots and warehouses, some refrigerated. They constructed hundreds of helicopter pads and scores of airfields, including huge jet strips at Danang and Bienhoa. Until their arrival, Saigon had been South Vietnam's only major port, and its antiquated facilities were able to handle only modest ships. Now, almost overnight, they built six new deep-draft harbors, among them a gigantic complex at Camranh Bay, which they completed at breakneck speed by towing prefabricated floating piers across the Pacific. They connected remote parts of the country with an intricate communications grid, and they linked Saigon to Washington with submarine cables and radio networks so efficient that U.S. embassy officials could dial the White House in seconds—and President Johnson could, as he did frequently, call to check on progress.

By 1967, a million tons of supplies a month were pouring into Vietnam to sustain the U.S. force—an average of a hundred pounds a day for every American there. An American infantryman could rely on the latest hardware. He was transported to the battle scene by helicopter and, if wounded, flown out aboard medical evacuation choppers known as dust-offs because of the dust kicked up by their rotors as they landed. His target had usually been "softened" beforehand by air strikes and artillery bombardments, and he could summon additional air and artillery assistance during a fight. Tanks and other armored vehicles often flanked him in action, and his unit carried the most up-to-date arms—mortars, machine guns, grenade and rocket launchers, and the M-16, a fully automatic rifle.

With the exception of the nuclear weapon, nearly every piece of equipment in America's mighty arsenal was sooner or later used in Vietnam. The skies were clogged with bombers, fighters, helicopters, and other airplanes, among them high-altitude B-52s and such contrivances as "Puff the Magic Dragon," a converted DC-3 transport outfitted with rapid-fire machine guns capable of raking targets at the rate of eighteen thousand rounds per minute. So dense was the air traffic, in fact, that South Vietnam's airports became the world's busiest. In addition to flying from bases inside the country, the air armada operated out of Guam and Thailand and from carriers in the South China Sea. And the U.S. flotilla deployed off Vietnam also included cruisers, destroyers, patrol boats, tankers, hospital ships, and light craft to penetrate the rivers and canals of the Mekong delta. Every service sought to be represented in Vietnam because, as American officers explained at the time, "it's the only war we got."

Vietnam also served as a laboratory for technology so sophisticated it made James Bond's dazzling gadgets seem obsolete by comparison. American scientists created an array of ultrasensitive devices to detect the enemy through heat, light, and sound refraction, and they even invented an electronic instrument that could smell guerrillas. They produced defoliants and herbicides to destroy jungles and wipe out rice and other crops on which the North Vietnamese and Vietcong relied for food. They perfected rockets like the "Walleye," an air-to-surface missile containing a television camera that enabled a pilot to adjust its course by scanning a screen in his cockpit. And there were bombs of nearly every size, shape, and explosive intensity, from blockbusters to phosphorous and napalm bombs that roasted their victims alive. Another devastating weapon were cluster bombs, whose hundreds of pellets burst out at high velocity to rip deep into the body of anyone within range. Designed for "surgical" raids against troop concentrations, the cluster bombs were frequently dropped by American aircraft on populated regions in both North and South Vietnam, killing or maiming thousands of civilians. General Harold K. Johnson, army chief of staff, once attributed the indiscriminate casualties to a lack of precise intelligence about targets. "We have not enough information," he said. "We act with ruthlessness, like a steamroller."

Along with importing guns and ammunition, oil, spare parts, and other war matériel, Westmoreland and his logistical experts inundated

Vietnam with the luxuries that have become necessities for U.S. forces far from home. Not only could American soldiers isolated on remote hilltop fire bases or in jungle camps look forward to receiving cigarettes and beer by helicopter, but choppers periodically flew in hot meals—and the menu at Thanksgiving and Christmas featured turkey, cranberry sauce, and candied yams. Those in the rear echelons patronized clubs and snack bars and that unique U.S. military institution, the Post Exchange. The main PX, located in the Saigon suburb of Cholon, was only slightly smaller than the New York Bloomingdale's, its counters laden with everything from sports clothes, cameras, tape recorders, and transistor radios to soap, shampoo, deodorant, and, of course, condoms. A GI finishing his tour in Vietnam could purchase an automobile or motorcycle for delivery back in the United States, and he might even be solicited by the representatives of Wall Street brokerage firms that had set up offices in Saigon to buy and sell stocks. The great American cornucopia inevitably spilled its wares into the local economy, and the streets of Saigon and other South Vietnamese cities were jammed with black markets that served, in effect, as a parallel PX—and they often hawked articles that were unavailable at the real PX.

All this power intoxicated the Americans who initially went to Vietnam with a proud and overweening sense of confidence. Whatever the objective of the war—and many could not define its purpose with any precision—they were certain that U.S. omnipotence would triumph. Philip Caputo, then a young marine lieutenant, recalled the feeling that he and his buddies shared as their battalion splashed ashore at Danang in the spring of 1965: "When we marched into the rice paddies on that damp March afternoon, we carried, along with our packs and rifles, the implicit convictions that the Vietcong would be quickly beaten."

Yet they—and the U.S. public—began to realize that the challenge was not so simple. The seemingly straightforward conflict soon degenerated into a protracted, exhausting, indecisive war of attrition that increasingly appeared to be futile. President Johnson nevertheless persisted with expressions of determination and optimism—and U.S. troops continued to fight and die as the war generated its own momentum. As the struggle lengthened, America's faith in its invincibility faded. As Caputo, mirroring the mood of U.S. soldiers in the field, added: "We kept the packs and rifles; the convictions, we lost."

At one point in the war, after U.S. aircraft had reduced a South Vietnamese province capital to rubble, an American army officer was quoted as explaining that "we had to destroy the town in order to save it." His remark accurately described the impact on Vietnam of the massive U.S. intervention. The United States, motivated by the loftiest intentions, did indeed rip South Vietnam's social fabric to shreds—and six years after the end of the war, when I returned there, the Communists had still not stitched the pieces together again. They predictably blamed the dislocations on American "imperialism," and their diagnosis was not entirely wrong.

As the war intensified in 1965, the U.S. bombing, shelling, and defoliation of rural areas drove peasants from their hamlets, creating a refugee problem of immense proportions. An estimated four million men, women, and children—roughly a quarter of South Vietnam's population—fled to the fringes of cities and towns in an attempt to survive. They were shunted into makeshift camps of squalid shanties, where primitive sewers bred dysentery, malaria, and other diseases. Thousands, desperate to eke out a living, drifted into Saigon, Danang, Bienhoa, and Vung Tau, cities that now acquired an almost medieval cast as beggars and hawkers roamed the streets, whining and tugging at Americans for money. For grotesque contrast, no place to my mind matched the *terrasse* of the Continental Palace Hotel, a classic reminder of the French colonial era, where limbless Vietnamese victims of the war would crawl like crabs across the handsome tile floor to accost American soldiers, construction workers, journalists, and visitors as they chatted and sipped their drinks under the ceiling fans.

The refugee influx into the cities was deliberately spurred in many instances by American strategists, who calculated that this "forced urbanization," as they termed it, would deny peasant support to the North Vietnamese and Vietcong, and thus hamper their ability to subsist in the countryside. Westmoreland believed this, as did his civilian deputy in charge of "pacification," Robert Komer, who asserted that the "process of degrading" the enemy would be accelerated by reducing its "population base." The theory was ambitiously translated into practice at the beginning of 1967, when thirty thousand American troops launched Operation Cedar Falls in Binh Duong province, a Communist stronghold near the Cambodian border north of Saigon. American aircraft bombed its hamlets and denuded its rice fields and surrounding jungles with herbicides before the infantry, accompanied by tanks and bulldozers, moved in to eradicate a reported enemy web of bunkers and tunnels. The sweep resulted in an exodus of some seven thousand inhabitants.

There and elsewhere, however, the North Vietnamese and Vietcong slipped back within months of being cleaned out of their sanctuaries. But the refugees, uprooted from the devastated land and fearful of renewed offensives, remained in the cities and towns—their disrupted, dispirited families aggravating the instability of South Vietnam's already fragile society. Without their farms, they were condemned to hopeless poverty, and the traditional social structure was further shattered as their children, tempted by the incredible affluence that the Americans had brought to Vietnam, defied time-honored vows of filial piety and broke away from their parents in a frenzied quest for easy wealth. For young women in particular, the primrose path to relative riches was irresistible.

During the French war, organized vice had been largely confined to the Saigon suburb of Cholon, where the Binh Xuyen gang and its local Chinese confederates directed casinos, brothels, and opium dens and kicked in a percentage of the profits to the puppet emperor Bao Dai. The French, sensitive to male frailty, also maintained an institution known as the Bordel Militaire de Campagne, or BMC, an authorized bordello that traveled with the troops. But the American establishment was too puritanical to sanction sex officially. Tawdry bars and nightclubs and "massage parlors" proliferated in Saigon, Danang, and wherever else American soldiers congregated, staffed mainly by poor peasant girls lured into prostitution by the prospect of earning more in a week than their fathers made in a year. Several distinguished U.S. diplomats and officers discreetly adopted Vietnamese consorts—usually elegant Saigon ladies who used the liaisons to elevate themselves into luxury and to take out insurance in the event of future disaster.

A lively narcotics traffic developed as well during the American war, the petty drug dealers often fronting for senior South Vietnamese government officials with access to heroin refined from opium grown in Laos. Among those allegedly involved in the trade were Prime Minister Nguyen Cao Ky and his successor, General Tran Thien Khiem, said to have funneled the proceeds from the business into their political machines. By 1971, according to Pentagon estimates, nearly 30 percent of American troops in Vietnam had experimented with either opium or heroin, and quantities of drugs were also being exported to the United States. Periodic attempts by American agents to smash the elaborate smuggling network were thwarted by their superiors in the U.S. mission, since a crackdown would have exposed nearly every prominent member of the Saigon regime. But the narcotics trade was only a small part of the economic corruption that pervaded the upper echelons of Saigon—and which essentially owed its phenomenal growth to the fact that the United States, in its rush to prosecute the war, pumped more money into South Vietnam than the country could absorb.

One day in 1966, I was appalled by an incident that still sears my memory. Nguyen Cao Ky had then embarked on a drive against corruption by condemning to death a Chinese merchant, Ta Vinh, on charges of illicit steel transactions. Eager to demonstrate his zeal, Ky had arranged for the supposed culprit's public execution in the square facing Saigon's central market, and I joined the crowd that had assembled to witness the gruesome sight. A chubby and surprisingly young man, Ta Vinh was dragged to the stake by Vietnamese soldiers as his wife and children, garbed in ritual white mourning dress, let loose bloodcurdling wails of despair. The spectators watched numbly as the firing squad performed its task, and dispersed just as silently when the episode ended. For they knew, the way everyone in Saigon knew everything, that Ky's campaign was a sham. He had wanted to make a dramatic gesture, and the Chinese businessmen of Cholon had delivered him a scapegoat in order to protect themselves. Indeed, Ta Vinh was the only miscreant arrested during Ky's hollow effort to stamp out fraud, and his punishment did nothing to discourage corruption. On the contrary, corruption spread wildly as the war escalated.

One of the devices for channeling American assistance to South Vietnam was the "commercial import program," under which American imports were sold locally in order to generate the currency that would pay the expenses of the Saigon government's bureaucracy and army. The system seemed to be rational on paper, but it went awry in practice. Entrepreneurs with the right connections obtained licenses to import such merchandise as television sets, motor scooters, and refrigerators, which they sold principally to urban Vietnamese who were themselves reaping profits from the American presence and could afford luxuries. So the aid revolved in a narrow circle, with only a pittance reaching the peasants, whose allegiance was deemed crucial to the success of the war. And even the necessities that trickled down to the rural areas were frequently diverted into shady schemes. For example, speculators hoarded imported American fertilizer and created artificial shortages that sent prices skyrocketing. One of the most notorious speculators was the brother-in-law of General Nguyen Van Thieu, who superseded Ky as South Vietnam's ruler. But he was a piker compared to Thieu himself, who carried away millions of dollars in gold when he fled Vietnam in April 1975.

Without an ideology or even a positive purpose to inspire loyalty, the Saigon leaders could only purchase fidelity—and they practiced a style of secular simony, trafficking in jobs that gave their subordinates the opportunity to make money. General Dang Van Quang, the Mekong delta commander, was therefore accorded the rice and opium franchise in his region; later, assigned to Saigon, he increased his considerable fortune by selling passports for upwards of twenty thousand dollars each. General Van Toan's infantry division, deployed among the cinnamon plantations near Dalat, devoted more of its time and energy to harvesting the precious spice than to fighting the enemy, while General Nguyen Huu Co, a defense minister, cashed in on lucrative real estate killings—and he even had the audacity to pocket the rent from the lease of government land to the U.S. army. Lesser South Vietnamese officers participated in the system as well, paying kickbacks to their superiors for a chance to share the plunder. The going rate for the post of district chief in 1967 was the equivalent of ten thousand dollars, payable to the corps commander. Officials in many regions also paid off local Vietcong chiefs, with whom they had arranged accommodations.

Despite the gossamer image that they projected in their silk *ao dais,* women played an important role in the corruption, using the positions of their husbands as a means to deal in gold, commodities, and property. Even today in Vietnam, the wives of Communist generals commandeer military aircraft to fly from Hanoi to Saigon in order to loot the former southern capital of its residual treasures.

Inflation soared to dizzying peaks during the war, and the dwindling value of the South Vietnamese piaster fueled an epic black market in currency that drained America of millions of dollars a year. Various remedies were introduced, like readjusting exchange rates and issuing special scrip to GIs, but to no avail. The United States was also bilked by imaginative "irregularities," as the euphemism went, such as fake invoices for supplies that were never delivered. At one point, for instance, American investigators estimated that the amount of cement earmarked for Vietnam in a single year could have paved over the entire country. And the theft from PXs and American warehouses was so extensive that not only cigarettes, whiskey, hair spray, and other consumer items but rifles, ammunition, helmets, and flak jackets were for sale on street corners. Whole consignments of furniture, typewriters, and fire extinguishers disappeared without a trace. Before he was caught, a Saigon truck driver spent two days vainly seeking a customer for a stolen computer worth more than $2 million.

To American officials under pressure to wage the war, however, the colossal waste was simply a factor in the equation. "The way we're squandering money here, we could probably buy off the Vietcong at five hundred dollars a head," I once said jokingly to Robert Komer.

"We've staffed it," he snapped back. "Twenty-five hundred dollars a head."

Judging from their destinies, though, numbers of senior South Vietnamese were either too honest or too incompetent to enrich themselves. General Tran Van Don arrived nearly penniless in the United States in 1975; Ky opened a modest liquor store in California despite his alleged gains, while Bui Diem, the ambassador to Washington, ended up running a Jewish delicatessen there.

But the graft and bribery corroded the Saigon regime less than did its almost total reliance on the United States. Even so, the South Vietnamese relationship with the Americans following the U.S. combat commitment in 1965 was peculiar, complex, and ambivalent.

Sensitive to Communist charges of "neocolonialism," the United States formally upheld the integrity of the Saigon government. With America's prestige and his own reputation at stake, however, Lyndon Johnson wanted the war prosecuted urgently and efficiently. So the concept of cooperation with the South Vietnamese evaporated—except to a few romantics like General Edward Lansdale, who was back in Vietnam in a vague advisory job, still clinging to the dream of counterinsurgency. Now it was an American war, with Americans drafting the military operations and American soldiers bearing the brunt of the fighting. Thousands more American "specialists" were also assigned to the countryside to supervise pacification programs ranging from training local self-defense units to distributing irrigation pumps to peasants and dispensing health care to children. The United States, in short, was determined to save South Vietnam despite the shaky Saigon leadership.

South Vietnamese officials, aware that their survival depended on the United States, quickly adapted to the overwhelming American presence. Province chiefs, for example, learned to curry favor with their American advisers by entertaining them with dinners and girls—and especially by furnishing them with glowing progress reports that served to win the Americans promotions. Many South Vietnamese army officers also retained a *mentalité de colonisé* from their days in the French forces, and they willingly submitted to American direction. General Buu Vien recalled after the war that nothing had boosted the morale of his colleagues more than the approbation of their U.S. advisers: "They never failed to mention how much they were appreciated by their American counterparts, as though appreciation by American advisers was evidence of their success."

This attitude characterized the highest echelons of the Saigon regime. Bui Diem observed after the war that Nguyen Van Thieu, the head of state, had "always considered the American factor the most important element—if not the vital one—in every problem he had to solve, whether it concerned the future of the country or his own political future."

Prime Minister Ky shared the feeling, and he basked in the approval of the Americans. At a conference in Honolulu in February 1966, for instance, he delivered an address before President Johnson in pure Great Society language, pledging to carry out a "social revolution" that would guarantee everyone in South Vietnam "respect and dignity, and a chance for himself and his children to live in an atmosphere where all is not disappointment, despair, and dejection." Elated by the echo of his own voice, Johnson leaned toward Ky after the speech and said: "Boy, you speak just like an American." Ky reveled in the praise—as did his American advisers, who had of course written the speech for him.

But while they recognized their reliance on the United States, the South Vietnamese leaders also perceived that they were abdicating their credibility to an enemy that could justifiably claim to represent Vietnamese nationalist legitimacy. They repeatedly tried to assert their sovereignty by defying the Americans in disputes that often resembled quarrels between an adolescent and a parent. They would sulk or rebel or maneuver mysteriously, their petulance betraying an uncomfortable sense of dependence and frustration with the growing American intrusion into their affairs. The more they resisted American guidance, however, the more the U.S. commanders bypassed them in the planning and pursuit of the war. Soon the Saigon government became little more than a facade, and its irrelevance augured its doom.

Johnson had improvised the Honolulu conference on the spur of the moment in order to divert media attention away from Senator Fulbright, who had scheduled televised hearings on Vietnam that, Johnson feared, would heighten the public doubts about the war. The meeting opened with neither adequate preparation nor even a precise agenda. Johnson, undaunted by such details, used it as a pulpit from which to exhort American and South Vietnamese officials to win the war—telling them in Texas style that he wanted "coonskins on the wall." He also extolled Ky, who returned to Vietnam, his vanity inflated, to upset the country's delicate political balance. Listening to the rhetoric and observing its aftermath, I was reminded of a similar sequence of events five years before, when Johnson, then vice-president, had unwittingly fueled Ngo Dinh Diem's delusions of grandeur by exalting him as the "Winston Churchill of Asia."

Ky owed his titular authority to a tacit accord with the generals who commanded South Vietnam's four military regions. They backed him as prime minister because he was acceptable to the United States, which furnished them with funds and supplies, and because he rarely meddled in their areas, where they ruled as virtual warlords. The arrangement suited the Americans, since the semblance of political harmony meant that they could "get on with the war." But Ky, presuming that President Johnson had mandated him to consolidate control, began to rock the boat—to the dismay of American officials in Saigon and Washington. After trying to manage Diem, Duong Van Minh, Nguyen Khanh, and an array of lesser South Vietnamese figures, they found themselves once again confused and tormented by yet another "puppet" pulling his own strings.

The trouble erupted in March 1966 when Ky sought to extend his sway over central Vietnam by dismissing General Nguyen Chanh Thi, the boss of the region. Both flamboyant characters who wore gaudy uniforms and sported sinister mustaches, the two young officers had been friends, and their rivalry seemed to typify the personal struggles for power that chronically afflicted South Vietnam. But their dispute mirrored more than individual ambition.

Under American pressure to confect a democratic image palatable to the U.S. public, Ky had earlier promised to retire in favor of an elected civilian government. But following his inspirational encounter with Johnson in Honolulu, he stalled, and various South Vietnamese factions demanded his resignation. Foremost among them were the militant Buddhists headed by Tri Quang, the monk who had mobilized the opposition to Diem three years before. Tri Quang directed the opposition from Hué, where he had cemented an alliance with General Nguyen Chanh Thi. Ky figured that he could bridle the Buddhists by ousting Thi—and American officials approved the tactic, explaining that it was a "step toward political stability" that would bolster the Saigon regime. They, and Ky, miscalculated.

Within days of Thi's removal, Buddhists streamed into the streets of Hué to demonstrate, and the protests spread south to other coastal cities. Dock workers and civil servants in Danang went on strike, and violence broke out in parts of Saigon as gangs of youths set fire to automobiles and smashed shop windows. The police, either bewildered or sympathetic to the crowds, did nothing to curb the agitation. Meanwhile, South Vietnamese military operations in the central provinces stopped as Thi's troops, joining the resistance, took over Hué and Danang in an apparent act of secession. South Vietnam soon seemed to be roiled by a civil war within a civil war, a spectacle that stupefied members of the U.S. mission in Saigon. Their Vietnamese protégés, for whom the United States had expended so much in blood and treasure, were behaving like ingrates. Westmoreland, baffled by Ky's motives, referred to his conduct as "foolishness," but other American officials were less charitable. One of them, unable to restrain his frustrated fury, exploded at me: "What are we doing here? We're fighting to save these people, and they're fighting each other!"

The chaos worsened in early April when Ky announced his intention to "liberate" Danang, which he claimed was in Communist hands. The allegation was patently ridiculous, since Danang had been heavily invested by U.S. marines for a year. Nevertheless, desperate to see order restored, Ambassador Lodge gave Ky American airplanes and pilots to transport four thousand South Vietnamese soldiers to Danang. Leading the operation himself, Ky landed to find Thi's dissident troops blocking the road into the city with machine guns. The U.S. marine commander, in charge of the airport, intervened to avert a clash, leaving the two forces deadlocked. After an afternoon of posturing, Ky finally flew back to Saigon and his men departed a few days later. His mission unaccomplished, he had "lost face."

The Buddhists, incensed by the way the Americans had helped Ky, now turned to denunciations of the United States. They sent a telegram to Lodge, assailing him for helping Ky to "suppress and wipe out the Vietnamese people," and they paraded through Hué with banners reading DOWN WITH THE CIA and END FOREIGN DOMINATION OF OUR COUNTRY. Ky thought these slogans were further proof of Communist complicity in the Buddhist movement, and his assertion might have been dismissed as hyperbole had it not been repeated by senior American officials and influential American journalists. McGeorge Bundy contended in a speech on April 8 that Tri Quang was conspiring with the Communists to seize power. By no coincidence, *The New York Times* columnist Cyrus L. Sulzberger simultaneously published the same accusation, having been briefed by William Porter, deputy U.S. ambassador, at whose house in Saigon he was then staying. Sulzberger also interviewed Ky, who persuaded him that the Communists had "deeply infiltrated" the Buddhist ranks in a maneuver to cut central Vietnam off from the rest of the country.

Like so much other information emanating from Saigon, the allegation was sheer fantasy. Not only had the Communists remained aloof from the disorder, but they later regretted their failure to profit from the turmoil. Ho Chi Minh's principal deputy, Le Duan, explained in a secret message to his southern comrades in July 1967 that they "had not taken the initiative in inciting the masses to arise" because their machinery in the cities of the region was "still weak." As a consequence, he admitted, "we lost an opportunity." He added, however, that the experience "taught us a lesson"—and the Communists began to construct an urban apparatus that became important, particularly in Hué, during the Tet offensive the following year.

A week after tarring the Buddhists as Communist agents and dupes, Ky abruptly zigzagged and acquiesced to their demands to resign following election of a constituent assembly of civilians, to be held within five months. Placated, Tri Quang urged his disciples in central Vietnam to cease demonstrating. The tumult subsided, but the lull was brief. Early in May, fearful of looking weak, Ky again reversed himself, proclaiming that he would not quit soon—and, indeed, expected to remain in office "for at least another year." With that, he dispatched a force of two thousand troops against his adversaries in Danang, this time without informing the U.S. embassy in Saigon or even consulting Nguyen Van Thieu, the chief of state.

The surprise move stunned the Americans, and the country itself also went into an uproar. Ky's units landed in Danang at dawn on May 14, killing and wounding more than twenty dissident soldiers in a battle that raged throughout the day. General Ton That Dinh, whom Ky had assigned to Danang to supplant Thi as regional commander, fled to Hué in a helicopter lent him by the U.S. marines. Ky thereupon gave the job of eliminating his opponents to Colonel Nguyen Ngoc Loan, a ruthless officer who would gain worldwide notoriety two years later, when he was photographed summarily executing a Vietcong suspect. Now, deploying tanks and armored cars, he systematically combed Danang street by street, slaying hundreds of rebel troops and more than a hundred civilians, most of whom had taken refuge in Buddhist temples. With South Vietnamese regulars fighting each other, the war against the Communists had become superfluous—and the internecine conflict nearly snared the Americans; the U.S. marine commander in Danang put six of his jets aloft to prevent Ky's aircraft from rocketing the last resistants in the city.

A few weeks later, having crushed the Danang dissidents, Ky prepared to assault Hué, still held by the insurgents. Having witnessed the final stage of the Danang resistance, I traveled to Hué aboard a local bus, negotiating my way past an army barricade erected along the coastal road to block rice, fuel, and other supplies from reaching the city. Hué, an imitation of Beijing built by Vietnam's ancient emperors in deference to their Chinese patrons, had been a placid, introspective, traditional town in contrast to raucous, crass, contemporary Saigon, a corrupt creation of Western imperialism. But now, beleaguered Hué was tense as it awaited attack. Squads of rebel soldiers straddled its intersections, and groups of youths roamed its streets, knives and grenades hanging from their belts. The American consulate bristled with barbed wire: a gang of young toughs had sacked the U.S. Information Service library a few days before in full view of the police. One American official speculated that the Buddhists and their supporters were targeting American installations in the hope of turning U.S. public opinion, weary of the Vietnamese political turmoil, against the Saigon regime. "They're making a mistake," he explained to me. "You don't put that kind of pressure on Uncle Sam and get away with it."

But nothing in Vietnam was that simple, as I discovered again during a visit to Tri Quang's headquarters at the Dieude temple, an ornate structure located near the Perfume River, which meanders through Hué. The scene was an unabashed blend of the spiritual and the temporal. Amid the tinkle of bells and the fragrance of incense, Buddhist nuns wearing shapeless gray cassocks chanted prayers in reedy voices as old women with betel-stained teeth prayed at altars laden with offerings of fruits and flowers. In the courtyard behind, a tiny cottage overflowed with monks and students briskly typing tracts and cranking out manifestos on a vintage mimeograph. And there, in a back room, was Tri Quang, seated on the floor in ritual saffron robe, apparently issuing directives to his acolytes—as if, I noted at the time, Cardinal Spellman were managing the New York mayoralty campaign from an alcove in St. Patrick's Cathedral. I could appreciate the caustic comments of Tri Quang's critics, who decried him for mixing piety and politics. Yet I could also imagine his appeal for the many Vietnamese who admired his bold challenge to the upstart Saigon regime—just as, throughout history, Asians had rallied behind mystical iconoclasts.

I had not seen Tri Quang since the Buddhist struggle against Diem three years earlier, and he still defied easy comprehension. Though his French was fluent, he spoke to me through a Vietnamese interpreter as a matter of principle, rambling on enigmatically. The primary aim of the Buddhists, he said, was to end "oppression" by installing a South Vietnamese government that would "satisfy the aspirations of the people." What sort of government? With what kind of leadership? With what programs? His dark eyes narrowed and he brushed aside such mundane details. "I am merely a monk," he replied. "Those are questions for politicians."

It gradually occurred to me that my attempt to pin Tri Quang down to specifics was pointless. He was not, despite his organizational talent, an ordinary political promoter armed with a positive platform or coherent plan, striving to acquire power. Instead, he seemed to personify a form of fundamentalism in his passionate effort to preserve Vietnam's venerable values, which both the Americans and the Communists were contaminating with their modern ideas and practices. Implicitly, too, he was a xenophobe, as hostile to an alien imprint on Vietnam as the mandarins had been who persecuted European missionaries and their Vietnamese Christian converts in centuries past. But his zeal could not stop the American and Communist machines that were, in different ways, tearing the country's social tapestry to shreds. So his struggle was doomed from the start—and, predictably, the Communists banished him to a monastery after they extended their authority over the whole of Vietnam in 1975.

By late May 1966, as the Buddhist movement appeared to be faltering, its militants resorted to last-ditch gestures. They staged parades, hunger strikes, and other demonstrations in Saigon, Danang, and elsewhere, and their initially peaceful protests quickly degenerated into riots when government troops dispersed them with tear gas and bayonets. In Hué, the same youths who had gutted the U.S. Information Service library went on to burn the vacated American consulate. Over a period of three weeks, at least ten Buddhist monks and nuns set themselves ablaze across the country—more than had committed suicide in the offensive against Diem in 1963. Tri Quang tried to calm the agitation, but the campaign he had inspired now eluded his control.

I witnessed the first in this series of self-immolations on the morning of May 29 at the Dieude temple in Hué, where I had met with Tri Quang a couple of days before. A Buddhist nun in her mid–fifties, Thanh Quang, had entered the temple compound at dawn, accompanied by a few friends. She assumed the lotus position as one friend doused her with gasoline. Then she lighted a match, immediately exploding into flame as another friend fed peppermint oil to the fire to suppress the stench of scorched flesh. By the time I arrived, her burning body was still erect, the hands clasped in prayer. The religious rite was fast becoming a political episode. As crowds of spectators knelt before her, appealing to Buddha to ease her suffering, reporters from the local radio station passed among them, recording their cries for later broadcast. Soon Tri Quang appeared to distribute to the foreign correspondents present copies of a letter that the nun had addressed to President Johnson, condemning America's "irresponsible" support for the Saigon regime. Tri Quang blamed Johnson for her death, and indicted him for having "masterminded the repression of the Vietnamese people." As more Buddhist suicides occurred, Johnson issued a statement calling them "tragic and unnecessary," and urged the South Vietnamese people to uphold the government—a clear signal that the United States would not abandon Ky and his entourage.

The insurgent officers in central Vietnam began to dissociate themselves from the Buddhist militants and make deals with Ky's intermediaries. Hué's defenses crumbled without them, and Ky's troops marched into the city in early June, subduing the handful of civilian dissidents who attempted to resist. The government soldiers embarked on an American-style public relations drive, giving band concerts and handing out candy to children, and they treated the vanquished opposition discreetly. General Thi was exiled to the United States with a generous allowance, and several Buddhist monks were allowed to remain, untouched, in their temples. But Colonel Loan, whom Ky had assigned to clean up Hué after his successful crackdown in Danang, displayed little mercy toward the regime's hard-core adversaries. He jailed hundreds of students and other rebels, many of whom were to languish in prison for years without trial. He also arrested Tri Quang, who had gone on a hunger strike, and transferred him to detention in a Saigon hospital.

The Buddhist movement never recovered from the defeat. Its crisis was only a squall amid the bigger storms that buffeted Vietnam, but it confirmed and clarified the future. The turmoil had been too close for the regime's comfort, dramatizing as it did the danger of factionalism when the enemy forces were expanding. The Americans, no longer willing to tolerate such political turbulence, tightened their hold on the Saigon government—expecting in return that the regime would permit them to wage the war as they saw fit. South Vietnam's dependence on the United States increased, and American officials ceased to make excuses for the shortcomings of their protégés. The new reality was expressed in an old epigram: "They may be sons-of-bitches, but they're our sons-of-bitches."

But Lyndon Johnson also wanted to preserve the image of legitimate South Vietnamese authority—largely to assuage public opinion in America, which had been horrified by the spectacle of Buddhist monks and nuns burning themselves alive. Johnson reckoned that a constitution followed by elections would solve the problem. Meeting with Ky in Guam in March 1967, he characteristically cast his request as a personal favor. "My birthday is in late August," he said. "The greatest birthday present you could give me is a national election."

Delegates to a constituent assembly in Saigon had earlier drafted a new constitution along American lines, assisted by John Roche, a scholarly White House aide; it provided for a bicameral legislature and a powerful president. Elections were now scheduled for the beginning of September, and Johnson, eager to publicize South Vietnam's dedication to "democracy," enlisted twenty-two U.S. congressmen, governors, business executives, and other dignitaries to serve as informal observers. Brought to Vietnam and toured around, they saw what their official guides wanted them to see—and their confusion was reflected in the malapropism of one of them, a Texas clergyman who kept referring to the country as "South Vietcong."

Though not flagrantly fraudulent, as elections in Ngo Dinh Diem's time had been, the contest could hardly be labeled fair—the word used by American officials to describe it. Civilian candidates were screened to disqualify anyone holding "pro-Communist" or "neutralist" views—a sanction that eliminated one mild politician who advocated a cease-fire— and they could campaign only by traveling together to certain areas in an airplane lent to them by the Saigon generals. Still, more than 80 percent of South Vietnam's registered voters turned out, though they went to the polls under subtle pressure. Their identity cards were punched as they cast ballots, so that those who abstained might later be arraigned for having obeyed the Vietcong's appeal to boycott the election.

Nevertheless, the election produced surprises. Propelled by his ambitious wife, General Nguyen Van Thieu, the figurehead chief of state, had challenged Ky for the presidency. His move alarmed American officials in Saigon, who feared that a feud between the two officers might split the South Vietnamese army. They tried to get Thieu to withdraw, but he refused. Eventually, his fellow generals arranged a compromise: they agreed to sponsor Thieu as president on condition that Ky, who would run for vice-president, be named chairman of a secret military council empowered to shape government policy from behind the scenes. Thieu agreed; later, he would shrewdly outwit his colleagues and concentrate authority in his own hands. But he performed miserably in the 1967 elections, and his slate mustered only 35 percent of the votes—most of them in outlying districts where local commanders managed the contests. Ky candidly explained in his memoirs that he would have won 60 or 70 percent of the vote by rigging the election had he been chosen to head the ticket: "I was the very person who organized and controlled the election. There was no reason for me to cheat in favor of Thieu and get the blame, when I had given up my own chance for the presidency."

Thieu's astonishingly poor performance was compounded by an unusually strong showing on the part of an obscure civilian, Truong Dinh Dzu, whom nobody had taken seriously. An unsavory lawyer who had once put his wife up as collateral for a loan, Dzu slipped through the net barring proponents of peace by keeping his mouth shut until his candidacy had been validated. He then campaigned with a dove as his emblem, urging negotiations with the Vietcong. He came in second with 17 percent of the vote—more a protest against military rule, it seemed at the time, than positive support for his platform. Embarrassed to have had such a runner-up, Thieu promptly arrested him on charges of illicit currency transactions, a felony for which half the Saigon population could have been indicted. Thieu also jailed a number of other dissident political figures—some of whom he reluctantly released at the behest of the U.S. embassy.

It was plain even then that the elections would do nothing to alter the course of the war. But Lyndon Johnson had his birthday gift in the form of a Saigon regime that could be displayed to the American public and to the world as a legal government. And his South Vietnamese allies, who had done their best to please him, could continue to count on lavish U.S. aid.

While the South Vietnamese generals squabbled among themselves, the Communists were also engaged in an internal controversy. And just as the Saigon regime's bickering affected its relations with the United States, so the dispute in the Hanoi hierarchy strained North Vietnam's relations with China. The quarrels differed vastly, however. The South Vietnamese were scrapping for personal power, while the Communist debate concerned the formulation of a strategy to cope with the immense American military commitment in Vietnam. And while internecine rivalries had virtually paralyzed the Saigon government, the wrangling in Hanoi scarcely diminished the ability of the North Vietnamese regime and the Vietcong to withstand the American challenge.

The key issue for the Vietnamese Communists was whether to match the American escalation by continuing to infiltrate big units into South Vietnam or to wage a less conventional conflict over a longer period. The Chinese, on whom they relied heavily for aid, were pressing them to follow the slower and more modest course, mainly for reasons related to China's own policies.

Though American officials repeatedly portrayed Mao Zedong as the guiding spirit behind the Communist "aggression" in Vietnam, Mao actually took a cautious approach to the war. He did not favor a peaceful settlement and, consistent with his hostility to U.S. "imperialism," exhorted the Vietnamese Communists to keep fighting. But his principal preoccupation was to prevent the war from expanding to the point where it might require direct Chinese intervention.

For one thing, Mao was then preparing to launch the Great Proletarian Cultural Revolution, his devastating purge of the Chinese Communist party, and he needed his army to help him carry out the political campaign at home. Also, a big war in Southeast Asia would compound the threat to Chinese national security, at a time when the Soviet Union was building up its forces along China's northern borders. No doubt, too, he wanted to avoid a conflict like the one in Korea, in which China had sustained horrendous casualties. And it may have been true, as Vietnamese Communists later claimed, that he wanted to use them as proxies in a war that would bleed the United States and also leave them too exhausted to resist Chinese domination. In September 1965, his defense minister, Lin Biao, published a long article urging Hanoi to minimize its risks by conducting a prudent protracted war: "Revolutionary armed forces should not fight with reckless disregard for the consequences when there is a great disparity between their own strength and the enemy's. If they do, they will suffer serious losses and bring heavy setbacks to the revolution. Guerrilla warfare is the only way to mobilize and apply the whole strength of the people against the enemy."

The Vietnamese Communists rebuffed the advice. "We cannot automatically apply the revolutionary experiences of other countries in our country," declared Le Duan, their party secretary-general, recalling that "each time we rose up to oppose foreign aggression, we took the offensive and not the defensive." So in late 1965 they decided on a conventional war designed "to win a decisive victory on the southern battlefield in a relatively short period." Spelling out the plan, General Nguyen Chi Thanh, the Communist commander in the south, emphasized that the first objective would be swiftly to annihilate the South Vietnamese army and hasten a U.S. withdrawal.

General Thanh died in the summer of 1967—killed not by American bombs, as was rumored at the time, but by cancer, in a Hanoi hospital. By then, with the enormous American military machine inflicting a murderous toll on their troops, his colleagues had begun to have second thoughts about the profligate expenditure of manpower. General Vo Nguyen Giap, who had paid a heavy price for his premature Red River offensive against the French in 1951, now argued for a less costly and more realistic timetable, estimating that success might take another fifteen or twenty years. The North Vietnamese leaders started to explore alternatives. Doubts also afflicted many senior American soldiers and civilians, as they observed the tenacity of the Communists, both in response to the U.S. bombing of the north and in their combat conduct on the ground in the south.

Operation Rolling Thunder, the American air strikes against North Vietnam, went on almost daily from March 1965 until November 1968, dropping a total of a million tons of bombs, rockets, and missiles—roughly eight hundred tons per day for three and a half years. During 1966 alone, according to an official Pentagon tabulation, the United States staged seven thousand air raids against roads, five thousand against vehicles, and more than a thousand against railway lines and yards in North Vietnam, hitting many of the same targets several times. One objective of Operation Rolling Thunder was to crack the morale of the Hanoi leaders, and compel them to call off the southern insurgency; the other was to weaken the Communists' fighting capacity by impeding the flow of their men and supplies to the south. But neither goal was even remotely achieved. In August 1966, General Westmoreland conceded that he saw "no indication that the resolve of the leadership in Hanoi has been reduced." Secretary of Defense McNamara, an architect of the air offensive, expressed the same conclusion more incisively a year later at a closed-door session of a subcommittee of the Senate Armed Services Committee. He asserted that "enemy operations in the south cannot, on the basis of any reports I have seen, be stopped by air bombardment—short, that is, of the virtual annihilation of North Vietnam and its people." McNamara antagonized the generals and their congressional supporters by speaking the unpalatable truth, and President Johnson was soon to ease him out of office.

Besides attacking Communist forces and convoys as they deployed to move from staging areas in the southern provinces of North Vietnam, the American air strikes were directed against the Ho Chi Minh Trail in Laos. Hundreds of American aircraft bombed the Laotian routes every day, their missions facilitated by electronic detection devices and other sophisticated gadgets. Covert teams of South Vietnamese, Cambodians, and Laotians, many led by American officers, were also insinuated into the region to provide the American bombers with information on enemy activities. Even so, the raids barely dented the southward movement of either Communist troops or supplies.

The needs of the Communist fighting forces were minimal. Unlike the American or South Vietnamese armies, they had no aircraft, tanks, or artillery, and they could do without fuel, spare parts, and shells—not to mention the beer, shaving cream, talcum powder, and other luxuries that were necessities for American soldiers. The North Vietnamese and

Vietcong needed no more than fifteen tons of supplies a day from the north in order to sustain their effort in the south. And since the Soviet Union and China were then furnishing North Vietnam with nearly six thousand tons of aid daily, only a tiny fraction had to trickle down the Ho Chi Minh Trail for the Communists to wage the war.

Nor were the U.S. air strikes effective against the infiltration of North Vietnamese combat divisions into the south. Though the bombing of the Ho Chi Minh Trail grew in intensity, American intelligence experts estimated that the annual infiltration rate soared from thirty-five thousand in 1965 to one hundred and fifty thousand by late 1967. And most of the North Vietnamese who died while making the march were victims of dysentery, malaria, and other diseases rather than U.S. bombs.

The trek was still a ghastly ordeal, as one Communist veteran, Tran Thi Truyen, vividly recalled to me during an interview in her native village outside Hanoi in 1981. She went south at the age of sixteen to serve as a nurse in a field hospital in southern Laos, near the South Vietnamese frontier. Like her comrades, she had carried a rifle, a shovel, and a sixty-pound knapsack containing clothes, food, and a few personal items. Her unit was driven by truck to the head of the trail, and proceeded from there by foot on its month-long journey.

The rainy season had just started, and the route was muddy. Occasional flash floods forced us to cling to trees and shrubs to keep from being washed away. The jungles were infested with leeches and other insects that swarmed all over us. We crossed deep rivers and streams, and there were the mountains, some so high that it was as if we were walking above the clouds. We sometimes needed ladders to scale their steep slopes, or we removed our sandals and climbed in our bare feet. Despite our hardships, the local tribesmen acting as guides tried to scare us with tales of bandits in the area. I was young, and I frightened easily.

Worse still, Truyen and her unit were constantly harassed by U.S. aircraft as they marched down the trail.

The Americans had denuded the jungles with their bombs, and there was no place to hide. They would light up the area with flares, then drop bombs everywhere. Each time they flew overhead, our commander ordered us to disperse and dig foxholes, but the bombs fell close, and I shook with fear. My heart would throb, and my whole body trembled inside as the bombs exploded. Even after the bombing had stopped, I couldn't focus my eyes, and my head ached for hours.

Truyen eventually reached her destination, a jungle clearing where the field hospital was to be set up. She and her comrades began by constructing an underground surgery eight feet deep, fortifying its ceiling with thick logs and a layer of dirt, on top of which they built a thatched hut as their dormitory. They also built a subterranean ward for patients and another as a storage room for medicine. The wounded started to arrive even before the construction was completed, carried in on bamboo stretchers over miles of rugged terrain, and surgeons operated by the light of oil lamps amid gory scenes that curdled Truyen's stomach.

I was inexperienced, and my first sight and smell of blood and pus so nauseated me that I vomited and couldn't work. Some of the wounded had lost arms or legs. Or their bellies had been ripped open by bomb fragments, and their intestines were spilling out. Others were horribly burned by napalm. Many, who had been lying injured in the jungle for days, were brought in with maggots crawling out of their infected wounds. And there were the malaria cases, who became delirious with fever and rampaged like madmen. I soon recovered from my shock and revulsion, and I did my best—until I also caught malaria and was sent home.

In North Vietnam, meanwhile, the regime managed the war effort by mobilizing the country's principal resource—people. The traffic destined for the south was never seriously interrupted as thousands of work teams, many composed of young women, repaired roads and rail communications; the rail lines to China, a vital link, were kept open by Chinese labor battalions; engineers rebuilt demolished bridges three or four times, replacing them during reconstruction with temporary spans of planks laid across boats or pontoons. If trucks were stalled by the bombing, peasants pushing bicycles outfitted with bamboo frames transported hundreds of pounds of cargo for miles, and porters gingerly balancing shoulder poles carried supplies over remarkably long distances. When American airplanes attacked North Vietnam's ports, longshoremen unloaded oil drums from Soviet and East European freighters onto barges and sampans which dispersed the barrels through an intricate web of canals and rivers into the countryside for safety. Statistics again tell the story. Even though the U.S. bombing campaign escalated drastically during the period, imports reaching North Vietnam by sea more than doubled to about 1.4 million tons between 1965 and 1967.

One of the illusions of those who advocated strategic bombing was that the air offensive could obliterate or at least slow down Communist war production. But that belief was an outmoded one, left over from World War II, when air raids failed to flatten the German economy. It also ignored the fact that North Vietnam, a simple agrarian society with limited manufacturing capability, was essentially a conduit through which Soviet and Chinese matériel passed on its way to the battlefield in the south. The destruction of its few factories scarcely deprived North Vietnam of the means to carry on the conflict. By the middle of 1967, for example, the American attacks had cut the country's capacity to generate electricity by 85 percent. Yet, as McNamara noted at the time, it was able to meet war needs by switching to some two thousand diesel-driven generators; North Vietnam's normal requirements were so small, he remarked, that all its installations combined generated only one fifth of the electricity produced by the Potomac Electric Power Company branch in Alexandria, Virginia.

The American investment in the bombing campaign was thus wildly disproportionate to the destruction it inflicted, and official American estimates dramatized. By late 1967, the United States had imposed some $300 million in damage on North Vietnam—but at a loss to the American air force of more than seven hundred aircraft valued at approximately $900 million.

The North Vietnamese developed one of the strongest air defense concentrations in the world, comprising eight thousand antiaircraft guns, more than two hundred surface-to-air missile batteries, a complex radar system, and computerized control centers, all provided by the Soviet Union. The entire structure earned the respect of American pilots, who had not expected such withering flak. "Ninety-nine percent of the time as I dropped bombs," one of them recollected after the war, "somebody was shooting at me."

The Communists focused as well on civil defense, so that the U.S. raids caused fewer casualties than might have been expected from the tonnage of bombs dropped. Individual shelters resembling manholes dotted city streets, and peasants dug elaborate networks of trenches and tunnels that stretched from their villages into the fields, enabling them to cultivate their crops between air attacks. The Hanoi government also decentralized its administration and evacuated thousands of people from urban areas. The massive dislocations created severe scarcities of food and other commodities, and conditions might have been appalling had the Soviet Union and China not provided assistance. Their aid, apart from weapons, amounted to some $300 million in 1967 alone—not much in contrast to the billions in U.S. help consumed by South Vietnam, but still crucial.

Despite their resilience, the North Vietnamese were not immune to pain and fear. The U.S. air offensive probably killed a hundred thousand civilians and, at an early stage, Prime Minister Pham Van Dong told a British journalist in an unusual outburst of emotion that "I'm not acting when I say that I am obliged to cry—literally cry—at the suffering and the losses." The region just to the north of the seventeenth parallel, where North Vietnamese units assembled to move south, was a special target of American aircraft. Years after the war, an inhabitant of the area, Ho Thanh Dam, recollected the day in July 1967 when they struck Vinh Quang, his village:

> The bombing started at about eight o'clock in the morning and lasted for hours. At the first sound of explosions, we rushed into the tunnels, but not everyone made it. During a pause in the attack, some of us climbed out to see what we could do, and the scene was terrifying. Bodies had been torn to pieces—limbs hanging from trees or scattered around the ground. Then the bombing began again, this time with napalm, and the village went up in flames. The napalm hit me, and I must have gone crazy. I felt as if I were burning all over, like charcoal, and I lost consciousness. Comrades took me to the hospital, and my wounds didn't begin to heal until six months later. More than two hundred people died in the raid, including my mother, my sister-in-law, and three nephews. They were buried alive when their tunnel collapsed.

As a practical strategy, however, the bombing backfired. American planners had predicted that it would drive the enemy to capitulation, yet not only did the North Vietnamese accept the sacrifices, but the raids rekindled their nationalistic zeal, so that many who may have disliked Communist rule joined the resistance to alien attack. In Hanoi in 1981, I even discerned a certain nostalgia for the war. Ton That Tung, a prominent physician, compared the élan of those years to the country's present gloominess: "There was extraordinary fervor then. The Americans thought that the more bombs they dropped, the quicker we would fall to our knees and surrender. But the bombs heightened rather than dampened our spirit. Now, since the end of the war and without the bombs dropping, we have lost much of that fervor. We complain about food and housing shortages—complaints never heard during the war, when nobody cared what they ate or how they slept. The change is strange and paradoxical."

Communist troops fighting in the south also displayed great stamina, despite dreadful hardships. As diaries and notes discovered on their corpses revealed, they suffered from the heat and humidity, disease and fatigue—and hunger constantly clawed those in the mountains and jungles far from South Vietnam's populated littoral, where they could forage for food. The steady pounding of American artillery and aircraft unnerved them, and many were sad and homesick away from their families. An unfinished letter to his mother signed by Mai Van Hung, a young North Vietnamese soldier killed near Pleiku in late 1965, probably shared the sentiments of numbers of his comrades: "How devastating and poignant this war is! It has stolen the vernal spring of our lives, we fledglings who knew nothing except our school-books. I didn't expect to be so wretched. If I see you again in the future, I will tell you everything in detail. If not, please calm your grief and do not mourn me."

The chances were that Hung's other letters, if he wrote any, rarely or never reached his mother—as I speculated after talking with North Vietnamese veterans. One retired captain told me, for instance, that he had no contact with his wife or parents during his first six years in the south, and then exchanged messages with them only once a year over the next three years. Nor were the dead shipped home, as I also learned in the north, where village cemeteries feature a war monument flanked by rows of neat white tombs bearing the names, but not the bodies, of those killed in action. Families received only cursory reports of the deaths of their husbands or sons during the war—a tragedy for the Vietnamese, with their close kinship ties. The experience of Hoang Thi Thu, an unusually outspoken peasant whom I interviewed in a hamlet near Hanoi in 1981, was undoubtedly shared by other war widows:

I didn't receive a single letter from my husband after he went south. I wrote to him often, but I don't know whether he ever got my letters. Then, one day, I was suddenly handed an official notice saying that he had been killed, without any details of how he died. I was shattered by the news, and I've been miserable ever since. Sometimes I think that I'm going out of my mind, as if my soul has departed from my body. I can't hear anything. I can't concentrate on anything. Yes, he died for the country, but it's been very painful for me, extremely painful.

Still, the North Vietnamese and Vietcong forces were formidable foes, as the Americans who fought against them consistently acknowledged. "I wish they were on our side," was a comment commonly uttered by American officers. Among the thousands of prisoners taken during the war, few showed signs of contrition. In that respect, they differed drastically from Germans captured in World War II or Chinese Communists in the Korean war. Numbers of enemy troops in those conflicts could be induced to surrender because they had lost confidence in their cause. But Konrad Kellen, a RAND Corporation expert who interrogated North Vietnamese and Vietcong prisoners, found their convictions unshaken after they had laid down their arms. "Neither our military actions nor our political or psychological warfare efforts seem to have made an appreciable dent on the enemy's overall motivation or morale," he concluded. At a time when official American statements brimmed with optimism, he predicted that the Communists were "unlikely to yield, let alone disintegrate," under American pressure: "The thought of compromise in the current struggle, even in return for concessions, seems alien to these men. They see the war entirely as one of defense of their country against the invading Americans, who, in turn, are seen merely as successors to the French."

Big North Vietnamese and Vietcong units went into actual combat infrequently—sometimes only once or twice a year. Their commanders knew that they could not match superior U.S. military might in frontal clashes. They also preferred to engage in hit-and-run maneuvers, thereby retaining the initiative so that they could choose the terrain for battle. And, by avoiding direct confrontations, they hoped that the Americans would eventually exhaust themselves in grueling and often fruitless search-and-destroy operations.

As the war dragged on, a major challenge for the Communist leaders was to buoy up the spirit of their men. The process has been labeled "indoctrination," implying that the enemy troops were subjected to some mysterious sort of totalitarian "brainwashing." But the notion is specious. The North Vietnamese and Vietcong regulars had a tradition of opposition to foreign intervention. They had been raised on legends of Vietnam's resistance to Chinese rule, and their fathers or uncles or older brothers had fought against the French. They were thus convinced from the start of the righteousness of their mission, and it was unnecessary to persuade or coerce them into subscribing to the validity of the war against the United States and its Saigon government "puppets."

I asked a high-level North Vietnamese officer in Hanoi after the war to explain frankly how his comrades had been able to make such sacrifices during the conflict. "You must understand the depth of our patriotism," he replied, and went on to spout familiar slogans about Vietnamese fidelity to independence and sovereignty. Yet North Vietnamese and Vietcong prisoners interrogated during the war almost unanimously expressed the same line, and they were sincere. "I knew that I might be killed, but I was committed to the sacred salvation of the nation," said a North Vietnamese private under questioning, and another recalled discussions with his comrades on the subject: "Sometimes we sat and talked about seeing our loved ones again. But we all realized that the country had been invaded, and that to get home sooner, we had to fight the war. As long as the war continued, we agreed, we could not put our own happiness above our duty."

Like any soldiers, though, they grieved over the deaths of buddies and yearned for their families, and their perseverance had to be bolstered. They also had to be rewarded or punished for courage or cowardice in battle, or penalized for such infractions as chasing girls or stealing chickens. To perform these and similar functions, indispensable cadres stiffened every North Vietnamese and Vietcong unit. The system, borrowed from the Chinese Communist army, was based on the notion of a *cadre*—a framework to steel a unit. But the system could be no better than the cadres themselves, who were supposed to combine the roles of personal confessor, surrogate parent, and ideological tutor to the troops. So important were they that Ho Chi Minh once declared: "Success or failure depends on whether our cadres are good or bad."

The cadres were usually Communist party members and often Vietminh veterans of the war against the French—seasoned revolutionaries with a lifetime of experience behind them. Most of those assigned to Vietcong detachments were native southerners who had hidden in the south after the 1954 partition or had gone north and returned later. Tensions occasionally arose later, when North Vietnamese cadres were infiltrated into the ranks of the Vietcong. Many dynamic northerners lacked the patience to deal with the slower pace of their southern comrades, and some were too sectarian to adjust to the political climate of the south, where much of the population was hostile to Communist doctrine. After the war, a senior North Vietnamese official candidly disclosed to me that regional differences had been a problem, recalling that "it wasn't easy to find and train northerners to adapt to conditions in the south."

But most of the cadres, whatever their origin, earned the respect and admiration of the troops. North Vietnamese and Vietcong prisoners interrogated during the war repeatedly evoked the image of "big brother" to describe their cadres, who from their viewpoint resembled trustworthy, loyal, honest, courteous, kind, cheerful, and wholly virtuous scoutmasters. In contrast to South Vietnamese army officers, who regarded themselves as a privileged class, the Communist cadres ate and slept with the men, joined them in battle, and shared their hardships. They invited ordinary soldiers to debate and even criticize operational plans so that, as a North Vietnamese private recollected, "we always knew why we were fighting." Another testified to the effectiveness of his unit's cadre: "Twelve of the eighteen men in our company were killed during an enemy sweep, including the commander and the cadre himself. But we survivors weren't scared or demoralized, and nobody thought of defecting—probably because of the way the cadre had motivated us."

Along with encouraging troops or listening to their troubles cadres monitored them closely—like Orwellian "big brothers." This practice was partly intended to prevent malingering and desertion, and it also safeguarded against such violations of Communist puritanism as flirtations between soldiers and peasant girls. Its more serious purpose was to deprive individuals of privacy and, as all armies do, reinforce their fidelity to the unit. A further refinement of the collective approach, again acquired from the Chinese Communists, were three-man cells whose members assumed responsibility for each other. The device worked well in combat, where soldiers rely on their buddies for help. In particular, North Vietnamese and Vietcong troops chronically worried about being left wounded on the battlefield, and an obligation of their teammates was to rescue them.

Yet other mechanisms employed to cement the Communist forces were criticism and self-criticism forums, also learned from the Chinese. As in group therapy sessions, officers and men alike were licensed to denounce each other candidly or blame themselves for mistakes; again, judging from prisoner interrogations, the procedure usually contributed to cohesion. A North Vietnamese sergeant explained, for example, that discipline in his company invariably improved after he had submitted to the barbs of his troops, and a Vietcong private compared his confessions of error before his comrades to looking at himself in a mirror, saying that "I was able to see the dirt on my face and clean it up." But the

Communists were not always lenient. They executed informers and traitors, sometimes summarily, and they harshly punished soldiers for gratuitously molesting peasants whose cooperation they needed. Yet they could also be flexible, as in the case of a noncommissioned Vietcong officer who threatened to retire to his native village to marry his childhood sweetheart. After considerable haggling, they appointed him to a sedentary clerical job in the village. A captured Communist cadre explained philosophically: "We observed the principle that nobody is perfect."

North Vietnamese and Vietcong troops resorted to various maneuvers to offset their military inferiority. They tried to "cling to the enemy's belt"—their term for engaging in close combat so that the Americans could call in air and artillery strikes only at the risk of endangering their own men. They were constantly darting out of tunnels and bunkers to ambush American patrols, and they also relied on an assortment of ingenious mines and booby traps. Nevertheless, they sustained ghastly losses—less often in battle than as a consequence of the bombing of "free fire zones," sectors that the Americans declared open to indiscriminate air raids, or "harassment and interdiction," the relentless shelling of supposedly hostile areas by U.S. artillery. Nor could they easily withstand massive American search-and-destroy drives such as Operation Cedar Falls, launched at the beginning of 1967.

The sweep, conducted by sixteen thousand American and an equal number of South Vietnamese troops, was designed to wipe out a Communist stronghold northwest of Saigon known as the Iron Triangle. After evacuating at least ten thousand civilians, the U.S. forces bombed and shelled the area, then leveled its four principal villages in an effort to eliminate the Communist base which the Vietminh had built twenty years before during the war against the French. Forewarned, most of the Vietcong soldiers fled to nearby Cambodia, leaving some seven hundred dead, and those who stayed to cover the retreat were badly mauled. Dang Xuan Teo, a Vietcong guerrilla interviewed in Vietnam after the war, recalled how for days the Americans besieged him and his comrades in a tunnel, where they barely survived on roots and leaves until, one night, they finally managed to escape. The U.S. command hailed the operation as a triumph. But, by the end of the year, the Communists had returned to the devastated region and reconstructed the sanctuary, which they used as a springboard for their assault against Saigon in the Tet offensive of early 1968.

The same pattern was repeated again and again throughout Vietnam during the war, with the Americans conquering territory that could not be held. The war was not a classic conflict between armies pushing back the enemy as they advanced across fronts, but a test of endurance in which the side able to last longer would prevail. A key to the struggle lay in mobilizing people—or at least reducing their opposition—by persuasion or coercion or a mixture of both.

General Westmoreland never understood this reality. He refused to recognize that the Communists might represent a tempting alternative to a rural population eager for political, economic, and social change; he simplistically dismissed them as "bully boys," who could be defeated in a conventional war—the only kind he knew how to wage. Sir Robert Thompson, the British counterinsurgency adviser to the Saigon government, saw more clearly that time was working against the United States and its South Vietnamese allies unless they could isolate the Vietcong from peasant support. Pleading for a more modest antiguerrilla approach, he cautioned the Americans against squandering their resources in attempts to wear out the enemy in big battles. The Communists could deadlock the conflict and exhaust the U.S. forces, he warned; in a revolutionary war, "you lose if you do not win."

The Communists did in fact pursue a protracted struggle, and made horrendous sacrifices in lives to attain their long-range objective. They sent more than a hundred thousand North Vietnamese regulars into the south every year after 1966; at least a half million of their troops died in action; yet there were always fresh recruits to replace the casualties from their pool of some two million men. Overwhelming American firepower piled up mounds of enemy dead—grotesquely termed the body count in official parlance—but the tactical triumphs failed to add up to a strategic victory. Westmoreland's war of attrition, calculated to grind down the North Vietnamese and Vietcong, instead wore out his own forces—and, in the process, gradually exhausted the patience of the American public. The Communists were prepared to go on and on, and they had factored their human costs into the equation.

There was no "typical" U.S. soldier in Vietnam, despite the stereotype of the "grunt" promoted by the news media, politicians, and even veterans themselves. The three million Americans who served there went through many varied experiences—partly because the quality of the war varied in different areas of the country, and partly because its nature changed over time.

American units in the Mekong delta slogged week after week across paddies, occasionally tangling with Vietcong guerrillas, while other units clashed with North Vietnamese regiments in big engagements in the highlands. Still others were continually peppered by snipers as they patrolled the perimeters of sprawling U.S. installations at Danang and Bienhoa and Camranh, and many more spent seemingly endless periods at lonely hilltop batteries, firing artillery shells at real or presumed enemy concentrations. Air force pilots could return from dangerous missions over North Vietnam to the relative comfort of their bases, and some lucky GIs drew assignments in Saigon, where the military bureaucracy resembled a miniature Pentagon.

But Vietnam was unique among American wars in at least two respects: under a rotation schedule, draftees were committed for only a year—which meant, for many, that survival became their main preoccupation; but in a war without front lines, few could feel safe anywhere. A survey conducted for the Veterans Administration and published in 1980 underscored the point statistically: of the veterans sampled, most had been exposed to "combat," which meant that they had come under some kind of attack. But in reality, only a minority had actually clashed with large North Vietnamese units or Vietcong irregulars, run into mines or booby traps, or been ambushed. Yet 76 percent had been on the receiving end of enemy mortars or rockets, and 56 percent had seen Americans killed or wounded. While infantrymen obviously faced greater risks, headquarters typists were also vulnerable.

In many ways, the American troops sent to Vietnam were no less ideological than their North Vietnamese and Vietcong adversaries. Exhorted by Kennedy and Johnson to join in the crusade to halt the spread of global Communism, they firmly believed in the sanctity of their cause. Also, their fathers had fought in World War II, and they felt it was their generation's turn to do its duty. They knew the United States had never been defeated in a war, and their impulses were stimulated and dramatized by the exploits of movie and television heroes—a factor that emerges repeatedly in their personal recollections. William Ehrhart, a former marine sergeant, emphasized the influence on him of what he called the "John Wayne syndrome," and another veteran, Dale Reich, imagined himself to be "a soldier like John Wayne, a dashing GI who feared nothing and either emerged with the medals and the girl, or died heroically." In *Born on the Fourth of July,* an account of his service, Ron Kovic recalled his decision to enlist in the marines after two recruiters had stirringly addressed his senior high school class: "As I shook their hands and stared up into their eyes, I couldn't help but feel that I was shaking hands with John Wayne and Audie Murphy."

According to the 1980 Veterans Administration study, most Vietnam veterans did not lose their patriotic pride after the conclusion of the war. Looking back, 71 percent of those polled said that they were "glad" to have gone to Vietnam; 74 percent claimed to have "enjoyed" their tour there; 66 percent expressed a willingness to serve again. But these responses, though astonishing, do not necessarily contradict the more familiar notion that ordinary U.S. soldiers became increasingly disillusioned as the war dragged on. For as the prospect of victory dimmed, their zeal was eroded by frustration, and they sought to attribute blame for their disappointment. In the retrospective survey, 82 percent complained that they had been sent into a conflict which "the political leaders in Washington would not let them win"—a sentiment shared by Americans as a whole, which has doubtless contributed to their declining faith in their public institutions. Yet no nation, least of all the United States, readily admits to failure. So the veterans and civilians who viewed the war as a tragedy could also subscribe to President Reagan's description of its purpose as "noble."

As they waged the war, however, U.S. troops were gradually disenchanted less by grand strategic flaws than by the accumulation of their own experiences. I have compiled dozens of these experiences, either from direct interviews or from memoirs, and the stories could fill volumes. But perhaps the bits and pieces that follow add up to a credible set of impressions.

Most GIs sent to Vietnam after the first American forces arrived in 1965 went as individual replacements rather than in units. Consequently, from the start many of them were overcome by loneliness. When he reached one of the American division headquarters along with a handful of other men, Dale Reich was randomly assigned to a company whose members accepted him without comment: "The old clichés about camaraderie under fire did not seem to apply. . . . I was crushed by the combination of slipping one step closer to combat, and finding no one to pat me on the back and assure me that I would survive. Instead, I found that even my fellow soldiers had no real interest in my welfare."

The solitude was intensified by a feeling that they were in an alien and probably hostile environment. William Ehrhart had fantasized before leaving home that it would be like the scenes of World War II he had seen in the movies—French girls and Italian kids spilling into the streets to hail their liberators with wine and flowers. But Vietnam was taut and tense. Charles Sabatier, a draftee from Texas, had scarcely landed in Saigon when he noticed that the windows of the green U.S. army bus that transported him to his camp were screened with wire mesh as a precaution against grenade assaults. "I thought we were in a friendly country, and now I'm told that people might run up and throw grenades into the bus. And I thought, Oh my God, they're going to try to kill me. There I was, twenty years old, and suddenly I realized that I might not live to be twenty-one or twenty-two."

Vietnam confused and confounded innocent young Americans. Many, persuaded they were there as saviors, sincerely treated the Vietnamese with concern and kindness, providing them with hygiene, roads, wells, and other benefits as part of programs that one U.S. general called the velvet glove. But they were also chronically apprehensive and rightly suspected that any Vietnamese might be hostile. They were told that some areas belonged to the Vietcong and others to the Saigon regime, but they never trusted such flimsy intelligence, as a former marine captain, E. J. Banks, recalled:

> You never knew who was the enemy and who was the friend. They all looked alike. They all dressed alike. They were all Vietnamese. Some of them were Vietcong. Here's a woman of twenty-two or twenty-three. She is pregnant, and she tells an interrogator that her husband works in Danang and isn't a Vietcong. But she watches your men walk down a trail and get killed or wounded by a booby trap. She knows the booby trap is there, but she doesn't warn them. Maybe she planted it herself. It wasn't like the San Francisco Forty-Niners on one side of the field and the Cincinnati Bengals on the other. The enemy was all around you.

Soon after taking over the region around Danang in the spring of 1965, the U.S. marines embarked on "cordon-and-search" missions, later to be given the quaint title of "county fair" operations. In theory, they were supposed to surround a group of hamlets, then distribute food and dispense medical care to the inhabitants while probing for Vietcong cadres. In practice, as Ehrhart described them, the operations were less benign: "We would go through a village before dawn, rousting everybody out of bed, and kicking down doors and dragging them out if they didn't move fast enough. They all had underground bunkers inside their huts to protect themselves against bombing and shelling. But to us the bunkers were Vietcong hiding places, and we'd blow them up with dynamite—and blow up the huts too. If we spotted extra rice lying around, we'd confiscate it to keep them from giving it to the Vietcong."

As the peasants emerged, Ehrhart continued, they were "herded like cattle into a barbed wire compound, and left to sit there in the hot sun for the rest of the day, with no shade." Meanwhile, several South

Vietnamese policemen with an American interrogator and his interpreter would pass through the crowd, selecting people to be taken to a nearby tent for questioning about the Vietcong presence in the vicinity: "If they had the wrong identity card, or if the police held a grudge against them, they'd be beaten pretty badly, maybe tortured. Or they might be hauled off to jail, and God knows what happened to them. At the end of the day, the villagers would be turned loose. Their homes had been wrecked, their chickens killed, their rice confiscated—and if they weren't pro-Vietcong before we got there, they sure as hell were by the time we left."

These were routine missions, not outrageous atrocities like the Mylai massacre that occurred in March 1968. Yet, in village after village, a fear of the unknown engulfed American soldiers. Mark Smith, a veteran of the First Cavalry Division, was fascinated by Vietnam's beauty from the start. In coastal Binh Dinh province north of Saigon, his operational area, the lush green mountains rose from a plain of rice fields divided with such geometrical precision as to suggest that the peasants who had landscaped the scene were natural mathematicians. But he felt intimidated by the "subtle, incomprehensible" villages—"whole societies right in front of us, yet impenetrable even after we had entered them, never understanding anything or seeing anything understandable, the people staring at us as if we were from Mars."

Approaching a hard-core Vietcong village could be explosive, however, as two marine companies discovered in early 1967 at Thuybo, a complex of hamlets straddling an intersection of rivers about a dozen miles south of Danang. Captain E. J. Banks, commanding the sweep, had expected only a minor engagement, even though the sector had been designated as "unfriendly." But, on that hot and humid morning, the enemy fire intensified as his men advanced slowly across rice fields toward the tree line shrouding the village. By dark, they had suffered heavy casualties, and only one helicopter managed to get through to evacuate the wounded. What began as a small-scale operation would degenerate into three murderous days of fighting, as so many operations in Vietnam did. A marine private, Jack Hill, later recollected his own experience during the encounter: "They started with snipers, and then their thirty calibers opened up, sounding like ten or fifteen jackhammers going off at the same time. Our guys were falling everywhere. We spread out and dug in, waiting for the word to go forward. But we couldn't move. We were pinned down, all day and all night. It was raining something pitiful, and we couldn't see nothing. So we just lay there, waiting and waiting and hearing our partners dying, big guys dying and crying for their mothers, asking to be shot because they couldn't take it no more."

Hill's squad finally entered the village at dawn. The enemy had evaporated, leaving not even a cartridge shell. The peasants, mostly old men and women, were running around in panic, screaming and denying any connection with the Vietcong. Disregarding them, the marines combed the place, burning huts and blowing up underground shelters: "Our emotions were very low because we'd lost a lot of friends. The death rate was ridiculous for such an operation. So when we went through those hutches, we gave it to them, and whoever was in a hole was going to get it. And whatever was moving was going to move no more—especially after three days of blood and guts in the mud."

Interviewed in Thuybo after the war, a local Communist cadre depicted the episode as a holocaust, claiming that the marines had deliberately slaughtered one hundred and forty-five civilians, including women and children. Captain Banks rejected the charge, contending that not more than fifteen peasants had been killed—"as if it had been a robbery and gunfight on a city street and several bystanders were hit." The truth will never be known. The only reality about death in Vietnam was its regularity, not its cause.

Another reality that frustrated U.S. troops in Vietnam was the enemy's ability to return to villages that had supposedly been cleaned out. They could never "liberate" territory, but found themselves going back again and again to fight the same battles in the same areas with the same unsatisfactory results. Their repeated offensives during 1967 in Binh Dinh province, a Communist stronghold since the French war, illustrated the problem. They conducted at least four massive drives into the region—operations with names like Masher, White Wing, and Pershing—and inflicted nearly eleven thousand casualties on the North Vietnamese and Vietcong. But apart from its principal towns, the province remained in Communist hands.

For most GIs in combat zones, patrols with no fancy operational names were a daily ordeal. Ehrhart recollected the normal experience of his marine unit as it plodded across rice fields and through jungles in the region near Danang: "You carried fifty to seventy pounds of equipment, and it was tough going, particularly in forested areas. Often you'd have to pull yourself along from one tree branch to the next, or we'd have to help each other by gripping hands. And you couldn't see anything, so you didn't know what was there around you. Of course, squads were sent out to flank the main column, but they would disappear from sight. Nobody wanted an assignment to the flanking squads because it was pretty hairy."

The heat and rain and insects were almost worse than the enemy. Drenched in sweat, the men waded through flooded paddies and plantations, stopping from time to time to pick leeches out of their boots. They might reach for a cigarette only to find the pack soaked. And at the end of the day, as Ehrhart recalled, they had nothing to look forward to except the next day.

> You dug a hole right beside where you were going to sleep, and put up a one-man poncho tent. Unless something happened, you'd wake up in the morning with your mouth tasting rotten and your clothes still wet. You'd eat, maybe for a half hour or forty-five minutes, and then you'd be off again, not thinking very much. In retrospect, it amazes me how ordinary that kind of life became. You're sitting there at six o'clock in the morning, a cigarette hanging out of your mouth, pulling on your boots, and you're in the middle of nowhere. Suddenly you realize, I'm not supposed to live this way, but then you're surprised that it seems so natural.

American combat units often patrolled for months without drawing even stray Vietcong sniper fire, and as Mark Smith remembered thinking at the time, "It was better to get into a fight than just walk around sweating." To him, indeed, battle was exhilarating.

> When you made contact with the enemy, you went from the most horrible boredom to the most intense excitement I've ever known in my life. You couldn't remain detached. Someone was trying to kill you and you were trying to kill someone, and it was like every thrill hitting you all at once. If I felt safe in a fight, below the line of fire, I almost didn't want it to end. But even in a severe fight, when I didn't feel safe, there was a distinct beauty to it—a sense of exultation, the bullets cracking around your head and the tracers flying so close that they would blind you for a moment.

But there was none of that romantic agony for many GIs as the unseen enemy harassed them with mines, booby traps, and mortars. Ronald J. Glasser, an army doctor, compiled some of their combat experiences in a book entitled *365 Days,* describing the kind of search-and-destroy mission that killed and crippled American soldiers every day in Vietnam—

without bringing the United States any nearer to its vague and elusive goal of victory.

By early morning, a suffocating dry heat hung over the rice fields, making it nearly impossible to breathe. The men chewed salt tablets as they walked, trying as well as they could to shelter the metal parts of their weapons from the sun. "A little before noon, the point man, plodding along a dusty rise, sweating under his flak vest, stepped on a pressure-detonated 105-mm shell, and for ten meters all around the road lifted itself into the air, shearing off his legs as it blew up around him. The rest of the patrol threw themselves on the ground." That evening, the company was mortared—only two rounds, but enough to keep the men awake despite their exhaustion. The heat continued to hang over them as they lay on the ground, smoking marijuana or just looking vacantly up at the empty sky. It was the fifth night that week they had been hit. They would suffer more losses the next morning, when they began sweeping again.

They moved out on line, humping through the gathering heat, chewing salt pills as they had the day before, looking out over the same shimmering landscape. A little after ten o'clock, they began moving through a hedgerow. A trooper tripped a wire and detonated a claymore set up to blow behind him. It took down three others, killing two right off and leaving the third to die later. The survivors rested around the bodies till the dust-offs came in and took out the casualties, then started up again.

Soon afterward, one of the platoons entered a tangled jungle area. The thick overhead foliage filtered out almost all the sunlight, making it difficult to see, while the matting of vines and bushes held onto the heat, magnifying it until the men felt that they were moving through an airless oven. The sweat poured off them as they trod cautiously. At places the growth was so thick that they slung their weapons and pulled the vines apart with their bare hands. Thorns caught onto their fatigues and equipment, and they had to tear themselves loose. Scratched and bleeding, they pushed on.

Three quarters of the way through the tangle, a trooper brushed against a two-inch vine, and a grenade slung at chest height went off, shattering the right side of his head and body. The medic, working down in the dim light, managed to stop the major bleeders, but could do nothing about the shattered arm and the partly destroyed skull.

Nearby troopers took hold of the unconscious soldier and, half carrying, half dragging him, pulled him the rest of the way through the tangle.

The Communists invented an extraordinarily lethal arsenal of mines and booby traps. The "Bouncing Betty" was so called by GIs because it leaped out of the earth, exploding as its firing device was triggered. More destructive were mortar and artillery shells hung from trees, nestled in shrubbery, or buried under the mud floors of Vietnamese huts. Others included booby-trapped grenades tripped by wires and fragmentation mines detonated by enemy guerrillas crouched in the jungle; and there were primitive snares, like sharpened bamboo staves hidden in holes. Cautious and fearful, GIs constantly attempted to second-guess the mines, as Tim O'Brien wrote in his memoir of the war, *If I Die in a Combat Zone*:

Should you put your foot to that flat rock or the clump of weeds to its rear? Paddy dike or water? You wish you were Tarzan, able to swing with the vines. You try to trace the footprints of the man to your front. You give it up when he curses you for following too closely; better one man dead than two. The moment-to-moment, step-by-step decision-making preys on your mind. The effect is sometimes paralysis. You are slow to rise from rest breaks. You walk like a wooden man . . . with your eyes pinned to the dirt, spine arched, and you are shivering, shoulders hunched.

It was less a fear of death that nagged the American soldiers, as one of O'Brien's buddies put it, than the absurd combination of certainty and uncertainty—the certainty that the mines were everywhere, and the uncertainty about how to move or sit in order to avoid them. The Vietcong had so many ways to plant and camouflage mines, he mused. "I'm ready to go home," he added.

So were many GIs as the war floundered, and their original sense of purpose became clouded by doubt. Looking back, Ehrhart spoke for others:

After a few months, it began to seem crazy, but you didn't dare to draw conclusions that might point in terrifying directions. Maybe we Americans weren't the guys in white hats, riding white horses. Maybe we shouldn't be in Vietnam. Maybe I'd gotten my ass out in these bushes for nothing. Still, it never occurred to me to lay down my rifle and quit. Instead, you develop a survival mentality. You stop thinking about what you're doing, and you count days. I knew that I was in Vietnam for three hundred and ninety-five days, and if I was still alive at the end of those three hundred and ninety-five days, I'd go home and forget the whole thing. That's the way you operated.

Protests spread in the United States against the war in Vietnam. Many, like this one, expressed the view that the war was subverting Lyndon Johnson's progressive social and economic programs. But American blacks were not united in their attitude toward the war.

Though President Johnson had not only his cabinet but a large staff of advisers, he relied heavily on a few old cronies, like Abe Fortas (center) and Clark Clifford, both successful Washington lawyers.

Johnson distrusted the joint chiefs of staff but heeded them because of their influence in Congress. He posed in 1964 with (left to right): Marine General Wallace Greene; Admiral David McDonald; Air Force General Curtis LeMay; Air Force General Earle Wheeler, chairman; and Army General Harold Johnson.

One of Johnson's visible and vocal critics was Senator John Stennis of Mississippi, a member of the Senate Armed Services Committee. Johnson took him seriously when Stennis demanded tougher action, believing he reflected the mood of most Americans.

By 1967, Defense Secretary McNamara had begun to realize that the bombing of North Vietnam was not producing the desired results. He came under increasing pressure from the military establishment and its supporters in Congress.

In October 1966, President Johnson made a swift trip to South Vietnam, where he told American soldiers in his Texas drawl to "nail the coonskin to the wall." Here he decorates a soldier at Camranh Bay, with General Westmoreland, U.S. commander in Vietnam, behind him.

President Johnson encouraged peace explorations but often thwarted them. British Prime Minister Wilson (right) undertook such an effort with Soviet Prime Minister Kosygin (left), who visited London in 1966. The attempt collapsed after Johnson raised the ante for a settlement.

Many key decisions were made by Johnson (back to camera) after informal discussions with his aides at a luncheon held every Tuesday in a White House dining room. He always made up his own mind but was continually seeking consensus to validate his moves.

A massive protest against the Vietnam war was staged in front of the Pentagon in October 1967. Among those who participated were the playwright Arthur Miller and the novelist Norman Mailer. The demonstration angered and troubled the president.

A large proportion of Americans supported the war—even though, by 1967, a majority believed it to have been a mistake. Many Americans wanted the United States to get out of Vietnam, but at the same time they did not want to lose a war for the first time in their country's history.

We have reached an important point, when the end begins to come into view.

—William Westmoreland

A feeling is widely and strongly held that "the Establishment" is out of its mind . . . that we are trying to impose some U.S. image on distant peoples we cannot understand, and that we are carrying the thing to absurd lengths. Related to this feeling is the increased polarization that is taking place in the United States, with seeds of the worst split in our people in more than a century.

—John McNaughton

By the beginning of 1966, Vietnam had become an obsession for Lyndon Johnson—the "center of our concerns," as he put it in his State of the Union message. Yet he had no intention of quitting or even compromising. He still believed the United States was strong and prosperous enough to produce both guns and butter. He had also persuaded himself that making any concessions to North Vietnam would provide his right-wing opponents with the pretext to sabotage his Great Society. So he reaffirmed his pledge to persevere: "We will stay until aggression has stopped," he intoned, "because in Asia and around the world are countries whose independence rests, in large measure, on confidence in America's word and in America's protection."

But Johnson sensed that the war was poisoning his administration—and might eventually tilt the nation against him unless he could show rapid progress. One of his closest aides, Jack Valenti, described the gloom that seemed to be enveloping the White House: "Vietnam was a fungus, slowly spreading its suffocating crust over the great plans of the president, both here and overseas. No matter what we turned our hands and minds to, there was Vietnam, its contagion infecting everything that it touched, and it seemed to touch everything."

Actually, the nearly two hundred thousand American soldiers sent to Vietnam during 1965 had made a critical difference—at least in conventional military terms. The marines had secured the sector around Danang and gone on to stage the first big American drive of the war in August, crippling a Vietcong regiment in the vicinity. Two months later, a U.S. airborne division crushed three North Vietnamese regiments in the Ia Drang valley, a dense jungle area near Pleiku, and prevented a Communist sweep from the central highlands down to the populated coast. The Ia Drang operation, Silver Bayonet, demonstrated for the first time the effectiveness of pitching large units into action by helicopter, and it also proved that B-52s, designed for strategic bombing, could be deployed to give tactical support to ground forces. Though more than three hundred Americans died in the battle, the engagement cost the Communists nearly two thousand men, and the favorable ratio of casualties prompted General Westmoreland to assert that his search-and-destroy missions could gradually grind down the enemy—on condition that he be given the battalions to do the job.

But his concept was flawed. The "kill ratio" would scarcely gratify Americans back home, who refused to equate the lives of their boys with those of the enemy. So Westmoreland's policy of attrition was doomed from the start, since U.S. opinion would eventually react against increasing American losses, no matter how many North Vietnamese regulars and Vietcong guerrillas were wiped out. Westmoreland's determination to defend all of South Vietnam rather than hold selected enclaves would also frustrate his own forces eventually. One U.S. officer later likened it to "Primo Carnera going after Willie Pep in a pigsty ten miles square."

By the end of the year, the Communists were building up their strength in South Vietnam at twice the rate of the U.S. escalation. Westmoreland reckoned that he would need more men than he had originally anticipated, both to cope with the immediate threat and to shift to the offensive in 1966. His request for a virtually open-ended troop commitment put the president in a dilemma: Johnson wanted to win the war, but he hoped to keep the investment within politically acceptable bounds. As usual, Johnson sent Robert McNamara to Vietnam to appraise the situation.

Until late November 1965, McNamara had believed firmly in the American crusade in Vietnam. But his attitude altered perceptibly during his quick trip to Saigon at this juncture. The U.S. combat performance impressed him, yet he was shaken by the evidence that North Vietnamese infiltration into the south had risen so dramatically—and would surely continue. Discarding his customary display of public optimism, he candidly told correspondents in Saigon that "it will be a long war," and returned to Washington to offer Johnson a bleak set of options.

The current plan to boost the number of American troops in Vietnam to some three hundred thousand by late 1966 would merely serve to avert disaster—in which case, he advised, the best approach was to seek a "compromise solution" through negotiations. On the other hand, the United States could "stick with our stated objectives" by providing "what it takes"—a total of at least six hundred thousand men by the beginning of 1968. But, McNamara cautioned, even that "will not guarantee success." For one thing, it might raise the American casualty rate to a thousand deaths a month. And, he figured, the odds were "about even" that nothing better would be attained than "a military standoff at a much higher level," along with the potential danger of "active Chinese intervention." In short, the future held out the unalluring possibility of a deadlock that might explode into a wider war.

Johnson fretted about domestic dissent as he pondered his choices. Student opposition to the war was spreading in response to larger draft quotas. Two young American protesters, emulating the Vietnamese Buddhists, committed suicide by self-immolation in early November, one in front of the Pentagon and the other at the United Nations, and a crowd of twenty thousand marched on the White House to clamor for peace. Surveys disclosed that an overwhelming majority of Americans favored a fresh cease-fire initiative—though nearly the same proportion approved dynamic action if the effort failed. "The weakest chink in our armor is American public opinion," Johnson warned his staff. "Our people won't stand firm in the face of heavy losses, and they can bring down the government."

Aware of that hazard, McNamara urged Johnson to stop the American air strikes against North Vietnam for three or four weeks before committing more troops to the conflict. This would give the Communists a "face-saving chance" to consider a diplomatic settlement, he argued, and it would also show America and the world that the administration did not intend to escalate "without having tried, through a pause, to end the war"—or at least make it appear that "we did our best to end it." Johnson was skeptical; a Communist rebuff would hand his generals and their right-wing supporters a pretext to demand even stronger military moves. Nevertheless, he consulted his key aides—among them Rusk, Ball, and McGeorge Bundy—as well as Clark Clifford, and, with dubious propriety, Abe Fortas, now a Supreme Court justice.

After a week of preliminary talks, the advisers assembled in the White House cabinet room on December 17 for two final days of debate. Johnson, hunched forward earnestly, opened the first session by announcing his readiness to "take any gamble" that might produce results. Clasping and unclasping his hands, he listened as the others spoke in turn. McNamara pressed hard for flexibility. "The military solution to the problem is not certain, one out of three or one in two," he said.

"Ultimately we must find alternative solutions. We must perforce find a diplomatic solution."

"What you are saying," Johnson interjected, "is that no matter what we do militarily, there is no sure victory."

"That's right," McNamara replied. They had been too optimistic in believing that American power alone would work. "We need to explore other means. Our military action approach is an unacceptable way to a successful conclusion."

Ball and Bundy concurred, and so did Rusk, who saw only one chance in twenty that a bombing halt would lead to a negotiated settlement; but it ought to be tried, if only for propaganda purposes. "You must think about the morale of the American people if the other side keeps pushing," he explained to Johnson. "We must be able to say that all has been done."

Fortas disagreed. The initiative would advertise America's "lack of certainty," thereby causing the public to worry about the administration's "depth of conviction." Besides, the venture was "ambivalent and ambiguous"; no prior arrangements had been made that signaled a positive outcome. Failure would create "renewed pressure for drastic action" and thwart future negotiating possibilities.

Clark Clifford had briefly harbored doubts a year earlier, but now he backed Fortas, arguing with the skill and precision that made him one of Washington's highest-priced lawyers. The North Vietnamese would reject any proposed settlement until they realized that they could not win, and they were far from that stage, he said. They would interpret a bombing halt as a "sign of weakness," undertaken only in reply to public pressure, and they would estimate that they could wear down the Americans as they had the French. Also, a "clearly unproductive" peace bid would be widely viewed as a "gimmick," demeaning to the president's prestige.

Chatting with Valenti during a break, Johnson confessed his bewilderment. He tried to put himself in Ho Chi Minh's shoes, but he was still baffled. "I don't know him," Johnson explained. "I don't know his ancestry or his customs or his beliefs. It is tough, very tough."

As the second day of conversations with his advisers wore on, Johnson abruptly reached a decision—perhaps more by intuition than by logic. He sighed, stood up, stretched, looked solemnly at the men around the table, and then, almost casually, addressed McNamara. "We'll take the pause," he said, and strode from the room.

The bombing halt began on Christmas morning and lasted for thirty-seven days, an interval Johnson used to promote a spectacular "peace offensive." He sent emissaries like Vice-President Hubert Humphrey, McGeorge Bundy, and Ambassador-at-Large Averell Harriman to more than forty countries to persuade their leaders of his sincerity. He also promulgated a fourteen-point program inviting the North Vietnamese to enter into "negotiations without preconditions."

"We have put everything into the basket of peace except the surrender of South Vietnam," Dean Rusk said. But he privately advised Ambassador Lodge to see the ambitious diplomatic operation for what it really was—an exercise in public relations. His cable to Lodge on December 28 even struck an uncharacteristically cynical note: "The prospect of large-scale reinforcements in men and defense budget increases for the next eighteen-month period requires solid preparation of the American public. A crucial element will be a clear demonstration that we have explored fully every alternative but that the aggressor has left us no choice."

Rusk nevertheless directed Henry Byroade, the U.S. ambassador to Burma, to inform his North Vietnamese counterpart in Rangoon that the bombing pause might be extended if the Communists reciprocated "by making a serious contribution toward peace." A Hanoi Radio broadcast denounced the American initiative as a "trick," and asserted that no political settlement was possible until the Johnson administration halted the air raids "unconditionally and for good." But the statement did not rule out future talks, an omission that some American officials construed positively—"like the flicker of an eyelid in a Trollope novel," one of them said.

The American commanders in Vietnam were not deterred by the diplomatic drive. After a one-day Christmas cease-fire on the ground, they intensified the war. Early in January, they launched the "biggest attack" to date against the Vietcong in the area near Saigon, and later in the month, as part of a thrust into Quangngai province, they staged the "largest amphibious operation" since the Inchon landing in Korea. Meanwhile, fresh American forces continued to arrive. These moves were not designed to foil the "peace" maneuvers, since Johnson monitored them closely himself, but they did little to generate an atmosphere of conciliation. Nor did Johnson's State of the Union address, delivered to Congress on January 12: "The days may become months and the months may become years, but we will stay as long as aggression commands us to battle."

Real or contrived, the diplomatic endeavor went nowhere, and Johnson resumed the bombing of North Vietnam at the end of January. Hanoi's man in Rangoon broke off contact with Ambassador Byroade, and eleven months passed before another U.S. official met with a North Vietnamese representative. Johnson's critics blamed him for the failure, but the Communist leaders shared responsibility. Like him, they were reluctant to negotiate seriously until they had improved their military position in South Vietnam. They spelled out this "very complicated" problem of war and diplomacy in an internal document that strangely resembled a White House memorandum. They could sit down at the conference table with their enemies, it concluded, only after they had destroyed "as much of their potential as possible" and could "force them into submission." But in contrast to the president, they did not have to cope with the vagaries of congressional, media, and public opinion.

On a trip back from Asia to Washington in early 1966, I asked several members of Congress for their views on the war. Most of them seemed to be unsure; one of them expressed the prevailing sentiment when he confided to me that he would probably make up his mind "when the casualties in my constituency become significant." But a few more concerned senators and representatives were beginning to ponder Vietnam. One group, troubled by the danger of a costlier conflict, leaned toward restraint. Another favored tougher action. Both factions vexed Johnson, who detested even the faintest hint of dissent. His reactions varied, however, according to his perception of their power.

He was chronically alarmed by hard-liners such as Senator John Stennis of Mississippi, a key member of the Armed Services Committee, who maintained close ties to the Pentagon brass. Stennis had originally had grave reservations about an American commitment to Southeast Asia, but he had come to believe that, once involved, the United States ought to mobilize its full military might to win. Johnson believed that Stennis reflected a significant segment of public opinion, which worried about an expanded conflict yet recoiled from the thought of an American setback. So Johnson repeatedly sought to placate Stennis and his ilk, sometimes by capitulating to their demands and sometimes by conceding enough to the generals and admirals to assure them of his intention to push on to victory.

Increasingly, too, Johnson surrounded himself with congressional loyalists like Senators Gale McGee of Wyoming and Fred Harris of Oklahoma, rewarding them with pledges of patronage and invitations to his informal White House suppers. He patched up an old quarrel with Senator Paul Douglas of Illinois, whose staunch anti-Communism would be an asset, promising to help Douglas's campaign for re-election. By contrast, Johnson did not hesitate to bring the immense weight of the presidency to bear against liberal dissidents. One victim of his wrath was Senator Vance Hartke of Indiana, an ardent Johnson enthusiast who had begun to have misgivings about the war.

Late in January 1966, Hartke signaled his doubts to Johnson in a letter cosigned by fourteen of his Senate colleagues—among them Eugene McCarthy, the junior senator from Minnesota. The mild message proposed only that the president refrain from resuming air strikes against North Vietnam and continue to explore a possible diplomatic settlement. To Johnson it was a case of *lèse majesté*. He excoriated Hartke publicly as "obstreperous" and privately as a "prick"; going even further, he saw to it that several of the senator's protégés were dismissed from their federal jobs. Punishing Hartke, he figured, would serve as a warning to others. But soon he had to cope with a far more formidable adversary, Robert Kennedy, now the junior senator from New York.

McNamara, an intimate friend and godfather to one of his sons, had confided to Kennedy his own sense of foreboding about the war in the hope that Kennedy could encourage Johnson to stonewall the joint chiefs of staff, who were then clamoring for renewed bombing. Kennedy sent Johnson a copy of *Never Call Retreat*, one of the volumes in a history of the Civil War by Bruce Catton, with a handwritten note suggesting that Johnson might derive "some comfort" from the marked passages—which showed that Abraham Lincoln had faced "identical problems and situations." Kennedy meant to indicate that Lincoln had resisted pressure from his generals and Johnson ought to do the same. But Johnson interpreted the gesture as an expression of support. On January 31, the day the bombing raids over North Vietnam resumed, Kennedy moved toward a break with Johnson over the war. The president's decision, he said in a florid speech, "may become the first in a series of steps on a road from which there is no turning back—a road that leads to catastrophe for all mankind." The issue soon exacerbated Johnson's obsessive hatred of the Kennedy clan. If he had "lost" Vietnam, he told Doris Kearns years later, "there would be Robert Kennedy out in front leading the fight against me, telling everyone that I had betrayed John Kennedy's commitment to South Vietnam. That I had let a democracy fall into the hands of the Communists. That I was a coward. An unmanly man. A man without a spine. Oh, I could see it coming all right. Every night when I fell asleep I would see myself tied to the ground in the middle of a long, open space. In the distance I could hear the voices of thousands of people. They were all shouting at me and running toward me: 'Coward! Traitor! Weakling!' "

Senator Fulbright was another annoyance, relentlessly heckling and needling Johnson, his Rhodes scholar's eloquence couched in an Arkansas drawl. He was a friend turned foe, which to Johnson made him more reprehensible than someone like Wayne Morse, who had at least been a consistent, predictable critic. Johnson was especially troubled by Fulbright's forum, the Senate Foreign Relations Committee, which began nationally televised hearings on the war policy in early 1966. The hearings so disturbed Johnson that on February 4 he tried to upstage them by suddenly announcing his departure next day for Honolulu to confer with the South Vietnamese leaders. Further to divert public attention away from the unpalatable military side of the war, Johnson directed the participants at the Honolulu meeting to concentrate on economic, social, and political projects for South Vietnam—the "pacification" programs that had by then become largely subordinated to the fighting. Back in Washington, though, he authorized such aides as Dean Rusk and Maxwell Taylor to appear before Fulbright, whose interrogations of administration supporters and opponents continued throughout February, a political theater in peculiar contrast to the battle scenes flashing across the nation's television screens every evening.

The Senate testimony yielded few revelations. Skeptics like George Kennan warned that the "preoccupation" with Vietnam was undermining America's global obligations while Rusk, chain-smoking under the glare of the lights, again portrayed the conflict as part of a worldwide struggle to stop "the steady extension of Communist power through force and threat." Still, the hearings provoked Americans to think about the war, and raised important questions.

Fulbright seemed to become more and more haunted by the war as the months passed. In April, he delivered a series of lectures at Johns Hopkins University where, a year earlier, Johnson had offered Ho Chi Minh a huge aid package in exchange for submission. The United States, declared Fulbright, was "in danger of losing its perspective on what exactly is within the realm of its power and what is beyond it." In displaying an "arrogance of power," he went on, "we are not living up to our capacity and promise as a civilized example for the world." Johnson, who believed Fulbright had personally smeared him as "arrogant," riposted by labeling the senator and other foes of the war as a bunch of "nervous Nellies" who lacked the courage to drive on to victory.

Still another nuisance was the venerable newspaper columnist Walter Lippmann, who exerted enormous influence on Washington insiders, and, through them, the rest of the nation. Johnson had promised him that the war would not be escalated, but now Lippmann felt deceived, and their relationship degenerated into an acrimonious feud. Johnson resorted to snide and salacious remarks about Lippmann, even accusing him of aiding and abetting the enemy, and Lippmann responded with equal rancor, privately calling Johnson "the most disagreeable individual ever to have occupied the White House." He also delivered an unusually angry tirade against Johnson in his column of February 3: the president had "never defined our national purpose except in the vaguest, most ambiguous generalities about aggression and freedom," he wrote. "Gestures, propaganda, public relations, and bombing and more bombing will not work." He predicted that Johnson would eventually find himself "in a dead-end street" unless he revised his Vietnam policy. And, with acute prescience, he foresaw domestic turmoil: "The division of the country will simply grow as the casualties and costs increase, and the attainment of our aims and the end of the fighting continue to elude us."

The economic costs of the war were climbing even as Lippmann wrote. In July 1965, when Johnson granted General Westmoreland forty-four combat battalions, he had calculated that the conflict would require roughly $2 billion for the year ahead. But the real figure ran to four times that amount—and worse was yet to come. As McNamara planned the military budget for the fiscal year ending in June 1967, he estimated that annual expenditures on Vietnam would range from $11 billion to $17 billion. As it turned out, the war consumed $21 billion that year, and the price continued to rise.

Compared to past conflicts, the war was not costly. By the middle of 1967, it was absorbing only about 3 percent of America's gross national product, the country's total output of goods and services—compared to 48 percent for World War II and 12 percent for the Korean war at their peaks. But the economic burden of Vietnam, though relatively modest, frightened Johnson. He feared that even the slightest accommodation to the war would compel him to sacrifice some of his domestic programs—and, more critically, awaken the public to the costs of the commitment. He wanted to wage the war without paying for it—just as he repeatedly refused to admit that he was escalating the conflict whenever he raised the troop level or stepped up the bombing. So he procrastinated, juggling and faking and concealing the statistics in a desperate attempt to avoid increasing taxes, the only way he could foot the bill. The subterfuge worked until the summer of 1967, when the numbers could no longer be fudged. Early in August, prodded by his economic specialists and outside business advisers, Johnson reluctantly proposed a 10 percent tax surcharge on individual and corporate incomes. Congress delayed passage of the proposal for nearly a year, and the budget deficit, which had soared to almost $10 billion for fiscal 1967, skyrocketed to triple that figure the following year. The inflation spiral that was eventually to cripple the United States and the rest of the world had begun its dizzy ascent.

Johnson was correct to have anticipated an adverse reaction to the tax increase. Approval for his handling of the war dwindled steadily from the summer of 1965. Now, for the first time, opinion crossed a significant barrier: a survey published in October 1967 showed that 46 percent of the public regarded the commitment to Vietnam as a "mistake," while 44 percent continued to back it. Still, the overwhelming majority of Americans opposed withdrawal and favored tougher attacks against North Vietnam. The studies disclosed another phenomenon: endorsement of the war was strongest among the college-educated, upper-income middle classes whose sons were least likely to be conscripted for combat under the deferment system. Even so, the confused and uncertain national mood at the time was probably best summed up by the housewife who told a pollster: "I want to get out, but I don't want to give up."

After the war, many politicians, generals, and even journalists reproached the news media for having disenchanted the American people. Westmoreland implied, for instance, that it was through American reporters in Vietnam that "the strategists in Hanoi indirectly manipulated our open society, and hence our political system." But the press, with all its shortcomings, tended to follow rather than lead the U.S. public, whose opinions were usually shaped more by such events as the tax surcharge or the death of a local boy than by television broadcasts and newspaper commentaries.

The experience of *Time* and *Life* magazines exemplified the change that information organizations underwent when their editors, along with everyone else, gradually perceived the futility of the war.

During the early 1960s, when I served as their senior correspondent in Southeast Asia, the sister publications paid only occasional attention to Vietnam, often treating it condescendingly as an exotic area of colorful people with unpronounceable names. Henry Luce, the boss, was passionately concerned with China, his birthplace, but in the spring of 1960, when we traveled together in Asia, he spurned my suggestion to visit Vietnam. His principal worry, he snapped at me in his staccato style, was "the danger of bombs falling on Chicago." As the American intervention in Vietnam grew, however, his top editors could not ignore the war. They opened a bureau in Saigon—where, until American combat troops landed in Vietnam, only the wire services and *The New York Times* had maintained permanent offices. Frequently, though, the magazines distorted the dispatches of their reporters and relied instead on guidance from White House, State Department, and Pentagon officials—and from the president himself. True to their tradition, *Time* and *Life* stood up for America.

Luce's successor, Hedley Donovan, went to Vietnam in late 1965 to see for himself, and his reactions were predictable. After the usual round of official briefings and a look at the battlefield, he wrote in *Life* that "the war is worth winning" and that victory was within sight. Eighteen months later, following another trip, his views began to alter. He now observed the widening gap between the official U.S. claims of progress and the realities of the situation, and his doubts were further intensified by what his correspondents told him—most notably Frank McCulloch, Saigon bureau chief and a rugged former marine sergeant who had long before understood the hopelessness of the American cause. Back home, Donovan also listened to his Long Island neighbors, solid conservative citizens who were troubled by rising casualties and higher taxes for a war that seemed to be going nowhere. He ventilated his misgivings to a New York University graduating class; if America failed in Vietnam, he said, he and other optimists ought to avoid recrimination and "admit that we had attempted something beyond our powers."

Then, under his direction, the magazines took a quantum leap. In October 1967, a *Life* editorial enunciated a new corporate policy toward the war. The United States had gone into Vietnam for "honorable and sensible purposes," it declared, but the undertaking had proved to be "harder, longer, more complicated" than America's leaders foresaw. No longer was the conflict "worth winning," as Donovan had written. On the contrary, the commitment was "not absolutely imperative" to the defense of strategic U.S. interests—and thus a difficult challenge "to ask young Americans to die for." "Hedley Donovan has betrayed me," complained Lyndon Johnson, as if the magazine had assaulted him personally. Two years later *Life*'s editors were to illustrate the Vietnam tragedy even more starkly by publishing, in a single issue, the portraits of some of the two hundred and fifty young Americans who had died in Vietnam in one routine week; the faces staring out of the pages were a dramatic reminder that anonymous casualty figures were in fact the sons, brothers, and husbands of neighbors.

Johnson had already gone to battle with the august and authoritative *New York Times* at the end of 1966. After much deliberation, the North Vietnamese leaders had finally decided to permit an American journalist to visit North Vietnam, and, on the advice of Wilfred Burchett, a pro-Communist Australian writer, they selected Harrison Salisbury, the *Times*'s assistant managing editor. The U.S. air strikes against North Vietnam had recently been stepped up and Johnson had insisted that the bombing was aimed strictly at military objectives. Salisbury reported differently. In a series of detailed dispatches he disclosed that cities and towns had been hit and many civilians killed. His accounts confronted the administration with what a Pentagon spokesman, Phil Goulding, called a "credibility disaster."

As Goulding later conceded, Salisbury's stories presented a "reasonably accurate picture" of the bomb damage—though Salisbury had initially failed to attribute his information to Communist sources, and he conveyed the wrong impression that the United States was indiscriminately trying to destroy North Vietnam. But the Johnson administration was concerned less with the truth than with the effect of the report on opinion. Administration officials had been trying to depict the air offensive as a "surgical" endeavor that miraculously spared North Vietnamese people, knowing full well the raids frequently struck civilian targets. So, as Goulding put it, the Salisbury dispatches made the Johnson entourage appear to be "a liar and deceiver."

For a while in early 1967 it seemed that Salisbury had replaced Ho Chi Minh as the administration's prime adversary. Hundreds of Pentagon researchers were assigned to prepare line-by-line rebuttals, and their findings were leaked to rival newspapers like *The Washington Post*, which triumphantly reported that Salisbury's accounts matched a Communist "propaganda pamphlet." The *Post*'s chief diplomatic correspondent, Chalmers Roberts, who often took his cue from senior government figures, embellished the campaign against him by calling Salisbury's invitation to Hanoi a new enemy weapon—as "clearly conceived" as the Vietcong's "poison-tipped bamboo spikes." An advisory board composed largely of publishers overruled a jury of newspaper editors that had voted to award Salisbury the Pulitzer prize. And Johnson himself entered the controversy to refute Salisbury; the bombing, said the president, was "the most careful, self-limited air war in history."

Despite the fuss over Salisbury's articles, however, the U.S. news media trailed behind public opinion—and Congress lagged even farther. The legislature's main instrument was its constitutional authority to appropriate money for the war, but senators and representatives repelled by the Vietnam conflict consistently balked at using that prerogative, lest they be charged with shunning their patriotic obligation to furnish funds to the fighting men in the field. The president could also penalize them for dissent by withholding federal grants from their constituencies or denying federal jobs to their friends. Indeed, Johnson even co-opted many congressmen merely by inviting them to bask in the pomp and glory of White House functions—just as medieval monarchs tamed unruly barons in the splendor of their castles. For all their qualms about the war, members of Congress were long on rhetoric and short on action.

In February 1966, for example, Senator Wayne Morse introduced an amendment to repeal the Tonkin Gulf resolution, whose passage only he and Ernest Gruening of Alaska had opposed nineteen months earlier. Morse, a skilled parliamentarian, maneuvered to prolong Senate debate on the subject for two weeks. Several senators joined him—among them Mike Mansfield, the majority leader, and Richard Russell of Georgia, who rose to deplore the "very great grant of power" conferred by the resolution on the president. But the country was at war—or, as Mansfield said as he motioned to shelve the bill, "we are in too deep now." As a result, only five senators backed Morse. Gruening then introduced a bill to bar draftees from Vietnam without congressional approval; he mustered only Morse's vote besides his own.

During the seven-year span from July 1966 through July 1973, Congress recorded one hundred and thirteen votes on proposals related to the war. But its first limitation on U.S. military activities in Southeast Asia was not imposed until 1969—a restriction on American troop deployments in Cambodia and Laos—and it directed its full opposition to a continued commitment in the region only in August 1973, when it voted to stop all bombing throughout Indochina. By then, the U.S. combat forces had been withdrawn and the American prisoners of war held in Hanoi had come home; the argument that "our boys" needed support had lost its validity.

Lyndon Johnson was never confronted by more than token resistance on Capitol Hill to his Vietnam policies. His own aides, though, were increasingly dismayed. In an effort to placate those among them who favored diplomatic flexibility, Johnson approved attempts to start negotiations with North Vietnam. The quest for peace stumbled through a series of secret and often ambiguous maneuvers, some of which briefly seemed to be promising. In many instances, the search for a settlement was conducted by intermediaries who took their dreams for reality in what one cynic dubbed "the race for the Nobel prize."

One of the entrants in the obstacle course was Chester Ronning, a seasoned Canadian diplomat who went to Washington in January 1966 with a suggestion. Having recently been named Canada's "special representative" to both North and South Vietnam, he offered to use his "good offices" to get discussions going with the Communists. He had criticized U.S. policy, and American officials distrusted him. But William Bundy, assistant secretary of state, reluctantly gave him the green light.

After several delays, Ronning met in Hanoi in March with North Vietnam's Prime Minister Pham Van Dong, whose refrain sounded familiar: the regime refused to be bombed to the conference table and would "talk" only when the United States had "unconditionally" ceased its air strikes. The "talks," Pham Van Dong indicated, could eventually develop into formal "negotiations" based on his earlier proposals— which included the demand that the Vietcong be accorded a political role in the south. It was unclear whether the Communists might relax some of these terms, but the American officials who studied Ronning's account of the meeting were really uninterested in clarifying nuances. For one thing, they were not about to recommend an unequivocal halt to the bombing for the sake of vague conversations. For another they feared that any transactions with the North Vietnamese would exacerbate the Saigon government's troubles. The Ronning channel dried up.

Ronning's effort was supplanted by another venture, code-named Marigold, and initiated by Janusz Lewandowski, Polish delegate to the moribund International Control Commission. In late June 1966, Lewandowski saw Giovanni D'Orlandi, the urbane Italian ambassador in Saigon. He had just met with Ho Chi Minh, the Polish diplomat claimed, and he was carrying what he described as a "very specific peace offer." The North Vietnamese were receptive to a "political compromise" and would go "quite a long way" toward such a "settlement." D'Orlandi gathered that the Poles were acting on behalf of the Soviet Union, which wanted an end to the war in order to prevent North Vietnam from edging closer to China. He passed the message on to Ambassador Lodge, who spelled out the intriguing details in a cable to Dean Rusk.

As Lewandowski explained it, the North Vietnamese had dropped their demand that South Vietnam become a neutral state, and they would even tolerate its present government—though they preferred "someone other" than the truculent Nguyen Cao Ky as its head. They had watered down their idea of what the Vietcong would do in the south, requiring only that its representatives "take part" in negotiations, and their attitude toward the American presence in Vietnam had changed drastically. No longer did they insist on an immediate American withdrawal, but were ready to discuss a "reasonable calendar." And they were prepared to accept a "suspension" of the U.S. air strikes against the north as a prelude to talks.

Ambassador-at-Large Averell Harriman had recently been appointed by Johnson to run the "peace shop," as some administration insiders snidely named the search for a diplomatic settlement in Vietnam. He and his deputy, Chester Cooper, a former CIA analyst, were tantalized by Lewandowski's report, and they set diplomatic wheels in motion. Lodge met with Lewandowski in Saigon and other U.S. officials contacted their counterparts elsewhere in the world. Lewandowski meanwhile showed the North Vietnamese his own version of the U.S. position—including, among its points, America's willingness to "take into account" the Vietcong's interests in an eventual political solution to the war. At the end of November, he reported to Lodge that they had agreed to preliminary discussions with American officials in Warsaw—in what would be the first direct encounter with the enemy. Despite misgivings about Lewandowski's formulation, the word went out from Washington to John Gronouski, American ambassador in Warsaw, to arrange for the sessions.

But the administration's military and diplomatic departments had not been synchronized. American aircraft had been striking targets within ten miles of Hanoi since the summer, and they hit oil depots and railroad yards even closer to the city during the first two weeks of December. Polish officials, presumably in touch with the North Vietnamese, warned that continued attacks would jeopardize the Warsaw talks. Harriman and Cooper, until then unaware of the scheduled raids, appealed to Johnson for a pause, and they were backed by McNamara. But Rusk cautioned against a trap, and he was seconded by Walt Rostow, who had recently succeeded McGeorge Bundy as head of the president's national security council staff. On December 6, Johnson vetoed a bombing halt, and the North Vietnamese canceled the Warsaw rendezvous a week later.

So Marigold wilted—or perhaps it was never destined to bloom. A European Communist defector later alleged that Lewandowski had been acting on his own; Wilfred Burchett also dismissed the initiative as inconsequential, saying that "well-meaning friends" of North Vietnam had unilaterally tried to put together a deal. Johnson later brushed aside the episode, saying that "the simple truth was that the North Vietnamese were not ready to talk with us," and John McNaughton of the Pentagon concluded that the ambiguous overture had been "like making smoke signals in a high wind." But to Chester Cooper, patiently scouting every hint of a bargain, it was Johnson who had not been ready to talk—unless, of course, the enemy submitted to his terms.

Johnson similarly sidestepped another possibility, proposed by a pair of private U.S. citizens, Harry Ashmore and William Baggs, who visited Hanoi in January 1967 at the invitation of Ho Chi Minh. Both were newspapermen associated with the Center for the Study of Democratic Institutions, a liberal California think tank, and they were briefed by State Department officials before their departure. They met with Ho for two hours, and he sounded receptive—implying that all issues were negotiable once the United States stopped bombing and ceased the buildup in the south. This was hardly a major breakthrough, but the amateur emissaries discovered to their chagrin back in Washington that neither Johnson nor anyone else showed the slightest interest. Johnson refused to see them, saying that he could not talk with "everybody who's been over there talking with Ho"—as if Americans were flocking to Hanoi. But to assuage Fulbright, whom Ashmore and Baggs had consulted, the president ordered Bill Bundy and Harriman to help the two men draft a message telling Ho that the administration would enter into "secret discussions at any time, without conditions." And the message suggested, as evidence of "good faith," that both sides display "some reciprocal restraint" to indicate that they would not use the negotiating period to gain a "military advantage."

Without informing Ashmore and Baggs, however, Johnson pre-empted their message with a tougher letter of his own. He would not halt the bombing or make any other conciliatory gestures, Johnson told Ho Chi Minh, until he was "assured" that the North Vietnamese infiltration into the south had stopped. Johnson stiffened his line, he later explained, because the North Vietnamese were then taking advantage of a temporary truce over Tet, the lunar New Year holiday, to move men and supplies southward. Ho predictably rejected Johnson's demand—and the exploration ended, leaving Ashmore and Baggs to charge the administration with "duplicity." Johnson had drastically revised the U.S. negotiating position, and the two free-lance intermediaries were not the only ones who were baffled and disappointed.

An earlier plan devised by Johnson's aides—the so-called Phase A–Phase B formula—proposed that the United States would first suspend its air raids against North Vietnam and then, without necessarily publicizing it, the Americans and Communists would both gradually restrict their military actions in South Vietnam and withdraw. The idea was to give the Hanoi leaders an opportunity to retreat without "losing face."

The scheme did not preclude negotiations, but Johnson wanted to avoid a repetition of the Korean experience, when U.S. soldiers died as cease-fire discussions dragged on. Besides, he considered the proposal generous, since he reckoned that America was winning the war.

In his letter to Ho, however, Johnson completely reversed the two-phase formula. Now, he insisted, the Communists would have to wind down the conflict before the United States halted the bombing. Or, as he put it, he was not going to stop the air strikes "merely for talks," but to promote "a long step toward peace itself."

Britain's Prime Minister Harold Wilson, who planned to entertain Aleksei Kosygin in London for a week in early February 1967, believed that his Soviet counterpart could be persuaded to urge the North Vietnamese to compromise. Wilson presumed that the Soviets favored a settlement to prevent their Chinese rivals from increasing their influence in Southeast Asia. He also speculated that the North Vietnamese, then upset by the convulsions of Mao's Cultural Revolution, might be leaning toward the Soviet Union. But Johnson, resentful of Wilson's criticism of America's bombing strategy, was also worried that Wilson might claim credit if the effort yielded results. Still, the president could not afford to alienate an ally—who would surely intimate that a chance for peace had been missed. So he accepted Wilson's proposal to bring Kosygin into the game. Chester Cooper, whom the British trusted, flew to London to serve as liaison man in the operation—code-named Sunflower.

Kosygin seemed eager to cooperate. A British intelligence tap on his telephone recorded his prediction to Leonid Brezhnev, the Soviet Communist party boss in Moscow, that a "great possibility" for a deal was in the offing. His optimism did not guarantee a solution, since the North Vietnamese could be stubborn, even to their Communist patrons, yet the prospects looked promising.

But Johnson and his entourage proceeded with a rare combination of ineptitude and intransigence. They sent Cooper to London without informing him of Johnson's strong letter to Ho. So Cooper advised Wilson that the two-phase formula still represented the American approach, though in fact it was now obsolete. The hope was, Cooper explained, that the halt in bombing for the Tet truce could be prolonged indefinitely if the North Vietnamese responded positively through Kosygin.

Cooper and David Bruce, the American ambassador in London, with guidance from Washington, drafted an outline for the U.S. proposal. It appeared to Wilson to match a separate message that Johnson had sent him, and he handed the document to Kosygin. Cooper, assuming that the operation was on track, went to the theater—leaving word where he could be found, just in case. Midway through the first act of *Fiddler on the Roof*, an usherette roused him. Walt Rostow was telephoning from Washington. The negotiating script had been amended. A new, tougher version was being cabled.

Wilson was staggered. Johnson had switched policy just as the Soviets, for the first time in the war, were consenting to risk their own precarious influence in Hanoi and act as brokers. Not only would the aggressive Chinese taunt them for cooperating with the West, but Kosygin's own prestige in Moscow might be in jeopardy. Wilson fired off a furious personal cable to Johnson, blaming him for "a hell of a situation." Johnson, equally testy, replied that Wilson had modified the verb tense in the proposal, thereby weakening his demand that the North Vietnamese stop their infiltration before the American air strikes ceased.

Wilson, Cooper, and Bruce, desperate to benefit from Kosygin's last few hours in London, hammered out a fresh formula: the United States would continue the bombing pause past Tet, in exchange for which North Vietnamese forces poised to go south would remain in place. They sent it to Washington for approval on February 12, a Sunday, as Wilson asked Kosygin to stand by. Responding late that night, Johnson agreed—on condition that the North Vietnamese accept by Monday afternoon, London time. The deadline was "ridiculous," Bruce told Rusk by telephone—to no avail. The North Vietnamese kept silent. Kosygin went home. And on February 13 Johnson resumed the air raids over North Vietnam. Wilson would afterward deplore the waste of a "historic opportunity"—though it was, in reality, simply another refusal by the belligerents to shift to the conference table before they had improved their battlefield postures.

Henry Kissinger learned the same reality later in 1967, when he made his diplomatic debut in the Vietnam drama. Then a Harvard professor, he became involved accidentally in June at an international gathering in Paris where he encountered Herbert Marcovich, a French biologist. Marcovich mentioned that a French friend of his, Raymond Aubrac, an official of the Food and Agriculture Organization, knew Ho Chi Minh personally—having housed him when Ho was negotiating with the French at Fontainebleau in 1946. Marcovich suggested that the acquaintance might contribute to a political settlement. Kissinger transmitted the idea to the State Department, which agreed. With Kissinger as their

American connection, Aubrac and Marcovich flew to Hanoi in July in a new, unofficial operation, code-named Pennsylvania.

They had a courtesy meeting with Ho, who was old and ill and no longer managed daily affairs; then they discussed substance with Pham Van Dong. He listened carefully as they offered yet another variation of the proposal for a cessation of the U.S. air strikes in exchange for assurances that the Communists would not use the bombing pause to gain a military advantage. Pham Van Dong again demanded an "unconditional" bombing halt as a prelude to negotiations, but he sounded a few moderate notes. The air offensive could be ended without a public announcement because, as he put it, "we do not want to humiliate" the Americans. And, though North Vietnam's goal was a political role for the Vietcong in the south, he envisaged a "broad coalition" in Saigon that could include, "without consideration of past activities," members of the "puppet" government as well as "puppet" army officers. Pham Van Dong, sincere or not, dangled visions of national reconciliation before his two French visitors, saying: "The essential thing is to forget the past."

Aubrac and Marcovich reported to Kissinger in Paris. He transmitted their account to Johnson, who immediately sent a message back through them to Pham Van Dong, officially endorsing the proposal they had made in Hanoi—in diplomatic shorthand, the "no advantage" formula. Johnson even made this milder approach public in a speech in San Antonio in late September. He was willing to stop all air strikes "when this will lead promptly to discussions"—assuming, of course, that North Vietnam "would not take advantage of the bombing cessation or limitation" to strengthen its forces in the south.

A semantic minuet followed. Wilfred Burchett wrote from Hanoi that the Communists were "in no mood for concessions or bargaining"—and would agree only to "talks" and not "negotiations" in exchange for a bombing halt. The North Vietnamese foreign minister, Nguyen Duy Trinh, had said in January that talks "could" start if the air raids stopped; now, in December, he changed the tense—saying that his government "will" talk after the bombing had ceased unconditionally. Soon afterward, Clark Clifford, about to become secretary of defense, responded to this minute move with a tiny step. Testifying before a Senate committee, he interpreted the "no advantage" phrase liberally, suggesting that the administration would not object to the North Vietnamese transporting "the normal amount of goods, munitions, and men" into the south during a cease-fire.

But the nuanced dialogue was a smoke screen. Even as he clamored for peace, Johnson was intensifying the bombing campaign—targeting, for the first time, sites near the center of Hanoi and close to the heart of Haiphong. And the Communists were also escalating—their infiltration into the south was up to some twenty thousand men a month in preparation for a major offensive. The diplomatic explorations would go on, but the protagonists were edging toward a "fight and talk" strategy.

In the middle of 1966, the joint chiefs of staff reckoned that they would have to boost the total American force in Vietnam to more than a half-million men within the next eighteen months. A call-up of the reserves was required; otherwise, they warned, the United States could not easily maintain its international defense obligations. But Johnson once again declined to mobilize the reserves—like taxes, a measure that would spotlight the costs of the conflict and, he feared, sour American public opinion. The cheaper alternative was to step up the U.S. air strikes against North Vietnam. The Pentagon brass also favored fiercer bombing, but Robert McNamara's enthusiasm had cooled off as his confidence in the war effort itself eroded.

It had been "McNamara's war" for a long time, a cause he had promoted tirelessly since the start of President Kennedy's tenure in office. He had viewed the struggle during the early 1960s almost exclusively in quantitative terms, calculating that the United States could win simply by committing its superior resources effectively. Now, however, his faith was slipping.

I first discerned the change in February 1966 at the Honolulu conference, when he invited a few reporters into his hotel room for a rare private briefing. His face seemed to be grayer and his patent leather hair thinner, and his voice lacked the authority it had once projected when he would point briskly to graphs and flip-charts to prove his rosy appraisals. Johnson had launched the sustained U.S. air offensive against North Vietnam exactly a year before; but, McNamara told us, the raids had not succeeded—and could not. A rural society could not be blasted into submission, he said with unusual emotion: "No amount of bombing can end the war."

By these discreet private hints to journalists, McNamara was seeking to circulate his concerns through Washington. For the joint chiefs of staff were then pressing for an ambitious bombing program. They could obliterate almost every oil installation, bridge, airfield, railroad, power plant, port facility, and factory in North Vietnam, they argued, and thus hasten the end of the war. McNamara partly approved their recommendations, at least on paper—for a devious motive: he was certain that the raids would be ineffectual, and only by demonstrating the failure could he subdue the generals and admirals and their congressional confederates, and persuade Johnson the struggle must be ended by diplomatic means.

As usual, Johnson procrastinated, ever fearful that China might intervene or that a Soviet ship might accidentally be hit, igniting World War III. In June 1967, he authorized air attacks against petroleum storage sites near Hanoi and Haiphong, which U.S. military spokesmen initially hailed as devastating—"the most significant, the most important strike of the war," one officer said. The facts indicated otherwise. Though temporarily inconvenienced, the North Vietnamese had not been deprived of fuel, much of which they had dispersed to concealed spots elsewhere; their troop and supply movements into the south continued unabated; and, as a CIA report later disclosed, they cleverly took advantage of the raids to extract larger doses of aid from China and the Soviet Union. True to McNamara's expectations, neither their will nor their ability to carry on the fight had been shaken.

Among the factors that influenced McNamara were the changing attitudes of his civilian aides—men like John McNaughton and Adam Yarmolinsky, whose zest for the war was fast evaporating. Searching for fresh ideas, they canvassed several prominent scholars, including Jerome Wiesner of MIT and George Kistiakowsky of Harvard, both former presidential science advisers, who in turn assembled forty-seven of their academic colleagues at a school in Wellesley, Massachusetts, for deliberations throughout the summer of 1966. The group emerged with what would be called the Jason study, named for a division of the Institute of Defense Analyses, the think tank that had organized the conference, and its blunt conclusions further confirmed McNamara's mounting reservations about the direction of U.S. policy in Vietnam.

The bombing campaign, the study said, was having "no measurable direct effect" on enemy military activities—and it restated the familiar reasons for that evaluation: North Vietnam was "basically a subsistence agricultural economy" that presented an "unrewarding target" for air raids; the volume of supplies sent south was too small to be stopped by air strikes and, in any case, the country had ample manpower to keep its primitive logistical network intact; intelligence estimates showed that infiltration into the south had risen since the bombing began and could continue to increase; and Chinese and Soviet assistance was more than compensating for the damage being inflicted. As for the effect of the air offensive on the morale of the North Vietnamese leadership and population, the report's observation simply underscored the testimony of nearly every foreign visitor to Hanoi within the past year. "The bombing clearly strengthened popular support of the regime by engendering patriotic and nationalistic enthusiasm to resist the attacks."

The scholars, under some obligation to offer a positive alternative to their thoroughly negative assessment, endorsed an idea originally suggested by McNamara—to stretch an electronic fence for roughly a hundred miles through the area separating the two zones of Vietnam that would block enemy traffic from the north into the south. It could be outfitted with the latest detection devices and sophisticated mines, and it would be monitored on the ground and from the air by up-to-date acoustical and photographic equipment. Despite objections from Westmoreland and other officers, construction of the barrier began soon afterward, but the project quickly turned out to be absurd, and it was abandoned.

In October 1966, back in Vietnam for the first time in nearly a year, McNamara again lapsed into divergent public and private statements. Progress "has exceeded our expectations," he assured the news media—but, he informed Johnson confidentially, he was only "a little less pessimistic" than he had been on his last trip because "we have by and large blunted" the enemy initiative. Still, he added grimly, he saw "no reasonable way to bring the war to an end soon." Though they were suffering huge casualties, the North Vietnamese and Vietcong could "more than replace" their losses through recruitment and infiltration, which had not been slowed down by the bombing. The Saigon government seemed more solid, yet the "pacification" effort had "gone backward." The Communist presence had spread, so that its political apparatus "thrives in most of the country," and "full security exists nowhere"—not even in areas supposedly under American control. Worst of all, South Vietnam's leadership and population were apathetic, corrupt, and undisciplined, and there appeared to be no prospect of stirring them out of their torpor. "This important war must be fought and won by the Vietnamese themselves. We have known this from the beginning. But the discouraging truth is that, as was the case in 1961 and 1963 and 1965, we have not found the formula, the catalyst, for training and inspiring them into effective action."

McNamara now advocated a drastic change of approach. He urged that the U.S. air offensive against North Vietnam be "stabilized"—contending that bigger raids would not deter the enemy and might, among other dangers, raise the "serious risk of drawing us into open war with China." He suggested limiting American troop increases—arguing that the total U.S. force in South Vietnam be kept at fewer than a half-million men, well below the seven hundred thousand in Westmoreland's schedule. He recommended a more vigorous pacification drive—and warned that tough reforms had to be imposed to prompt the Saigon regime to improve its performance. Above all, he proposed "credible" gestures aimed at inducing the Communists to negotiate—such as a total bombing halt, or a "realistic plan" to give the Vietcong a political voice in the south.

This was not a prescription for surrender but a scenario for restraint. Hold the line, buy time, minimize the costs and hazards of the war, McNamara was saying, and the American public will support a protracted struggle that promises neither defeat nor victory yet might, eventually, finish satisfactorily.

The joint chiefs of staff reacted with predictable anger. They rejected McNamara's grim assessment and claimed that the situation had "improved substantially over the past year." Nor would they agree to a curb on the air campaign against North Vietnam. The air attacks were America's "trump card"—not to be bargained away except for an equivalent concession, such as an end to "aggression" in South Vietnam. Finally, pleading for stronger action, they asserted that "the American people, our allies and our enemies alike, are increasingly uncertain as to our resolution to pursue the war to a successful conclusion."

From their own viewpoint, the professional soldiers had a logical case. Trained to wage a conventional conflict on the plains of central Europe, they had not originally been disposed to intervene in Vietnam. Once involved, however, they wanted to win—though their definition of victory was cloudy. Now, with McNamara's zeal dissipating, they were alarmed lest impending high-level decisions foil a proper war effort. Transmitting their "unequivocal" sense of concern to Johnson, they again pressed him to make "more effective and extensive use of our air and naval superiority"—and, as they put it, deliver North Vietnam a "sharp knock."

Late in October 1966, Johnson journeyed to Manila for another planning conference with the South Vietnamese leaders, coupling his official sessions with prodigious feats of optimistic oratory. One day, surreptitiously absenting himself from the meetings, he flew to the vast American base at Camranh Bay—the first incumbent president to visit Vietnam. There he plunged into a crowd of stunned GIs, exhorting them to "nail the coonskin to the wall." But despite his verbal exuberance, Johnson waffled. Gravely disappointing the joint chiefs of staff, he opted for McNamara's modest plan to scale down the rate of escalation—yet the decision, like all his decisions, was subject to change. Meanwhile, he sought comfort in the upbeat accounts handed him by aides like Walt Rostow and Robert Komer, who was soon to become head of pacification programs in Vietnam.

Komer, a former CIA analyst, was a shrewd and energetic bureaucrat whose sensitive antennae were tuned to Johnson's desires. Once, after producing an implausibly buoyant "progress" report on Vietnam for the White House, he was discussing its contents with a group of correspondents. "Come on, Bob," said one of the journalists, "you know damned well that the situation isn't that good." Komer, undaunted, replied in his nasal twang: "Listen, the president didn't ask for a 'situation' report, he asked for a 'progress' report. And that's what I've given him—not a report on the situation, but a report on the progress we've made."

Thus, in a "prognosis" for the future, Komer concluded in late 1966 that "slow, painful, and incredibly expensive though it may be—we're beginning to 'win' the war." This did not mean, he added prudently, that "we're going to win." But, he asserted, "we are successfully countering" North Vietnamese infiltration, and Vietcong strength in the south "has probably already peaked out." The "trend line" showed, therefore, that the Communists might conceivably "find it wiser to negotiate" than to continue defying U.S. might. Like all hopeful forecasts, however, this one hedged. Could the Americans and their South Vietnamese allies "mount a maximum effort" in the year ahead? Was the United States "prepared to stick it out as long as necessary"? Or would the American public tire of the war? Komer left those questions unanswered, but Lyndon Johnson had a positive response. By the beginning of 1967, more than six thousand U.S. soldiers had already been killed in Vietnam. Yet, Johnson proclaimed in his State of the Union address to Congress, he would still "stand firm."

A nagging debate over strategy divided the Johnson administration during the first half of 1967, and though observers identified the squabbling factions as "hawks" and "doves," the distinction was an oversimplification. Nobody of any stature within the president's circle at the time said openly or even privately that the U.S. bombing should stop and American forces be withdrawn if there were parallel concessions on the Communist side. Partisans of such an approach would only begin to emerge after the Tet offensive of 1968, when the domestic political price of the war had apparently become unbearable. So the quarrel that poisoned the Johnson administration was between those who advocated an extremely tough campaign against the enemy and those who were less belligerent—with many straddling the two positions.

Nor could the dispute be portrayed as a straightforward rivalry between soldiers and civilians. The most pugnacious hard-liners were naturally the top soldiers, whose business it was to wage war—the joint chiefs of staff and the top operational officers, notably Westmoreland and Admiral Sharp, the commander for the Pacific. But their key supporter in the executive branch was a civilian, Walt Rostow, the sound of whose saber rattled throughout Washington. This group also included Dean Rusk, who equated flexibility with capitulation, as well as several CIA officials. The skeptics, on the other hand, mainly comprised McNamara and his civilian aides at the Pentagon, who were backed at the State Department by Averell Harriman and his "peace shop." A number of CIA analysts shared their misgivings, and among their cautious sympathizers were some lower-ranking generals in Vietnam who had learned the futility of the conflict from direct experience. In between, meanwhile, were middle-level bureaucrats such as William Bundy. And there was Lyndon Johnson himself, who swung from depths of doubt to peaks of ferocity. Whenever possible, however, he deferred decisions.

A different pattern prevailed on Capitol Hill, where Johnson faced two small opposition blocs on the Vietnam issue. One, crystallized around Senator Fulbright and his Foreign Relations Committee, was pushing for a way out of the war. The other, centered on Senator Stennis and the Senate Armed Services Committee, wanted stronger action. Johnson knew that most congressmen would toe the administration line. He was irritated by Fulbright, whom he mocked as "Senator Halfbright," but he dared not taunt Stennis and his followers, who might tar him with being timid toward Communism. One of his priorities was to appease the conservatives—without becoming their captive.

By 1967 Johnson had been escalating the war steadily for eighteen months with dismal results. A CIA summary of the air strikes against North Vietnam during 1966 told him part of the story: hundreds of bridges had been wrecked, but virtually all of them had been rebuilt or bypassed. Thousands of freight cars, trucks, and other vehicles had been destroyed, but North Vietnamese traffic was moving smoothly. Roughly three quarters of the country's oil storage facilities had been eliminated, but there were no fuel shortages. The bombing had cost the United States nearly ten dollars for every dollar's worth of damage inflicted.

The morale of the Communists had not been weakened, and they were continuing to supply their forces in the south.

The knee-jerk reaction of the generals and admirals was to demand more bombing. "Bomb, bomb, bomb—that's all they know," Johnson grumbled, yet kept authorizing new targets, hoping to mollify the senior officers and their congressional cronies. But after every new attack, they raised the ante. In April 1967, for instance, when Johnson permitted raids against power transformers, ammunition dumps, and other objectives near Hanoi and Haiphong, the assaults barely hindered the enemy, and soon the joint chiefs had convinced Johnson to approve further bombing. Throughout this dialogue, they issued statements extolling the air campaign as "highly effective."

In the spring of 1967, back home for consultations, General Westmoreland acceded to Johnson's request to be optimistic in public, affirming in a series of speeches and interviews that the evidence pointed to "steady and encouraging success." Behind closed doors, however, he warned Johnson that "the war could go on indefinitely" unless he found "a way to halt North Vietnamese infiltration" and unless the Vietcong organization seriously began "to disintegrate," a prospect he considered "unlikely." What he wanted was more men, and even then he saw no rapid success. Like a corporation executive presenting a production schedule to the chairman of the board, he reeled off the numbers for Johnson.

Under the current plan—to deploy a total of four hundred and seventy thousand U.S. troops in Vietnam by late 1967—he could "do little better than hold our own." Increase the force by a hundred thousand and, he estimated, "the war could well go on for three years." Add yet another hundred thousand: he could shrink the schedule to two years. After all, Westmoreland explained, "we are fighting a war of attrition in Southeast Asia."

But this was not quite the same as manufacturing shoes or automobiles. "When we add divisions, can't the enemy add divisions, and if so, where does it all end?" Johnson asked. Westmoreland conceded it "likely" that the Communists would put in more troops. Johnson, haunted by the memory of the Chinese pouring into Korea, envisioned a similar disaster in Vietnam. "At what point," he pressed, "does the enemy ask for volunteers?" Westmoreland could only reply: "That is a good question." Johnson did not need an answer. "I'm not going to spit in China's face," he later confided to an aide.

Just as he strung along the joint chiefs of staff by extending their bombing targets inch by inch, so Johnson ultimately gave Westmoreland a troop increment of only forty-five thousand men, while leaving open the possibility of sending others. And the bureaucrats re-enacted their routine of churning out fresh contingency plans. One was a bold recommendation by Rostow for invading North Vietnam. Mercifully, it was shelved, but Rostow persisted with the proposal—even claiming years after the war that it might have been the key to victory.

One of the most perceptive documents was an unsolicited analysis drafted by Alain Enthoven, a senior assistant to McNamara. An expert on European defense issues, Enthoven dealt only tangentially with Vietnam at the Pentagon. He was, so to speak, an inside observer, with no personal or professional ax to grind. The real force confronting the United States in Vietnam, he wrote, was less Communism than "the strongest political current in the world today—nationalism." That force had welded the North Vietnamese together through more than twenty years of almost uninterrupted fighting, and, he predicted, it would inspire them to "continue to endure great hardship." Thus the American bombing would not "hurt them so badly as to destroy their society or, more to the point, their hope of conquering all Vietnam." The basic challenge for America, therefore, was to promote an "equally strong" sense of nationalism in the south. Without that, "we will have lost everything we have invested . . . no matter what military success we may achieve."

Domestic U.S. opinion was crucial, Enthoven went on. The struggle was "a race between, on the one hand, the development of a viable South Vietnam and, on the other, a gradual loss in public support, or even tolerance, for the war" among Americans at home. The Communists were betting that America's patience would wear thin. To avoid that, the administration had to arrest the U.S. public's declining support for the war while accelerating South Vietnam's development. "Our horse," Enthoven stressed, "must finish first."

But how could the American public be persuaded to back the commitment? For one thing, Enthoven argued, American casualties had to be held down. More significantly, the "diversion of the national wealth from badly needed domestic programs" had to be curbed, and it was vital to stop the "ominous history" of relentless escalation. Above all, Americans had to be given some sense of when the war would end. Only then could they be expected to make sacrifices.

Vietnam was already so saturated with American soldiers chasing an elusive enemy that a U.S. battalion's "kill rate" averaged less than one Vietcong per day, Enthoven observed. Besides, Americans could not cope with pacification, which required "political and economic progress" under Saigon government sponsorship rather than "military victories." And, he cautioned, a big U.S. buildup would ultimately weaken South Vietnam. "If we continue to add forces and to Americanize the war, we will only erode whatever incentives the South Vietnamese people may now have to help themselves in this fight. Similarly, it would be a further sign to the South Vietnamese leaders that we will carry any load, regardless of their actions."

Enthoven concluded that "we're up against an enemy who just may have found a dangerously clever strategy for licking the United States": to "wait us out," keeping their losses at "a level low enough to be sustained indefinitely, but high enough to tempt us to increase our forces to the point of U.S. public rejection of the war."

A similar mood of foreboding clouded other civilians in the Defense Department. In contrast to their military colleagues, the civilians were not fettered with a rigorous belief that firepower yielded results. Nor did they fear that their careers hinged on proving that bullets and bombs would succeed. So they could assess the situation more dispassionately— or at least express their misgivings more candidly. At that stage, though, they were still in what Leslie Gelb, then a young Pentagon analyst, later termed a "twilight zone"—they had not yet reconciled their private pessimism with the official policy of optimism.

In many instances, these bureaucrats would return home in the evening to face puzzled or even defiant wives and children. Gelb's wife, who often would have watched the war on the television news before his arrival, would greet him with the question: "What are you guys doing out there?" Others had college-age sons and daughters who attended "teach-ins" or participated in antiwar demonstrations, and disputes now poisoned the dinner conversation. John McNaughton, a certified hardliner a year earlier, was disturbed enough to say to McNamara that "a feeling is widely and strongly held" around the country that " 'the Establishment' is out of its mind." The pervasive opinion was, as McNaughton described it, "that we are trying to impose some U.S. image on distant peoples we cannot understand, and that we are carrying the thing to absurd lengths." What loomed was "the worst split in our people in more than a century," compounded by the government's increasing isolation from the public. McNaughton noted sadly that McGeorge Bundy, George Ball, and Bill Moyers, all of whom had at least had the guts to voice misgivings about the war, had resigned. And, he asked ominously, "Who next?"

McNamara would be next—but not until months later. Yet his opponents were already mobilizing against him, and they began to close ranks in May 1967, when he once again set forth his recommendations for a future policy in Vietnam.

The Communists were not going to negotiate until after the U.S. elections in November 1968, he now estimated—and neither moderation nor escalation would change their minds. Confronted by "imperfect alternatives," the United States ought to adopt what amounted to a holding operation. He proposed that the air campaign against North Vietnam be limited to bombings of enemy staging areas and infiltration routes in the southernmost provinces, and he emphasized the importance of promoting the pacification programs in South Vietnam more energetically. And he urged that the administration cool the domestic controversy over the war by avoiding such explosive issues as the call-up of the army reserve.

The plan enraged the joint chiefs of staff, who saw it as nothing less than "defeatism." Reams of memos flew from their Pentagon offices across the Potomac to the White House, the Congress, and various other government departments, restating and refining every earlier argument they had advanced. Their outburst inflamed the strategy debate afresh, and Washington's paper mills shattered all previous records as different bureaus responded. Johnson, caught in the cross fire, reacted as he usually did: he compromised and improvised. He rejected McNamara's proposal to curb the air offensive but maintained most of his former restrictions on the bombing, and he also rebuffed Westmoreland's request for a large troop increase. But the generals and admirals would not accept the setback without a fight, especially when they could deploy their big guns on Capitol Hill.

John Cornelius Stennis of Mississippi, then celebrating his twentieth year in the Senate, was a classic southern conservative Democrat of his generation. On the domestic front, he had implacably resisted civil rights and other liberal legislation, while in foreign affairs he distrusted international entanglements. Coupled with his insularity, however, was a firm conviction that, once involved in conflict abroad, the United States could consider nothing less than victory. He had been uneasy in early 1954, when the French were pressing the Eisenhower administration to rescue them from defeat in Indochina, fearing that "we will move to a point from which there will be no return." But after Lyndon Johnson's troop commitment in 1965, he saw the course without reservations. Despite "many regrets that we are in there," he said, America's present "purpose is to win"—and he demanded that Johnson's Great Society programs be "relegated to the rear" in order to release the resources to crush the enemy and achieve "peace with honor."

Stennis's views endeared him to the Pentagon's senior soldiers. They also admired him for his tangible influence. As a dynamic veteran of the Senate Armed Services Committee, he could bargain on their behalf in the congressional marketplace, gaining them advantages through intricate legislative deals. Either directly or through leaks to the press, they would apprise him and his like-minded colleagues of their requirements and grievances, certain at least of sympathy and frequently of action. So, late in the spring of 1967, they complained to him about McNamara and others, and Stennis scheduled closed hearings of the Preparedness Subcommittee of the Armed Services Committee for August to investigate the alleged attempts by "unskilled civilian amateurs" to shackle the "professional military experts."

Henry Kissinger and his two French intermediaries, Marcovich and Aubrac, were then scouting peace possibilities with a North Vietnamese representative in Paris, and the question of the air campaign was an important item on their agenda. But for Johnson, Stennis was a higher priority. On August 9, the day that the hearings opened, he eased the restrictions on bombing and permitted U.S. aircraft to hit previously prohibited targets within the city limits of Hanoi and Haiphong as well as near the Chinese border. As the subcommittee sessions went on, the raids proliferated. On August 20, American airplanes flew more than two hundred sorties, the largest daily number to date in the war. The next day, Johnson's nightmare came near to becoming reality when the Chinese shot down two U.S. aircraft that had accidentally crossed their frontier. Stennis was not deterred.

Beginning with Admiral Sharp, who had flown in from Honolulu, a procession of top navy, army, and air force officers testified, each elaborating variations on the same theme—the absolute necessity to continue and even expand the air war against North Vietnam. They pointed to graphs and charts and statistical tables, and claimed, among other things, that the bombing had until now prevented the Communists from doubling their forces in the south, which would have compelled the United States to deploy an additional eight hundred thousand troops at a cost of $75 billion "just to hold our own." If the raids were not more effective, it was because the administration had imposed "overly restrictive controls" that had spared important targets, escalating the attacks too gradually and giving the enemy time to build up "formidable air defenses." To halt or curb the air campaign, therefore, would be a "disaster."

McNamara, whose turn came at the end of August, also showed up at the hearings with an arsenal of graphs and statistics. Facing him in the chamber besides Stennis were Senators Henry Jackson, Stuart Symington, and Strom Thurmond, all partial to the military establishment. McNamara welcomed the inquiry, figuring that by influencing these men he could deflate the generals and admirals; sensing that the president preferred to remain aloof from the proceeding in order to preserve his flexibility, he had not cleared his presentation in advance with Johnson; so, very much alone, he tried to defend the strategy that the president had approved.

In his precise, professorial, faintly patronizing style, he stressed that the bombing of North Vietnam had been conceived only as a "supplement" to the conflict in the south, not as a "substitute for the arduous ground war." But, discarding his own earlier optimistic expectations, he had little positive to say for the air raids. They had not reduced the movement of enemy supplies into South Vietnam, since the Communists needed only fifteen tons a day to fight—and "even if the quantity were five times that amount, it could be transported by only a few trucks." They had not seriously damaged the economy of North Vietnam, which "is agrarian and simple"—and whose population was unfamiliar with "the modern comforts and conveniences that most of us in the Western world take for granted." They had not broken morale, since the North Vietnamese were "accustomed to discipline and are no strangers to deprivation and death"—and "continue to respond to the political direction" of their leaders. As for the leaders themselves, nothing offered "any confidence that they can be bombed to the negotiating table." The sole strategy for knocking the North Vietnamese out of the war from the air, McNamara concluded, would be some form of genocide: "Enemy operations in the south cannot, on the basis of any reports I have seen, be stopped by air bombardment—short, that is, of the virtual annihilation of North Vietnam and its people."

Stennis and his associates were not swayed. Indeed, their verdict had been reached before the hearings had opened. Civilian authority, they asserted in a final report, had "consistently overruled the unanimous recommendations of military commanders and the joint chiefs of staff," who had repeatedly proposed "systematic, timely, and hard-hitting" actions. Their simple prescription was to put the soldiers in charge.

Lyndon Johnson was not about to yield his constitutional prerogatives as commander in chief to a cabal of right-wing politicians and soldiers. But the hearings unsettled him. He privately denounced the senators for attempting to drive him deeper into the war, yet he wanted to avoid a collision with them, especially when opinion surveys told him that most Americans favored tougher measures—their mood pungently expressed in the bumper sticker that demanded, WIN OR GET OUT. Once again, his expedient was appeasement.

Violating his own cautious instincts, he approved air strikes against fifty-seven new North Vietnamese targets—nearly half of them in heavily populated areas and some in the sensitive zone near the Chinese border. He also invited General Earle Wheeler, chairman of the joint chiefs of staff, to participate regularly in his Tuesday luncheons at the White House—where, in a second-floor dining room decorated with a mural of Cornwallis surrendering at Yorktown, he and his inner circle deliberated policy. And he decided to dump McNamara.

McNamara had been a model cabinet officer for Johnson—able, conscientious, discreet, and, above all, loyal. But Johnson was ruthless, and McNamara had become a liability. Not only had he put Johnson on the spot by antagonizing the Stennis faction, but he relentlessly clung to the same line at the White House. In front of Rusk, Rostow, Wheeler, and the others at a Tuesday luncheon in late October, he bluntly told Johnson that the current strategy in Vietnam was "dangerous, costly, and unsatisfactory," and he also produced a memorandum recommending steps to "stabilize our efforts": maintain the air strikes against North Vietnam at the present level for the next two months, then halt the bombing—partly to invite a Communist response, or at least demonstrate that the United States was "not blocking negotiations." Stop building up the American combat force in the south, and study ways to reduce casualties—while drafting plans to give the South Vietnamese "greater responsibility for their own security."

Johnson, always in quest of a consensus, circulated McNamara's memo in some instances without identifying the author. The reactions were overwhelmingly negative. General Maxwell Taylor, now a special consultant, warned that the proposed "pullback" would "probably degenerate into a pullout." Westmoreland and Ellsworth Bunker, who had replaced Lodge as ambassador in Saigon, were equally hostile, while Rusk, though receptive to the idea that the South Vietnamese should do more, opposed a bombing pause that would eliminate the "incentive for peace." Abe Fortas and Clark Clifford, invited to comment, were also unfavorable. The "duty" of the administration, said Fortas, was to fulfill what he believed to be the desire of the American people—"namely, to prevent North Vietnamese domination of South Vietnam by military force or subversion." Clifford, whose attitude was to change sharply only a few months hence, reacted even more strongly. McNamara's plan, he wrote to Johnson, would "retard the possibility of concluding the conflict rather than accelerating it"—and, in his flamboyant courtroom manner, he imagined North Vietnam's response to the "stabilization" of America's strategy: "The chortles of unholy glee issuing from Hanoi would be audible in every capital of the world. Is this evidence of our zeal and courage to stay the course? Of course not! It would be interpreted to be exactly what it is. A resigned and discouraged effort to find a way out of a conflict for which we had lost our will and dedication."

Typically, Johnson had sought a consensus in order to confirm his own inclination, which was to reject McNamara's proposals. An "unrequited" bombing halt, he said in December, would "be read in both Hanoi and the United States as a sign of weakening will"—as would the "so-called policy of stabilization" on the ground in South Vietnam. So, given a vote of no-confidence, McNamara had to go. But the disagreement over Vietnam had been complicated by another, related factor that may have been more crucial for Johnson. The other element was Robert Kennedy.

Johnson feared and loathed the Kennedys. Now, Bobby had become a strident critic of the war—and, worse yet, his switch was paying off. A poll of presidential potentialities conducted in July 1967 showed Kennedy trailing Johnson by 39 percent to 45 percent; a survey in October showed Kennedy ahead by a margin of 20 percent. In Johnson's eyes, the logic of the situation was crystal-clear: Kennedy had persuaded his intimate friend McNamara to turn against the war—which meant, quite plainly, that McNamara had been persuaded to double-cross Johnson. "Every day," Johnson later recalled, "Bobby would call up McNamara, telling him that the war was terrible and immoral, and that he had to leave." The pressure on McNamara grew to such a pitch, according to Johnson, that he came close to a nervous breakdown—and one consequence, the president implied, was his confrontation with the Stennis subcommittee.

McNamara's dismissal has never been elucidated. Johnson's version, as he recounted it to Doris Kearns, was that McNamara came close to "cracking," and it would have been "a damn unfair thing to force him to stay" in the administration. So they discussed alternatives and, Johnson said, he got McNamara the presidency of the World Bank—"the only job he really wanted then." But Arthur Schlesinger, Jr., basing his information on a conversation between McNamara and Kennedy, has a different account: that McNamara, unaware that Johnson had procured him the World Bank post, learned of his ouster from the press. In any case, Johnson replaced him with Clark Clifford, an old crony whom he could trust—or so he thought at the time.

McNamara left the government a disillusioned man, and he made no attempt to conceal his anguish at a farewell luncheon at the State Department in late February 1968, just before his official departure. Among those present, along with Rusk, Clifford, and other senior officials, was Harry McPherson, a Johnson aide, who recalled to me his own astonishment at McNamara's display of emotion: "He reeled off the familiar statistics—how we had dropped more bombs on Vietnam than on all of Europe during World War II. Then his voice broke, and there were tears in his eyes as he spoke of the futility, the crushing futility, of the air war. The rest of us sat silently—I for one with my mouth open, listening to the secretary of defense talk that way about a campaign for which he had, ultimately, been responsible. I was pretty shocked."

In Vietnam itself, Westmoreland resolutely pursued his strategy of attrition, with a series of search-and-destroy operations code-named Junction City and Francis Marion and Kingfisher; and the enemy "body count" mounted astronomically. By the end of 1967, the U.S. troop presence was up to nearly a half million, an increase of a hundred thousand during the year, and American soldiers killed in action exceeded nine thousand—bringing total battlefield deaths for the past two years to more than fifteen thousand. More than a million and a half tons of bombs had been dropped since the air strikes began, on both the north and the south. But the war was deadlocked. General Fred Weyand, one of Westmoreland's field commanders, grimly measured the progress for a visiting Washington official: "Before I came out here a year ago, I thought we were at zero. I was wrong. We were at minus fifty. Now we're at zero."

Equally worrisome to Johnson was the domestic weariness with the war—especially on the eve of an election year. He had tried to placate the right-wingers by scuttling McNamara, yet they continued to press him for further escalation. Their impatience was not unlike the mood of the public, whose disillusionment with the war appeared to reflect displeasure with Johnson's leadership more than with the commitment itself. Meanwhile, Johnson was alienating his progressive constituency, which had supported him for his civil rights and social programs. Allard Lowenstein, a liberal activist, had been laboring since the summer to get an antiwar Democrat to challenge Johnson in the presidential race. Bobby Kennedy demurred, figuring that the moment was not ripe. But Senator Eugene McCarthy of Minnesota, an iconoclastic figure, announced on November 30, 1967, that he would run against Johnson in the primaries as an opposition candidate to the war. Johnson saw McCarthy for what he was—a stalking horse for Kennedy—and the sight heightened his sense of beleaguerment. The street demonstrations were also enraging him; during one particularly noisy period of protests, he harried an aide, "How can I hit them in the nuts? Tell me how I can hit them in the nuts."

Johnson railed against "gutless" bureaucrats who leaked "defeatist" information to "simpleton" reporters; "it's gotten so," he told a visitor to the White House, "you can't have intercourse with your wife without it being spread around by traitors." But in contrast to Richard Nixon, who was to organize agents to harass or spy on dissenters, Johnson believed that he could reform his adversaries—and he mounted an impressive public relations machine.

One of Rostow's assistants monitored congressional speeches, deluging critics with "correct" information supplied by a special White House research team. To help Americans get the "facts," Rostow himself chaired a "psychological strategy committee," which released favorable government reports on the war to the media. Its equivalent in Saigon, run by Barry Zorthian and a cast of hundreds, fed correspondents everything from statistics to captured enemy documents, nearly all designed to prove that the war was being won. And Johnson personally participated in the effort, touring military bases and naval installations around the country to promote optimism and confidence.

As presidents do in moments of crisis, he sought comfort from distinguished outsiders as well. His aides saw to it that a "citizens' committee" was formed of more than a hundred prestigious Americans, including former Presidents Truman and Eisenhower, to rally public opinion behind the administration. Another group, dubbed the "wise men," included elder statesmen like former Secretary of State Dean Acheson, retired Ambassador Robert Murphy, and the prominent New York banker John McCloy. Convened in early November at the State Department, they were handed reports and briefed orally, and they predictably endorsed Johnson's policy without the faintest awareness that in a few months events would compel them to reverse their views and stimulate fresh decisions.

On the theory that battle-scarred soldiers were irresistible, Johnson summoned Westmoreland home in mid-November to revive the country's flagging spirit. Westmoreland later recollected that he had compunctions about fulfilling the public relations task, but he obeyed orders. His tour schedule was meticulously planned to give him broad exposure—except to critics who might pose pernicious questions. Carefully steered away from Senator Fulbright and his ilk, Westmoreland met with the more sympathetic Senate and House Armed Services Committees, and he attended a White House banquet to which Johnson had invited the tamer members of Congress. Westmoreland performed perfectly throughout, never uttering a gloomy word. "The ranks of the Vietcong are thinning steadily," he assured a gathering at the Pentagon, and he promised a National Press Club audience that "we have reached an important point when the end begins to come into view." And he defied the Communists to stage a massive attack. "I hope they try something," he told a *Time* interviewer, "because we are looking for a fight."

So were the Communists in Vietnam. Their leaders had been planning a major offensive since the summer—and, by the fall, their paper mills were working overtime, instructing military units and political cadres to prepare for a huge drive that would throw the Americans and the Saigon regime into "utmost confusion." The present juncture, said one directive, was a "golden opportunity" to "liberate" hamlets and villages, towns, cities, and South Vietnam "as a whole." In Hanoi following the war, a retired North Vietnamese officer recalled to me that he and his comrades were told to prepare for the drive because "Uncle Ho was very old and we had to liberate the south before his death." The massive attack erupted on Tet, the lunar New Year, and for Lyndon Johnson it brought the end into view.

14 Tet

A wounded GI being helped by his buddies during the battle of Hué in 1968. The toughest fighting occurred at the Citadel, which the Communists held tenaciously. American artillery and aircraft also bombed and shelled the city.

Early in 1968, American marines were besieged by a massive Communist force at Khesanh, in the northern part of South Vietnam. To President Johnson and other Americans, the siege was reminiscent of the Vietminh encirclement of the French at Dienbienphu.

Johnson followed the course of the battle at Khesanh on a sand table constructed in the White House situation room. He is seen here with Walt Rostow (right), his national security adviser, George Christian (left), his press secretary, and General Robert Ginsburg.

Communist officers prepared a major strike to take place during Tet, the Vietnamese lunar New Year, at the end of January 1968. The offensive was to be carried out mainly by southern Vietcong units, except in the northern provinces, where North Vietnamese troops were deployed.

A squad of Vietcong commandos succeeded in smashing into the U.S. embassy compound in Saigon as the Tet offensive started. They killed five Americans. Ambassador Ellsworth Bunker (in white shirt) looks at one of the Vietcong casualties afterward.

A girl discovers the corpse of a relative following the battle of Hué. The bodies of nearly 3,000 South Vietnamese executed by the Communists were exhumed, including soldiers, officials, and civilians suspected of government sympathies.

Colonel Nguyen Ngoc Loan, South Vietnam's police chief, summarily executes a Vietcong suspect in Saigon. A filmed version of the startling event was shown on international television.

A North Vietnamese soldier killed during the battle for Hué. As often occurred, his body was looted for valuables by South Vietnamese troops. The North Vietnamese sustained heavy losses, having uncharacteristically tried to hold Hué against superior U.S. firepower.

South Vietnamese soldiers carry a casualty of the fighting in Saigon during the Tet offensive. The Communists struck towns and cities throughout South Vietnam, expecting the assaults to inspire uprisings by the urban population.

In mid-March, having observed Senator McCarthy's showing, New York Senator Robert Kennedy entered the presidential race. The polls at the time showed that he was more popular than Johnson—and his appearance in the contest alarmed the president.

Senator Eugene McCarthy of Minnesota became a leading opponent of the war in 1967. He lost to President Johnson in the March 1968 New Hampshire primary by only 300 votes.

In an effort to change Johnson's commitment to the war, Clark Clifford mobilized a group of elder statesmen, the "wise men." In front of Johnson (left to right) are former Ambassador Henry Cabot Lodge, former Secretary of State Dean Acheson, and retired General Omar Bradley.

On the evening of March 31, 1968, Johnson stunned the nation by announcing that he would not run for re-election. He appeared to have been defeated by recent events in Vietnam. In fact, he had been pondering the decision for many months.

In all honesty, we didn't achieve our main objective, which was to spur uprisings throughout the south. Still, we inflicted heavy casualties on the Americans and their puppets, and that was a big gain for us. As for making an impact in the United States, it had not been our intention—but it turned out to be a fortunate result.

—Tran Do

I have concluded that I should not permit the presidency to become involved in the partisan divisions that are developing in this political year. . . . Accordingly, I shall not seek, and I will not accept, the nomination of my party for another term as your president.

—Lyndon Johnson

After years of viewing the war on television, Americans at home had become accustomed to a familiar pattern of images. Columns of troops, disgorged from hovering helicopters, cut through dense jungles or plodded across muddy rice fields toward faraway villages, occasionally stumbling onto mines or booby traps, or drawing fire from hidden guerrillas. Artillery shelled distant targets from lonely bases, and aircraft bombed the vast countryside, billows of flame and smoke rising in their wake. The screen often portrayed human agony in scenes of the wounded and dying on both sides, and the ordeal of civilians trapped by the combat. But mostly it transmitted the grueling reality of the struggle—remote, repetitious, monotonous—punctuated periodically by moments of horror.

On the evening of January 31, 1968, the spectacle suddenly changed. Now, Americans saw a drastically different kind of war. The night before, nearly seventy thousand Communist soldiers had launched a surprise offensive of extraordinary intensity and astonishing scope. Violating a truce that they themselves had pledged to observe during Tet, the lunar New Year, they surged into more than a hundred cities and towns, including Saigon, audaciously shifting the war for the first time from its rural setting to a new arena—South Vietnam's supposedly impregnable urban areas.

The carefully coordinated series of attacks exploded around the country like a string of firecrackers. Following an abortive foray against the coastal city of Nhatrang, the Communists struck at Hoi An, Danang, Quinhon, and other seaside enclaves presumed to have been beyond their reach, and they even rocketed the huge American complex at

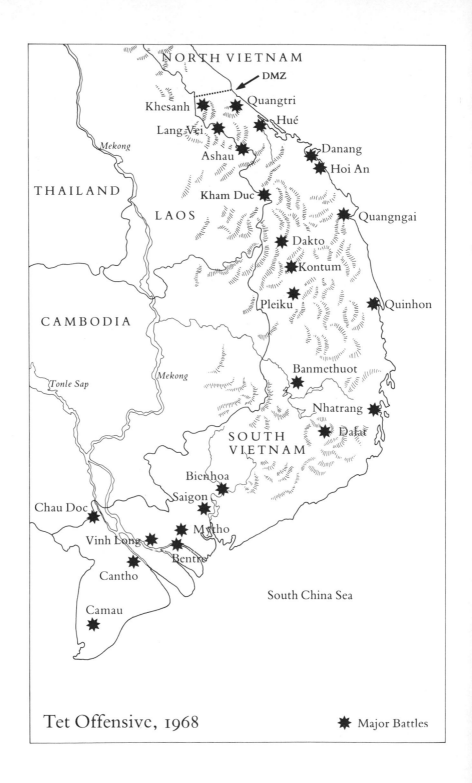

Tet Offensive, 1968

★ Major Battles

Camranh Bay. They stormed the highland towns of Banmethuot, Kontum, and Pleiku, and they hit Dalat, the mountain resort that by tacit accommodation had been spared the conflict. Simultaneously, they invaded thirteen of the sixteen provincial capitals of the populous Mekong delta, among them Mytho, Cantho, Bentre, and Soctrang, and they seized control of scores of district seats, disrupting the Saigon regime's fragile pacification programs. They fought stubbornly, sometimes blindly, and frequently abandoned their flexible tactics to defend untenable positions. In many places, they were swiftly crushed by overwhelming American and South Vietnamese military power, its destructive capacity brought to bear with uncommon fury—and often indiscriminately. They also displayed unprecedented brutality, slaughtering minor government functionaries and other innocuous figures as well as harmless foreign doctors, schoolteachers, and missionaries. Nowhere was the battle fiercer than in Hué, which Communist units held for twenty-five days, committing ghastly atrocities during the initial phase of their occupation.

The Communists staged their boldest stroke against the Saigon region, deploying some four thousand men, most of them in small teams. One of their key objectives was the U.S. embassy, situated in the heart of the sprawling metropolis, which was assaulted in the early morning darkness of January 31. An American officer, later assessing the operation by the standards of a conventional soldier, derided it as a "piddling platoon action." The feat stunned U.S. and world opinion.

The U.S. embassy, an ugly concrete pile shielded by thick walls, was an eyesore in the neighborhood of handsome pastel buildings of the French colonial vintage. Going back in 1981, I noticed that the compound had been taken over by Vietnam's government-owned oil exploration corporation—an enterprise that evidently did little business, since its doors were tightly shut. But during the war, with the Stars and Stripes flying above its ramparts, the enclosure represented the unshakable American presence in Vietnam.

The nineteen Vietcong commandos assigned to the job began their preparations three months earlier. As a gesture of confidence, the United States had recently transferred full responsibility for the defense of Saigon to the South Vietnamese authorities, whose notions of security were notoriously lax. Accordingly, the commandos easily moved arms, ammunition, and explosives into Saigon from their base near a rubber plantation thirty miles to the north, concealing the shipments in truckloads of rice and tomatoes. Inside the city, they stored the matériel in an automobile repair shop whose proprietor, suspected by the South Vietnamese to be an enemy agent, had somehow eluded jail. Nor was American security much better. The Vietcong squad had evidently relied for guidance on a clandestine confederate who had worked for years in the U.S. mission as a chauffeur, nicknamed Satchmo. He was to die during the attack, a Soviet machine gun beside him.

The commandos, jammed into a truck and a taxicab, pulled up in front of the embassy at nearly three o'clock in the morning. Vaulting from the vehicles, they quickly blasted a hole in the wall and rushed into the compound, automatic weapons blazing. Within five minutes, they had killed four GIs and another one shortly thereafter. Four Saigon policemen, theoretically on guard outside, fled as soon as the shooting started. Ambassador Ellsworth Bunker, asleep at his residence a few blocks away, was hustled off to safety at the home of a subordinate. The ranking American diplomat inside the chancery building, Allen Wendt, a junior economic specialist doing routine night duty, locked himself in the fortified code room. A half hour later, a shocked State Department official telephoned from Washington, where it was midafternoon of the previous day. News of the attack had just come over the Associated Press teletype, and Lyndon Johnson was frantically demanding information.

WAR HITS SAIGON, screamed the front-page headline of Washington's afternoon tabloid *The News*. But newspaper accounts paled beside the television coverage, which that evening projected the episode, in all its vivid confusion, into the living rooms of fifty million Americans. There, on color screens, dead bodies lay amid the rubble and rattle of automatic gunfire as dazed American soldiers and civilians ran back and forth trying to flush out the assailants. One man raced past the camera to a villa behind the chancery building to toss a pistol up to Colonel George Jacobson on the second floor. The senior embassy official shot the last of the enemy commandos as he crept up the stairs.

Nearly six and a half hours after the action began, the Americans declared the site secure, and General Westmoreland appeared to speak to reporters. Dressed in starched fatigues, he delivered a televised statement as stiff as his uniform. The Communists had "very deceitfully" taken advantage of the Tet truce "to create maximum consternation," he intoned, concluding optimistically that their "well-laid plans went afoul."

But as they watched Westmoreland's reassuring performance on their television screens, Americans at home could also see the carnage wrought by the offensive in the vicinity of Saigon. The Communists had hurled a division against the U.S. base at Bienhoa, north of the capital, and they had attacked Westmoreland's own headquarters as well as the South Vietnamese general staff offices, both situated at the Saigon airport. Their rockets ripped into Locbinh, the suburban center of General Weyand's corps command, blowing an ammunition dump sky-high, and they blocked roads to prevent American and South Vietnamese reinforcements from entering Saigon. In undertaking so widespread a drive, however, the Communists had stretched themselves thin, and inside the capital their squads continued to assault police posts, army barracks, prisons, and other installations with almost hopeless desperation. Nevertheless, the dimensions of their offensive dazzled American officers; one of them, as he tracked the assaults on a map of the Saigon region, thought it resembled a pinball machine, lighting up with each raid.

Hardly had television crews finished covering the fight for the U.S. embassy than another skirmish erupted nearby. American and South Vietnamese units, their dead lying in the street, were blasting an enemy band of thirteen men and a woman barricaded inside an apartment house after a reckless bid to break into the presidential palace, the most heavily fortified building in the capital. Not far off, cameras concentrated on the siege of Saigon's main radio station, grabbed by Vietcong commandos during the night. That evening, as they watched the battle on television, American audiences heard the staccato voice of a correspondent on the spot, doing his best to explain the chaotic images. "There are an undisclosed number of Vietcong inside," he sputtered. "They're surrounded by South Vietnamese troops, and they're pinned down inside."

Western correspondents could not, of course, report from the Communist side during the offensive. Years after the war, though, a Vietcong veteran of the operation against the Saigon radio station, Dang Xuan Teo, related his version of the episode—and his account revealed, among other things, the ability of the Communists to prepare a campaign of such magnitude without detection by either the U.S. or South Vietnamese authorities.

A slim, sinewy man, Teo had escaped death or capture in early 1966, when a massive American force, during Operation Cedar Falls, bombed and bulldozed the Vietcong sanctuary in the so called Iron Triangle, an area of jungles and rubber plantations near the Cambodian border north of Saigon. But there, as in other regions from which they had been eliminated, the Communists gradually rebuilt their strength, and, within eighteen months, they were poised to spring on the capital. In November 1967, Teo's commanders directed him to train a fourteen-man squad to attack the radio station, terming the job a "once-in-a-lifetime" assignment. They were to seize the building and hold it for two hours, after which Vietcong regulars would relieve them. The members of the team sensed that it would probably be, for most of them at least, an "end-of-a-lifetime" mission.

Teo understood the difficulties involved. The radio station, a crucial communications facility, had been a prime objective in every attempt to overthrow the Saigon regime. Having studied the coups, Teo knew that his commandos could easily overcome the platoon of government troops guarding the station and gain control of the place. "The real problem," he recalled, "would be to occupy it until help arrived."

Teo celebrated the Tet holiday two days early, paying respect to his departed ancestors in ritual fashion. Then he went into action. Years before, Vietcong agents had acquired a villa two hundred yards from the radio station, stocking its cellar with weapons for terrorist activities and other contingencies, such as the present assault. Teo's comrades, infiltrating into the city separately on buses, trucks, and motor scooters, assembled at the villa—where they discovered to their dismay that the wooden gunstocks had been eaten through by termites. It was too late to obtain fresh arms. They wrapped rags around the guns as substitute stocks. At three o'clock on the morning of January 31, just as other Vietcong squads were attacking elsewhere, they started off.

They burst into the courtyard of the radio station by ramming a car filled with dynamite through its gate. Then, pouring into the building, they quickly annihilated a platoon of guards, most of whom were sleeping. The fighting was over within ten minutes, and they were in control. At that stage, however, the operation began to go wrong. They had brought along tapes recorded beforehand to broadcast a proclamation announcing the liberation of Saigon and other propaganda. But the attack triggered a signal that cut the station off from a transmitter fourteen miles away, and they never went on the air. Instead, South Vietnamese government technicians at the transmitter played an incongruous medley of Viennese waltzes, Beatles tunes, and Vietnamese military marches—the only music available at the transmitter site. Nor did the relief force of Vietcong regulars arrive on schedule. By daylight, the Communist commandos were trapped inside the station by South Vietnamese troops and, as Teo recalled, their prospects looked dim. "We were down to eight men. We still had some explosives, but our ammunition supply was depleted. We didn't know whether to continue to hold the place or destroy it. The comrades decided that I should try to get away, report to our superiors, and return with orders. I managed to escape. Soon afterward, though, they detonated the explosives, blowing up the building and sacrificing themselves." American television audiences could see the aftermath on their screens: grinning and giggling South Vietnamese soldiers scavenged the Vietcong corpses for money and other valuables, looted the radio station itself, and stole any equipment still intact.

But the most memorable image of the upheaval in Saigon—and one of the most searing spectacles of the whole war—was imprinted the next day on a street corner in the city. General Nguyen Ngoc Loan, chief of South Vietnam's national police, was the crude cop who had brutally crushed the dissident Buddhist movement in Hué two years earlier. Now his mood was even fiercer: Communist invaders had killed several of his men, including one gunned down with his wife and children in their house—and Loan was roaming the capital in an attempt to stiffen its defenses.

That morning, Eddie Adams, an Associated Press photographer, and Vo Suu, a Vietnamese cameraman employed by the National Broadcasting Company, had been cruising around the shattered town. Near the An Quang temple, they spotted a patrol of government troops with a captive in tow. He wore black shorts and a checkered sports shirt, and his hands were bound behind him. The soldiers marched him up to Loan, who drew his revolver and waved the bystanders away. Without hesitation, Loan stretched out his right arm, placed the short snout of the weapon against the prisoner's head, and squeezed the trigger. The man grimaced—then, almost in slow motion, his legs crumpled beneath him as he seemed to sit down backward, blood gushing from his head as it hit the pavement. Not a word was spoken. It all happened instantly, with hardly a sound except for the crack of Loan's gun, the click of Adams's shutter, and the whir of Vo Suu's camera.

At the "five o'clock follies," as correspondents in Saigon called the regular afternoon briefings held in the U.S. Information Service auditorium, Westmoreland exuded his usual confidence. But his report was smothered the next morning in America's newspapers, whose front pages featured the grisly photograph of Loan executing the Vietcong captive. And the next evening, NBC broadcast its exclusive film of the event—slightly edited, to spare television viewers the spurt of blood bursting from the prisoner's head.

Meanwhile, the most bitter battle of the entire war was unfolding in Hué, the lovely old town of temples and palaces, reconstructed by the emperor Gia Long in the nineteenth century to replicate the seat of his Chinese patron in Beijing. Communist forces crashed into the city from three directions in the early hours of January 31, meeting little resistance from the government division based there. They ran up the yellow-starred Vietcong flag atop the Citadel, an ancient fortress in the center of town, and then their political cadres proceeded to organize the worst bloodbath of the conflict.

Five months before, as they began to prepare for the assault, Communist planners and their intelligence agents inside the city meticulously compiled two lists. One detailed nearly two hundred targets, ranging from such installations as government bureaus and police posts to the home of the district chief's concubine. The other contained the names of "cruel tyrants and reactionary elements," a rubric covering civilian functionaries, army officers, and nearly anybody else linked to the South Vietnamese regime as well as uncooperative merchants, intellectuals, and clergymen. Instructions were also issued to arrest Americans and other foreigners except for the French—presumably because President de Gaulle had publicly criticized U.S. policy in Vietnam.

Vietcong teams, armed with these directives, conducted house-to-house searches immediately after seizing control of Hué, and they were merciless. During the months and years that followed, the remains of approximately three thousand people were exhumed in nearby river-beds, coastal salt flats, and jungle clearings. The victims had been shot or clubbed to death, or buried alive. Paradoxically, the American public barely noticed these atrocities, preoccupied as it was by the incident at Mylai—in which American soldiers had massacred a hundred Vietnamese peasants, women and children among them. Revisiting Vietnam in 1981, I was able to elicit little credible evidence from the Communists to clarify the episode.

General Tran Do, a senior Communist architect of the Tet offensive, flatly denied that the Hué atrocities had ever occurred, contending that films and photographs of the corpses had been "fabricated." In Hué itself, a Communist official claimed that the exhumed bodies were mostly of Vietcong cadres and sympathizers slain by the South Vietnamese army after the fight for the city. He also blamed most of the civilian casualties during the battle on American bombing. But he hinted that his comrades had participated in at least a share of the killing—resorting to familiar Communist jargon to explain that the "angry" citizens of Hué had liquidated local "despots" in the same way that "they would get rid of poisonous snakes who, if allowed to live, would commit further crimes." Balanced accounts have made it clear, however, that the Communist butchery in Hué did take place—perhaps on an even larger scale than reported during the war.

Captured in the home of Vietnamese friends, Stephen Miller of the U.S. Information Service was shot in a field behind a Catholic seminary. Dr. Horst Günther Krainick, a German physician teaching at the local medical school, was seized with his wife and two other German doctors, and their bodies were found in a shallow pit. Despite their instructions to spare the French, the Communists arrested two Benedictine missionaries, shot one of them, and buried the other alive. They also killed Father Buu Dong, a popular Vietnamese Catholic priest who had entertained Vietcong agents in his rectory, where he kept a portrait of Ho Chi Minh—telling parishioners that he prayed for Ho because "he is our friend too." Many Vietnamese with only the flimsiest ties to the Saigon regime suffered as well.

Pham Van Tuong, a part-time janitor at a government office, was gunned down in his front yard along with his two small children. Mrs. Nguyen Thi Lao, a cigarette vendor, was presumably executed because her sister worked in a government bureau. Anyone resisting arrest was promptly killed, but those who surrendered to the Communists often fared no better. Five South Vietnamese officers, who emerged from their hiding place without a fight, were taken to a high school playground and each shot in the head. Many people disappeared after submitting to Vietcong promises of a quick release, as one woman later recalled: "The Communists came to our house and questioned my father, who was an elderly official about to retire. Then they went away, returning afterward to say that he had to attend a study session that would last only ten days. My mother and I were worried because the Communists had arrested his father in just that way in 1946. Like his father, my father never came back."

Clandestine South Vietnamese teams slipped into Hué after the Communist occupation to assassinate suspected enemy collaborators; they threw many of the bodies into common graves with the Vietcong's victims. The city's entire population suffered in one way or another from the ordeal and Trinh Cong Son, a poet who survived the holocaust, later expressed his sentiments in an ironically macabre ballad.

I saw, I saw, I saw holes and trenches
Full of the corpses of my brothers and sisters.
Mothers, clap for joy over war.
Sisters, clap and cheer for peace.
Everyone clap for vengeance.
Everyone clap instead of repentance.

On February 24, South Vietnamese troops ripped the Vietcong flag down from the south wall of the Citadel, hoisting the government's red and yellow banner in its place. Many were natives of Hué whose families had been ravaged by the Communists, and they had fought well. But three U.S. marine battalions played the decisive role in the liberation of the city. Myron Harrington, then commanding a hundred-man company, remembered afterward his apprehensions as a truck convoy transported his unit toward the battle from Phu Bai, a marine base to the south: "I could feel a knot developing in my stomach. Not so much from fear—though a helluva lot of fear was there—but because we were new to this type of situation. We were accustomed to jungles and open rice fields, and now we would be fighting in a city, like it was Europe during World War II. One of the beautiful things about the marines is that they adapt quickly, but we were going to take a number of casualties learning some basic lessons in this experience."

Leaving their vehicles, the marines crossed the Perfume River aboard landing craft as Communist troops peppered the boats from both shores. The weather was cold and clammy, and the low overcast made tactical air support almost impossible. They entered Hué from the north, cautiously threading through its streets as they headed toward the Citadel to bolster another marine unit already there. Harrington was prudent, but the scene appalled and frightened him: "My first impression was of desolation, utter devastation. There were burnt-out tanks and trucks, and upturned automobiles still smoldering. Bodies lay everywhere, most of them civilians. The smoke and stench blended, like in some kind of horror movie—except that it lacked weird music. You felt that something could happen at any minute, that they would jump out and start shooting from every side. Right away I realized that we weren't going to a little picnic."

Harrington's orders, received soon after reaching the marine command post near the Citadel, were to take a fortified tower located along the east wall that was bristling with North Vietnamese and Vietcong troops. The next morning, he launched a frontal assault with two platoons and a tank. Artillery and mortars had shelled the target in advance, but his men faced an implacable enemy. As one of the platoons moved out, a round hit its radio operator, breaking Harrington's contact with his right flank from the start. "Needless to say, we continued. The marines, super guys, crawled and crept toward the wall and up the tower, clearing the North Vietnamese and Vietcong from their spider holes one by one with hand grenades and rifle fire. At one stage, we began to draw fire from buildings nearby, and that caused us problems for several days. But our artillery neutralized it, and we finally took the tower, which gave us the high ground, the critical terrain that marines always try to gain."

The marines could now direct artillery against the Citadel, their forward observer giving the batteries such precise readings that the shells often fell within twenty-five yards of their position inside the fortress. But the battle went on for another ten days as they pushed ahead into the intricate recesses of the old structure, and, Harrington recalled, the combat became increasingly close, almost intimate.

> As a marine, I had to admire the courage and discipline of the North Vietnamese and the Vietcong, but no more than I did my own men. We were both in a face-to-face, eyeball-to-eyeball confrontation. Sometimes they were only twenty or thirty yards from us, and once we killed a sniper only ten yards away. After a while, survival was the name of the game as you sat there in the semidarkness, with the firing going on constantly, like at a rifle range. And the horrible smell. You tasted it as you ate your rations, as if you were eating death. It permeated your clothes, which you couldn't wash because water was very scarce. You couldn't bathe or shave either. My strategy was to keep as many of my marines alive as possible, and yet accomplish our mission. You went through the full range of emotions, seeing your buddies being hit, but you couldn't feel sorry for them because you had the others to think about. It was dreary, and still we weren't depressed. We were doing our job—successfully.

During the fight for the Citadel, as in the other battles for South Vietnam's towns and cities at the time, ubiquitous television crews were present—filming for overnight transmission to millions of American viewers the extraordinary drama of their husbands, sons, and brothers in action. In one segment, showing Harrington's company firing from behind a stone wall at an unseen enemy, a grimy marine paused for a few moments to reply wearily to a correspondent's questions.

> *What's the hardest part of it?*
> Not knowing where they are—that's the worst thing. Riding around, running in sewers, the gutter, anywhere. Could be anywhere. Just hope you can stay alive, day to day. Everybody just wants to go back home and go to school. That's about it.
> *Have you lost any friends?*
> Quite a few. We lost one the other day. The whole thing stinks, really.

Seventeen members of Harrington's company lost their lives in the struggle for the Citadel, and nearly one hundred and fifty U.S. marines were killed during the entire Hué battle, as well as four hundred South Vietnamese troops. An estimated five thousand Communist soldiers met their death—most of them annihilated by American air and artillery strikes that also inflicted a heavy toll on the civilian population. Reflecting on the engagement in an interview after the war, Harrington evoked a phrase coined elsewhere in South Vietnam during the Tet offensive. "Did we have to destroy the town in order to save it? Well, I don't think that the North Vietnamese and Vietcong were about to give it up even if we'd surrounded Hué and tried to starve them out. We had to go in and get them. There was no other way, except to dig them out. But we didn't go in there simply to show how great our weapons were, how much destructive power we possessed. We did our best to avoid malicious damage. Yet, when we had to destroy a house, we destroyed it."

Early in March, the U.S. command reported that some two thousand American and four thousand South Vietnamese soldiers had died since the start of the Tet offensive a month before. Westmoreland's intelligence officers reckoned as well that fifty thousand enemy troops had been killed, and, despite their spotty record, the estimate was plausible—as I gathered from Dr. Duong Quynh Hoa, a prominent Communist figure, in 1981 at her villa in Ho Chi Minh City.

"We lost our best people," she said mournfully, recalling that Vietcong military units composed mostly of indigenous southerners had borne the brunt of the fighting and suffered the heaviest casualties. Over the next year, she went on, the southern Communist political organization was to be badly battered by the CIA's Phoenix program, a covert campaign designed to uproot the Vietcong's rural structure. So growing numbers of North Vietnamese agents were sent south to fill the vacuum. They rebuilt the southern Communist apparatus, and they remained after the war to manage it—often antagonizing their southern comrades, who, despite an abstract commitment to national cohesion, clung to their regional identity. Many southerners viewed them as rigid, doctrinaire, alien, and even corrupt carpetbaggers, and Dr. Hoa made no secret of her loathing for them. "They behave as if they had conquered us," she told me.

Soldiers, whatever their convictions, cannot be inspired to plunge into ambitious military ventures without the assurance of success. As they prepared for the gigantic Tet campaign, Communist cadres conducted a vigorous propaganda program designed to persuade the North Vietnamese and Vietcong forces that their goal was within grasp. They advised the troops in a series of directives and meetings that the "general offensive and uprising" represented a "golden opportunity" to liberate South Vietnam, and promised them that the restive southern population would join in the struggle to crush the American "aggressors" and topple the "tyrannical" Saigon administration. Ho Chi Minh, then old and ailing, threw his enormous prestige behind the effort. Just before Christmas, in his first public appearance in four months, he addressed a rally in Hanoi and urged the people of both Vietnams to achieve "even greater feats of battle" during the year ahead. On January 1, 1968, Hanoi Radio broadcast a poem he had written to dramatize the special urgency of the moment.

This spring far outshines previous springs.
Of triumphs throughout the land come happy tidings.
Forward!
Total victory shall be ours!

The passionate exhortations, coupled with the frenzied enemy attacks, prompted General Westmoreland to portray the Tet blitzkrieg as a desperate "go-for-broke" bid by the enemy to avert inevitable defeat— not unlike the Battle of the Bulge staged by the Germans during the final days of World War II. Some American analysts also interpreted the dynamic enemy push as primarily an attempt to dismay the American people, whose support of the war seemed to be waning. But the Communist decision was characteristically more complicated, as General Vo Nguyen Giap, the principal architect of the campaign, explained in an interview in Hanoi after the war: "For us, you know, there is no such thing as a single strategy. Ours is always a synthesis, simultaneously military, political, and diplomatic—which is why, quite clearly, the Tet offensive had multiple objectives."

In September 1967, Giap had published a lengthy appraisal of the current situation in Vietnam. He conspicuously avoided any mention of the imminent Tet campaign, then being planned secretly. But his assessment furnished clues to the Communist motives for the offensive—and, paradoxically, resembled the judgments that many skeptical American officials in Washington were beginning to reach about the war at the same time.

Giap implicitly conceded that the struggle was deadlocked—at least on the battlefield. The Communists lacked the strength to match America's superior firepower, while the U.S. forces were too dispersed in protecting their bases and other installations to pursue the elusive North Vietnamese and Vietcong troops. In Giap's estimation, however, the impasse favored the Communists. The United States could not escalate the conflict without committing additional soldiers and matériel, and could not boost its investment without reducing both its global defense responsibilities and its domestic economic and social programs. Thus, he concluded, the United States was overextended—its resources strained by a little war that had grown into a big war.

Giap's long-range strategy was to continue to bleed the Americans until they agreed to a settlement that satisfied the Hanoi regime. For that reason, the Communists were willing to endure terrible casualties during the Tet campaign, as they did throughout the war. The Tet offensive was not intended to be a decisive operation, but one episode in a protracted war that might last "five, ten, or twenty years." Essentially, Giap was repeating to the United States what Ho Chi Minh had warned the French a generation before: "You can kill ten of my men for every one I kill of yours. But even at those odds, you will lose and I will win."

A collateral concept in Giap's grand design stemmed from his perception that the United States and its South Vietnamese clients were inextricably interdependent. Though the South Vietnamese "puppets" relied completely for their survival on the Americans, they nevertheless played a vital role by defending U.S. facilities, fulfilling police functions, managing pacification projects, and performing other static duties. Above all, their veneer of sovereignty cloaked what the Communists derisively called a neocolonial relationship. In short, there was no way for either ally to wage the war alone.

But Giap was persuaded that the alliance was inherently unstable, and would eventually disintegrate as the United States increased the pressure on the Saigon government to prosecute the war more effectively. He was equally convinced that latent anti-American sentiment pervading South Vietnam could be exacerbated and exploited. One of the Communist goals of the Tet offensive was to drive a wedge between the Americans and the South Vietnamese—a goal that was discernible from the start of the operation.

By attacking the American embassy, for example, the Communists sought to demonstrate to the South Vietnamese people that the United States was vulnerable despite its immense power. They assaulted the cities and towns in the expectation that part of the southern regime's urban administration would turn against the Americans. And their attempt to disrupt the pacification effort was aimed as well to attract rural officials to their side. They also believed that South Vietnam was ripe for revolution, and that weary government soldiers, dislocated peasants, frustrated religious factions, fractious youths, and other unhappy elements of the southern population would rise in opposition to the Saigon authorities and the Americans.

President Johnson's aides, no less parochial, were persuaded that the Communists planned their actions to resonate in the United States. On one occasion, for instance, Walt Rostow assured his staff that a Vietcong strike against a remote village had been calculated to coincide with a Senate debate on U.S. appropriations for Vietnam—as if tacticians in Hanoi consulted the *Congressional Record* before deploying their units. But the Communists fundamentally conceived the Tet offensive to sway South Vietnamese opinion rather than influence American opinion. Nor was it timed to the U.S. presidential election of November 1968. Giap's blueprint clearly relegated the political scene in America to a secondary place in the Communist strategy. He routinely praised the U.S. antiwar movement for its "sympathy and support," yet he emphasized that the "decisive" arena was Vietnam itself, where Communist success hinged on "changing the balance of power in our favor." Similarly, he dismissed the election as merely a reshuffle "in the hierarchy of the capitalist ruling class" that would not alter the "nature" of America's "aggressive imperialism."

For all their propaganda promises of impending victory, however, the Communists were realistic enough to chart the Tet campaign with maximum and minimum objectives in mind. Ideally, of course, they hoped to topple the Saigon regime and promote the formation of a neutralist coalition government dominated by their Vietcong surrogates, which would expel the Americans and put Vietnam on the path to reunification under Communist control. But they reckoned on improving their position even if the offensive failed to fulfill that ambitious goal.

They estimated that President Johnson, confronted by the disarray of the Tet outbreaks, would finally stop bombing North Vietnam and thus submit to beginning negotiations on their terms. So, at the very least, they were hoping to propel the war into the phase of simultaneous fighting and talking—a classic Communist maneuver. One of their motives was to project the impression, especially to the South Vietnamese population, that they were conciliatory. But more importantly, the ploy would weaken the alliance between South Vietnam and the United States by arousing in the Saigon regime's senior officers the fear and suspicion that the Americans might abandon them if the enemy agreed to an accommodation—as was indeed to occur in October 1972, when Henry Kissinger and his North Vietnamese counterpart, Le Duc Tho, reached a compromise at the expense of the Thieu government.

On the eve of the Tet offensive, therefore, the Communists added a diplomatic dimension to their plan. Until then, they had insisted, peace talks could not start before the Americans met several conditions. But now the North Vietnamese foreign minister, Nguyen Duy Trinh, issued a more tempting offer. At a reception in Hanoi on December 30, 1967, he declared that the Communists "will" open discussions with the United States once the air strikes against North Vietnam were halted. This was, with variations, a repetition of the gesture made by Ho Chi Minh almost exactly fourteen years earlier, when he proposed negotiations to the French as both their armies braced for the showdown battle at Dienbienphu.

Now as then, the Communists were gambling—"We cannot anticipate all specific conditions and situations that will develop," one of their internal directives explained. But, they stressed, the risks would be worth the wager if "we are highly determined in our actions" and learn to adapt to events "in the process" of the combat.

The Tet offensive had actually started in September 1967, when Communist troops launched a series of attacks against a string of isolated American garrisons scattered across the highlands of central Vietnam and along the Laotian and Cambodian frontiers. Westmoreland had just told a group of American correspondents in Saigon that "a sense of despair" pervaded the enemy ranks as their losses mounted, but his description of them scarcely fit the facts. Deployed in regiments and even divisions, the Communist forces were equipped with superb new Soviet automatic rifles, flamethrowers, and backpack radios as well as mortars, rockets, and big antiaircraft guns, and they struck with extraordinary precision. Their first target was Conthien, a small U.S. marine fire base located atop a barren hill south of the porous boundary separating the two Vietnams. Then they hit Locninh and Songbe, a pair of American outposts near the Cambodian border north of Saigon. And, in early November, they began the largest engagement of the war to date, a battle that raged for twenty-two days around Dakto, a dense jungle region in the mountains above Pleiku.

Westmoreland was delighted. The Communists were at long last waging his brand of big conventional conflict where he wanted to fight—in the hinterlands far from South Vietnam's cities—and his stupendous military machine could show dramatic results. The firepower he brought to bear was unprecedented, awesome, almost beyond the bounds of imagination. At Conthien alone, nearly eight hundred B-52 flights dropped twenty-two thousand tons of bombs as fighter-bombers and warships in the South China Sea also pummeled the area, reducing its gentle slopes to a bleak landscape of craters and charred tree stumps. The jungles surrounding Dakto were pounded by three hundred B-52 missions, more than two thousand fighter-bomber assaults, and one hundred and seventy thousand artillery shells, and chemical warfare units denuded the few remaining shreds of foliage with herbicides. The staggering North Vietnamese and Vietcong losses over the three-month period boosted the estimated number of Communist troops killed in action during the year to some ninety thousand, inspiring Westmoreland to proclaim on a visit to Washington in November that "the enemy's hopes are bankrupt."

Back in Vietnam six weeks later, however, he focused on an even larger battle looming around Khesanh, a rolling region as lovely as the hills of Tuscany. Khesanh straddled Route 9, an old French road linking the Vietnamese coast to the Laotian market towns along the Mekong. A small camp had been built there by the U.S. special forces to recruit and train local mountain tribesmen, and Westmoreland began to expand it during the summer as a springboard against Communist sanctuaries in Laos—a proposed move that President Johnson would afterward reject. Westmoreland stockpiled the base with ammunition and other matériel, refurbished its primitive airstrip, and sent in a U.S. marine battalion to bulwark its defenses. But Khesanh instead became the site of a huge confrontation whose significance was to be debated long after the war had ended. The battle dragged on for two months, and became almost daily fare for American television viewers already satiated by the spectacle of the Tet offensive shattering South Vietnam's cities and towns.

Late in 1967, an accumulation of U.S. intelligence reports indicated that four North Vietnamese infantry divisions, stiffened by two artillery regiments and armored units—a total of forty thousand men—were converging on Khesanh. Westmoreland moved six thousand U.S. marines into the sector, and he drafted plans to deluge the enemy from the air in a bombing cascade appropriately code-named Operation Niagara. He also instructed his aides to study the feasibility of using tactical nuclear weapons—until a directive from Washington cut short the research out of fear that if the press found out about it, the protests against the war at home would increase. Westmoreland later denounced the ban, arguing that the use of nuclear weapons could conceivably have compelled the Communists to capitulate, in the same way that two atomic bombs "had spoken convincingly" to the Japanese leaders during World War II—a complaint that showed how narrowly he perceived the conflict.

Westmoreland estimated that the Communists were closing in on Khesanh as part of a broad maneuver designed to grab South Vietnam's northernmost provinces prior to negotiations—just as they had thrown themselves against the French at Dienbienphu in order to buttress their bargaining posture at the Geneva Conference of 1954. American officers in Vietnam suddenly began to read the available literature on Dienbienphu. Westmoreland also assembled his staff to listen to a lecture on the French experience, but he shut off discussion of the subject after hearing the grim account. "We are not, repeat not, going to be defeated at Khesanh," he announced. "I will tolerate no talking or even thinking to the contrary."

The Dienbienphu analogy was preposterous. The French had been trapped in an inaccessible valley with only a few artillery pieces, while the Americans had a formidable array of howitzers and mortars at Khesanh as well as long-range guns capable of blasting the enemy positions from outside the perimeter. In contrast to the French, who had lacked aircraft, the U.S. force could rely on a formidable fleet of helicopters and cargo planes to carry in supplies and replacements, and to evacuate the wounded. Above all, the besieged marines were able to count on the B-52s, which would drench the surrounding North Vietnamese and Vietcong troops with a total of more than seventy-five thousand tons of explosives over a nine-week span—the deadliest deluge of firepower ever unloaded on a tactical target in the history of warfare.

The ratio of American to Communist casualties was also to highlight the difference between Dienbienphu and Khesanh. Approximately eight thousand Vietminh and two thousand French army soldiers died at Dienbienphu. But the struggle for Khesanh cost the Communists at least ten thousand lives in exchange for fewer than five hundred U.S. marines killed in action. In Hanoi after the war, a Communist veteran of the battle recalled the carnage inflicted on his comrades, disclosing to me that some North Vietnamese and Vietcong units suffered as much as 90 percent losses under the relentless downpour of American bombs, napalm, and artillery shells. Giap, who was rarely troubled by heavy human tolls, flew to the front late in January 1968 to inspect the situation personally—and he nearly became a casualty himself when a flight of thirty-six B-52s dropped a thousand tons of bombs near his field headquarters. Westmoreland had ordered the air strike after his electronic experts suspected, from intercepting enemy radio traffic, that a prominent Communist figure might be in the area.

Despite the obvious differences, the superficial resemblance between Khesanh and Dienbienphu was irresistible to American observers and officials alike. "The parallels are there for all to see," Walter Cronkite informed a CBS radio audience in early February. Marvin Kalb, the CBS correspondent at the State Department, reported that the "historical ghost" of the French disaster was "casting a long shadow over Washington." They and their colleagues were afterward criticized by Westmoreland and others for having jazzed up the comparison, but the journalists were merely echoing military and civilian sources in Washington and Saigon. Even before the encounter began, Walt Rostow had discerned from captured enemy documents that the Communists were deploying to "re-enact a new Dienbienphu." Once the fighting started, Westmoreland called the Khesanh clash a "vain attempt" by the North Vietnamese "to restage Dienbienphu."

The specter of Dienbienphu haunted nobody more than it did Lyndon Johnson. In 1954, as a senior member of the Senate Armed Services Committee, he had opposed U.S. intervention to rescue the beleaguered French bastion. Now he feared a repetition of that catastrophe at Khesanh—only this time the devastated terrain would be littered with American dead and wounded. On a trip to Australia to commemorate the recently deceased prime minister, he warned the Australian cabinet that the Communists planned to resort to "kamikaze tactics" in the weeks ahead—"a wave of suicide attacks," as he put it. By late January, with the battle raging, Khesanh became his obsession. Pentagon specialists had constructed a sand-table model of the Khesanh plateau in the basement situation room of the White House and Johnson, dressed in a bathrobe, would prowl around the chamber during the night—reading the latest teletype messages from the field, peering at aerial photos, requesting casualty figures. In one of the oddest demands ever imposed by a president on his top officers, he insisted that the joint chiefs of staff sign a formal declaration of faith in Westmoreland's ability to hold Khesanh. Ordering the statement from General Earle Wheeler, the chairman, Johnson said: "I don't want any damn Dinbinphoo."

Actually, the Communists had never regarded Khesanh to be another Dienbienphu—or so several of their soldiers explained to me after the war. Perhaps, having failed to overrun the U.S. garrison, they were naturally trying to discount the significance of the engagement. For the same reason, Giap sounded implausible when he later contended that

Khesanh assumed an inflated importance only because the Americans chose to make it a test of their prestige. But a lower-ranking Communist officer, who had fought at Dienbienphu and Khesanh, underlined a point that seemed to me to be credible: "At Dienbienphu, the French and ourselves massed for what we both expected to be a final battle. The Americans, however, were strong everywhere in the south. Thus we realized from the beginning that we could not beat them decisively in a single encounter like Khesanh."

Why, then, did the North Vietnamese and Vietcong forces submit to such horrendous losses at Khesanh? Nearly every Communist officer to whom I posed the question offered roughly the same answer. The battles at Khesanh and elsewhere in the hinterlands before and during the Tet offensive were intended to draw the Americans away from South Vietnam's population centers, thereby leaving them naked to assault. Many American experts shared that view at the time. Retired Brigadier General S. L. A. Marshall, a noted commentator on military affairs, perceived Khesanh to be "just a feint." An official American military history of the period also concluded that the Communists had besieged the base "in order to divert a major portion of our resources to a remote area" while they attacked the country's cities and towns. Major General Lowell English, a U.S. marine commander at Khesanh, similarly decried Westmoreland's decision to hold the bastion—calling it "a trap" laid by the enemy "to force you into the expenditure of absolutely unreasonable amounts of men and matériel to defend a piece of terrain that wasn't worth a damn."

But Westmoreland fell for the enemy ruse. From the start of the Tet offensive, he dismissed the Communist onslaught against the cities as simply "a diversionary effort" contrived to distract attention away from Khesanh and the northern regions of South Vietnam. His exaggerated focus on Khesanh was finally punctured a few days after he ended his tour in Vietnam in June, when the fortress was abandoned—a withdrawal conducted in secret to avoid jarring the American people, who had been told that U.S. marines were dying to secure the "crucial anchor" of the defense chain in the sector.

The Khesanh fiasco was overshadowed, however, by allegations that Westmoreland had either misinterpreted or deliberately doctored intelligence reports prior to the Tet outbreaks. Sam Adams, then a young CIA analyst, later accused Westmoreland and his staff of scaling down estimates of Communist strength in an attempt to justify their contention that they were making progress in the war. His own research led Adams to calculate that the total North Vietnamese and Vietcong force in South

Vietnam on the eve of Tet comprised some six hundred thousand men. He charged Westmoreland and his aides with shrinking the real figure by excluding guerrillas, cadres, and other auxiliaries from the enemy roster. The simmering controversy boiled up into a bitter legal stew in 1982, when Westmoreland sued CBS and Adams for defaming him in a television documentary inspired by the indictment. But the actual issue in the dispute was clouded.

Rival American agencies in Vietnam had regularly transmitted divergent sets of statistics back to Washington, invariably selecting the data that served their particular interests. Westmoreland played this numbers game. But it is doubtful that his deception deprived Lyndon Johnson of the facts, as Adams alleged. Johnson always had alternative sources of information. Thus, if he chose to share Westmoreland's rosy outlook, he did so because he needed all the optimistic evidence he could muster to show his domestic critics that the war was being won.

Even so, Westmoreland and the U.S. military establishment in Vietnam were clearly caught off guard by the Tet offensive. A West Point textbook on the war, published years later, attributed the "complete surprise" achieved by the Communists to a U.S. "intelligence failure ranking with Pearl Harbor." American intelligence specialists reached roughly the same conclusion in March 1968, after going to Saigon to conduct an official investigation. "The intensity, coordination, and timing" of the attacks "were not fully anticipated," they found—adding that another "major unexpected element" had been the Communists' ability to hit so many targets simultaneously. But above all, U.S. officers had been lulled into a false sense of security because illusory reports on North Vietnamese and Vietcong casualties, infiltration, recruitment, and morale "had downgraded our image of the enemy."

Communist defectors and prisoners, captured documents, electronic espionage devices, and covert agents provided American experts with piles of information. But, like medieval scholars interpreting theological scriptures, various intelligence specialists detected different meanings in the material. So, as early as December 20, 1967, Westmoreland warned Washington to expect a "maximum effort" by the enemy—while Admiral Sharp deemed the prospect of an offensive "remote." In any case, Westmoreland expected that the main action would be centered on South Vietnam's northernmost provinces, and he shifted troops to the region. He also envisioned the onslaught coming before Tet, presuming that the Communists would not court the risk of alienating the population by violating a truce they themselves had proclaimed for the sacred holiday.

Unfamiliar with Vietnam's past, very few Americans knew that one of the most famous exploits in the nation's history occurred during Tet of 1789, when the Emperor Quang Trung deceptively routed a Chinese occupation army celebrating the festival in Hanoi. Nor did they understand that the Vietnamese, after centuries of internecine turmoil, were inured to duplicity.

Westmoreland later acknowledged his misjudgment, admitting that he had not anticipated the "true nature or the scope" of the enemy attacks—yet he at least took the precaution of putting his forces on the alert. But South Vietnamese President Nguyen Van Thieu, disregarding the potential danger, furloughed most of his troops for the holiday and went off with his wife to her family's home in the Mekong delta town of Mytho.

If the Americans and their allies were napping before the Tet upheaval, the Communists also blundered. "We have been guilty of many errors and shortcomings," their initial appraisal of the campaign confessed, deploring such deficiencies as their failure to inspire the South Vietnamese population to rebel or their inability to rally Saigon government soldiers and officials to their banners. Many North Vietnamese and Vietcong troops were plainly disenchanted by the realization that, despite their enormous sacrifices during the campaign, they still faced a long struggle ahead. Official reports expressed alarm at the erosion of morale among those who had "lost confidence" in the Communist leadership and had become "doubtful of victory, pessimistic, and display shirking attitudes."

Tran Van Tra, a senior Communist general in the south at the time, candidly admitted in a military history published in Hanoi in 1982 that the offensive had been misconceived from the start. "During Tet of 1968," he wrote, "we did not correctly evaluate the specific balance of forces between ourselves and the enemy, did not fully realize that the enemy still had considerable capabilities and that our capabilities were limited." The Communists had set objectives "that were beyond our actual strength," founded "in part on an illusion based on our subjective desires." Thus, he went on, "we suffered large losses in matériel and manpower, especially cadres at various echelons, which clearly weakened us." As a result, "we were not only unable to retain the gains we had made but had to overcome a myriad of difficulties in 1969 and 1970 so that the revolution could stand firm in the storm."

Revisiting Vietnam after the war, I was astonished by the number of Communist veterans who retained bad memories of the Tet episode—and openly recalled to me their disappointment at its outcome. Dr.

Duong Quynh Hoa, at the time a secret Vietcong operative in Saigon, had joined the commandos invading the capital. In retrospect, she bluntly denounced the venture as a "grievous miscalculation" by the Hanoi hierarchy, which in her view had wantonly squandered the southern insurgent movement. Captain Tran Dinh Thong, a North Vietnamese regular, was equally frank. He remembered feeling "depressed and worried about the future" after the abortive operation, and he blamed its planners for having "incorrectly" surveyed the situation beforehand. Even General Tran Do conceded that the attacks had not been a resounding triumph. Indeed, he explained to me, the Tet campaign went in an unexpected direction: "In all honesty, we didn't achieve our main objective, which was to spur uprisings throughout the south. Still, we inflicted heavy casualties on the Americans and their puppets, and that was a big gain for us. As for making an impact in the United States, it had not been our intention—but it turned out to be a fortunate result."

After the war, in an angry tirade against the press, General Westmoreland alleged that voluminous, lurid, and distorted newspaper and particularly television reports of the Tet attacks had transformed a devastating Communist military defeat in Vietnam into a "psychological victory" for the enemy. Peter Braestrup, who covered Vietnam for *The Washington Post*, leveled the same charge in his book *Big Story*, contending that "crisis journalism" had rarely "veered so widely from reality" than it did in describing and interpreting events during that period. But public opinion surveys conducted at the time made it plain that, whatever the quality of the reporting from Vietnam, the momentous Tet episode scarcely altered American attitudes toward the war.

American opinion toward the war was far more complicated than it appeared to be on graphs and charts. Public "support" for the war had been slipping steadily for two years prior to Tet—a trend influenced by the mounting casualties, rising taxes, and, especially, the feeling that there was no end in view. For a brief moment after the Tet offensive began, Americans rallied round the flag in a predictable display of patriotic fervor. But their mood of despair quickly returned as the fighting dragged on, and their endorsement of the conflict resumed its downward spiral.

What this slide in "support" specifically meant was that, by late 1967, a plurality of Americans had concluded that the United States had "made a mistake" in committing combat troops to Vietnam. This sentiment was often analyzed wrongly, however. A common assumption was that "antiwar" signified "pro-peace." But that was not always the case. On the contrary, most Americans were dispirited because they felt that President Johnson was not prosecuting the war dynamically enough. Their attitude, summed up succinctly, seemed to say: "It was an error for us to have gotten involved in Vietnam in the first place. But now that we're there, let's win—or get out."

A survey conducted in November 1967, for example, indicated that while 44 percent of Americans favored a complete or gradual withdrawal from Vietnam, 55 percent wanted a tougher policy—and they included a handful who advocated the use of nuclear weapons. In February 1968, while the Tet offensive was raging, 53 percent favored stronger military operations, even at the risk of a clash with the Soviet Union or China, compared to only 24 percent who preferred to see the war wound down. Interestingly, much the same sentiment prevailed after the war: a study carried out in 1980 found that 65 percent of Americans believed that "the trouble in Vietnam was that our troops were asked to fight a war that we could never win."

But the spectacular offensive in Vietnam trapped Lyndon Johnson at a crucial juncture. His popularity had been dwindling for years—partly because of the war, but also because the electorate's faith in his economic and social programs had faded. When he entered office in late 1963, eight out of ten Americans had liked his policies. By 1967, in contrast, only four out of ten citizens gave him a positive score. Then came Tet, and his ratings plummeted—as if Vietnam were a burning fuse that had suddenly ignited an explosion of dissent.

During the six weeks following the initial Communist attacks, public approval of his overall performance dropped from 48 percent to 36 percent—and, more dramatically, endorsement for his handling of the war fell from 40 percent to 26 percent. The country's trust in his authority had evaporated. His credibility—the key to a president's capacity to govern—was gone.

More important, perhaps, Johnson was being abandoned by the vocal elements of the population—the media commentators, business executives, educators, clergymen, and other "elites," whose voices resonated more forcefully in Washington than did those of Middle America. These opinion leaders had already begun to express misgivings about the war. But now they were concluding that the futile conflict, which threatened to divide and torment the nation internally as well as dissipate its global assets, was no longer worth the effort. Closer to the corridors of power, they had been slower than the public to lose confidence in the president.

Once they changed, however, their influence weighed heavily on politicians, administration officials, and Johnson himself. To Johnson and his aides at the time, the precise texture of the growing opposition was not easily discernible—nor did it matter. They were traumatized by the evidence that the administration had become isolated in an election year.

The Tet offensive stunned Johnson. Having swallowed most of the reports claiming that the Communists had been defanged, he had never imagined that they could attack the U.S. embassy in Saigon or assault the cities of South Vietnam. But he concealed his emotions. On the morning of January 31, after a fitful night of checking the torrent of messages from Saigon, his first reaction, typically, was to orchestrate a public relations drive designed to promote optimism. He ordered Westmoreland to hold daily briefings for U.S. correspondents in Vietnam in order to "reassure the public here that you have the situation under control," and he told the White House press corps that the Communist operation had been a "complete failure." He also instructed Dean Rusk, Robert McNamara, Walt Rostow, and other prominent aides to thump the same theme in newspaper and television interviews during the ensuing weeks.

Art Buchwald satirically flattened the news-management campaign from the start. His syndicated column of February 6 portrayed a confident General George Armstrong Custer boasting that "the battle of Little Big Horn had just turned the corner," and the Sioux were "on the run." Other press comments were more somber. An unusually blunt editorial in the usually subdued *Wall Street Journal* warned that "the American people should be getting ready to accept, if they haven't already, the prospect that the whole Vietnam effort may be doomed." But the news media were yet to strike an even worse blow against Johnson.

Walter Cronkite was the nation's most reliable journalistic personality—a figure who "by a mere inflection of his deep baritone voice or by a lifting of his well-known bushy eyebrows . . . might well change the vote of thousands of people," as one politician had extravagantly put it. Moreover, Cronkite was apple-pie American, a Missouri boy who expressed the mood of the heartland as much as he presumably influenced its pulse beat. His views on the war had mostly been balanced, nearly bland. Now, on the evening of February 27, he delivered a fresh verdict. Just back from Saigon, he rejected the official forecasts of victory, predicting instead that it seemed "more certain than ever that the bloody experience of Vietnam is to end in a stalemate." The broadcast shocked and depressed Johnson, who assumed that Cronkite's despondent comment would steer public opinion even farther away from support for the war. But Cronkite, like all other journalists, was lagging behind the American public—reflecting rather than shaping its attitudes.

Not only Vietnam was nagging the Johnson administration. The North Koreans had recently seized the *Pueblo*, a U.S. intelligence ship, and there were hints of growing tensions over Berlin and in the Middle East. The strain even began to affect Rusk, the personification of southern courtesy. At one briefing, pressed by newsmen to explain the American failure to detect the Tet offensive in advance, he flared up with unaccustomed fury: "Whose side are you on? Now, I'm secretary of state of the United States, and I'm on our side! None of your papers or your broadcasting apparatuses are worth a damn unless the United States succeeds. They are trivial compared to that question. So I don't know why people have to be probing for the things that one can bitch about, when there are two thousand stories on the same day about things that are more constructive."

Yet not even Rusk, one of the hardest of the hard-liners, was impervious to doubt. Years afterward, when we talked about the impact of the Tet events on the American public, he remembered having sympathized with his chagrined kinfolk in Cherokee County, Georgia. "Dean," they had pleaded at the time, "if you can't tell us when this war is going to end, well then maybe we just ought to chuck it." And, recalling their words to me, he added: "The fact was that we could not, in any good faith, tell them."

How could Johnson continue to kindle the nation's enthusiasm for the war when, even to many of his own aides, it had become an outrage? Harry McPherson, a fellow Texan, and one of his speechwriters and confidants—a sensitive young lawyer whom Johnson, with only daughters, had almost adopted—sat at a desk in the White House only steps away from the radios and teletypes receiving Westmoreland's assurances of a decisive Communist setback. He could consult Rostow, forever upbeat. Still, McPherson recalled, he saw the truth on the television screen: "I watched the invasion of the American embassy compound, and the terrible sight of General Loan killing the Vietcong captive. You got a sense of the awfulness, the endlessness, of the war—and, though it sounds naive, the unethical quality of a war in which a prisoner is shot at point-blank range. I put aside the confidential cables. I was more persuaded by the tube and by the newspapers. I was fed up with the optimism that seemed to flow without stopping from Saigon."

Much of the optimism that flowed from Saigon was confected—a deliberate attempt by Westmoreland to justify his earlier expressions of confidence. Richard Holbrooke, then a young U.S. official and later to be a senior State Department figure, was sent to Vietnam at the time in a group assigned to appraise the situation. Years afterward, Holbrooke recalled his impressions of the mood then pervading the American mission. Ambassador Ellsworth Bunker, a laconic Vermonter, was characteristically calm. But Westmoreland was "dispirited, deeply shaken, almost a broken man"—a person totally different from his upbeat messages to Washington. In subsequent years, Westmoreland would assert that he had never wavered, that the press had betrayed him. As Holbrooke observed him, however, he was "stunned that the Communists had been able to coordinate so many attacks in such secrecy."

Johnson meanwhile fixed his gaze on the battlefield. Especially preoccupied by the plight of Khesanh, he offered to send Westmoreland reinforcements. But Westmoreland, aware that fresh troop arrivals would contradict his optimistic assertions, demurred. What followed was an intricate dialogue between Washington and Saigon that mirrored the situation in the two capitals. Johnson was primarily concerned with domestic opinion, while Westmoreland was trying to protect his reputation as a soldier. The exchange also revealed the machinations of the U.S. military bureaucracy—and it would, in the weeks ahead, lead to decisions that were to reverse the course of the war.

General Earle Wheeler, chairman of the joint chiefs of staff, cabled Westmoreland on February 8 to warn him that the president was "not prepared to accept a defeat"—adding: "If you need more troops, ask for them." Westmoreland, still sanguine, responded that he might need a division and a half in April if conditions in South Vietnam's northern areas worsened. Wheeler prodded him, pointing out that Johnson, for "psychological and political" reasons, could not afford to allow the Communists to hoist their flag over any part of South Vietnam. "Please understand that I am not trying to sell you on the deployment of additional forces," Wheeler explained—but he was doing exactly that. He cautioned Westmoreland that the conflict had entered a "critical phase," and he urged him to request "what you believe is required under the circumstances."

It now dawned on Westmoreland what he was being obliquely ordered to ask for more men, and, in soldierly fashion, he obeyed. Wheeler, interposing himself as Westmoreland's surrogate, raised the issue with Johnson at a White House meeting on February 11, a Sunday. Wheeler explained that Westmoreland was not expressing a "firm demand" for additional troops and could cope without them, but more forces would give him the "increased capability to regain the initiative and go on the offensive at an appropriate time."

Wheeler then told Westmoreland what he had told Johnson—and, thus prompted, Westmoreland officially requested more men. Discarding his earlier optimism, he even injected a note of panic in his message. "A setback is fully possible if I am not reinforced," he said. "I desperately need reinforcements. Time is of the essence."

A shrewd military bureaucrat, Wheeler was plainly promoting a clever ploy on behalf of the joint chiefs. For, in forwarding Westmoreland's formal request to Johnson, he emphasized that dispatching additional troops to Vietnam would severely deplete America's total armed forces—unless more than a hundred thousand U.S. army and marine reservists were simultaneously recalled to service. In sum, Wheeler had taken advantage of the Tet emergency to coax Westmoreland into asking for more men so that the joint chiefs could press Johnson to mobilize the reserves—a step he had repeatedly avoided.

Johnson, seeing through the transparent scheme, was even less inclined to test public opinion now than he had been before. He consigned the issue of the reservists to "study," and instead approved an additional contingent of only some ten thousand troops for Vietnam. But Westmoreland, his appetite whetted, resorted to a typical military gambit.

He fashioned a fresh analysis of Communist strategy, and tailored it to accommodate his appeal for more men. Until now, he said, the United States had been conducting a limited war on the assumption that the Communists were waging a "protracted" struggle. But the war had become a "new ball game." The Communists had switched to an ambitious bid to "achieve a quick victory" and were sustaining heavy losses in the attempt. Only with "adequate" reinforcements could he "capitalize" on their casualties, and "materially shorten the war."

By no coincidence, Westmoreland's conversion suited Wheeler and his colleagues. They had long brooded about Vietnam's effect on America's global security obligations. For two years, Johnson had been fighting a costly war without harnessing the United States to its imperatives. And, because he had refused to call up the reserves, army units in Europe and elsewhere, their officers and noncoms sent to Vietnam, were skeletal. The only combat-ready division defending the United States, the 82nd Airborne, had been stripped to one third its strength to provide troops for the war. The marine corps could not attract enough recruits. Draftees could be conscripted to replenish the ranks, but they lacked the experience to serve as leaders and technicians—and enlisting them in large numbers also posed domestic political problems. Ironically,

Wheeler and the joint chiefs essentially concurred in General Giap's assessment: the conflict was bleeding America.

At that stage, as Westmoreland put it later, Wheeler "conned" him into a grandiose project. On February 23, Wheeler flew to Saigon and inflated Westmoreland's hopes. He pointed out that McNamara was due to be replaced as secretary of defense by Clark Clifford, a proponent of toughness. It seemed likely, Wheeler intimated, that Johnson would concede to mobilizing the reserves, approve U.S. ground attacks against the Communist sanctuaries in Cambodia and Laos, and perhaps even authorize American incursions into enemy staging areas in the southern part of North Vietnam. In reality, the chances of Johnson endorsing all or any of these moves were remote, but the gullible Westmoreland took Wheeler at his word. He submitted to Wheeler's suggestion that they draw up a huge troop request to cover the requirements of both Vietnam and America's worldwide responsibilities.

This consisted of three "force packages" totaling about two hundred and six thousand men. Approximately one hundred and eight thousand, earmarked for Vietnam, would reach there by May 1. The rest would be deployed in September and December if needed, or else assigned to strengthen the nation's anemic armed forces in other places. The whole project hinged on Johnson's assent. Or as Westmoreland, speaking in Pentagon jargon, later described it to me, the concept was "a contingency plan based on the assumption of a decision."

Back in Washington to lobby for the gigantic troop increase, Wheeler omitted any mention of invading Cambodia and Laos or beefing up America's international military presence. Instead, he portrayed Westmoreland as an imperiled field commander whose position might collapse unless he received reinforcements rapidly. Flatly contradicting Westmoreland's optimism, he reported to Johnson that the Tet offensive had been "a near thing," and he cautioned that the enemy's "major, powerful, nationwide assault has by no means run its course." The only way to avert a catastrophe in Vietnam, he asserted, was to send out more men—which meant, of course, mobilizing the reserves.

Clark Clifford, who listened to Wheeler deliver his report to Johnson at a White House meeting on February 28, would remember it as "so somber, so discouraging, to the point where it was really shocking." He was especially shaken by the effect the account had on Johnson. The president, he said, was "as worried as I have ever seen him."

Vietnam now confronted Johnson with the biggest challenge he had faced since he agonized over the decision to commit U.S. combat troops three years before. To fulfill Wheeler's request for more men, he would have to place the nation on a virtual war footing in an election year, amid growing protests against his management of the conflict. But to rebuff Wheeler was to renounce victory and perhaps even risk defeat. Johnson could not make a judgment without a full-scale examination of the options. He turned to Clifford. Directing him to conduct a new study, he said plaintively: "Give me the lesser of the evils."

Tall, dapper, charming, and eloquent, Clark Clifford was one of the most distinguished lawyers in Washington. A Kansan then in his early sixties, he had served as a young counsel to President Truman—quitting to start a private practice that now earned him a half-million dollars a year representing corporations, foreign regimes, and other affluent clients. He owed his colossal success, in part, to an extraordinary range of contacts. He knew everybody worth knowing—from bankers and business executives to labor leaders and journalists, diplomats, bureaucrats, congressmen, cabinet officers, and the president. These friends and acquaintances fed him information vital to his craft of wielding influence effectively. He also derived strength from his independence. Having already acquired wealth, prestige, and power, he did not need a prominent public post to promote himself. So he was almost doing Johnson a favor by joining the administration, and he felt that he could speak out more frankly than other members of the White House entourage.

Except for a passing moment of uneasiness in 1965, Clifford had consistently championed the administration's policy in Vietnam, and Johnson expected him to be a steadier defense secretary than Robert McNamara. But even though Clifford continued to sound tough, doubts had begun to creep into his mind in the late summer of 1967, when Johnson sent him abroad to persuade a number of America's allies to commit more men to the war effort. The leaders of countries like Thailand, the Philippines, Australia, and New Zealand—the "dominoes" supposedly threatened by Communism—refused to increase their token troop contributions. Clifford returned home "puzzled, troubled, concerned"—now beginning to think, as he wrote afterward, that perhaps "our assessment of the danger to the stability of Southeast Asia and the Western Pacific was exaggerated." His misgivings were heightened further after he entered the Pentagon on March 1, 1968.

Clifford's appointment initially dismayed several of the civilian officials at the Pentagon. They regarded him as a dilettante whom Johnson had picked solely for his fidelity, and they were particularly upset by his hard-line reputation. Some, fearing that he would plunge the country deeper into the war, even contemplated resignation. But they finally figured that their best bet was to proselytize him, as they had McNamara. The man who labored hardest at that task was Paul Warnke, assistant secretary for international security affairs, whose office focused on the political aspects of defense issues. A measure of his achievement was to be apparent later, when he became Clifford's law partner. Later, too, Westmoreland excoriated him as a "persistent rebel" whose "spell" transformed Clifford into a "dove and defeatist."

Oddly enough, Warnke had barely known Clifford until then, even though they were both top Washington attorneys. Warnke, a partner in the prestigious firm of Covington and Burling, had been a litigator rather than a political broker and lobbyist like Clifford. Already close to fifty, he had gone into the government for the first time the year before as a respite from the law, and he quickly perceived that the struggle in Vietnam had reached a deadlock in which American soldiers would continue to die fruitlessly because, however many battles they won, they could not win the war. He had helped to bring McNamara around to that view. Now his job was to educate Clifford. If he failed, he would quit.

Johnson had handed Clifford a brutal schedule. He wanted recommendations on the request for troops no later than March 4. Clifford convened his study group at the Pentagon on February 28, two days before he was due to be sworn into office. Its thirteen members included Rusk, Rostow, Wheeler, Warnke, and Maxwell Taylor, as well as Henry Fowler, secretary of the treasury, and McNamara, in a valedictory role.

Predictably putting forth a grand geopolitical analysis, Rostow argued for firm action in Vietnam to deter "aggression . . . in the Middle East, elsewhere in Asia, and perhaps even Europe"—and, during the weeks ahead, he also pressed Johnson to approve American forays into North Vietnam and Laos. Wheeler and Taylor seconded this dynamic approach, while McNamara contended that the only alternative was a negotiated settlement. Fowler meanwhile introduced a sobering thought. A force buildup, he explained, would raise the costs of waging the war and thus require cuts in domestic social programs, other military expenditures, and foreign aid. Even so, a tax increase would be necessary, but its passage by Congress was improbable. Severe economic and financial difficulties menaced the nation unless the administration could inspire the population to make sacrifices—an implausible prospect in an election year.

Clifford realized immediately that the dilemma extended far beyond the narrow subject of troop deployments. He faced nothing less than a sweeping re-evaluation of America's whole policy toward Vietnam. Instead of merely appraising the need for men and matériel, he would have to propose "the most intelligent thing to do for the country. . . . Try though we would to stay with the assignment of devising means to meet the military's request, fundamental questions began to recur over and over."

Working at breakneck speed to meet the deadline, various government departments generated memorandums to be fed into the report to Johnson. Warnke, commissioned by Clifford to draft the document, assumed that his new boss would "do what we all thought ought to be done" if guided properly. His staff, composed mostly of young civilian and military officials frustrated by the futility of the war, could not doctor the assessments sent in by other agencies. But they had considerable editorial latitude to shape the direction of the study, and they saw this as a unique opportunity to effect a major change. One of them, Morton Halperin, later recalled that "we were going to write what we thought even if that meant we all got fired"—and they completed a draft that, in his words, "really attacked the fundamental motives" of U.S. policy in Vietnam.

Warnke read the draft to Clifford at a meeting on March 1 attended by Wheeler and others, and it painted an unalluring picture of the situation. Since the Communists could match any increase in American troop strength, it said, the escalation suggested by Wheeler and Westmoreland promised "no early end to the conflict." Instead, the strategy would "entail substantial costs" in Vietnam and especially in the United States—where the subordination of economic and social expenditures to military outlays "runs great risks of provoking a domestic crisis of unprecedented proportions." Moreover, a large influx of additional American soldiers would encourage the Saigon regime to believe that the United States "will continue to fight its war while it engages in backroom politics and permits widespread corruption." Warnke therefore proposed that U.S. units in South Vietnam be pulled back to defending the populated areas along the coast. And he urged that the South Vietnamese army be trained and equipped as a more effective force.

Warnke's presentation naturally appalled Wheeler, and the joint chiefs rapidly responded with demands for vigorous action. Westmoreland again called for U.S. incursions into Laos, while Admiral Sharp advocated more intensive bombing of North Vietnam, asserting that toughness was "the only policy that the Communists understand." But their vagueness disturbed Clifford. One afternoon after the war, as we sat in his lavish Washington law office appropriately looking down on the White House, he recollected his attempts at the time to extract precise replies from Wheeler and his colleagues. "How long would it take to succeed in Vietnam? They didn't know. How many more troops would it take? They couldn't say. Were two hundred thousand the answer? They weren't sure. Might they need more? Yes, they might need more. Could the enemy build up in exchange? Probably. So what was the plan to win the war? Well, the only plan was that attrition would wear out the Communists, and they would have had enough. Was there any indication that we've reached that point? No, there wasn't."

By early March, Clifford told me, he had quietly turned against the war—having concluded that "all we were going to do was waste our treasure and the lives of our men out there in the jungles." From then on, he was convinced, America's aim should be to curb its involvement in Vietnam and to disengage gradually. But the final verdict would rest with the president, and Clifford knew as a skilled political operator that he had to proceed prudently. He did not want to jolt Johnson. Nor could he afford to antagonize Wheeler and the joint chiefs of staff.

On March 4, after an exhausting weekend of polishing, Clifford sent his recommendations to the White House. They were far more cautious than Warnke's original proposals. But despite his disappointment, Warnke understood that the process of reaching decisions was extremely complex. The report would set the agenda for an internal debate, stimulating the president to pose questions. Its real purpose, Warnke later explained, was to divert Johnson's attention away from the specific issue of troop requests and "to get him to focus on the wider questions."

Though it contained something for everyone, Clifford's report tilted toward the moderates. It sought to placate the joint chiefs by favoring a call-up of the reserves to cope with "possible contingencies worldwide," but it spurned their appeal for a bigger U.S. combat role in Vietnam, stating bluntly that "there is no reason to believe" that the Communists could be beaten by "an additional two hundred thousand American troops, or double or triple that quantity." Moreover, the document featured two proposals that had always been anathema to the military establishment: flatly ruling out the prospect of victory, it suggested that Westmoreland be directed not to try "either to destroy the enemy forces or to rout them completely"—implying that American units might instead be withdrawn to coastal enclaves; and it further proposed that the South Vietnamese be warned in no uncertain terms that continued U.S. assistance would be predicated on a marked improvement in their performance. Thus, for the first time, the Saigon regime was to be put on notice that American patience was limited.

Johnson's reaction was mixed. He found the report unduly pessimistic and, as he recorded in his memoirs, preferred to rely on Westmoreland rather than on "many people in Washington, especially Pentagon civilians." But he was sensitive to the "growing criticism" of the war coming "from the press and from vocal citizens." So he decided to defer a decision. Nevertheless, his outlook began to shift. He had almost been ready to raise taxes, mobilize the reserves, and pour more men into Vietnam. Now, though he had not yet defined a new attitude, his mind was changing.

At that stage, Rusk approached him with an idea. Rusk, primarily pained by the gloomy mood at home, had come to believe that America's confidence in the president's policies might be restored by curtailing the bombing of North Vietnam as a prerequisite to inviting the Communists to negotiate. If they agreed, Johnson would be seen as an apostle of peace; if not, as seemed more likely, he had a justification for stronger American military moves. In any case, the experiment would be cheap, since monsoon rains normally reduced air operations during that period anyway. Outlining the project at Johnson's regular Tuesday luncheon on March 5, Rusk recommended that the gesture be uncomplicated by stated conditions in order to avoid "theological debates about words." Or as he put it: "Just take the action, and see whether anybody is able to make anything out of it."

Both Clifford and Warnke objected, fearing that its almost certain rejection by the Communists would furnish the joint chiefs of staff with the pretext to demand an intensification of the war. Johnson also greeted the notion coolly, having halted the bombing eight different times over the past three years without results. But he soon reconsidered, partly because he needed some sort of peace proposal to appease public opinion and because he trusted Rusk—"a deliberate man, a judicious man, a careful man" who would not steer him into a crazy scheme. He tucked the idea away for future use.

Though Johnson had virtually shelved the troop request concocted by Wheeler and Westmoreland, news of their bid for more men began to filter up to Capitol Hill. Senator Robert Kennedy heard the story from Daniel Ellsberg, a young Defense Department official, and he publicly criticized the proposed deployment on the Senate floor. Other senators, among them William Fulbright and Gaylord Nelson, also denounced any escalation, while Mike Mansfield, the Senate majority leader, declared that "we are in the wrong place, fighting the wrong war." As they spoke out, a more important switch was occurring less openly in Congress. The hard-line senators, like John Stennis and Henry Jackson, who had consistently underwritten the military establishment, now began to see the hopelessness of the struggle. They quietly imparted their views to Clifford, and also voiced their opinions to Wheeler, warning that they could not subscribe to bigger force commitments as long as the administration refused to pursue a winning strategy.

On March 8, sensing that the tide was running against them, Wheeler advised Westmoreland to cease making optimistic statements to the press if he expected Congress to back their plea for a larger manpower investment in Vietnam. The rebuke startled Westmoreland, who naively replied that he was merely appraising the situation objectively. The next day, effectively announcing defeat on the Washington front, Wheeler again cabled Westmoreland: "I do not wish to shunt my troubles on you. However, I must tell you frankly that there is strong resistance from all quarters to putting more ground force units into South Vietnam. . . . You should not count on an affirmative decision for such additional forces."

The seeds of a sensational newspaper revelation had meanwhile been planted on the evening of March 1 at the elegant Georgetown home of William Moorhead, a Pennsylvania congressman. Moorhead had thrown a party for the Washington chapter of Skull and Bones, the Yale secret society, whose members included Edwin Dale, a *New York Times* reporter, and Townsend Hoopes, under secretary of the air force. Hoopes, who had turned against the war, hinted to Dale that a faction at the Pentagon was forming to resist a troop buildup in Vietnam. Dale passed the tip to his *Times* colleagues Neil Sheehan and Hedrick Smith, both former Vietnam correspondents now covering defense and diplomatic affairs. Tapping their sources, they stitched together the details within a week. On March 10, a Sunday, the *Times* published their dispatch on page one under a three-column headline.

WESTMORELAND REQUESTS
206,000 MORE MEN, STIRRING
DEBATE IN ADMINISTRATION

The story was incomplete, lacking as it did the fact that Wheeler wanted half the force to fulfill America's security obligations elsewhere in the world. Even so, it posed a central question that now was being asked with increasing frequency in Congress and across the United States. If the Tet battles had crippled the Communists—as Johnson,

Westmoreland, and other senior administration figures continued to proclaim—why were another two hundred thousand Americans needed in Vietnam? Characteristically, the president widened his already gaping credibility gap into a veritable canyon by instructing his press secretary, George Christian, to say that "no specific request" for troops had reached the White House. Johnson, privately furious at the *Times* disclosure, traced its origin to Hoopes, whom he would repeatedly deride during the months ahead. "Hoopees! Hoopees! Who the hell is Hoopees? Here I take four million people out of poverty, and all I ever hear about is Hoopees."

The *Times* was not the only news medium to torment Johnson. Shortly afterward, Rusk appeared before Fulbright's Foreign Relations Committee to testify for eleven hours over a two-day period. The spectacle was broadcast on television during the day and taped excerpts were replayed to larger audiences in the evening, and though Rusk acquitted himself well under Fulbright's relentless grilling, the marathon hearing gave the public a unique insight into the mounting congressional dissidence against the administration's Vietnam policies.

On the second day of the hearing, another drama was taking place in New Hampshire, the site of the election year's first presidential primary election. Until then, Johnson had managed to prevent Vietnam from becoming a domestic political issue, largely by mustering bipartisan backing for the war and thus reducing his critics to an apparent handful of either right- or left-wing extremists with only marginal influence. Senator Eugene McCarthy, the sole Democrat who planned to challenge Johnson on the issue in the primaries, was somewhat more respectable. Yet he was an eccentric without broad appeal, whose ratings in the polls by the middle of February showed him gaining fewer than 20 percent of the votes in New Hampshire. Johnson's name was absent from the ballot, since he had not yet formally entered the race. But his activists had organized a write-in campaign on his behalf, implying in their advertisements that a vote for McCarthy was a vote for the enemy: "The Communists in Vietnam are watching the New Hampshire primary."

The results were staggering. Of the fifty thousand votes cast for the Democratic party contenders, McCarthy received only three hundred fewer than Johnson. A maverick senator had successfully defied an incumbent president and master politician in a performance that electrified the country. Interestingly, though, New Hampshire citizens had strongly endorsed McCarthy as a protest against Johnson rather than as a gesture of approval for a peace platform. Studies conducted later indicated that many of McCarthy's supporters favored the war, but had registered dissatisfaction with the administration—and a large proportion of them voted in the November national election for George Wallace, a ferocious anti-Communist. Or perhaps many mistook Eugene McCarthy for the late Senator Joe McCarthy, the fanatical Red-baiter who had died in 1957.

McCarthy may have been a symbol. Four days later, however, Bobby Kennedy announced his candidacy, and he was real. Moreover, he made it plain that he intended to use the war as an issue to defeat Johnson. Two days before throwing his hat into the ring, he approached Clifford with a proposition for the president: he would stay out of the race on condition that Johnson confess publicly that the administration's Vietnam policy had been an error and appoint a commission including himself to recommend a new course. The idea was both arrogant and devious. For Johnson to accept would signify, in effect, the abdication of his authority as chief executive. To spurn it, though, meant the opposition of a formidable foe bearing a magical name and launching a challenge at a time when he, Johnson, could not have been more vulnerable.

Not only did he reject Kennedy, but he defiantly struck shrill notes in his speeches on Vietnam. "We shall and we are going to win," he harangued a business group on March 17, and he sounded even more strident in an address to a convention of farmers in Minneapolis the next day. In recalling every crisis of the century, from the sinking of the *Lusitania* and the attack on Pearl Harbor to the Berlin blockade, his hoarse voice rasped out the peroration. "The time has come when we ought to stand up and be counted, when we ought to support our leaders, our government, our men, and our allies until aggression is stopped, wherever it has occurred."

The Wisconsin primary was scheduled for April 2, and Johnson, on the ballot, faced serious opposition from both Kennedy and McCarthy. His advisers foresaw not only his doom, but the doom of the Democratic party. One of them, James L. Rowe, a party insider since the Roosevelt era, sent him a tough memorandum. In contrast to Kennedy and McCarthy, who had become the peace candidates, he had become "the war candidate." So he had to "do something exciting and dramatic" to recapture the peace issue. Intransigence was not the answer. "Hardly anyone today is interested in winning the war," Rowe told him. "Everyone wants to get out, and the only question is how."

The message sank in. On March 20, the morning after Rowe's memo reached him, Johnson telephoned Clifford and said: "I've got to get me a peace proposal."

Three days later, Johnson secretly dispatched Wheeler to the Philippines to inform Westmoreland not to expect the additional forces he had requested the month before. The president would furnish only thirteen thousand five hundred more American troops, and it was up to Westmoreland to inspire the South Vietnamese to make a greater effort. The Saigon regime had only recently begun, under pressure, to conscript eighteen-year-olds—while, ironically, American draftees of the same age had been fighting the war for nearly three years.

In good times, Lyndon Johnson could be cheerful, expansive, generous. But now he felt alone and beleaguered, a bound Prometheus being ravaged by real or imagined vultures. His former press secretary and protégé, Bill Moyers, found him insulated inside the White House, paranoiacally blaming all his woes on political and personal rivals. Henry Brandon, a British correspondent, was stunned by his appearance. He looked exhausted—his face ashen, his eyes sunken, his skin flabby, and yet, underneath, his expression was taut. To Clark Clifford, his old confidant, Johnson had suddenly become cranky and suspicious. In only a few weeks, he recollected, "the bloom was off our relationship."

Harry McPherson, who observed the two men closely at the time, later analyzed the interplay between them. He recalled that over the past year, as Vietnam increasingly obsessed him, Johnson had come to depend primarily on three faithful advisers—Rusk, Rostow, and McNamara. Then McNamara defected, and Johnson turned to Clifford, counting on him for a fresh perspective coupled with the total devotion he expected from all his associates. But as he examined the crisis from inside the government, Clifford changed, and as he changed he no longer seemed to Johnson to be loyal. Johnson was disappointed, and he felt he had been deceived by an intimate and valued friend. So, McPherson concluded, Johnson began to tune Clifford on and off—sometimes consulting him, sometimes ignoring him, sometimes treating him with an excessive politeness contrived to illustrate the distance that separated them.

Johnson had no intention by now of enlarging the war, but neither did he intend to quit. Nor was he ready to stop the American air strikes against North Vietnam in return for possible talks with the Communists, since he thought that would endanger the forces still besieged at Khesanh. His strategy, in short, was simply to "hang in there."

Clifford's dream, in contrast, was to reshape Johnson's entire approach to the war and to put him on the path to an honorable withdrawal from Vietnam. But Clifford's ideas for winding down the U.S. commitment were just as fuzzy as Johnson's conviction that, by holding on, the situation would somehow improve. He regarded Rusk's suggestion for a partial pause in the air raids to be a gimmick. He believed instead that the peace process might be started by a full bombing halt, which would show the Communists the administration's sincere desire for a compromise. "The baby has to crawl before the baby can walk," Clifford argued.

By late March, however, Clifford had barely dented Johnson's attitude. He and his assistants at the Pentagon, desperate, contemplated wholesale resignation. But, deciding that such a bold protest would wreck the administration and shatter the country, Clifford cast around for a dose of "stiff medicine" to purge Johnson's thinking. He found the prescription in the elder statesmen—the "wise men"—who had endorsed the president's policies only five months before.

It was a measure of Johnson's sense of his own inadequacy that, for all his crude populist affectations, he curried the respect and admiration of the Eastern establishment—the distinguished group that alternated between prestigious public positions and lucrative private pursuits. So he consented to Clifford's proposal to reconvene the "wise men." But it was also a reflection of Clifford's conspiratorial skill that he knew in advance, having made a few telephone calls, that many of these prominent figures had turned against the war since their last session in November. Johnson might have guessed as much himself. Dean Acheson, secretary of state under Truman and a key member of the group, had already urged him to search for a way out of the war, and he had heard a similar plea from Arthur Goldberg, his envoy to the United Nations, who was due to attend the meeting as well.

The group, numbering fourteen, assembled at the State Department for dinner on the evening of March 25. Among those present, besides Acheson and Goldberg, were George Ball, McGeorge Bundy, Henry Cabot Lodge, and Abe Fortas, all veterans of past Vietnam debates, as well as newcomers to the subject like Douglas Dillon, the New York banker who had served both Eisenhower and Kennedy, John J. McCloy, and Robert Murphy, a seasoned diplomat. The conclave also included Maxwell Taylor and two other retired generals, Omar Bradley of World War II vintage, and Matthew Ridgway, the U.S. commander during the Korean conflict. Rusk, Rostow, and Wheeler were there along with Clifford. Clifford outlined the three choices facing the president: he could escalate the war with more troops and heavier bombing; he could continue on the present course; or he could curb the air raids and deploy American forces around South Vietnam's populated areas while preparing the Saigon regime to take over the fighting.

Three official specialists then appeared to deliver briefings, and one of them, Philip Habib, a deputy assistant secretary of state and outspoken Brooklynite, pulled no punches. He described the corruption and ineptitude that riddled the South Vietnamese government and army, and he guessed that it might take five or ten years to achieve any real progress— an assessment that stupefied the group. Acheson, the most prestigious person there, bluntly set the tone: the administration had to find a way out of the war.

The "wise men," considerably wiser, met the next day for lunch with Johnson, and he interrogated them one by one. Their replies astounded him. They all favored disengagement from the war, except for Bradley, Murphy, Fortas, and Taylor. Acheson, who sat at Johnson's right in the White House family dining room, talked the most—and he talked candidly. Here was this patrician figure, who had persuaded Truman to finance the French conflict in Indochina nearly two decades before, now renouncing the cause he had upheld solidly since then. The basic problem in South Vietnam, he said, was the Saigon regime's lack of popular support, and the same problem plagued the administration, which also lacked popular support for the struggle. When one of the others objected to his portrayal of American policy as an effort to impose a military solution on the Communists, Acheson erupted: "What in the name of God have we got five hundred thousand troops out there for—chasing girls? You know damned well this is what we're trying to do—to force the enemy to sue for peace. It won't happen—at least not in any time the American people will permit."

"Somebody poisoned the well," Johnson growled after his prominent advisers had left. Infuriated, he ordered a search for the culprit. He called in two of the government specialists who had briefed the group, and instructed them to replay their comments to him. But he could not locate Habib, who had left town. In his memoirs, however, Johnson conceded that the elder statesmen had swayed him profoundly. "If they had been so deeply influenced by the reports of the Tet offensive," he wrote, "what must the average citizen in the country be thinking?" America had collapsed on the home front rather than on the battlefield, he felt. "I remained convinced that the blow to morale was more of our own doing than anything the enemy had accomplished with its army. We were defeating ourselves."

Clifford was elated. But he still had to steer Johnson toward an actual decision to "de-escalate" the war. For weeks, Clifford had been recruiting confederates around Washington. Indeed, he told me, he had fancied himself to be a character like the Scarlet Pimpernel, covertly enlisting plotters during the French Revolution, whispering, "Is he with us?" He sensed a kindred spirit in Harry McPherson, the president's speech-writer. In late February, they had both attended McNamara's farewell luncheon at the State Department, and Clifford was touched by McPherson's sympathetic reaction to McNamara's emotional outburst against the war. That afternoon, back at his office, Clifford telephoned McPherson. "Old boy, I noticed you today, and it seems to me that we're on the same side. I think we should form a partnership. You be the partner in the White House, and I'll be the partner at the Pentagon. You tell me what goes on over there, and I'll tell you what happens here—and together we'll get the country and our president out of this mess."

Their chance arose toward the end of March, as McPherson grappled with a speech on Vietnam that Johnson had directed him to write weeks earlier. Gone are the days when Abraham Lincoln could scratch a few remarks on the back of an envelope on the way to Gettysburg. Preparing a presidential address has become a vast collective enterprise. Various government bureaus contribute ideas, which are discussed at meeting after meeting before a version is shown to the president, who invariably bucks it back for revisions, and the officials meet again and again to discuss it afresh. So McPherson had gone through five or six drafts by the last week of March, feeling like "an engineer assembling an erector set." Soon, though, Clifford would begin to register his views.

He and Rusk were still wrangling over the issue of halting the bombing raids over North Vietnam. But the details of the issue, almost talmudic in their complexity, had become less important than the tone of the address—its delivery now scheduled for the evening of March 31. Several of Johnson's advisers had submitted their versions, and the speech at that stage still rang with Churchillian phrases pledging the United States to keep fighting. Three days before the deadline, however, Clifford met at the State Department with Rusk, Rostow, William Bundy, and McPherson, and he insisted on a complete overhaul. To broadcast the speech in its present form, he warned, would be a "tragic error." It was a "hard-nosed" lecture on war, not the peace pronounce-ment that the president needed. "For example, the first sentence read, 'I want to talk to you about the war in Vietnam.' I wanted that changed to 'I want to talk to you about peace in Vietnam.' What I wanted to do—and did—was to turn it around."

Clifford also wanted the speech to announce a full or partial bombing halt as a first step toward winching down the war—but his concern with its absence from the text was misplaced. Johnson, who often conferred separately with his various advisers, had already indicated to Rusk that he intended to include the proposal in his address. Even Rostow favored a limited curb on the air strikes.

McPherson returned to his typewriter to punch out yet another, more conciliatory draft. He marked it Speech 1A, and sent it to Johnson, whose desk by this time was littered with a dozen or more versions. The next morning, as McPherson related the story to me, Johnson telephoned him. " 'I don't like what you say there on page three,' he said. I looked very quickly to see which draft he was talking about. It was 1A, the alternate version. We were on track."

On the morning of March 30, the day before the deadline, Johnson assembled his advisers at the White House for a drafting session that stretched into the evening. Coatless, his necktie loosened, Johnson hunched over the text, scrutinizing every word. The speech now announced a partial U.S. bombing halt, but Clifford watched Johnson like a lawyer, questioning any nuance that might offer a pretext to resume the air strikes. The address still lacked a peroration, however, and McPherson offered to write one swiftly. Johnson stopped him. "Don't worry," he said, "I may have a little ending of my own." With that, he strode from the room.

"Good Lord," McPherson said to Clifford, "is he going to quit?" And, he recalled, "Clifford looked at me as if I were out of my mind."

McPherson confirmed his instinct the next day, a Sunday, when he returned to the White House to learn that Johnson was closeted in the family quarters with Horace Busby, a close friend and former aide. McPherson spent the day polishing the address, which Johnson was to deliver on television at nine o'clock that evening. Late in the afternoon, Johnson telephoned to ask his opinion of the speech. "It's pretty good," McPherson answered, adding that he was pleased and proud it had been changed.

"I've got an ending," Johnson said.

"So I've heard," McPherson responded.

"What do you think?"

"I'm very sorry, Mr. President."

"Okay," Johnson replied, accentuating his Texas drawl, "so long, pardner."

The scene in Johnson's bedchamber that afternoon was tumultuous as Busby put the finishing touches on the most dramatic paragraphs of the speech—the president's statement that he would not run for re-election. Johnson ambled around the room, talking almost continually on the telephone, trailing its long cord behind him and occasionally using a free hand to play with his baby grandson, who was crawling about. Personal friends, guests at the White House, wandered in and out, and Johnson's valets bustled back and forth, selecting his clothes for the evening performance. A pair of U.S. navy doctors appeared at one point to scrape Johnson's hands, which suffered from a benign kind of skin disease. He summoned Clifford, among others, to show him the relevant passages of the address. Clifford was dumbfounded. "I've made up my mind," said Johnson. "I'm actually going to do it."

Johnson had nearly announced a decision to leave the presidency in his State of the Union message to Congress in January, before the Tet offensive. In September, he had sent George Christian, his press secretary, to Texas to ask Governor John Connally, an old and devoted associate, how he might withdraw his candidacy gracefully, but Connally had skirted the question. Early in the year, Johnson had also invited Busby to draft a statement on the subject for him, but Busby had persuaded him to reconsider, saying that the country should not have a lame-duck president for so long. Thus, though the war punctured Johnson's popularity, he was not entirely a casualty of the Tet offensive.

Johnson had survived a severe heart attack in 1955, but he worried that a second might leave him crippled in office, like Woodrow Wilson, and his wife, Lady Bird, feared worse—his death before another term ended. Johnson also believed that, having promoted more progressive social and economic legislation than any U.S. leader since Roosevelt, he probably had exhausted his political capital with Congress. Over lunch one day in early March, he assured McPherson and Joseph Califano, another aide, that Congress would refuse him the honeymoon year that it usually grants new presidents. "We're like an old couple who've known each other too long," he said. "We've yelled at each other and begged from each other too often, and I would never get that year." And there was Vietnam.

As he spoke to the nation on the evening of March 31, 1968, only the impact of Vietnam seemed to matter: "I have concluded that I should not permit the presidency to become involved in the partisan divisions that are developing in this political year. . . . Accordingly, I shall not seek, and I will not accept, the nomination of my party for another term as your president."

Johnson also announced he was restricting U.S. air strikes to the area below the twentieth parallel, as Rusk had proposed, thereby sparing 90 percent of North Vietnamese territory. He authorized Averell Harriman to open negotiations whenever the Communists were ready. But he did not state specifically that he would refrain from resuming the bombing if the talks with the enemy failed to make progress. Nor did he say clearly and categorically that he would not increase the American force in Vietnam beyond the nearly five hundred and fifty thousand troops already committed. He seemed to have left the door ajar to the possibility of renewed escalation, and the generals and admirals and their pugnacious supporters never abandoned the hope of tougher action. During the months ahead, however, Clifford would maneuver to prevent the conflict from intensifying again, assuming the responsibility, often without Johnson's authorization, of "interpreting" the lame-duck president's intentions. Clifford could definitively declare by September 1968 that Vietnam was no longer "an unlimited drain on our resources," adding that "the so-called 'bottomless pit' has been capped."

Consistent with their plan to fight and talk simultaneously, the Communists had decided even before Johnson's abdication speech to begin discussions. And, now aware of the shift in American public opinion, they figured on making a big impact in the United States. In the middle of March, they invited Walter Cronkite to Hanoi, aiming to use him to convey their new approach to his vast American television audience. But Cronkite declined; it might seem that he was being rewarded for his criticism of the war. Charles Collingwood, a seasoned CBS correspondent, went in his place. In an interview with him on April 5, Foreign Minister Nguyen Duy Trinh stated that North Vietnam was prepared to meet with an American delegation.

The U.S. diplomats were headed by Harriman and the North Vietnamese by Xuan Thuy, a second-rank Communist veteran. The conference opened in Paris on May 10 in a mood of euphoria—hope ran so high among the American officials, in fact, that they chose hotel rooms in the expectation that a settlement was only months away. But the dialogue reached an impasse within weeks as the spokesmen for both sides repeated the same arguments. The United States insisted on the withdrawal of the North Vietnamese forces inside South Vietnam—a demand rejected by the Communists, who insisted in their turn that the Saigon regime be reshuffled to include Vietcong representatives.

The frustrating talks were to drag on for another five years. More Americans would be killed in Vietnam than had died there previously. And the United States itself would be torn apart by the worst internal upheavals in a century.

15 Nixon's War

On President Nixon's orders, national security adviser Kissinger entered into secret
negotiations with Le Duc Tho (at right), a senior member of the North Vietnamese
regime. Both sides were reluctant to make concessions, but Kissinger admired Le Duc
Tho's determination and tenacity.

Vice-President Humphrey won the Democratic nomination for president at the Chicago convention in August 1968 that was convulsed by a large antiwar wing of the party. Lame-duck President Johnson leaned on Humphrey to support administration policy.

Outside the convention hall, Chicago police confront antiwar demonstrators. Not until late September did Humphrey break away from Johnson in an effort to win over the antiwar voters, but by then it was too late.

President-elect Nixon introduces Kissinger, his choice as national security adviser, to the press in December 1968. Kissinger had joined Nixon a month earlier, having previously worked for Governor Nelson Rockefeller of New York.

Nixon with his advisers (left to right): Secretary of State William Rogers, Secretary of Defense Melvin Laird, and Henry Kissinger, his national security adviser. Laird, a former Wisconsin congressman, was sensitive to the American public's opposition to the war. He coined the term "Vietnamization" to describe the process by which U.S. troops would be replaced by South Vietnamese forces.

Ho Chi Minh (left) died at the age of seventy-nine in September 1969. He had earlier retired from the day-to-day management of North Vietnam's affairs, ceding authority to a collective leadership headed by Le Duan, senior member of the Communist party politburo, and Pham Van Dong (right), prime minister of North Vietnam.

American forces in Cambodia in May 1970. Even though they were soon withdrawn, their incursion triggered enormous antiwar demonstrations in the United States. Four students were killed by national guardsmen at Kent State University in Ohio.

Protests against the war amplified, as seen in this demonstration in New York. But the president claimed that he had the support of the "silent majority" of Americans, and opinion polls showed he was not entirely wrong.

In order to show that the public backed his policies, Nixon encouraged demonstrations by such groups as these New York "hard hats"—construction workers who staged a lunchtime rally calling for victory in Vietnam.

By the early 1970s, antiwar sentiment at home was beginning to affect GIs in Vietnam (below). Nixon was withdrawing American forces, and the remaining soldiers lost their zeal for a war that seemed to be winding down.

Americans, whatever their attitude toward the war, were stunned in 1969 by the revelation of a massacre of South Vietnamese peasants by U.S. troops at the village of Mylai.

The Phoenix program, an effort to uproot the Vietcong structure in the South Vietnamese countryside, was conducted under CIA auspices. Many thousands of Vietnamese were killed, yet the program was ineffective in many respects. Vietnamese Communists later acknowledged that it had weakened the Vietcong.

A major test of "Vietnamization" took place in February 1971, when South Vietnamese forces invaded Laos without American advisers. They performed poorly. Larry Burrows, the Life photographer who had been covering Vietnam for a decade, was killed during the operation.

Prince Sihanouk (left), head of the Cambodian government in exile from 1970 to 1975, is seen on a visit to Hanoi in 1973 with Prime Minister Pham Van Dong (center) and Defense Minister General Vo Nguyen Giap.

In Cambodia, a coup d'état *was staged against Prince Norodom Sihanouk by General Lon Nol, his defense minister (seen here), in March 1970. Sihanouk was in Moscow at the time, trying to persuade the Soviet government to help him evict the Vietnamese from Cambodia.*

Late in February 1972, President Nixon met with Mao Zedong in Beijing. Nixon's historic trip was demoralizing to the North Vietnamese; they saw their ally consorting with their enemy.

The North Vietnamese staged a major offensive against South Vietnam in the spring of 1972, presumably to improve their final negotiating position. The South Vietnamese city of Quangtri, scene of fierce fighting, was reduced to rubble.

In May 1972, Nixon attended a summit meeting in Moscow with Leonid Brezhnev, the Soviet Communist party leader. Brezhnev welcomed Nixon even though the United States was then intensifying its bombing of North Vietnam.

During the Christmas season of 1972, Nixon ordered the bombing of Hanoi and Haiphong to force the North Vietnamese to agree to a settlement. Though the tonnage of bombs dropped was heavy, it was aimed at military targets, and civilian casualties were lighter than reported at the time.

In Paris on January 27, 1973, the United States, North Vietnam, South Vietnam, and the Vietcong, then called the Provisional Revolutionary Government, officially signed a cease-fire accord. A political settlement was to follow.

I will not be the first president of the United States to lose a war.
—Richard Nixon

What interests me is what you can do with power.
—Henry Kissinger

L yndon Johnson and Richard Nixon shared several traits. Both of them, born and raised in lace curtain obscurity, had clawed their way to prominence, often resorting to devious means to overcome obstacles. As Westerners, both oscillated between envy and disdain for the Ivy Leaguers from New York and Boston who supposedly comprised the power elite. And though both were seasoned politicians, whose hides should have been thickened in the rough-and-tumble of the Washington arena, neither ever learned to react gracefully to criticism. But they differed in at least one important respect. While Johnson, the earthy extrovert, constantly sought solace in the company of cronies and advisers, relying on their real or contrived consensus for reassurance, Nixon, by contrast, was a dour, humorless figure who fancied himself a solitary giant, like Winston Churchill or Charles de Gaulle or Mao Zedong.

Just as the Vietnam war shattered Johnson, so it eventually contributed to Nixon's downfall. Johnson had sunk deeper and deeper into the quagmire of Southeast Asia until his senior aides turned against him, fearing that the American public's frustrations with the endless struggle might wreck the Democratic party—as indeed it did. Nixon, on the other hand, was largely responsible for his own doom. The domestic opposition to the conflict that grew during his first term in office exacerbated his sense of beleaguered isolation, prompting him to sanction the accumulation of offenses that became Watergate. His White House chief of staff, H. R. Haldeman, later wrote that "without the Vietnam war there would have been no Watergate"—asserting that Nixon might be "revered today" as a brilliant president had the scandal remained submerged. Given his record, however, Nixon seemed to be destined for disrepute. His political career began as it ended, with deliberate duplicity designed for one purpose: to win. "If you can't lie," he once confided to a friend, "you'll never go anywhere."

A native of southern California, he was graduated from Duke University Law School and served as a naval officer in the Pacific during World War II—afterward, like Johnson, inflating his combat role. In 1946, local

Republicans picked him to challenge the incumbent congressman, Jerry Voorhis, a wealthy and idealistic New Deal liberal. Nixon triumphed after smearing Voorhis as a Communist sympathizer—the same tactic he was to employ in his race for the Senate four years later, when he pinned the label of "pink lady" on his Democratic opponent, Helen Gahagan Douglas. By then he had stoked the anti-Communist hysteria of the period by pursuing Alger Hiss, the distinguished former State Department official alleged to have been a Communist agent, who was convicted of perjury.

Nixon's crusade against the "Red menace" seemed to be motivated less by ideology than by opportunism. He derived satisfaction from nailing Hiss because, as he divulged afterward, the case gave him "nationwide publicity." As vice-president during Eisenhower's first term, he endorsed Senator Joe McCarthy's wild witch-hunts—shifting only after McCarthy slandered Eisenhower and became a liability to the Republican party. Even so, Nixon later looked back on McCarthy with affection and indulgence, describing him as "a casualty in the great struggle of our times."

Nixon initially strayed into foreign affairs—a field in which he eventually claimed to be an expert—for domestic political reasons. Along with other right-wing Republicans, he seized on the Communist conquest of China in 1949 to blast the Truman administration, contending that Mao Zedong's victory was a "direct result" of President Truman's decision to withhold U.S. aid from Chiang Kai-shek, the Chinese Nationalist leader. He kept up the attack after Truman dismissed General Douglas MacArthur, the flamboyant American commander during the Korean war who had insisted on extending the conflict into China. Nixon excoriated Truman's move as "appeasement," and he sponsored a resolution in Congress calling for MacArthur's reinstatement. Arguing for the intensive bombing of Communist installations inside China, he invoked a phrase that resonated through his oratory two decades later, when he tried to blast the North Vietnamese into a compromise settlement of the Vietnam war: "Our broad objective, of course, is peace with honor."

Apart from his naval service, Nixon had never been abroad. Then, in 1953, sent by Eisenhower on a seventy-three-day tour of Asia, he discovered the world. Greeted sumptuously by Asian leaders, masters of the art of lavish welcomes, he acquired the taste for pomp and pageantry that he would later introduce to his presidency, when he garbed the White House guards in Ruritanian splendor. He also began to regard himself as a statesman of international stature, though his observations during the trip tended to confirm his preconceptions rather than open his eyes to fresh vistas. A brief visit to Vietnam, where he talked with French soldiers fighting against Ho Chi Minh's legions, stiffened his conviction that France deserved assistance in its desperate effort to block the advance of global Communism. The next year, however, he characteristically zigzagged when Eisenhower's advisers assembled to discuss actual ways to rescue the besieged French garrison at Dienbienphu.

Admiral Arthur Radford, chairman of the joint chiefs of staff, had floated the notion that the United States might save the French by deploying three tactical atomic weapons against the Communists. Nixon, along with Secretary of State John Foster Dulles and others, supported Radford—and, in a public speech at the time, he even raised the possibility of making a direct American troop commitment to Vietnam should the French be defeated. But he backtracked after Eisenhower ruled out any form of U.S. intervention without British participation. Still, the idea of wielding force stuck in his mind, and it repeatedly punctuated his later denunciations of Lyndon Johnson's reluctance to escalate the Vietnam war rapidly. Writing in the *Reader's Digest* in August 1964, for example, he cautioned that Asia's entire fate hinged on the outcome in Vietnam, and he appealed for tougher action: "All that is needed, in short, is the will to win—and the courage to use our power—now."

On March 31, 1968, when Lyndon Johnson announced his decision to retire, he claimed that he wanted to withdraw from "the partisan divisions that are developing in this political year" in order to devote himself to a dispassionate quest for peace in Vietnam. As the race for the presidency gathered momentum, however, he began to feel that his abdication might not be irrevocable; perhaps the Democrats would clamor for him to run again when they held their convention in Chicago in August. So he continued to maneuver from behind the scenes, indicating that he was willing to be drafted. Above all, he was determined to block the nomination of a candidate who would transgress his Vietnam policy by proposing greater concessions to the Communists, such as a total halt to the bombing of North Vietnam. He suspected that Vice-President Hubert Humphrey, his logical heir, favored that course as the only way to triumph over Senator Eugene McCarthy's strident antiwar faction, which threatened to fracture the party. But Johnson preferred a Republican successor—even the repugnant Nixon—to a Democrat who would disavow him.

Chicago resembled riotous Saigon when the Democrats assembled there in late August. Some ten thousand antiwar protesters had converged on the city, most of them white youths, their groups a mélange of left-wing extremists, moderate dissidents, and hippies simply out to create chaos. Mayor Richard Daley had mobilized an equal number of police and national guardsmen to maintain security, but one of his aides only increased the tension from the start when he impugned the crowd as "revolutionaries bent on the destruction of America." Army, navy, and air force intelligence services had also infiltrated the demonstration with covert agents—including a team, disguised as a television crew, to photograph the youngsters for the federal records. Clandestine CIA operatives were present as well, despite regulations that prohibit them from functioning inside the United States.

At first no more disorderly than a campus pantie raid, the events on the streets of Chicago suddenly flared into violence on August 28, when police and guardsmen tried to prevent the demonstrators from marching on the International Amphitheater where the Democratic convention was being held. They chased the kids through the downtown area, attacking them with clubs, rifle butts, and tear gas while the youths, some waving Vietcong flags, riposted with rocks and bottles. Hundreds were arrested, yet thousands reappeared the next day at a rally in Grant Park to hear Tom Hayden, a radical organizer who later married Jane Fonda, warn that the battles were only beginning. Television made the most of the spectacle, and Sam Brown, a McCarthy activist, afterward looked back on the Chicago episode as a disaster that alienated many Americans sympathetic to the antiwar movement. "Instead of nice young people ringing doorbells," he said, "the public saw the image of mobs shouting obscenities and disrupting the city."

Vice-President Humphrey and his staff, anticipating trouble at the convention, had drafted a compromise platform on the Vietnam war. Among other things, it called for a complete cessation of the U.S. air strikes against North Vietnam and the transfer of more responsibility to the South Vietnamese. The language seemed to satisfy the late Robert Kennedy's supporters as well as such Johnson loyalists as Dean Rusk and Walt Rostow—all of whom realized that Richard Nixon, by then the Republican nominee, would be the sole beneficiary of discord within the Democratic ranks. For a moment it looked as if a consensus had been achieved. But then Humphrey telephoned Johnson in Texas to obtain his approval, and he got a typically petulant response. The compromise, Johnson growled, was a personal affront to him: "This plank just undercuts our whole policy and, by God, the Democratic party ought not be doing that to me. And you ought not be doing it. You've been a part of this policy."

Humphrey capitulated. He introduced a Vietnam platform conforming to Johnson's dictates. Other factions thereupon presented rival versions, and an unprecedented three-hour debate ensued—the speakers constantly interrupted as emotional antiwar delegates snaked through the convention hall, chanting slogans against the administration. The Johnson plank, under Humphrey's sponsorship, finally passed by a slim margin as its foes unleashed a torrent of protests. Members of the New York delegation, wearing black armbands, rose to sing "We Shall Overcome."

Humphrey soon sensed his blunder. As he acknowledged afterward, he should have defied Johnson, struck a bargain with the Kennedy contingent, and isolated the stubborn McCarthy fringe, thus reunifying the Democrats. But he did not declare his independence until the end of September in Salt Lake City, where he delivered the speech that he had wanted to give at the convention—advocating a total bombing halt and the "de-Americanization" of the war as "an acceptable risk for peace."

The discussions in Paris, which had been dormant, were now awakened by the North Vietnamese. They offered to broaden the talks to include both Saigon government and Vietcong representatives if, in exchange, the U.S. air raids against North Vietnam were unconditionally stopped. The overture was partly intended to confer official status on the Vietcong, which would presumably damage the morale of the South Vietnamese regime, but it was also designed to boost Humphrey, whom the Communists preferred to Nixon, despite their scorn for all American politicians.

The gesture put Johnson on the spot. To agree to the proposal would mean, in effect, to endorse the conciliatory platform he had spurned on the eve of the Democratic party convention. He was reluctant as well to appear to be playing politics with the war just before the election. But to reject the proposal might earn him a dark place in the history books as a president who, during his last days in office, rebuffed a chance for peace. On the evening of October 31, in a televised address to the nation, he announced a complete halt to the bombing of North Vietnam.

Humphrey's supporters have contended for years that the Democrats would have beaten Nixon if Johnson had adopted a moderate position earlier. After all, Nixon and his running mate, Governor Spiro T. Agnew of Maryland, were to nose out Humphrey and his vice-presidential candidate, Senator Edmund Muskie of Maine, by only a half-million votes—less than a 1 percent difference. But Nixon would have won by a larger margin if not for the third candidate in the race, George Wallace, governor of Alabama, who also appealed to hard-line opinion.

Republican aspirants for the presidency had smelled blood late in 1967, when the public's impatience with Johnson's conduct of the war eroded his popularity. Governor George Romney of Michigan, the first Republican to enter the presidential contest formally, vowed to get the United States out of Vietnam with its reputation intact, and Governor Nelson Rockefeller of New York echoed the same theme. Nixon, striving to match their promises, similarly emphasized during the primary campaigns that, if elected, he would "end the war and win the peace." One day in March 1968, after Nixon had addressed an audience of New Hampshire textile workers, a young wire-service reporter put a jazzy lead on his account of the routine speech. Nixon, he wrote, possessed a "secret plan" for Vietnam.

The sensational dispatch hit television screens that evening and newspaper headlines the following morning, and it eventually became a historical fact. But it was a canard. Nixon, at that juncture, had no plan for Vietnam—secret or otherwise. As one of his assistants recalled, he was then only pondering an "approach" derived from his experience during the Eisenhower administration.

Having observed Johnson's futile escalations, candidate Nixon ruled out a "military victory" in Vietnam. But, as he later put it, he had no intention of becoming "the first president of the United States to lose a war." He figured instead that he could scare the North Vietnamese into submission by borrowing a tactic devised by Eisenhower at the beginning of 1953. In Korea at that time, the Chinese and Korean Communists were simultaneously talking and fighting—deliberately stalling at the conference table while they strived to improve their stance on the battlefield. Eisenhower hinted through intermediaries that he might resort to atomic weapons unless the negotiations moved forward, and the prospects for an armistice quickly brightened. Now, with the discussions in Paris languishing, Nixon reckoned that he could emulate his former boss. As he explained the idea to Haldeman, he would threaten the North Vietnamese with annihilation.

I call it the Madman Theory, Bob. I want the North Vietnamese to believe that I've reached the point where I might do anything to stop the war. We'll just slip the word to them that, "for God's sake, you know Nixon is obsessed about Communists. We can't restrain him when he's angry—and he has his hand on the nuclear button"—and Ho Chi Minh himself will be in Paris in two days begging for peace.

As he toyed with the notion, Nixon also contemplated the possibilities of persuading the Soviet Union and perhaps even China to press North Vietnam to acquiesce to an acceptable solution of the war. In a radio speech he had intended to deliver on the evening of March 31—then canceled because Lyndon Johnson announced his retirement that night— he wrote that "if the Soviets were disposed to see the war ended and a compromise settlement negotiated, they have the means to move Ho Chi Minh to the conference table." Now he estimated that he could make it worth their while to intercede on his behalf.

It took no particular prescience to surmise that the Soviet Union was fed up with the war. Its massive aid program to North Vietnam, a region outside its true realm of interest, was draining its domestic economy. Besides, the conflict was botching Soviet hopes of improving relations with the United States. But like America, the Soviet Union was mired in Southeast Asia for essentially symbolic reasons. To abandon their Vietnamese comrades would expose the Soviets to charges, especially from their Chinese rivals, of betraying the worldwide struggle against U.S. imperialism. Nixon estimated, therefore, that they would jump at the opportunity to help him make peace. Moreover, he would induce them to cooperate with such advantages as modern technology, wheat, and an agreement to harness strategic nuclear weapons—all more vital to basic Soviet needs than Vietnam. Cooperation, however, would have to be global; the Russians could not expect arms control or trade unless they contributed to reducing tensions in other areas, like the Middle East, Berlin, and Vietnam. Nixon called the concept "linkage."

As for a Chinese connection, Nixon had long been toying with a somewhat different view. He had once been the darling of Chiang Kai-shek; indeed, he had made a fool of himself during his televised debates with John F. Kennedy in 1960 by arguing that the Nationalist-held islands of Quemoy and Matsu were crucial to U.S. security. But he had matured by late 1967, when he wrote in *Foreign Affairs* that Communist China could no longer be left "forever outside the family of nations . . . to live in angry isolation." A year later, with the Sino-Soviet dispute heating up, he began to perceive that Mao Zedong might be receptive to a rapprochement with America as a counterweight to the Russians. Triangular diplomacy would give both the United States and China added leverage in their dealings with the Soviet Union. And here, too, Nixon anticipated that the Chinese might reciprocate by persuading their Vietnamese allies to compromise.

At the end of 1968, as Nixon prepared to move into the White House, these geopolitical considerations were still abstract speculations. To translate them into reality would require a diplomatic giant. By sheer impulse, he selected Henry Kissinger.

Then forty-five, Kissinger personified human complexity—his characteristics ranging from brilliance and wit to sensitivity, melancholy, abrasiveness, and savagery. As he adapted to Nixon's court, with its arcane and unsavory intrigues, he was also to acquire a talent for duplicity. He was not, as he liked to pretend, the innocent scholar fallen among fierce competitors for influence; he had flourished in an academic jungle at least as hostile as the upper echelons of government. For he was driven by inexhaustible, almost primeval ambition. "What interests me," he confessed to the journalist Oriana Fallaci, "is what you can do with power."

He had landed in New York in 1938 with his family, Jewish refugees from Nazi Germany, a timid adolescent whose highest aspiration was to become an accountant. Drafted into the infantry during World War II, he was spotted by Fritz Kraemer, another German immigrant, who recruited him for the U.S. military administration that would run postwar Germany. Kissinger excelled in the occupation army, and he afterward heeded Kraemer's advice: he went to Harvard, where he found a new mentor in William Yandell Elliott, a patrician professor of government, who named him head of a summer seminar for promising foreign officials. Thus Kissinger began to weave a web of global contacts, cultivating those who succeeded and discarding the failures. As a celebrity years later, he snubbed a minor European civil servant who had once attended the seminar. "Henry, don't you remember your old friends?" the man remonstrated. "The secret of my success," Kissinger replied, "is to forget my old friends."

Though he had graduated with top honors and an award for his doctoral dissertation, Kissinger's peers initially denied him a Harvard professorship because, they felt, he would use rather than serve the university. Elliott recommended him for a staff job at the Council on Foreign Relations in New York, and the assignment catapulted him into loftier spheres. He wrote *Nuclear Weapons and Foreign Policy,* an argument for a limited atomic strategy, which made the 1958 best-seller lists and established him as a major defense specialist. He also widened his spectrum of prestigious acquaintances to include a new patron, Nelson Rockefeller, who hired him as an adviser. Now Harvard granted him a tenured position on its faculty, but Cambridge became only a base as he sallied forth in search of bigger conquests.

He made little headway with the Kennedy set, which was already overloaded with intellectuals like McGeorge Bundy, John Kenneth Galbraith, and Arthur Schlesinger, Jr.—and in addition, they could not abide Kissinger's awkward solemnity. He went slightly further with Johnson, for whom he conducted Operation Pennsylvania, one of several abortive attempts to lure the North Vietnamese into negotiations. By early 1968 he had returned to advising Rockefeller, who was scrambling at the time to become the Republican presidential candidate. Kissinger would probably have had no alternative, if Rockefeller failed, to going back to the dreariness of teaching at Harvard. He could not plausibly switch to the Democrats, and working for Nixon was out of the question.

Kissinger had met Nixon only briefly, at a cocktail party at Clare Boothe Luce's elegant Manhattan apartment late in 1967. He later recalled that Nixon seemed more "thoughtful" than he had expected, and claimed that until then he had shared the orthodox anti-Nixon Harvard bias. In fact, he displayed nothing but contempt for Nixon during the ensuing months. On the eve of the Republican convention in July 1968, for example, he described Nixon as "the most dangerous, of all the men running, to have as president." Nixon's nomination drove him to despondency; the country, he feared, was about to be taken over by an anti-Communist fanatic. Over the next few weeks, however, ambition spurred him to reconsider. He began to ingratiate himself with the Nixon camp while keeping in contact with the Democrats.

Johnson was then considering the halt in the bombing of North Vietnam—a step that might swing the antiwar liberals back into supporting Humphrey. As Humphrey's fortunes rose, Kissinger maintained his ties with the Democrats. But through one of Nixon's foreign policy aides, Richard Allen, he got in touch with the Republicans, offering to furnish them with covert information on Johnson's moves. A clandestine channel was set up through Nixon's campaign manager, John Mitchell, and Kissinger guided the Republicans secretly on the Vietnam issue for nearly two months—thus supplying Nixon with the ammunition to blast Humphrey for "playing politics with the war." Kissinger glosses over the episode in his memoirs, recalling that "only one question was ever put to me by the Nixon organization." Nixon, by contrast, says in his memoirs that he received three substantial messages from Kissinger. Whatever the truth, Kissinger's subterfuge earned him Nixon's admiration and gratitude. Kissinger was soon to acquire his most important patron.

Other intrigues were going on—among them one involving Anna Chennault, the Chinese-born widow of General Claire Chennault, commander of the Flying Tigers during World War II. A Republican activist, she recommended to South Vietnamese President Nguyen Van Thieu that he object to the last-minute halt in the bombing of North Vietnam, a maneuver which she hoped would foil the Democrats and help Nixon. She also urged Thieu to procrastinate on the matter of participation in the Paris talks, explaining that firmer American support for his cause would be forthcoming after Nixon entered the White House. Her conduit to Thieu was Bui Diem, his ambassador to the United States. But Johnson was tracking her every move. Both the FBI and the CIA were tapping her telephone conversations with Bui Diem, intercepting the cable traffic to and from the South Vietnamese embassy in Washington, and spying on Thieu through an electronic device installed in his Saigon office. Nixon believed that he was being bugged as well—especially after Johnson bluntly warned him against relying on Madame Chennault's machinations.

Stiffened by the messages from Chennault, Thieu balked at sending diplomats to Paris until four days before Nixon's inauguration on January 20, 1969. His pretext was alleged displeasure with the seating accommodations for an expanded conference, which accorded formal rank to the Vietcong delegation. He directed Bui Diem to inform the lame-duck Johnson administration that "even the appearance" of the Vietcong as a distinct entity was unacceptable, calling the proposed table arrangement a "Communist trap" that would disrupt his regime and demoralize his army. Weeks of farcical haggling yielded a compromise, but Thieu's boycott had been prompted by more than guile. He foresaw that recognition of the Vietcong as a partner in the negotiations would inevitably give it official status inimical to his claim to exclusive legitimacy. At that stage, however, Nixon and Kissinger had no inkling of the frustrations that Thieu would eventually cause them. Their priority was to get the North Vietnamese to concede to their terms for peace.

On the morning of November 25, 1968, responding to a telephone summons, Kissinger went to President-elect Nixon's headquarters at the Hotel Pierre in New York. The two men had not met during Kissinger's months as a secret informer. They chatted—and Kissinger departed, uncertain what Nixon had in mind for him. The next day, he learned from John Mitchell that Nixon wanted him as national security adviser. At another meeting with Nixon a day later, Kissinger accepted. But, to keep on good terms with them, he went through the motions of consulting Rockefeller and a few Harvard colleagues.

A president who concentrates on domestic social, economic, and racial problems faces the long and tedious business of bargaining with legislators, lobbyists, and even rival factions within his own cabinet, often without achieving rapid results. But the international arena is glittery and immediate; a politician can resemble a statesman as he circles the globe amid the glamour of summit meetings with world leaders. Unlike Johnson, who would have preferred to focus on internal issues, Nixon intended to devote himself primarily to foreign affairs. And Nixon, even more than Johnson, distrusted the State Department and the CIA—which in his opinion were staffed by Ivy League liberals who had disdained or disregarded him in the past. The center of authority, he believed, ought to be the White House. Kissinger agreed. In his Harvard doctoral dissertation, published as *A World Restored,* he had stressed that officialdom was by its very nature opposed to the formulation of bold and imaginative decisions: "The essence of bureaucracy is its quest for safety; its success is calculability. Profound policy thrives on perpetual creation, on a constant redefinition of goals. . . . Bureaucracies are designed to execute, not to conceive."

During the transition period, as he organized his administration, Nixon directed Kissinger to "revitalize" the national security council—and gave him the latitude to assemble his own team. Kissinger's recruits included Colonel Alexander Haig, then back from military duty in Vietnam; Anthony Lake, a foreign service officer with Vietnam experience; and Morton Halperin, a deputy assistant secretary of defense who had helped to tilt Clark Clifford against the war. Relying on a blueprint largely drafted by Halperin, they began to revamp the decision-making apparatus so as to curb the influence of the State Department, the Pentagon, and the CIA. The new structure was shaped to put Kissinger in charge of an array of government committees, thus assuring his control over the recommendations flowing to the president. Roger Morris, a member of the Kissinger group, was to call the renovation "a seizure of power unprecedented in modern American foreign policy."

Nixon's secretary of defense, Melvin Laird, was to be a difficult obstacle to the new setup. Nixon had chosen him because, as a veteran Republican congressman, Laird could sway friends on Capitol Hill. But because he had his own constituency, Laird felt he deserved his own direct access to the president. Kissinger soon fixed that by opening up an indirect channel from the White House to the joint chiefs of staff, thereby circumventing Laird.

Excluding the secretary of state, William Rogers, was easier. Nixon had picked Rogers, an affable lawyer who had been Eisenhower's attorney general, because his unfamiliarity with international affairs guaranteed the direction of policy from the White House. Rogers's lack of interest in the subject was confirmed as early as Inauguration Day. While the major figures in the new administration were attending ceremonies, lowlier officials deposited on Rogers's desk a fat volume containing position papers on all the major issues. "You don't expect me to read all this stuff, do you?" remarked Rogers when he noticed the book. The comment swiftly reached Kissinger's aides, one of whom later recalled to me: "From then on, we knew that we wouldn't have any trouble with State."

In that same month of January 1969, *Foreign Affairs* published an article on Vietnam by Kissinger, written before he joined Nixon, which eloquently outlined his views on the war. He argued that General Westmoreland's strategy of attrition was futile, since the Communists could sustain far higher casualties than the United States and would therefore "win" as long as they did not "lose." He also minimized the significance of the military setback suffered by the Communists during the Tet offensive: its impact on the American public placed limits on further U.S. escalation and made "inevitable" the need for a diplomatic solution to the war. The question was how to reach a settlement.

Kissinger's negotiating script was not especially original. He favored a separation of the military and political issues, as Johnson had. The Americans and North Vietnamese would deal only with such military matters as a cease-fire and the mutual withdrawal of their troops from the south, leaving it to the Saigon regime and the Vietcong to hammer out a political agreement. He could appreciate the complexity of the diplomacy, which required that the United States reach an accommodation with its adversaries without antagonizing its allies—neither of whom showed any signs of compromising. And he foresaw possible future obstacles, which were indeed to become crucial. While conceding that the South Vietnamese government should have a "major voice" in the discussions, he drew the line at its right to veto an accord—a hint that the United States might force its ally to accept if it looked attractive. He also sensed that the North Vietnamese might turn out to be intransigent, in which case he advocated that America continue to maintain a presence in Vietnam on a reduced scale.

Kissinger, like Nixon, believed that the war had to be ended "honorably" for the sake of America's global prestige. Like Nixon, moreover, he was not averse to deploying force to compel the North Vietnamese to acquiesce. But they differed in at least two important respects at the start of their liaison. Though he subscribed to Nixon's "linkage" concept, Kissinger seemed to be less sanguine than was his boss about the ability or willingness of the Soviet leaders to compel Ho Chi Minh to be compliant. Indeed, he was wary of exerting too much pressure on the

Soviets, lest their cooperation on Vietnam become a precondition to the resolution of such cosmic problems as the control of nuclear arms. Nor did Kissinger and Nixon share the same hopes for South Vietnam's ultimate fate. Perhaps, as presidents do, Nixon mused on his place in history—or he may have feared a revival of the "who-lost-China" squabble that had caused such an upheaval in American politics during the 1950s. So, while he ruled out victory in Vietnam, he also refused to contemplate defeat, and he envisioned a durable peace agreement rather than just an armistice. Kissinger, by contrast, merely hoped for an agreement that would give the Saigon government a "reasonable" chance to survive—a "decent interval," as he later said privately.

No sooner was he installed in the White House than Kissinger directed his staff to canvass American officials in Washington and Saigon for their appraisals of the prospects for Vietnam. The bundle of confidential reports, like similar surveys conducted over the years, revealed sharp divergences. Senior officers asserted that the South Vietnamese army was making "rapid strides," while civilian analysts doubted that the Saigon leadership would "ever constitute an effective political or military counter to the Vietcong." Pentagon and CIA experts disputed the size of the Communist force in the south, and the contributors to the study were deeply divided over the value of the bombing of North Vietnam that Johnson had stopped. Nobody, however, discerned much light at the end of the tunnel. The "bulls" judged from their computers that it would take 8.3 years for the Saigon regime to gain the allegiance of some four million South Vietnamese living in enemy or contested areas; the "bears" foresaw that objective attainable in 13.4 years.

An introduction to the massive document, written by one of Kissinger's assistants, underlined its "emphatic differences"—and that was the artful aim of the exercise. Kissinger had deliberately had the disparate estimates compiled in order to dramatize to Nixon the divisions among the Vietnam specialists. Implicitly, Nixon could now feel free to act without reference to the bureaucrats, and he did. His first target was Cambodia.

Prince Norodom Sihanouk, the Cambodian ruler, was acutely conscious of his uncomfortable location: flanked by Vietnam and Thailand, hated neighbors that had invaded Cambodia time and again through the centuries. He was continually contriving schemes to preserve his nation's fragile neutrality. In 1954, after wangling independence from France, he bid for American protection. When the United States swung its weight behind South Vietnam, he shifted toward China and later broke the American connection completely. Gradually, expecting the

Vietnamese Communists to prevail, he consented to allowing them supply routes and bases in the Cambodian frontier zone near South Vietnam; the Chinese, he calculated, would restrain them from violating his sovereignty. But by late 1967, his maneuvers were faltering. China had sunk into the isolation of Mao Zedong's Cultural Revolution. The North Vietnamese and Vietcong forces, bracing for the Tet offensive, were building up inside Cambodia. And General Westmoreland was pressing President Johnson to approve American ground assaults against the enemy's Cambodian sanctuaries.

At that juncture, Sihanouk began to switch again by repairing his diplomatic relations with the United States. He invited Jacqueline Kennedy to visit Cambodia's wondrous Angkor temples, welcoming her with all the panoply of a state dignitary. Then, in an interview with me published in the *Washington Post* on December 29, 1967, he advanced a formula to discourage the Vietnamese Communists, deflate Westmoreland, and minimize the encroachments on Cambodian territory: he would grant the United States the right of "hot pursuit" against the North Vietnamese and Vietcong in Cambodia—as long as no Cambodians were harmed. He also suggested that President Johnson send a special envoy to Cambodia to discuss the situation, mentioning Senator Mike Mansfield, "a just and courageous man whom we consider a friend." Plainly trying to prevent Cambodia from becoming a battlefield, Sihanouk said: "We are a country caught between the hammer and the anvil, a country that would very much like to remain the last haven of peace in Southeast Asia."

In January 1968, an official American mission arrived in Phnompenh, headed by Chester Bowles, the U.S. ambassador to India. Sihanouk told Bowles in private what he had told me in public. He was "not opposed to hot pursuit in uninhabited areas," which "would be liberating us from the Vietcong." But Lyndon Johnson was then reluctant to expand the war. Nothing came of the offer. American intrusions into Cambodia continued to be limited to so-called Daniel Boone squads—covert teams of U.S. volunteers and local mercenaries wearing either black peasant pajamas or unidentifiable uniforms, assigned to gather intelligence or to sabotage enemy installations.

Within a week of Nixon's inauguration, however, the appeal for U.S. action against the North Vietnamese and Vietcong presence in Cambodia was resurrected by General Earle Wheeler, chairman of the joint chiefs of staff. He was seconded by Westmoreland's successor, General Creighton Abrams, who calculated that the Communists had recently moved forty thousand fresh troops into the Cambodian bases and were supplying them largely by sea through the port of Sihanoukville, on the Gulf of Siam. Abrams recommended a "short-duration" raid by B-52s against the Cambodian sanctuaries, which presumably concealed the elusive Communist headquarters—the Central Office for South Vietnam, or COSVN. He contended that no Cambodian civilians inhabited the sector, so that the project would not transgress Sihanouk's "hot pursuit" restriction. Classified documents published later were to disclose that Abrams and other top officers, knowing the targeted areas to be populated by civilians, had secretly conceded that "some Cambodian casualties would be sustained in the operation." State Department and CIA analysts also doubted Cambodia's logistical significance, arguing instead that the Ho Chi Minh Trail threading through Laos was more important to the Communists.

Nixon initially waffled. But late in February, he ordered the bombing of Cambodia in retaliation for a renewed Communist offensive in South Vietnam. The impulsive decision worried Kissinger, Rogers, and Laird for practical rather than ethical reasons. Kissinger was concerned about embarking on the venture without preparing for the diplomatic consequences; Rogers feared its potential effect on private peace talks; and Laird was alarmed by the possible impact on congressional, media, and public opinion. Himself a seasoned politician, Nixon could appreciate Laird's reservations. He delayed. Still, he was determined to launch the air strikes. On March 16, meeting with Kissinger, Rogers, Laird, and Wheeler in Washington, he insisted that the "only way" to get the Communists to negotiate was "to do something on the military front . . . something they will understand." The Cambodian bombing began the next day.

Dubbed Menu, the "short-duration" operation in fact was to go on continuously for fourteen months, and it conformed to the conviction Nixon had held since 1950, when he had asserted that "peace with honor" could be attained in Korea by attacking China. Now, though, he was adjusting to circumstances. He would have preferred to resume the strategic bombing of North Vietnam, since hitting the Cambodian sanctuaries was simply tactical. But such a step might have disrupted the discussions in Paris and given the Communists an excuse to denounce him. Thus his strikes against Cambodia were essentially an oblique threat, intended to signal to the North Vietnamese his readiness to resort to tougher measures unless they let up—just as Eisenhower had tamed the Chinese by rattling atomic weapons.

A key ingredient in the operation was total secrecy. Nixon and Kissinger realized that by admitting to bombing raids against a country whose neutrality they professed to respect, they might cause an international crisis. Their silence was therefore calculated to avert protests from Sihanouk, and it succeeded. Not only did he shut eyes to the bombing, but soon his army was furnishing the Americans with intelligence on the Vietnamese Communist bases. Nor did the North Vietnamese complain, since their objection would have indirectly confirmed the illicit deployment of their troops on Cambodian soil.

But another consideration motivated Nixon's blackout. Still in the honeymoon period that favors all new presidents, he feared that disclosures of the bombing would reawaken antiwar sentiment at home, which had abated at the time. Accordingly, an elaborate dual reporting system was introduced at the Pentagon to divert information on the air strikes from normal channels. The secretary of the air force and the air force chief of staff, along with many government specialists responsible for Cambodia, were not told of the details. Nixon, Kissinger, and Laird briefed a few sympathetic members of Congress but kept the legislature as a whole uninformed. The subject was supposedly sealed against leaks.

In May, however, an enterprising *New York Times* correspondent, William Beecher, revealed the bombings in Cambodia. His scoop aroused no public reaction, but it outraged Nixon and Kissinger. They consulted J. Edgar Hoover, director of the FBI, and wiretaps of dubious legality were placed on the telephones of four journalists and thirteen officials, including members of Kissinger's own staff. Hoover quoted Kissinger as saying that the administration "will destroy whoever did this." The first abuses of authority, later to emerge as the Watergate scandal, had begun.

Officially acknowledged in 1973, this clandestine bombing campaign was also to fuel the clamor in Congress for Nixon's impeachment. In testimony before a Senate committee, several distinguished lawyers agreed that Nixon had exceeded his constitutional prerogatives, and they supported proposed legislation to curb the president's ability to wage war. One among them, ironically, was Nicholas Katzenbach, who as attorney general in the previous administration had defended Johnson's right to commit U.S. forces to Vietnam under the Tonkin Gulf resolution.

The Cambodian bombing failed to deter the North Vietnamese. And the other part of Nixon's original scheme—to induce the Soviet Union to act as intermediary—was equally unsuccessful. Kissinger first essayed this approach in March, when he conceived of an assignment for Cyrus Vance, a former deputy defense secretary who had participated in the

Paris talks. Vance was to go to Moscow to open preliminary discussions with the Soviets on the control of strategic weapons, making it plain that their help in concluding the Vietnam war would facilitate an arms deal. While there, Vance would also arrange through Soviet auspices to meet discreetly with a senior North Vietnamese to underscore Nixon's eagerness to reach a compromise. In an attempt to organize Vance's mission, Kissinger conferred with Anatoly Dobrynin, the veteran Soviet ambassador in Washington, warning him that the United States would intensify the war unless a settlement could be achieved. So Nixon and Kissinger had set out to translate the "linkage" theory into reality.

Nothing happened. Either the Soviets could not exert any real leverage on the North Vietnamese or, more likely, they never tried. They knew that Ho Chi Minh and his comrades would tilt toward the Chinese to resist Soviet pressure. Late in 1969, as Nixon's patience wore thin, Kissinger again cautioned Dobrynin, telling him ominously that "the train has just left the station and is now headed down the track." But Dobrynin parried the threat; his superiors in Moscow, he said, wanted to improve relations with the United States regardless of Vietnam. They were not going to become snared in the "linkage" trap.

Nixon fell back on other alternatives. One, to be called Vietnamization, would enable the United States to pull its combat troops out of Vietnam by transferring responsibility for the war to the South Vietnamese. The other was to negotiate directly and secretly with the North Vietnamese, thereby circumventing the Saigon government, whose leaders feared that any accord with the Communists would undermine them. But these two efforts seemed to be incompatible, even contradictory. Why should the Communists conciliate if the U.S. forces were being withdrawn? Time was on their side. They were not troubled by an anguished public. From every indication, the Saigon regime would crumble if the Americans quit South Vietnam. So they had only to wait until the Americans departed, then overwhelm the South Vietnamese— as they nearly had before Lyndon Johnson intervened with ground units in the spring of 1965.

The answer was that Nixon had no intention of retreating entirely from Vietnam—not, at least, during his presidency. To placate public opinion at home, he wanted an agreement that would gain the release of the American prisoners, then numbering about four hundred, being held in brutal conditions in North Vietnamese jails. For the same reason, he envisioned the removal from South Vietnam of the more than half-million GIs sent there during the Johnson administration. Meanwhile, he would stiffen the South Vietnamese army with advisers, equipment, and a shield of B-52s and other aircraft to prevent a Communist takeover. Thus, by assuring South Vietnam's security, he would not be the first American president to lose a war.

Nixon advanced the idea informally to reporters in July 1969, during a stop in Guam on the first leg of a round-the-world journey, and soon his publicists elevated the notion to a "doctrine." In the past, Nixon said, the United States had committed men as well as money and matériel to protect nations against Communism. From now on, countries receiving American military and economic assistance would have to furnish their own troops. Nixon later explained that this was "not a formula for getting America *out* of Asia, but one that provided the only sound basis for America's staying *in* and continuing to play a responsible role." In short, by shifting the human burden to local surrogates, the United States could project its global power at a cost tolerable to Americans. The policy was not tailored exclusively for Vietnam. Nixon was then beginning to lavish a sophisticated arsenal on the Shah of Iran to make him the pivot of U.S. defenses in the Middle East.

Opinion surveys conducted in the spring of 1969 showed that most Americans were willing to give Nixon a chance to cope with Vietnam. But Nixon realized that his approval ratings would slip fast unless he made progress in bringing the boys home. Signs of impatience were already visible in Congress, which the Democrats dominated. Senator Mike Mansfield, the Democratic majority leader who had muted his misgivings during the Johnson era, was now speaking out, along with familiar Democratic critics like William Fulbright and Edward Kennedy, and even Republicans urged Nixon to act rapidly. The Senate Republican whip, Hugh Scott of Pennsylvania, called for the unilateral withdrawal from Vietnam of a "substantial number" of American troops, and his plea was echoed by such party colleagues as Jacob Javits of New York and Charles Percy of Illinois. Secretary of Defense Laird, attuned to the mood on Capitol Hill from his years in the House, also lobbied Nixon.

Nixon started by hinting that some GIs might be repatriated in the months ahead. Then, on May 14, in his first major address on Vietnam, he appealed to the public to trust him. He rejected either a "purely military solution on the battlefield" or a compromise "that would amount to a disguised American defeat" and suggested instead that "the time has come for new initiatives." But he offered little more than a rehash of Johnson's old proposal for the mutual withdrawal of American and North Vietnamese forces from South Vietnam—giving it a fresh look by suggesting a simultaneous pullout over a one-year period. On his instructions, Kissinger staged a "good guy–bad buy" charade: he briefed Dobrynin about the speech in advance, warning him that the petulant Nixon would "escalate the war" if the Soviets "didn't produce a settlement."

The response from the North Vietnamese was predictably negative, as it would be again and again on the same point. They were not going to redeploy their troops to the north, since the Vietcong alone was no match for the Saigon government army. And though for diplomatic purposes they maintained the fiction that they were not involved in the south, they considered it their right to resist foreign intruders anywhere in Vietnam. At that stage, their principal demand was the resignation of South Vietnam's President Thieu in favor of a coalition regime that included the Vietcong—which, they well knew, Nixon would never accept. But they were hardly in a hurry to negotiate seriously; better to let Nixon stew in the pressure cooker of mounting antiwar sentiment in the United States.

And indeed it was true that Nixon could not afford to delay at least token American troop withdrawals. General Abrams was depressed by the prospect. But he adjusted, supplanting Westmoreland's huge search-and-destroy sweeps with small unit actions. Thieu was jittery, but, reconciling himself to the fact that he had no choice, he complied. Nixon arranged a meeting with him in early June on Midway island—the forlorn atoll being a safer place than Washington, where antiwar demonstrations might have greeted Thieu. The Midway sessions ended with Nixon announcing the repatriation of twenty-five thousand Americans—and he added another forty thousand to the redeployment schedule in three months.

By now, Laird was pressing for a timetable to shrink the U.S. force in Vietnam to roughly two hundred and six thousand men by the end of 1971. He also calculated these anticipated troop reductions into the Pentagon budgetary procedure, thereby making it difficult to interrupt them without upsetting the defense establishment's entire financial equilibrium. In an interview years later, Laird recalled to me that he had joined the Nixon cabinet convinced that the American people were "fed up with the war," and he was alarmed as well by its debilitating effect on U.S. security obligations in Europe and elsewhere. Looking back, I believe that his contribution to America's departure from Vietnam has been underestimated.

Laird's eagerness to disengage in Vietnam annoyed Kissinger, who spoke differently to different people. He assured his liberal Harvard friends that he was working to extract the United States from Vietnam, adding that he had no desire to end up like Walt Rostow, whose toughness on the war issue had earned him excommunication from the ranks of Ivy League intellectuals. But to Nixon he cautioned against hasty "de-escalation," arguing that a strong American presence in Vietnam "remains one of our few bargaining weapons," and again in September he warned Nixon that he was "deeply disturbed" by the administration's course. He doubted the ability of South Vietnamese soldiers to replace GIs, whose withdrawal would become like "salted peanuts" to the American public: "the more U.S. troops come home, the more will be demanded." Thus, he reasoned, the enemy had only to "wait us out." He recommended instead that the North Vietnamese be bombed and their ports mined unless they agreed to respect Thieu's regime in Saigon. "I can't believe," Kissinger said to his staff, "that a fourth-rate power like North Vietnam doesn't have a breaking point."

Without Laird's knowledge, in September 1969 Kissinger picked a few assistants to prepare a plan for inflicting what he called a "savage, punishing" blow against North Vietnam. Three of the aides, after drafting the details, dissented. Lawrence Lynn, a former Pentagon official, criticized its military aspects. Anthony Lake and Roger Morris, contending that the North Vietnamese could not be broken, argued for an immediate settlement to reduce American casualties and perhaps salvage something. They proposed that the North Vietnamese and Vietcong be permitted to remain in the areas of South Vietnam they already held, and the peaceful formation of a coalition regime in Saigon be encouraged. Otherwise, they predicted, "we see the president sinking deeper into the Johnsonian bog." Kissinger forwarded the attack project to Nixon anyway, but Laird intervened. The bombing strikes against North Vietnam would exacerbate domestic opposition to the war and postpone "Vietnamization," Laird argued. Nixon shelved the idea—for the time being. "I'm not sure we're ready for this," he said.

Laird concocted the unwieldy term Vietnamization as an improvement on "de-Americanizing." He had visited Vietnam in March, a defense secretary assessing the situation through the eyes of a politician. The U.S. electorate, he told Nixon on his return, would "not be satisfied with less" than the "eventual disengagement of American men from combat." So it was "essential to decide now to initiate the removal from Southeast Asia of some U.S. military personnel." As for the South Vietnamese, they could be equipped and trained to defend themselves. Nixon found confirmation of Laird's appraisal in the sanguine view of Sir Robert Thompson, the British guerrilla warfare specialist, who advised him that the Saigon regime had the capacity, with continuing

American aid, to hold its own. Thompson also steeled Nixon's resolve to stand firm with an apocalyptic admonition: "The future of Western civilization is at stake in the way you handle yourselves in Vietnam."

Communist intractability and Nixon's growing inflexibility meanwhile nourished each other. In his 1969 *Foreign Affairs* article, Kissinger had described the Johnson administration's vain attempts to negotiate as having been "marked by the classic Vietnamese syndrome: optimism alternating with bewilderment; euphoria giving way to frustration." Now, in 1969, he and Nixon were on the threshold of the same experience, which was to go on for the next three years.

The Soviet avenue to Hanoi had turned out to be a blind alley. Then, on August 4, Kissinger was stymied at his first secret meeting in Paris with a Communist representative, Xuan Thuy, the chief North Vietnamese delegate. The two men repeated positions that both sides had already spurned—Kissinger proposing the mutual withdrawal of U.S. and North Vietnamese troops and Xuan Thuy insisting on the dissolution of the Saigon government. Jean Sainteny, the former French colonial official who had tried to avert the Indochina war nearly a half century before, had set up the rendezvous in his apartment, and now he performed another service for the Americans. In July, he had transmitted a letter to his old friend Ho Chi Minh from Nixon, who urged that they "move forward at the conference table" to settle "this tragic war." But Nixon also asked Sainteny to deliver an ultimatum to the North Vietnamese. Unless a diplomatic breakthrough occurred by November 1— the first anniversary of Johnson's bombing halt—he would resort "to measures of great consequence and force."

Ho Chi Minh's answer, which did not reach Washington until August 30, merely reiterated the public Communist line—prompting Nixon to call it a "cold rebuff." Ho may not have written the reply to Nixon. His secretary, Tuu Ky, recalled to me in Hanoi in 1981 that Ho's heart had begun to fail in early 1969, and by late August he could no longer work. On September 2, Ho died at the age of seventy-nine.

Ho's death inspired a burst of emotional mourning in North Vietnam, and a pledge by his successors to carry on the struggle "until there is not a single aggressor in the country." His mantle now fell on old warriors like Le Duan, Pham Van Dong, and Vo Nguyen Giap, nationalists who had been fighting against Westerners for most of their adult lives. Like Ho, they regarded the defeat of the United States and its South Vietnamese allies to be a sacred duty, not a matter for compromise or, even less, capitulation to Nixon's conditions. So the prospects were remote that they would buckle. But Nixon was proceeding, as Johnson had, on the assumption that he could compel them to forsake their goal of national reunification and concede to a Vietnam permanently divided, another Germany or Korea.

For a brief moment, Nixon appeared to have checked domestic dissidence. In September he announced a second troop withdrawal as well as a reduction in draft calls, the latter calculated to quell antiwar protests by students returning to college campuses. He also labored to convince legislative critics of his sincerity, silencing even Senator Fulbright. An opinion poll conducted in October gave his approach to Vietnam an extraordinary approval rating of 71 percent.

Still, opponents of the war on Capitol Hill soon renewed their demands for fresh initiatives—some persuaded that Ho Chi Minh's death offered an opportunity for a faster peace, others spurred by purely partisan motives. On September 25, Senator Charles Goodell, a maverick New York Republican, proposed legislation to bring all the GIs home by the end of 1970. Ten similar resolutions were introduced in Congress over the next three weeks by such senators as Mark Hatfield, Frank Church, Claiborne Pell, and Jacob Javits, and Fulbright started to speak out again. Nixon denounced their gestures as harmful to his bargaining posture. But despite considerable public support, he could not stop the antiwar momentum from spreading among the vocal elements of the population—the press commentators, educators, corporation executives, labor leaders, clergy, and other prominent personalities whose attitudes get into the newspapers and onto television screens.

Late in the summer of 1969, various different antiwar factions were contemplating nationwide protests. Sam Brown, a twenty-five-year-old former divinity student who had campaigned for Senator Eugene McCarthy, concluded that moderate antiwar demonstrations ought to be concentrated in communities rather than on campuses so that, as he later explained, "the heartland folks felt it belonged to them." He and other young militants thereupon organized a series of "moratoriums," to begin in various parts of the country on October 15 and to be repeated during the following months. This plan quickly won endorsement from university faculties, religious associations, civil rights groups, and others, including national and local political figures. The North Vietnamese, acknowledging the importance of the U.S. home front for the first time, broadcast a letter signed by Pham Van Dong acclaiming the protests as a "noble reflection" of the American public's desire to save its sons "from a useless death in Vietnam."

Despite Nixon's dream of commanding a tight ship, his entourage responded diversely to these forthcoming demonstrations. Laird, anxious to ease the tension, declared that Vietnamization had become the administration's "highest priority." He also invented new jargon to signal a decline in U.S. casualties, saying that American troops in Vietnam were shifting from "maximum pressure" on the enemy to "protective reaction." By contrast, Vice-President Agnew inflamed passions. He flayed the protesters for their refusal to repudiate Pham Van Dong's letter, implied they were Communist dupes or worse, and, in a barrage of sophomoric adjectives, later called them "an effete corps of impudent snobs who characterize themselves as intellectuals."

Nixon's outlook was not far from Agnew's. According to Raymond Price, one of his closest aides, Nixon fancied himself a victim of the same "fashionable" Eastern establishment that had undermined Johnson. He believed, as Price put it, that "he was defending the traditional values of Middle America against the media and academic elites who were glorifying rebellion." Nixon feared as well that the demonstrations would undermine his credibility, since he could not plausibly meet his November 1 deadline to resort to "measures of great consequence and force" against North Vietnam without sending the United States into convulsions. He had to rally American public opinion behind him dramatically.

The first "moratorium," as *Time* remarked, infused "new respectability and popularity" into the antiwar resistance. It was largely a sober, almost melancholy manifestation of middle-class concern, with none of the violence that had attended the Democratic convention in Chicago. A quarter of a million people converged on Washington, thousands of them following the widow of Martin Luther King, Jr., in a candlelit procession through the capital. Huge crowds assembled peaceably in New York, Boston, Miami, Detroit, and other cities to listen to speakers ranging from familiar opponents of the war like Dr. Benjamin Spock and David Dellinger to former Supreme Court Justice Arthur Goldberg and Ambassador Averell Harriman, who told a gathering on Long Island that Nixon "is going to have to pay attention." But Nixon feigned indifference. "Under no circumstances will I be affected," he had said earlier, adding that policy "made in the streets" equaled "anarchy." On October 15, he directed an assistant to put out the word that he had been conducting "business as usual."

In fact, behind his pose of casual contempt, Nixon was alarmed. Besides pre-empting his ultimatum to North Vietnam—or at least the bluff—the demonstrations had besieged him in the White House, just as dissidence had beleaguered Johnson. His term had more than three years to run, and he had to extricate himself. He ordered his staff to draft a rebuttal, to be delivered on November 3, 1969, nearly two weeks before the next "moratorium."

The quintessential Nixon speech pulled him through the crisis with flying colors. In it, he succinctly spelled out his "plan to end the war." He would strengthen the South Vietnamese to defend themselves as American forces were gradually withdrawn. He was ready to compromise with the Communists, on condition that they recognize the Saigon government, and he warned that he would take "strong and effective measures" if they intensified their military actions. But all this required time, which brought him to the core of his address—a plea for public backing. The world's confidence in American leadership hinged on the outcome in Vietnam. "And so tonight," he intoned, "to you, the great silent majority of my fellow Americans—I ask for your support. Let us be united for peace. Let us be united against defeat. Because let us understand: North Vietnam cannot defeat or humiliate the United States. Only Americans can do that."

The response to the presidential address, orchestrated by the Republican party apparatus through its county machines, was overwhelmingly favorable. Telephone calls of sympathy jammed the White House switchboard, and thousands of positive telegrams and letters flowed into Washington. Deluged by similar messages, a bipartisan majority of Congress registered approval of the president's Vietnam strategy. Nixon's ratings in the polls soared. Delighted, he told his aides: "We've got those liberal bastards on the run now, and we're going to keep them on the run."

To spare Nixon the appearance of indignity, the job of pursuing the "liberals" was entrusted to Agnew. The vice-president began by assailing the news media as "a small and unelected elite" that "do not—I repeat not—represent the view of America." The Democrats counterattacked, Hubert Humphrey denouncing this diatribe as an appeal to the public's "baser instinct." Television network executives howled, but, fearing the administration's possible influence on the issuance and renewal of station licenses, caution became their guide.

The "moratorium" of November 15 was even bigger than the demonstrations of the month before. By now, the American public was being exposed to disclosures that raised uncomfortable moral questions about the war. Colonel Robert Rheault and his special forces team were charged with the summary execution of a suspected Vietcong spy, the alleged murder being labeled in official jargon as "termination with extreme prejudice." And the U.S. army indicted Lieutenant William Calley and Sergeant David Mitchell for the massacre of South Vietnamese civilians at Mylai, a village in coastal Quangngai province. But Nixon's shrewd pitch to the "silent majority" had been successful—for the present, anyway—in containing the antiwar movement. Henceforth, though, the war in Vietnam was to be "Nixon's war."

Some thirty thousand Americans had been killed in Vietnam by the time Nixon entered office—and nearly ten thousand were to perish there during his first year as president. The Communists greeted him with a series of attacks that stretched through the spring of 1969, causing heavy U.S. casualties. In May, continuing their massive search-and-destroy drives into the hinterlands, American forces fought one of the fiercest battles of the war to capture Apbia mountain, located in the Ashau valley a mile from the Laotian border. The peak, gruesomely nicknamed "Hamburger Hill" because the clash ground up so many GIs, was reoccupied by the North Vietnamese a month later, and the human cost of the futile engagement further roused criticism of the war at home. Soon afterward, as a grim reminder that the war was far from finished, *Life* published photographs of the two hundred and forty-two young Americans slain in a single week. Official spokesmen tried to justify the value of dynamic actions, but General Abrams was quietly instructed to scale down the military effort. For different motives, the Hanoi hierarchy sent similar orders to its field commanders.

By early 1970, about two thirds of the estimated one hundred and twenty-five thousand Communist regulars in the south were North Vietnamese, deployed to replace the main-force Vietcong troops devastated during the Tet offensive two years earlier. For all their skill in battle, the northerners were handicapped politically by their unfamiliarity with the region. The Vietcong political structure was also suffering, largely as a consequence of the Phoenix program, one of the more controversial American operations of the war. Conceived by the CIA three years before, Phoenix was basically another American solution grafted onto a South Vietnamese problem. The Saigon government intelligence services, responsible for uprooting Vietcong agents, were typically a tangle of rival groups competing with each other for power and graft. By centralizing these factions under sound management, the American theory went, the rural apparatus on which the Vietcong relied for recruits, food, money, and asylum could be crushed. So Phoenix was created as a cooperative enterprise—its title a rough translation of *phung hoang*, a mythical Vietnamese bird endowed with omnipotent attributes. Saigon government military, police, and civilian officials, trained by U.S. army advisers, were supposed to penetrate the peasant population to gather information and to arrest or slay Communist cadres. In 1969, according to the wondrously precise statistics released by the American mission in Saigon, 19,534 Vietcong organizers, propagandists, tax collectors, and the like were listed as having been "neutralized"—6,187 of them killed.

The Phoenix operation aroused an outcry from American antiwar activists, who labeled it "mass murder." But several Americans involved in Phoenix described it instead as a program riddled with inefficiency, corruption, and abuse. South Vietnamese officials, interested only in promoting themselves, balked at working together, robbed much of the U.S. aid appropriated for the exercise, and were so receptive to bribes that 70 percent of the Vietcong suspects captured bought back their freedom. Worse yet, Phoenix required village authorities to fulfill monthly quotas, which they did by classifying anyone killed in a skirmish as a member of the Vietcong—thereby distorting the figures of "enemy" dead. They also rounded up innocent peasants in order to inflate police blotters, then spared those who could pay them off, and they frequently tortured villagers on no more evidence than the accusation of jealous neighbors. Looking back on his experience in one district, Lieutenant Colonel Stuart Herrington recalled that "no single endeavor caused more grief and frustration" for an American adviser like himself.

Thus I was inclined to discount the claim advanced during the war by William Colby, the CIA executive who ran Phoenix, that the endeavor as a whole, despite its flaws and excesses, eliminated some sixty thousand authentic Vietcong agents. My perspective changed after the war, however, when top Communist figures in Vietnam confirmed Colby's assessment. Madame Nguyen Thi Dinh, a veteran Vietcong leader, told me that Phoenix had been "very dangerous," adding: "We never feared a division of troops, but the infiltration of a couple of guys into our ranks created tremendous difficulties for us." To Colonel Bui Tin, a senior officer, it had been a "devious and cruel" operation that cost "the loss of thousands of our cadres," and the deputy Communist commander in the south at the time, General Tran Do, called it "extremely destructive." Nguyen Co Thach, Vietnam's foreign minister after 1975, admitted that the Phoenix effort "wiped out many of our bases" in South Vietnam, compelling numbers of North Vietnamese and Vietcong troops to retreat to sanctuaries in Cambodia.

Early in 1970, aware that the battlefield was deadlocked, the Communists began to revamp their strategy. With Nixon under pressure at home to remove the GIs from Vietnam, time seemed to be on their side.

Nevertheless, they faced grave uncertainties. The unpredictable Nixon might halt U.S. troop withdrawals. Nor could they be sure of defeating the South Vietnamese army, which in any case would continue to be stiffened by American advisers, equipment, and the formidable fleet of B-52 bombers. One possible option was to drop their demand that Thieu's regime be dissolved and agree to some kind of political compromise with him. But they rejected that alternative because, as Foreign Minister Thach confided to me in 1981, they felt too weak to make such a concession. Instead, they retrenched by switching back to small operations, promising that the "protracted" struggle would eventually regain momentum.

Morale was a problem, especially among the southern Vietcong insurgents who had borne the brunt of the fighting, only to be told that victory was still a distant dream. Thousands surrendered to the Saigon regime, or simply returned to their native villages. The Vietcong's rural machinery had been badly damaged, either as a result of the Phoenix program or because peasant sympathizers fled to urban refugee camps to escape the horrendous American bombing of the countryside. The South Vietnamese government, realizing that U.S. troops would not remain in Vietnam forever, was also beginning to improve its "pacification" performance by promoting land reform and arming local militia. General Giap adapted to these developments as he planned ahead. He foresaw the war becoming, ultimately, a conventional conflict, with big divisions clashing in showdown battles. "Great strides" would be made, he wrote in January 1970, "only through *regular war* in which the main forces fight in a concentrated manner" (his italics).

While Nixon could not plausibly point to dramatic progress after a year in office, he was nevertheless moving in a fresh direction in Vietnam. The Communists had lost much of their steam, the South Vietnamese were showing signs of assuming responsibility for themselves, and he had repatriated more than a hundred thousand young Americans and promised to bring home another hundred and fifty thousand over the next year. But in the spring of 1970, determined to demonstrate his power, he plunged into a crazy sequence of events in Cambodia.

Prince Sihanouk's charisma was fading. The Cambodian economy was in shambles, drained partly by his extravagances and the cupidity of his court, and also because his attempts to raise revenues by building hotels and a gambling casino had gone awry. Though the peasants still revered him as a *devaraja*, a god-king descended from the sacred serpent of the Mekong, he had alienated the middle classes of Phnompenh, his capital. Envious of Saigon and Bangkok, flourishing on American dollars, they yearned to share in the wealth lavished by the United States on its Southeast Asian clients. The ragtag Cambodian army was particularly disaffected. Senior Cambodian officers were nostalgic for the days before Sihanouk's mercurial neutralism deprived them of American military aid. Along with the prime minister, General Lon Nol, many of them had privately profited from shipping weapons and other supplies from the port of Sihanoukville to the North Vietnamese and Vietcong bases near the Vietnam border. But the lure of renewed U.S. assistance was more attractive, and they dreamed of shifting squarely into the American camp. Besides, their relations with the Vietnamese Communists had deteriorated.

Early in 1969, after Sihanouk acquiesced to the American bombing of their sanctuaries, the North Vietnamese had expected him to swing against them completely. They had been arming and training guerrillas of the Khmer Rouge—the Cambodian Communist movement—in North Vietnam. To exert pressure on Sihanouk, they infiltrated a Khmer Rouge force of some twelve thousand back into Cambodia, spurring an incipient civil war. As the tension mounted, so did Sihanouk's denunciations of the Vietnamese Communists. But he and his top soldiers differed in their prescription for the dilemma. They believed, naively, that they could count on the United States to help them evict their hated neighbors. He believed, naively, that he could get them to quit his territory through diplomatic maneuvers.

But no crisis could deter Sihanouk from his annual "cure" for obesity at a clinic on the Côte d'Azur. He departed for France in January 1970, complacently entrusting Cambodia to Lon Nol and the deputy prime minister, Prince Sisowath Sirik Matak, a cousin belonging to a rival royal clan. The two men, neither very brainy, blundered from the start by assuming that they could effectively crack down on the Vietnamese Communist presence in Sihanouk's absence. Beginning in March, they exhorted Cambodian youths to sack the North Vietnamese and Vietcong legations in Phnompenh, and followed the riots with an ultimatum to the Vietnamese Communists to leave their remote Cambodian bases. Soon Cambodian mobs were running amok, slaughtering innocent Vietnamese civilian residents in an explosion of primeval ethnic passion that portended horrors yet to come. Lon Nol and especially Sirik Matak, hoping to benefit from the chaos, now contemplated Sihanouk's ouster. Allegations to the contrary, there is no firm evidence to substantiate the speculation that CIA agents encouraged them—though contacts with

American operatives may have inspired their wishful thinking that the United States favored a *coup d'état*.

In Paris at this juncture, Sihanouk erred. As he acknowledged later, he should have rushed home, where he could have deployed his immense prestige and skill to reimpose his authority. But his mother warned him that danger awaited his return, and he chose instead to go to Moscow to enlist Soviet support to eject the North Vietnamese and Vietcong from Cambodia. Accomplishing nothing there, he decided to fly to Beijing for the same purpose. On March 18, as they drove to the Moscow airport, Soviet Prime Minister Aleksei Kosygin informed him that he had been deposed by his opponents that morning. Sihanouk had once observed Emperor Bao Dai on the Côte d'Azur, and the memory of the deposed ruler wasting in luxurious exile haunted him. Rather than seek a safe haven in France, he proceeded to China.

The French had set up the eighteen-year-old Sihanouk as their puppet ruler in 1941, when they controlled Cambodia as a colonial protectorate, and they felt a special responsibility for him. Now, after his overthrow, they began to ponder the possibility of an international initiative to reinstall him in Phnompenh. There was a precedent for the idea. In 1964, the major powers had acted in concert to reinstate Prince Souvanna Phouma, prime minister of Laos, who had been toppled by an army colonel. The French now suggested the Cambodian problem be considered at a new version of the Geneva Conference of 1954, which had confirmed Cambodia's independence. Some French officials even envisioned the expansion of such a meeting to discuss peace for Vietnam.

Both the North and South Vietnamese regimes, reluctant to allow other nations to dictate their fate, promptly rejected the proposal. By contrast, the idea struck a chord in Britain, which with the Soviet Union had served as cochairman of the earlier Geneva conclave. Negative noises emanated from the Kremlin, but a positive response was advanced by the Polish foreign minister, Stefan Jedrychowski, an oblique signal that the Soviets were not totally averse to the notion. The Chinese ambassador had stayed on in Phnompenh, also a hint that the Chinese might be receptive to an accommodation.

In Washington, meanwhile, senior State Department figures urged flexibility. Marshall Green, assistant secretary of state for Far Eastern affairs, recommended that the French proposal be explored—or, in any case, that military moves that would impede American troop withdrawals from Vietnam be avoided. Secretary of State William Rogers was equally prudent. On March 23, he assured reporters of America's respect for "the neutrality, sovereignty, and independence" of Cambodia, adding that events there "will not cause the war to be widened in any way." Melvin Laird, as usual sensitive to American public opinion, also favored restraint.

Sihanouk, by now in Beijing, characteristically zigzagged. One of his first gestures was to see an old acquaintance, Ambassador Etienne Manac'h of France, in an effort to keep his lines open to the West. But shortly afterward, his regal pride affronted by the Lon Nol regime's vulgar attacks against himself and his family, he publicly announced the creation of a coalition with his former Communist foes to "liberate our motherland." Years later, after the Khmer Rouge had killed several of his children, he still justified his impetuous political decision as having been a personal necessity. His soprano voice rising emotionally, he told me: "I had to avenge myself against Lon Nol. He was my minister, my officer, and he betrayed me."

Cambodia was being convulsed by anarchy in late March 1970. Rival Cambodian gangs were hacking each other to pieces, in some instances celebrating their prowess by eating the hearts and livers of their victims. Cambodian vigilantes organized by police and other officials were murdering local Vietnamese, including women and infants. North Vietnamese and Vietcong troops and their Khmer Rouge confederates were pushing the Cambodian army back into the interior as South Vietnamese units covertly penetrated the border areas accompanied by their U.S. advisers—despite a Pentagon directive prohibiting Americans from crossing the boundary. The hapless Lon Nol, realizing that he had unleashed the furies, decried all foreign intrusion and asserted Cambodia's "strict neutrality." Then, reversing himself on April 14, he broadcast a desperate appeal for outside help. American officials in Phnompenh had prompted the plea as a device to lend legitimacy to a forthcoming U.S. step. For Nixon had secretly decided to aid Lon Nol a month earlier—indeed, even before Sihanouk had been overthrown.

The complicated and often confused machinations that went on inside the Nixon administration during that period have not been—and may never be—fully clarified. Kissinger has noted, however, that "historians rarely do justice to the psychological stress on a policy-maker," and Nixon's mood at the time was certainly a factor. He was more than usually tense, defiant, isolated. The Senate had just enraged him by rejecting in succession two of his candidates for a vacant Supreme Court seat. He was infuriated by press revelations of a covert American bombing campaign against the Communists in Laos, whose "neutrality" the United States theoretically honored. His testiness was also aggravated when Kissinger returned from a first futile round of secret talks in Paris with Le Duc Tho, the new high-ranking North Vietnamese negotiator. And, among other challenges to his authority, there was Cambodia. Much has been made of his infatuation then with the film *Patton*, starring George C. Scott as the lonely, stubborn, aggressive general whose daring risks had won decisive battles in World War II. Nixon watched the movie again and again, and made his aides watch it with him, pointing out to them with admiration Patton's disregard for his critics.

But more tangible motives also propelled Nixon toward Cambodia. With the Communists swiftly closing in on Phnompenh, he feared that the whole country would "go down the drain" unless he acted. General Abrams and other senior officers were warning him as well that another large U.S. troop withdrawal, imperative for domestic political reasons, would jeopardize the American forces remaining in South Vietnam unless the enemy sanctuaries in Cambodia could be eliminated. Nor had Nixon abandoned his original belief that a spectacular manifestation of American power would, by showing the North Vietnamese leaders that "we were still serious about our commitment in Vietnam," drive them to an acceptable compromise at the conference table. Nevertheless, he edged toward direct American intervention gradually—and deceptively.

"We don't anticipate that any request will be made," replied Secretary of State Rogers on March 23, when a reporter asked him whether the United States might grant military assistance to Lon Nol. But Rogers was excluded from the decisions being made at the White House. Six days earlier, on the eve of Sihanouk's ouster, Kissinger had told Nixon that Lon Nol intended to enlarge the Cambodian army by ten thousand men. Two days later, with Sihanouk gone, Nixon instructed Kissinger to "get a plan to aid the new government." Secret orders went out to the American mission in Saigon to furnish Lon Nol's force with weapons captured from the Communists. Dissident Cambodian soldiers, trained by the Americans in Vietnam for clandestine operations in Cambodia, were flown to Phnompenh. To cut the State Department out of the picture further, Nixon directed the CIA to beef up its staff in the Cambodian capital.

By late April, different aides were giving Nixon different advice. General Abrams and his military colleagues in Saigon and Washington were predictably pressing for vigorous measures. Laird, by contrast, was worried. And Rogers, again thinking that he could speak for the administration, told a congressional subcommittee that the administration had "no incentive to escalate" the war into Cambodia because that would jeopardize the Vietnamization program. Kissinger, at first ambivalent, shifted to adjust to Nixon's hardening attitude. CIA analysts, whose only function was to forecast, estimated that American and South Vietnamese infantry would be required to rescue Lon Nol, but however much an allied drive into Cambodia harmed the Communists, "it probably would not prevent them from continuing the struggle."

Anxiety pervaded Capitol Hill, where Senators Frank Church and John Sherman Cooper began to draft legislation to forbid American fighting men from entering Cambodia. On April 20, 1970, Nixon announced the withdrawal of another hundred and fifty thousand U.S. troops from Vietnam within a year—adding that "we finally have in sight the just peace we are seeking." Two days later, at five o'clock in the morning, he dictated a memorandum to Kissinger declaring that "we need a bold move in Cambodia to show that we stand with Lon Nol." Though Lon Nol might collapse anyway, "we must do something symbolic" for the only Cambodian regime in twenty-five years with "the guts to take a pro-Western and pro-American stand."

The question was how to proceed. Laird, reconciled to Nixon's determination to "do something," tried to minimize the action. He favored a foray against Communist bases in the "Parrot's Beak," a narrow Cambodian frontier area, to be conducted by only South Vietnamese forces and their American advisers. The recommendation, as Nixon later described it, was "the most pusillanimous little nitpicker I ever saw." He wanted to stage "the big play"—going for "all the marbles," since he expected "a hell of an uproar at home" whatever he did. He indirectly encouraged General Abrams to propose intervention by American combat units as well. Abrams broadened the targets to include sanctuaries in the "Fish Hook" border region, farther north, where he also claimed to have located the legendary Communist headquarters, COSVN. On Sunday night, April 26, Nixon decided to "go for broke" with the entire "package."

Despite Nixon's solicitude for Lon Nol, the Cambodian leader was neither consulted nor even informed in advance of the American project to invade his country. To his dismay, he learned of the operation only after it had started from Lloyd Rives, head of the U.S. mission in Phnompenh—who himself had learned of it only from Nixon's speech broadcast by the "Voice of America." But the deeper issue revolved around Nixon's constitutional prerogatives, a matter that in different guise was to spell his ultimate downfall. Lon Nol's approval notwithstanding, it was doubtful if Nixon had the authority to broaden the war without congressional authority—just as it was doubtful that he had the power to begin, in secrecy, the bombing of Cambodia the year before. Almost as an afterthought, he assigned the task of preparing a legal justification to William Rehnquist, an assistant attorney general, who came up with the argument that the law mandated presidents to deploy troops "in conflict with foreign powers at their own initiative."

Nor did Nixon seem to be conforming to the "doctrine" he had enunciated in Guam, which was to spare GIs from battles on alien soil. One of Nixon's speech writers, William Safire, raised this point during a briefing session with Kissinger, who exploded: "We wrote the goddam doctrine, we can change it!"

Kissinger was under tremendous pressure. Several members of his staff, hostile to the Cambodian venture, were about to quit. He was concerned about his connections with Harvard, where antiwar fever ran high. At the same time, he had to appear belligerent to retain his place in Nixon's inner circle. According to William Watts, one of his aides, Kissinger received a telephone call one evening during this period from Nixon, who at critical moments frequently sought the company of his crony, Charles "Bebe" Rebozo. Nixon, sounding drunk, passed the telephone to Rebozo, who said: "The president wants you to know if this doesn't work, Henry, it's your ass." Watts, who was monitoring the conversation for Kissinger, heard Nixon add in a slurred voice: "Ain't that right, Bebe?"

Nixon unveiled the Cambodian "incursion" on the evening of April 30, 1970, in a televised address that was, as Kissinger derisively put it later, "vintage Nixon." He could have depicted the operation as a minor tactic, designed merely to crush the Communist bases in order to bring the boys home faster. But, consonant with his pugnacious paranoia, he chose instead to be pious and strident, to respond defiantly to his critics, and to defend an overblown reaction to what he perceived as a challenge to America's global credibility. Resorting to coarse jingoism, he had spurned "all political considerations," he said, preferring to follow his conscience rather than "be a two-term president at the cost of seeing America become a second-rate power." International equilibrium hinged on the Cambodian venture: "If, when the chips are down, the world's most powerful nation, the United States of America, acts like a pitiful helpless giant, the forces of totalitarianism and anarchy will threaten free nations and free institutions throughout the world."

An allied force of twenty thousand men, supported by American aircraft, were attacking the two main North Vietnamese and Vietcong bases in Cambodia as Nixon spoke. The South Vietnamese had initially crossed the border two days before. The drive against COSVN, the Communist headquarters supposedly situated in the "Fish Hook," turned out to be quixotic. Instead of the miniature Pentagon imagined by official U.S. spokesmen, American troops found a scattering of empty huts, their occupants having fled weeks before in anticipation of the assault. Meanwhile, Nixon's claims of success for the campaign as a whole were debatable. As usual, the computers compiled impressive statistics of the enemy arms, ammunition, food, and other supplies destroyed; and indeed the damage inflicted on the Communist logistical apparatus was a benefit, for it relieved the military pressure on the heavily populated region around Saigon, thereby giving the South Vietnamese a bit of additional time to prepare replacements for the withdrawing American troops.

But the triumph was temporary and, in long-range terms, illusory. The Communists were soon able to supplant their lost equipment from the vast stocks furnished by the Soviet Union and China. They also shifted their strategic focus to the northern provinces of South Vietnam, where they were to move toward the conventional conflict forecast by General Giap. More critically for the future, the United States was now going to be responsible for the flimsy Lon Nol regime in addition to propping up the shaky Saigon government. Nixon had promised only a couple of weeks earlier that "the just peace we are seeking" was in sight, yet he had expanded the war. The antiwar movement at home, which he had skillfully subdued, suddenly erupted again in the biggest protests to date.

A large proportion of the American people, traditionally loyal to the president in crucial moments, supported the Cambodian incursions. Once again, however, the opinion leaders set the pace. Press commentators lashed out at Nixon, with *The New York Times* calling the action a "virtual renunciation" of his pledge to end the war and the *Wall Street Journal* warning against "deeper entrapment" in Southeast Asia. Educators, clergymen, lawyers, businessmen, and others protested. Nixon's secretary of the interior, Walter Hickel, publicly objected and was later fired, and more than two hundred State Department employees registered their dissatisfaction in a public petition. In many instances, top administration figures were stunned by the anguish of their children. A poignant scene occurred at the home of one senior official who had strenuously worked against the Cambodian offensive from behind the scenes. His two sons, unaware of their father's exertions, denounced him over dinner—and walked out of the house.

Nixon went into a rampage even before the full storm of domestic opposition had burst, almost as if he relished the coming onslaught. At the Pentagon on the morning after the invasion, he interrupted a briefing and embarrassed the officers present by exhorting them in foul language to "blow the hell out" of the Communist sanctuaries in Cambodia. Out in the corridor, he also uncorked a diatribe against antiwar students, whose fresh round of demonstrations had not yet even occurred. Not knowing that his remarks were being taped, he branded the youths as "bums blowing up campuses." He later advised his staff on how to deal with congressional critics: "Don't worry about divisiveness. Having drawn the sword, don't take it out—stick it in hard. . . . Hit 'em in the gut. No defensiveness."

Universities and colleges across the country were then seething over one issue or another, but Cambodia suddenly crystallized the unrest, and disaster struck at Kent State University in Ohio. There, as elsewhere, antiwar students had attacked the reserve officers training building. Echoing Nixon's inflammatory rhetoric, Governor James Rhodes assailed the rioters as "worse than the brownshirts" and vowed to "eradicate" them. He ordered national guardsmen onto the campus to impose order. On May 4, 1970, nettled by the demonstrators, they shot a volley of rifle fire into the crowd, killing four youths. The administration initially reacted to this event with wanton insensitivity. Nixon's press secretary, Ron Ziegler, whose statements were carefully programmed, referred to the deaths as a reminder that "when dissent turns to violence, it invites tragedy."

Kissinger was torn. On the one hand, he was chagrined by the resignation of four of his aides, who urged him to quit as well. A group of Harvard colleagues also came to Washington to tell him personally of their revulsion, and he felt that the angry meeting marked his final rupture with the academic community. In an interview with me years later, he blamed Nixon for failing to find "the language of respect and compassion that might have created a bridge at least to the more reasonable elements of the antiwar movement." But according to Nixon's recollections, Kissinger "took a particularly hard line" at the time, stressing that "we had to make it clear that our foreign policy was not made by street protests." Roger Morris, one of the assistants who left his staff, recalled that Kissinger was chronically alarmed by demonstrations, which summoned up the Nazi mobs of Germany during his childhood.

The Kent State killings sparked protests across the country. More than four hundred universities and colleges shut down as students and professors staged strikes, and nearly a hundred thousand demonstrators marched on Washington, encircling the White House and other government buildings. The spectacle briefly sobered Nixon. One night, accompanied only by his valet, he drove to the Lincoln Memorial, where young dissidents were conducting a nocturnal vigil. He treated them to a clumsy and condescending monologue, which he made public in an awkward attempt to display his benevolence. But not long afterward, when several senators nearly succeeded in restricting his military activities in Cambodia, he decided to stop "screwing around" with his congressional adversaries and other foes. He ordered the formation of a covert team headed by Tom Huston, a former army intelligence specialist, to improve the surveillance of domestic critics. During later investigation into Nixon's alleged violations of the law, Senator Sam Ervin of North Carolina called the Huston project evidence of a "Gestapo mentality," and Huston himself warned Nixon that the internal espionage was illicit. Nixon afterward contended, however, that "when the president does it, that means it is not illegal."

Nixon had campaigned for election on a pledge to "end the war and win the peace." But after nearly a year and a half in office, he seemed to have gone in the opposite direction. He had extended the war beyond Vietnam into Cambodia, and he had brought the war home with greater intensity. And despite his pretension of toughness, he was not going to extricate himself without offering significant concessions to the Communists.

16 The Peace That Never Was

North Vietnamese troops enter Saigon in April 1975. South Vietnamese army resistance was light. American officials had tried various ways to work out a last-minute settlement, but were unsuccessful.

American prisoners of war released in Hanoi following the cease-fire agreement, most of whom were pilots. They had been held in a jail they derisively called the "Hanoi Hilton."

A South Vietnamese band serenades Saigon government troops released from captivity by the Communists following the cease-fire. The question of the status of political prisoners had been a sticking point in the armistice negotiations.

Air Force Captain Ronald Bliss, a former prisoner, is greeted by his wife, Charlene, as he arrives in San Antonio. He had been shot down over North Vietnam in 1966 and held captive in Hanoi for seven years.

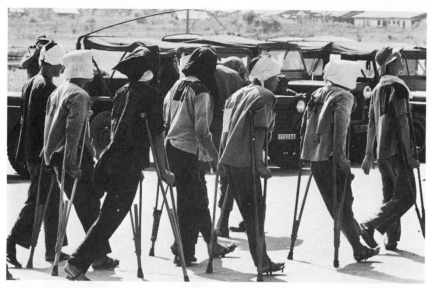

North Vietnamese prisoners released in the south after the armistice accord. Prisoners on both sides were treated badly in this undeclared war, fought outside the rules of the Geneva Convention.

Despite the armistice, both sides skirmished to gain territory that could be used as a lever in further negotiations for a political settlement. South Vietnam's President Nguyen Van Thieu (center), who had opposed the cease-fire agreement, urged his army to grab territory.

Under the cease-fire agreement, South Vietnamese villages controlled by the Vietcong were permitted to declare their allegiance—and did so by flying the Vietcong flag.

Billions of dollars' worth of American military equipment was discarded as junk following the cease-fire. Under the agreement, however, the United States was permitted to give South Vietnam matériel as replacements.

On August 9, 1974, President Nixon resigned rather than face impeachment. With his resignation, Congress moved quickly to protest against continued American involvement in Southeast Asia—one effect of which was to curb further aid to the South Vietnamese regime.

Commanders of the North
Vietnamese forces rolling
southward into Danang
were surprised by the
speed with which the
South Vietnamese forces
crumbled before their
onslaught. President
Thieu had demoralized his
own officers with confused
instructions.

General Van Tien Dung,
field commander of the
North Vietnamese forces
that staged the final
offensive in early 1975.
Dung soon replaced Giap
as defense minister.

Phnompenh, capital of Cambodia, came under heavy shelling in early 1975 as Communist forces closed in. Here the dead lie sprawled in a marketplace directly hit by a bomb.

Thousands of refugees flee southward in late April 1975. Refugees entering Saigon were checked to prevent Vietcong infiltration, but such precautions proved futile.

At Nhatrang, a city in central Vietnam, an American official punches a Vietnamese trying to board an evacuation airplane. Nhatrang was overrun almost immediately after this photograph was taken.

Ambassador Graham Martin, a veteran diplomat, was among the last American officials to leave Saigon in 1973. He had been optimistic that the southern regions of South Vietnam could be defended, and was slow to put an evacuation plan into effect.

The first North Vietnamese soldiers and tanks arrive at the presidential palace in Saigon, where General Duong Van Minh, the temporary president, was waiting. Minh surrendered to Colonel Bui Tin, the ranking North Vietnamese officer—actually a correspondent for a Hanoi military newspaper.

Americans and selected South Vietnamese file to the roof of an American embassy building in Saigon to board a helicopter to the safety zone. The choppers flew to American aircraft carriers deployed off the coast.

We have finally achieved peace with honor.

—Richard Nixon

Today, America can regain the sense of pride that existed before Vietnam. But it cannot be achieved by refighting a war that is finished. . . . These events, tragic as they are, portend neither the end of the world nor of America's leadership in the world.

—Gerald Ford

On February 21, 1970, in a dingy little house located in an industrial Paris suburb, Henry Kissinger met secretly for the first time with a North Vietnamese figure who was to be his tenacious diplomatic adversary for the next three years. Le Duc Tho, a gray, austere, aloof man then in his late fifties, had none of the charm of Ho Chi Minh, the flair of Vo Nguyen Giap, or the warmth of Pham Van Dong. Like his senior comrades, he was of middle-class origin. The son of a functionary in the French colonial administration of Vietnam, he had attended French schools before joining the struggle for independence. He helped to found the Indochinese Communist party, was a charter member of the Vietminh, and spent years either in jail or fleeing from the police. As the top Vietminh commissar for southern Vietnam during the war against France, Le Duc Tho continued to be chiefly responsible for that region after the United States intervened to underwrite the Saigon regime, hiding in jungles or remote villages as he supervised the growing insurgency. He was one of the few Communist leaders who refused to be interviewed when I visited Hanoi after the war. To Westerners, his career is largely a mystery.

So, as their marathon dialogue began, Kissinger faced a specimen he had never before encountered—a professional revolutionary for whom negotiations were a form of protracted guerrilla warfare. The exasperating haggling over trivial details was to test Kissinger's endurance, and he not only displayed remarkable stamina but developed a perverse respect for Le Duc Tho's determination. "I don't look back on our meetings with any great joy," Kissinger confessed to me afterward, "yet he was a person of substance and discipline who defended the position he represented with dedication."

It seems peculiar in retrospect that Kissinger and Le Duc Tho should have resorted to clandestine talks on the outskirts of Paris while a formal peace conference was being held within the city. But they shared an obsession for secrecy, and they both saw practical advantages in the covert approach.

From Kissinger's viewpoint, the surreptitious discussions enhanced his flexibility. He could bypass the Washington bureaucracy he detested, even to the extent of cutting out Secretary of State William Rogers and Defense Secretary Melvin Laird, who were only informed of the conversations a year after they had started. He was also able to plug leaks to the press—except when he himself managed the news by slipping selected tidbits to his favorite reporters. And there was the delicate matter of relations with South Vietnamese President Nguyen Van Thieu. Though Nixon and Kissinger had sworn to him that no peace agreement would be concluded without his assent, they realized that Thieu stood to lose the most from a compromise deal with North Vietnam. Thus, while they briefed him on the bilateral negotiations, he was kept at a distance. Thieu was aware of this maneuver, but since he relied on American aid for survival, his options were limited.

The North Vietnamese, despite their avowed solidarity with the Vietcong, also welcomed this chance to negotiate without their southern comrades interfering in the bargaining process. The northerners, as well, calculated that, by talking directly with Kissinger, they might drive a wedge between the United States and the Saigon regime—or, at least, exacerbate Thieu's suspicions. At the time, stymied militarily, they hoped to gain at the negotiating table what they had not won on the battlefield.

Unlike Kissinger, to whom Nixon had given considerable latitude, Le Duc Tho had to check his every step with the collective leadership that had taken over in Hanoi after Ho Chi Minh's death in September 1969. The two men therefore held only three sessions between February and April 1970—with no visible results. But they had no intention of quitting. They resembled a couple of boxers in the early rounds of a match, sparring to size each other up, both knowing that neither could score a quick knockout. Nevertheless, they were under different time pressures. With tolerance for the war dwindling in the United States, Kissinger could not negotiate forever. The North Vietnamese, untrammeled by domestic dissidence, were prepared to talk endlessly.

Le Duc Tho began by insisting, as his comrades had previously, that a peace settlement must simultaneously resolve the military and political issues; an armistice had to be related to the replacement of the present Saigon regime with a coalition government containing Vietcong representatives. The package was unrealistic: no American president could appear to be scuttling an ally to appease an enemy. Yet the North Vietnamese were to cling to this condition for two years. In 1954, after beating the French, they had been virtually compelled by the major powers at the Geneva Conference to stop fighting in the expectation that nationwide elections would assure their control over all of Vietnam. But the big powers, including their Soviet and Chinese allies, tacitly conspired to cancel the elections soon afterward, thus depriving them of probable victory. They were not about to repeat that mistake.

Kissinger proposed a slight variation on the mutual withdrawal plan he had presented the summer before to Xuan Thuy, head of the North Vietnamese diplomatic delegation in Paris, who had since been superseded by Le Duc Tho. Kissinger suggested, as a "face-saving" device, that North Vietnamese combat units in the south be accorded "legal" status separate from that of the Americans: they could be repatriated to the north without a public announcement from Hanoi as long as they were in fact pulled out. Le Duc Tho predictably spurned the idea, as Xuan Thuy had. The North Vietnamese regarded their military presence in the south as imperative, since Vietcong forces alone were too weak to resist the Saigon regime's superior army. Besides, they were wedded to the principle that, as Vietnam's only legitimate nationalists, they had the right to deploy their troops anywhere in the country. After all, their soldiers were defending sacred Vietnamese soil; to equate them in any way with the American "aggressors" was an outrage.

Though they parried Kissinger's gambit, the Communists sensed a softening of the American position. In Hanoi after the war, one of Le Duc Tho's senior aides read to me excerpts from his official diary of the talks. Kissinger's offer to consider the North Vietnamese and American forces in South Vietnam differently, he had noted, suggested that the United States would eventually retreat from its requirement that the northern troops be removed from the south. Kissinger had no such thought in mind at that stage, but the Communist perception was prescient.

By the late summer of 1970, American combat units had been pulled out of Cambodia, and the domestic turmoil aggravated by the incursions seemed to have abated. But the relative calm was fragile, particularly in the academic community. Hardly a week passed without sporadic student protests, and returning veterans were beginning to participate in the demonstrations. A special commission appointed by Nixon to assess the unrest in universities and colleges reported that the country was "so polarized" that campuses might again explode in a fresh cycle of violence and repression, which would jeopardize "the very survival of the nation." The commission, directed by William Scranton, former Republican governor of Pennsylvania, called the divisions splitting American society "as deep as any since the Civil War" and contended that "nothing is more important than an end to the war" in Vietnam. The public appeared to share that attitude. Surveys showed that increasing numbers of Americans wanted a firm deadline for a U.S. troop withdrawal from Southeast Asia, whatever the risks for the Saigon government. The hope found expression on Capitol Hill, where the Senate only narrowly defeated a bill sponsored by Senators George McGovern of South Dakota and Mark Hatfield of Oregon to bring all the GIs home by December 31, 1971.

Vice-President Spiro Agnew, acting as Nixon's lightning rod, flailed the opposition senators as "radical liberals" and even excoriated the Scranton group for its "neutrality" in recommending national reconciliation. Nixon, meanwhile, oscillated between bravado and alarm. On the one hand, convinced that the "silent majority" would continue to back him under almost any circumstances, he boasted that he could resume the bombing of North Vietnam with impunity. On the other hand, troubled by the erosion of his popularity, he privately expressed the fear that he might be denied a second term. What especially rattled him was a growing disaffection among conservative politicians, the pillars of his support in Washington and in county courthouses across America, who were worried that the interminable war would go against them in the congressional elections in November. He was not disturbed by the McGoverns and Hatfields; they had nothing better to suggest, he said, than a "bug-out." "But," he confided to Kissinger, "when the Right starts wanting to get out, for whatever reason, that's *our* problem."

Richard Nixon's dilemma in Southeast Asia was in many ways worse than Lyndon Johnson's chronic nightmare. Nixon had expanded the war into Cambodia, and the North Vietnamese, in response, had extended their grip over Laos. Instead of dealing solely with Vietnam, a daunting challenge in itself, Nixon had assumed responsibility for all of Indochina. He also had to maintain the momentum of GI withdrawals, yet without any guarantee that the South Vietnamese army could improve rapidly enough to compensate for the departing U.S. troops. As the size of the American force shrank, moreover, the United States would inevitably lose leverage in bargaining with North Vietnam. Clearly, Nixon and Kissinger desperately needed a drastic new initiative.

They dredged up the notion of a "standstill cease-fire," one idea among many that had been buried in the bureaucratic files for years: the two sides would stop shooting and remain in place while an international conference hammered out an equitable settlement. The plan scared Thieu, who envisioned the North Vietnamese troops staying indefinitely in the southern regions they occupied. And Nixon had never liked the formula, which he regarded as dangerous to the Saigon regime. Kissinger had also voiced reservations in his *Foreign Affairs* article two years before, observing that the plan would probably result in a partition of South Vietnam. In addition, he had cautioned that with such a formal cessation of hostilities, the belligerents would then base their claims on the amount and location of the real estate they dominated.

But Nixon and Kissinger lacked room to maneuver in late 1970. Domestic dissent, again bubbling, threatened to boil over unless they ended the war. Le Duc Tho had made it plain, however, that the North Vietnamese troops were not going to pull out of the south, even if all the Americans departed. As far as the Communists were concerned, a mutual withdrawal scheme was no more negotiable now than it had been when Lyndon Johnson's advisers concocted it. Thus Nixon and Kissinger turned to the "standstill cease-fire" idea.

Nixon unveiled the plan in a televised address on October 7, 1970, having told reporters it would be "the most comprehensive statement ever made on this subject since the beginning of this difficult war." He stressed that he had already repatriated one hundred and sixty-five thousand GIs from Vietnam and would bring home another ninety thousand by the following spring. The scheme earned instant praise in Congress, where even such antiwar stalwarts as McGovern, Hatfield, and Fulbright lent their names to a resolution of approval. The press applauded, with the usually skeptical *Wall Street Journal* hailing the approach as "so appealing and so sane that only the most unreasonable critics could object to it." This positive reaction seems to have been a combination of relief at Nixon's moderate tone and sincere hope for the success of his effort. Once again, Nixon had foiled his opponents.

But apart from its value as a domestic political ploy, would the offer hasten a conclusion to the war? Nixon had flamboyantly billed his statement as "the most comprehensive" ever made on the war until then, but in his memoirs he conspicuously omitted any explanation of its purpose—nor, indeed, did he even mention the speech. Kissinger recalled the initiative in his memoirs, recollecting that after meeting with Xuan Thuy in Paris a week before Nixon's address, he was pessimistic about its chances. At the time, however, Kissinger intimated to his aides that the cease-fire proposal was actually a disguised concession of major proportions, intended to convey to the North Vietnamese that the United States had scrapped the mutual withdrawal requirement: their forces could remain in place only if they dropped their demand that Thieu be jettisoned. Some members of Kissinger's staff stick by that version to this day, putting the onus on the Communists for their refusal to take up the offer. The North Vietnamese did in fact reject the truce plan and again insisted that no progress was possible until the Thieu regime ceded authority to a coalition government in Saigon that "favors peace, independence, and democracy." But their rebuff was not gratuitous; they had valid motives for spurning the offer.

Nixon had sidestepped the phrase "mutual withdrawal" in his speech, thereby creating an impression of new flexibility—and for that reason won acclaim. But his language was deceptive. He said that the removal of the American forces from Vietnam would be "based on principles" that he had "previously" outlined. One of these principles was, of course, the mutual withdrawal of both American and North Vietnamese troops. A day later, speaking to reporters during a trip to Georgia, he bluntly confirmed that he had not diluted this policy. His offer of "a total withdrawal of all our forces," he said, was contingent on "mutual withdrawal on the other side."

It could be argued that Nixon felt constrained to restate the mutual withdrawal policy openly so as to avoid demoralizing the Saigon regime, which trembled at any suggestion that the Americans might switch strategy on an issue vital to its security. But Kissinger made no effort to hint privately to the North Vietnamese that American policy was shifting. At that point, in fact, there was no change. The "standstill cease-fire" offer was nothing more than a tranquilizer to placate the American public on the eve of congressional elections. Kissinger saw it in just that context—a device that "at a minimum . . . would give us some temporary relief from public pressures." Strangely, however, he scolded North Vietnam for dismissing it, and still does, when in fact they shared his view that it was merely window dressing.

I have digressed into this apparently theoretical exegesis in order to raise a crucial question that aroused controversy then and has ever since. The United States and North Vietnam were to reach an agreement, in October 1972, after Kissinger had dropped the mutual withdrawal theme and Le Duc Tho had dropped the demand for Thieu's resignation. Could the same agreement have been reached two years earlier? Kissinger has asserted that the Communists were implacable at that time and even refused to budge when he began to ease his stance shortly afterward. The North Vietnamese contended later, as they did then, that

Nixon's cease-fire proposal of 1970 was a "trick," allowing that they might have acquiesced in it had it been authentic. This is one of those speculative what-could-have-beens of history, unlikely to be elucidated as long as the participants in the negotiations hold each other responsible for the failure to achieve a settlement sooner. My own feeling, though, is that both were at fault—Kissinger for not making the truce offer a real concession and Le Duc Tho for not pressing him to explore its possibilities. In reality, neither was ready for an accommodation. The Vietnam tragedy is the story of squandered opportunities.

The diplomacy of Vietnam had seesawed in a similar pattern since the start of the struggle. Neither side was willing to deal from weakness, hoping for a stronger battlefield position to improve its bargaining posture. Nor was either side eager to compromise from current strength, reckoning that an even stronger battlefield position would enable it to dictate terms. Now the two sides were stalled. At the beginning of 1971, however, a debacle augured a break in the deadlock.

Nixon and Kissinger foresaw a massive Communist drive unfolding in 1972, timed to influence American voters during the presidential election campaign. Accordingly, they expected a big North Vietnamese logistical move during the early months of 1971, before the rains made the transport of supplies difficult. The U.S. commanders in Saigon and their colleagues in the Pentagon assumed that the enemy buildup could be thwarted by cutting the Ho Chi Minh Trail, the web of roads and jungle paths in the Laotian panhandle. A congressional amendment, passed after the Cambodian incursion of 1970, barred American ground troops from entering Cambodia and Laos, so the job would have to be performed by the South Vietnamese infantry with U.S. air support. Given the code name Lamson 719, for an ancient Vietnamese triumph over China, this trial of Vietnamization got under way on February 8, 1971. As Kissinger was to describe it later, "the operation, conceived in doubt and assailed by skepticism, proceeded in confusion."

The blunders were monumental. The South Vietnamese had never been tested in major deployments, especially without accompanying American advisers. American planners had estimated that the thrust would require four seasoned U.S. divisions—roughly sixty thousand men—but the Saigon regime assigned to the attack an inexperienced force only half that size. The objective, the Laotian town of Tchepone, situated about twenty miles inside the border, was a trap within easy range of North Vietnamese and Vietcong units. Thieu, a model of pusillanimity, ordered his officers to stop their soldiers when they had taken a total of three thousand casualties, so that the South Vietnamese army stopped less than halfway to its target. And, as if it mattered, scant attention was paid to Prince Souvanna Phouma, prime minister of Laos, who protested in vain against the violation of his country's neutrality. His complaints were chronic; international agreements notwithstanding, the benighted land had for years been an unpublicized sideshow to the war in Vietnam.

Tchepone, already wrecked by earlier American air strikes, was now reduced to rubble by U.S. bombers. Some South Vietnamese troops finally captured the worthless target, but most were pinned down by Communist artillery in shelling and ground assaults. In March, Alexander Haig was sent by Kissinger to survey the situation. He reported that Thieu's commanders were reluctant to continue fighting; the task now, said Haig in soldierly style, was for the South Vietnamese to retreat "in an orderly and tactically sound fashion." But the retreat had already been going on for weeks, and it was a virtual rout. With the North Vietnamese in pursuit, government soldiers clawed their way back to Vietnam along a route littered with corpses and ruined vehicles, walking when their trucks ran out of fuel. They tried to crowd onto the American helicopters sent to evacuate the wounded, and many dangled from the skids, their bodies ripped to shreds as the choppers skimmed jungle treetops. Four American photographers died when one helicopter crashed, among them Larry Burrows of *Life*, who had been covering the war in Vietnam for nearly a decade. We had first worked together for the magazine in France in 1950.

The operation not only failed to destroy North Vietnam's Ho Chi Minh Trail, but exposed the South Vietnamese army's deficiencies. The government's top officers had been tutored by Americans for ten or fifteen years, many at training schools in the United States, yet they had learned little. In part, they had been taught conventional methods unsuited to the war in their own country, but, more significantly, they represented a regime that rewarded fidelity rather than competence. Thieu, like his predecessors, lived in constant dread of a *coup d'état*. He wanted loyalty above all else, and his military subordinates conformed, realizing that promotions were won in Saigon, not in battle. And vital to advancement was the avoidance of risks, even at the price of defeat. The glory of death in action paled beside the wealth and prestige to be acquired by genuflecting to authority. The prospects for Vietnamization therefore seemed bleak.

"Tonight I can report that Vietnamization has succeeded," proclaimed President Nixon in a televised speech on April 7, 1971. He could hardly say otherwise without acknowledging that his policy was failing, and as usual he attacked the news media for focusing on a few horrible scenes during the Laos operation. He later recalled that Kissinger had shared his optimism. But Kissinger concluded afterward that the venture had fallen "far short of our expectations" and blamed the fumble on myopic American planning, poor South Vietnamese execution, and even Nixon's warped leadership—everyone, characteristically, except himself.

Whatever the truth, the Laotian episode ignited different passions in Saigon and the United States. In Saigon, where rumors ripened and spread with the speed and extravagance of tropical vegetation, accounts of the setback in Laos were exaggerated. Nevertheless, the distorted tales struck a nerve, especially among young people, who saw the South Vietnamese army falter in its first big test. They were becoming skittish at the likelihood of a future without the presence of the United States, and their uneasiness sparked anti-American outbursts. Students demonstrated in front of American offices and sabotaged American vehicles, and they pasted up posters such as one showing Nixon astride a mound of dead South Vietnamese soldiers, its message alleging that Vietnamization meant the sacrifice of Vietnam by America. Minor traffic accidents involving GIs and Vietnamese flared up into major confrontations, and resentment against the United States began to be apparent even within Thieu's inner circle. One of his confidants was now Hoang Duc Nha, a young cousin who had returned from school in the United States with a smart-aleck manner and an animus toward Americans. "The Americans are businessmen," he warned Thieu. "They'll sell you out if you can no longer assure them of a profit."

The growing rancor toward the United States among urban South Vietnamese was mirrored in the sense of futility that seeped through the ranks of the American armed forces, its most serious symptom a growing narcotics addiction, which one official study linked to "idleness, loneliness, anxiety, and frustration." The U.S. command in Saigon estimated that sixty-five thousand GIs were on drugs in 1970. Fred Hickey, a helicopter pilot at the time, later recalled that almost entire American units, including officers, were "doing heroin." "The majority of people were high all the time," he said. "For ten dollars you could get a vial of pure heroin the size of a cigarette butt, and you could get liquid opium, speed, acid, anything you wanted. You could trade a box of Tide for a carton of prepacked, prerolled marijuana cigarettes soaked in opium." The American military authorities introduced measures to halt the epidemic. "They harassed everybody," Hickey went on, "making them take urine analysis tests any time, day or night. They had no regard for human dignity."

And there was "fragging"—fragmentation grenade attacks by men against their officers. More than two hundred incidents were recorded in 1970, and Hickey recalled the case of one lieutenant whose arrogance and incompetence antagonized his men. "The first time, they booby-trapped his hooch with a smoke grenade, yellow smoke, which was a warning. But he didn't take any heed. Then they tried another, red smoke, which said the next one was going to be a hand grenade or a white phosphorous grenade. He obviously didn't believe it. The last one was a hand grenade, and he was eliminated and replaced. Grenades leave no fingerprints. Nobody's going to go to jail."

As morale deteriorated in Hickey's unit, the GIs split into factions, "the red-necks from Texas and the Deep South who hated the California and New York liberals, and vice versa." Racial tensions mounted. "The blacks were moving into their black power thing, and they got militant. They removed any black who wasn't militant, then they moved in on the whites." A minor civil war erupted within the First Cavalry Division based at Bienhoa, and the ringleaders were arrested. But the friction would begin again, sometimes instigated by "juicers," alcoholics high on drugs, who would pick fights. "Everybody seemed to be at everybody else's throat," Hickey continued. "You had to speak softly, mind your own business, sleep with a weapon at all times, and only trust your closest buddies, nobody else. I had a knife attached to my boot."

The U.S. commanders knew that the answer to the problem was to end the war and repatriate the GIs, for whom the conflict had become as pointless as it had for the rest of the American people. In March 1971, a poll reported that public confidence in Nixon had dropped to 50 percent, the lowest rating since he entered office. Support for his conduct of the war slid to 34 percent, another survey stated, with 51 percent of Americans persuaded that the conflict was "morally wrong."

Street protests resumed in America, now spearheaded by Vietnam veterans, and two hundred thousand demonstrators marched on Washington to stage a huge rally in late April. One of the most eloquent speakers was John Kerry, a former naval officer later to be elected lieutenant governor of Massachusetts, who said that his fellow veterans were determined to "reach out and destroy the last vestige of this barbaric war." The House of Representatives, usually prudent, began to stir as the Democratic whip, Thomas P. "Tip" O'Neill, prompted a group of colleagues to urge the repatriation of all GIs by the close of the year. On June 22, Majority Leader Mike Mansfield prevailed on the Senate to pass a similar resolution that, while not legally binding on the president, reflected the climate on Capitol Hill.

Remarkably subdued, Nixon replied to the antiwar sentiment by saying that "while everybody has a right to protest peacefully, policy in this country is not made by protests." But his fury was rekindled on June 13, when *The New York Times* began publishing lengthy excerpts from the "Pentagon Papers," the news media's inevitable nickname for a mammoth collection of confidential government memorandums on the war that had been compiled and analyzed by Defense Department officials during the Johnson administration. Why the archive was commissioned in 1967 by Robert McNamara, then secretary of defense, has never been made clear. Among other explanations, former Secretary of State Dean Rusk and others have speculated that McNamara aimed to give the record on Vietnam to his friend Robert Kennedy, who was contemplating a bid for the presidency at the time.

The appearance of the documents shocked Nixon, since any disclosure of squabbles and duplicity within the government—even the Johnson administration—might damage the public's faith in his own leadership. When the Supreme Court denied his appeal to stop their publication, he staged a tantrum: "I want to know who is behind this and I want the most complete investigation that can be conducted. . . . I don't want excuses. I want results. I want it done, whatever the costs." Kissinger, equally appalled, worried that the "hemorrhage of state secrets" would cramp his delicate diplomatic endeavors—especially his covert talks with the North Vietnamese and his tentative early maneuvers toward China. Uneasy among the right-wing zealots in the Nixon entourage, Kissinger may have also felt tainted because of his acquaintance with Daniel Ellsberg, the former bureaucrat who confessed to having purloined the classified material.

Ellsberg, just turned forty, was a familiar figure in the Vietnam cast of characters. Lean, nervous, and volatile, he was a *summa cum laude* graduate of Harvard who had become one of the Pentagon "whiz kids," the brilliant young scholars recruited by McNamara. When our paths first crossed in 1966 in Saigon, where he belonged to a special counterinsurgency team headed by Edward Lansdale, he was a fervent believer in the war who hotly disputed my lack of enthusiasm. Four years later, when we met again in Cambridge, Massachusetts, he had become an ardent foe of the war who seemed to be disappointed by my detachment from it. Kissinger had consulted him for ideas on Vietnam during the transition period before Nixon took office, but now, after the publication of the documents, maligned him to Nixon as a "fanatic" and a "drug abuser." Attorney General John Mitchell suggested that Ellsberg might be part of a Communist "conspiracy," and there was even apprehension inside the White House that his action could inspire conservative officials to leak information about the plans that Nixon and Kissinger were formulating for rapprochements with the Soviet Union and China.

For all their alarm about national security, however, Nixon and his staff discerned benefits in the Pentagon Papers crisis. Just as he had used the Alger Hiss case to vault to the forefront of the anti-Communist crusade two decades before, so he could use the Ellsberg flap to discredit leftists, liberals, and other adversaries of the Vietnam war—and, by extension, Democrats and everybody else he deemed inimical. Egil "Bud" Krogh, an earnest young White House assistant, put it succinctly: "Anyone who opposes us, we'll destroy. As a matter of fact, anyone who doesn't support us, we'll destroy."

On Nixon's instructions to organize an investigation of Ellsberg, Krogh and a young lawyer, David Young, were appointed to manage a clandestine unit jokingly known as the "plumbers," because its theoretical task was to plug "leaks." Nixon's special counsel, Charles Colson, helped to broaden the group with clandestine experts like E. Howard Hunt, formerly of the CIA, and G. Gordon Liddy, a retired FBI agent. Soon their activities ranged from the smelly to the illicit. Colson composed a list of some two hundred Nixon "enemies," among them: Gregory Peck, Carol Channing, Joe Namath, President Derek Bok of Harvard, and several journalists, including me. After Nixon proposed a campaign to blame the Democrats for the Vietnam war, Hunt faked two State Department cables purporting to implicate John F. Kennedy in the murder of South Vietnamese President Ngo Dinh Diem. The forgeries were to be planted with William Lambert, a *Life* writer, but the magazine folded before he could verify their authenticity. Hunt and his team broke into the California home of Ellsberg's psychiatrist, Lewis Fielding—an act for which they were eventually convicted, along with Krogh, Colson, and John Ehrlichman, Nixon's assistant for domestic affairs. And, of course, the Democratic national committee headquarters in the Watergate building was on the agenda. Thus Nixon's chief of staff, H. R. Haldeman, was to write that "without the Vietnam war there would have been no Watergate."

The Watergate trauma lay ahead, but Nixon was profoundly depressed by the middle of 1971. He had failed to persuade the public, the press, the politicians, or the judiciary to share his indignation over the Ellsberg affair. Overcome by self-pity, a typical mood, he felt victimized by the antiwar demon and its sympathizers in the news media; they were poisoning American opinion. He knew that the venom was Vietnam, yet he had no antidote. He would occasionally toy with the wild notion of blasting North Vietnam to bits and then pulling out, horrifying Kissinger and even Haig with bloodcurdling descriptions of his fantasy holocaust. Then, regaining his composure, he would studiously ponder negotiating possibilities.

Kissinger had resumed his discussions with the North Vietnamese in Paris in late May 1971, and the intermittent talks dragged on inconclusively into the next year—the main obstacle being the eventual status of the Saigon regime. Once again, the Americans were strapped by the same dilemma that had limited them throughout the war: despite their immense power, they had little control over internal South Vietnamese politics. Thieu was the stumbling block, but they could not plausibly supplant him with a compromise figure acceptable to the Communists. For one thing, Nixon and Kissinger remembered the chaos that had convulsed South Vietnam following Diem's ouster, which the United States had encouraged. They also realized that, by submitting to the Communists, they would make themselves hostage to further enemy demands. And they feared that Thieu might, under extreme pressure, threaten to pull down the Saigon government structure and accuse them of betrayal. The specter of an ignominious finale in Vietnam haunted Kissinger. A humiliating collapse would shatter America's global credibility, he believed, and, as he put it, "leave deep scars on our society, fueling impulses for recrimination." Constantly on his mind was the tragedy of the Weimar Republic, a member of his staff later recalled, the democracy that had eventually been ripped asunder by the tensions that divided Germany after its defeat in World War I.

The Communists were to claim later that Nixon and Kissinger missed a chance for a settlement in 1971, when Vice-President Nguyen Cao Ky and General Duong Van Minh were each considering the possibility of challenging Thieu for the presidency of South Vietnam in an election scheduled for October 3. Le Duc Tho suggested to Kissinger that the United States "stop supporting" Thieu, who would presumably be defeated in a three-way contest by a rival willing to work out a political accommodation with the Vietcong. Thus, the Communist thesis went, Thieu would have been deposed legally, thereby satisfying North Vietnam's demand that he be removed as the prerequisite to an overall agreement. As it turned out, however, Thieu found a pretext to disqualify Ky's candidacy. Minh, knowing he would lose, dropped out of the race, and Thieu won another term with no opposition. So, the Communists alleged afterward, Nixon and Kissinger had squandered an opportunity for peace.

The charge contained an element of truth. The CIA, acting on orders from Washington, furnished Thieu with funds to finance his campaign. The U.S. mission in Saigon did little to dissuade Thieu from eliminating Ky, though Ambassador Ellsworth Bunker reportedly tried to bribe Minh to run in order to make the exercise look "democratic." Nevertheless, it is doubtful that a real challenge to Thieu would have made a difference. In the first place, there was no guarantee that either Ky or Minh could have beaten Thieu, whose loyal army and police units were capable of mobilizing votes in his favor. Nor was it certain that either Ky or Minh would have been congenial toward the Vietcong; both realized that continuing American aid depended on their pursuit of a tough anti-Communist course. At that stage, too, Thieu appeared to Nixon and Kissinger to represent stability; the last thing they wanted were fresh convulsions in Saigon.

By early 1972, Nixon could justly claim that he was fulfilling his pledge to reduce the U.S. combat role in Vietnam. He had withdrawn more than four hundred thousand GIs since he entered office, and American battle deaths were down to fewer than ten a week. To show the American public his earnest desire for peace, he also revealed for the first time that Kissinger had been talking secretly with the North Vietnamese. But his effort to pacify domestic opinion had drawbacks. Like a bridge player losing his trump cards, Kissinger was being deprived of his "negotiating assets" as the American force in Vietnam shrank. Moreover, the troop withdrawals made it increasingly probable that U.S. aid to the Saigon regime would sooner or later be drastically cut; congressmen could no longer be shamed into voting appropriations for Vietnam with the argument that "our boys in the field" had to be supported. For broader diplomatic purposes, Nixon and Kissinger were then planning dramatic new overtures to China and the Soviet Union. The paths to peace in Vietnam might run through Beijing and Moscow. They set out to explore those routes.

As the war escalated after 1965, the North Vietnamese had relied more and more on help from the Soviet Union and China. They needed Soviet surface-to-air missiles, radar, communications equipment, and other sophisticated military matériel to counter the American bombing, and they depended on Chinese rice to feed their population. Disputes between the Soviet Union and China complicated these aid programs. Mao Zedong, after the tumultuous Cultural Revolution of the late 1960s, had elevated himself to the stature of Marx and Lenin in the pantheon of Communist deities, and he refused to cooperate with Soviet "revisionists," even in supporting their Vietnamese comrades. Among other things, he denied the Russians the use of Chinese airfields as well as the right to fly supplies to Vietnam over China, telling the Kremlin leaders, "Frankly speaking, we do not trust you."

Much as they deplored the quarrel between their Communist patrons—and occasionally tried to patch it up—the North Vietnamese improvised ways to turn it to their advantage. They were in the forefront of a classic "national liberation" war against the United States—the kind of textbook struggle that propagandists in Moscow and Beijing extolled with passionate monotony. Whatever the differences between them, the Soviets and Chinese were both committed to underwriting the struggle, lest they appear to be "soft on imperialism" to factions within their own countries and to the various foreign revolutionary movements whose allegiance they were competing to win. By playing the Russians and Chinese off against one another, the North Vietnamese were therefore able to get each to furnish them with the support they required.

It was a tricky game, however. The time would come when the Communist giants developed priorities more important to them than Vietnam; they would not hesitate to put their own interests first. That time was fast approaching at the start of the 1970s, as each sought a rapprochement with the United States. Nixon and Kissinger were perceptive and nimble enough to grasp the opportunity to improve America's security, and a crucial factor was working in their favor: a Republican administration could accommodate to the Communist powers without the domestic risk of triggering right-wing denunciations.

A seismic shock had jolted the Chinese on August 20, 1968, when Soviet and Warsaw Pact forces invaded Czechoslovakia to crush Alexander Dubček's reformist government. The Soviet Communist party boss, Leonid Brezhnev, had issued a "doctrine" warning that the Soviet Union might intervene in any Communist country whose policies deviated from its standards. Brezhnev's statement had coincided with a massive buildup of Soviet forces along China's northern and western frontiers. Early in March 1969, Soviet and Chinese patrols clashed on an uninhabited island in the frozen Ussuri River, a desolate spot marking the boundary between Manchuria and the Soviet Union's easternmost Maritime Provinces. Larger engagements broke out in other border regions during the next few months. Mao Zedong, to whom any relationship with the Americans had once represented a breach of the Communist faith, now contemplated a reconciliation with the United States in order to offset the Soviet menace.

A long and complicated mating dance followed. Finally, on February 21, 1972, Nixon landed in Beijing, announcing with his usual rhetorical overkill that his spectacular breakthrough to China was "the week that changed the world." Nixon and Kissinger finished their ceremonial chat with Mao, then plunged into substantive discussions with Zhou Enlai, the suave and skillful Chinese prime minister. Vietnam was high on the agenda. The Chinese, who had previously hoped that a long war there would bleed both their American enemies and their feisty Vietnamese neighbors, thereby opening Southeast Asia to their influence, now feared that the deterioration of American power would deprive them of a counterweight to the Soviet Union. They wanted a rapid end to the conflict. Still, they had to avoid making gestures that might drive Vietnamese Communists into the arms of the Soviets, who sought a chance to flank China on the south. Moreover, Zhou had to avoid arousing his radical Chinese rivals, who were ready to seize on the Vietnam issue as a pretext to attack him and other pragmatists in Beijing. As Kissinger recalled, Zhou ambiguously urged an early peace, but without endorsing North Vietnam's political demands.

To the North Vietnamese, Nixon's visit to Beijing evoked nightmare memories of China's "sellout" at the 1954 Geneva Conference—a betrayal that had condemned them to the battlefield for the next decade. It seemed inadmissible for their Chinese allies to be entertaining their enemy at all. Worse yet, the United States and China were negotiating their fate "behind our back," as they complained afterward. According to the North Vietnamese account, the Chinese had advised them four months earlier to defer the question of Thieu's status, and concede instead to a quick agreement aimed at getting the last American troops out of Vietnam. The North Vietnamese had interpreted the suggestion to mean that they ought to abandon their struggle to reunify Vietnam. Indeed, Mao had pointed to the similarity of their objective and his dream of conquering Taiwan: just as China could not take over the island, so the North Vietnamese were not strong enough to gain control of the south. "Where the broom cannot reach," he had said, "the dust is not swept away." Chinese duplicity, as the North Vietnamese saw it, was further confirmed by the Shanghai Communiqué that climaxed the Nixon trip. Nixon promised to reduce the U.S. military presence on Taiwan "as the tension in the area diminishes"—a clear indication, to Hanoi's analysts, that the fix was in: an American withdrawal from the island in exchange for peace in Vietnam. The North Vietnamese propaganda chief, Hoang Tung, soon admitted that "our fighting has become very difficult" as a result of the Sino-American deal.

Their efforts to promote restraint in Vietnam notwithstanding, the Chinese had actually increased their aid to North Vietnam in late 1971, primarily to keep pace with the Soviet Union, which was furnishing the Hanoi regime with heavy equipment, including tanks and other armored vehicles. The buildup presaged a new Communist offensive, and information reaching the U.S. command in Saigon indicated that it would be big. As early as November 1971, truck convoys were sighted on the Ho Chi Minh Trail, now a road network, presumably transporting matériel to three North Vietnamese divisions deployed along the border between Cambodia and South Vietnam. Enemy units were also massing above the demilitarized zone separating North and South Vietnam, and Communist statements signaled a major onslaught. General Vo Nguyen Giap published an article in December calling for dynamic attacks, and other Communist declarations echoed that theme.

Nixon, reluctant to jeopardize his trip to China, had exerted no pressure on the Chinese to curb the North Vietnamese. But he sent a tough message to Brezhnev, whom he was planning to meet in Moscow in the spring of 1972, warning that their encounter might be canceled if the Russians allowed the North Vietnamese to embark on ventures "designed to humiliate us." Brezhnev's reply was vague and uncooperative, again revealing indirectly that he had limited leverage over his comrades in Hanoi.

Just as they had misread the Tet offensive of 1968 as a "go-for-broke" operation, many Americans were to see the forthcoming Communist push in Vietnam as another enemy attempt to gain a swift decision. But such a strategy was alien to the Communists. They viewed each engagement as a step in a series of encounters, winning some and losing some, until eventually the tide would turn in their favor. Giap, displaying his erudition as a historian, underlined this long-range process in an interview at the time: "The battle that will decide the future of our people began more than twenty-five years ago. A battle, no matter how important it may be, whether Issus or Hastings, Philippi or Belle-Alliance, can only represent the high point of a developing situation."

Thus the Communists had several motives in mind as they prepared their action in early 1972. They hoped to influence the American presidential election campaign, then starting, and they also figured on assuring themselves of continued Soviet and Chinese support by demonstrating their fighting ability. But above all, the new drive was inextricably linked to a central issue: how the balance of forces in South Vietnam related to the negotiations with the Americans. And, once again, it reflected the adherence of the Communists to the belief that military success dictates diplomatic success. If they inflicted a crushing defeat on the Saigon government army, they could prove the failure of Vietnamization and convince the United States that an agreement on their terms was the only way out. Battlefield victories were the key factor "for the attainment of a political settlement," declared a Vietcong magazine called *Tien Phong*, or *Vanguard*, adding: "When the head passes through, the tail will follow easily."

On March 30, 1972, the Communists struck in three successive waves, committing a total of one hundred and twenty thousand North Vietnamese regulars and thousands of Vietcong guerrillas to a synchronized operation: the first wave rolled over South Vietnam's northern provinces while the second swept across the central highlands to the coast and the third hit the area above Saigon. The Mekong delta, though spared the brunt of the offensive, was to suffer most severely from its consequences. Despite the advance intelligence they had received, American and South Vietnamese commanders were stunned by the magnitude and duration of the actions, which also shocked top administration officials in Washington. Five weeks before, Secretary of Defense Laird had told members of Congress that nationwide North Vietnamese and Vietcong assaults were "not a serious possibility." General Westmoreland, then army chief of staff, foresaw a Communist drive fading "in a matter of days" because "the staying power of the enemy is not great." The battles, of unprecedented fury in some places, were to last into June, causing frightful military and civilian casualties on both sides.

The Communists staged their most dynamic attacks against the northern provinces. Equipped with Soviet artillery, rockets, and tanks, some fifteen thousand North Vietnamese troops converged on the area in a three-pronged pincer—eastward from Laos, up from Cambodia through the Ashau valley, and directly down from North Vietnam across the demilitarized zone. The senior Saigon government officer in the region, General Hoang Xuan Lam, an incompetent largely responsible for the South Vietnamese debacle in Laos the year before, had been given the command by Thieu as a reward for loyalty. Thieu waffled before replacing him with a more effective figure, General Ngo Quang Truong. But Truong could not rally one of his two divisions, a raw unit that panicked in the face of the onslaught. The Communists captured the province capital of Quangtri on May 1 and held it until September, thereby dominating the whole northern sector. They refrained from pushing on to Hué, partly because they could not supply their forces and also because their drive had an essentially political purpose.

The coastal route south from Quangtri became known as the "highway of terror" as it was pounded by North Vietnamese artillery and American aircraft and warships, which killed and maimed thousands of fleeing civilians and government soldiers. A South Vietnamese army sergeant, Nguyen Tho Hang, recalled being trapped with his unit in a bunker in Quangtri under Communist shelling so relentless that "we couldn't even raise our heads." Ordered to evacuate the city, he packed into a jeep with five or six comrades, and drove toward Hué.

First, we had trouble getting out of town because the streets were blocked by rubble from destroyed buildings. Then the road was crowded with so many people, civilians and soldiers, that we could only crawl along. It was like everybody in the area was on that road, and Communist shells were exploding everywhere. A shell fell about five yards in front of our jeep, damaging a tire and wounding a comrade in the leg. We abandoned the jeep and ran. The comrade couldn't run. We left him behind, and he was later killed. Soon we saw Communist tanks. I ran toward the sea, then doubled back, and finally got to a safe place. I had run all day, without stopping, and my feet were covered with blisters.

The Communists showed relative restraint in the central highlands, where they besieged the town of Kontum, even though a South Vietnamese division fled rather than fight. In coastal Binh Dinh province, the North Vietnamese seized three district capitals after local self-defense units failed to receive support from the region commander, whose performance was described by an American adviser in the area as "disgraceful." General Nguyen Van Toan, another of Thieu's cronies, had spent most of the war reaping fat profits from the cinnamon trade in the sector. Nearly forty thousand South Korean troops deployed in Binh Dinh as part of the allied force displayed complacency rather than their usual brutal zeal, having been ordered to avoid combat because the war was winding down.

Near the Cambodian border north of Saigon, by contrast, a bitter battle raged for Anloc, the capital of Binh Long province. A force of three thousand North Vietnamese, spearheaded by forty tanks, stormed Anloc on April 13 and almost seized the town. Repulsed by government troops, who sustained heavy casualties, the Communists began a siege. Their artillery shelled the town around the clock. Thieu proclaimed Anloc to be a symbol of South Vietnam's resistance. He diverted a division from the Mekong delta to the battle and even pitched his own palace guard into the fight. But in the end Anloc owed its survival to

American help. American helicopters airlifted supplies to the town's defenders and carried out the wounded while B-52s bombed enemy positions in the vicinity.

The action in the Mekong delta was light compared to massive battles elsewhere. But in this densely populated area of fertile rice fields, the real prize to be won in the war, the Communists made significant progress during the offensive. They had counted on the inexorable arithmetic of the war in order to extend their hold over the region.

By now, only six thousand of the seventy thousand Americans remaining in Vietnam were combat troops, and their activities were restricted. The Saigon regime had more than a million men under arms, about half of them regulars and the rest in various local units—a force superior in firepower that outnumbered the enemy by a ratio of about five to one. Even so, Thieu's army was stretched thin, which gave the Communists the edge they hoped to exploit in the Mekong delta. For as Thieu rushed his big battalions away from the area to check the North Vietnamese offensive in other parts of the country, Vietcong guerrillas rapidly filled the vacuum left by their redeployment. Within two months, guerrillas overran or occupied more than a hundred abandoned government posts in the region, and pacification programs crumbled in several key provinces, such as Chuong Thien and Dinh Tuong. If a truce was to freeze the two sides in place pending a final political settlement, the Communists wanted to control as much of the rich and populous Mekong delta as possible.

Figuring that domestic American pressures would prevent Nixon from reintroducing American forces in Vietnam, they were also out to cripple the Vietnamization effort. Pham Van Dong publicly stated that it was necessary to prove the failure of Vietnamization to prove to Nixon that "he has everything to lose except the honorable exit we are determined to enable him to make." Melvin Laird, who had a vested interest in seeing Vietnamization work, acclaimed the South Vietnamese military performance as "astonishingly successful." Nixon expressed the same optimism in public, but he was privately glum. With the U.S. forces virtually out of action in Vietnam, America's position and prestige hinged on the Saigon regime—"the weak link in our whole chain," as he noted in his diary. "The real problem," he wrote, "is that the enemy is willing to sacrifice in order to win, while the South Vietnamese simply aren't willing to pay that much of a price in order to avoid losing."

Nixon's observation was not original. It merely restated the dilemma that had confounded the United States since the very beginning of its intervention in Vietnam. The Communists were prepared to accept appalling casualties for the sake of minimal gains. Their losses in this 1972 drive probably ran to fifty thousand dead and at least as many wounded. They had not crushed the South Vietnamese army, shattered the Saigon government, or permanently acquired territory. But, at an astronomical cost in human life, they had laid the groundwork for an eventual political deal and rehearsed a future offensive. And, by puncturing the illusion of Vietnamization, they clouded the period ahead with grave uncertainties.

Though the South Vietnamese troops often displayed uncommon courage, they would have collapsed without American air support and advisers to stiffen their ranks. In the south alone, B-52 bombers flew nearly five thousand sorties during the offensive, pulverizing the enemy around Anloc and in the vicinity of Quangtri. The American advisers frequently took command of government units that would have been otherwise routed. This critical reliance on the United States heightened Thieu's anxiety that an American departure would leave him naked, especially if Nixon and Kissinger allowed the North Vietnamese to remain in the south. It also stiffened Nixon's conviction that to quit Vietnam unconditionally would doom the Saigon regime—and his own reputation.

Nixon noted in his diary that "all the air power in the world," including strikes against Hanoi and Haiphong, would not save South Vietnam "if the South Vietnamese aren't able to hold on the ground." But a day after the Communist offensive began, he ordered B-52s and other U.S. aircraft to hit targets in North Vietnam. It was not the first time he had authorized raids against the north. Since 1970, American bombers had been flying so-called "protective reaction" missions under the pretext of accompanying reconnaissance airplanes. Now, however, the strikes were to be massive. He soon lapsed into his Patton mood: "The damned war would be over now," he told aides, had he followed his instincts and resumed the sustained bombing of North Vietnam when he invaded Cambodia two years before. He also delighted the joint chiefs of staff by directing them to dust off their old blueprints for blasting the Hanoi area and mining Haiphong harbor, both of which had been placed off limits by Lyndon Johnson. Nixon now asserted that only "decisive action" against the north would stop the Communists in the south. In reality, his military initiative had a dual psychological purpose: he wanted to reassure Thieu that, whatever the shape of a future agreement, America would continue to protect him; and he wanted to show the Communists that he was ready to bomb North Vietnam again if they violated an eventual settlement. He was putting the "madman theory" into practice.

The crucial question at the moment was the potential Soviet reaction. Nixon was due to meet Brezhnev in Moscow later in the spring to discuss such cosmic issues as the control of nuclear weapons. Kissinger had scheduled a secret trip to Moscow to arrange the encounter, but he and Nixon differed sharply over how to proceed. Nixon, obsessed by Vietnam, was prepared to cancel the meeting unless Brezhnev persuaded the North Vietnamese to accede to an acceptable peace. "Whatever else happens, we cannot lose this war," Nixon insisted. "The summit isn't worth a damn if the price for it is losing in Vietnam." He told Kissinger to warn Brezhnev that Vietnam alone would determine America's relations with the Soviet Union; if Brezhnev proved to be recalcitrant, he added, Kissinger "should just pack up and come home." Kissinger, while endorsing a strong approach to North Vietnam, favored more flexibility toward the Russians. He feared that a cancellation of the talks between Nixon and Brezhnev would jeopardize the international power balance. Besides, he doubted the degree of Soviet influence in Hanoi. Unlike Nixon, he had ceased to believe in the concept of "linkage."

Kissinger's mission to Moscow, seen in retrospect, should destroy the notion that governments function smoothly and rationally. He landed there on April 20 without informing the U.S. ambassador, Jacob Beam, who represented the hated State Department. He then met with Brezhnev while his assistant, Alexander Haig, in the White House, relayed feverish admonitions to hang tough from Nixon, who was ensconced with his friend Bebe Rebozo at Camp David, the presidential retreat in Maryland. Disobeying instructions, Kissinger strayed from the subject of Vietnam and discussed arms control with Brezhnev, who, he concluded, was eager for a summit meeting "at almost any cost." As for Vietnam, he repeated past American offers, but added that the North Vietnamese troops that had invaded the south for the present offensive must be withdrawn.

This new proposal subsequently inspired much nuanced hairsplitting. Many historians regard Kissinger's "demand" to have been a major American concession in disguise. They submit that, by requiring North Vietnam to pull back only the troops sent south for the 1972 offensive, he was actually permitting the northerners already in South Vietnam to remain there—thus finally dropping the futile "mutual withdrawal" formula. Dismissing that analysis as "pure nonsense," Kissinger claims in his memoirs that the "standstill cease-fire" scheme had superseded the "mutual withdrawal" idea long before, and that his suggestion to Brezhnev, designed to be relayed on to Hanoi, was merely confected to keep the Russians involved in the Vietnam negotiations. A key to the bargaining process, however, was how the Vietnamese Communists interpreted Kissinger's proposal. They rebuffed it at the time, understandably refusing to disengage six or seven crack divisions in the middle of a massive drive. However, as one of their senior officials told me after the war, they again sensed that the Americans would ultimately scrap the mutual withdrawal condition. But, the official recalled, they would not be satisfied that Kissinger had discarded it explicitly.

Kissinger, back from Moscow, was confident that Nixon's forthcoming summit meeting with Brezhnev would yield a landmark strategic arms control treaty. But Nixon was transfixed by Vietnam to the exclusion of everything else. He decided to unleash B-52s against the area around Hanoi and Haiphong over the weekend starting May 5, whatever the outcome of talks between Kissinger and Le Duc Tho, planned to take place in Paris three days earlier. Consistent with his view since the Korean war, Nixon felt that "peace with honor" could be achieved only by bombing. He also suspected that the Communists were stalling in hopes of making a deal with the Democratic "supporters of Hanoi" in Congress after the November election. Privately reproaching Kissinger as being "obsessed" with the need for a negotiated settlement, he dispatched him to Paris with an ultimatum for the North Vietnamese: "Settle or else!"

The session with Le Duc Tho, held outside Paris the day after the Communists captured the city of Quangtri, produced only strident rhetoric. Kissinger was fretful. He shared Nixon's resolve to be tough, but he worried that Brezhnev might withdraw his invitation to Moscow, and he dreaded a rupture with China as well. He was trying to rebuild his good relations with Ivy League colleagues, and he also repeated to close aides his fear of becoming "this administration's Walt Rostow," who was banished to an unacceptable place like the University of Texas.

By the morning of May 8, Nixon had decided to mine Haiphong harbor and intensify the bombing of North Vietnam elsewhere. He planned to announce this that evening, and his aides, canvassed by Kissinger beforehand for the record, reacted predictably. Laird dissented, arguing that South Vietnam was the main arena. CIA director Richard Helms was also opposed; the agency's analysts doubted, as they always had, that air strikes would deter the North Vietnamese. Agnew was enthusiastic, and Lyndon Johnson's old Democratic party pal, John

Connally, now Nixon's secretary of the treasury, asserted that the president had to "show his guts and leadership on this one." Nixon, surprisingly moderate in his televised speech, offered the Communists somewhat more supple proposals. He conspicuously omitted any mention of the mutual withdrawal formula, but said that U.S. forces remaining in Vietnam would pull out within four months of a cease-fire and the release of American prisoners of war. An internal political settlement could be negotiated "between the Vietnamese themselves."

As the air strikes and harbor mining began, Nixon and especially Kissinger nervously awaited the thunder from the Kremlin. All they heard was a routine statement of reproval and a mild protest against the bombing of a Soviet freighter in Haiphong harbor. The Soviet foreign trade minister, Nikolai Patolichev, then in Washington, instead posed for photographs with Nixon at the White House. As a *Washington Post* diplomatic correspondent at the time, I received a signal from a Soviet embassy official, who suggested an urgent meeting in a local cafeteria. "We've done a lot for those Vietnamese," he said, "but we're not going to let them spoil our relations with the United States." The Moscow summit was on.

Nixon emerged from his biggest foreign policy crisis to date with public approbation. Though twenty-two thousand letters and telegrams that poured into the White House favoring his actions against North Vietnam were not completely voluntary, having been organized by the Republican national committee, the opinion polls nevertheless showed his approval rating up to nearly 60 percent. But he was politician enough to know that Americans always back the president in a pinch, and that his support would slip, particularly on Capitol Hill. Among the other legislation making headway, the Senate passed an amendment on July 24 prescribing a total U.S. troop withdrawal from Vietnam contingent only on the release of the American prisoners of war. So, as Kissinger sourly observed, the Communists merely had to wait until "Congress voted us out of the war."

The North Vietnamese also faced problems. For one thing, they were bothered by Nixon's trip to Moscow just as they had been by his journey to Beijing. Hanoi's official newspaper, *Nhan Dan,* plaintively warned the Communist giants that concern for their "immediate and narrow interests" was a betrayal of their "lofty internationalist duties" and would damage the "world revolutionary movement." Nor did the U.S. political scene offer the North Vietnamese much cause for comfort. An antiwar figure, Senator George McGovern, had won the Democratic nomination for president, and his appeals for peace had propaganda value. But the Communists soon realized that, with the Democrats split over his candidacy, McGovern's chances of winning were slim. They would have to deal with a re-elected Nixon—now, after successfully brandishing force, more certain than ever that military might was the answer.

As they contemplated their next step, however, the Vietnamese Communists were fundamentally riveted on the situation in Vietnam itself. They had not crushed the United States and its South Vietnamese allies in a showdown battle, as they had beaten the French force at Dienbienphu; thus they were in no position to dictate the peace. On the other hand, their spring offensive had netted them gains in the Mekong delta and other regions. They could have phased back to guerrilla tactics and pressed for a coalition government in Saigon, in which case they would have to contend with a more belligerent Nixon, who was not about to dump Thieu. Or they could concede to a temporary compromise by discarding their insistence on Thieu's removal, in which case the Americans would go home, leaving them the opportunity to resume their struggle at a later stage. They decided to compromise. But they had the same options years before, so why now? Because now they expected explicit U.S. recognition of their right to maintain North Vietnamese troops in the south—the key to their future bid for power.

Despite their cries of outrage against Nixon, the North Vietnamese had promptly resumed their talks with Kissinger. On August 1, Le Duc Tho returned to Paris with his earlier demands diluted. To Kissinger, he appeared for the first time to be moderating his previous requirement that the political and military issues be resolved in one package. Moreover, he seemed to hint that Thieu's abdication was no longer a prerequisite for an accommodation. A speech by Pham Van Dong not long afterward made no mention of Thieu, and intelligence reports further indicated that Communist cadres in the south were being told to prepare for a settlement. Among other things, the cadres were directed to extend their reach over as much territory and as many people as possible in anticipation of a truce. Under a "leopard spot" arrangement, the Saigon regime and the Vietcong would hold the areas they controlled at the time of the cease-fire, pending a final settlement.

The Communists, having set the American presidential election as their deadline, showed increasing flexibility in September. Then, on October 8, 1972, came the climax.

The secret rendezvous for the meetings in France had been shifted to a pleasant house near Paris, this one at Gif-sur-Yvette, the former home of the painter Fernand Léger, who had willed it to the French Communist party on his death in 1955. Le Duc Tho presumed that the Americans "were in a rush" to reach an agreement before the presidential election. He thereupon opened with "a very realistic and very simple proposal": the United States and North Vietnam would between them arrange a cease-fire, American troop withdrawal, prisoner exchanges, and other military matters; political problems would be left to the opposing Vietnamese sides, which would form an interim body, later entitled a "council of national reconciliation," composed of Saigon government, Communist, and ambiguous "neutral" representatives—its task, to supervise eventual elections and, in theory, achieve permanent peace. In the interval, the Saigon regime and the Vietcong would continue as distinct entities, their respective armies remaining in the areas each controlled, the pattern as crazy as the spots on a leopard.

The proposal was "very simple" in one respect: it would hasten the American departure from Vietnam. But as a practical arrangement, at least for the Saigon regime's security, it was flimsy. Nothing in it guaranteed that the council of reconciliation would actually be created, much less lead to a durable peace. On the contrary, the two Vietnamese forces would probably go on fighting it out, the Communists from a superior military posture. Kissinger explicitly acquiesced in the presence of North Vietnamese troops in the south, extracting only a vague pledge that they would not be resupplied. But he had no choice. A North Vietnamese withdrawal had been "unobtainable through ten years of war," as he later explained. "We could not make it a condition for a final settlement. We had long passed that threshold."

The breakthrough, though incomplete, elated Kissinger. But he had more trouble with his own staff than with Le Duc Tho. His specialist on Vietnam, John Negroponte, argued that the Communists' offer was badly flawed; by leaving the enemy forces intact, it left the situation "basically unresolved." He and other aides scrutinized the text word by word, even looking for subtle differences between the English and Vietnamese versions. Kissinger exploded. They were "nit-picking," he shouted. "You don't understand. I want to meet their terms. I want to reach an agreement. I want to end this war before the election. It can be done, and it will be done." Turning his wrath on Negroponte, he added: "What do you want us to do? Stay there forever?"

Kissinger, aware that real estate meant strength, urgently cabled Thieu to "seize as much territory as possible," especially in the populated Saigon region. Orders meanwhile went out from the Pentagon for crash deliveries of military equipment to the Saigon government, an operation dubbed Enhance Plus—its purpose to furnish Thieu with hardware that, under the agreement, could be replaced. Matériel worth some $2 billion was flown to South Vietnam from such American aid recipients as Taiwan, South Korea, and the Philippines, which were to receive more modern weapons in exchange. The program, completed in six weeks, gave the Saigon regime the fourth largest air force in the world. To circumvent a clause in the draft accord that required the dismantling of U.S. bases in South Vietnam, the American installations were swiftly and secretly transferred to South Vietnamese ownership. Even so, Thieu began to panic.

Then forty-eight, Thieu was the youngest of five children of a small landowner in coastal Phamrang province, a barren area that spawns people as rugged as its rocky soil. After attending a French missionary school in Hué, he had served briefly as a village chief under the Vietminh but saw brighter prospects in the French colonial army, in which he earned a commission in 1949. He was an able officer. Ambition spurred him to marry into a prominent Vietnamese Catholic family; he converted to Catholicism himself, like the *collaborateurs* of the nineteenth century. Following the French defeat, he attracted the attention of his American military advisers, who sent him to train in the United States. His subsequent career was almost exclusively political. He plotted and juggled incessantly, finally becoming president in 1967, after which he plotted and juggled incessantly. Stubborn and indecisive, suspicious, cunning, yet often naive, he bought the fidelity of subordinates by tolerating their corruption, governing through his own instincts and the counsel of an astrologer. His attitude toward the Americans was ambivalent. He was certain that they—and the stars—held the key to his fate. But he distrusted them just as profoundly as he did everyone else.

Nixon was now equally ambivalent toward Thieu. During the summer, as the Communists seemed to be edging toward a compromise, he sent Haig to Saigon to assure Thieu that "under no circumstances" would South Vietnam's security be traded away. But in early October, with Kissinger poised in Paris for a possible breakthrough, Nixon insisted that Thieu, implacably opposed to any deal whatsoever, be pressed to accept a settlement, remarking that "the tail can't wag the dog." Kissinger himself flew to Saigon after a session with Le Duc Tho to obtain Thieu's approval of the draft accord, and again Nixon's messages were mixed. He told Thieu in a letter that he saw "no reasonable alternative" to the agreement, adding that the Communists would face "the most serious consequences" if they violated it; but meanwhile he cautioned Kissinger to be gentle: "Thieu's acceptance must be wholehearted so that the charge cannot be made that we forced him into a settlement. . . . It cannot be a shotgun marriage."

On October 21, four days after ironing out a few details with Kissinger in Paris, the North Vietnamese officially approved the proposed accord, and Nixon promptly acknowledged their assent. Kissinger, who was scheduled to initial the document in Hanoi at the end of the month, went to Saigon to get Thieu's concurrence. Accompanied only by Ambassador Ellsworth Bunker, he met in the presidential palace with Thieu, who was attended by his flashy cousin Hoang Duc Nha. The talks, which began placidly, soon degenerated into melodrama.

Kissinger blundered from the start by handing Thieu an English-language copy of the agreement, thereby wounding his national pride. Thieu in turn antagonized Kissinger by rudely canceling one of their meetings, ostensibly to study the document. Then Kissinger scared Thieu by showing him an interview that Pham Van Dong had just given Arnaud de Borchgrave of *Newsweek*, in which the North Vietnamese prime minister, trying to exert pressure on Thieu, described him as having been "overtaken by events," and said that he envisioned the planned "council of reconciliation" to be a "coalition of transition." The word "coalition" enraged Thieu. He and Nha now accused the United States of colluding with the Soviet Union and China to subvert their regime. Weeping, they protested that the Americans were paving the way for the Communists to grab power in Saigon. They also objected to the presence of North Vietnamese troops in the south and contended that the demilitarized zone dividing the two parts of the country should be a secure border. In short, they wanted to unravel the whole agreement and have South Vietnam recognized as a sovereign state—thus nullifying the entire Communist struggle for reunification. That, however, was the supreme irony of the moment. Having fought a war to defend South Vietnam's independence, the United States was now denying its legitimacy.

Kissinger, himself inclined to rages, reported to Nixon that Thieu's terms "verge on insanity." Nixon shifted once again. He cabled Thieu, threatening to cut off American assistance to South Vietnam, and warned him that his intransigence "would have the most serious effects upon my ability to continue support for you." He also ordered Kissinger to "push Thieu as far as possible," even to the extent of threatening that the United States would sign a separate treaty with the North Vietnamese. The notion of having the CIA organize a coup to oust Thieu wafted through the White House. Chronically distrustful, Thieu sensed the danger, but he refused to budge. Kissinger went home. "In twenty-four hours," as one of his aides recalled, "the bottom fell out."

At this stage, Nixon backtracked yet again. To scuttle Thieu, he feared, would lead to a Communist takeover of Vietnam. So he decided to stop hectoring him, reckoning that Thieu would acquiesce once he realized that Congress, which reconvened in January, might cut off his aid. Perhaps, as Kissinger suspected, Nixon was being badgered by White House hard-liners like H. R. Haldeman and John Ehrlichman, who equated compromise with capitulation. He knew as well that Nixon was quite capable of a complete flip—scrapping the accord and blasting North Vietnam to bits. Kissinger's priority was to salvage the agreement.

Amid these complications, Nixon had proposed to North Vietnam that the signing of the accord be delayed because "the difficulties in Saigon have proved somewhat more complex than originally anticipated." But the difficulties in Saigon worsened. On October 24, Thieu publicly denounced the draft treaty and told his forces that the Communist apparatus in the south "must be wiped out quickly and mercilessly." His call for action gave the North Vietnamese the pretext to test America's professed desire to end the war. Two days later, they broadcast a summary of the proposed settlement and charged the United States with attempts to "sabotage" it. Kissinger, aiming both to reassure them of America's sincerity and to convey to Thieu the administration's dedication to a compromise, made his television debut that afternoon in a press conference attended by hundreds of reporters in the packed White House press room: "We believe that peace is at hand," he declared. "We believe that an agreement is within sight."

As Kissinger admitted afterward, his misguided statement inflated expectations in the United States. It also upset Nixon, who felt that it showed weakness toward the Communists and also would stiffen Thieu's intransigence. Virtually disavowing Kissinger, he publicly declared that the agreement contained "differences that must be resolved." Nixon then began to zigzag around Thieu again. "We are going to have to put him through the wringer," he noted. But on November 14, a week after his landslide re-election, he gave Thieu his "absolute assurance" that he would "take swift and severe retaliatory action" should the North Vietnamese violate the agreement. At the same time, he directed Kissinger to submit to Le Duc Tho the sixty-nine amendments to the draft agreement which had been proposed by Thieu. Kissinger, who regarded the changes as "preposterous," faced a dilemma. Nixon was hustling him to terminate the war before the inauguration on January 20, but confronting Le Duc Tho with Thieu's grievances might abort the embryonic accord. Kissinger's relations with Nixon grew taut. Haldeman and Ehrlichman were also sniping at him for seeking publicity. And genuine diplomatic problems were still unresolved, such as a schedule for the exchange of prisoners and the creation of a credible mechanism to monitor the cease-fire.

Kissinger and Le Duc Tho hardened their positions as their talks dragged on into December. Now the Communist hierarchy in Hanoi felt, as an official there recalled to me, that the Americans were maneuvering to rewrite the draft. On December 13, Le Duc Tho suspended the deadlocked sessions and returned to Hanoi for consultations. Kissinger, for his part, recommended two options to Nixon: either intensify the bombing of North Vietnam immediately to compel the Communists to talk "seriously," or wait until January to resume negotiations, displaying real toughness if the discussions failed then. According to Nixon's account, Kissinger's attitude toward the Communists was apoplectic: "They're just a bunch of shits. Tawdry, filthy shits."

Nixon, again in one of his Patton moods, needed no advice from Kissinger. On December 14, he sent an ultimatum to North Vietnam to begin talking "seriously" within seventy-two hours—or else. He simultaneously ordered Admiral Thomas Moorer, chairman of the joint chiefs of staff, to prepare massive air attacks against railroads, power plants, radio transmitters, and other installations around Hanoi as well as docks and shipyards in Haiphong. He was lifting the restrictions, as the joint chiefs had requested for years, and he told Moorer: "I don't want any more of this crap about the fact that we couldn't hit this target or that one. This is your chance to use military power to win this war, and if you don't, I'll hold you responsible." Kissinger meanwhile put out a sweet-and-sour statement. The settlement was "99 percent completed" but, he asserted, "we will not be blackmailed into an agreement. We will not be stampeded into an agreement, and, if I may say so, we will not be charmed into an agreement until its conditions are right." The Communists echoed a similar line. Apart from "a very small number" of technicalities, said Xuan Thuy in Paris, the draft still contained differences of "fundamental importance."

Rather than explore the differences further, Nixon gave the signal for a new operation, Linebacker Two. Starting on December 18, B-52 and other American aircraft flew nearly three thousand sorties for the next eleven days, excluding Christmas Day, mainly over the heavily populated corridor that stretched sixty miles between Hanoi and Haiphong.

They dropped some forty thousand tons of bombs in the most concentrated air offensive of the war against North Vietnam—and the episode still arouses controversy.

The public response in the United States was relatively muted; with almost all the American troops home, the war had ceased to be a national torment. Congress, adjourned for the holidays, seemed to be split along partisan lines, with the Democratic majorities in both chambers planning moves to end the American involvement in Vietnam after the recess. By contrast, news commentators reacted with outrage. A *New York Times* editorial excoriated Nixon's reversion to"Stone Age barbarism," and the *Washington Post* called his assaults "savage and senseless." The revulsion abroad was widespread. Pope Paul VI told an audience at the Vatican that the bombing of "blessed" Vietnam was causing him "daily grief."

The dispatches of a lone French correspondent on the spot, cited in many American newspaper, television, and radio accounts, referred repeatedly to the "carpet bombing" of downtown areas in Haiphong and Hanoi. But Malcolm Browne of *The New York Times* reported from Hanoi soon afterward that the damage had been "grossly overstated," and other foreign journalists corroborated his testimony. So did Tran Duy Hung, mayor of Hanoi. American antiwar activists visiting the city during the attacks urged the mayor to claim a death toll of ten thousand. He refused, saying that his government's credibility was at stake. The official North Vietnamese figure for civilian fatalities for the period was 1,318 in Hanoi and 305 in Haiphong—hardly the equivalent of the Americans' incendiary bombing of Tokyo in March 1945, for example, when nearly eighty-four thousand people were killed in a single night. The comparison is, of course, irrelevant, except that the Christmas bombings of Hanoi have been depicted as another Hiroshima.

One argument advanced to explain the low casualties is that the populations of Hanoi and Haiphong were by then largely evacuated to the countryside. But that thesis skirts the fact, as I observed in 1981, that most of the buildings in both cities were neither demolished nor reconstructed. In fact, the B-52s were programmed to spare civilians, and they pinpointed their targets with extraordinary precision. Nevertheless, some bombs did stray, with ghastly results. I interviewed survivors in the Kham Thien district of Hanoi, a neighborhood located near a railway yard, where more than two hundred died. A young woman, Nguyen Thi Duc, broke down in tears as she recalled the deaths of her mother, two brothers, sister, and brother-in-law when their house was struck. At the Bach Mai hospital, situated near an airfield, Dr. Nguyen Luan related how he had amputated the limbs of victims in order to extricate them from the rubble. Of the one hundred patients and staff in the hospital at the time, eighteen were killed.

The American military costs were not inconsequential. The North Vietnamese shot down twenty-six U.S. aircraft, among them fifteen B–52s, and ninety-three pilots and crew members were lost, thirty-one of them captured. By December 30, when the bombing stopped, the Americans had exhausted their targets and the Communists had run out of surface-to-air missiles, having launched more than twelve hundred during the period. Four days earlier, replying to an American message, the North Vietnamese signaled their willingness to talk again as soon as the bombing halted. Kissinger and Le Duc Tho resumed their meetings on January 8, 1973, resolving their differences the next day—Nixon's sixtieth birthday. Nixon had already sent an ultimatum to Thieu: "You must decide now whether you desire to continue our alliance or whether you want me to seek a settlement with the enemy which serves U.S. interests alone." Thieu caved in. He realized that he could not, as he put it, "allow myself the luxury" of resisting America.

"We have finally achieved peace with honor," intoned Nixon. But the peace agreement, formally signed in Paris on January 27, 1973, scarcely differed from the draft hammered out in October. Nixon's dynamic bombing campaign had been superfluous—at least as an instrument of diplomacy. His purpose, however, had not been diplomatic. He had wanted to reassure Thieu and to warn the Communists that he would not hesitate to bomb North Vietnam again should the armistice break down. The "madman theory" was no abstraction.

At that juncture, all the peace settlement accomplished was to stop the conflict pending a political solution, which might never be achieved. The Saigon regime gained time—a "decent interval"—in which to resist the Communist challenge. But the Communists were not going to evaporate. Unlike the Geneva agreement of 1954, which had required their army to regroup in the north, this accord authorized both their northern and southern forces to remain in whatever areas of the south they controlled. Thus the situation—a Communist commentator called it "half war and half peace"—was almost certain to erupt in renewed fighting. It took no particular prescience to anticipate that eventuality. Writing for *The New Republic* from Paris at the time, I noted that the present phase "may only be an interlude that precedes the beginning of what could become the third Indochina war." The key, I added, was "whether the struggle that lies ahead can be waged without American involvement."

For Nixon—and for much of the public in the United States—the war would not be finally finished until the American prisoners held in North Vietnam came home. Since 1961, nearly nine thousand U.S. airplanes and helicopters had been lost in action over Cambodia, Laos, and the two Vietnams. Some two thousand pilots and crew members had been killed, more than a thousand were missing, and the captives in Communist hands numbered close to six hundred. The first Americans to be freed under the cease-fire agreement emerged on February 12, 1973; they included Robinson Risner, an air force colonel, who had been incarcerated in Hanoi for seven and half years. Flown to Clark Field in the Philippines along with a hundred other airmen in the initial group released, Risner showed his spit and polish when he was summoned to the telephone to speak with the president: "This is Colonel Risner, sir, reporting for duty."

There was no glory, however, in the ordeal of Risner and other Americans kept in the "Hanoi Hilton" and other jails. Though the North Vietnamese had acceded to the Geneva Convention of 1949, which holds that prisoners of war are "victims of events" who merit "decent and humane treatment," they followed the Soviet lead in making an exception for "crimes against humanity"—their portrayal of the U.S. bombing of their country. They confined many of the Americans to solitary cells for long periods, submitting them to such brutalities as a rope torture that yanked their limbs out of joint. They abused the captives for declining to broadcast prepared antiwar statements—often excerpted from the American press—or for rejecting other requests for "cooperation." Admiral James Bond Stockdale, a navy pilot downed in 1965, noted that the hardiest survivors were not necessarily the strong political or religious types, but the "plucky little guys" who refused to be "reasonable" toward their Communist tormentors. Yet, as Stockdale observed, "The pain and the loneliness were shallow complaints compared to finding yourself stripped of all entitlement to reputation, love, or honor at home."

The American public, exposed to accounts of these agonies, was not consoled by the knowledge that the Vietnamese on both sides could be just as cruel to each other. South Vietnamese and Vietcong prisoners were frequently savaged by their respective captors. Thieu's jails bulged with critics of his regime, many of them innocuous, and the Communists were no more lenient toward their dissenters. But all that was irrelevant. As the last Americans left Hanoi in March, the prevailing sentiments in the United States were relief that the war had ended and revulsion toward the very subject of Vietnam. American news organizations closed their offices or drastically reduced their staffs in Saigon, exorcising Vietnam from newspaper headlines and television screens. Even so, Nixon still feared the residual antiwar protesters. Fulfilling a long-standing promise, he invited Thieu to the continental United States for the first time, but limited him to a small "family dinner" at his personal retreat in San Clemente, California. Vice-President Agnew, assigned to welcome Thieu in Washington, found that very few dignitaries were willing to attend the ceremonies.

Congress now began to disengage America totally from Southeast Asia. Nixon had hinted on March 15 that the United States might again intervene in Vietnam to prevent reported Communist violations of the truce, and his new secretary of defense, Elliot Richardson, said somewhat more explicitly that "we cannot rule out" that eventuality. But on June 4, the Senate acted to prevent such a move by approving a bill sponsored by Senators Clifford Case of New Jersey and Frank Church of Idaho to block funds for any U.S. military activities in Indochina, and the House of Representatives endorsed the legislation. Nixon and Kissinger frantically lobbied to get the ban extended until August 15 to enable American aircraft to continue bombing in Cambodia, which had not been included in the cease-fire agreement. By then, Nixon had been publicly accused by his special counsel, John Dean, of covering up various illegalities within his administration, and another aide, Alexander Butterfield, had disclosed the existence of tapes recording White House conversations which were to substantiate Dean's charges. Nixon's presidency was crumbling as the Watergate revelations came thick and fast, and the votes on Capitol Hill deprived the Saigon regime of recourse to direct American help in the event of impending disaster.

Kissinger and others have suggested that Watergate, by turning Congress against Nixon, spelled the end for Indochina. But the argument is simplistic. The Watergate scandal did indeed ruin Nixon, thereby propelling Congress into asserting its prerogatives in foreign policy, as frequently occurs when the executive branch is weakened. But given the public's antipathy toward Vietnam at the time, it is doubtful that the United States could have regenerated a commitment to rescue Thieu's government. The Vietnamese Communists, through political or military means or a mixture of both, were determined eventually to gain power in Saigon. And Thieu, inept and corrupt, was unable to stop them—especially without the Americans.

The CIA reported in April that the North Vietnamese presence in the south numbered roughly one hundred and fifty thousand men—essentially the same as the year before. Kissinger, by contrast, thought that illicit infiltration from the north was swelling the enemy ranks in the south. Whatever the facts, Kissinger met again with Le Duc Tho in Paris, and they issued a joint pledge to respect the truce. But neither Thieu nor the Communists intended to honor the armistice. Kissinger realized then that "only a miracle" could salvage the Saigon government. He was even gloomier about Cambodia, where the Lon Nol regime held little more than Phnompenh, the capital. Earlier he had dismissed Le Duc Tho's plea that North Vietnam lacked the influence to persuade the Cambodian Communists to stop fighting. As later events were to prove, Le Duc Tho was telling the truth.

Ambassador Graham Martin, who arrived in Saigon in April to head the diminished American mission, did not share Kissinger's pessimism. Anachronistically, he was still inspired by the crusade to save Southeast Asia. But he had been given the assignment because he was expendable—the ideal "fall guy" whose probable failure to maintain an American presence in Indochina would not cause any political damage. Astonishingly, neither Nixon nor Kissinger mentions him, even in passing, in their memoirs.

A North Carolinian, then sixty-one, Martin had begun his government service in the Roosevelt era as an aide to Averell Harriman, an important political figure in the New Deal, who later promoted his diplomatic career. Martin, who spent eight years in the U.S. embassy in Paris after World War II, was a fierce anti-Communist liberal. He was no stereotype, however. As ambassador in Bangkok during the 1960s, he squelched an attempt by the American military establishment to inflate its functions there by deploying U.S. troops to check a minor insurgency in Thailand. But Martin was miscast for Vietnam. His wife's son had died in the war, which left him with a heavy emotional burden. Physically frail following an automobile accident, he could not travel around the country. And his prickly style was ill-suited to coping with Thieu, who desperately needed to be nursed, reassured, restrained.

Thieu's regime was in relatively sturdy shape at the start of the truce. His army, equipped with last-minute deliveries of American weapons and still receiving U.S. aid, controlled roughly 75 percent of South Vietnam's territory and about 85 percent of its population. But Thieu was jittery. The armistice was merely a "phase" in the war, he repeatedly affirmed, and he conspicuously avoided the word "peace" in his pronouncements. Spurning American counsel to broaden his base of support so that he could prevail in any coming political contest with the Communists, he instead cracked down on dissidents. In any case, he could not reform his regime without disrupting the system of bribes and kickbacks that guaranteed him the loyalty of his officers. His biggest mistake, however, was to launch military operations aimed at seizing areas occupied by the North Vietnamese and Vietcong in the Mekong delta and along the Cambodian border. Though initially successful, these efforts soon taxed the regime's resources. Still, he was confident that Nixon would save him from real trouble. "You have my assurance," Nixon had written in January, "that we will respond with full force should the settlement be violated by North Vietnam."

The Communists, eager to win the sympathy of the weary southern population, had hailed the cease-fire in their propaganda as an opportunity for all Vietnamese to bury their differences in "peace and love." But they needed the truce as a respite to rebuild their strength; like Thieu, they anticipated renewed struggles. Their internal debates during that period have been described in a remarkable book by General Tran Van Tra, one of the top commanders in the south, an account that was banned almost immediately after its publication in Ho Chi Minh City in March 1982, when he himself disappeared from sight. The document, copies of which were smuggled out of Vietnam, matches other evidence that Tra, who was dedicated to the cause of Communism in the south, may have been purged for criticizing his northern comrades.

A sinewy soldier then in his mid-fifties, Tra was a native of Quang-ngai, a coastal province in central Vietnam. He had quit his job on the railroad in his early twenties to join the Vietminh resistance against the French, and had become a senior officer in the south. Sent to the north when Vietnam was partitioned in 1954, he trained in the Soviet Union and China and trekked down the Ho Chi Minh Trail nine years later to assume responsibility for the Vietcong organization in the Mekong delta, using the code name Anh Tu, his family's third son. He commanded the attack against Saigon during the Tet offensive of 1968, and he entered the city legally, following the cease-fire, to serve on an armistice commission.

Summoned to Hanoi in March 1973, he attended a high-level meeting at which the Communist leaders pondered the future. They concurred that their present problems in the south were serious. The South Vietnamese force, now more than a million men armed with American aircraft, artillery, and tanks, was retaking key sectors, while the Communists had not recovered from their massive spring offensive of 1972. "Our troops were exhausted and their units in disarray," wrote Tra. "We had not been able to make up our losses. We were short of manpower as well as food and ammunition, and coping with the enemy was very difficult." Vietcong cadres in some places were confused, numbers of them actually behaving passively toward the Saigon government in the belief that they had to observe the cease-fire.

At this rate, disaster loomed for the Communists. Their spies inside the Saigon regime informed them that Thieu had developed a plan for the next two years to keep grabbing territory until he felt secure enough to authorize an election—the results of which would, of course, confirm him as South Vietnam's sole authority. He would then scrap the tattered cease-fire agreement openly and proceed to mop up the Communist remnants just as Diem had liquidated the Vietminh survivors after he consolidated his power. The clock would be turned back to the dark days of the 1950s, when the southern Communist movement was nearly extinguished.

On the other hand, the party leaders in Hanoi figured, the Saigon government army was handicapped by the absence of the B-52s and the American military advisers. They also calculated that it would be years before the South Vietnamese troops were trained properly. Thus they concluded that "the path of revolution in the south is the path of revolutionary violence." But they emphasized prudence and flexibility; a premature push could end in catastrophe. As he contemplated the strategy, Tran Van Tra reflected on the ambitious Tet offensive of 1968, when "an illusion based on our subjective desires" had propelled the Communists into their costly campaign against South Vietnam's towns and cities. Had that drive been planned "scientifically," he wrote, "the future of the revolution would certainly have been far different."

The Communist commanders now instructed their forces to attack only where they were clearly superior to Thieu's troops, their ultimate objective to tilt the military balance in their favor. Meanwhile, they embarked on a huge logistical program designed to create a springboard for an eventual offensive of vast proportions. To move large trucks, tanks, and armored vehicles into position to strike a final blow at Saigon, their labor battalions began hacking through jungles and cutting across mountains to build an all-weather highway from Quangtri province on the central coast down into the Mekong delta—a project destined to stretch their total road network to more than twelve thousand miles. They also started construction of an oil pipeline, three thousand miles long, to reach from Quangtri to the town of Locninh, their main headquarters, seventy-five miles northwest of Saigon. And they laid out a modern radio grid, centered in Locninh, that enabled them to communicate directly with Hanoi and with their field units. General Van Tien Dung, later to lead the operation against Saigon, resorted to purple metaphors to describe the operation: "Strong ropes inching gradually, day by day, around the neck, arms, and legs of a demon, awaiting the order to jerk tight and bring the creature's life to an end."

That the Communists could undertake such a stupendous enterprise testified to the failure of American bombings to destroy the equipment and fuel that they had amassed in North Vietnam over the preceding years. For they were not getting new supplies: Pham Van Dong and Le Duan, the party secretary-general, were rebuffed in both Moscow and Beijing in October 1973 when they asked for additional Soviet and Chinese military aid. Zhou Enlai, the Chinese prime minister, told Pham Van Dong: "It would be best for Vietnam and the rest of Indochina to relax for, say, five or ten years."

North Vietnamese and Vietcong units lay low during the rainy summer of 1973, then cautiously went into action in the autumn. Instead of staging big assaults, they hit at the Saigon government's weak spots—small airfields, remote outposts, and storage facilities. By the late spring of 1974, Tran Van Tra estimated, they had recaptured all the territory in the Mekong delta lost to the South Vietnamese army following the truce. But they were counting on developments apart from military operations to help them.

The Saigon scene, chronically volatile, was again boiling up. Despite Thieu's rigorous police measures, assorted political and religious factions were denouncing him, and their agitation was symptomatic of deeper problems nagging the society. The millions of refugees who had poured into the cities for safety had survived and even prospered by catering to the Americans as secretaries, maids, prostitutes, cabdrivers, shoeshine boys, and in other such roles. But the jobs had gone with the American departure. Neither the United States nor the Saigon government had focused on laying down a durable industrial or commercial foundation for Vietnam's city-dwellers, the war having generated a false sense of affluence. The economic disintegration was also aggravated by soaring prices, partly a consequence of the Arab oil embargo triggered by the war in the Middle East late in 1973.

South Vietnam's crumbling economy eroded army morale, which had been surprisingly high until then. A survey conducted during the summer of 1974 by the U.S. mission in Saigon found that more than 90 percent of the soldiers were not receiving enough in wages and allowances to sustain their families. Inflation was only one cause, however. Corruption was now exceeding all bounds as commanders robbed payrolls and embezzled other funds. Quartermaster units often insisted on bribes in exchange for delivering rice and other supplies to troops, and even demanded cash to furnish the fighting men with ammunition, gasoline, and spare parts. Officers frequently raised the money by squeezing local villagers, whose support they alienated in the process, and many traded with the Communists privately. The American report cautioned that the "deterioration" had to be halted "if the South Vietnamese military is to be considered a viable force." Ambassador Martin dismissed the warning with a tired cliché: "a little corruption oils the machinery." There was nothing he could do, in any case. Thieu's wife and cronies and their wives, indifferent to the danger, were reaping fortunes in real estate and other deals, and they set the code of misconduct for the entire officialdom. Or as an old Vietnamese adage put it: "A house leaks from the roof."

The roof collapsed in the United States on August 9, 1974, when Nixon resigned rather than face impeachment proceedings. One of his last acts as president had been to sign into law a bill that imposed a ceiling of $1 billion on American military aid to South Vietnam for the next eleven months. A couple of days after his departure, the House of Representatives voted to trim the actual appropriation to $700 million. Nixon's successor, Gerald Ford, hastily assured Thieu in a personal letter that "our support will be adequate." Ambassador Martin and others were to assert that the cuts in U.S. assistance had prevented the South Vietnamese from resisting the Communists effectively, but a Pentagon study later noted that only about two fifths of the $700 million allocated actually reached Vietnam; the rest was committed to equipment that awaited shipment or had not yet been spent.

Back in the south during the summer of 1974, General Tran Van Tra sat snugly in his command post near Locninh, drafting strategy as torrential tropical rains lashed the surrounding rice fields and jungles. He calculated victory in 1976—on condition that the Communists moved dynamically during the "pivotal" dry season ahead. Like any good officer, he weighed the hazards and opportunities. Thieu's troops had to be prevented from forming solid lines of defense in coastal redoubts, which would require driving them swiftly into isolated pockets that could be eliminated one by one. Their airfields would also have to be hit hard, lest their tactical bombers get off the ground. Above all, the eventual push on Saigon, the prize, had to be carried out swiftly and meticulously "to avoid a fight for each street and house" that would, as

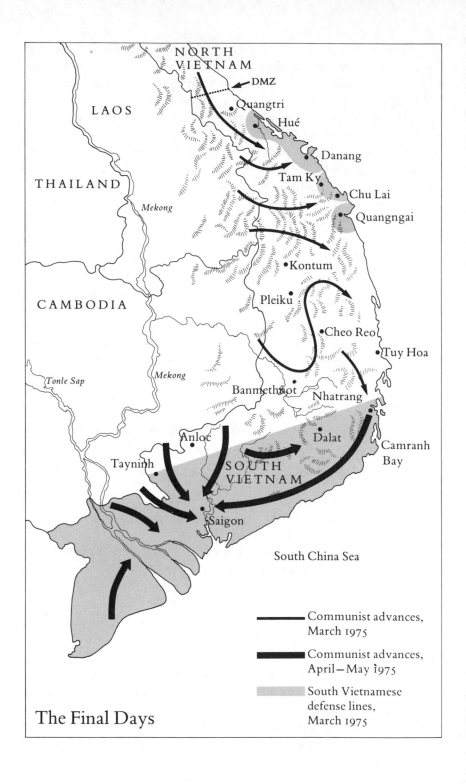

NORTH VIETNAM

LAOS

DMZ

•Quangtri

Hué

Danang

THAILAND

Tam Ky

Chu Lai

Quangngai

Mekong

CAMBODIA

•Kontum

•Pleiku

•Cheo Reo

•Tuy Hoa

Tonle Sap

Mekong

Banmethuot

Nhatrang

Anloc

Dalat

Camranh
Bay

Tayninh

SOUTH
VIETNAM

Saigon

South China Sea

Communist advances,
March 1975

Communist advances,
April–May 1975

South Vietnamese
defense lines,
March 1975

The Final Days

he wrote, "turn the city into rubble and create difficulties" for the Communist assault force. He drew up a plan to attack the capital from five directions. The north and northwest, with their open terrain, offered the best approach for tanks and battalions. The south and west—a maze of rivers, canals, and swamps—would be slow going.

Tra returned to Hanoi late in October 1974 to promote his plan, noting that the Ho Chi Minh Trail was a "far cry" from the primitive web of paths he had first descended more than a decade earlier. Now, traveling by car, he cruised along a modern highway dotted with truck rest and service areas, oil tanks, machine shops, and other installations, all protected by hilltop antiaircraft emplacements.

Once in Hanoi, his attempt to win approval for his project resembled the efforts of American generals in Washington to lobby for their programs. Tra proposed an immediate attack against Route 14, which traverses Phuoc Long, a mountainous province about sixty miles north of Saigon. Control of the road would signify virtual control of the province, he pointed out. The South Vietnamese army would therefore be denied a vital area between central Vietnam and the Mekong delta. The Communists would also gain a springboard for an eventual assault against Saigon from the north, and the city could be captured during the dry season of 1976—perhaps even before the anniversary of Ho Chi Minh's birthday in May. But Kissinger's nemesis, Le Duc Tho, now back at his old job of managing policy for the south, was reluctant to gamble. He preferred to continue with the logistical buildup into 1976 before initiating major military ventures; any offensive might be prolonged, and neither the Soviet Union nor China was likely to replenish North Vietnam's arsenal. General Van Tien Dung, the second-ranking North Vietnamese officer after Giap, concurred. Rather than risk resources at this time, he urged continued small-scale attacks until the moment was ripe for a bigger drive.

Undaunted, Tra carried his case to Le Duan, a consistent advocate of energetic action in South Vietnam, who worked out a compromise. Tra could launch his operation in Phuoc Long province, but only with limited forces. Beginning their attacks in the middle of December, the Communist troops seized the key junction on Route 14 the day after Christmas. On January 6, 1975, they hoisted their flag over Phuoc Binh, the province capital, the first regional seat of importance taken by the Communists since the capture three years before of Quangtri, which the Saigon regime had later regained. The garrison defending Phuoc Binh was no match for the eight thousand North Vietnamese regulars who pulverized the town with artillery and rocket fire before storming its perimeter. Fearful of flying within range of Communist antiaircraft guns, South Vietnamese pilots could not operate like the B-52s that had unloaded their bombs from an altitude of six miles.

Stunned by the loss of Phuoc Binh, members of the Saigon regime were doubly shocked by the almost inaudible American reaction to the defeat. Le Duan, encouraged, now urged a more aggressive schedule: bolder actions "to create conditions for a general uprising in 1976," with a bid for complete victory sooner "if opportunities present themselves." So the strategy was to be improvised, with each new step determined by the results of the last one. A crucial question was whether the United States might intervene, but the grizzled Communist leaders, the dream of a lifetime within their grasp, refused to be pessimistic. Pham Van Dong, then nearly seventy, had been struggling for a half century. Addressing his comrades at one meeting in Hanoi, he conceded that American bombers might return. But only U.S. combat troops would make a difference, and, he quipped: "They won't come back even if we offered them candy."

In November 1974, anxious to avert disaster in Indochina, Kissinger had resorted to diplomacy. He raised the issue of Vietnam during President Ford's meeting with Brezhnev at Vladivostok, then broached the subject of Cambodia with the Chinese during a quick trip to Beijing. In both instances, the likelihood of better relations with the United States was offered as an incentive, but at both sessions he drew a blank. The Communist superpowers, having decided that the Saigon regime was doomed, were now preoccupied with their coming rivalry for increased influence in Southeast Asia. The Chinese had accelerated their aid to the Cambodian Communists, who were advancing on Phnompenh, while the Soviets, in hope of retaining a foothold in the country, still recognized the Lon Nol regime. They had also renewed their assistance to the North Vietnamese. General Viktor Kulikov, chief of the Soviet armed forces, had in fact rushed to Hanoi in December with promises of fresh matériel, and his pledge had influenced their decision to forge ahead fast. Their next target was to be Banmethuot, capital of Darlac province, a squalid town situated on a plateau in the central highlands of South Vietnam.

They entrusted the operation to General Van Tien Dung, at fifty-eight the youngest of the politburo members and the only one with authentic proletarian antecedents. A peasant boy from the area near Hanoi, he had worked in a French textile factory before joining the Communist party in the 1930s. Giap adopted him as a protégé, and he rose rapidly in rank; as the Vietminh army's chief of staff, he orchestrated the immense logistical achievement that crushed the French at Dienbienphu. In contrast to Giap, a spinner of brilliant and often erratic theories, Dung was a solid if uninspired officer—an adversary befitting the American military bureaucrats who had directed the U.S. war effort. He later succeeded Giap as defense minister, and he had acquired new trappings of authority when I interviewed him in Hanoi in 1981. Dressed in glittering Soviet-style regalia, a swagger stick tucked under his arm, he arrived at his office in a black Russian limousine as aides snapped to attention. During our chat, however, he displayed much of the charm and wit that pervades *Our Great Spring Victory*, his account of the conquest of South Vietnam.

Dung, having moved four divisions into central Vietnam, set up his command post in a jungle clearing "whose dry leaves covered the ground like a yellow carpet." General Pham Van Phu, the inept government commander of the region, knew that the element of surprise gave the Communists an advantage even though their forces were equal in size. Aware of his edge, Dung uncorked his attacks on March 1 with a feint toward Phu's headquarters at Pleiku. Phu braced for the main assault there, but Dung instead cut the road to Banmethuot, thereby isolating its meager garrison of only a thousand defenders. Within a week, three North Vietnamese divisions were converging on Banmethuot. They struck before dawn on March 10, their tanks slamming into the town following an artillery barrage. The battle was over by five o'clock in the afternoon—many South Vietnamese troops fleeing with their families, who traditionally lived with the army.

At first Thieu decided to "lighten the top and keep the bottom" by abandoning the northern provinces of South Vietnam. He instructed Phu to evacuate Pleiku and Kontum, another highland town. Phu promptly evacuated himself, by air, leaving two hundred thousand leaderless men, women, and children to straggle down a treacherous mountain road to the coast as the Communists shelled them. And the situation was worse along the coast. Reversing his earlier decision, Thieu now insisted that Hué be held to the last man. But the Communists severed the highway south of the city, its only escape route. Remembering the Communist slaughter of civilians during the Tet offensive in 1968, the population of Hué panicked.

By late March, more than a million refugees were streaming toward Danang, which was itself being bottled up as Communist forces attacked farther south along the littoral at Chulai and Quangngai. On March 25, the day Hué fell, North Vietnamese rockets ripped into downtown Danang, Vietnam's second largest city. Within three days, thirty-five thousand Communists were poised in its suburbs, while terrified citizens jammed the airport, the docks, and the beaches, attempting to flee. Thousands waded into the sea, among them mothers clutching babies; many drowned or were trampled to death as they fought to reach barges and fishing boats; sometimes South Vietnamese soldiers shot civilians to make room for themselves. On March 29, Edward Daley, president of World Airways, flew a jumbo jet into Danang. Frenzied mobs crowded the runway, and nearly three hundred Vietnamese clambered aboard in ten minutes, virtually all of them men. Others, clinging to the rear stairway, fell to their deaths. The next day, Easter Sunday, the Communists marched into Danang.

Six days earlier, the Communist leaders in Hanoi had transmitted a secret message to General Dung at his command post near Banmethuot, informing him that their new timetable was to "liberate" the south before the rains began in May. Their principal concern was to get to Saigon as quickly as possible, before the South Vietnamese forces regrouped to defend it. They directed Dung to divert his troops from the coast, where they were approaching Nhatrang, and to aim them directly at the southern capital. Dung thereupon transferred his headquarters to Locninh to be closer to Saigon. There, in a bamboo shack on the outskirts of town, he was joined by Tran Van Tra and Pham Hung, the senior politburo member stationed in the south. On April 7, as Dung and his comrades were conducting a planning session, they heard the roar of a motorcycle outside. The rider was a tall figure in a blue shirt and khaki pants, a black leather bag slung over his shoulder. Le Duc Tho had arrived from Hanoi to monitor the final phase, entitled the Ho Chi Minh Campaign. Dung would take charge, with Hung as chief political commissar and Tra and Le Duc An, a northern officer, their deputies. The offensive against Saigon was to be launched no later than the last week of April. "From then on," Tra recalled, "we were racing the clock."

John Gunther Dean, U.S. ambassador to Cambodia, was by then arranging to evacuate the American embassy staff and selected Cambodians by helicopter to an aircraft carrier in the Gulf of Thailand. The logistics of evacuation in Vietnam were staggering by comparison. The potential victims of a Communist takeover numbered, in addition to six thousand Americans, more than a hundred thousand Vietnamese now or formerly employed by various American agencies—who, with their kin, swelled the total to nearly a million. An exodus of that magnitude from the north of the country to the south had been carried out with relative smoothness over a three-month period in 1954, but the present circumstances were drastically different. The imminent danger was that frenzied government troops might massacre the Americans and their Vietnamese cohorts to prevent them from departing.

Ambassador Martin was to explain later that it was a desire to avoid panic that restrained him from ordering rescue operations sooner than the final hour. But he was also paralyzed by a bureaucratic mentality that, for example, denied evacuation to local employees of the International Business Machine subsidiary on the grounds that they had to stay to process the Saigon government payroll. Until late April, his procrastination was essentially prompted by a conviction that the Saigon area could be defended. And he believed that the key to holding firm was some $700 million in supplemental American aid to mobilize fresh South Vietnamese units, a recommendation advanced by General Fred Weyand, the last U.S. commander in Vietnam. Martin telephoned his friends on Capitol Hill from Saigon, begging for the money. Kissinger, in a similar appeal to the Senate Appropriations Committee on April 15, contended that the funds would bolster the Saigon regime's ability to negotiate with the Communists on terms "more consistent with self-determination."

Implicit in these pleas was a maneuver to shift the onus to Congress for South Vietnam's almost certain collapse. And indeed, in subsequent years Kissinger, Martin, and others did blame the legislature for the catastrophe. Yet the politicians were simply reflecting the opinion of the overwhelming majority of Americans, who favored no further aid to the Saigon government. President Ford, himself a former congressman, probably perceived the national mood better than his administration officials did. On April 23, speaking at Tulane University in New Orleans, he relegated Vietnam to the history books: "Today, Americans can regain the sense of pride that existed before Vietnam. But it cannot be achieved by refighting a war that is finished. . . . These events, tragic as they are, portend neither the end of the world ,nor of America's leadership in the world."

With their irrepressible appetite for intrigue, prominent South Vietnamese now became ever more deeply immersed in plots to oust Thieu, in the hope that the Communists might concede to a political accommodation, and assorted foreign intermediaries intruded into the conspiracies. Thomas Polgar, CIA chief in Saigon, suggested a coup, but the idea was flatly rejected by William Colby, the agency's director, who saw America's complicity in the downfall of Ngo Dinh Diem as a grievous error. General Tran Van Don, now defense minister, was colluding with the French ambassador to install General Duong Van Minh, a figure presumably acceptable to the Communists. Robert Shaplen of *The New Yorker*, who after decades of reporting from Vietnam had developed a proprietary interest in the country, was promoting Nguyen Cao Ky. Thieu, not waiting to be booted out, resigned on April 21. He left for Taiwan four days later, after bitterly describing his desertion by the United States "an inhumane act by an inhumane ally."

By now, forty thousand North Vietnamese troops had overrun Xuan-loc, thirty-five miles northeast of Saigon on the road to Bienhoa airfield. The battle had raged for two weeks—the only engagement during the government's last phase in which its forces fought well, as their aircraft inflicted heavy casualties on the Communists with such devastating weapons as cluster bombs. Speeding forward after the breakthrough, the North Vietnamese divisions turned the corner at Bienhoa and headed south for Saigon.

There, under intense pressure from Washington, the U.S. mission had finally set in motion its emergency withdrawal plans. Some fifty thousand Americans and Vietnamese had departed during the previous weeks. On April 29, with the Communists rocketing the Saigon airport, the ultimate alternative was Option IV—the largest helicopter evacuation on record. Over a span of eighteen hours, shuttling back and forth between the city and aircraft carriers riding offshore, a fleet of seventy marine choppers lifted more than a thousand Americans and nearly six thousand Vietnamese out of the beleaguered capital—two thousand of them from the U.S. embassy compound.

The operation, conducted in an atmosphere of desperation, was close to miraculous. The original plan had been for buses to pick up the Americans and Vietnamese designated for departure at appointed places around the city and to deliver them to various helicopter pads. But the procedure quickly broke down. Mobs of hysterical Vietnamese, clamoring to be evacuated, blocked the buses. Thousands surged toward the takeoff spots, screaming to be saved. Rumors of impending Communist shelling swept through the crowd and exacerbated the panic; in fact, the North Vietnamese were deliberately holding their fire, no longer seeing any gain in gratuitous slaughter. Martin, sanguine to the end, had declined to ship out his personal belongings, including his collection of Asian curios. Now, feverish with pneumonia, he no longer mattered. Admiral Noel Gayler, the commander for the Pacific, had flown in to take charge. Accompanied by his wife, clutching his embassy flag, Martin climbed to the chancery roof to board a helicopter. By dawn on April 30, its streets deserted, Saigon awaited the Communists.

Thieu had abdicated to Tran Van Huong, his decrepit vice-president, who swiftly shunted his tattered authority to General Minh, supposedly the man to placate the Communists. But the Communists were not to be appeased. On the night of April 29, sweeping down from Bienhoa, their forward columns had driven into the outskirts of Saigon, clashing along the way with a few South Vietnamese units. By morning, they were inside the capital, headed for the government army garrison, the police headquarters, the radio station, and other vital targets. An armored squadron, coming in from the north, rumbled down Hong Thap Tu Street and turned left onto Thong Nhut Boulevard to face the presidential palace. As the tanks rolled through the gates into the spacious courtyard, one of the crew rushed up the stairs to unfurl the red and yellow Vietcong flag from a balcony. General Minh and his improvised cabinet, dressed in business suits, were gathered in an ornate reception chamber on the second floor. It was eleven o'clock, and they had been there for hours.

Colonel Bui Tin, deputy editor of *Quan Doi Nhan Dan*, the North Vietnamese army newspaper, was covering the campaign as a correspondent. Having reported the capture of Banmethuot, Danang, and Xuanloc, he was eager to witness the "liberation" of Saigon, and had joined the armored spearhead at Bienhoa. Now, riding a tank into the palace grounds, he prepared to play a dual role. As a journalist, he wanted to record the capitulation. But as the ranking officer with the unit, his first duty was to take the surrender.

"I have been waiting since early this morning to transfer power to you," announced General Minh as Bui Tin entered the room.

"There is no question of your transferring power," replied Bui Tin. "Your power has crumbled. You cannot give up what you do not have."

A burst of gunfire erupted outside, and several of Minh's ministers ducked. Their nervousness provided Bui Tin with the pretext to deliver a short speech: "Our men are merely celebrating. You have nothing to fear. Between Vietnamese, there are no victors and no vanquished. Only the Americans have been beaten. If you are patriots, consider this a moment of joy. The war for our country is over."

Leaving the chamber, Bui Tin roamed through the building until he found Thieu's private office. He sat down at the desk and composed his dispatch, datelining it: The Puppet Presidential Palace. Now in his fifties, he had enlisted in the Vietminh just thirty years before. He had fought as a regular in the Red River valley and at Dienbienphu, and he had trekked the length of the Ho Chi Minh Trail, shuddering under the American bombing. Twelve hours earlier, on a bridge at the entrance to Saigon, he had survived a tank skirmish. He finished his article and strolled into the park behind the palace. Stretching out on the grass, he gazed at the sky, exalted.

Chronology
Cast of Principal Characters
Notes on Sources
Acknowledgments
Photo Credits
Index

Chronology

*Indicates events unrelated to Vietnam but
useful as reference points.*

208
B.C.
Trieu Da, a renegade Chinese general, conquers Au Lac in the
northern mountains of Vietnam, establishes a capital, and proclaims himself emperor of "Nam Viet."

1st
century
B.C.
Han dynasty expands and incorporates Nam Viet into the Chinese
empire as the province of Giao Chi.

A.D. 40
Trung sisters lead insurrection against the Chinese and set up an independent state.

800
★ Charlemagne crowned emperor of the West by Pope Leo III.

967
Emperor Dinh Bo Linh ascends throne, calling his state Dai Co
Viet. Period of independence follows.

1066
★ Norman invasion of England.

1428
The Chinese recognize Vietnam's independence by signing an accord after nearly a decade of revolt led by Emperor Le Loi.

1460–
98
Le Thanh Tong rules Vietnam. Introduces comprehensive legal
code and other reforms; extends dominion southward.

1545
Civil strife roils Vietnam, splitting the country for nearly two centuries.

1607
★ First permanent English settlement in America, at Jamestown, Virginia.

1627   Alexandre de Rhodes, French missionary, adapts Vietnamese language to Roman alphabet. Paves way for further French influence
        in Vietnam.

1772   Start of Tayson rebellion. Ruling Nguyen clan unseated. French
        missionary activity spreads.

1776   ★ American Declaration of Independence signed, July 4.

1787   Pigneau de Béhaine, French missionary, enlists support of Louis
        XVI to help a pretender to the throne, Nguyen Anh, regain control. France agrees to send men and matériel in exchange for exclusive commercial privileges, but later reneges.

1789   ★ French Revolution begins.

1802   ★ Napoleon becomes consul for life.

        Gia Long (Nguyen Anh) becomes emperor of Vietnam and unifies
        the country.

1820   Captain John White of Salem, Massachusetts, is first American to
        set foot in Vietnam.

1841   ★ Britain defeats China in the first Opium War and extracts trade
        concessions from the Chinese.

1843   Permanent French fleet deployed in Asian waters.

1847   Clash between French forces and Vietnamese mandarins at the city
        of Tourane, now Danang.
        Tu Duc ascends throne with plans to eliminate Christianity in Vietnam.

1848   ★ Revolutions throughout Europe.

1852   ★ Napoleon III takes power in France; endorses series of expeditions
        to Vietnam to protect missionaries and gain trade concessions.

1861   French forces capture Saigon.

        ★ Civil war erupts in America.

1862   Tu Duc signs treaty with French granting them broad religious,
        economic, and political concessions.

1863   French control extends to Cambodia.

1870	★ Third Republic is formed in France following the Franco-Prussian War and the overthrow of Napoleon III.
1873	French inroads into Tonkin begin.
1879	Cochinchina's first French civilian governor is appointed.
1883	France establishes a "protectorate" over Annam and Tonkin, and rules Cochinchina as a colony.
1887	France creates Indochinese Union composed of Cochinchina, Annam, Tonkin, and Cambodia.
1890	Ho Chi Minh is born in central Vietnam.
1911	Ho leaves Vietnam, not to return for thirty years.
1914	★ World War I breaks out in Europe. Some hundred thousand Vietnamese go to France in labor battalions.
1915	★ Panama Canal opens.
1918	★ Russian Revolution begins in October. Ho Chi Minh, then known as Nguyen Ai Quoc, arrives in Paris; remains there for the next seven years.
1919	Ho tries to petition President Woodrow Wilson, at the Versailles peace conference, for self-determination in Vietnam.
1920	Ho joins newly formed French Communist party in December.
1924	Ho leaves Paris for Moscow, becomes full-time Communist agent. Later goes to Canton as assistant to Mikhail Borodin, Soviet representative in China.
1930	Ho and comrades form Indochinese Communist party in Hong Kong.
1932	Bao Dai, theoretically emperor since 1925, returns to Vietnam from school in France to ascend throne under French tutelage.
1936	Popular Front government in France sponsors short-lived liberal reforms in Vietnam.
1939	★ World War II begins in September as Germans invade Poland.
1940	★ France falls to Germany in June. Marshal Philippe Pétain sets up

French government in Vichy. General Charles de Gaulle, in London, forms Free French forces.

In September, Japan occupies Indochina, but leaves the French colonial administration intact.

1941   Ho returns to Vietnam covertly, forms the Vietminh to fight both Japan and France.
        ★ Japanese attack Pearl Harbor, December 7.

1944   ★ Allied forces invade Europe, June 6.
        Vo Nguyen Giap forms Vietminh army.
        ★ General de Gaulle establishes provisional French government in Algiers, returns to Paris in August.

1945   Japanese take over French administration throughout Indochina, March 9.
        Bao Dai proclaims the independence of Vietnam under Japanese auspices, March 11.
        ★ President Roosevelt dies on April 12. Harry Truman becomes president of the United States.
        ★ Germany surrenders, May 8.
        At Potsdam Conference in July, Allied leaders assign British to disarm Japanese in southern Vietnam; Chinese Nationalists to perform the same function north of the sixteenth parallel.
        ★ Japan capitulates, August 15, after the United States drops atomic bombs on Hiroshima and Nagasaki.
        Japanese transfer power in Indochina to the Vietminh, August 18.
        Bao Dai abdicates on August 23.
        Ho proclaims provisional government in Hanoi on August 29, with Bao Dai as supreme counselor.
        Japan formally surrenders to the Allies. Ho declares the independence of Vietnam, September 2.
        British forces under General Douglas Gracey land in Saigon on September 13; soon return authority to the French.
        Lieutenant Colonel A. Peter Dewey of the OSS is killed in Saigon, September 26, the first American to die in Vietnam.
        Indochinese Communist party dissolved in November, replaced by Association for Marxist Studies as Ho tries to broaden his base.
        Throughout the period, some two million Vietnamese die of famine in the north.

1946   China agrees to withdraw forces from Vietnam, and France concedes its extraterritorial rights in China.
        French and Vietminh reach accord in March; France recognizes Vietnam as a "free state" within the French Union. French troops authorized to return to the north to replace the Chinese. A referendum to determine whether Tonkin, Annam, and Cochinchina should be reunited.

In May, Ho Chi Minh goes to Fontainebleau for negotiations.

Admiral Thierry d'Argenlieu, French high commissioner for Indochina, violates March agreement by proclaiming a separate government for Cochinchina in June.

Negotiations at Fontainebleau break down in September, but Ho signs *modus vivendi* covering economic issues and agreeing to cessation of hostilities. He returns to Vietnam.

Amid growing tensions, French warships bombard Haiphong, November 23.

Vietminh forces withdraw from Hanoi in December after attacking French garrisons. Ho Chi Minh creates a rural base. The war has begun.

1947   ★ George Kennan of the State Department, writing under the pseudonym "X," publishes the concept of "containment" in *Foreign Affairs*.

★ U.S. Congress votes funds on May 15 to aid Greece and Turkey to combat Communist insurgency and terrorism, according to a policy soon known as the Truman Doctrine.

★ On June 5, Secretary of State George Marshall outlines aid program to Europe, later called the Marshall Plan.

Bao Dai, living in Hong Kong, offers to negotiate with France to achieve Vietnam's independence and unity.

★ Britain grants independence to India and Pakistan in August.

Bao Dai initials understandings with French High Commissioner Emile Bollaert in December, recognizing Vietnamese independence within limits.

1948   ★ Soviet Union blockades land routes to Berlin in April. United States and Britain fly food and coal into the city until the blockade is lifted in September 1949.

★ Harry Truman narrowly defeats Thomas Dewey for the presidency on November 2.

1949   Bao Dai and President Vincent Auriol of France sign the Elysée Agreement on March 8, making Vietnam an "associated state" within the French Union. France retains control of Vietnam's defense and finances.

Bao Dai returns to Vietnam in April after three years of self-imposed exile.

★ North Atlantic Treaty Organization (NATO) formed by the United States, Canada, and ten Western European nations, August 24.

★ Chinese Communists complete the conquest of China on October 1; Mao Zedong proclaims the establishment of the People's Republic of China.

1950 Ho Chi Minh declares on January 14 that the Democratic Republic of Vietnam is the only legal government. It is recognized by the Soviet Union and China, but also establishes diplomatic relations with Marshal Tito's Yugoslavia, prompting some American officials to suggest that Ho is not a Soviet "puppet."

United States and Britain recognize Bao Dai's government, February 7. Chinese Communists, now at the Vietnamese border, begin to provide modern weapons to the Vietminh.

* On June 26, North Korea invades South Korea. President Truman, without consulting Congress, commits American troops to the war under United Nations auspices.

Truman signs legislation granting $15 million in military aid to the French for the war in Indochina, July 26.

French defeated at Caobang, a key post on the Chinese border. General Jean de Lattre de Tassigny named French military commander and high commissioner for Indochina, December 6.

1951 Ho Chi Minh creates the Lao Dong, or Workers party, in February as a substitute for the Communist party, ostensibly dissolved in 1945.

* Truman dismisses General Douglas MacArthur, the American commander in Korea, for unauthorized statements, April 11.

* Cease-fire talks begin in Korea in July, though fighting continues for the next two years.

1952 General Giap's offensive in the Red River valley blunted by de Lattre.

De Lattre dies in Paris, January 11.

* United States explodes first hydrogen device in the Pacific, November 1.

* Dwight D. Eisenhower elected president of the United States, November 4.

1953 * Joseph Stalin, the Soviet leader, dies on March 5.

* Armistice agreement signed in Korea, July 27.

France grants Laos full independence as a member of the French Union in October. Majority of the French National Assembly expresses hope for a negotiated settlement to the Indochina war.

Prince Norodom Sihanouk takes command of the Cambodian army on November 9; declares Cambodia's independence from France.

French forces reoccupy Dienbienphu.

Ho Chi Minh tells a Swedish newspaperman that he is ready to discuss French peace proposals.

Vietminh forces push into Laos in December.

1954 On January 25, foreign ministers of United States, Britain, France, and Soviet Union meet in Berlin; agree that a conference on Korea and Indochina should be held in April.

Battle of Dienbienphu begins, March 13; French defeated at Dienbienphu, May 7.

Eisenhower decides in April against American intervention to help France in Indochina after Britain rejects his proposal for concerted action.

Indochina phase of the Geneva Conference opens on May 8, with Britain and Soviet Union as cochairmen.

★ Government of Prime Minister Joseph Laniel falls in Paris in June.

Bao Dai selects Ngo Dinh Diem as prime minister, June 16.

Pierre Mendès-France, invested as prime minister of France, June 17, pledges to achieve a cease-fire in Indochina within a month; goes to Bern to negotiate secretly with Zhou Enlai, Chinese foreign minister.

Diem returns to Saigon, July 7.

Agreements reached at Geneva in July call for cessation of hostilities in Vietnam, Cambodia, and Laos. Provisional demarcation line at seventeenth parallel divides Vietnam pending political settlement to be achieved through nationwide elections. Final declaration accepted orally by all participants at the conference except United States, which states it will not disturb the agreements but would view renewed aggression with concern. Bao Dai's government denounces agreements.

The Southeast Asia Treaty Organization (SEATO) formed, September 8, by United States, Britain, France, Australia, New Zealand, Pakistan, Thailand, and Philippines.

French forces leave Hanoi, October 9.

General J. Lawton Collins, Eisenhower's special envoy, arrives in Saigon to affirm American support for Diem, including $100 million in aid. Hundreds of thousands of refugees flee from the north to the south with help of U.S. navy.

1955   United States begins to funnel aid directly to Saigon government in January, agrees to train South Vietnamese army.

Diem crushes the Binh Xuyen sect in April.

Period ends for French forces and their Vietnamese auxiliaries to deploy to the south, and for Vietminh troops to regroup in the north.

Diem rejects the Geneva accords and refuses to participate in nationwide elections on July 16, a decision backed by the United States.

Ho Chi Minh, in Moscow in July, accepts Soviet aid, having earlier negotiated in Beijing for Chinese assistance.

Diem defeats Bao Dai in a referendum, October 23, becomes chief of state; proclaims the Republic of Vietnam, with himself as president, October 26.

In December, massive land reform programs begin in North Vietnam, with landlords tried before "people's tribunals."

1956   Prince Sihanouk, now Cambodian prime minister, asserts his intention in April to pursue a neutralist policy.
Diem begins crackdown on Vietminh suspects and other dissidents.
* Soviet Union crushes October uprisings in Hungary and Poland.
* Britain, France, and Israel launch the Suez war in November.

1957   In January, Soviet Union, favoring a permanent division of the country, proposes that North and South Vietnam be admitted to United Nations as separate states.
Diem arrives in U.S. for ten-day visit on May 8. President Eisenhower reaffirms support for his regime.
Communist insurgent activity in South Vietnam begins in October in accordance with decision reached in Hanoi to organize thirty-seven armed companies in Mekong delta. During the year, guerrillas assassinated more than four hundred minor South Vietnamese officials.

1958   Communists form a coordinated command structure in eastern Mekong delta in June.
Prince Souvanna Phouma dissolves his neutralist government in Laos on July 22; succeeded by Phoui Sananikone, who with American support adopts anti-Communist stance.

1959   A plot to overthrow Sihanouk uncovered in February, with a CIA agent involved.
North Vietnam forms Group 559 in May, to begin infiltrating cadres and weapons into South Vietnam via the Ho Chi Minh Trail.
Group 759 organized in July by Communists to send supplies to the south by sea.
Major Dale Buis and Sergeant Chester Ovnand killed by guerrillas at Bienhoa on July 8, the first Americans to die in what would be called the Vietnam Era.
Diem promulgates law authorizing intense repression of Communist suspects and other dissidents in August.
Hanoi leadership creates Group 959 in September to furnish weapons and other supplies to Communist insurgents in Laos.
* In December, Charles de Gaulle takes power in France; establishes Fifth Republic.

1960   North Vietnam imposes universal military conscription in April.
Eighteen prominent South Vietnamese petition Diem to reform his government.
Captain Kong Le stages *coup d'état* in Laos in August, hands power back to Souvanna Phouma. General Phoumi Nosavan, with CIA help, forms opposition faction in southern Laos.
Lao Dong congress opens in Hanoi, September 5; stresses need to combat Diem regime.

* John F. Kennedy defeats Richard Nixon for the presidency, November 8.

South Vietnamese army units unsuccessfully attempt to overthrow Diem, November 11.

Hanoi leaders form National Liberation Front for South Vietnam, December 20, which Saigon regime dubs the "Vietcong," meaning Communist Vietnamese.

Crisis erupts in Laos in late December as General Phouma attacks Vientiane. Soviet aircraft fly supplies to Souvanna Phouma's neutralist faction.

1961   As he leaves office, Eisenhower warns Kennedy that Laos is the major crisis in Southeast Asia.

In March, Kennedy asserts American support for the sovereignty of Laos, while Britain and Soviet Union propose an international conference to resolve the crisis.

* American-backed attempt to overthrow Fidel Castro fails at the Bay of Pigs in April.

Vice-President Lyndon Johnson visits South Vietnam in May; proposes additional American aid to Diem regime.

Geneva conference on Laos opens, May 16; later creates neutral coalition headed by Souvanna Phouma.

* Kennedy meets Soviet Prime Minister Nikita Khrushchev in Vienna, June 4.

Maxwell Taylor and Walt Rostow visit Vietnam in October; recommend American combat troop intervention disguised as flood relief. Kennedy spurns idea, but decides to give Diem more equipment and advisers.

1962   American Military Assistance Command formed in South Vietnam, February 6. By mid-1962, American advisers increased from 700 to 12,000.

Two South Vietnamese pilots bomb Diem's palace, February 27, but Diem and his family survive.

In May, Communists form battalion-size units in central Vietnam.

Geneva accords on Laos signed, July 23.

* Kennedy forces the Soviets to withdraw missiles from Cuba in October.

American and Saigon governments promote strategic hamlet program.

1963   Vietcong units defeat South Vietnamese at the battle of Ap Bac, January 2.

Ho Chi Minh and Chinese President Liu Shaoji denounce "revisionism," May 1, indicating North Vietnamese shift toward China.

South Vietnamese troops and police shoot at Buddhist demonstrators in Hué, May 8. Crisis intensifies as Buddhist monk commits suicide by self-immolation in June.

South Vietnamese General Tran Van Don informs Lucien Conein, a CIA agent, on July 4 that officers are plotting against Diem.

Ngo Dinh Nhu's forces attack Buddhist temples, August 21.

Ambassador Henry Cabot Lodge arrives in Saigon, August 22, replacing Frederick Nolting. On August 24, Washington recommends that Nhu be removed; also suggests American support for mutinous generals against Diem; Lodge concurs.

Kennedy criticizes Diem in a television interview, September 2.

Duong Van Minh and other generals stage coup against Diem and Nhu, November 1; Diem and Nhu are murdered after their surrender next day.

* On November 22, Kennedy assassinated in Dallas; succeeded by Lyndon Johnson.

By year-end, 15,000 American military advisers are in South Vietnam, which has received $500 million in aid during the year. Communist leadership in Hanoi decides to step up the struggle in the south.

1964   General Nguyen Khanh seizes power in Saigon, January 30; arrests four ruling generals but allows Minh to remain as figurehead chief of state.

Secretary of Defense Robert McNamara visits Vietnam in March; vows support for Khanh.

Dean Rusk, McNamara, and others confer in Honolulu, June 2, on increased aid to South Vietnam. Pentagon strategists refine plans for bombing North Vietnam.

Covert South Vietnamese maritime operations begin against North Vietnam in July.

North Vietnamese patrol boats attack the *Maddox,* an American destroyer in the Tonkin Gulf, August 2. A doubtful second incident reported two days later. American aircraft bomb North Vietnam for the first time later this month.

Congress passes the Tonkin Gulf resolution on August 7, giving Johnson extraordinary power to act in Southeast Asia.

* China explodes its first atomic bomb in October.

* Khrushchev ousted, October 14; replaced by Leonid Brezhnev and Aleksei Kosygin.

Vietcong attack Bienhoa air base, October 30, but Johnson rejects proposal for retaliatory raids against North Vietnam.

* Lyndon Johnson defeats Barry Goldwater for the presidency, November 3.

In November, Saigon convulsed by rioters protesting Khanh's rule. Taylor, now ambassador, urges Khanh to leave the country.

Vietcong terrorists bomb American military billet in Saigon, December 24. Johnson again rejects proposal for raids against North Vietnam.

1965   Johnson's national security adviser, McGeorge Bundy, arrives in Saigon on February 4, as Soviet Prime Minister Aleksei Kosygin arrives in Hanoi.

Vietcong stage attacks against American installations, February 7. Johnson authorizes Flaming Dart, American air raids against North Vietnam.

Dr. Phan Huy Quat forms government in Saigon, February 18; General Khanh leaves the country.

Operation Rolling Thunder, sustained American bombing of North Vietnam, begins on February 24.

Two marine battalions land to defend Danang airfield, March 8, the first American combat troops in Vietnam.

Johnson, at Johns Hopkins University, April 7, offers Ho Chi Minh participation in a Southeast Asian development plan in exchange for peace.

North Vietnamese Prime Minister Pham Van Dong rejects Johnson's proposal, April 8; says settlement must be based on Vietcong program.

Air Vice Marshal Nguyen Cao Ky takes over as prime minister of a military regime in Saigon, June 11.

American command in Saigon reports on June 26 that Vietcong have put five South Vietnamese combat regiments and nine battalions out of action in recent months.

Johnson reappoints Lodge ambassador to South Vietnam, July 8, to replace Taylor. Eighteen American combat battalions now in the country.

Johnson approves Westmoreland's request, July 28, for forty-four additional combat battalions.

In September, Chinese Defense Minister Lin Biao, in "Long Live the Victory of People's War!," indicates China will not intervene directly in Vietnam. Mao Zedong begins the Great Proletarian Cultural Revolution.

American forces defeat North Vietnamese units in the Ia Drang valley in October, the first big conventional clash of the war.

By December, American troop strength in Vietnam reaches nearly 200,000.

Johnson suspends bombing of North Vietnam on December 25 in an attempt to induce the Communists to negotiate.

1966   Johnson resumes bombing, January 31.

Johnson and South Vietnamese leaders issue a communiqué, February 8, in Honolulu, emphasizing need for pacification in South Vietnam.

Buddhist demonstrators against Saigon regime in Hué and Danang, March 10. Government troops take over Danang, May 23. Government troops take over Hué, June 16.

American aircraft bomb oil depots near Hanoi and Haiphong, June 29.

President de Gaulle of France visits Cambodia in September; calls for American withdrawal from Vietnam.

American and South Vietnamese leaders conclude conference in Manila, October 25.

American troop strength in Vietnam reaches nearly 400,000 by year-end.

1967   North Vietnamese Foreign Minister Nguyen Duy Trinh says on January 28 United States must stop bombing North Vietnam before talks can begin.

Johnson ends two-day meeting on Guam, March 21, with Thieu and Ky. North Vietnamese reveal exchange of letters between Johnson and Ho Chi Minh.

Westmoreland confers with Johnson in Washington, April 27; addresses Congress next day.

Ellsworth Bunker arrives in Saigon to replace Lodge as ambassador, May 1.

* Johnson completes two days of talks with Soviet Prime Minister Kosygin, June 25, at Glassboro, New Jersey.

McNamara, testifying before a Senate subcommittee in August, asserts American bombing of North Vietnam is ineffective.

In South Vietnam, Thieu elected president, Ky vice-president, September 3.

Communists begin major actions in September. Westmoreland starts to fortify Khesanh.

Johnson, in San Antonio on September 29, says United States will stop bombing in exchange for "productive discussions."

Westmoreland, in the United States in November, exudes optimism.

Foreign Minister Trinh says on December 29 that North Vietnam "will" talk once the United States halts its bombing.

American troop strength in Vietnam approaches 500,000 by year-end. Domestic protests against the war rise.

1968   In January, Sihanouk tells Johnson's emissary, Chester Bowles, that he will not stop American forces from pursuing the Vietcong over the Cambodian border.

* USS *Pueblo* seized by North Koreans, January 23.

Tet offensive begins, January 31, as North Vietnamese and Vietcong attack South Vietnamese cities and towns.

American and South Vietnamese troops recapture Hué on February 25 after twenty-six days of fighting.

General Earle Wheeler, chairman of the joint chiefs of staff, brings request from Westmoreland in Saigon for 206,000 additional American troops.

Clark Clifford, succeeding McNamara as secretary of defense, begins study of troop request; soon favors rejection of buildup.

* Senator Eugene McCarthy of Minnesota nearly defeats Johnson in New Hampshire primary.
* Senator Robert F. Kennedy of New York announces candidacy for president, March 16.

  Westmoreland appointed army chief of staff, replaced in Vietnam by General Creighton Abrams.

  On March 25, "wise men" meet in Washington; advise Johnson against further escalation.

  On March 31, Johnson announces partial bombing halt, offers talks, and says he will not run for re-election.
* Martin Luther King, Jr., assassinated in Memphis, April 4.

  North Vietnamese diplomats arrive in Paris in mid-May for talks with American delegation headed by Averell Harriman.
* Senator Robert F. Kennedy assassinated in Los Angeles, June 5, after winning the California primary.
* Richard Nixon wins Republican nomination for president in Miami, August 8.
* Vice-President Hubert Humphrey wins Democratic nomination for president in Chicago amid riots outside the convention hall.

  Johnson stops all bombing of North Vietnam.
* Nixon elected president of the United States, November 5, with Spiro Agnew as vice-president.
* Henry Kissinger chosen by Nixon as national security adviser, December 2.

  American troop strength in Vietnam at year-end is 540,000.

1969 In January, Paris talks expanded to include Saigon government and Vietcong representatives.

Nixon begins secret bombing of Cambodia, March 18.

Secretary of Defense Melvin Laird invents term "Vietnamization" in March to cover American troop withdrawals.

Nixon proposes simultaneous withdrawal from South Vietnam of American and North Vietnamese forces, May 14.

Nixon, with Thieu on Midway, June 8, announces withdrawal of 25,000 American troops from Vietnam.

Nixon unveils "Nixon Doctrine" in Guam on July 25.

In August, Kissinger meets covertly in Paris with North Vietnamese negotiator Xuan Thuy.

Ho Chi Minh dies in Hanoi at age of seventy-nine, September 3.

Massive antiwar demonstrations in Washington, October 15.

Nixon delivers "silent majority" speech on November 3.

Another big antiwar demonstration in Washington, November 15.

On November 16, revelation of the Mylai massacre, which took place the year before.

American troop strength in Vietnam reduced by 60,000 by December.

1970 Kissinger begins secret talks in Paris with Le Duc Tho, February 20.

Sihanouk overthrown in Cambodia by Lon Nol and Sisowath Sirik Matak, March 18.

Nixon announces, April 30, that American and South Vietnamese forces have attacked Communist sanctuaries in Cambodia.

Large antiwar protests spread across the United States. National guardsmen kill four students at Kent State University in Ohio on May 4.

Nixon proposes "standstill cease-fire," October 7, but repeats mutual-withdrawal formula next day.

American combat deaths in Vietnam during last week in October numbered twenty-four, lowest toll since October 1965.

On November 12, Lieutenant William Calley goes on trial at Fort Benning, Georgia, for his part in the Mylai massacre.

American troop strength in Vietnam down to 280,000 men at year-end.

1971 In February, South Vietnamese forces begin incursions in Laos against the Ho Chi Minh Trail.

Lieutenant Calley convicted, March 29, of premeditated murder of South Vietnamese civilians at Mylai.

* The New York Times begins publishing Pentagon Papers on June 13. Supreme Court upholds its right to do so.

* On July 15, Nixon announces Kissinger's trip to China.

* Nixon's chief of staff, John Ehrlichman, organizes the "plumbers," July 17, to investigate Daniel Ellsberg, who made the Pentagon Papers public.

Thieu re-elected president of South Vietnam, October 3.

American troop strength in Vietnam down to 140,000 men in December.

1972 Nixon reveals on January 25 that Kissinger has been negotiating secretly with the North Vietnamese.

* Nixon arrives in China, February 21.

North Vietnam launches offensive across the demilitarized zone, March 30.

On April 15, Nixon authorizes bombing of area near Hanoi and Haiphong.

* Kissinger goes to Moscow, April 20, to prepare Nixon's summit meeting with Brezhnev on May 20.

North Vietnamese capture the city of Quangtri, May 1.

On May 8, Nixon announces mining of Haiphong harbor and intensification of American bombing of North Vietnam.

* Five men arrested, June 17, for breaking into Democratic National Committee offices at Watergate complex in Washington, D.C.

Kissinger meets again with Le Duc Tho in Paris, August 1; senses progress. In Saigon, mid-August, senses Thieu's reluctance to accept cease-fire accord.

Thieu opposes draft agreement in meeting with Kissinger's assistant, Alexander Haig, October 4.

Breakthrough at Paris meeting between Kissinger and Le Duc Tho, October 8. Back in Saigon in mid-October, Kissinger finds Thieu implacably opposed to agreement.

Hanoi radio broadcasts details of the agreement in an effort to pressure Kissinger. But he is anxious to reassure North Vietnam; declares that "peace is at hand."

* Nixon re-elected, November 7, defeating Senator George McGovern by a landslide.

Kissinger resumes talks with Le Duc Tho, November 20; presents him with sixty-nine amendments to agreement demanded by Thieu. Fresh talks between Kissinger and Le Duc Tho begin again in December and break down.

On December 18, Nixon orders bombing of areas around Hanoi and Haiphong; raids continue for eleven days. Communists agree to resume diplomatic talks when bombing stops.

1973   Kissinger and Le Duc Tho resume talks, January 8; finally initial agreement, January 23.

Cease-fire agreements formally signed in Paris, January 27. Secretary of Defense Laird announces that draft in the United States has ended.

Last American troops leave Vietnam, March 29.

Last American prisoners of war released in Hanoi, April 1.

* Nixon aides H. R. Haldeman, John Ehrlichman, and John Dean and Attorney General Richard Kleindienst resign, April 30, amid charges that the administration obstructed justice.

Graham Martin sworn in as ambassador to South Vietnam, June 24, replacing Ellsworth Bunker.

* John Dean, former White House counsel, tells a special Senate committee, June 25, that Nixon tried to cover up the Watergate affair. Alexander Butterfield, former Nixon aide, discloses to committee, July 13, existence of tapes of White House conversations.

On July 16, Senate Armed Services Committee begins hearings on the secret bombing of Cambodia.

United States stops bombing Cambodia, August 14, in accordance with congressional prohibition.

* On August 22, Nixon announces appointment of Kissinger as secretary of state to replace Rogers.

* Agnew resigns, October 10; replaced by Representative Gerald Ford as vice-president.

* On November 7, Congress overrides Nixon's veto of law limiting the president's right to wage war.

1974   Thieu declares in January that the war has begun again.

* House Judiciary Committee opens impeachment hearings on Nixon, May 9.

Communist buildup of men and supplies proceeds in South Vietnam in June.

* Supreme Court rules, July 24, that Nixon must turn over White House tapes to Leon Jaworski, Watergate special prosecutor; House Judiciary Committee votes, July 30, to recommend impeaching Nixon on three counts.
* Nixon resigns, August 9; replaced by Ford.
* Ford pardons Nixon, September 8, for all federal crimes that he "committed or may have committed."

Communists review plans in September to resume fighting during the coming dry season.

1975   Communists capture Phuoc Long province, north of Saigon, January 6.

North Vietnamese General Van Tien Dung goes south to take command of Communist forces, February 5.

Communists capture Banmethuot, March 11.

Thieu meets with his commanders at Camranh, March 15; orders northern provinces of South Vietnam abandoned.

Thieu reverses himself, orders Hué held at all costs, March 20. But the city falls to the Communists five days later.

Communists capture Danang, March 30.

On March 31, politburo in Hanoi directs General Dung to push toward Saigon in the "Ho Chi Minh Campaign."

Le Duc Tho arrives at Communist headquarters at Locninh, April 7, to oversee offensive.

In Cambodia, Phnompenh falls to the Khmer Rouge, April 17.

Communists capture Xuan Loc, April 21, last South Vietnamese defense line before Saigon.

President Ford, speaking in New Orleans on April 23, calls the war "finished."

Thieu leaves Saigon for Taiwan, April 25. Vice-President Tran Van Huong transfers authority as chief of state to General Duong Van Minh, April 28.

Option IV, evacuation of last Americans from Saigon, begins, April 29. Ambassador Martin departs.

Communist forces capture Saigon, April 30. Colonel Bui Tin takes surrender from Minh.

U.S. merchant ship *Mayaguez* seized by Cambodian Communists in Gulf of Siam, May 12. American aircraft bomb Cambodia. Thirty-eight U.S. marines die in rescue of thirty-nine seamen.

1976   * Jimmy Carter elected president of the United States, November 2.

1977   On January 21, the day after his inauguration, Carter pardons most of 10,000 Vietnam war draft evaders.

Assistant Secretary of State Richard Holbrooke begins talks with Vietnamese officials in March to explore U.S. recognition of Vietnam.

1978   Vietnam joins Comecon, the East European economic communi-
            ty, in June.
            In July, tensions between Vietnam and Cambodia build up; rela-
            tions between Vietnam and China deteriorate.
            In October, United States postpones plans to normalize relations
            with Vietnam.
            In November, Vietnam and Soviet Union sign a friendship pact,
            which the Chinese term a "threat to the security" of Southeast
            Asia. Vietnam starts to repress its ethnic Chinese minority. Thou-
            sands flee the country.
          * Carter announces full-scale diplomatic relations between the United
            States and China, December 15.
            Vietnam invades Cambodia, December 25.
            Thousands of "boat people" begin to flee Vietnam in December.

1979   China invades Vietnam in February.

1980   * Ronald Reagan elected president of the United States,
            November 4.

1982   Vietnam veterans memorial unveiled in Washington, D.C., No-
            vember 11.

Cast of Principal Characters

Bao Dai

Last emperor of Vietnam. Succeeded his father in 1925 at the age of twelve, but did not ascend throne until 1932. Cooperated with Japanese during World War II. Abdicated in 1945 to join Vietminh briefly; went into exile and returned under the French to rule as chief of state 1949–55, when Ngo Dinh Diem ousted him in a referendum. Has since lived in France.

Bui Diem

South Vietnamese ambassador to United States 1966–72, and later roving envoy for President Nguyen Van Thieu. Northerner by birth, he fled to the south in 1954 and published an English-language newspaper in Saigon before joining the South Vietnamese government.

Bui Tin

Deputy editor of *Quan Doi Nhan Dan*, official North Vietnamese army newspaper, published in Hanoi. Veteran Communist officer, he took the surrender from the crumbling Saigon regime on April 30, 1975.

Duong Van Minh

Known as "Big Minh" because of his size, he was trained by French and later became the senior army officer when Ngo Dinh Diem established his government in 1955. Led the coup against Diem in November 1963 and was himself toppled two months afterward. Took over South Vietnamese regime in April 1975 and surrendered to Communists. Was permitted to immigrate to France in 1983.

Gia Long

Scion of the Nguyen clan (rivals of the Trinh dynasty), he launched a campaign to gain control of all Vietnam in the late eighteenth century and proclaimed himself emperor in 1802. His cause was

helped by Pigneau de Béhaine, a French missionary. Originally named Nguyen Anh, adopted name
Gia Long on ascension to throne. He died in 1819.

Ho Chi Minh

Born Nguyen Tat Thanh in 1890, he left his native
province in central Vietnam as a youth and traveled the world; moved to Paris in 1917, remaining
there for seven years; joined the infant French
Communist party in 1920; went to Moscow four
years later and became a Communist agent. Used a
number of aliases, the best known of them,
Nguyen Ai Quoc, "Nguyen the Patriot." Founded
the Indochinese Communist party in Hong Kong
in 1930, but did not return to Vietnam until 1941,
when he created the Vietminh and adopted his
most famous alias, Ho Chi Minh, "He Who En-
lightens." Proclaimed Vietnam's independence
from France in September 1945, then fought the
French for the next nine years, finally defeating
them at Dienbienphu. President of North Vietnam—the Democratic Republic of Vietnam—from
1945 until his death in September 1969.

Hoang Duc Nha

Cousin and special adviser to South Vietnamese
President Nguyen Van Thieu, he became increasingly influential after 1972, when Thieu was under
pressure to sign a cease-fire agreement. Immigrated
to the United States and took up residence in Con-
necticut.

Le Duan

Born in 1908 in the central Vietnamese province of
Quangtri; quit his job as a railroad employee to become a professional revolutionary; rose rapidly in
the Communist hierarchy. By 1959, was secretary-
general of the Lao Dong (Workers party); later
succeeded Ho Chi Minh as the most powerful figure in Vietnam. Operating under the alias Ba,
"Second Son," he took a particular interest in the
insurgency in South Vietnam.

Le Duc Tho

Born about 1912 in northern Vietnam. A founder
of the Indochinese Communist party who played
an important part in building its structure. Given
responsibility for directing the insurgency in the
south; at the same time, negotiated with Henry
Kissinger. Rejected the Nobel Peace Prize, which

	he and Kissinger were awarded for achieving the cease-fire agreement in January 1973.
Le Loi	Led a guerrilla war in the early fifteenth century against the Chinese, defeating them in 1418 and establishing the longest dynasty in Vietnamese history, which ruled until 1804. By then, Vietnam was divided by rebellions and rival clans.
Le Thanh Tong	Ascended the throne of Vietnam in 1460 and ruled for thirty-seven years. The greatest of the Le dynasty emperors, he gave Vietnam a legal code and other reforms; also extended Vietnamese rule southward by conquering the kingdom of Champa in the central part of the peninsula.
Minh Mang	Successor to Gia Long; enthroned in 1819 and ruled for twenty-one years. Published edicts banning Catholic missionaries, which furnished France with a pretext to plan to conquer Vietnam.
Ngo Dinh Diem	Intense anti-Communist nationalist from a Catholic family of central Vietnam. Returned from exile in the United States in 1954 to become prime minister to Bao Dai, whom he ousted the next year in a rigged referendum. Rejected the elections prescribed under the 1954 Geneva agreement. Overthrown and murdered by his own generals in November 1963.
Ngo Dinh Nhu	Diem's younger brother and chief political adviser. Organized regime's secret political movement, the Can Lao. Assassinated along with Diem in 1963.
Madame Ngo Dinh Nhu	Born Tran Le Xuan, daughter of a Frenchified family in Hanoi. Became the "first lady" of South Vietnam, since Diem was a bachelor. Her strident manner provoked opposition to the regime. Retired to Rome in 1964.
Ngo Dinh Thuc	Oldest of the Ngo brothers and archbishop of Hué. Did much to antagonize the Buddhists; later excommunicated by the Vatican for religious extremism.
Nguyen Cao Ky	Prime minister of South Vietnam, 1965–67, and its figurehead vice-president until 1971. A flamboyant

pilot and originally the most dynamic of South Vietnam's young officers, but eased out of power by Nguyen Van Thieu. Fled to California and opened a liquor store in 1975.

Nguyen Co Thach   Foreign minister of Vietnam since its reunification in 1975. An able diplomat, he served as one of Le Duc Tho's deputies during the Paris negotiations; after 1977, tried to establish diplomatic relations with the United States, but talks failed.

Nguyen Huu Tho   Chairman of the National Liberation Front (the Vietcong) for South Vietnam, founded in December 1960. Saigon lawyer, jailed under the Diem regime for political dissidence; innocuous figure who took directives from the Communist party central committee in Hanoi.

Nguyen Khanh   South Vietnamese general who became prime minister in January 1964, when he overthrew the officers who had overthrown Diem. Lasted in office little more than a year.

Nguyen Van Thieu   Born in 1924 in central Vietnam; served briefly in the Vietminh before joining Vietnamese army created by French; trained in France and later in United States and maneuvered to become president of South Vietnam in 1967. Indecisive and distrustful, was unable to rule after 1973; fled Vietnam just before the fall of Saigon in late April 1975. Lived thereafter in Britain.

Pham Van Dong   Son of a mandarin, born in central Vietnam in 1908; became involved in nationalist politics as a student in Hanoi; fled to China, where he met Ho Chi Minh and was one of the founders of Indochinese Communist party. Skilled administrator who led Vietminh delegation to 1954 Geneva Conference; served as Ho's prime minister from 1950 onward; retained that post after reunification of Vietnam in 1975.

Phan Boi Chau   Born in 1867, one of the most influential of the modern Vietnamese nationalists. Sentenced to life imprisonment by the French in 1925 but permitted to live under house arrest in Hué, where he inspired younger nationalists. He died in 1940.

Phan Thanh Giang	Distinguished mandarin, sent to Paris by Tu Duc in 1863 to negotiate a compromise with French. After the French violated agreement, he committed suicide; in a farewell message, pledged his sons never to collaborate with France.
Thieu Tri	Successor to Minh Mang; ascended the throne in 1841 and ruled for six years. Reign coincided with the Opium War, first major effort by British to open China to trade, which spurred the French to press for similar concessions in Vietnam.
Tran Do	Deputy commander of Communist forces in South Vietnam and instrumental in the 1968 Tet offensive. Spent most of his time in the south, constantly moving his headquarters to avoid American bombs.
Tran Kim Tuyen	A Catholic, trained as a physician. Left North Vietnam in 1954 to become head of Ngo Dinh Nhu's covert police and intelligence operations, set up with CIA help. Later plotted to overthrow the South Vietnamese regime, but played no part in the coup, having been exiled beforehand by Nhu. Escaped to Britain in 1975, where he opened a rooming house in Cambridge.
Tran Van Don	Born in France in 1917, son of a doctor. Returned to Vietnam to train at a French military school for Vietnamese officers; after fighting with French against Vietminh, became a senior officer in Diem regime; was one of the organizers of the coup to oust Diem. Escaped to United States in 1975; has worked as a headwaiter and real estate salesman.
Tran Van Tra	Born in central Vietnam in 1918; worked on the railroad before joining Vietminh. Became a deputy commander of the Communist forces in the south and directed attack against Saigon during 1968 Tet offensive. His written history of final offensive in 1975 was banned in reunified Vietnam, and it is believed he was purged for criticizing the Communist party leadership.
Tri Quang	Buddhist monk who organized opposition to South Vietnamese regime in 1963 and again in 1966. Put under house arrest when the Communists took control of Vietnam in 1975.

Trieu Da	Chinese general who organized a rebellion against China and set up one of the earliest Vietnamese states, in 208 B.C., calling it Nam Viet. The state held out against China for a hundred years, but was conquered.
Trung sisters	Two aristocrats, Trung Trac and Trung Nhi, led the first major Vietnamese insurrection against Chinese rule, in A.D. 40. Their kingdom, which reached from southern China to the region around Hué, was soon reconquered by the Chinese. The Vietnamese still revere them as goddesses.
Truong Chinh	Born in 1908, son of a schoolteacher; one of the founders of the Indochinese Communist party. Inspired by Mao Zedong's celebrated Long March, changed his name from Dang Xuan Khu to Truong Chinh, "Long March." Held responsible for excesses of land reform in North Vietnam in 1955, but emerged from demotion and continued as major Communist theoretician.
Tu Duc	Ruled Vietnam, 1848–83; xenophobic and insular emperor who promulgated harsh laws against Catholics, which provided France with the pretext to invade Vietnam. Reign effectively spelled the end of Vietnamese independence.
Van Tien Dung	One of the few authentic peasants in the Communist hierarchy, born in 1917. Became a protégé of Vo Nguyen Giap and handled logistics at battle of Dienbienphu; directed offensive against Saigon in 1975; became defense minister of reunified Vietnam.
Vo Nguyen Giap	Modern Vietnam's foremost military figure, born in 1912 in central Vietnam. Taught high school and studied law at University of Hanoi while engaging in Communist activities; created the Vietminh military organization that defeated French at Dienbienphu; continued as chief Communist strategist in the war against the United States and South Vietnam. Virtually retired from public life after 1975.
Xuan Thuy	Foreign minister of North Vietnam, 1963–65; headed delegation at Paris peace talks in 1968; negotiated with Kissinger as Le Duc Tho's deputy.

The French

Georges Thierry d'Argenlieu

First high commissioner to Indochina after World War II. Born in 1884, a Carmelite monk and naval officer who rose to rank of admiral; maneuvered to thwart an agreement between France and the Vietminh; died in 1964.

Georges Bidault

Perennial political figure of the Fourth Republic and foreign minister at the time of Geneva Conference in 1954. Took a tough position toward Vietminh, but resigned when his government fell, giving way to Pierre Mendès-France.

Léon Blum

Socialist prime minister during the 1930s and again after World War II. Initially sympathetic to Vietnamese nationalist cause, later less so, largely because of pressures from conservative elements in his ruling coalition.

Emile Bollaert

High commissioner for Indochina, March 1947–October 1948; civil servant with no experience in foreign affairs who was more concerned with domestic politics in France than with Vietnam itself.

Christian de La Croix de Castries

Dashing cavalry colonel with impressive military record in World War II; assigned to command French garrison at Dienbienphu.

Jean Cédile

Member of General Charles de Gaulle's Free French forces who was parachuted into southern Vietnam in August 1945 to negotiate with Vietminh; became a partisan of a strong French presence in Indochina.

Léonard Charner

Career naval officer, born in 1797; commanded a force that consolidated French position around Saigon in 1861; returned to France and was elected to the Senate.

Georges Clemenceau

Radical politician, born in 1841, who fiercely opposed colonial ventures in Asia on grounds that France's real interests lay in Europe. Reached the peak of his fame as prime minister during World War I, when he was known as "The Tiger."

René Cogny	A chief aide to Henri Navarre; contributed to planning that locked the French garrison into its untenable position at Dienbienphu. Later served as French government representative in Morocco.
Paul Doumer	Liberal politician, born in 1857; became governor-general of Indochina in 1897 and in the next five years made it a profitable economic venture, building roads and bridges and raising revenues by creating an opium monopoly. Elected president of France in 1931; assassinated while in office a year later.
Jean Dupuis	Merchant and explorer living in China who organized his own force to seize part of Hanoi from the Vietnamese in 1873, an attack that gave France a pretext to intervene.
Jules Ferry	"Jules-the-Tonkinese," leading French imperialist of late nineteenth century who believed that France's industrial growth depended on colonial markets and sources of raw materials. Elected prime minister in 1879; died in 1893.
Francis Garnier	Naval officer and explorer who participated in French expedition up the Mekong from Cambodia into China. Killed during a skirmish in Tonkin in 1873, when he was thirty-four; his romantic exploits fired French imperialists.
Charles Rigault de Genouilly	Career naval officer who commanded an expedition to Asia in 1858 and staged an attack against Tourane. As minister of the navy, a vigorous advocate of French intervention in Indochina.
Pierre Benoît de La Grandière	Appointed governor of Cochinchina in 1863, when he was fifty-six; extended French rule through the southern region and into Cambodia. Conceived of the Mekong expedition; died in 1876.
François Guizot	Born in 1787, a prominent figure in King Louis Philippe's government and a noted historian. Originally opposed French imperial ventures in Asia, arguing that Europe was more important, but deployed a fleet off the China coast. Died in 1874.
Joseph Laniel	Prime minister of France in 1954, at time of French defeat at Dienbienphu; a typical Fourth Republic

politician, unable to resist public protests against the war in Indochina.

Jean de Lattre de Tassigny	Military and civilian commander in Indochina, 1950–51; inspired his forces to inflict heavy defeats on the Vietminh, but these were temporary. Died in 1952.
Jacques Philippe Leclerc	*Nom de guerre* of Philippe de Hauteclocque, born in 1902. Led armored division that liberated Paris from the Germans in 1944. A year later, as commander in Indochina, defeated Vietminh in southern Vietnam but recognized need for a negotiated settlement.
Dominique Lefèbvre	Nineteenth-century missionary who conspired to replace Emperor Thieu Tri with a monarch more receptive to Christianity. His presumed arrest by the Vietnamese gave the French pretext to attack Tourane in 1847.
Pierre Mendès-France	Maverick political figure who warned against involvement in Indochina. Elected prime minister in June 1954 during the Geneva Conference and met a self-imposed deadline to reach an armistice there. Ousted from office soon after; died in 1982.
Charles Marie Le Myre de Vilers	First civilian governor of Indochina, 1879–83. Relatively enlightened compared to previous military governors; during his tenure, Cochinchina was completely pacified and began to be developed economically.
Napoleon III	Born in 1808, nephew of Napoleon Bonaparte. Proclaimed himself emperor after staging a coup in 1851. His wife, Eugénie, a devout Catholic, urged him to promote Christianity in Indochina, but he hesitated because of domestic commitments. Died in 1873.
Henri Navarre	Commander of the French forces in Indochina; chose to fight at Dienbienphu, a site he selected as part of a strategy to assault the Vietminh from various bases and also to protect Laos.
Paul Louis Philastre	A "native affairs" officer sympathetic to the Vietnamese; openly decried French "aggression," but negotiated treaty that in 1879 gave France control over Indochina.

Pierre Pigneau de Béhaine	Eighteenth-century missionary in Vietnam who dreamed of building an empire for France in Asia. Befriended Nguyen Anh, later the Emperor Gia Long, and negotiated a treaty on his behalf in 1787 with Louis XVI.
Léon Pignon	High commissioner for Indochina, 1948–50; earlier had been an adviser to d'Argenlieu; strongly opposed compromise with the Vietminh, but resisted giving latitude to the Bao Dai regime.
Alexandre de Rhodes	Seventeenth-century Jesuit missionary who perfected *quoc ngu,* transcribing the Chinese characters used to write Vietnamese into the Roman alphabet. Conceived of training Vietnamese priests to propagate Christianity.
Jean Sainteny	A former banker in Hanoi, sent to Vietnam in 1945 to negotiate on behalf of France with Ho Chi Minh, whom he befriended. Arranged the secret talks between Kissinger and Le Duc Tho in Paris in 1972.
Etienne Valluy	Successor to Leclerc in 1946 as commander in Indochina. Issued orders to attack Vietminh only five weeks after France had negotiated an agreement with Ho Chi Minh.

The Americans

Dean Acheson	Secretary of state, 1949–52; persuaded Truman to begin furnishing aid to the French then fighting in Indochina. In 1968, urged Johnson to stop escalating the war and to seek a negotiated solution. He died in 1971.
Spiro Agnew	Governor of Maryland, 1967–68. Chosen by Nixon as vice-president in 1968. Resigned in October 1973 following his indictment for tax evasion. During the Nixon administration he denounced antiwar critics in the most vitriolic terms.
George Ball	Lawyer who served as a senior State Department official in Kennedy and Johnson administrations. Consistently argued against the deepening American involvement in Vietnam.

Chester Bowles	Critic of American commitment to Vietnam; removed from post of under secretary of state by Kennedy in 1963 and sent to India as ambassador. Conducted a mission to Cambodia in 1968 to repair relations with Prince Norodom Sihanouk.
McGeorge Bundy	Harvard professor and dean who joined Kennedy administration in 1961 as head of national security council staff, a post he continued to hold under Johnson until 1966. One of the "wise men" who urged Johnson to de-escalate the war in 1968.
William Bundy	Brother of McGeorge, served with CIA for ten years until 1961, when he shifted to Defense Department during the Kennedy administration. Later, as assistant secretary of state for Far Eastern affairs under Johnson, played a key role in formulating Vietnam policy.
Ellsworth Bunker	Born in 1894, alternated between private enterprise and government service. American ambassador in Saigon, 1967–73.
Frank Church	Senator from Idaho, 1957–81, chairman of Foreign Relations Committee, 1975–81; incurred the wrath of Johnson by criticizing American involvement in Vietnam.
Clark Clifford	Distinguished Washington lawyer, appointed secretary of defense by Johnson in 1968 to replace Robert McNamara; quickly maneuvered to steer Johnson away from further escalation of the war.
Lucien Conein	French-born CIA agent who served as liaison between Ambassador Henry Cabot Lodge and the South Vietnamese generals who overthrew Diem in 1963. Previously served in Vietnam with the OSS at end of World War II.
A. Peter Dewey	Lieutenant colonel in the OSS, assigned to Saigon in 1945; accidentally killed by the Vietminh in September; first American to die in Vietnam.
John Foster Dulles	Secretary of state, 1953–59, and strong anti-Communist who favored full support for the French in Indochina; he failed to dissuade them from compromising with the Vietminh at 1954 Geneva Conference; died in 1959.

Elbridge Durbrow	Ambassador to South Vietnam, 1957–61; outwardly voiced confidence in Diem regime but privately warned of its lack of effectiveness.
Dwight D. Eisenhower	President, 1953–61; decided against intervening to help France at Dienbienphu, but had furnished aid to French before then, and endorsed support for Diem after 1955. He died in 1969.
Daniel Ellsberg	Defense Department official who served in Vietnam in 1967; participated in the group that compiled the "Pentagon Papers" and later purloined the documents and gave them to *The New York Times,* which published them in 1971.
Gerald R. Ford	Named vice-president following Agnew's resignation; became president after Nixon's resignation in 1974; had been Republican minority leader of House of Representatives, 1965–73.
J. William Fulbright	Senator from Arkansas, 1945–79; as chairman of Foreign Relations Committee, managed the Tonkin Gulf resolution, which in 1964 gave Johnson the power to commit American forces to Southeast Asia. He soon turned against the war, and held hearings criticizing the conflict.
Alexander Haig	After commanding an infantry division in Vietnam, he joined Kissinger's national security council staff in 1969. Was used to negotiate with President Thieu during final phase of the cease-fire talks in 1972, and served briefly as secretary of state (1981–82) in Reagan administration.
Morton Halperin	Young Defense Department official during Johnson administration who became a principal aide to Henry Kissinger. Suspected of giving information to the press, he had his telephone tapped by the FBI. He brought suit against Kissinger following his resignation from the government.
Paul Harkins	General in charge of military advisory mission to South Vietnam in 1963; opposed the coup against Diem; acquired notoriety for insistence on optimistic reporting from his officers.

W. Averell Harriman	Served as assistant secretary of state for Far Eastern affairs, 1961–63, and was instrumental in authorizing American support for the overthrow of Diem. Headed delegation to Paris peace talks in 1968, when he was seventy-seven years old.
Roger Hilsman	Harriman's successor as assistant secretary of state for Far Eastern affairs (1963–64) and an advocate of counterinsurgency in Vietnam. Played a key role in promoting the coup against Diem and resigned from the government soon after Johnson took office.
Hubert H. Humphrey	Senator from Minnesota, 1948–64; became vice-president under Johnson; ran for the presidency as the Democratic candidate in 1968, losing by a narrow margin to Richard Nixon. His supporters claimed that he was defeated by Johnson's reluctance to halt the bombing of North Vietnam. He died in 1978.
Lyndon B. Johnson	Senator from Texas, 1949–61, when he became Kennedy's vice-president. Entered the White House after Kennedy's assassination in November 1963; chose not to run again in 1968. He died in 1973.
George Kennan	Specialist in Russian and Soviet affairs, was head of State Department's policy-planning staff in the late 1940s when he conceived of "containment" to block Soviet expansion. This concept, he later explained, had not been designed to apply to places like Vietnam.
John F. Kennedy	Elected president in 1960 after serving since 1953 as senator from Massachusetts; was assassinated in November 1963, three weeks after the murder of Diem.
Robert F. Kennedy	Attorney general in his brother John's administration, served as senator from New York from 1965 until his assassination in June 1968. His decision to run for presidency on Democratic ticket alarmed Johnson.

Henry Kissinger	Appointed national security adviser by Nixon in 1969; in that capacity he negotiated with Le Duc Tho until the Paris peace settlement was achieved in January 1973. Nixon later appointed him secretary of state, a position he continued to hold under President Ford, 1973–77.
Robert Komer	Nicknamed the "Blowtorch" because of his dynamism, he managed the pacification programs in Vietnam in 1967 and 1968; became a senior Defense Department official in the Carter administration.
Melvin Laird	Republican congressman from Wisconsin, 1953–69; secretary of defense (1969–72) in Nixon administration; strongly favored American troop withdrawal from Vietnam and invented the term "Vietnamization."
Edward Lansdale	Air force officer during World War II; in 1955, under CIA auspices, served as an adviser to Diem. Returned to Vietnam in 1966 as a special assistant to Ambassadors Henry Cabot Lodge and Ellsworth Bunker.
Henry Cabot Lodge	Born in 1902, grandson of an illustrious senator, he held several important public posts, among them senator from Massachusetts and ambassador to the United Nations during the Eisenhower administration. Served two tours as ambassador to Vietnam, the first, 1963–64, the second, 1965–67; played a key role in the overthrow of the Diem regime.
Robert McNamara	As secretary of defense for seven years, 1961–68, was a senior policymaker of the Vietnam war. A Ford Motor Company executive from 1946 until he joined the Kennedy administration in 1961, he resigned in 1968 to become president of the World Bank when disenchanted with the war.
Mike Mansfield	Mining engineer who later taught political science at the University of Montana before his election to Congress; was a senator from Montana, 1952–76. An early supporter of Diem who later turned against the war. Carter appointed him ambassador

to Japan, a post he continued to hold in the Reagan administration.

Graham Martin

Last American ambassador to South Vietnam, from 1973 until the fall of Saigon in 1975. Former newspaperman, he held several high diplomatic posts, including ambassador to Thailand and to Italy.

Wayne Morse

Senator from Oregon, 1945–69, he was a maverick who early on almost single-handedly opposed the Vietnam war. Only he and Senator Ernest Gruening of Alaska voted against the Tonkin Gulf resolution in August 1964. He died in 1974.

Richard M. Nixon

Elected to Congress from California following service in navy during World War II. Served two terms as vice-president under Eisenhower, 1952–60, but defeated for presidency by John Kennedy. Won presidential elections in 1968 and 1972 but forced by the Watergate scandal to resign in August 1974.

Frederick Nolting

Scholarly diplomat from Virginia who spent most of his career in Europe before Kennedy appointed him ambassador to South Vietnam in 1961. Served in Saigon until the summer of 1963; embittered by American complicity in the overthrow of Diem, he resigned to go into banking.

Charlton Ogburn

One of the handful of State Department officials who during the late 1940s and early 1950s warned against American involvement in Southeast Asia. He later became a successful writer.

Archimedes Patti

OSS officer during World War II who was assigned to assist Ho Chi Minh's guerrillas fight the Japanese. Spent several months with Ho in Hanoi in late 1945 and helped him to draft the Vietnamese declaration of independence.

Arthur Radford

Admiral and chairman of joint chiefs of staff, 1953–57, and a strong partisan of American intervention to rescue French at Dienbienphu; overruled by Eisenhower.

Matthew Ridgway	General and chief of staff of army during Eisenhower administration; strongly opposed American involvement in Vietnam. Believed that United States could not conduct a land war in Asia. Had commanded U.S. forces in Korea in 1950 and 1951 and also served as allied commander in Europe for two years thereafter.
Franklin D. Roosevelt	President from 1933 until his death in 1945; paid little attention to Indochina during World War II, considering the region to be a military rather than political problem.
Walt W. Rostow	Went from a distinguished academic position at the Massachusetts Institute of Technology to a top State Department job during the Kennedy administration. As Johnson's national security adviser (1966–68), he was a partisan of forceful action in Vietnam.
Dean Rusk	Secretary of state, 1961–68, under Kennedy and Johnson; devoted more years to Vietnam than any other senior American official, having faced the problem as assistant secretary of state for Far Eastern affairs as early as 1950; consistently favored strong American involvement, arguing that "aggression" had to be stopped.
Walter Bedell Smith	General who served as under secretary of state, 1953–54; in that capacity headed American delegation at 1954 Geneva Conference.
Maxwell Taylor	Kennedy's favorite general; served as chairman of joint chiefs of staff, 1962–64; recommended a deeper American commitment to Vietnam in 1961. Johnson appointed him ambassador to South Vietnam in 1964, a post he held for more than a year.
Harry S. Truman	As president, 1945–52, took the first step toward involving United States in Vietnam when he agreed to Dean Acheson's proposal to aid French in 1949. His move to help Greece and Turkey against Communist threats, known as the Truman Doctrine, was an early phase in the containment policy. He died in 1972.
Cyrus Vance	Deputy secretary of defense under Robert McNamara, 1964–67, afterward becoming Averell Harri-

man's chief associate at the Paris peace talks that began in 1968. As secretary of state (1977–80) in the Carter administration, favored diplomatic relations with Communist regime in Vietnam.

Paul Warnke

Washington lawyer who joined Defense Department as general counsel in 1966 and became assistant secretary of defense a year later. He helped to turn Clark Clifford against the war.

William Westmoreland

Appointed head of military advisory mission to Vietnam in 1964 by Johnson; until his departure in 1968, commanded U.S. combat forces in the country. Later became chief of staff of the army.

Earle Wheeler

Chairman of joint chiefs of staff, 1964–70, and principal military figure in Washington overseeing the Vietnam war; excelled as a military politician to advance the interests of the Pentagon.

Others

Leonid Brezhnev

Secretary-general of the Soviet Communist party, 1964–83; invited Nixon to summit meeting in Moscow in spring of 1972, even though United States had intensified its bombing of North Vietnam.

Anthony Eden

British foreign secretary who served along with Vyacheslav Molotov as cochairman of Geneva Conference of 1954. Instrumental in persuading Prime Minister Winston Churchill to reject Eisenhower's suggestion for joint intervention to help the French at Dienbienphu. He died in 1977.

Douglas Gracey

Commander in charge of the British force that entered Saigon in September 1945 to disarm the Japanese; against orders, released and armed interned French troops in the city, thereby triggering clashes between the French and the Vietminh.

Aleksei Kosygin

Soviet prime minister from 1964 until his death in 1980; traveled to Hanoi in February 1965 in an attempt to persuade the North Vietnamese to negotiate with the United States, a visit that was aborted when American bombing of the north began.

Lon Nol	As Cambodian defense minister, he led *coup d'état* that ousted Prince Norodom Sihanouk from power in March 1970, an event that opened the way for American and South Vietnamese incursions into Cambodia. Went into exile in Hawaii when the Communists took over in 1975.
Mao Zedong	Chinese Communist party chairman; first warned North Vietnamese against negotiating with the United States, then invited Nixon to Beijing in February 1972. He died in 1976.
Vyacheslav Molotov	Cochairman with Eden of the 1954 Geneva Conference; delivered verdict that compelled Vietnamese Communists to settle for less than their objectives; agreed to cancel Vietnamese elections two years later, again disappointing the Hanoi leaders.
Souvanna Phouma	Prince who was made prime minister of Laos in 1962 following a conference at Geneva; held the post until the Communist takeover in 1975. Laos, occupied by North Vietnamese troops and bombed by the United States, was a devastated victim of the war in Vietnam.
Pol Pot	Pseudonym of Cambodian Communist leader who slaughtered an estimated two million of his people in an effort to make Cambodia an agricultural utopia; ousted from power after the Vietnamese invasion in late 1978, he continued to wage a guerrilla war.
Norodom Sihanouk	Enthroned as king of Cambodia by the French in 1941, later abdicated; maneuvered tirelessly to preserve Cambodia's neutrality, but was overthrown while on a trip to France in March 1970. Later lived in China and North Korea, and tried to regain power in Cambodia.
Robert Thompson	British officer and scholar who, after directing counterinsurgency efforts in Malaya, arrived in South Vietnam in the early 1960s to undertake the same task as an adviser to Diem; later an unofficial adviser to Nixon.

Zhou Enlai   As China's foreign minister, reached compromise in Geneva in 1954 with Mendès-France that ended the French war in Indochina; with Kissinger, as prime minister, arranged Nixon's visit to Beijing in February 1972. In both instances, incurred the wrath of North Vietnamese, who accused him of conniving with their enemies. He died in 1976.

Notes on Sources

The material for this book has been derived from three principal sources: my experiences and observations as a journalist covering the war; the interviews conducted within recent years for *Vietnam: A Television History*; and the vast body of literature published on the subject.

Having preserved the voluminous notes I had gathered during more than thirty years as a reporter, I was able to recapture the past—as one might from a diary. The notes were invaluable in at least two important respects. They helped me to evoke the atmosphere of certain periods, to reconstruct events as they were seen and felt then, rather than relying on my own dim memories or on the often faded or distorted recollections of participants. And they provided me with the attitudes expressed at the time by officials and others, many of whom revised their earlier views to conform to later policies and patterns.

Whenever possible, I have cited people by name in the text. In instances where statements are quoted anonymously, it is that I judged an attribution to be superfluous—or simply because my notes are incomplete.

To have depended solely on information gathered contemporaneously would have of course been grossly inadequate for this effort to present a comprehensive history. For one thing, several episodes were complicated and confused as they occurred and had to be unraveled afterward to be understood and described in their context. Also, the process of reaching decisions in Washington, Saigon, and especially Hanoi was shrouded in secrecy impenetrable to an outsider. But above all, the military, political, social, economic, and human dimensions of the conflict were too big for any single individual to encompass as the struggle unfolded. In particular, it was extremely difficult to report on the Communist side during the war, since captured documents, propaganda, and interrogations of prisoners or defectors furnished only part of the story. I believe that the North Vietnamese and Vietcong leaders made a serious error in denying access to the Western news media.

The scope of this history owes much to the interviews for the companion television project conducted by my associates and myself over a span of some three years in the United States, Europe, and Vietnam. The cast of characters ranges from ordinary soldiers and civilians to the major figures on both sides. Nearly every leader whose cooperation we requested agreed to speak on camera, and preliminary talks with them were frequently as useful for the book as for their filmed interviews. They are quoted by name in the text, thus obviating the need for footnotes. I approached them with an awareness that their recollections might be self-serving; persons formerly in positions of authority tend to justify their conduct, especially when the strategies they promoted still arouse controversy. But it was elementary journalism to check their accounts with their assistants and rivals and by consulting the enormous documentation that has emerged since the war. This is not to suggest that the record is complete. I regret the refusal of Robert McNamara, Le Duc Tho, and Nguyen Van Thieu to be interviewed personally. However, their aides did speak with me, and I was able to use other sources recently made public.

My seven weeks in Vietnam from late January through March 1981 afforded me a unique opportunity to study the conflict from an angle largely neglected until now because of the regime's reluctance to open its doors to Western writers. Obtaining a visa entailed more than a year of negotiations, often through intermediaries, with the Vietnamese missions in London and Paris, and at the United Nations in New York. The trip was finally approved, presumably because the Vietnamese authorities were eager to tell their side of the story, and officials in Vietnam received my television colleagues and me hospitably. It would be naive to assume, however, that a reporter can function freely in a totalitarian state like present-day Vietnam. But, having operated under rigid conditions in the Soviet Union, China, and other Communist societies, I found the Vietnamese by comparison to be surprisingly candid, especially in private conversations. I was struck by the extent to which older Vietnamese Communists, who began their revolutionary careers in the struggle against French colonial rule, still showed the imprint of French cultural influence.

Besides having been the first television war, Vietnam was also "the first Xerox war," to borrow Professor Lawrence Lichty's phrase. A stupendous amount of paper was generated during the conflict, and much of it is not yet sorted out. The most compact collection of documents covering the period through 1968 is *The Pentagon Papers*, edited by Mike Gravel, 5 vols. (Boston: Beacon Press, 1971). Many key documents are also included in *Vietnam: The Definitive Documentation of Human Decisions*, edited by Gareth Porter, 2 vols. (Stanfordville, N.Y.: Earl Coleman Enterprises, 1979). A handy reference is *Background Information Relating to Southeast Asia and Vietnam*, 7th ed., Senate Committee on Foreign Relations (Washington: U.S. Government Printing Office, 1975). Another useful guide to events from 1961 through 1973 is *South Vietnam: U.S.–Communist Confrontation in Southeast Asia*, 7 vols. (New York: Facts on File, 1966–1973). One of the most valuable studies of the formulation of Vietnam policy during the Kennedy and Johnson administrations, alas unpublished, has been prepared by William Gibbon with the assistance of Patricia McAdams for the Congressional Research Service. I consulted material as well at the John F. Kennedy Library in Boston and at the Lyndon B. Johnson Library at the University of Texas in Austin.

An interesting document, unfortunately written in jargon, is the Communist history of the war—*Vietnam: The Anti–U.S. Resistance for National Salvation 1954–1975: Military Events* (Hanoi: People's Army Publishing House, 1980), which has been translated into English by the Joint Publications Research Service, Arlington, Virginia. Material on the Communist side of the war is also available at the Indochina Archive, University of California, Berkeley; Department of Asian Studies, Cornell University, Ithaca, New York; and the RAND Corporation, Santa Monica, California.

Documents, whatever their origin, ought to be approached with caution. They frequently reflect the efforts of military and civilian bureaucrats to advance their own proposals, and often do not represent policy. The final American decisions were invariably made by the president, often for a variety of motives that are not always spelled out in memorandums—or even elucidated in memoirs. On the Communist side, the politburo in Hanoi directed policy, and few of its deliberations have been made public. The decisions of the South Vietnamese government tended to be made on a personal rather than institutional basis. Thus it was crucial for the purposes of this history that I supplement the available documentation with interviews, bearing in mind that the participants in the war were rarely models of dispassionate objectivity.

Chapter 1: The War Nobody Won

As should be apparent from the narrative, much of the material in this chapter comes from my direct observation. I was startled to discover that the name of Chester M. Ovnand, one of the first two American servicemen to be killed during the Vietnam era, is misspelled "Ovnard" on the Vietnam Memorial; officials at the Pentagon promise that the indignity will be corrected.

The discussion of "manifest destiny" as a factor in U.S. foreign policy is partly based on an interview with Professor Daniel Bell of Harvard as well as on his article "The End of American Exceptionalism," in *The Public Interest*, No. 41, Fall 1975. A lucid and persuasive account of American imperialism is contained in Ernest R. May, *"Lessons" of the Past* (New York: Oxford University Press, 1973; London: Oxford University Press, 1974). A comprehensive quantitative survey of present American views on Vietnam is Louis Harris and Associates, "Myths and Realities: A Study of Attitudes Toward Vietnam Era Veterans," conducted for the Veterans Administration, July 1980. The literature on the problems of Vietnam veterans is extensive; among many documents, I consulted Arthur Egendorf, "Research on Vietnam Veterans: Major Themes and Implications for Post-War Healing," an unpublished manuscript. An important book on the subject is Gloria Emerson, *Winners and Losers: Battles, Retreats, Gains, Losses and Ruins from Long War* (New York: Random House, 1976).

Colonel Harry G. Summers, Jr., explained his ideas on American strategy in Vietnam to me in personal interviews. His appraisal is amplified in his book, *On Strategy: The Vietnam War in Context* (Carlyle, Pa.: U.S. War College, 1981), and also in his unpublished paper, "The U.S. Army Institutional Response to Vietnam," delivered at an International Military History Symposium on August 4, 1982. I recommend four other postwar studies: Anthony Lake, ed., *The Legacy of Vietnam* (New York: New York University Press, 1976); W. Scott Thompson and Donaldson D. Frizell, eds., *The Lessons of Vietnam* (New York: Crane, Russak, 1977); Richard A. Hunt and Richard H. Shultz, Jr., *Lessons from an Unconventional War* (New York: Pergamon Press, 1982); and Drew Middleton, "Vietnam and the Military Mind," *The New York Times Magazine*, January 10, 1982. Numerous opinion polls have been published describing the impact of Vietnam on American attitudes toward Central America. I have referred to three: "Poll Shows a Majority Want U.S. to Stay Out of Salvador," *The New York Times*, March 21, 1982; "Majority in Poll Oppose Reagan on El Salvador," *Washington Post*, March 24, 1982; and "Poll Finds a Majority Fears Entanglement in Central America," *Washington Post*, May 25, 1983. For a comparison of early American sentiment toward Vietnam, the authoritative work on the subject is John E. Mueller, *War, Presidents and Public Opinion* (New York: John Wiley, 1973). I frequently consulted Mueller as well as other public opinion specialists, among them Ben Wattenberg, in doing my research.

The description of Vietnam today is based on my own visit there in 1981. I published accounts of my trip in considerably different form in "Hanoi: The Problems of Peace," *The Atlantic*, August 1981, and in "Saigon: 'Liberated' But Still Capitalist," *The Atlantic*, November 1981. I also recommend William Shawcross, "In a Grim Country," *New York Review of Books*, September 24, 1981. For an account of life in postwar Vietnam by a Vietnamese who escaped to the United States, see Nguyen Long, with Harry H. Kendell, *After Saigon Fell* (Berkeley: University of California Press, 1981). The repression of human rights in Vietnam has been described in the annual reports of Amnesty International as well as in several other studies, among them Ginette Sagan and Stephen Denney, *Violations of Human Rights in the Socialist Republic of Vietnam* (Palo Alto, Calif.: Aurora Foundation, 1983) and *Charter 78: The Prison System in South Vietnam*, Que Me, Paris, 1978. The experience of one man in a "re-education" camp is related in Nguyen Ngoc Ngan, *The Will of Heaven* (New York: E. P. Dutton, 1981). A solid journalistic report on the Indochinese refugees is Barry Wain, *The Refused* (New York: Simon & Schuster, 1981).

For information on the Cambodian genocide, I have relied on several Cambodian sources, among them my friend Kiri Tith. Two recent accounts of the situation in Cambodia by Elizabeth Becker are "Recovery After Pol Pot Relapses to Poverty," *Washington Post*, February 28, 1983, and "Cambodia Blames Ousted Leader, Not Party," *Washington Post*, March 1, 1983.

The material in this chapter comes entirely from published sources. Tribute ought to be paid to Joseph Buttinger, an American who researched the history of Vietnam long before the subject evoked any interest in the United States. Buttinger was critical of both the French colonialists and the Vietnamese Communists, and his style is somewhat cranky. But his books are readable and credible. For this chapter I have drawn from *The Smaller Dragon: A Political History of Vietnam* (New York: Frederick A. Praeger; London: Stevens & Sons, 1958). A sound look at the region in general is Georges Coedes, *The Making of Southeast Asia* (Berkeley: University of California Press, 1964; London: Routledge & Kegan Paul, 1965); an introduction to the area is Stanley Karnow, *Southeast Asia* (New York: Life World Library, 1962). Kavalam M. Pannikar, a wise and distinguished Indian diplomat, has written perceptively of the Western impact on Asia in a classic book, *Asia and Western Dominance* (New York: John Day, n.d.). I recommend two books with a Marxist tilt, both superbly researched: Jean Chesneaux, *Contribution à l'histoire de la nation Vietnamienne* (Paris: Editions Sociales, 1955), and Le Thanh Khoi, *Le Viêt-nam, histoire et civilisation* (Paris: Editions de Minuit, 1955).

The early period of French colonialism is solidly described in: John Cady, *The Roots of French Imperialism in Asia* (Ithaca: Cornell University Press, 1954; London: Oxford University Press, 1954); Thomas E. Ennis, *French Policy and Developments in Indochina* (Chicago: University of Chicago Press, 1956); Henri Marc and Pierre Cony, *Indochine française* (Paris: Editions France-Empire, 1946); Milton E. Osborne, *The French Presence in Cochinchina and Cambodia: Rule and Response (1859–1905)* (Ithaca: Cornell University Press, 1969); and Charles Robequain, *L'Indochine française* (Paris: Armand Colin, 1935). Other accounts, somewhat on the colorful side, are: Charles Gosselin, *L'Empire d'Annam* (Paris: Perrin, 1904); Georges Grandjean, *L'Epopée jaune* (Paris: Société française d'éditions littéraires et techniques, E. Malfere, 1929); and Tao Kim Hai, *L'Indochine française* (Tours: Maison Mame, n.d.). A splendid book of old French photographs is Georges Buis and Charles Daney, *Quand les Français decouvraient l'Indochine* (Paris: Editions Herscher, 1981).

The role of the French missionaries in Indochina is rather luridly portrayed in Tao Kim Hai, mentioned above, and in Just-Jean Etienne, *Souvenirs et récits d'un ancien missionaire à la Cochinchine et au Tong-King* (Tours: Maison Mame, 1864). Osborne, cited above, contains a serious analysis of the attraction of Christianity for many Vietnamese, as does Etienne Vo-duc-Hanh, *La Place du Catholicisme dans les relations entre la France et le Viêt-Nam de 1851 à 1870* (Leiden: Brill, 1969).

The parliamentary debates over the early French involvement in Indochina were loud and lusty. For the reader diligent enough to pursue the details, I recommend the *Annales de la Chambre des Députés* for October 30, October 31, and December 7, 1883, and March 30, 1885. Jules Ferry, the leading French imperialist of his time, makes his case in *Le Tonkin et la mère-patrie* (Paris: Victor-Havard, 1890).

Chapter 3: The Heritage of Vietnamese Nationalism

Not until the early 1950s, when I began to report from Paris on the French war in Indochina, did I acquire some very sketchy notions of the Vietnamese nationalist movement. The little I learned at the time came not from books, but from a few members of the Vietnamese community in Paris. As I mention in the narrative, I met these Vietnamese, along with African nationalists, purely by chance: I rented a room in an apartment owned by Jean Longuet, the great-grandson of Karl Marx, whose father, a prominent socialist leader of the 1920s, had been a vigorous opponent of colonialism. The apartment in the Rue Cassini, near the Paris Observatory, had belonged to Balzac, and under the auspices of Longuet *fils*, a smooth article with no particular political leanings, it became a meeting place for various nationalists. Partly because of these connections, my boss at the *Time* and *Life* bureau, Frank White, assigned me to cover the nationalist "beat," among my other duties. It was in that capacity that I had the extraordinary opportunity to retrace Ho Chi Minh's footsteps through Paris, described in the narrative. I saved my original notes—a lesson for young reporters who jot their observations on the backs of envelopes.

During my visit to Vietnam in 1981, I sought out several elderly Vietnamese Communists to ask them to recapture their recollections of their experiences in the nationalist movement. The Museum of the Revolution in Hanoi also features a good many souvenirs from early nationalist times. The literature of the period is rich, but I will cite only a limited number of the published materials for reasons of space.

The books by Buttinger, Chesneaux, and Le Thanh Khoi already mentioned emphasize the important point that a Vietnamese national identity, sharpened as a result of repeated wars with China, existed for several centuries before the European arrival. A contemporary Vietnamese Communist writer, Nguyen Khac Vien, underlines the same theme in *Tradition and Revolution in Vietnam* (Berkeley: Indochina Resource Center, 1974). Two fine accounts of traditional Vietnamese society under the impact of French colonialism are Ngo Vinh Long, *Before the Revolution: The Vietnamese Peasants Under the French* (Cambridge: MIT Press, 1973) and Alexander Woodside, *Community and Revolution in Modern Vietnam* (Boston: Houghton Mifflin, 1976). Osborne, already cited, contains a fascinating description of the *collaborateurs*, the Vietnamese who were drawn into the French colonial orbit.

Paul Doumer, the governor general who made Indochina a profitable venture for France, has told his story in florid *belle époque* style in *L'Indo-Chine française: Souvenirs* (Paris: Vuibert et Nony, 1905). Joseph Buttinger also relates the story with a critical eye in *Vietnam: A Dragon Embattled*, Vol. I, *From Colonialism to the Vietminh* (New York: Frederick A. Praeger; London: Pall Mall, 1967). How the French colonial administration organized the opium business is recounted in Alfred W. McCoy, *The Politics of Heroin in Southeast Asia* (New York: Harper & Row, 1972). For some of the flavor of French colonial life in Indochina, I recommend M. Franklin Kline, *Official Guide for Shippers and Travellers to the Principal Ports of the World*, issued by the Osaka Shosen Kaisha, Osaka, Japan. Kline, who was my father-in-law, published his weighty guide annually from 1913 until his retirement in 1934. It contains several quaint chapters, illustrated lavishly, on the comforts of Saigon, Hanoi, and Haiphong. Despite the complacency of the French about their Asian possession, a few French writers warned of the potential dangers that lay ahead in Indochina unless the colonial system was liberalized. One of the earliest of these warnings came from Jean Ajalbert, *Les Nuages sur l'Indochine* (Paris: Louis-Michaud, 1912). A later book, which caused a sensation on its publication, was Andrée Viollis, *Indochine S.O.S.*, with a preface by André Malraux (Paris: Gallimard, 1935). Because of its influence on French public opinion, *Indochine S.O.S.* is the only foreign book displayed in the Museum of the Revolution in Hanoi.

Two landmark works on the rise of modern Vietnamese nationalism are by David G. Marr: *Vietnamese Anticolonialism 1885–1925* (Berkeley: University of California Press, 1971) and *Vietnamese Tradition on Trial 1920–1945* (Berkeley: University of California Press, 1981). Again, Buttinger, Chesneaux, and Le Thanh Khoi make important contributions, as do Ellen J. Hammer, *The Struggle for Indochina* (Stanford: Stanford University Press; London: Oxford University Press, 1954) and John T. McAlister, Jr., *Vietnam: The Origins of Revolution* (New York: Alfred A. Knopf, 1969). A massive research job with a Marxist slant is Thomas Hodgkin, *Vietnam: The Revolutionary Path* (New York: St. Martin's Press, 1981). Some interesting material on the relationship between the Soviet Union and the burgeoning Vietnamese Communist movement can be found in Charles B. McLane, *Soviet Strategies in Southeast Asia* (Princeton: Princeton University Press, 1966).

Separating fact from fancy in the life of Ho Chi Minh is not easy. The most readable book on Ho is Jean Lacouture, trans. Peter Wiles, *Ho Chi Minh: A Political Biography* (New York: Random House; London: Allen Lane, 1968). A slim volume, which seems to me to merit attention, is by a former OSS agent who knew Ho personally—Charles Fenn, *Ho Chi Minh: a Biographical Introduction* (New York: Charles Scribner's Sons; London: Studio Vista, 1973). Ho himself can be read in Nguyên-Aï-Quôc, *Le Procès de la colonisation française* (Paris: Librairie du Travail, 1923); Ho Chi Minh, *Selected Works,* vols. I–IV (Hanoi: Foreign Languages Publishing House, 1960–62); and Ho Chi Minh, *Prison Diary* (Hanoi: Foreign Languages Publishing House, 1966). I collected some interesting anecdotes on Ho during my 1981 visit to Hanoi from Hoang Quang Viet, one of the early Vietminh leaders; Hoang Tung, chief party propagandist and the editor of *Nhan Dan*, the official Communist party newspaper; and Ho's secretary, Tuu Ky. A colorful article on Ho's numerous aliases is "His Many Names and Travels," in *Vietnam Courier*, No. 5, Hanoi, 1981.

Chapter 4: The War with the French

The narrative features eyewitness accounts by many Vietnamese who recalled to me in interviews their memories of World War II and its aftermath in Vietnam. Several former OSS officers also contributed their recollections, among them Lucien Conein, Archimedes L. A. Patti, and Frank White. The role of the OSS is also described in R. Harris Smith, *OSS: The Secret History of America's First Central Intelligence Agency* (Berkeley: University of California Press, 1972); *Causes, Origins, and Lessons of the Vietnam War*, Senate Committee on Foreign Relations (Washington, D.C.: U.S. Government Printing Office, 1973); and Archimedes L. A. Patti, *Why Viet Nam? Prelude to America's Albatross* (Berkeley: University of California Press, 1980). Unfortunately, the OSS documents of the period, held by the CIA, have not yet been declassified. The background to American policy toward Indochina at the time can be found in *Foreign Relations of the United States, 1944–1947*, Department of State (Washington, D.C.: U.S. Government Printing Office, 1972) and in *The Pentagon Papers*, Vol. I. Several interesting documents are also contained in the Porter collection. I have also read the British dispatches from Saigon in a collection of declassified British Foreign Office documents from the period.

The most vivid and credible account of the period, albeit written from a French viewpoint, is Philippe Devillers, *Histoire du Viêt-Nam de 1940 à 1952* (Paris: Editions du Seuil, 1953). Another important book on the period is Jean Sainteny, *Histoire d'une paix manquée* (Paris: Amiot-Dumont, 1953). A short but dramatic French account of the outbreak of hostilities is Jean Julien Fonde, "Il y a vingt-cinq ans à Hanoi," from *La Revue militaire générale*, Paris, 1972. Two polemical volumes on French policy at the time are Alfred Georges, *Charles de Gaulle et la guerre d'Indochine* (Paris: Nouvelles Editions Latines, 1974), and Claude de Boisanger, *On pouvait eviter la guerre d'Indochine: Souvenirs 1941–1945* (Paris: Librairie d'Amérique et d'Orient, 1971). Buttinger's second volume of *Vietnam: A Dragon Embattled*, subtitled *Vietnam at War*, tells the story well.

Chesneaux and Hodgkin present the Vietminh point of view in detail. The most authoritative Vietminh account, however, is General Vo Nguyen Giap, *Unforgettable Days* (Hanoi: Foreign Languages Publishing House, 1978). I am especially indebted to my friend and colleague Robert Trumbull, of *The New York Times*, one of the most talented correspondents to cover Asia, for his reminiscences of Ho Chi Minh during the late 1940s. Some of his recollections are in his book, *The Scrutable East* (New York: David McKay, 1964).

From 1950 through 1954, the period covered in this chapter, the French struggle to retain Indochina intensified and collapsed as America's indirect involvement in the region deepened. My dispatches from Paris during those years are woven into the narrative. I spent considerable time in the French National Assembly, listening to tedious debates on the war as successive governments of the Fourth Republic repeatedly promised progress. The same theme was repeated at regular military briefings by aristocratic young French officers in custom-tailored uniforms as their comrades died in droves in the jungles and rice fields of Indochina. The climax came when Pierre Mendès-France became prime minister in 1954, an event I reported in detail.

The aforementioned books by Buttinger, Chesneaux, Devillers, and Hammer are valuable. The corruption that pervaded Vietnam during the French war is dramatically told by the French journalist Lucien Bodard in *The Quicksand War: Prelude to Vietnam* (Boston: Atlantic-Little, Brown; London: Faber & Faber, 1967). Bao Dai's autobiography, poignant and pathetic, is *Le Dragon d'Annam* (Paris: Plon, 1980). S. J. Perelman's improbable encounter with Bao Dai appears in *Westward Ha!* (New York: Simon & Schuster, 1948). A highly critical description of different aspects of the French war is compiled in a special issue, August-September 1953, of *Les Temps Modernes*, the French monthly magazine directed by Jean-Paul Sartre.

The French war can be refought in the memoirs of France's defeated politicians and generals. The works, many of them polemical and self-justifying, include General Paul Ely, *L'Indochine dans la tourmente* (Paris: Plon, 1964); Joseph Laniel, *Le Drame indochinois: De Dien-Bien-Phu au pari de Genève* (Paris: Plon, 1957); General Henri Navarre, *Agonie de l'Indochine* (Paris: Plon, 1956); and General Yves Gras, *Histoire de la guerre d'Indochine* (Paris: Plon, 1979). The best writer on the French war, however, was Bernard Fall, who in addition to his many articles produced two superb books: *Street Without Joy: Insurgency in Indochina 1946–1963* (Harrisburg, Pa.: Stackpole Books, 1961; rev. ed., 1963) and *Hell in a Very Small Place: The Siege of Dien Bien Phu* (Philadelphia: J. B. Lippincott Co., 1966; London: Pall Mall, 1967). To add a personal note, Fall was unusually generous in sharing his knowledge and wisdom with reporters like myself. The battle of Dienbienphu has also been described dramatically by Jules Roy, *The Battle of Dien Bien Phu,* trans. Robert Baldick (New York: Harper & Row; London: Faber & Faber, 1965). The authoritative Communist account is Vo Nguyen Giap, *Dien Bien Phu* (Hanoi: Foreign Languages Publishing House, 1962). I also interviewed several Vietminh veterans of Dienbienphu in Vietnam in 1981.

Two other accounts of the French war are worth mentioning: Edgar O'Ballance, *The Indo-China War 1945–1954: A Study in Guerrilla Warfare* (London: Faber & Faber, 1964) and Robert J. O'Neill, *General Giap* (New York, Frederick A. Praeger; London: Cassell, 1969). A solid study of the Vietminh is Bernard

Fall, *The Viet-Minh Regime*, Ithaca, Cornell University Southeast Asia Program, 1956. A rare study of internal Vietnamese politics during the French war, which I acquired on the black market in Ho Chi Minh City in 1981, is Pierre Dabezies, "*Forces politiques au Viêtnam,*" mimeographed, undated. A classic on the period is Paul Mus, *Viêt-Nam: Sociologie d'une guerre* (Paris: Editions du Seuil, 1950). This basic book on Vietnam has never been translated into English.

The definitive work on the Geneva Conference of 1954, in my opinion, is François Joyaux, *La Chine et le règlement du premier conflit d'Indochine* (Paris: Publications de la Sorbonne, 1979). Based on hitherto classified French foreign ministry documents, it discloses the secret negotiations between Mendès-France and Zhou Enlai to settle the war at the expense of the Vietminh. A primary source is Sir Anthony Eden, *Full Circle: Memoirs of Sir Anthony Eden* (Boston and London: Cassell, 1960). Other books on the conference are Victor Bator, *Vietnam: A Diplomatic Tragedy* (Dobbs Ferry, N.Y.: Oceana Publications, 1965); Philippe Devillers and Jean Lacouture, *End of a War: Indochina 1954*, trans. Alexander Lieven and Adam Roberts (New York: Frederick A. Praeger; London: Pall Mall, 1969); and Melvin Gurtov, *The First Vietnam Crisis* (New York: Columbia University Press, 1967). Also, Jean Lacouture, *Pierre Mendès-France* (Paris: Editions du Seuil, 1981). China and Vietnam have revealed their differences at Geneva; the arguments of the two sides are contained in *The Truth About Vietnam-China Relations Over the Last Thirty Years* (Hanoi: Ministry of Foreign Affairs, 1979) and Hoang Van Hoanh, "Distortion of Facts about Militant Friendship between Viet Nam and China Is Impermissible," *Beijing Review*, No. 49, December 7, 1979. U. Alexis Johnson, a senior member of the American delegation at Geneva, very kindly showed me his unpublished memoir on the conference. Other American documents that pertain to the conference are contained in *Foreign Relations of the United States, 1952–1954*, Department of State, 2 vols. (Washington, D.C.: U.S. Government Printing Office, 1981). Prime Minister Pham Van Dong furnished me with the Vietminh version of the Geneva negotiations during an interview in Hanoi in 1981.

A sound account of the start of the American involvement in Vietnam during the French war is Robert Blum, *Drawing the Line: The Origin of the American Containment Policy in East Asia* (New York: W. W. Norton, 1982). Other documents on the period are contained in *The Pentagon Papers*, vol. I, in Porter, and in the declassified State Department papers just cited. To put the Indochina war into the context of the times, see Harry S. Truman, *Memoirs*, 2 vols. (Garden City, N.Y.: Doubleday; London: Hodder & Stoughton, 1956); Dwight D. Eisenhower, *Mandate for Change* (Garden City, N.Y.: London: Heinemann, 1963); Townsend Hoopes, *The Devil and John Foster Dulles* (Boston: Atlantic-Little, Brown, 1973); and Daniel Yergin, *Shattered Peace* (Boston: Houghton Mifflin, 1977).

I first met Ngo Dinh Diem in Paris in the late spring of 1954, after Bao Dai had appointed him prime minister. The introduction was arranged by Ton That Thien, then a student in France and later to become director of the Vietnam News Agency; Thien now teaches at McGill University in Montreal, and we have remained in contact. During the years after that meeting, I was largely involved in covering the Algerian war as well as other news in Europe and the Middle East. Then, in the spring of 1959, I was appointed bureau chief for *Time* and *Life* magazines in Hong Kong, with responsibility for covering China and Southeast Asia. I made my first trip to Vietnam that summer, at a time when the entire foreign press corps either stationed in Saigon or visiting the city could sit around a small table in the Hôtel Caravelle bar. Access to sources was relatively easy in those early years. But with the rise of the Vietcong insurgency and the mounting dissension in Saigon, the Diem regime became increasingly sensitive to the news media—as did the American mission under Ambassador Frederick Nolting. Nevertheless, there were always enough American military and civilian officials, as well as members of the Diem government, to talk with; many of those I recall are cited in the acknowledgments.

Buttinger's second volume of *Vietnam: a Dragon Embattled* is valuable for the period. Other first-rate books focused on Vietnam itself are: Denis Bloodworth, *An Eye for the Dragon* (New York: Farrar, Straus & Giroux; London: Secker & Warburg, 1970); Bernard Fall, *The Two Viet-Nams: A Political and Military Analysis* (New York: Frederick A. Praeger, 1963; London: Pall Mall, 1964); David Halberstam, *The Making of a Quagmire* (New York: Random House; London: Bodley Head, 1964); Gerald C. Hickey, *Village in Vietnam* (New Haven: Yale University Press, 1964); Donald Lancaste, *The Emancipation of French Indochina* (New York and London: Oxford University Press, 1961); Edward G. Lansdale, *In the Midst of Wars* (New York: Harper & Row, 1972); Nguyen Qui Hung, *Neuf ans de dictature au Sud Viêtnam* (Saigon: privately printed, 1964); Nguyen Thai, *Is South Vietnam Viable?* (Manila: Carmelo & Bauermann, 1962); Jeffrey Race, *War Comes to Long An* (Berkeley: University of California Press, 1972); Robert G. Scigliano, *South Vietnam: Nation Under Stress* (Boston: Houghton Mifflin, 1964); Robert Shaplen, *The Lost Revolution* (New York: Harper & Row, 1965; London: Andre Deutsch, 1966); Tran Van Don, *Our Endless War* (San Rafael, Calif.: Presidio Press, 1978); James Trullinger, *Village at War* (New York: Longman, 1980); and Denis Warner, *The Last Confucian* (New York: Macmillan, 1963; London: Angus & Robertson, 1964). The best novel on the period—and still the best novel on Vietnam—is Graham Greene, *The Quiet American* (London: Heinemann, 1955; New York: Viking Press, 1956).

Fall, cited above, describes North Vietnam during this period. Also see P. J. Honey, *Communism in North Vietnam* (Cambridge: MIT Press, 1963). The first Western book on the Communist insurgent movement is Douglas Pike, *Viet*

Cong: The Organization and Techniques of the National Liberation Front of South Vietnam (Cambridge: MIT Press, 1966). The memoir of a prominent Vietcong leader in the south is Nguyen Thi Dinh, *No Other Road to Take*, trans. Mai V. Elliott, Ithaca, Cornell University Department of Asian Studies, June 1976. The Communist military history published in Vietnam in 1980 also furnishes fresh insights into the beginnings of the Vietcong insurgency, making it clear that the Hanoi leadership played the predominant role in encouraging military action in the south. This was confirmed in an interview with General Giap on French television in February 1983, and also during my interviews in Vietnam.

Among the most perceptive studies of the Vietcong were those undertaken by the RAND Corporation. Though they had little impact on either American or South Vietnamese government policy, they remain valuable for students of the period. Among them are W. P. Davison, *Some Observations on Viet Cong Operations in the Villages*, RM-5267/2-ISA/ARPA (July 1967); John C. Donnell, *Viet Cong Recruitment: Why and How Men Join*, RM-5486/1-ISA/ARPA (December 1967); Nathan Leites, *The Viet Cong Style of Politics*, RM-5487 (May 1968); J. J. Zasloff, *Origins of the Insurgency in South Vietnam, 1954–1960*, RM-5163/2-ISA/ARPA (May 1968); J. J. Zasloff, *Political Motivation of the Viet Cong and the Vietminh Regroupees*, RM-4703/2-ISA/ARPA (May 1968). I have consulted the raw RAND data, and also interviewed many Vietcong prisoners or defectors myself.

The documents on policy-making in the Eisenhower and Kennedy administrations during this period can be found in *The Pentagon Papers* and in the Porter collection. Among the many books on the Kennedy administration, those that touch most directly on Vietnam are George Ball, *The Past Has Another Pattern* (New York: W. W. Norton, 1982); Roger Hilsman, *To Move a Nation* (Garden City, N.Y.: Doubleday, 1967); and Arthur Schlesinger, Jr., *A Thousand Days* (Boston: Houghton Mifflin; London: Andre Deutsch, 1965). I have interviewed many of the principal figures in the Kennedy administration, who are cited in the narrative.

Chapter 7: *Vietnam Is the Place*

Since I was in Vietnam during the early 1960s, my contacts with members of the Kennedy entourage in Washington were limited. But I have interviewed many of the principals in preparing this book: Dean Rusk, Averell Harriman, Maxwell Taylor, McGeorge Bundy, William Bundy, Roger Hilsman, George Ball, Michael Forrestal, Edward Lansdale, Arthur Schlesinger, Jr., and Paul Kattenburg. Documents on the period are in *The Pentagon Papers* and in the Porter collection as well as in *Vietnam Commitments 1961*, Department of State (Washington, D.C.: U.S. Government Printing Office, 1972).

An extremely perceptive analysis of the deepening American commitment to Vietnam, for these and later years, is Leslie H. Gelb and Richard K. Betts, *The*

Irony of Vietnam: The System Worked (Washington, D.C.: Brookings Institution, 1979). George Herring has written an excellent short history, *America's Longest War* (New York and Chichester: John Wiley, 1979). David Halberstam describes the period with verve in *The Best and the Brightest* (New York: Random House, 1972). On the situation inside Vietnam, two RAND Corporation studies by Gerald Hickey are valuable: "Accommodation and Coalition in South Vietnam," P-4213 (January 1970) and "Accommodation in South Vietnam: The Key to Sociopolitical Solidarity," P-3707 (October 1967). I was helped in Vietnam during those years by Hickey and other RAND specialists, among them John Donnell and Joseph Zasloff. My key South Vietnamese contacts included Ton That Thien, Vu Van Thai, Nguyen Thai, and the late Dang Duc Khoi. It was during this period that I first met Colonel Pham Ngoc Thao, then province chief in Bentre, who I learned later was a secret Communist agent. I also interviewed Ngo Dinh Diem and his brother Nhu, and Madame Nhu.

Chapter 8: The End of Diem

Through a combination of circumstances, I was able to observe the overthrow of Ngo Dinh Diem closely. I was initially introduced to the incipient conspiracy as early as January 1961 by Dr. Tran Kim Tuyen, then head of Diem's covert intelligence apparatus. Tuyen, alarmed by the growing internal dissidence, had begun to press Diem and Nhu for reforms, and he considered it to be in his interest to divulge his activities to an American reporter. He was briefly "exiled" to Hong Kong in 1963, where we kept in contact, though he had been overtaken by events at that stage. Another early conspirator was Colonel Pham Ngoc Thao, an inveterate plotter, who kept me informed—or perhaps misinformed. I fit the pieces together afterward from interviews with Henry Cabot Lodge, William Trueheart, Lucien Conein, Duong Van Minh, Tran Van Don, Le Van Kim, Dang Duc Khoi, and others at the Saigon end, and with Kennedy administration officials of the period, among them Dean Rusk, McGeorge Bundy, Averell Harriman, George Ball, Maxwell Taylor, Roger Hilsman, Michael Forrestal, and Paul Kattenburg. Interesting sources on the Diem regime's secret contacts with Hanoi were Tran Van Dinh, who claims to have acted as an intermediary, and Mieczyslaw Maneli, a Polish diplomat who later defected to the United States.

The essential documents are in *The Pentagon Papers* and the Porter collection. A congressional probe that adds little is U.S. Senate Committee on Foreign Relations, *U.S. Involvement in the Overthrow of Diem, 1963* (Washington, D.C.: U.S. Government Printing Office, 1972). Tran Van Don has told his story in *Our Endless War* (San Rafael, Calif.: Presidio Press, 1978). Maneli recounts his activities in *War of the Vanquished* (New York: Harper & Row, 1971). A fine description of the contemporary atmosphere is contained in John Mecklin, *Mission in Torment* (Garden City, N.Y.: Doubleday, 1965). There is also Robert

Shaplen, *Time Out of Hand: Revolution and Reaction in Southeast Asia* (New York: Harper & Row, 1969). The Washington scene is portrayed in aforementioned books by George Ball, Roger Hilsman, and Arthur Schlesinger, Jr. Among the many accounts of the Buddhist crisis are Erich Wulff, "The Buddhist Revolt," *The New Republic*, August 31, 1963, and passages in Buttinger's second volume of *Vietnam: A Dragon Embattled*.

Chapter 9: The Commitments Deepen

The Lyndon Johnson story must inevitably begin with his own memoirs, however apologetic they may be—*The Vantage Point: Perspectives of the Presidency, 1963–1969* (New York: Holt, Rinehart & Winston, 1971). Of the many books on Johnson, the two that I found most useful were Doris Kearns, *Lyndon Johnson and the American Dream* (New York: Harper & Row, 1976) and Merle Miller, *Lyndon: An Oral Biography* (New York: G. P. Putnam, 1980). The atmosphere inside the Johnson administration is described in several books that cover this and later periods, among them: Harry C. McPherson, Jr., *A Political Education* (Boston: Atlantic-Little, Brown, 1971); Jack Valenti, *A Very Human President* (New York: W. W. Norton, 1975); Lady Bird Johnson, *A White House Diary* (New York: Holt, Rinehart and Winston, 1971); Maxwell Taylor, *Swords and Ploughshares* (New York: W. W. Norton, 1972); and Henry F. Graff, *The Tuesday Cabinet: Deliberation and Decision on Peace and War Under Lyndon B. Johnson* (Englewood Cliffs, N.J.: Prentice-Hall, 1970). Among the many critiques of Johnson are Tom Wicker, *JFK and LBJ: The Influence of Personality upon Politics* (New York: William Morrow, 1968), and Eric F. Goldman, *The Tragedy of Lyndon Johnson* (New York: Dell; London: MacDonald & Evans, 1969).

Gelb and Betts, cited above, offer acute insights into Johnson's policy toward Vietnam, and Herring's history is also useful. Two other books of value are Philip L. Geyelin, *Lyndon B. Johnson and the World* (New York: Frederick A. Praeger, 1966) and Henry Brandon, *Anatomy of Error: The Inside Story of the Asian War on the Potomac, 1954–1969* (Boston: Gambit, 1969; London: Andre Deutsch, 1970). Other works that cover this and other periods are: Guenter Lewy, *America in Vietnam* (New York and London: Oxford University Press, 1978); George McTurnan Kahin and John W. Lewis, *The United States in Vietnam* (New York: Dial Press, 1967); Marvin Kalb and Elie Abel, *Roots of Involvement* (New York: W. W. Norton, 1971); Paul Kattenburg, *The Vietnam Trauma in American Foreign Policy, 1945–75* (New Brunswick, N.J.: Transaction Books, 1980); and Daniel Ellsberg, *Papers on the War* (New York: Simon & Schuster, 1972). Again, the relevant documents are in *The Pentagon Papers* and in the Porter collection. A brilliant essay is James Thomson, Jr., "How Vietnam Could Happen: An Autopsy," *The Atlantic*, April 1968. I also recommend Halberstam's *The Best and the Brightest*; Ernest B. Furguson, *Westmoreland, the Inevitable General* (Boston: Little, Brown, 1968); and Henry L. Trewhitt, *McNamara: His Ordeal in the Pentagon* (New York: Harper & Row, 1971). My sources for the Communist side are cited in the narrative.

Chapter 10: Disorder and Decision

I relied heavily for advice regarding the Tonkin Gulf incident on William B. Bader, who uncovered much of the truth on the controversial events as a staff member of the Senate Foreign Relations Committee. Ray Cline, former deputy director of the CIA, was helpful on the subject in addition to the passages quoted in the narrative. I am indebted to the late Ralph Johnson of the CIA, who provided me with information on the clandestine South Vietnamese operations as well as details on the activities of Tucker Gougelmann, the covert adviser to the commandos. My thanks also to Anthony Austin of *The New York Times*, who has described the Tonkin Gulf affair in his vivid book, *The President's War* (Philadelphia: J. B. Lippincott, 1971). Other published works on the incident are Joseph C. Goulden, *Truth Is the First Casualty* (Chicago: Rand McNally, 1969); Eugene C. Windchy, *Tonkin Gulf* (Garden City, N.Y.: Doubleday, 1971); *The Gulf of Tonkin, 1964 Incidents*, Senate Committee on Foreign Relations (Washington, D.C.: U.S. Government Printing Office, 1968). A good biography of Fulbright is by Haynes Johnson and Bernard Gwertzman, *Fulbright: The Dissenter* (Garden City, N.Y.: Doubleday, 1968). Everett Alvarez, the first American pilot shot down over North Vietnam, described his experience in an interview. Communist accounts of the incident come from interviews with Prime Minister Pham Van Dong and other figures in Vietnam.

I covered the events in Saigon at the time, and then interviewed several of the South Vietnamese personalities mentioned in the narrative. I later interviewed Nguyen Khanh, Nguyen Cao Ky, and Bui Diem, as well as other Saigon government political figures, along with Maxwell Taylor and other members of the U.S. mission in Saigon. Books containing good accounts of events in South Vietnam are Frances FitzGerald, *Fire in the Lake* (Boston: Atlantic-Little, Brown, 1972) and Shaplen's *The Lost Revolution*. An excellent guide to North Vietnamese policies is William J. Duiker, *The Communist Road to Power* (Boulder, Col.: Westview Press, 1981), which covers these and subsequent years. Many of the essential documents are in *The Pentagon Papers* and the Porter collection.

Chapter 11: LBJ Goes to War

The Washington figures interviewed for this chapter include Dean Rusk, McGeorge Bundy, William Bundy, George Ball, Walt Rostow, Bill Moyers, Jack Valenti, Paul Warnke, Cyrus Vance, and General Harold K. Johnson. I am indebted to Bui Diem for his account of attitudes inside the Saigon regime; General William C. Westmoreland was also interviewed. The Communist personalities interviewed include Prime Minister Pham Van Dong and General Tran Do, the deputy Vietcong commander in the south, as well as others cited in the narrative.

The most comprehensive book on this period is Larry Berman, *Planning a Tragedy: The Americanization of the War in Vietnam* (New York: W. W. Norton, 1982). I also recommend Douglas Kinnard, *The War Managers* (Hanover, N.H.: University Press of New England, 1977), as well as several authors mentioned in connection with earlier chapters, among them Doris Kearns, Merle Miller, George Ball, Henry Brandon, Philip Geyelin, George Herring, and John Mueller. In addition to William Duiker, cited above, two other studies of the Communist side are Donald S. Zagoria, *Vietnam Triangle* (New York: Pegasus, 1967) and W. R. Smyser, *The Independent Vietnamese: Vietnamese Communism Between Russia and China, 1956–69*, Athens, Ohio University Papers in International Studies, 1980. *The Pentagon Papers* and the Porter collection also contain relevant documents.

Chapter 12: Escalation

I observed firsthand the Americanization of the war as it unfolded after the spring of 1965. In addition to my notes of the period, I relied on several books and reports, among them: General William C. Westmoreland, *A Soldier Reports* (Garden City, N.Y.: Doubleday, 1976); Westmoreland, *Report on the War in Vietnam: Section II, Report on Operations in South Vietnam, January 1964–June 1968* (Washington, D.C.: U.S. Government Printing Office, 1969); Jack Shulimson and Major Charles M. Johnson, *U.S. Marines in Vietnam: The Landing and the Buildup, 1965*, Washington, D.C.: History and Museums Division, Headquarters, U.S. Marine Corps, 1978; Edward Hymoff, *First Marine Division, Vietnam* (New York: M. W. Lads, 1967); Hymoff, *The First Air Cavalry Division, Vietnam* (New York: M. W. Lads, 1967); U.S. Military Assistance Command, Vietnam, *1967 Wrap-Up: A Year of Progress*, Saigon, 1968; and *Aggression from the North: The Record of North Vietnam's Campaign to Conquer South Vietnam*, Department of State (Washington, D.C.: U.S. Government Printing Office, 1962).

The Communist side of the war is contained in North Vietnam's military history cited in connection with earlier chapters. Communist strategy is outlined in General Vo Nguyen Giap, *Big Victory, Big Task* (New York: Frederick A. Praeger, 1967). Two superb studies by Konrad Kellen of the RAND Corporation on the Communist forces are *A Profile of the PAVN Soldier in South Vietnam*, RM-5013-ISA/ARPA (June 1966), and *Conversations wtih Enemy Soldiers in Late 1968/Early 1969: A Study of Motivation and Morale*, RM-6131/1-ISA/ARPA (September 1970). See also William Darryl Henderson, *Why the Vietcong Fought* (Westport, Conn.: Greenwood, 1979).

Interviews in Vietnam after the war yielded several accounts of life under the American bombing. An excellent study on the subject is Jon M. Van Dyke,

North Vietnam's Strategy for Survival (Palo Alto, Calif.: Pacific Books, 1972). Among the other important books on the bombing are James Clay Thompson, *Rolling Thunder* (Chapel Hill: University of North Carolina Press, 1980); Raphael Littauer and Norman Uphoff, eds., *The Air War in Indochina* (Boston: Beacon Press, 1972); and National Research Council, *The Effects of Herbicides in South Vietnam* (Washington, D.C.: National Academy of Sciences, 1974).

A critical collection of anecdotes on the American military involvement is Cincinnatus, *Self-Destruction: The Disintegration and Decay of the United States Army During the Vietnam Era* (New York: W. W. Norton, 1978). A reporter's critical account of one episode in the war is Jonathan Schell, *The Village of Ben Suc* (New York: Random House, 1967). A correspondent's account that deserves attention is Ward Just, *To What End: Report from Vietnam* (Boston: Houghton Mifflin, 1968). Probably the best reporter's account of the war on the ground is Michael Herr, *Dispatches* (New York: Alfred A. Knopf, 1978).

A number of interviews with North Vietnamese, Vietcong, and Saigon government soldiers, conducted after the war, try to convey their experiences. Several American veterans were also interviewed. And I depended on accounts produced by GIs themselves, and recommend the following: Mark Baker, *Nam: The Vietnam War in the Words of the Men and Women Who Fought There* (New York: William Morrow, 1981); Philip Caputo, *A Rumor of War* (New York: Holt, Rinehart & Winston, 1977); Frederick Downs, *The Killing Zone: My Life in the Vietnam War* (New York: W. W. Norton, 1978); Ron Kovic, *Born on the Fourth of July* (New York: McGraw-Hill, 1976); Tim O'Brien, *If I Die in a Combat Zone, Box Me Up and Ship Me Home* (New York: Dell, 1973); Al Santoli, *Everything We Had: An Oral History of the Vietnam War by Thirty-Three American Soldiers Who Fought It* (New York: Random House, 1981); Samuel Vance, *The Courageous and the Proud* (New York: W. W. Norton, 1970); James Webb, *Fields of Fire* (Englewood Cliffs, N.J.: Prentice-Hall, 1978); Francis J. West, Jr., *Small Unit Action in Vietnam: Summer 1966* (New York: Arno Press, 1967); and West, *The Village* (New York: Harper & Row, 1972).

Chapter 13: Debate, Diplomacy, Doubt

During the years covered in this chapter, I shuttled between Hong Kong and Vietnam, with trips to Washington as well as to Manila and Honolulu to cover the conferences held in those cities. I also visited Phnompenh from time to time, partly because of events in Cambodia and also to report insofar as was possible on the Communist side from my contacts with North Vietnamese, Vietcong, and Soviet diplomats stationed there. I was helped considerably by Wilfred Burchett, the pro-Communist Australian journalist, who usually imparted more information in private conversations than he did in print.

A comprehensive account of the various will-of-the-wisp negotiating endeavors during the Johnson administration is by David Kraslow and Stuart H. Lorry, *The Secret Search for Peace in Vietnam* (New York: Random House, 1968). Some of these efforts are related with charm and wit by Chester L. Cooper, a gentleman of charm and wit, in *The Lost Crusade* (New York: Dodd, Mead; 1970).

Dean Rusk, George Ball, McGeorge Bundy, William Bundy, Paul Warnke, Alain Enthoven, Leslie Gelb, Harry McPherson, and other members of the Johnson administration have provided me with valuable details on the Washington scene during this period—including Robert McNamara's disaffection with the war. The relevant documents are in *The Pentagon Papers* and the Porter collection. During those days, I saw Senators Mike Mansfield and J. William Fulbright and their staffs on my visits to Washington. A good account of the evolution of Robert Kennedy's thinking on the war comes from Arthur M. Schlesinger, Jr., *Robert Kennedy and His Times* (Boston: Houghton Mifflin, 1976). Other valuable books on the period, already cited, are Gelb and Betts, Herring, and Mueller. For the Harrison Salisbury fuss, see Salisbury's book *Behind the Lines: Hanoi, December 23, 1966–January 7, 1967* (New York: Harper & Row; London: Secker & Warburg, 1967), as well as Phil G. Goulding, *Confirm or Deny: Informing the People on National Security* (New York: Harper & Row, 1970).

Chapter 14: Tet

Apart from my own notes, I have relied on two outstanding books on this period: Don Oberdorfer, *Tet!* (Garden City, N.Y.: Doubleday, 1971), and Herbert Schandler, *The Unmaking of a President* (Princeton: Princeton University Press, 1977). Oberdorfer returned to Vietnam to reconstruct the events of Tet as they occurred there, while Schandler conducted several interviews to re-create the events that led to President Johnson's decision to stop escalating the war. I have been able to go beyond these books, particularly in interviews with Communist veterans of the Tet offensive, among them General Tran Do, the deputy commander in the south; Dr. Duong Quynh Hoa, a covert Vietcong agent in Saigon; and Captain Tran Dinh Thong, a North Vietnamese regular during the battle of Khesanh. I am especially indebted to David Elliott for his analysis of the Communist strategy during Tet—a thesis generally supported by Duiker.

I have also interviewed several key figures in the Johnson administration, most notably Clark Clifford, Harry McPherson, Dean Rusk, Walt Rostow, and George Christian. In addition to *The Pentagon Papers* and the Porter collection, books on the period include Robert Pisor, *The End of the Line: The Siege of Khe Sanh* (New York: W. W. Norton, 1982); Townsend Hoopes, *The Limits of Intervention* (New York: David McKay, 1970); and the works cited earlier by

Lyndon Johnson, Lady Bird Johnson, Doris Kearns, Merle Miller, Herring, and Gelb and Betts. A provocative book on the role of the news media is Peter Braestrup, *Big Story,* 2 vols. (Boulder, Col.: Westview Press, 1977).

Chapter 15: Nixon's War

I covered the Nixon administration as a diplomatic correspondent for the *Washington Post* and briefly as a special correspondent for NBC News before becoming associate editor of *The New Republic.* No longer based in Asia during this period, I revisited Vietnam, Cambodia, and Laos on assignment. My notes from those years have served me for this chapter. The principal documents are Richard Nixon, *RN: The Memoirs of Richard Nixon,* 2 vols. (New York: Warner Books, 1979) and Henry Kissinger, *White House Years* (Boston: Little, Brown; London: Weidenfeld & Nicolson, 1979), which often relate different versions of the same events.

Among the other books I have consulted are John Ehrlichman, *Witness to Power* (New York: Simon & Schuster, 1982); H. R. Haldeman, *The Ends of Power* (New York: Times Books, 1978); William Safire, *Before the Fall: An Inside View of the Pre-Watergate White House* (Garden City, N.Y.: Doubleday, 1975); Fawn M. Brodie, *Richard Nixon* (New York: W. W. Norton, 1981); David Wise, *The Politics of Lying* (New York: Random House, 1973); J. Anthony Lukas, *Nightmare: The Underside of the Nixon Years* (New York: Viking Press, 1976); and Tad Szulc, *The Illusion of Peace: Foreign Policy in the Nixon Years* (New York: Viking Press, 1978). Nixon's earlier views on Vietnam are in "Asia After Vietnam," *Foreign Affairs,* October 1967. Kissinger's article, referred to in the narrative, is "The Vietnam Negotiations," *Foreign Affairs,* January 1969.

In addition to my interviews with him, I consulted several books on Kissinger, among them Marvin Kalb and Bernard Kalb, *Kissinger* (Boston: Little, Brown; London: Hutchinson, 1974); Roger Morris, *Uncertain Greatness: Henry Kissinger and American Foreign Policy* (New York: Harper & Row; London: Quartet, 1977); John Stoessinger, *Kissinger: The Anguish of Power* (New York: W. W. Norton, 1976); and Seymour M. Hersh, *The Price of Power: Kissinger in the Nixon White House* (New York: Summit Books, 1983). A valuable guide to Kissinger's view of the world is Henry Kissinger, *A World Restored* (New York: Grosset & Dunlap, 1964). Henry hangs himself in Oriana Fallaci, *Interview with History,* trans. John Shepley (New York: Liveright, 1976).

An excellent corrective to Kissinger's own account of the Vietnam negotiations is Allan E. Goodman, *The Lost Peace* (Stanford, Calif.: Hoover Institution, 1978). I was helped in reconstructing my narrative of the negotiations by several of Kissinger's former assistants, among them Winston Lord, William Sullivan, Anthony Lake, Morton Halperin, Peter Rodman, and John Negroponte. For the Communist version of the negotiations, I am grateful to Nguyen Co Thach, the present foreign minister of Vietnam, and to Dang Nghiem Bai, the Vietnamese official who kept notes for Le Duc Tho during the talks. William Duiker's *The Communist Road to Power,* cited in connection with earlier chapters, provides acute insights into the policies of the Hanoi leaders. Some important Communist documents are contained in the Porter collection.

For the situation in South Vietnam during this period, see Douglas S. Blaufarb, *The Counterinsurgency Era* (New York: The Free Press; London: Collier-Macmillan, 1977), and Stuart A. Herrington, *Silence Was a Weapon: The Vietnam War in the Villages* (Novato, Calif.: Presidio Press, 1982).

The passages on Cambodia are partly based on my talks with Prince Sihanouk in Beijing in the spring of 1973. The comprehensive book on Cambodia during the Nixon years is William Shawcross, *Sideshow* (New York: Simon & Schuster, 1979). Kissinger's rebuttal to Shawcross can be found in his *Years of Upheaval* (Boston: Little, Brown, 1982). Much of the flavor of Cambodia during the period is described in Charles Meyer, *Derrière le sourire Khmer* (Paris: Plon, 1971). The story of the French attempt at negotiations comes from conversations with Etienne Manac'h and Marc Menguy, both of the French ministry of foreign affairs.

Chapter 16: The Peace That Never Was

Much of my own reporting during this period from Washington, Paris, and Saigon appeared in *The New Republic.* Essential reading are the Nixon and Kissinger memoirs cited above—both to be approached with caution. Allan Goodman, cited in the notes for Chapter 15, is excellent. Members of the Kissinger staff generously helped me. My references for Nixon's trip to China are drawn from research for Stanley Karnow, *Mao and China: From Revolution to Revolution* (New York: Viking Press, 1972). I am grateful to Richard Solomon, formerly the China specialist on Kissinger's national security council staff, for his guidance over the years. See also the Kalbs and Hersh on Kissinger as well as other books mentioned earlier, among them Ehrlichman, Haldeman, Safire, Lukas, and others. A provocative study of the news media coverage of Nixon's bombing of North Vietnam is Martin Herz, *The Prestige Press and the Christmas Bombing, 1972* (Washington, D.C.: Ethics and Public Policy Center, 1980).

The most vivid reading on the final period is Frank Snepp, *Decent Interval: An Insider's Account of Saigon's Indecent End* (New York: Random House, 1977). I am grateful to Stuart A. Herrington for allowing me to consult the manuscript of his book on the period, to be published by Presidio Press. A novel that captures the flavor of the time is Bernard and Marvin Kalb, *The Last Ambassador* (Boston: Little, Brown, 1981). The debacle is also recounted in Alan Dawson, *55 Days: The Fall of South Vietnam* (Englewood Cliffs, N.J.: Prentice-Hall, 1977). Graham Martin's account of his conduct is contained in *Hearing before the Special Subcommittee on Investigations, Committee on International Relations, House of Representatives* (Washington, D.C.: U.S. Government Printing Office, 1976).

I interviewed several Communist veterans of the final offensive, most notably Colonel Bui Tin, who took the surrender from the interim South Vietnamese regime. The two authoritative Communist accounts published are General Van Tien Dung, *Our Great Spring Victory* (New York: Monthly Review Press, 1977), and General Tran Van Tra, *Vietnam: History of the Bulwark B2 Theatre,* Vol. 5, *Concluding the 30-Years War,* translated by the Joint Publications Research Service in Arlington, Virginia (Ho Chi Minh City: Van Nghe Publishing House, 1982). The two accounts differ in several important respects. Tra's version has been removed from circulation, and Tra himself has dropped out of sight—evidence that the Communists regard the Dung account as official.

An excellent compilation of the views and experiences on the South Vietnamese side is Stephen T. Hosmer, Konrad Kellen, and Brian M. Jenkins for the RAND Corporation, *The Fall of South Vietnam: Statements by Vietnamese Military and Civilian Leaders,* a report prepared for Historian, Office of the Secretary of Defense, R-2208-OSD (HIST) (December 1978). I am indebted to Bui Diem, former South Vietnamese ambassador in Washington, for giving me his original contribution to the report.

Acknowledgments

The views expressed in this book are mine. However, I could not have completed a work of such magnitude without the help of many people, including those who assisted me in years past.

At The Viking Press, I am indebted to Nanette Kritzalis, managing editor, and Susan Shapiro, copy editor, as well as Melissa Browne, Altie Karper, Ruth Randall, and Theodora Rosenbaum; and to Richard Adelson, Beth Tondreau, and Gene Waller in design and production for their skill in getting the book into print rapidly and accurately. My thanks as well to the design staff of WGBH: Douglass Scott, Jeffrey Bell, Deborah Paddock, Eileen Ryan, and Christopher Pullman.

I did much of my research while serving as chief correspondent for "Vietnam: A Television History," a thirteen-part documentary series produced under the auspices of WGBH, Boston, in cooperation with Central Independent Television of Britain and Antenne-2 of France. Peter McGhee, director for national programming at WGBH, deserves to be thanked for his strong support and guidance. My thanks, too, to the producers, associate producers, and others involved in the television project: Elizabeth Deane, Austin Hoyt, Andrew Pearson, Henri de Turenne, Martin Smith, Serge Gordey, Marilyn Hornbeck, Bruce Palling, Karan Sheldon, Tuggelin Yourgrau, Judith Vecchione, Jan Langmack, Kenn Rabin, Alison Smith, Carol Hayward, Jacques Weissgerber, Eric Handley, Eric Neudel, Bradley Borum, Janet Hayman, Mavis Smull, Kay Matschullat, Raye Farr, Maureen Fahey, Cynthia Meagher Kuhn, John Waite, Nicole Jouve, and Sara Altherr.

My special gratitude goes to Richard Holbrooke and David Aaron, who read and commented on parts of the manuscript. Leslie Gelb provided me with important insights, and I relied on Ronald Goldfarb for his expert counsel. I also owe particular thanks to Bui Diem, Bui Tin, Ton That Thien, Douglas Pike, and Kwoh Yu-pei. Numerous colleagues as well as officials, veterans, and others on both sides in the war must be thanked for submitting to interviews or for furnishing me with advice and information. Many helped me during my decades as a correspondent; some are no longer alive. I have tried to remember most of them in the following list:

Chloe Aaron, Morton Abramowitz, Sam Adams, Everett Alvarez, Desaix Anderson, R. W. Apple, Peter Arnett, Anthony Austin, Dorothy Avery; William Bader, George Ball, E. J. Banks, Bao Dai, Daniel Bell, Charles Benoit, Claude Bernard, Richard Betts, Homer Bigart, Douglas Blaufarb, Herbert Bleuchel, Robert Blum, Lucien Bodard, Arnaud de Borchgrave, Chester Bowles, Peter Braestrup, Pierre Brochand, Dean Brown, Sam Brown, Malcolm Browne, Kevin Buckley, Everett Bumgartner, McGeorge Bundy, William Bundy, Ellsworth Bunker, Wilfred Burchett, Larry Burrows, Russell Burrows, Horace Busby; Clifford Case, Alexander Casella, Anne Chamberlin, Sisouk Na Champassak, John Chancellor, Jean-François Chauvel, George Christian, Clark Clifford, Ray Cline, Sloan Coffin, William Colby, J. Lawton Collins, John Condon, Lucien Conein, Lawrence Connell, Chester Cooper, William Corson, Sterling Cottrell; Jean Daniel, Dan Davidson, Dang Duc Khoi, Dang Van Son, Dang Xuan Teo, Ted Danielson, Louis Dauge, Orrin DeForrest, David Dellinger, Vincent Demma, William Depuy, Philippe Devillers, Doan Doc Luu, John Dominis, John Donnell, Tom Dooley, Joseph Duffey, William Duiker, John Michael Dunne, Duong Duc Hong, Duong Quynh Hoa, Duong Van Minh, Elbridge Durbrow, Tillman Durdin, Fred Dutton; William Ehrhart, David Elliott, Daniel Ellsberg, Gloria Emerson, Alain Enthoven; Horst Faas, Bernard Fall, Dorothy Fall, James Fallows, Loren Fessler, Frances FitzGerald, Philip Foisie, Gerald Ford, Michael Forrestal, Henry Fowler, J. William Fulbright; Philip Geyelin, William Gibbon, Vernon Gillespie, David Ginsburg, Guido Goldman, Allan Goodman, Jean-Yves Gory, Marshall Green, H. D. S. Greenway, Peter Grose, Jean-Louis Guillaud; Ha Van Lau, Philip Habib, David Halberstam, Morton Halperin, Averell Harriman, John Hasey, Myron Harrington, David Harris, Gilbert Harrison, George Herring, Stuart Herrington, Seymour Hersh, Gerald Hickey, Charles Hill, Jack Hill, Roger Hilsman, Hoang Duc Nha, Hoang Quoc Viet, David Hudson, Hue Tam To Tai, Thomas Hughes; Harold Isaacs; Campbell James, Brian Jenkins, Harold K. Johnson, Ralph Johnson, U. Alexis Johnson, Craig Johnstone, Ward Just; George Kahin, Robert Kaiser, Bernard Kalb, Marvin Kalb, Peter Kalischer, Harold Kaplan, Paul Kattenburg, Jack Keegan, Konrad Kellen, Robert Kennedy, John Kerry, Randolph Kidder, Eva Kim, Douglas Kinnard, Henry Kissinger, George Kistiakowsky, Robert Komer, Henry Koren,

Joseph Kraft; Jean Lacouture, Fred Ladd, Melvin Laird, Anthony Lake, Edward Lansdale, Kermit Lansner, Vint Lawrence, Le Chan, Scott Leavitt, Lee Lescaze, Herbert Levin, Anthony Lewis, Guenter Lewy, Henry Cabot Lodge, Winston Lord, James Lowenstein, Van S. Lung; Patricia McAdams, John McAlister, Douglas MacArthur II, Eugene McCarthy, Stephen McClintic, Paul McCloskey, Robert McCloskey, Frank McCulloch, Clay McManaway, Harry McPherson, Mieczyslaw Maneli, Robert Manning, Mike Mansfield, Carl Marcy, Murray Marder, Graham Martin, Leonard Maynard, John Mecklin, Joseph Mendenhall, Marc Menguy, Jill Merrill, Stuart Methven, Charles Meyer, Paul Miles, Abbot Low Moffet, Charles Mohr, Robert Montague, Kenneth Moorefield, Thomas Moorer, Richard Moose, Hans Morgenthau, Roger Morris, Bill Moyers, John Mueller; John Negroponte, Gaylord Nelson, Ron Nessen, Ngo Dinh Diem, Ngo Dinh Luyen, Ngo Dinh Nhu, Madame Ngo Dinh Nhu, Ngo Minh Khoi, Ngo Vinh Long, Nguyen Cao Ky, Nguyen Chanh Thi, Nguyen Co Thach, Nguyen Cong Thanh, Nguyen Huu Tho, Nguyen Khac Vien, Nguyen Khanh, Nguyen Ngoc Linh, Nguyen Phuong Nam, Nguyen Thai, Nguyen Thi Binh, Nguyen Thi Dinh, Nguyen Tho Hang, Frederick Nolting, Phoumi Nosavan; Don Oberdorfer, Charlton Ogburn, Milton Orshefsky, John Osborne; Daniel Passent, Archimedes Patti, William Payeff, Jean-Louis Petit, Pham Ngoc Thao, Pham Van Dong, Pham Xuan An, Rufus Phillips, Souvanna Phouma, Walter Pincus, Anthony Poe, Jean-Claude Pomonti, François Ponchaud, Sam Popkin, Gareth Porter, William Porter, Mark Pratt, Ray Price; Jeffrey Race, Edward Regan, Jack Reynolds, Elliot Richardson, David Riesman, Robinson Risner, Lloyd Rives, Peter Rodman, Jerry Rose, Harry Rosenfeld, Walt Rostow, Dean Rusk, Bayard Rustin; Charles Sabatier, Pierre Salinger, David Sanford, Jean Sauvageot, Herbert Schandler, Jerrold Schecter, Thomas Schelling, Arthur Schlesinger, Jr., Frank Scotten, Blair Seaborn, Ted Serong, Robert Shaplen, William Shawcross, Neil Sheehan, Susan Sheehan, Norodom Sihanouk, Hedrick Smith, Mark Smith, Terrence Smith, Richard Smyser, Frank Snepp, Ray Snyder, Richard Solomon, Souphanouvang, Richard Steadman, Laurence Stern, Richard Stilwell, William Sullivan, François Sully, Harry Summers, Emory Swank, Carlton Swift, Tad Szulc; George Tanham, Maxwell Taylor, Ralph Thomas, James Thomson, Ton That Tung, Hugh Tovar, Sid Towle, Tran Ding Thong, Tran Do, Tran Duy Hung, Tran Kim Tuyen, Tran Ngoc Chau, Tran Ngoc Lieng, Tran Nhat Bang, Tran Thi Truyen, Tran Van Dinh, Tran Van Do, Tran Van Don, Tran Van Ngo, William Trueheart, Robert Trumbull, Tuu Ky; Leonard Unger, Warren

Unna; Jack Valenti, Mai Thu Van, Van Tien Dung, John Paul Vann, Vo Nguyen Giap, Vu Quoc Uy, Vu Van Thai; Denis Warner, Paul Warnke, Ben Wattenberg, William Watts, William Westmoreland, Frank White, Allen Whiting, M. G. M. Wilde, Sam Wilson, Frank Wisner, Grant Wolfkill, Alexander Woodside, André Wormser, Michael Wrigley; Adam Yarmolinsky, Charles Yost, Andrew Young, Earl Young, Gordon Young, Kenneth Young, Stephen Young; Donald Zagoria, Joseph Zasloff, Barry Zorthian, Victor Zorza.

Photo Credits

Chapter 1

p. 2 (top): Philip Jones Griffiths, Magnum; (bottom): Penelope Breese, Gamma-Liaison. p. 3 (top): Philip Jones Griffiths, Magnum; (bottom): Jean-Louis Atlan, Sygma. p. 4 (top): J. P. Laffont, Sygma; (bottom): Leonard Freed, Magnum. p. 5 (top): Philip Jones Griffiths, Magnum; (bottom): T. Terzani, Sygma. p. 6 (top): Marc Riboud, Magnum; (bottom) and p. 7 (both): Jean-Claude Labbé, Gamma-Liaison. p. 8 (both): Philip Jones Griffiths, Magnum.

Chapter 2

p. 47: M. Petit, *La France au Tonkin et en Chine,* n.d. p. 48 (top): Churchill, *A Collection of Voyages and Travels, . . .* 6 vols., London, 1746, vol. 6, Samuel Baron, "A Description of the Kingdom of Tonqueen."; (bottom): Séminaire des Missions Etrangères. p. 49 (top): Lefèbvre de Béhaine; (bottom): Séminaire des Missions Etrangères. p. 50 (top): J. Crawfurd, *Journal of an Embassy from the Governor-General of India to the Courts of Siam and Cochin China;* 2 vols., London, 1830, vol. 2; (bottom left): J. Barrow, *A Voyage to Cochinchina,* London, 1806; (bottom right): Gaston de Chaigneau. p. 51 (top left): Service Historique de la Marine, France; (top right): Séminaire des Missions Etrangères; (bottom): Musée d'Histoire Naturelle, France. p. 52 (top): F. Garnier, *Voyage d'Exploration de Indo-Chine,* . . . Paris, 1873; (bottom): Musée Indochinois du Trocadéro. p. 53: Musée de l'Armée. p. 54 (top): *Tour du Monde,* 1877, vol. 2; (bottom left): Bettmann Archive; (bottom right): Musée de l'Armée.

Chapter 3

p. 89: Maurice Durand Collection of Vietnamese Art, Yale University Library. p. 90: Société de Géographie. p. 91: Albert Kahn Collection, Département des Hauts-de-Seine. p. 92 (top): Archives Nationales de France; (bottom): Sipahioglu, Gamma-Liaison. p. 93 (top): Black Star; (bottom): Ngo Vinh Long Collection. p. 94 (top): D. Seylan Collection; (bottom): Bonneville, Gamma-Liaison. p. 95 (top): Albert Kahn Collection, Département des Hauts-de-Seine; (bottom): P. Doumer, *L'Indo-Chine Française: Souvenirs,* Paris, 1905. p. 96 (top): Maurice Durand Collection of Vietnamese Art, Yale University Library; (bottom): *L'Illustration,* Sygma.

Chapter 4

p. 128: Wide World. p. 129 (top): Patti Collection; (bottom) Courtesy Mrs. Nancy Pierrepont. p. 130 (top): Wide World; (bottom): Ngo Vinh Long Collection. p. 131 (both):

Imperial War Museum, London. p. 132 (top): Keystone; (bottom): Roger-Viollet. p. 133 (top): Eastfoto; (bottom): Patti Collection. p. 134 (top): Jack Birns, *Life* magazine, © 1949 Time Inc.; (bottom): Jack Birns, *Life* magazine, © 1950 Time Inc.

Chapter 5

p. 161: Black Star. p. 162 (both): Bettmann Archive. p. 163 (top): Al Hirschfeld; (bottom): Roger-Viollet. p. 164 (top): François Sully, Black Star; (bottom): *Paris-Match*. p. 165 (top): Howard Sochurek, *Life* magazine, © 1954 Time Inc.; (bottom) *Paris-Match*. p. 166 (both): Service Presse Information. p. 167 (top): Service Presse Information; (bottom left): Wide World; (bottom right): Frank Scherschel, *Life* magazine, © 1954 Time Inc. p. 168 (top): Service Presse Information; (bottom): National Park Service, Dwight D. Eisenhower Library.

Chapter 6

p. 206: Howard Sochurek, *Life* magazine, © 1955 Time Inc. p. 207 (top): Howard Sochurek, *Life* magazine, © 1954 Time Inc.; (bottom): Wide World. p. 208 (both): Howard Sochurek, *Life* magazine, © 1955 Time Inc. p. 209 (top): Edward G. Lansdale Collection, Hoover Institution Archives, Stanford University; (bottom): Michigan State University Archives & Historical Collections. p. 210 (top): Black Star; (bottom): Co Rentmeester, *Life* magazine, © 1967 Time Inc. p. 211 (top left): Wide World; (top right): Eastfoto; (bottom): Wide World. p. 212 (top): Black Star; (bottom): Ngo Vinh Long Collection.

Chapter 7

p. 240: Howard Sochurek, *Life* magazine, © 1962 Time Inc. p. 241 (top): Fred Ward, Black Star. p. 242 (top): Larry Burrows, *Life* magazine, © 1963 Time Inc; (bottom): François Sully, Black Star. p. 243 (top and bottom right): Larry Burrows, *Life* magazine, © 1962 Time Inc.; (bottom left): Burt Glinn, Magnum. p. 244 (both): Eastfoto. p. 245 (top): Wide World; (bottom): United Press International. p. 246 (top): François Sully, Black Star; (bottom): Gilles Caron, Gamma-Liaison.

Chapter 8

p. 270: Larry Burrows, *Life* magazine, © 1963 Time Inc. p. 271 (top): Wide World; (bottom): United Press International. p. 272 (top): Wide World; (bottom): François Sully. p. 273 (top): Stephen Markbreiter, Black Star. p. 274 (top): Larry Burrows, Larry Burrows Collection; (bottom): United Press International. p. 275 (both): Wide World. p. 276 (top): United Press International; (bottom): John F. Kennedy Library.

Chapter 9

p. 312: Larry Burrows, Larry Burrows Collection. p. 313 (top): Wide World; (bottom): Lyndon B. Johnson Library. p. 314 (both): Larry Burrows, Larry Burrows Collection. p. 315 (top): Larry Burrows, Larry Burrows Collection; (bottom): Lyndon B. Johnson Library. p. 316 (top): Harry Redl, Black Star; (bottom) Larry Burrows, Larry Burrows Collection. p. 317 (both): United Press International. p. 318 (top): Russ Melcher, Black Star; (bottom): Library of Congress.

Chapter 10

p. 349: Lyndon B. Johnson Library. p. 350 (both): Wide World. p. 351 (top): Lyndon B. Johnson Library; (bottom): United Press International. p. 352 (top): Sovfoto; (bottom): Max Scheler, Black Star. p. 353: James Pickerell, Black Star. p. 354 (both): François Sully. p. 355: United Press International. p. 356 (top): François Sully; (bottom): United Press International.

Chapter 11

p. 387: Larry Burrows, *Life* magazine, © 1965 Time Inc. p. 388 (top): Charles Bonnay, Black Star; (bottom): Lyndon B. Johnson Library. p. 389 (both): François Sully. p. 390 (top): United Press International; (bottom): Sovfoto. p. 391 (both): United Press International. p. 392 (top): Lyndon B. Johnson Library; (bottom): United Press International. p. 394: Eastfoto.

Chapter 12

p. 427: Larry Burrows, *Life* magazine, © Time Inc. p. 428: Black Star. p. 429: United Press International. p. 430 (top): René Burri, Magnum; (bottom): Bruno Barbey, Magnum. p. 431 (both): United Press International. p. 432: Marc Riboud. p. 433 (top): Marc Riboud, Magnum; (bottom): Sovfoto. p. 434 (top): United Press International; (bottom): Larry Burrows, *Life* magazine, © 1966 Time Inc.

Chapter 13

p. 474: Michael Abramson, Liaison. p. 475 (both): Lyndon B. Johnson Library. p. 476 (top left and right): Dennis Brack, Black Star; (bottom) United Press International. p. 477 (top): United Press International; (bottom): Lyndon B. Johnson Library. p. 478 (both): United Press International.

Chapter 14

p. 515: Donald McCullin, Magnum. p. 516 (top): Robert Ellison, Black Star; (bottom): Lyndon B. Johnson Library. p. 517 (top): Eastfoto; (bottom): Dick Swanson, *Life* magazine, © 1968 Times Inc. p. 518 (top): Larry Burrows, *Life* magazine, © 1969 Time Inc.; (bottom): Wide World. p. 519: Donald McCullin, Magnum. p. 520 (top): Larry Burrows, Larry Burrows Collection; (bottom): Cornell Capa, Magnum. p. 521: Cornell Capa, Magnum. p. 522 (both): Lyndon B. Johnson Library.

Chapter 15

p. 567: Gamma-Liaison. p. 568 (top): Fred Ward, Black Star; (bottom): Wide World. p. 569 (top): United Press International; (bottom): Nixon Project, National Archives. p. 570 (top): Marc Riboud, Magnum; (bottom): United Press International. p. 571 (top): Black Star; (bottom): United Press International. p. 572 (top left): Ronald Haeberle, *Life* magazine, © 1968 Time Inc.; (top right): Charles Bonnay, Gamma-Liaison; (bottom): Paul Schultzer, Time-Life Picture Agency, © 1965 Time Inc. p. 573 (top): United Press International; (bottom): Sipa Press, Black Star. p. 574 (top): Philip Jones Griffiths, Magnum; (bottom): Magnum. p. 575 (top): Claude Lafotan, Gamma-Liaison; (bottom): Charlon, Gamma-Liaison. p. 576 (top): Roger Pic, Gamma-Liaison; (bottom): Yves Billy, Sygma.

Chapter 16

p. 613: Buffon-Darquenne, Sygma. p. 614 (top): Wide World; (bottom): Dieter Ludwig, Gamma-Liaison. p. 615: United Press International. p. 616 (top): René Burri, Magnum; (bottom): Geneviève Chauvel, Sygma. p. 617: Gamma-Liaison. p. 618 (top): United Press International; (bottom) Mark Godfrey, Archive Pictures Inc. p. 619 (top): Sygma; (bottom): Alain Nogues, Sygma. p. 620 (top): Christine Spengler, Liaison; (bottom) Dieter Ludwig, Gamma-Liaison. p. 621 (both): United Press International. p. 622 (top): Buffon-Darquenne, Sygma; (bottom): United Press International.

Index

European Defense Community, 192, 193
Ewalt, Jack, 25
Expressen (newspaper), 193, 194

Faifo, 57, 59
Fall, Bernard, 185
Fallaci, Oriana, 141, 584
Faure, Edgar, 220
Felt, Adm. Harry, 262, 268, 286, 299, 304
Ferry, Jules, 55, 83–84, 85, 86–87, 97–98
Fielding, Lewis, 634
First Cavalry Division, 468, 632
Flexible response policy, 14, 250
Fonda, Jane, 580
Fontainebleau conference (1946), 154–55
Ford, Gerald, 661, 667
Ford, Harold, 403
Foreign Affairs, 175, 583, 588, 597, 627
Foreign Relations Committee (U.S. Senate), 249, 373, 374, 375, 418, 486, 503, 558
Forrestal, Michael, 287, 288
Fortas, Abe, 420, 426, 481, 510, 561, 562
Fosdick, Raymond, 178
Fowler, Henry, 553
France: in Asia, 58; in Vietnam (seventeenth-eighteenth centuries), 60–65; (nineteenth century), 67–78; (early twentieth century), 110–18; (1940–45), 140, 143, 144; (1945–54), 143–60, 171–75, 180, 181, 183–91, 194–98, 201–204
Franco-Prussian War (1870), 83
Free Khmer, 200, 202
French Concession (Shanghai), 71
French Revolution, 64
French Union, 153, 154
Freycinet, Charles de, 87
Front for National Salvation, 218
Fuerbringer, Otto, 297
Fulbright, J. William: and Tonkin Gulf resolution, 359, 374, 376; and war policy, 20, 418, 422–23, 444, 486, 503, 556, 594, 598, 627

Gagelin, François Isidore, 67
Gallieni, Gen. Joseph, 107
Gama, Vasco da, 57
Garnier, Lt. Francis, 79–80, 81, 82
Gates, Gen. Horatio, 64
Gayler, Adm. Noel, 668
Gelb, Leslie, 20, 506

Geneva accords and Conference (1954) 10, 43, 198–204, 213–14, 219, 224, 250, 253, 363, 625, 638, 654
Geneva Convention (1949), 655
de Genouilly, Adm. Charles Rigault, 69, 74–76
Gia Long, Emperor (Nguyen Anh), 62, 63, 64, 65, 66, 106
Giap, Gen. Vo Nguyen. *See* Vo Nguyen Giap
Gilpatric, Roswell, 287
Giscard d'Estaing, Valéry, 61
Glasser, Ronald, 470–72
Gloire, 69
Goa, 57
Goldberg, Arthur, 561, 599
Goldwater, Barry, 320, 357–58, 369, 395
Goodell, Charles, 598
Goodwin, Richard, 418
Gougelmann, Tucker, 365
Goulding, Phil, 490
Gracey, Maj. Gen. Douglas, 139, 148–49
La Grandière, Adm. Pierre-Paul-Marie-Benoît de, 78, 79
Grant, Ulysses S., 359
Great Britain: and French rule in Vietnam, 150; and Geneva Conference (1954), 198–204; in Vietnam (1945), 147–48
Great Society, 320, 321, 357, 479
Green, Marshall, 605
Greene, Graham, 220
Griffith, R. Allen, 188
Gronouski, John, 493
Gruening, Ernest, 20, 375, 376, 491
Guizot, François, 68

Habib, Philip, 562
Haig, Gen. Alexander, 22, 587, 630, 635, 644
Haiphong, 31, 41, 80, 81, 156–57, 652–53
Halberstam, David, 260, 296
Haldeman, H. R., 577, 582, 634, 651, 652
Halperin, Morton, 554, 587
"Hamburger Hill," 601
Ham Nghi, Emperor, 87, 108
Han dynasty (China), 99, 100
Hanoi, 41–42, 58, 80–81, 84, 104, 135, 144–45, 146, 151–52, 157–58, 652–53
Hanoi, University of, 115, 142
"Hanoi Hilton," 373, 655
Harkins, Gen. Paul, 258, 288, 289, 290, 291, 297, 298, 299–300, 304, 325, 345
Harmand, François, 85, 86

Taylor, Gen. Maxwell, 250, 251;
ambassador (1964–65), 345, 346, 347,
378; assessment by (1961), 251–52; on
bombing, 402, 409. 410; and Diem
overthrow, 287–99 passim; and domino
theory, 399; and Khanh, 347, 378–79,
380, 382–83; and Khanh overthrow,
384–86; and Ky and Thieu, 382–83; on
Saigon regime, 406, 407, 410; on troop
buildup, 397, 403, 415–16, 417, 419–20,
423; war review by, 19; and "wise
men," 561, 562
Tayson rebellion, 61–62, 64
Tchepone, 629–30
Teo, Dang Xuan. See Dang Xuan Teo
Tet offensive (1968), 155, 523–45, 639
Thach, Nguyen Co. See Nguyen Co
Thach
Thai, 98, 142
Thai Binh, 145–46
Thanh, Gen. Nguyen Chi. See Nguyen
Chi Thanh
Thanh Nien Cach Mang Dong Chi Hoi
(Revolutionary Youth League), 123
Thanh Quang, 449
Thanh Thai, 119, 215
Thant, U, 377
Thao, Col. Pham Ngoc. See Pham Ngoc
Thao
Thau Chin. See Ho Chi Minh
Thi, Gen. Nguyen Chanh. See Nguyen
Chanh Thi
Thien, Maj. Tran Cuu. See Tran Cuu
Thien
Thieu, Gen. Nguyen Van. See Nguyen
Van Thieu
Thieu Tri, Emperor, 68–70
Tho, 142
Tho, Maj. Lam Quang. See Lam Quang
Tho
Thompson, Sir Robert, 256, 464, 596–97
Thorez, Maurice, 152, 159
303 Committee, 364
365 Days (Glasser), 470
Thuc, Ngo Dinh. See Ngo Dinh Thuc
Thurmond, Strom, 509
Thuybo, 468–69
Thuyet, Ton That. See Ton That Thuyet
Ticonderoga, 366, 368, 369, 370, 372
Tien Phong (Vangard magazine), 640
Time, 10, 11, 14, 38, 297, 488–89, 514,
599
Times of Vietnam, 296

Tito, Marshal, 136, 176
Tocqueville, Alexis de, 12
Tokyo, 653
Tonkin, 57, 81, 82, 84, 85, 86, 88, 104, 116
Tonkin Gulf, 365–66
Tonkin Gulf incident, 366–73
Tonkin Gulf resolution, 22, 344–45, 358,
360–63, 374–76, 491
Tonsonhut airport, 258, 259
Ton That Dinh, Gen., 447; in Diem
overthrow, 291–308 passim
Ton That Thuyet, 87, 108, 109
Ton That Tung, 30, 458–59
Tot Dong, 104
Tourane, 57, 63, 69–75. See also Danang
Tra, Gen. Tran Van. See Tran Van Tra
Tran Cuu Thien, Maj., 231
Tran Dinh Thong, Capt., 545
Tran Do, Gen., 400–401, 523, 530, 545,
602
Tran Duy Hung, 144–45, 158, 653
Tran Hung Dao, 101
Tran Kim Tuyen, 230, 237, 280, 284
Tran Luc. See Ho Chi Minh
Tran Quoc Buu, 298
Tran Thien Khiem, Gen., 284, 290, 291,
294, 336–37, 379, 381, 440
Tran Thi Truyen, 455–56
Tran Trong Kim, 144
Tran Van Bo, 227–30
Tran Van Chuong, 266, 285, 296
Tran Van Don, Gen., 282; defense
minister (1975), 667; in Diem
overthrow, 282–310 passim; and Khanh,
337, 338, 339; refugee, 447
Tran Van Giau, 122, 150
Tran Van Huong, 381–82, 383–84, 669
Tran Van Huu, 180
Tran Van Khiem, 267
Tran Van Le Chi, 267
Tran Van Le Xuan. See Ngo Dinh Nhu,
Madame
Tran Van Tra, Gen., 544, 658–59, 660,
661, 663, 666
Trieu Au, 100
Trieu Da, 99
Trinh (Vietnamese dynasty), 58, 62, 106
Trinh Cong Son, 531
Trinh Trang, Emperor, 60
Tri Quang, 279, 280, 286, 298, 339, 379,
380, 445, 447, 448–49, 450
Trotsky, Leon, 122
Trueheart, William, 280–81

Truman, Harry S., 14, 43, 137, 169, 177, 320, 359, 513
Truman Doctrine, 170
Trung Nhi, 100
Trung Trac, 100
Truong, Gen. Ngo Quang. *See* Ngo Quang Truong
Truong Chinh, 32, 226
Truong Cong Dinh, 107
Truong Dinh Dzu, 451–52
Truong Uong Cuc. *See* COSVN
Truong Vinh Ky, Petrus, 114
Truyen, Tran Thi. *See* Tran Thi Truyen
Tu Duc, Emperor, 70–71, 75–79, 80–81, 82, 84, 85, 107
Tung, Col. Le Quang. *See* Le Quang Tung
Turner Joy, 369, 370
Tuu Ky, 597
Tuyen, Tran Kim. *See* Tran Kim Tuyen
Tuyet Lan. *See* Ho Chi Minh
Twining, Gen. Nathan, 197

Ugly American, The (Lederer and Burdick), 220
Union of Soviet Socialist Republics: and China, 328–29, 636–37; and U.S., 248, 328, 369, 639, 644–45; and Vietnam (1945–54), 152, 160, 169, 191–92, 193, 202–204; in 1954–60, 224; in 1964–68, 377, 411–12, 457; in 1969–75, 583, 593, 636, 638–39; after 1975, 32–33
United Nations, 33, 46, 377
United States: and Cambodia, 44, 45–46, 605–12; and China, 13–14, 43, 583, 636; and France in Indochina, 136, 147, 152, 170, 171–72; and global role, 14–15; and imperialism, 12–13; and Laos, 491; and manifest destiny, 12; and Philippines, 13; and Vietnam (1945–54), 169–72, 176–80, 196–98; in 1954–60, 214, 218–22, 224–25, 235–37; in 1960–63, 248–51, 253, 268–69, 278, 280–81, 286–90, 292–94; in 1964–68, 323, 324–27, 337–38, 340–48, 377–78, 386, 396–400, 403–407, 413–26; in 1969–75, 582–83, 593–94, 600; after 1975, 28, 33
University of Oriental Workers (Moscow), 122–23
Ussuri, River, 637

Valenti, Jack, 322, 479, 482
Valluy, Gen. Etienne, 155, 156, 157, 184

Van Ba. *See* Ho Chi Minh
Vance, Cyrus, 28, 425, 592–93
Vandenberg, Arthur, 177
Vann, Lt. Col. John Paul, 260, 261, 262
Van Tien Dung, Gen., 660, 663, 664–65
Van Toan, Gen., 442
Venice, 56, 57
Victorieuse, 69
Vientiane, 189
Vietcong: assassinations by, 238; at Bienhoa (1964), 402; at Binh Gia (1964), 407–408; and Brinks Hotel bombing (1964), 408–409; cadres, 462, 647; motivation, 254, 461; name, 10, 230; in National Liberation Front, 238–39; in 1965, 421–22; in 1968: *see* Tet offensive; in 1971, 635–36; in 1972, 640, 642; in 1973–74, 660; and North Vietnamese support, 330, 401, 419; and peace talks, 581, 586, 624, 625; and peasants, 232, 328; and Phoenix program, 601–602, 603; at Pleiku (1965), 411–12; and strategic hamlets, 256–57, 323–24; tactics of, 259, 460, 463, 642; Taylor on, 406; in Tet offensive (1968), 525–45, 601, 603
Vietminh: founded (1941), 126–27; as nationalist front, 140; in 1941–45, 140–44; in 1945–47, 145–60; in 1947–54, 182–86, 190–91, 194–98, 331, 540; in 1954–60, 226–27. *See also* Vietcong
Vietnam: Chinese control (third–fifteenth centuries), 83, 99–104; Chinese occupation of north (1945–46), 150–53; European contacts (seventeenth century), 57–58; French conquest (nineteenth century), 71–88; French control (nineteenth–twentieth centuries), 108–18; French missionary activity (seventeenth–nineteenth centuries), 60–65, 67–71; French return (1945), 150–51; French withdrawal (1954), 219, 220, 224; independent (fifteenth–nineteenth centuries), 104–108; nationalist movement (nineteenth–twentieth centuries), 108–109, 110–13; united (since 1975), 29–43; war of independence (1945–54), 169–205 *passim. See also* North Vietnam; South Vietnam for 1954–75
Vietnam, Democratic Republic of, 147–60, 169, 175, 176